MACROECONOMICS
THEORY AND POLICY IN CANADA

THIRD EDITION

David A. Wilton
University of Waterloo
David M. Prescott
University of Guelph

Addison-Wesley Publishers

Don Mills, Ontario • Reading, Massachusetts
Menlo Park, California • New York • Wokingham,
England • Amsterdam • Bonn • Sydney
Singapore • Tokyo • Madrid • San Juan

Acquisitions Editor: Shirley Tessier
Coordinating Editor: Kateri Lanthier
Copy Editor: Gail Copeland
Art and Design: Anthony Leung
Text Formatting: Tony Gordon Ltd.

Canadian Cataloguing in Publication Data

Wilton, David A.
Macroeconomics: theory and policy in Canada

3rd ed.
Includes bibliographical references and index.
ISBN 0-201-52776-6

1. Macroeconomics. 2. Canada - Economic policy - 1971- .* 3. Canada - Economic conditions - 1971- .* I. Prescott, David Martin, 1948- II. Title.

HC115.W57 1992 339'.0971 C92-093938-4

ISBN 0-201-52776-6

A B C D E F — ALG — 97 96 95 94 93 92

Printed and bound in Canada.

Table of Contents

Preface

In response to suggestions from many instructors, we have substantially revised and re-organized the third edition of *Macroeconomics: Theory and Policy in Canada.* Besides updating all of the statistical data, we have included two new theoretical chapters on the aggregate demand-aggregate supply (*AD-AS*) model and have added new sections to most chapters to reflect recent theoretical and policy developments, such as real business cycle theory and the Bank of Canada's price targets for the 1990s.

The major addition to *Macroeconomics* is a block of three chapters (7, 8, and 9) that provides a thorough treatment of the aggregate demand and supply model. Chapter 7 begins by developing the aggregate demand curve and the classical long-run aggregate supply curve. After investigating the comparative static results of this model, a short-run aggregate supply curve is derived based on the assumption that nominal wages are contractually fixed in the short run. The contractually fixed nominal wage rate is assumed to depend on the expected price level.

Chapter 8 is devoted entirely to examining the significant role that price expectations play in determining how the economy reacts to disturbances. We present a detailed analysis of adaptive and rational expectations models, and in a case study we test these two models of expectations formation by examining Canadian evidence on inflation forecasts. The new classical price surprise supply curve is derived and the controversial policy ineffectiveness proposition is explained and discussed. Real business cycle theory is also presented in Chapter 8 and a case study looks at Canadian evidence on four theories of the business cycle -- Keynesian, monetarist, new classical, and real business cycle theories. Finally, in an appendix we present an explanation of the signal extraction problem and its relationship to the new classical theory of the short-run aggregate supply function.

Chapter 9 returns to the practical policy issues posed by demand and supply shocks. The argument for and against demand management policies are presented for both types of shocks. An interesting feature of this analysis is the macroeconomic implications of cost of living allowance (COLA) clauses that are incorporated into many Canadian wage contracts. We explain how COLA clauses reduce the output and employment effects from demand shocks but amplify the output and employment effects of negative supply shocks.

To make room for this extended treatment of the *AD-AS* model, we have streamlined our treatment of the Keynesian cross and *IS-LM* models (three chapters in the second edition have been compressed into two chapters in the third edition) and have removed two of the *IS-LM-PEP* chapters (dealing with demand and supply shocks). The *IS-LM-PEP* model is used to study the problem of inflation and the *AD-AS* model is used to study the effects of shocks and various stabilization policy options.

Besides the new theoretical chapters on the *AD-AS* model and the necessary updating of statistical data, there are substantial revisions and improvements to other chapters. For example, Chapter 10 includes sections on recent new Keynesian theoretical developments, including a discussion of the cost of adjusting prices, efficiency wage models, insider-outsider models, and hysteresis effects. Rather than devoting one separate chapter to policy developments in Canada, we have integrated our discussion of Canadian policy directly into the relevant chapters. For example, our extended discussion of Canadian monetary policy now appears in the same chapter in which we analyze the theoretical implications of anti-inflation monetary policy under different expectational assumptions.

This text is designed for a second-year Canadian macroeconomics course, with the only prerequisite being an introductory economics course. Since we review the National Accounts, the Keynesian cross model, the multiplier process and the basic *AD-AS* model, even this prerequisite is not binding. While we develop our basic models in diagrammatic form, the algebraic counterpart for the *IS-LM* model is also provided in Chapter 5, for which only high school algebra is required. There is no calculus requirement to use this text, although students with calculus will find footnotes pointing out shortcuts in the analysis.

The length of this book reflects the fact that some Canadian universities offer full-year macroeconomics courses. For one-semester courses, a number of chapters will have to be omitted. If balance-of-payments adjustments are covered in another course, Chapters 6 and 12 could be omitted. Similarly, if a subsequent course covers the money, consumption, and investment "components" of a macroeconomic model, then Chapters 15-17 could be omitted. Alternatively, one could include either the balance of payments chapters and/or the "components" chapters and omit either the block of chapters dealing with the *AD-AS* model (Chapters 7-9) or the block of chapters dealing with the *IS-LM-PEP* model (Chapters 10-14).

It is a pleasure to acknowledge our indebtedness to those who have contributed to the publication of the various editions of this book. First we must thank our own teachers who shaped our understanding of macroeconomics: E. Domar, A.G. Hines, E. Kuh, R.G. Lipsey, C. McIvor, F. Modigliani, P.A. Samuelson, R.M. Solow, G.R. Sparks, R.W. Thompson, and J. Williamson. In particular, our intellectual debt to Richard Lipsey is enormous. It is Lipsey's integration of the Phillips curve into the *IS-LM* framework that forms the basis of the *IS-LM-PEP* model developed and used in Part IV of this book.

We would also like to thank the following people for their comments on the chapters and drafts of the various editions of this text:

E. Adomait (University of Guelph)
S. Alam (University of Calgary)
I. Anderson (University of Saskatchewan)
F. Atkins (University of Calgary)
B. Bernanke (Princeton University)
R. Bodkin (University of Ottawa)
L. Christofides (University of Guelph)
P. Davenport (University of Alberta)
S. Drugge (University of Alberta)
C. Fader (Wilfrid Laurier University)
S. Ferris (Carleton University)
D. Foot (University of Toronto)
E. Forget (University of Manitoba)
B. Forster (University of Wyoming)
D. Hum (University of Manitoba)
S. Kardasz (University of Waterloo)
D. Laidler (University of Western Ontario)
B. Lewis (Wilfrid Laurier University)
R. Milbourne (formerly of Queen's University)
F. Millerd (Wilfrid Laurier University)
T. Myatt (University of New Brunswick)
T. Nguyen (University of Waterloo)
E. Nosal (University of Waterloo)
J. Pesando (University of Toronto)
N. Ridler (University of New Brunswick)
A. Robertson (Wilfrid Laurier University)
B. Scarfe (University of Regina)
B. Scarth (McMaster University)
P. Sephton (University of New Brunswick)
S. Sheffrin (University of California, Davis)
J. Smithin (York University)
A.M.C. Waterman (University of Manitoba)
R. Wirick (University of Western Ontario)

The comments and suggestions we have received have undoubtedly helped us to improve the clarity and content of the book, but none of the above individuals should be held responsible for any deficiencies in the third edition.

Finally, we would like to thank Gail Copeland, Kateri Lanthier, Brian McGuinness, and Shirley Tessier at Addison-Wesley for their friendly cooperation and assistance in preparing the third edition.

Part 1

CHAPTER 1

Introduction

Canada's Frail Economy Viewed as Most Important Problem: Fully six-in-ten Canadian citizens (60 percent) cite some facet of the economy as being the most important problem facing the country today. Forty-three percent mention inflation or a related economic problem, while 17 percent specifically state that unemployment is the nation's principal problem at present [January 1991].[1]

The Gallup research organization regularly asks Canadians what is *the* most important problem facing the country. Inflation, the economy, and unemployment have been the dominant responses to this question since the early 1970s (see Figure 1.1). From 1973 to 1982, inflation and the economy, considered as one problem,[2] was the most frequent response, with about one-half of those interviewed selecting it as the most important problem facing the country; in three 1974 Gallup poll surveys, 70 percent of those interviewed claimed that inflation, high prices, and the economy was *the most important* problem facing the country. From 1983 to 1989, unemployment held the top position in this Gallup poll; in 1984 and 1985 over one-half of those interviewed responded that unemployment was *the* most important problem facing the country. With one brief exception (1988–89), a *macroeconomic* problem was cited by more than 50 percent of all respondents as *the* most important problem facing the country; in most years inflation, the economy, and unemployment received 60 percent to 80 percent of all responses.

---

1 *The Gallup Report*, Press Release, 14 January, 1991.

2 Unfortunately, the Gallup poll lumps together answers involving inflation, high prices, and the economy.

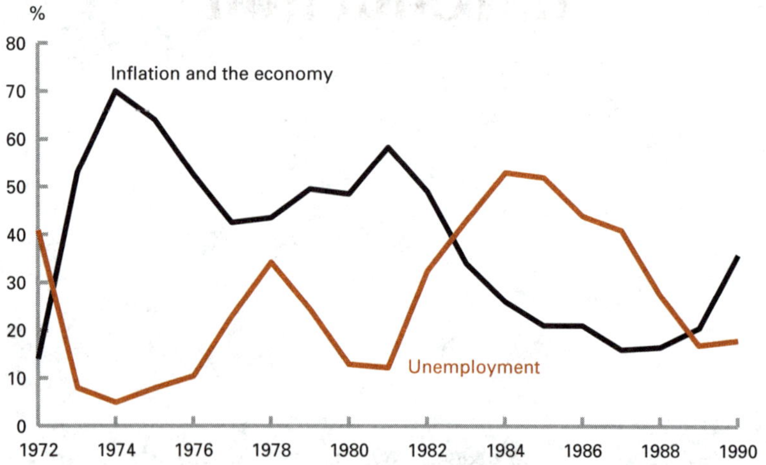

Figure 1.1 Gallup poll responses (1972–90) to the question: "What is the most important problem facing the country?"

Source: The Gallup Poll of Canada, *The Gallup Report* (Toronto: Canadian Institute of Public Opinion).

The reason why inflation dominated public opinion surveys from 1973 to 1982 is rather obvious. Double-digit inflation hit the Canadian economy in the mid-1970s and during the years from 1973 to 1982 the Canadian inflation rate averaged 9.6 percent. However, in 1982 the unemployment rate jumped from 7.5 percent to 11.0 percent, and remained above 10 percent for the next four years. Not surprisingly, in early 1983 unemployment overtook inflation in public opinion polls as the most important problem facing Canadians. In short, public opinion concerning the major problems facing the country has mirrored movements in two key macroeconomic variables — the inflation rate and the unemployment rate.

Besides long bouts of double-digit inflation and double-digit unemployment, a number of other macroeconomic problems emerged during the 1970s and 1980s. In 1980–81 the prime interest rate charged by banks shot up to 20 percent, "double" double-digit. Although the prime interest rate fell to less than 10 percent in 1987, it climbed back to almost 15 percent in 1990. The value of the Canadian dollar in the foreign exchange market also behaved like a yoyo: $1.03 U.S. in October 1976, $0.69 U.S. in February 1986 (a record low) and back up to $0.87 in August 1990. Then there was the tremendous "run up" of federal government debt during the 1980s, reaching $400 billion in 1991. Since

1982, the federal government deficit has exceeded $20 billion each year, with a record high deficit of $31.4 billion in 1985.

This roller coaster ride of the economy in the 1970s and 1980s stands in stark contrast to the economic tranquillity and prosperity of the 1960s. During the 1960s the unemployment rate was typically less than 5 percent (for example, 3.4 percent in 1966), the inflation rate averaged 2.5 percent, and the prime interest rate hovered around 6 percent. With the exception of the year 1967, for eight successive years (1962–69) *real* output increased by at least 5.2 percent per year (in 1967 the growth rate dipped to 3.3 percent). For the 1960s decade as a whole, the federal government enjoyed a surplus of revenues over expenditures. The Canadian economic record of the 1960s ("the good old days") provides a startling contrast to the turbulent 1970s and 1980s. Given our recent bouts of high inflation, high unemployment, high interest rates, and record high government deficits, macroeconomics certainly has a lot of explaining to do.

Output, Unemployment, Inflation, and Interest Rates

Having indicated the scope and importance of macroeconomics, we briefly review several key concepts from your introductory economics course and describe in a little more detail the historical record of the Canadian economy during the 1960–90 period. Unlike *micro*economics which studies the *individual* components of the economic system (such as individual consumer behaviour, the demand for corn flakes, and the supply-price decision of the profit-maximizing firm), *macro*economics is concerned with economic *aggregates* and the *overall* performance of the economy. In macroeconomics, the myriad different types of goods and services that are produced within the economy are *aggregated* into one giant output or product market. In the macroeconomic arena, output is just output (not hamburgers, hot dogs, pizza, and chicken wings) and attention is focused on aggregate issues. For example, is there sufficient aggregate demand to employ the economy's total labour force? On the other hand, it is the microeconomist's job to analyze how much of each particular type of good will be bought and sold, the role of relative prices, and the allocation of resources to different industries.

The major economic aggregates that macroeconomics seeks to explain are the total level of output within the economy, the unemployment rate, the inflation rate, and the interest rate. Figures 1.2, 1.3, and 1.4 present annual data for gross domestic product, the unemployment rate, the annual percentage change in the consumer price index, and the prime interest rate for the 1960–90 period. Each of these key macroeconomic variables will be discussed in turn.

Gross Domestic Product

Gross domestic product (GDP) represents the value of all final goods and services produced in the economy during a given interval of time. Each individual item produced within the economy is multiplied by its price tag and the total value is added together with that for all other final goods and services produced. In 1990 the value of goods and services produced in the Canada totalled \$678 billion, in comparison with only \$39 billion in 1960.

Although GDP has increased at a very rapid pace since 1960, much of this increase can simply be attributed to inflation (see Figure 1.4). A much more meaningful measure of total output is obtained by removing the general effects of inflation and evaluating each year's output in terms of a common set of prices. For example, if we measure the value of goods and services produced in 1990 in terms of the price tags that existed in *1986* (a benchmark year selected by Statistics Canada), then 1990 GDP is only \$571 billion (not \$678 billion). This new calculated value, obtained by imposing 1986 price tags on the quantity of goods and services produced in 1990, measures 1990 GDP in *constant* 1986 dollars — that is, dollars that have a *constant* level of purchasing power equal to that which prevailed in 1986. To avoid confusion, our original value for 1990 GDP (\$678 billion), measured in terms of *current* 1990 prices, will be referred to as *current* dollar (or *nominal*) output.

Re-evaluating 1960 GDP in terms of 1986 price tags, we find that the 1960 GDP of \$39 billion *current* dollars was equivalent to \$164 billion *constant* 1986 dollars; the *constant* 1986 dollar GDP value in 1960 is 4.2 times higher that the *current* dollar value because a 1960 dollar has 4.2 times the purchasing power of a 1986 dollar. Even though *current* dollar GDP increased by a factor of 17.4 between 1960 and 1990 (from \$39 to \$678 billion), in real *constant* dollar terms GDP increased by a factor of only 3.5 during the 1960–90 period (from \$164 to \$571 billion 1986 *constant* dollars). By correcting for the general effects of inflation, the *constant* dollar GDP magnitude records the *real* value of goods and services produced, and can be utilized to determine the overall growth rate within the economy.

In Figure 1.2(a) we have plotted *real* GDP expressed in *constant* 1986 dollars for the 1960–90 period; we have used a logarithmic vertical scale where equal vertical distances (such as 200 to 300 and 400 to 600) represent equal percentage changes (50 percent). Over this 30-year period, real output (GDP) has grown at an average annual rate of 4.2 percent. The major reasons for this growth in real output are increased supplies of factor inputs (labour and capital), as well as improved technology and greater labour productivity. During the 1960–90 period employment increased from 5.96 million to 12.57 million workers, an average annual increase of 2.5 percent. With respect to improved technology and greater labour productivity, real output per worker (measured in 1986 dollars) increased from $27,562 in 1960 to $45,398 in 1990, an average annual labour productivity increase of 1.7 percent. Thus increases in

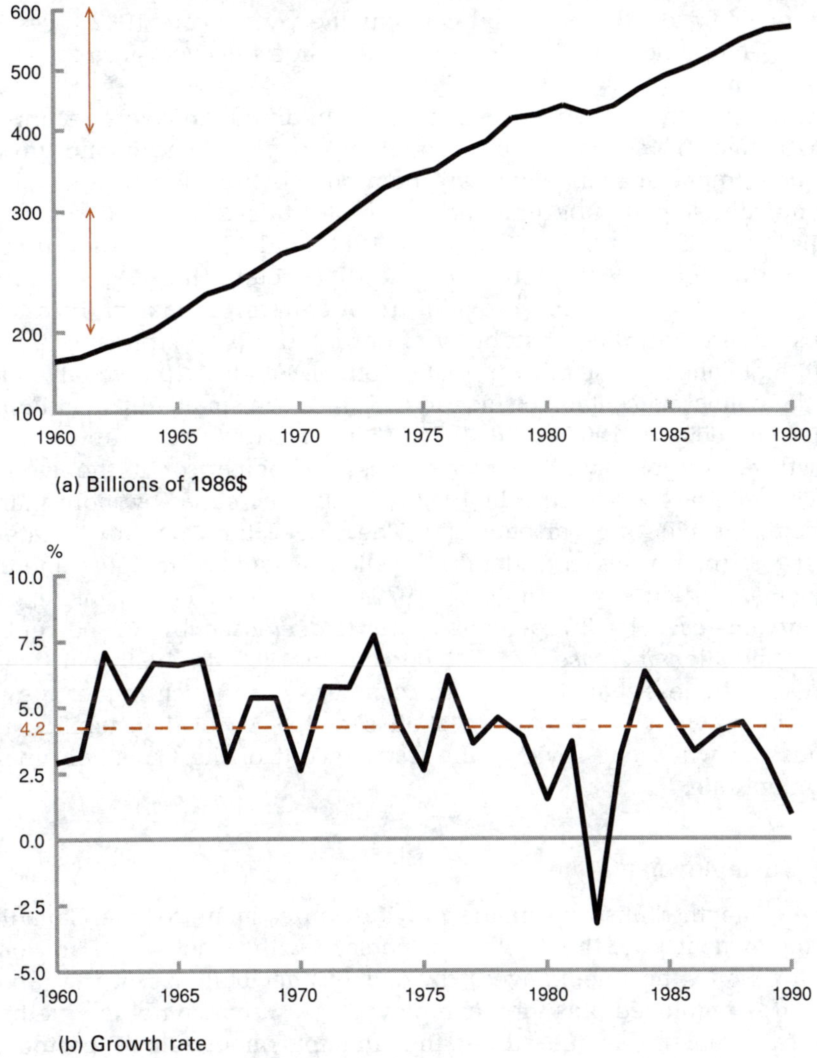

Figure 1.2 Gross domestic product, 1960–90

employment (2.5 percent) and increases in labour productivity (1.7 percent) account for the average growth rate in real output (4.2 percent).

This average annual 4.2 percent growth rate, however, conceals an important negative trend — a flattening out of the slope of the GDP line in Figure 1.2(a) around the year 1975. Compared to a 5.2 percent average annual growth rate from 1960 to 1974, the Canadian economy grew by only 3.3 percent (on average) during the 1975–90 period. As discussed below, this latter period contains the very severe 1982 recession when real GDP declined by 3.2 percent, the largest decline since the Great Depression.

Although the Canadian economy maintained an average annual growth rate of 4.2 percent over the 1960–90 period, economic growth has been quite uneven. There are numerous bumps and wiggles along the upward-sloping GDP line. For example, this GDP line takes small "dips" in 1960–61, 1967, 1970, 1975, 1980, and 1990; and then there's a big "dip" in 1982 (to better see the dips, rotate the page a quarter turn in a clockwise manner). Macroeconomics has traditionally focused on the cyclical instability of output and (un)employment.

To highlight the instability in real output, in Figure 1.2(b) we have plotted the annual percentage change in real GDP. The small "dips" in Figure 1.2(a) (in 1960–61, 1967, 1970, 1975, 1980, and 1990) show up as "low" growth rates (typically 2.5 percent or less, in comparison to the average growth rate of 4.2 percent). In 1982 real GDP *decreased* by more than 3 percent, the big "dip" in panel (a). The plot of the GDP growth rate in Figure 1.2(b) reveals considerable cyclical instability in the Canadian economy, particularly during the 1970s and 1980s. For example, real output *increased* by 3.7 percent in 1981, *decreased* by 3.2 percent in 1982, and then *increased* by 3.2 percent in 1983. In 1990 real output increased by less than 1 percent in comparison to much higher growth rates in previous years. As we shall see, this cyclical instability also stands out when one reviews the track record of the Canadian unemployment rate.

The Unemployment Rate

Once a month Statistics Canada provides an estimate for the Canadian unemployment rate: the number of persons without jobs who are looking for work (the unemployed) divided by the total size of the labour force (the employed plus the unemployed). (A discussion of the methodological problems in measuring the unemployment rate is postponed until Chapter 3.) Figure 1.3 presents the Canadian unemployment rate for the 1960–90 period.

The cyclical instability of the Canadian economy during this 30-year period is clearly evident from this plot of the unemployment rate. Following a recession in 1960–61 (with unemployment rates of 7 percent),

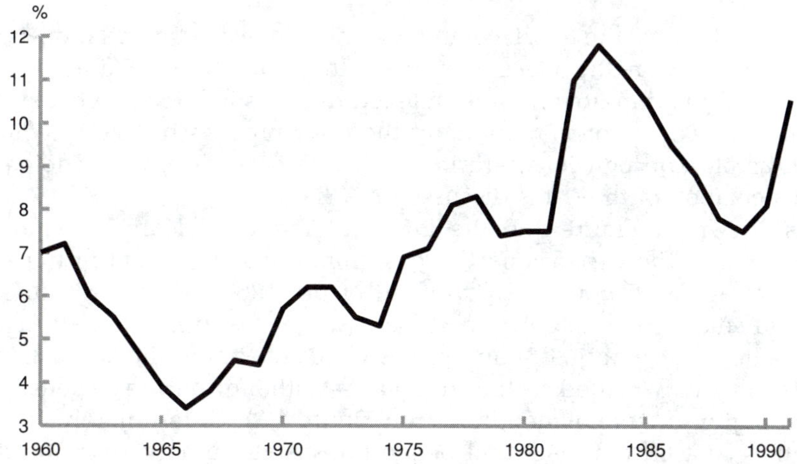

Figure 1.3 Unemployment rate in Canada, 1960–91

the vigorous economic expansion of the 1960s drove the unemployment rate down to 3.4 percent in 1966 and at the end of the 1960s the unemployment rate still remained well under 5 percent. In 1969–70 the Canadian government imposed a restrictive monetary policy (see Figure 1.5), sending the Canadian economy into a recession and the unemployment rate back up to 6.2 percent in 1971. A period of economic growth during the 1972–74 period, fostered by expansionary monetary policy, brought the unemployment rate back down to 5.3 percent in 1974. From 1975 through 1981 the unemployment rate drifted upwards but exhibited only minor variation, ranging from 6.9 percent in 1975 to 8.3 percent in 1978. Faced with continuing double-digit inflation, in the early 1980s the Bank of Canada instituted a very tight monetary policy (see Figure 1.5) and the unemployment rate jumped over to 12 percent in 1983, the highest rate since the 1930s. During the next six years real GDP grew at an average rate of 4.3 percent (see Figure 1.2(b)) and the unemployment rate drifted downwards, bottoming out at 7.5 percent in 1989. With inflation still a problem in 1989–90, the Bank of Canada once again instituted another dose of tight monetary policy (see Figure 1.5) and the Canadian unemployment rate climbed back up to 10.5 percent (as of March 1991).

As is clear from Figure 1.3, during the 1970s and 1980s the unemployment rate trended upwards and was characterized by much wider fluctuations. Successive recessions have witnessed higher peak unemployment rates, and the *minimum* unemployment rate during the expansion of the 1980s was higher than the *maximum* unemployment rate during the recession of the early 1960s.

The Inflation Rate

By far and away the most commonly used measure of inflation is the *rate of change* in the Consumer Price Index (CPI) (see Figure 1.4). In 1974 the Canadian government indexed the personal income tax system to the CPI (see Chapter 3); many of the government's transfer payments (such as old age pensions) are indexed to the CPI. (The methodology of the calculation of the CPI is discussed in Chapter 3.)

As shown in Figure 1.4, the inflation rate was clearly moving upwards during the expansionary 1960s, from about 1 percent in the early 1960s to almost 5 percent by the end of the 1960s. From 1969 to 1970 the Canadian government pursued a restrictive anti-inflationary monetary policy (see Figure 1.5) and in the words of Prime Minister Trudeau, "inflation was wrestled to the ground" — although at the expense of a much higher unemployment rate (see Figure 1.3). Unfortunately, in 1973 inflation "got off the mat" and began to escalate rapidly, reaching double-digit rates in 1974–75. Notwithstanding the imposition of wage and price controls from 1975 to 1978 and the Bank of Canada's conversion to monetarism in 1975 (see Chapter 14), the Canadian inflation rate stabilized at 8 percent to 9 percent in the latter half of the 1970s. With the inflation rate again drifting upwards in the early 1980s (hitting 12.5 percent in 1981), the Bank of Canada implemented a very tight monetary policy, which produced the worst recession since the 1930s. Given unemployment rates in the 11–12 percent range, the inflation rate quickly moderated to 5.8 percent in 1983 and 4.4 percent in 1984, the lowest

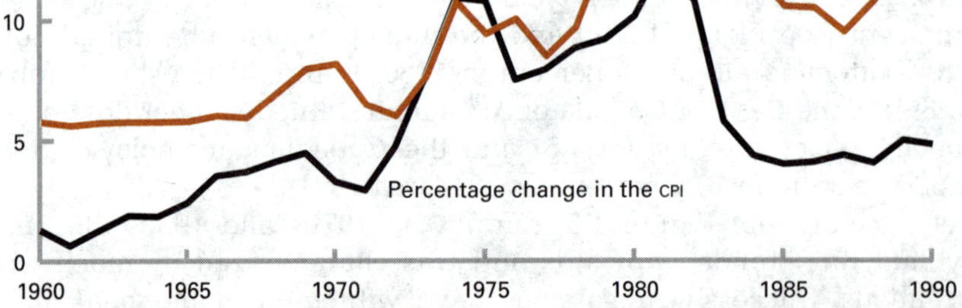

Figure 1.4 Inflation and interest rates, 1960–90

The Inflation Rate

By far and away the most commonly used measure of inflation is the *rate of change* in the Consumer Price Index (CPI) (see Figure 1.4). In 1974 the Canadian government indexed the personal income tax system to the CPI (see Chapter 3); many of the government's transfer payments (such as old age pensions) are indexed to the CPI. (The methodology of the calculation of the CPI is discussed in Chapter 3.)

As shown in Figure 1.4, the inflation rate was clearly moving upwards during the expansionary 1960s, from about 1 percent in the early 1960s to almost 5 percent by the end of the 1960s. From 1969 to 1970 the Canadian government pursued a restrictive anti-inflationary monetary policy (see Figure 1.5) and in the words of Prime Minister Trudeau, "inflation was wrestled to the ground" — although at the expense of a much higher unemployment rate (see Figure 1.3). Unfortunately, in 1973 inflation "got off the mat" and began to escalate rapidly, reaching double-digit rates in 1974–75. Notwithstanding the imposition of wage and price controls from 1975 to 1978 and the Bank of Canada's conversion to monetarism in 1975 (see Chapter 14), the Canadian inflation rate stabilized at 8 percent to 9 percent in the latter half of the 1970s. With the inflation rate again drifting upwards in the early 1980s (hitting 12.5 percent in 1981), the Bank of Canada implemented a very tight monetary policy, which produced the worst recession since the 1930s. Given unemployment rates in the 11–12 percent range, the inflation rate quickly moderated to 5.8 percent in 1983 and 4.4 percent in 1984, the lowest

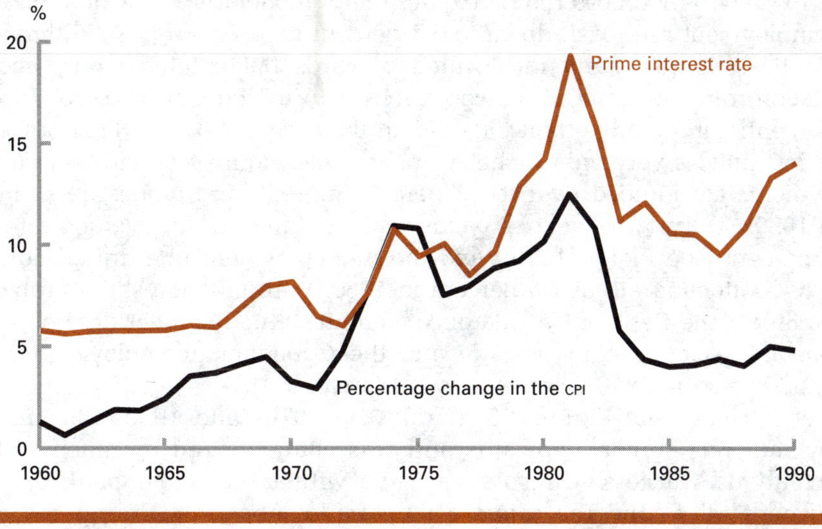

Figure 1.4 Inflation and interest rates, 1960–90

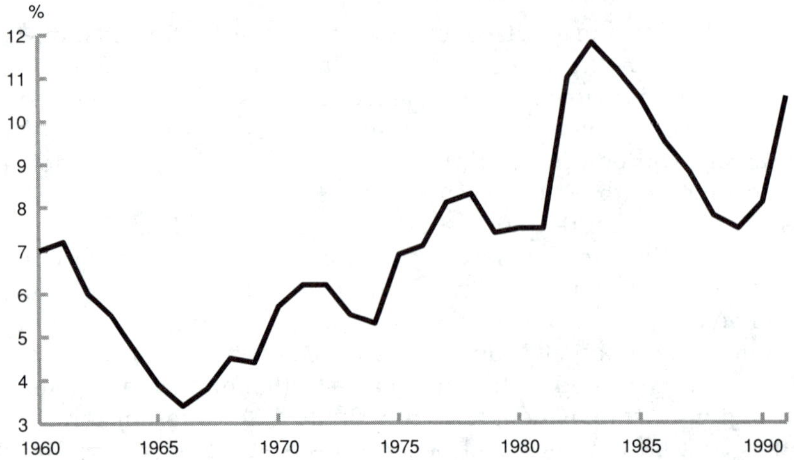

Figure 1.3 Unemployment rate in Canada, 1960–91

the vigorous economic expansion of the 1960s drove the unemployment rate down to 3.4 percent in 1966 and at the end of the 1960s the unemployment rate still remained well under 5 percent. In 1969–70 the Canadian government imposed a restrictive monetary policy (see Figure 1.5), sending the Canadian economy into a recession and the unemployment rate back up to 6.2 percent in 1971. A period of economic growth during the 1972–74 period, fostered by expansionary monetary policy, brought the unemployment rate back down to 5.3 percent in 1974. From 1975 through 1981 the unemployment rate drifted upwards but exhibited only minor variation, ranging from 6.9 percent in 1975 to 8.3 percent in 1978. Faced with continuing double-digit inflation, in the early 1980s the Bank of Canada instituted a very tight monetary policy (see Figure 1.5) and the unemployment rate jumped over to 12 percent in 1983, the highest rate since the 1930s. During the next six years real GDP grew at an average rate of 4.3 percent (see Figure 1.2(b)) and the unemployment rate drifted downwards, bottoming out at 7.5 percent in 1989. With inflation still a problem in 1989–90, the Bank of Canada once again instituted another dose of tight monetary policy (see Figure 1.5) and the Canadian unemployment rate climbed back up to 10.5 percent (as of March 1991).

As is clear from Figure 1.3, during the 1970s and 1980s the unemployment rate trended upwards and was characterized by much wider fluctuations. Successive recessions have witnessed higher peak unemployment rates, and the *minimum* unemployment rate during the expansion of the 1980s was higher than the *maximum* unemployment rate during the recession of the early 1960s.

inflation rate since 1971. For the next four years (1985–88) inflation fluctuated in the narrow interval between 4 percent and 4.4 percent. However, during the boom of the late 1980s, inflation rose to 5 percent in 1989, resulting in a further dose of a restrictive anti-inflationary monetary policy by the Bank of Canada.

Interest Rates

In Figure 1.4 we have also plotted the prime interest rate charged by banks. The interest rate spikes in 1969–70, 1980–81, and 1989–90 mark the three episodes of tight monetary policy (discussed above). Perhaps the most striking feature of interest rate movements is their very close association with movements in the inflation rate. Interest rates have followed the ups and downs of the inflation rate, rising in the 1974–82 period and falling in 1983. As we shall see in Chapter 3, there are very good economic reasons for a close association between interest rates and inflation rates. While the *spread* between interest rates and the inflation rate — often referred to as the *real interest rate* (see Chapter 3) — generally remained at less than 4 percent throughout the 1960s and 1970s, interest rates in the 1980s remained stubbornly high even though the inflation rate declined substantially. For example, in 1988 the interest rate of 11 percent was 7 percent higher than the inflation rate of 4 percent.

Other Macroeconomic Indicators

In Figure 1.5 we have plotted three other important macroeconomic indicators: the Canadian foreign exchange rate, the annual percentage change in the money supply, and the federal government budgetary position. As one can see in Figure 1.5(a), the government *fixed* the value of the Canadian dollar at $0.925 U.S. during the 1962–70 period. When the Canadian dollar was allowed to float in the foreign exchange market in June 1970, it remained relatively close to $1.00 U.S. until 1976. (Note that the Canadian dollar actually traded for *more* than $1.00 U.S. in 1974 and again in 1976.) However, from 1976 to 1986 it was all downhill; in early 1986 the Canadian dollar hit a low point of $0.69 U.S. Since 1986 the Canadian dollar has climbed back up, rising to $0.87 U.S. in 1990. Chapter 6 provides an extensive discussion of foreign exchange rates and an analysis of the macroeconomic implications of *fixed* versus *floating* foreign exchange rates (see also Chapter 12).

Turning to monetary and fiscal policy, Figure 1.5(b) presents the annual percentage change in the money supply during the 1960–90 period. Given the variability of the inflation rate over this period, we have plotted both the annual percentage change in the *nominal* money supply (M1) and the annual percentage change in the *real* money supply

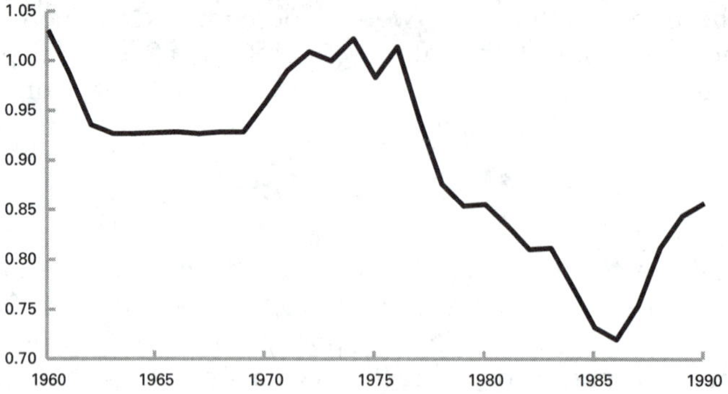

(a) Canadian exchange rate (in U.S.$)

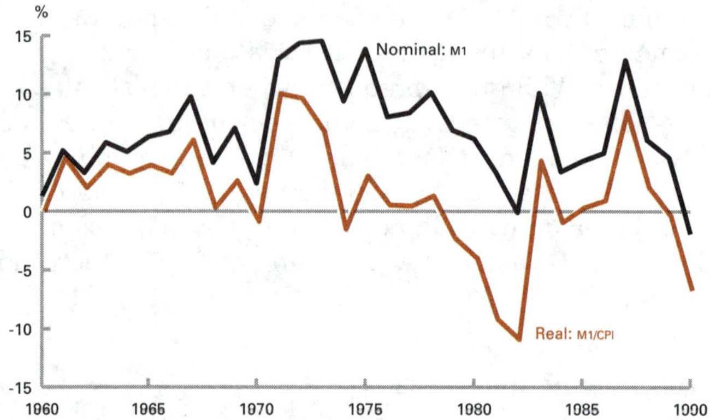

(b) Annual percentage change in the money supply

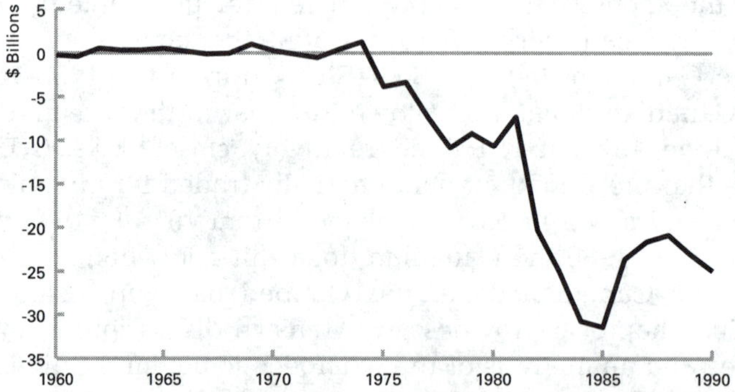

(c) Federal government budgetary position

Figure 1.5 Other macroeconomic indicators

(the percentage change in the nominal money supply minus the inflation rate).

After a decade of expansionary monetary policy and gradually increasing inflation rates, the Bank of Canada sharply curtailed the growth rate of the money supply in 1970 as the Trudeau government tried to "wrestle inflation to the ground." Having pushed the Canadian economy into a mini-recession in 1970–71 with its tight monetary policy, the Canadian government adopted a *very expansionary* monetary policy during the 1971–75 period (the nominal money supply increased, on average, by 14 percent each year). With all of this *extra* money sloshing around the economy, double-digit inflation broke out in 1974. In 1975 the Bank of Canada converted to a monetarist policy approach and committed itself to fighting inflation by *gradually* reducing the growth rate of the money supply (see Chapter 14). The growth rate of the money supply was curtailed sharply in 1981–82, forcing interest rates up to 20 percent (see Figure 1.4) and unemployment rates up to 12 percent (see Figure 1.3). With the inflation rate still running at 5 percent in the late 1980s, the Bank of Canada once again reduced the money supply (a negative change in the nominal money supply in 1990), precipitating another recession.

In Figure 1.5(c) we have plotted the surplus/deficit position (on a national accounts basis) for the federal government. As shown in this graph, the federal government generally ran a *surplus* of revenues over expenditures from 1964 to 1974, reaching a peak surplus of over $1.3 billion in 1974. However, since 1975 the government sector has been continually in a *deficit* position, with the deficits rapidly escalating in size during the 1982–85 period (reaching over $31 billion in 1985). These very large government deficits in the mid-1980s became a major public policy issue and a constraint on governments using fiscal policies. The issue of the size of the government deficit and debt (the accumulation of all past deficits) is discussed in Chapter 9.

Schools of Thought in Macroeconomics

In contrast to the economic tranquillity of the 1960s, the macroeconomic record of the 1970s, 1980s, and early 1990s raises a number of obvious questions:

1. Why does the unemployment rate now cycle between 7.5 percent and 12 percent? Why can't we get the unemployment rate back down to 4 or 5 percent?
2. What caused the outbreak of double-digit inflation in 1974? Why did it last for almost ten years? Is there anything that the government can do to prevent another outbreak of high inflation?

3. Is there any way to eliminate high inflation without going through a major recession, such as that which occurred in 1981–82 (with double-digit unemployment rates lasting until 1985)?
4. Will interest rates ever return to 6 percent?
5. Why can't the federal government balance its budget?

As is obvious from this series of rhetorical questions (and the Gallup poll results cited above), macroeconomics deals with many of the important issues and questions of the 1980s and 1990s.

Any subject that tackles such challenging questions is bound to generate a considerable amount of controversy. Contemporary macroeconomics is no exception. While there are numerous skirmishes among academic macroeconomists over rather abstract theoretical issues (such as *rational* inflation expectations, see Chapter 8), perhaps the major battleground in contemporary macroeconomics has been in the public policy arena. What role should the government play in attempting to navigate the economic system through troubled macroeconomic waters? Could some of the macroeconomic grief of the 1970s and 1980s have been avoided by a more "enlightened" government policy? If so, what were the major policy errors during this period? Do these policy errors account for the instability and upward trend in unemployment, inflation, and interest rates? In short, is there a better way for the government to run the economy? If not, is the Canadian economy totally at the mercy of uncontrollable external factors (such as the U.S. business cycle, U.S. monetary policy, and crises in the Middle East)?

On one side of this public policy debate are economists who take their inspiration from the British economist, John Maynard Keynes (1883–1946). Writing during the economic collapse of the 1930s, Keynes argued that government should take an active role in stabilizing the economic system (see Chapters 4 and 5 for a discussion of Keynesian economics). Keynes rejected the "classical" view that the free market system could be relied upon to maintain full employment (see Chapter 7 for a discussion of classical macroeconomics).

Followers of Keynes believe that by altering fiscal policy (changing government spending or tax rates) or monetary policy (changing the money supply), the government can moderate economic fluctuations and improve the overall performance of the economic system. The business cycle can be tamed by appropriate changes in government policy. In the words of Nobel laureate Franco Modigliani of the Massachusetts Institute of Technology (MIT), the central message of Keynesian economics is that a free enterprise system "*needs* to be stabilized, *can* be stabilized and therefore *should* be stabilized." From the 1940s to the early 1970s, this Keynesian view of an *activist, interventionist* government stabilization policy dominated macroeconomic thought.

However, the worsening economic muddle of the 1970s seriously undermined the Keynesian position that the judicious use of monetary and fiscal policies could maintain the economy on a high growth, low unemployment, and low inflation path. The prevailing Keynesian orthodoxy was strongly challenged by Milton Friedman, formerly of the University of Chicago and also a Nobel Prize winner. Given Friedman's belief that the growth rate in the money supply is the key determinant of macroeconomic activity, this new school of macroeconomic thought came to be known as *monetarism*.

To control inflation, monetarists stress the need to control the money supply. In addition, monetarists strongly argue against discretionary changes in monetary or fiscal policy for stabilization purposes. Given the "long and variable lags" of monetary policy and the difficulty in forecasting future economic events, monetarists question the ability of the government to implement a "correctly timed" Keynesian policy. Rather than run the risk of destabilizing the economy by implementing an "incorrectly timed" stabilization policy, monetarists believe that a *non-interventionist* policy approach is the safest course. Simply keep a steady hand on the policy levers — that is, keep the money supply growing at a steady low rate — and let the natural forces of the free market system take care of any economic problems. Like their classical predecessors, monetarists believe that the economic system is inherently stable and runs best when the government leaves it alone. It should be noted that Milton Friedman won an important convert to monetarism in 1975: Gerald Bouey, the Governor of the Bank of Canada.

During the 1980s monetarists were pushed off the centre of the macroeconomics stage by another group of even more conservative economists, calling themselves "new classical" economists. The leader of the new classical school of macroeconomics is Robert Lucas, also of the University of Chicago. While new classical economists share monetarist beliefs in a *non-interventionist* approach to government policy, new classical economists are very critical of the economic theory (or, more precisely, the lack of economic theory) behind Keynesian and monetarist macroeconomics. New classical economists stress that economic agents always optimize. Making economic decisions that are in their best interest, people are always in a state of equilibrium. There are no unexploited economic opportunities for government policy to capture. New classical macroeconomists assume that wages and prices are completely flexible.

As discussed in Chapter 8, a key new idea in the new classical approach to macroeconomics is the concept of *rational* expectations. Rational people are assumed to use all available information in forming their expectations of the future and rational people will not make any systematic forecasting errors (which the government might be able to exploit). In forming their expectations of the future, people will take into account the effects of the policy that they expect the government to implement. People will change their economic behaviour in *anticipation* of the government implementing a new policy, thus negating any effect when the policy is actually implemented. To borrow a football analogy, if the defense can predict what the offense will do, then by making appropriate defensive changes the offense will be completely nullified. New classical economists believe that *anticipated* government policy changes will have no effect on output or employment levels. Rational expectations seemed to drive the final nail in the Keynesian policymaker's coffin.

However, events of the 1980s called into question a key prediction of new classical macroeconomics. The Bank of Canada introduced a very restrictive monetary policy to eradicate double-digit inflation and the economy promptly plunged into the worst recession since the 1930s. This tight monetary policy of the 1980s (which was evident to anyone who read the financial press) clearly affected output and employment levels.

New classical economists responded by building *real* business cycle models, models which emphasized the importance of *real* factors (such as shifts in production technology) in explaining the business cycle. "New" Keynesians responded to the challenge of new classical macroeconomics by building models to explain why wages and prices may not quickly adjust to bring about market equilibrium, even when people act in their own best interests and form their expectations rationally (see Chapter 10). Under such circumstances, government policy may be able to smooth out some of the fluctuations in unemployment and output.

As is clear from the preceding discussion, much of the controversy in macroeconomics has been of a political economy nature: "liberal" Keynesians and "conservative" monetarists and new classical economists debating the appropriate role for government policy. An important objective of this textbook is to assess this important public policy debate between the followers of Keynes and the proponents of a laissez-faire approach to government policy. In developing simple models that will allow us to understand the interrelated problems of inflation, unemployment, and high interest rates, we pay particular attention to the key assumptions within the model that separate Keynesians from monetarists and new classical economists. Although there are important *theoretical* differences between the various schools of thought, many of the key differentiating assumptions and predictions are of an *empirical* nature. Throughout this textbook we will repeatedly use real world data, often in the form of special case studies, to illustrate the empirical validity of key theoretical assumptions or predictions of macroeconomic models. Theories that are contradicted by the "facts" are unlikely to improve our understanding of the macroeconomic system, or lead to the formulation of an "enlightened" government policy.

Outline of the Textbook

In Part 1 of the textbook we discuss a number of important conceptual issues concerning the measurement of income, output, inflation, and unemployment. Chapter 3 examines the economic costs and consequences of inflation and unemployment.

Part 2 of the book presents the basic models of Keynesian economics, beginning with a review of the *Keynesian cross* model and the multiplier process in Chapter 4. Interest rates and the money market are added to the model in Chapter 5, producing the *IS-LM* diagram (*IS* and *LM* are two curves in the diagram). The *IS-LM* model is used to illustrate Keynes's diagnosis of the causes of chronic unemployment, as well as Keynes's policy prescription (fiscal policy). Chapter 6 extends the *IS-LM* model to include balance of payments considerations (a *BP* curve) and the foreign exchange rate. Throughout these three chapters we assume *in*flexible wage and price levels, the key assumption of Keynesian economics.

Part 3 of the textbook permanently relaxes the assumption of *in*flexible price levels. Chapter 7 introduces the concept of aggregate supply and solves for the equilibrium price level using an aggregate demand and supply diagram; the implications of the classical flexible wage–price model are contrasted to the Keynesian fixed wage–price model. Chapter 8 considers the important role of price expectations in macroeconomics. Adaptive expectations and rational expectations models are contrasted, and the basic conclusions of new classical macroeconomics are presented. Using an aggregate demand and supply model, Chapter 9 reviews the various stabilization policy issues in the debate between Keynesian, monetarist, new classical, and new Keynesian economists over the appropriate role for fiscal and monetary policy.

Part 4 of the textbook turns to the problem of inflation. Chapter 10 analyzes the determinants of inflation, using the Price Expectations Phillips (*PEP*) curve as the key integrating concept, and concludes with a review of new Keynesian theory concerning why prices and wages may not be flexible. The next chapter incorporates the *PEP* curve into the *IS-LM* model, thereby providing an integrated *IS-LM-PEP* model of inflation, output, and unemployment. Chapter 12 is devoted to balance of payments adjustments for an open inflationary economy (the *IS-LM-BP-PEP* model). Chapter 13 tackles the elusive inflation–unemployment trade-off issue and completes our analysis of the long-run properties of the *IS-LM-PEP* model, paying particular attention to the long-run effects of monetary policy on inflation, interest rates, output, and unemployment. Chapter 14 explores the short-run adjustment costs associated with the implementation of an anti-inflationary restrictive monetary policy, and the potential usefulness of temporary wage and price controls.

Chapter 14 concludes with an examination of Canadian monetary policy in the 1970s and 1980s.

Part 5 of the book provides a more detailed discussion of some of the individual components of a macroeconomic model. Chapter 15 delves more deeply into the money market, providing a simple money supply model that illustrates how the Bank of Canada is able to control the money supply. In addition, Chapter 15 analyzes the demand side of the money market and compares several theoretical approaches to the demand for money. The final two chapters return to the market for goods and services. Chapters 16 and 17 review recent developments in consumption and investment theory.

CHAPTER 2

The National Income and Expenditure Accounts

Grown-ups love figures. When you tell them that you have made a new friend, they never ask you any questions about essential matters. They never say to you, What does his voice sound like? What games does he love best? Does he collect butterflies? Instead, they demand: How old is he? How many brothers has he? How much does he weigh? How much money does his father make? Only from these figures do they think they have learned anything about him.

Antoine de Saint-Exupéry[1]

As Disraeli, a former prime minister of Great Britain, once said, "There are lies, damn lies and statistics." While many may share Disraeli's skeptical view of statistics, without statistical information it would be impossible to formulate rational policies on important issues such as inflation, unemployment, the trade balance, interest rates, immigration, poverty, the environment, and a seemingly endless list of other public policy issues.[2] Canada's system of National Income and Expenditure Accounts provides an enormous amount of information on the economic health of the country. Although the system of national accounts does not in itself explain the country's economic performance, economists can use the information contained in the accounts to describe economic

1 Antoine de Saint-Exupéry, *The Little Prince* (New York: Harcourt Brace & World, 1943), pp.16–17.

2 During and just after World War II, the deficiency in available economic information became obvious. In 1945 the White Paper on Employment and Income outlined the government's economic objectives for the reconstruction period and a group was established to develop a set of National Income and Expenditure Accounts for Canada. Estimates of GDP were published regularly in the second half of the 1940s but it was not until 1952 that annual estimates for the period 1926–50 were available.

events. The data may show, for example, that a period of slow economic growth was accompanied by a drop in Canadian exports or a decline in business investment. In addition to merely describing economic events, the data contained in the national accounts are necessary for establishing important causal relationships between economic variables. Knowledge of these underlying economic relationships is essential if appropriate policy prescriptions are to be made. Economists often disagree over the nature of these underlying relationships and consequently different policy recommendations are proposed. Such disagreements can be settled only by an appeal to the facts, many of which are recorded in the national accounts. In this chapter we will describe the structure of the Canadian National Income and Expenditure Accounts and discuss some of the conceptual issues involved in measuring such concepts as national income.

The bottom line of the National Income and Expenditure Accounts is **gross domestic product** (GDP). One way to compute this number is to add up the expenditures that are made on currently produced final goods: this is the expenditure approach. During the process of producing these final goods, incomes are generated: employees earn wages and salaries, owners of stocks and bonds earn interest and dividends, and landlords receive rents. The final price tag of any item can always be broken down into the income payments — wages, rent, interest, and profits — that were paid out during the process of production. This breakdown of market prices into factor incomes — the income approach — ignores the effect of government subsidies and sales taxes, which are also reflected in market prices. (We will return to this point below.) Adding up all the income payments will always give the same total as adding up the total value of goods produced. If this were not so, part of the value of goods produced would mysteriously disappear from the economic system. The income approach to measuring economic activity also yields gross domestic product (GDP). By their definitions, the income and expenditure approaches must give identical estimates of current economic activity.

Expenditure Approach to GDP

First we should clarify an important point. GDP does not refer to the total value of all goods and services traded in the economy over a certain period of time, since this would greatly overestimate the level of economic activity. It is important to distinguish between *final* goods and *intermediate* goods.

Consider, for example, the manufacture of an automobile. A measure of the economic activity involved in producing this item is its market value. However, the production of the automobile involves many stages, some of which are separated by market transactions between different firms. Engine parts, tires, and cassette decks are all sold to the firm that finally assembles the car. If the value of these intermediate transactions were added together along with the value of the finished automobile we would obviously overestimate the value of economic activity involved. The value of the engine parts, tires, and cassette decks would all have been double-counted, once on their own account and again in the market value of the car itself.

To avoid this pitfall we distinguish between *final* goods, such as the automobile, which are primarily bought by households, and *intermediate* goods and services, which are purchased by firms and used up in the production process. Examples of intermediate goods and services are the electricity and advertising purchased by the Ford Motor Company and the paper bought by Addison-Wesley Publishers. The important feature of intermediate goods and services is that their value is fully incorporated into the price of the final product. This argument suggests that we are certainly safe in adding up the value of goods and services bought by households, since these items do not become part of another product — they are final goods and services. On the other hand, we should not include in GDP the goods and services bought by firms, because these are all intermediate goods and services whose value will be included in the final goods that firms sell.

Unfortunately, there is an exception to this straightforward classification. Firms' purchases of capital goods are included in GDP. For example, the cars purchased by a firm for the use of its sales representatives, or a new building constructed by a firm to store inventories are all included in GDP under the heading "Business Investment" in the national accounts. Since the lives of the car and the building are much greater than one year, the cost of the car and the building will not be fully reflected in the value of this year's output of final goods. (Firms do not charge very high prices in the first year of operation to recover the full cost of a new building.) Bear in mind, however, that national income accountants are interested in measuring *current* economic activity and regardless of whether the car (or new building) is used up entirely in the current year, economic activity took place to produce it. Consequently, purchases of capital goods are included in the current year's GDP. The reader might argue that, by classifying capital goods as final goods, double-counting will exist, since costs associated with that part of the car and building that are used up during the current production period (referred to as depreciation costs) certainly will be reflected in the market price of the final goods and services. Over several years the full cost of the car and the building will have been fully incorporated into the value of the firm's output of final goods through the inclusion of depreciation costs in the total costs of production. At that time, both the car and the building will have been counted twice in GDP; first when they are newly produced and second as they are used up in the production of other final goods. It is precisely for this reason that the word "gross" is used. In order to measure *net* economic activity in any given year we must subtract total depreciation costs from GDP. Over time, the subtraction of depreciation costs will remove the double counting in GDP that results from the inclusion of newly produced capital goods. We will meet the concept of depreciation again when we consider the income approach to the national accounts.

To recapitulate, gross domestic product measures the total value of market economic activity: the value of all *final* goods and services produced. The spending on these final goods can be categorized into a number of groups or expenditure components according to the nature of the item and the type of transaction involved. The four major categories are: personal expenditures; investment expenditures; government expenditures — goods and services purchased by the government; and net exports, which is the difference between Canada's exports and imports of currently produced goods and services. We will consider each of these separately. For reference, Table 2.1 shows some details of the GDP side of the National Income and Expenditure Accounts for 1990.

Table 2.1 Gross Domestic Product, 1990

	Billions of dollars		Percent of GDP
Personal expenditures		402.1	59.3
Goods	204.1		
Services	198.0		
Business investment		121.7	17.9
Residential construction	44.8		
Non-residential construction	36.3		
Machinery	43.2		
Value of physical change in inventories	2.6		
Government expenditure		149.3	22.0
Current	132.5		
Capital	16.8		
Exports		168.4	24.8
Imports		–165.5	24.4
Residual error		2.0	
Gross domestic product		677.9	

Personal Expenditure

By far the largest component of GDP is *personal expenditure* on goods and services. This spending amounted to $402.1 billion in 1990, which represented 59 percent of the value of GDP ($677.9 billion). Included in this total are such things as households' purchases of food, beer, sports equipment, textbooks, automobiles, and the services of hairdressers and dentists. Economists have found it useful to distinguish between total household *spending* on goods and services and total household *consumption* of goods and services. The former is recorded in the national accounts, while the latter refers to the quantity of consumer goods used up during the year. The difference between the two arises from the fact that some items that consumers purchased in the current year are not entirely consumed during the year. These items, such as automobiles and furniture, are called durable goods. A car that costs $10,000 and lasts ten years yields, on average, transportation services of $1,000 per year. A measure of actual household consumption, rather than spending, would include the amount households spend on services and non-durable goods plus that part of the stock of durable goods used up during the year. From a practical point of view, the calculation of household consumption, which requires an evaluation of the flow of services from existing durable goods, is more difficult than the calculation of household spending, which simply requires information on current expenditure. However, the reason the national accounts include current expenditure is that GDP is a measure of annual economic activity: the value of annual production of all goods and services. A car produced during the year should be included in this total regardless of the fact that it is fully consumed only after several years of use.

Business Investment

The second category of expenditure listed in Table 2.1 is *business investment*. It should be stressed that when we speak of "business investment" in this book, we mean the additions to the physical stock of capital goods. In general usage the word "investment" frequently refers to any action that is expected to give a return in the future. Thus, the purchase of gold bullion, Canada Savings Bonds, or a Tom Thomson painting may be considered investments. However, none of these actions represents the purchase of a newly produced item and therefore they do not represent current economic activity. Purchases of this type simply involve the exchange of assets between individuals, and while one of the traders concerned may consider he has made an investment, no new physical capital goods have been produced, and the transaction is not recorded in the national accounts. It follows from this that the buying of stocks or bonds, or the takeover of one firm by another, is not investment as we mean it here.

Three items have been recorded separately under the heading of "Business Investment" in the national accounts: (1) residential construction, (2) spending on plant and equipment, and (3) the value of the physical change in inventories. The first represents the value of new additions to the stock of residential buildings such as single detached houses, duplexes, and apartment buildings. It is a matter of convention that this item is recorded as business investment even though a good part is actually household expenditure. The second item, plant and equipment, refers to nonresidential construction such as office buildings, factories, and warehouses as well as machinery of all types, such as lathes, typewriters, and cars purchased by firms. The third item is the value of the physical change in inventories. This quantity can be either positive or negative. A positive number indicates that production during the year exceeded sales and inventories rose. If we measured total economic activity simply by adding up the various expenditure items, we would underestimate total annual production to the extent that inventories have accumulated. On the other hand, sales may exceed production, in which case inventory stocks would decline, and to measure current production we must subtract the change in inventories from the total value of sales.

The total of these three subcomponents is referred to as gross business investment. As pointed out above, the word "gross" indicates that no account has been taken of the fact that in producing the current year's output of goods and services, part of the capital stock wears out. *Net* business investment is equal to gross business investment less the investment required to replace the worn-out capital stock. Since it is gross business investment that is added to the other expenditure components, this total is referred to as *gross domestic product*. It is a gross measure of annual production because part of the national wealth, the stock of capital goods, is consumed during the process of production.

Government Expenditures

Since the services that the local, provincial, and federal governments supply are not sold in the marketplace, there is no price that can be used to value the productive activities of government. National income accountants therefore equate the value of this production to the costs of providing it. That is to say, the value of government output is defined by the value of inputs purchased by government. The national accounts distinguish between current and capital expenditures. Capital spending by governments consists chiefly of construction activities such as building schools, hospitals, roads, airports, and other capital projects. All levels of government are included but the investment spending of government business enterprises such as the Canadian National Railway is recorded under business investment. Current spending includes purchases of goods and services by all levels of government. These goods and services are required by, for example, schools, hospitals, and the armed services. The major cost incurred by government in providing services is wages and salaries paid to civil servants, teachers, nurses, police officers, military personnel, and other public employees. This expense is included in the "at cost" measure of government production.

It should be emphasized that government expenditures relate to purchases of *goods and services* only. Government spending on transfer payments such as family allowances, unemployment insurance, interest on the public debt and the like are not included. Unlike the money spent on teachers' salaries, for example, none of these outlays is for the production of goods or services and consequently there is no corresponding government production. The family allowance program, for instance, is a vehicle for transferring income from one group to another. The act of transferring this income is one of the services that the government provides, and it is valued in the national accounts at the cost, in terms of the materials (paper for the cheques) and personnel (civil servants who prepare the cheques), of providing this service. The dollar value of family allowances actually transferred does not represent any equivalent productive activity and is not entered into the national accounts under government expenditure or anywhere else. It is important therefore to distinguish between two concepts of total government spending. The first is the national accounts concept, which measures the contribution of government to total economic activity, and the second is total government spending for all purposes, much of which involves transferring income from one set of citizens — taxpayers — to another set of citizens — for example, the recipients of interest on the public debt, unemployment insurance, subsidies, and capital assistance. Certainly from a quantitative point of view the distinction is an important one. Table 2.1 shows that the contribution to total production of all levels of government was $149.3 billion in 1990, amounting to 22 percent of GDP. Total government spending, on the other hand, including transfers to the private sector, amounted to $29.3 billion, or 44 percent of GDP.

Imports and Exports

The Canadian economy is frequently referred to as being "open." By this it is meant that Canada has strong economic links to the rest of the world, the United States in particular. For example, in 1990 Canada exported 25 percent of that year's total production of goods and services and imported a similar quantity of foreign goods and services. In addition to the international flow of goods and services, Canadians also make an enormous number of international transactions of a purely financial nature. Canadians place funds in U.S. banks, and buy foreign governments' bonds, to list just a couple of examples. In Chapter 6 we will discuss more fully the balance of payments accounts that summarize Canada's international transactions. For the moment we will concern ourselves only with the international flows of goods and services, since the estimate of Canada's annual production of final goods and services must obviously include those that are produced in Canada and exported to foreigners. Similarly, Canadian expenditure on goods and services brought into the country must be excluded from the calculation of Canadian GDP.

Consider again the case of a car assembled in Canada. If part of the car, say the engine, has been imported into Canada, then the value of the car in the marketplace overstates the value of Canadian economic activity. The import content of the car should be subtracted from its market price in order to properly estimate domestic economic activity. It is extremely difficult to do this on a product-by-product basis. It is much easier to add up the value of imports as they enter the country. Since all imports must ultimately become final goods or services one way or another, the import-content adjustment to GDP is made by simply subtracting the annual value of imports from the total value of expenditure on final goods and services.

The final component of Table 2.1 is the *residual error*. This error arises because the two theoretically equivalent approaches to computing the value of annual production never agree in practice. Conceptually the income and expenditure methods should give identical numerical estimates but inevitably errors and omissions make this impossible. A simple resolution is adopted, namely, to take the average of the two totals. Tables 2.1 and 2.2 show that in 1990 the income approach yielded an estimate of GDP that exceeded the expenditure by \$4.0 billion. The two estimates are brought into line by adding half the difference (\$2.0 billion) to the expenditure total and subtracting a similar amount from the income total.

Expenditure Shares of GDP

It is convenient at this point to introduce a symbolic representation of the four major expenditure components of GDP. These are usually thought of as the sources of demand for the economy's output. Throughout the text the following symbols will apply: personal expenditure or consumption C, business investment I, government expenditures G, and net exports $X - M$, where X and M represent exports and imports, respectively. The following identity will play an important role in the models that will be developed in later chapters.

$$Z = C + I + G + (X - M), \tag{2.1}$$

where Z is aggregate expenditure on Canadian-produced goods and services.

Figure 2.1 shows how the ratios of these major expenditure components to GDP have varied over the period 1947–90. The vertical scales are identical for all of the graphs, which allows us to make comparisons between the variability of each series. *Personal expenditure*, or consumption, is by far the largest component of GDP. Just after World War II there was an enormous pent-up demand for new consumer goods. In the late 1940s, consumption accounted for nearly 68 percent of GDP. Then, right through to the early 1980s, the consumption share trended down to a low point of just below 56 percent. Since then, the consumption share has risen fairly quickly. It is interesting to note that the government share has been almost the mirror image of the consumption share. If government "crowds out" the private sector, it seems to be consumption that gets pushed aside by government. Throughout most of the period, government's share rose fairly smoothly and steadily. It is only since the early 1980s that the political pressure to reduce the size of government has had an effect on the government's expenditure, even though this pressure began much earlier. Figure 2.1 also shows clearly that *personal expenditure* and *government expenditure* are relatively stable components of aggregate demand.

As noted above, focusing on only government-produced goods and services seriously understates the increasing role of *total* government activity. In 1990 total government spending[3] was $295.3 billion, of which only $132.5 billion was spent on goods and services (the G component of GDP). Transfer payments to persons accounted for a further $83.2 billion. The fastest growing component of total government spending in recent years, however, has been the interest payments on government debt. High interest rates and the growing volume of government debt have combined to push interest payments made by all levels of government up to $63.4 billion in 1990. In turn, government revenues totalled $275.8 billion in 1990. Personal and corporate income taxes brought in $146.2 billion and a further $87.7 billion was collected through indirect taxes such as sales taxes. In 1990 total government

---

3 All levels of government, but excluding transfers from one level of government to another, for example, federal government transfers to provincial governments.

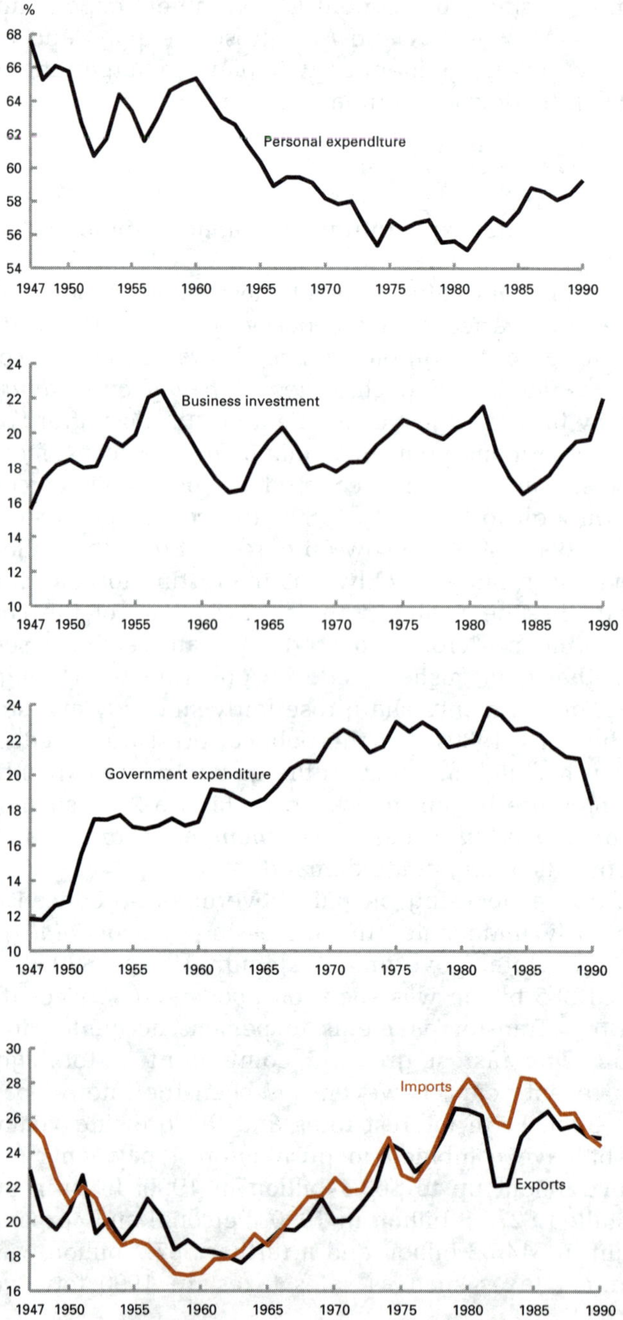

Figure 2.1 Percentage shares of expenditure components of GDP, 1947–90

revenues represented 41 percent of GDP, as compared with only 25 percent in 1950.

At the other extreme of variability are expenditures on *business investment*. The share of this component has not revealed any strong trend over the 44-year period (it starts low and finishes high, but the peak year was in 1957). The most noticeable feature of the investment graph is its relatively high variability compared to the other components. Generally, investment spending is procyclical, that is, its share rises during periods of economic expansion, such as the early 1970s and mid- to late 1980s, but shrinks during slumps, such as the early 1980s.

The shares of *imports* and *exports* have been plotted together so that the trade balance is apparent. For most years since World War II, imports have exceeded exports. Both imports and exports have grown rapidly since the mid-1960s, but there has been a levelling off in the past ten years.

The Income Approach to GDP

As we pointed out earlier, the value of any final product can be decomposed into the payments that are made to the owners of the factors of production. The production costs that determine the factory-gate price of a car, for example, are in fact the incomes received by the owners of the factors of production that make the car. These costs include wages and salaries paid to workers, interest income paid to individuals and firms that have made loans to the car manufacturer, and the car manufacturer's profits, which go to the owners in the form of dividends or retained earnings. The cost of intermediate goods bought by the car manufacturer, such as tires, can be broken down similarly into the incomes paid to the owners of the factors of tire production. The sum of these costs or incomes would give us the value of the car "at factor cost." The corresponding figure for the economy as a whole is called Net Domestic Income (NDI) at factor cost.

The first five lines of Table 2.2 show the breakdown of NDI into the various income components. The largest by far is *labour income*, which amounted to $383.2 billion, or 72.8 percent of NDI in 1990. Figure 2.2 shows the shares of the four major income components between 1960 and 1990. Both labour's share and the share accounted for by *interest and dividend income* have risen over this period. The interest and investment income component has almost tripled over this period. The main reason has been the steady upward trend in interest rates. The share of *unincorporated business income*, however, has shown a steady downward trend. Corporate *profits*, although highly variable, have shown no particular trend. Finally, Figure 2.2 demonstrates that labour's share of domestic income is countercyclical, while profits are procycli-

Table 2.2 Gross Domestic Product, 1990

	Billions of dollars
Add:	
Total labour income	383.2
Corporation pre-tax profits	47.9
Interest and investment income	57.9
Farm income	2.7
Nonfarm, unincorporated business income	37.2
Inventory valuation adjustment	–2.5
Equals:	
Net domestic income at factor cost	526.5
Add:	
Indirect taxes less subsidies	76.5
Capital consumption allowances	76.9
Residual error	–2.0
Equals:	
Gross domestic product at market prices	677.9

cal. Notice that *wages and salaries* account for their largest shares during economic slumps (1982, 1990), whereas the profit share is at a peak in boom times and at a low during recessions.

An item so far unexplained is the *inventory valuation adjustment*, which appears on line six of Table 2.2. Consider a year in which there is general inflation but the actual physical stock of inventories is unchanged. Let us consider a typical firm that has one unit of inventory at both the beginning and the end of the year. Suppose the initial price of this inventory is \$100 but inflation during the year raises the price of the inventory to, say, \$105. Since changes in the value of inventories are treated as income for the firm, the additional \$5 will show up as part of profits (the second item of Table 2.2) and hence it will contribute to net national income. However, in the expenditure version of the national accounts, the corresponding item is the value of the physical change in inventories. Since in our example there has been no *physical* change in inventories this item would be zero. This is appropriate since an objective of the national accounts is to measure the value of current economic activity. If inventories rise in value simply because of inflation but remain unchanged in physical quantity, then their rise in value does not represent economic activity and should not be included in GDP. The upshot is that an adjustment is required if the income and expenditure methods are to agree. In the present example, profits would be adjusted downwards by \$5; that is, the inventory valuation adjustment would be \$5. Table 2.2 shows that in 1990 the inventory valuation adjustment due

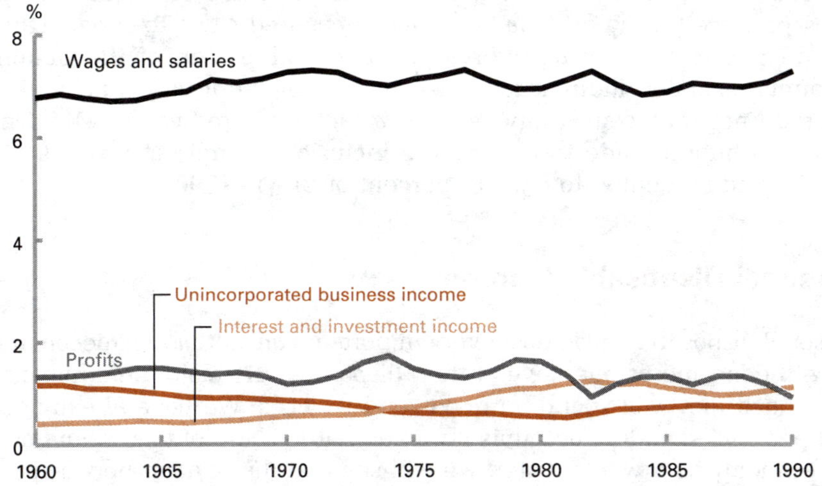

Figure 2.2 Shares of income components of NDI, 1960–90

to inflation amounted to $2.5 billion, which was subtracted from the total payment to factors of production to arrive at net domestic income.

To obtain GDP from NDI three adjustments have to be made. To explain this let us return to the example of the car. The incomes generated in producing the car sum to the factor cost of the car. This will differ from the market price on account of (1) depreciation costs, which cover the wear, tear, and obsolescence of the capital stock incurred during the car's production, (2) indirect taxes such as sales taxes levied on the car, and (3) any subsidies the manufacturer received from the government. We add the first two and subtract the third from the factor cost of the car to obtain its market price. At the aggregate level these three adjustments to net national income give us gross domestic product at market prices.

We argued earlier that GDP is a gross measure of current production and, over the long term, capital goods are double-counted — once on their own account when they are first produced, because capital goods are treated as final goods, and again in the value of the products that they help produce, because firms include the cost of capital depreciation in the price of the good or service produced. We now find that there is a second factor that causes GDP to exceed the value of current production (which is actually measured by net domestic income) — *indirect taxes*. Suppose, for example, that when the government raises an additional $1 billion in sales taxes the level of economic activity is unchanged. In this case GDP would rise by $1 billion because indirect taxes have increased, but total output would remain the same. The increased rate of sales tax drives up the market price of goods and services produced, thus artificially raising measured GDP. To repeat, there are no physical goods and services on the other side of the national accounts to match indirect taxes — only higher prices — and indirect taxes do not represent a payment for a factor of production. The artificial contribution made to GDP by the inclusion of indirect taxes is substantial and amounted to over 11 percent of GDP in 1990.

Personal Disposable Income

Personal disposable income is a very important concept in macroeconomics since the income people have at their disposal is the major determinant of how much they will spend on goods and services. We have already seen that personal spending accounts for a very large share of total spending in the economy as a whole. Later, we will see that the relation between personal disposable income and personal expenditure or consumption has played a major role in the development of modern macroeconomics.

In Table 2.3 the major sources of **personal income** are listed along with the deductions that the government takes out of this income. Personal income, net of these deductions, is equal to *personal disposable income*. The major sources of personal income are wages and salaries, which accounted for about 64 percent of the total in 1990. Interest, dividends, and other investment income is another important source, and

Table 2.3 Sources of Personal Income and Personal Disposable Income, 1990

	Millions of dollars
Add:	
Wages and salaries	383,244
Net farm income	2,708
Net income of nonfarm unincorporated business, including rent	37,221
Interest, dividends and miscellaneous investment income	87,814
Add current transfers:	
From government	83,461
From corporations	740
From nonresidents	907
Personal income	596,095
Subtract:	
Income taxes	99,647
Contributions to social insurance and government pensions	32,085
Other transfers to government	3,360
Personal disposable income	461,003

one which has grown considerably in recent years because of historically high interest rates. In 1990, this component accounted for 14.7 percent of personal income. Almost as important as investment income, are the **transfers** from government to individuals. In 1990, 14 percent of personal income came in the form of government assistance cheques such as family allowances and unemployment insurance. The last two items that make up personal income are relatively small. Transfers from corporations to persons include charitable donations and bad debts that are written off. Transfers from nonresidents include gifts.

The observant reader will have noticed that personal income, at $596.1 billion, actually exceeded NDI in 1990, which was only $526.5 billion (see Table 2.2). How can it be that the incomes actually received by persons exceeded the total amount of income that was generated through the production of goods and services? The reason for this is that there is a considerable amount of double-counting in personal income. Suppose, for example, that the only source of personal income is the income that is generated through productive activity and that all of this income (NDI) is paid out to persons.[4] In this case personal income will be exactly equal to NDI. Now if the government steps in and taxes individual incomes and then channels this money back to the same people in the form of family allowance cheques, personal income will rise because personal income includes all government transfers to persons. Personal income will now exceed NDI by the value of all family allowance cheques.

From the point of view of individual purchasing power, after-tax or disposable income is more important than personal income. As Table 2.3 shows, income taxes are the most important part of total government deductions, although compulsory contributions to social insurance and government pensions are also significant.

Real and Nominal GDP

In previous sections we have considered in some detail how the value of current economic activity is measured. In 1990 the market value of goods and services produced was $677.9 billion. This figure is sometimes referred to as GDP measured in current dollars because the goods and services are valued at current year prices. The corresponding figure for 1989 GDP was $651.6 billion. Again, this value of goods and services produced was evaluated at current prices, that is, the prices prevailing in 1989. The change in the value of GDP between 1989 and 1990 was

4 In fact not all of NDI is paid out to persons. In 1990 over $12 billion was kept by corporations as retained earnings to finance further expansion. In 1989 firms retained over $21 billion.

$26.3 billion, which represents 4 percent growth. A natural question to ask is, how much of this increase represents an increase in the physical quantity of goods and services produced and how much simply reflects increases in the prices of these goods and services? This is an important question because it is increases in the physical quantity of goods and services that create job opportunities for those entering the labour force and for those currently unemployed.

In order to separate these two factors economists distinguish between **nominal** GDP (GDP measured in current prices) and **real** GDP, which measures the physical quantity of goods and services produced annually. Obviously these *real* goods and services have to be evaluated in dollars, since we cannot add together apples and oranges. Table 2.4 illustrates how this would be done for a simple economy that produces just two items, shirts and haircuts.

In this hypothetical economy the value of nominal GDP rose by $80 or 160 percent over the period 1986–90. However, if the production of shirts and haircuts in 1990 is evaluated at 1986 prices we obtain a figure of $80, which represents real GDP in 1990 evaluated at 1986 prices. Real growth over this four-year period would be measured by the difference between $80 and $50, equalling 60 percent growth. Note that the actual output of shirts rose by 50 percent while the quantity of haircuts doubled. We would expect real GDP to rise by an amount somewhere between these two. Our actual measure of 60 percent lies closer to 50 percent than 100 percent because shirts have a higher price tag than haircuts and so the growth of shirt production is more heavily weighted than the growth in the number of haircuts.

Figure 2.3 shows how, in per capita terms, nominal and real GDP have changed over the years 1960–90. While the nominal per capita GDP series shows uninterrupted growth, the real GDP series identifies periods of strong physical growth, such as 1970–73, as well as years when the Canadian economy experienced recessions, such as 1975 and 1982–83. Without a correction for inflation, the change in nominal GDP can give a very misleading indication of the change in the production levels of goods and services. Because it is changes in real GDP that have a major influence on unemployment rates, economists prefer to use information on real GDP rather than nominal GDP for judging the economy's performance.

The Measurement of Inflation

In the next chapter many of the conceptual issues involved in the measurement of inflation and unemployment will be discussed. Since a comprehensive measure of the rate of inflation is implicit within the National Income and Expenditure Accounts, it is convenient to introduce this topic here.

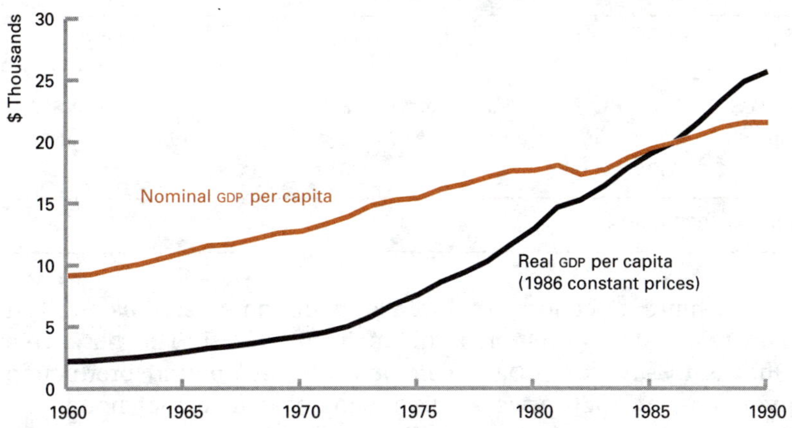

Figure 2.3 Real and nominal per capita GDP, 1960–90

If all of the thousands of individual prices in the economy changed by the same proportion over any given time interval, then we would have no difficulty at all in measuring the percentage change in the *general price level*; it would simply be identical to the individual price changes. In practice individual prices move by different amounts and not necessarily in the same direction. The change in the general price level is an average of the individual price changes.

One comprehensive measure of inflation is the GDP *implicit price index*. It is comprehensive in that the prices of consumer goods and services, investment goods, and exports all enter the calculation. In the previous section the distinction was made between nominal GDP, the value of currently produced goods and services evaluated at their current prices, and real GDP, the value of those same goods and services evaluated at their prices in some base period. Implicit in these calculations is an overall measure of the average change in prices from the base period to the current period. The argument begins with the observation that the value of a group of items can be expressed in terms of the product of a quantity measure and a price measure. Consider, for example, $5.00 worth of apples which cost 50¢ each. Obviously the value of the apples can be expressed as the product of 10 (quantity of apples) times 50¢ (the unit price of apples). This idea can be extended to the measurement of GDP. By dividing nominal GDP (current value) by real GDP (a measure of quantity) we obtain the unit price of GDP implied by our measure of physical quantity. The *ratio* of nominal to real GDP is consequently referred to as the GDP **implicit price index**.

Table 2.4 An Illustration of Real and Nominal GDP

1986 Nominal GDP	1990 Nominal GDP	1986 Real GDP*
4 shirts at $10 = $40	6 shirts at $15 = $ 90	6 shirts at $10 = $60
5 haircuts at $2 = $10	10 haircuts at $4 = $ 40	10 haircuts at $2 = $20
$50	$130	$80

*evaluated at 1986 prices

The shirt–haircut economy of Table 2.4 will again serve as an illustration. The relevant information is given in Table 2.5. The base year is 1986; that is to say, real GDP is calculated by evaluating production in any given year at 1986 prices. This means of course that nominal and real GDP have the same value in 1986, namely $50, so that their ratio is one. The unit price of real GDP is therefore unity in 1986. By 1990 nominal GDP reached $130. But measured in terms of 1986 prices, real GDP in 1990 was $80. The ratio of the value measure of GDP to the real or quantity measure of GDP gives the implicit unit price of GDP, which in 1990 was 1.625. Consequently, in this illustration, the unit price of GDP increased 62.5 percent over the period 1986–90. Note that this overall measure of inflation is a weighted average of the increases in the price of shirts (50 percent) and the price of haircuts (100 percent) and that the price of shirts is more heavily weighted because shirt production contributes more to GDP than haircuts.

At the present time, the constant dollar GDP series are calculated in terms of 1986 prices. Hence, constant dollar (real) and current GDP are identical in 1986 ($505.7 billion). Between 1986 and 1990 there were increases in both prices and output. The change in output is represented by real GDP, which is evaluated in constant 1986 prices. In 1990 GDP evaluated at 1986 prices amounted to $570.7 billion, which is 12.9 percent higher than the 1986 figure. As we have seen, current dollar GDP was $677.9 in 1990. This represents a change of 35.1 percent over the 1986 level, which includes the combined effects of price increases and the 12.9 percent increase in physical production. The average price increase over the four-year period is given by the implicit price index (IPI). The IPI is set at 100 in 1986. The value of the index in 1990 is given

Table 2.5 An Illustration of the GDP Implicit Price Index

	Nominal GDP	Real GDP	GDP Price Index
1986	$ 50	$50	1.0
1990	$130	$80	1.625

by the ratio of current to constant dollar GDP, that is, $100 \times (677.9 \div 570.7) = 118.8$. The implicit price index shows that prices rose 18.8 percent between 1986 and 1990.

The GDP implicit price index is the most comprehensive measure of inflation in that the prices of all Canadian-produced goods and services are included in the calculation. For many purposes the GDP implicit price index is too comprehensive. From the point of view of workers who are bargaining for increased wages to cover the higher cost of living, inflation means increases in the prices of the goods and services that they consume. A price index that includes the prices of capital equipment is not as useful as one that focuses on the items that a typical family purchases. The consumer price index (CPI) is designed to measure the rate of inflation that faces the typical consumer. As such, it is much more widely used than the more comprehensive GDP implicit price index. In the next chapter, which examines some of the conceptual issues that arise in the measurement of inflation and unemployment, we will take a closer look at the CPI, pointing out some of the advantages and disadvantages of this measure of inflation.

Key Concepts

gross domestic product (GDP)
net domestic income (NDI)
personal income
personal disposal income
government expenditures and transfers
real, nominal, and potential GDP
GDP implicit price index

Review Questions

1. Why is the distinction between intermediate goods and final goods important in the calculation of GDP?
2. How does the meaning of the word "investment" in the context of the National Income and Expenditure Accounts differ from its everyday meaning?
3. The value of goods and services produced by government cannot be measured by their market value because they are generally not

sold in a market. How is the value of government production determined? What is the justification for this method?

4. In 1990 all levels of government in Canada spent a total of $275.8 billion, but the national accounts (Table 2.1) show current and capital government expenditures were only $132.5 billion. How do you reconcile these figures?
5. The value of GDP includes the value of final goods and services produced for consumption, investment, and exports as well as by government. Why is it necessary to subtract imports into Canada from this total?
6. What is the distinction between gross and net investment? How is this related to the concepts of GDP and NDI?
7. Why is it important to distinguish between real and nominal GDP? Construct an example to illustrate how this distinction is made in practice.

CHAPTER 3

Inflation and Unemployment

> *Unemployment and inflation still preoccupy and perplex economists, statesmen, journalists, housewives and everyone else. The connection between them is the principal domestic economic burden of presidents and prime ministers, and the major area of controversy and ignorance in macroeconomics.*
>
> *James Tobin*[1]

In this chapter we examine the costs and consequences of inflation and unemployment, the two "most important problems facing this country today," according to Gallup poll surveys (see Chapter 1). While unemployment imposes unambiguous costs on individuals and society as a whole, the economic costs of inflation are more subtle and difficult to pin down. Before discussing the economic costs of inflation and unemployment, we briefly consider various conceptual problems that arise in measuring each.

Inflation

Even though the GDP implicit price index (which was discussed in the last chapter) is the most comprehensive measure of prices, it is not the most widely used. By far and away the most frequently employed measure of inflation is the *rate of change* in the **consumer price index** — CPI (see Figure 1.4). When the Canadian government indexed the personal income tax system in 1974 to avoid the increasing tax burden that would

1 J. Tobin, "Inflation and Unemployment," *American Economic Review*, March 1972, p. 1.

otherwise result during periods of inflation (see below), the CPI was chosen as the measuring rod for making the annual adjustments to the income tax system. In addition, many government transfer payments are indexed to the CPI and over one million Canadian workers have their wage rates directly tied to the CPI through a cost-of-living allowance (COLA) clause.

The objective of the consumer price index is to measure the cost of purchasing a given "basket" of consumer goods and services representative of the typical consumer's purchases. Statistics Canada collects information on the prices of over 600 separate items each month in 82 urban centres (with populations of 30,000 or more). Information on the expenditure patterns of Canadians is used to determine the particular weight attached to each item in the CPI.[2] Since the federal Goods and Services Tax (GST) and provincial sales taxes are included in the price, any increase in the GST (or provincial sales tax) will raise the overall level of the CPI, and increase the inflation rate for the year in which the sales tax increase takes place.

The use of a *fixed* set of weights for the individual items in the CPI basket avoids any potential problems arising from changes in the *mix* of goods purchased, which would affect the average price level. As real incomes rise over time, consumers likely shift their spending towards luxury items. For example, more meals may be eaten away from home. Since restaurant food costs more than home-prepared food, the average cost of food will rise over time simply as a result of changing spending patterns even if the prices of restaurant and home-prepared food do not change. The CPI avoids this difficulty by fixing the weight attached to the price of restaurant food at 5.04 percent and the weight attached to the price of food for home consumption at 13.01 percent. The CPI measures only price changes, and not changes in the mix of goods purchased. But this does not mean that the CPI is ideal for all purposes to which it is put. As noted above, the CPI is often used to measure the compensation that people require to offset the effects of inflation on the purchasing power of their incomes (COLA clauses are an example).

Two major difficulties arise when individual prices do not change at the *same* rate. First, people do not consume particular goods and services in exactly the same proportions. For example, low-income households spend a relatively large part of their incomes on food, so that the CPI weight for food is too low for low-income earners. Thus, in times of rapidly increasing food prices, the CPI will *under*state the rate of inflation for low-income earners.

The second difficulty arises from the fact that people respond to relative price changes by switching their spending patterns. When the

---

2 In 1986 the weights for the major components of the CPI were the following: housing (36.3 percent), transportation (18.3 percent), food (18.1 percent), recreation, reading and education (8.8 percent), clothing (8.7 percent), tobacco and alcohol (5.6 percent), and health and personal care (4.2 percent).

price of beef rises, consumers likely purchase close substitutes for beef, possibly pork or poultry. The full brunt of the rise in beef prices is therefore avoided. If consumers are compensated for the rise in beef prices to an extent determined by their original spending patterns, then they will have been *over*compensated to some degree. This argument depends on the assumption that the typical consumer spends his income in the best possible way. Given his income, there is no other bundle of goods that he can buy that gives greater satisfaction. Now if the price of beef rises and just enough additional income is given to the consumer so that he can buy his original choice of goods, he is certainly no worse off than before and most probably better off. At minimum he can buy the same bundle of goods as before; he can be no worse off. If he chooses to buy a different bundle of goods because the relative price of beef has increased (a new bundle with less beef), we know that he is now better off. Why? Because he freely chooses the second bundle in preference to the original bundle of goods (which he has enough income to purchase). The alternative bundle of goods must make him better off.

The CPI is not the ideal measure of inflation for particular groups in society whose spending patterns differ from the average Canadian's spending patterns, and it tends to *over*state the amount of compensation required to offset the effects of inflation when relative prices are changing. Nevertheless, the consumer price index, with its infrequent updating of the fixed weights, provides a reasonably good measure of how much more consumers must pay to purchase a *given* basket of goods and is almost universally used to describe the inflation process.

The Economic Costs and Consequences of Inflation

Turning to an analysis of the economic costs and consequences of inflation, let us begin by considering a *pure* inflation in which all prices (including wage rates) throughout the economy rise at the *same* rate. By abstracting from changes in relative prices (which occur regardless of whether there is general inflation or not), we are better able to understand the economic effects of inflation. Suppose that *all* prices thoughout the economy rise by 10 percent each year. What are the economic consequences of such a pure and steady inflation? Analysis of the economic costs of inflation leads to five important conclusions.

1. Inflation Diminishes the Value of Money

The real value of money is measured in terms of the *quantity* of goods and services a dollar can purchase. When prices rise, a dollar buys *fewer* goods in the marketplace; inflation diminishes the real value (purchasing power) of money. During the 1970s and 1980s, inflation almost quadrupled the level of the consumer price index (from 31 to 120). If the price of a lunch was $1.00 in 1970, inflation boosted the price to almost $4.00 in 1990. In 1970, $10 would buy ten lunches; in 1990 it didn't even buy three lunches!

2. Price Inflation Must Be Matched by Nominal Income Inflation

From our analysis of the national accounts in Chapter 2, we know that the value of all final goods produced within the economy must be distributed in the form of income payments to the various factors of production. Ignoring indirect taxes and depreciation, the sum of wages, interest, rent, and profits must be equal to the total value of goods produced. Thus if inflation increases the total value of all goods produced by 10 percent, then this additional 10 percent of total revenues must be distributed as increased income payments in the form of wages, interest, rent, or profits. If one side of the national accounts goes up by 10 percent, then the other side of the accounts must also go up by 10 percent. The inflation-induced increase in the value of all goods sold does not disappear from the economic system, but rather inflates total nominal income by 10 percent. *Price inflation must be matched by nominal income inflation.*

If all factor prices increase at the same rate, then each person's nominal income would rise by an amount exactly *equal* to the inflation rate. Such a pure inflation would have little effect on economic welfare. Each person would be able to purchase the same quantity of goods and services as before the inflation occurred. Real income and real purchasing power are not affected by pure inflation, as all prices and nominal incomes are rising at the same rate. Even if all individual incomes do not rise at the same rate, the national income accounts identity still remains valid in aggregate. Total nominal income must rise by an amount equal to the inflation rate. If one person receives an income increase that is *below* the inflation rate, some other person must receive an income increase that is *above* the inflation rate.

Our preceding analysis suggests that the *average* Canadian income earner has *not* been hurt by inflation. Is this in fact true? The ten years from 1972 through 1982 were the most inflationary period in Canadian history: the consumer price index rose by 151 percent during this ten-year period. How did the average Canadian income earner fare during this period of unprecedented double-digit inflation? In 1972 annual personal income per capita stood at $3,922. Ten years later, personal income per capita had risen to $13,214, an increase of 237 percent! During a period of unprecedented inflation, average income levels in Canada more than kept pace with rising prices.

Yet a large number of Canadians respond to opinion surveys stating that inflation is a major problem. Perhaps there is a simple psychological explanation: inflation may be subject to an optical illusion. Some people may see no connection between the prices of the things that they buy and the prices of the things that they sell (such as labour services). When prices rise for gasoline, beer, books, and rent, that's inflation (or theft)! But when wages rise, that's not inflation but rather one's well-deserved rewards for hard work. Some people may perceive only one-half of the inflation process and be blind to the other half — income earners may complain about the eroding effects of inflation, but fail to realize that without inflation their wages would be only a fraction of the size of their existing nominal values.

3. Output and Employment Do Not Depend on the Inflation Rate

The quantity of different goods bought and sold in the marketplace depends on *relative* prices, not on the actual level of prices. For example, the demand for a particular product, such as hamburgers, depends on the level of income and the relative price of hamburgers (relative to the prices of hot dogs, pizza, and chicken wings). If inflation raises all prices by 10 percent, the relative price of hamburgers does not change and the nominal income of consumers rises by 10 percent (as concluded previously). A 10 percent increase in all prices and nominal incomes has no effect on the quantity of hamburgers, hot dogs, pizza, and chicken wings demanded by consumers. Similarly, the quantity of goods supplied by firms depends on the price of the product relative to the cost of production. If prices and costs (such as wages) both rise by 10 percent, there will be no change in the quantity of goods supplied; the 10 percent increase in firm revenues from higher product prices will allow it to pay the 10 percent increase in production costs. As discussed in Chapter 7, it is the *real wage*, the nominal wage divided by the price level, that determines how many workers will be hired and how much output will be produced.

Inflation constantly changes the value of the dollar, the measuring rod for all prices (including factor prices). For example, from 1945 to 1990, consumer prices rose by a factor of 9.1 (almost 10 times)! Dollar prices in the 1990s are like 1940s prices quoted in dimes. Market transactions, however, depend on relative prices and real magnitudes, not on the length of the measuring rod. Economic decisions are unaffected by shifting all decimal points one place to the right (or left), or by thinking in terms of dimes rather than dollars. In a sense, inflation is like switching the unit of measurement from miles to kilometres — all the numerical distances increase but the real size of Canada and the relative distances between Halifax, Montreal, Winnipeg, and Vancouver do not change.

As discussed in Chapters 7, 11, and 13, a central proposition of modern macroeconomic theory is that the level of output and employment is independent of the general level of prices and the inflation rate. Living with a higher inflation rate neither increases nor decreases the level of real output and employment.

4. Interest Rates Will Reflect the Expected Inflation Rate

Will inflation have any effect on *real* wealth? For most components of personal wealth, the real value of the asset is unaffected by inflation. The prevailing market prices of houses, summer cottages, and automobiles will increase with the general inflation rate, and thus their *real* value should be unaffected by inflation. However, there is one category of wealth that would appear to be eroded in value by the process of inflation, namely, financial assets that are denoted in nominal dollar terms (such as bonds, savings accounts, and guaranteed investment certificates). Perhaps surprisingly, this assertion turns out to be incorrect. The interest rate paid on financial assets will reflect the inflation rate that is expected to prevail during the life of the financial asset, thus preserving the real value of the financial asset.

To illustrate this important point, suppose that I agree to loan you $1,000 for one year. Not being a particularly generous soul, I expect to receive an interest payment for giving up the use of my $1,000 for one year. Let's assume that we agree that 5 percent would be a suitable interest payment. Now, *if the inflation rate is zero*, at the end of the year the $1,000 repayment of the principal will allow me to purchase the same quantity of real goods that I might have purchased on the first day of the year. I take my $50 interest payment and everything is fine.

What happens if the inflation rate is not zero, but rather 10 percent? If I only charge you 5 percent for the use of my money for one year, at the end of the year you will return to me $1,050 ($1,000 principal plus $50 interest) but my real purchasing power will be reduced because of the 10 percent inflation rate. In fact, $1,050 one year later will only purchase $954 worth of real goods with inflated price tags (1,050 ÷ 1.1). Obviously you would have come out ahead on this transaction since you could have purchased $1,000 worth of real goods the day I lent you the money, and I can purchase only $954 worth of real goods the day you pay me back. Not only do I not receive an interest payment, I end up with less purchasing power than I had on the day I loaned you the $1,000. Consequently, rather than charging you 5 percent interest on the loan, I must increase the interest payment in order to maintain the real purchasing power of my $1,000 principal one year later. Given a 10 percent inflation rate, I would charge you 15 percent for the use of my money: 5 percent interest plus 10 percent to maintain the real purchasing power of my money.

Thus, the rate of interest charged by lenders and financial intermediaries will contain an **inflation premium** to reflect the **expected inflation rate** during the term of the loan. Defining the *real* interest rate RR as the interest rate that would prevail in a zero-inflation world, the *nominal* or market interest rate R will equal the real interest rate plus the expected inflation rate $\dot{P}^e$:

$$R = RR + \dot{P}^e \tag{3.1}$$

An increase in the *expected* inflation rate will cause an increase in the nominal interest rate. As illustrated in Figure 1.4, *nominal* interest rate movements have closely followed the inflation rate. In the 1960–67 period, inflation was less than 4 percent and interest rates were around 6 percent. When inflation peaked at over 12 percent in 1981, interest rates peaked at over 19 percent (and both fell together during the mid-1980s).

Commenting on high interest rates in late 1979, the Governor of the Bank of Canada said:

> I would first like to remind you that "it takes two to tango." If there is a borrower there must be a lender, and one needs to look at the situation from his side as well. Lenders are usually thought of as banks or other financial institutions but it is more accurate to regard those institutions as intermediaries. The true lenders are the savers, the Canadians who hold deposits with banks, trust companies, credit unions and caisses populaires, who have life insurance policies, who contribute to pension funds and who own bonds. To lenders, interest rates do not look all that high because they know that the interest they receive is in effect reduced by the declining purchasing power of the money they have loaned and will eventually get back. Of course borrowers know this too; they know that the real cost of borrowing is nowhere near as high as the level of interest rates makes it look.[3]

This fourth conclusion about inflation and interest rates also implies that the share of interest income in national income will rise when the expected inflation rate rises. Since total interest income is the product of the interest rate and the volume of loans outstanding, for a fixed volume of loans a jump in interest rates from 5 percent to 15 percent will cause a tripling of interest income. We have already seen in Chapter 2 that the share of interest and investment income in national income has continued to rise since the 1950s. There was a particularly steep rise in this share during the 1970s, which was due primarily to the increase in interest rates reflecting rising inflation expectations.

---

3 Statement prepared for the appearance of G.K. Bouey, Governor of the Bank of Canada, before the House of Commons Standing Committee on Finance, Trade and Economic Affairs, 25 October 1979, reprinted in *Bank of Canada Review*, November 1979, pp. 3–4.

5. The Foreign Exchange Rate Will Reflect the Inflation Rate

It is often asserted that unless inflation is brought under control, Canadian exports will be "priced out" of foreign markets and cheap imports will supplant domestic production. According to this argument, inflation must be fought to maintain our "competitive edge" against international competition and to protect domestic jobs. While this argument sounds convincing, to retain any validity it must be recast in relative inflation terms, comparing the Canadian inflation rate to international inflation rates. If Canadian and world prices are rising at the same rate, Canadian industries will not lose their "competitive edge."

Even if the Canadian inflation rate exceeds international inflation rates, the "competitive edge" argument overlooks the fact that the foreign exchange rate will tend to adjust to offset differences between inflation rates in various countries. As discussed in Chapter 6, if the Canadian inflation rate exceeds the foreign inflation rate, the resulting reduction in high-priced Canadian exports and increase in low-priced foreign imports will exert downward pressure on the Canadian dollar in foreign exchange markets. A depreciating Canadian dollar will cause the price of imported goods to rise and the price of Canadian exports to decline. The "competitive edge" that is lost through a relatively higher inflation rate will (eventually) be restored by a depreciation of the Canadian dollar. The *purchasing power parity theorem*, which is presented in Chapter 6, states that long-run movements in international exchange rates are directly determined by differences in inflation rates between trading countries. A freely fluctuating foreign exchange rate should maintain our "competitive edge" in those industries where Canada has a comparative advantage, irrespective of the inflation rate.

Unanticipated Inflation Can Play Havoc with the Economic System

Up to this point our analysis has been premised on the assumption that inflation is correctly anticipated. However, during the early stages of a new outbreak of inflation, or *dis*inflation (a reduction in the inflation rate), a sudden change in the rate of inflation may take most people by surprise; that is to say, there may be *un*anticipated inflation. Plans will have been made, and contracts will have been signed, on the basis of an incorrect expectation of inflation. The major consequences of such inflation miscalculations are *shifts* of income and wealth between various groups in society.

The distributional effects of unanticipated inflation are most pronounced in financial asset markets. When inflation is unanticipated, the inflation premium included in the interest rate will be incorrect and a transfer of purchasing power between the borrower and lender will occur. **Unexpected inflation** redistributes wealth from creditors to debtors, and unexpected disinflation redistributes wealth from debtors to creditors.

To illustrate the redistributional effects of an unexpected inflation rate, we return to our simple loan illustration. Assume that both the lender and the borrower anticipate a 10 percent inflation rate. In return for the use of $1,000 for one year, the borrower agrees to pay an interest rate of 15 percent, 5 percent real interest plus a 10 percent inflation premium. If the inflation rate turns out to be exactly 10 percent (as expected), at the end of the year the $1,150 proceeds from the loan will maintain the real purchasing power of the $1,000 principal and provide a $50 interest payment. However, if the actual inflation rate diverges from the 10 percent expected rate, the borrower must still return $1,150 to the lender at the end of the year. If the actual inflation rate turns out to be 20 percent, the $1,150 repayment would not permit the lender to purchase $1,000 worth of real goods at 20 percent inflated price tags. Given an unexpectedly *higher* inflation rate, the *borrower* clearly wins: the borrower can purchase $1,000 worth of real goods on the day the loan was made but returns less than $1,000 worth of real purchasing power to the lender at the end of the year. On the other hand, if the actual inflation rate turns out to be *lower* than anticipated, the *lender* would be the winner. For example, if the inflation rate unexpectedly fell to zero, the borrower would still have to repay $1,150 to the lender, which would represent $1,150 worth of real purchasing power since prices have not risen.

All financial assets and liabilities (such as bonds, savings accounts, guaranteed investment certificates, and mortgages) bear an interest rate that includes an inflation premium to offset the effects of *anticipated* inflation. To the extent that inflation is correctly anticipated, the inflation premium contained in interest rates preserves the real value of financial assets and liabilities. For example, as long as inflation is correctly anticipated, the interest earned on pension funds will preserve the real value of the principal invested and it will preserve the real value of the pension. However, *in*correctly anticipated inflation will generate a redistribution of purchasing power between borrowers and lenders. If *actual* inflation exceeds *expected inflation*, real purchasing power will be transferred from the lender to the borrower. Homeowners who negotiated 25-year mortgages at 6 percent during the tranquil 1960s (when inflation was expected to be 2 percent) were the big winners from the unexpected inflation of the 1970s. The market value of houses and the income levels of homeowners rose dramatically during the 1970s, whereas the 6 percent interest payments on the 25-year mortgage never changed. On the other hand, people who had their savings tied up in long-term 5 percent bonds suffered large financial losses from unexpected inflation during the 1970s (see Chapter 5 for a discussion of the effects of changing interest rates on the market value of bonds).

Unexpected inflation redistributes purchasing power from the lender to the borrower. Since the borrower's gain must be the lender's loss, the effects of unanticipated inflation are strictly distributional. There is *no aggregate loss* from unexpected inflation, only a redistribution of purchasing power between lenders and borrowers. Although the effects of unexpected inflation are distributional (my loss is your gain, and vice versa), the large and fortuitous shifts in purchasing power arising from unexpected inflation (disinflation) tend to turn the economic system into a giant roulette wheel. Each spin of unexpected inflation creates a new set of winners and losers. Undoubtedly the arbitrary consequences of unexpected inflation have created economic hardships and social tension. Even though for every loser there must be a winner, most people would rather not have to gamble their mortgage or pension savings on a spin of the unexpected-inflation roulette wheel.

However, we should emphasize that the villain is not the level of inflation, but rather the *uncertainty* of inflation. Redistribution of purchasing power between borrowers and lenders would still occur even if the inflation rate averaged out to 0 percent, but unpredictably fluctuated between –10 and +10 percent. It is the uncertainty of *future* inflation, not the actual level of inflation, that causes a redistribution of purchasing power.

In an environment of uncertain inflation, changes in *relative* prices, the basis of all economic decisions, are very difficult to determine. If you cannot predict the general inflation rate, you cannot tell whether the change in the price of a particular good represents a relative price change, or is just part of a general price increase attributable to inflation. You are forced to guess at the unpredictable inflation rate, pay your money, and take your chances. In a world of uncertain inflation, economic decision-making resembles a game of chance. The economic advantages of a stable, predictable inflation rate (be it 0, 5, or 10 percent) are overwhelming. Under such circumstances, relative price changes can be readily calculated and appropriate economic decisions taken.

The Economic Costs of a Stable Inflation Rate

In the preceding section we saw how *unexpected* (or uncertain) inflation can play havoc with the economic system. But even when it is expected, inflation has some undesirable consequences. Economists have identified three costs of a stable (predictable) inflation rate: the misallocation of resources caused by "shoe-leather" costs, "menu" costs, and tax distortions.

The "Shoe-Leather" Costs of Inflation

There is one component of wealth that is completely at the mercy of inflation: money pays a zero interest rate and therefore cannot be protected against inflation by an interest rate inflation premium. Inflation erodes the real purchasing power of money.

As discussed in Chapter 5, people typically choose to hold part of their wealth in the form of money to facilitate day-to-day transactions. Rather than walking to the bank to withdraw funds from a high-interest-earning savings account every time a purchase is made, people find it more convenient to forego the interest payments and hold cash balances. The time, trouble, and "shoe leather" associated with frequent trips to the bank outweigh the interest that could have been earned if one's cash balances were always invested in high-interest-earning savings accounts.

Inflation tips the balance towards more frequent trips to the bank. The higher the inflation rate, the larger the inflation premium in interest rates and the greater the opportunity cost of holding cash. Consequently, people will attempt to economize on their holdings of money as inflation rates rise, making more frequent trips to the bank to withdraw smaller and smaller amounts of money. Idle cash will be kept in high-interest-earning savings accounts for as many days of the year as possible. Thus inflation diverts scarce resources to the task of cash management. People will sacrifice time, energy, and "shoe leather" in an attempt to lessen the costs of holding money. Firms will hire more employees to work in the controller's office to manage and invest short-term funds. As such, inflation imposes an economic cost on society. Without inflation, some resources could be allocated to more socially productive uses.

Although the above theoretical argument is undoubtedly correct, the empirical consequences of this argument are likely very slight.[4] As Nobel laureate Robert Solow of MIT concluded, "A perfectly anticipated pure inflation imposes a small deadweight loss on society, mostly through a waste of effort directed toward economizing on the holding of money. . . . Not good, one is tempted to say, but no worse than a bad cold."[5]

The "Menu" Costs of Inflation

Economists have identified a second "deadweight loss" imposed by inflation. The higher the inflation rate, the more frequently prices within the economic system must be altered. In an inflationary world, scarce

---

4 For example, in 1990 the total amount of money (M1) per capita was approximately $1,450. Even if the 1990 inflation rate of 4.8 percent increased to 10 percent, and interest rates rose by 5 percent, there is only $72 extra forgone interest at stake for each person, or about 20¢ per day.

5 R.M. Solow, "The Intelligent Citizen's Guide to Inflation," *The Public Interest*, Winter 1975, p. 44.

resources must be diverted to the following types of activity: revising price tags, reprinting catalogues and restaurant menus, adjusting parking meters and vending machines. Inflation accelerates such "menu" price changes; without inflation some resources would be freed up for more productive uses.

In addition, the "menu" costs of adjusting prices likely differ from firm to firm. If the costs of adjusting prices are sufficiently large, a profit-maximizing firm may not initially adjust its prices (see Chapter 10). Thus firms with small "menu" costs will likely be quick to adjust their prices for inflation, whereas firms with large "menu" costs will probably be slower to adjust their prices for inflation. As a result, inflation will distort relative prices throughout the economy, causing resources to be misallocated.

Inflation-Induced Tax Distortions

As noted above, price inflation will be matched by nominal income inflation: the average income earner receives an income increase to offset the effects of inflation. But the government taxes nominal income. Does the average income earner suffer a decline in real after-tax income because the government taxes this inflation-induced increase in nominal income? Does inflation lead to increased government tax revenues (in real terms) and higher average income tax rates? If so, inflation, interacting with the income tax system, could distort economic decisions (people will try to evade these inflation-induced higher tax rates) and cause a misallocation of resources throughout the economy, a very *real* cost of inflation. We briefly examine the effects of inflation on the taxation of three different kinds of income: *labour*, *interest*, and *capital gains*.

Labour income

The Canadian income tax system is *progressive*: average and marginal tax rates *increase* as the level of income rises. In 1990 the federal income tax rate was 17 percent on taxable income up to $28,275, 26 percent on taxable income between $28,276 and $56,549, and 29 percent on taxable income of $56,550 or more (in addition, Canadians had to pay a federal income surtax and provincial income taxes). Even though one's real income might not be changing, an inflation-induced increase in nominal income can push a taxpayer into a higher tax bracket and lead to a higher average rate of taxation. Faced with a lower after-tax real wage rate, people may respond by altering labour supply behaviour, perhaps by working fewer hours.

To prevent such inflation-induced increases in income tax rates (often referred to as a "tax bracket creep"), in 1974 the Liberal government *indexed* the income tax system to the inflation rate: each year the tax brackets would move up by the annual inflation rate. During the next ten years the average and marginal rates of income tax for a given level of real income remained virtually constant. Without this inflation **indexation of the income tax system**, Canadian wage earners would have faced very much higher average and marginal tax rates, which would have caused serious distortions within the labour market.

In May 1985 the Conservative government modified the inflation indexation of the income tax system. In an attempt to generate more tax revenues to reduce the size of the federal deficit, the government limited tax indexation to annual inflation in excess of 3 percent. The tax brackets (for example, \$28,750 and \$56,550 in 1990) will not be adjusted upwards for the initial 3 percent inflation each year. Although wage earners are protected against tax bracket creep arising from annual inflation in excess of 3 percent, each year since 1985 the government has reaped the benefit of a small *unannounced* tax increase. Slowly, but surely, the initial 3 percent of the annual inflation rate has pushed some taxpayers into *higher* tax brackets and *raised* average and marginal tax rates (eight years of 3 percent inflation compounds into 30 percent of non-indexed inflation).

Interest income

Although labour income is partially protected against inflation under the Canadian income tax system, *interest income* is not protected against inflation. As discussed earlier in this chapter, the market (nominal) interest rate R includes an inflation premium. The real interest rate RR is obtained by subtracting the expected inflation rate $\dot{P}^e$ from the nominal interest rate.

$$RR = R - \dot{P}^e \tag{3.1a}$$

In a world of zero inflation, real and nominal interest rates would be identical (as they roughly were throughout the first half of this century). Inflation drives a wedge between the nominal interest rate and the real interest rate.

A *properly* indexed tax system would tax only real interest payments. Unfortunately our tax system taxes nominal interest payments. As a result, the government taxes the inflation premium contained in nominal interest rates, which may produce *negative* after-tax real returns.

To examine this inflation-induced tax problem, suppose that you face a marginal tax rate of t and receive nominal interest payments equal to R (which includes an inflation premium of $\dot{P}^e$ to offset expected inflation). After income tax is paid, you will be left with $(1 - t) \times R$. However, to determine your *real after-tax rate of return*, you must subtract the expected inflation rate to allow for the loss in purchasing power associated with inflation:

$$\text{Real after-tax rate of return} = (1 - t)R - \dot{P}^e = (1 - t)(RR + \dot{P}^e) - \dot{P}^e$$
$$= (1 - t)RR - t\dot{P}^e$$

For many very realistic values of t, RR, and $\dot{P}^e$, the real after-tax rate of return will be *negative*.

To illustrate, suppose that your marginal tax rate is 40 percent and the real rate of interest is 4 percent. The above formula suggests that your real after-tax rate of return will be negative for all inflation rates greater than 6 percent (which includes every year from 1973 through 1982). Suppose the inflation rate is 10 percent. Then the nominal interest rate R would be 14 percent (the real interest rate RR is assumed to be 4 percent) and your income tax payments would be 5.6 percent (14 × 40 percent). After income tax is paid, your net rate of return of 8.4 percent is less than the 10 percent inflation rate. Allowing for inflation and income taxes, there is a *negative* rate of return of 1.6 percent. In contrast, your after-tax return would be +2.4 percent if the inflation rate were *zero*. Inflation interacting with the income tax system has converted a net positive return into a net negative return!

This incorrect tax treatment of interest income in an inflationary world causes a number of distortions in financial markets and resource misallocation problems. Since lenders will be very reluctant to lend funds at negative real interest rates, they will demand much higher interest rates to allow them to pay the income tax on the inflation premium in nominal interest rates. To illustrate, suppose a lender demanded a +2.4 percent after-tax real rate of return. Given a 10 percent expected inflation rate and a 40 percent marginal tax rate, the lender will have to charge a nominal interest rate of 20.67 percent to net a +2.4 percent real after-tax rate of return: the lender will get to keep 60 percent of this 20.67 percent nominal return after paying income tax, which is 12.4 percent, and then must deduct 10 percent for expected inflation.[6] The incorrect tax treatment of interest income in an inflationary world has substantially raised the nominal interest rate the lender must charge, from 14 percent to over 20 percent. Besides raising interest rates, the incorrect tax treatment of interest income probably drives many lenders into the underground economy, where they lend funds privately without declaring any taxable interest income (thus depriving the government of income tax revenues).

Correcting the income tax system to eliminate these inflation-induced distortion effects on interest income is not nearly as straightforward as indexing the income tax system to offset the effects of inflation on lab-

---

6 To compute the appropriate interest rate to charge so that you will be able to pay the extra income tax associated with the inflation premium, you have to add the following additional factor to the nominal interest rate: $\dot{P}^e \times t / (1 - t)$.

our income. Although the appropriate taxable income concept is *real* interest income, people do not have financial records detailing the amount of real interest income received (as opposed to nominal interest received). The financial system would have to provide the taxpayer with two sets of computer records, detailing *both* nominal interest payments and real interest payments (the latter concept based on nominal interest rates less a suitable inflation adjustment). With the emergence of daily interest accounts, it would be very difficult for a person with a fluctuating bank account to determine the exact inflation premium to deduct from nominal interest payments, that is, to claim only real interest payments for tax purposes.

Capital gains

In 1972 the Liberal government introduced a tax on capital gains (prior to 1972, capital gains were not taxed). *One-half* of any capital gain on the sale of financial securities or personal property (excluding one's principal residence) must be included as taxable income, and taxed at the marginal rate. The Canadian tax system *does not* distinguish between *real* and *nominal* capital gains. To the extent that capital gains simply represented the effects of inflation, investors could again be faced with *negative* after-tax real returns.

To illustrate this inflation-induced tax problem, suppose your mother purchased shares of Acme Inc. for $100 each in 1981 and sold them for $120 in 1983. If her marginal tax rate was 40 percent, she would have had to pay $4 per share in capital gains tax (40 percent of one-half of $20), leaving her with an after-tax nominal return of $16, or 16 percent. But between 1981 and 1983, prices rose by 17 percent. Her real after-tax return was actually negative; $116 in 1983 had less purchasing power than $100 in 1981. The capital gains tax negated her real return.

Given that the capital gains tax applies to inflation gains as well as real gains, the after-tax real return on stocks can easily turn out to be negative. Investors fearing a negative after-tax real return might channel their funds away from securities markets, perhaps towards various tax shelters and loopholes. Again, inflation interacting with the income tax system distorts real returns and can cause a misallocation of resources. To avoid such distortions, the government should not tax the inflation component in capital gains.

Rather than exempting inflation capital gains from income taxation, in 1985 the Conservative government granted individual Canadians a *lifetime* capital gains exemption of $500,000, which was subsequently reduced to $100,000. In granting this large exemption for capital gains tax, no mention was made of any inflation distortion (the annual inflation rate was less than 4 percent in May 1985 when the exemption was introduced). The Conservative government simply argued that this exemption "will encourage more Canadians to invest in small and large businesses."

What Should be Done About Inflation?

Inflation, even when correctly anticipated, leads to some misallocation of resources (from shoe-leather costs, menu costs, and tax distortions). If inflation is not correctly anticipated, there will be redistributional effects, as well as additional resource misallocation problems.

During the 1980s and early 1990s the Bank of Canada championed the cause of price stability and warned Canadians about the dangers of living with inflation (even 4 percent annual inflation). John Crow, the Governor of the Bank of Canada, outlined the case for "price stability":

> All modern economies have a monetary foundation. We use money so that transactions may be carried out in the most efficient and least costly way possible. To secure fully the economic benefits this provides, our economies need a monetary standard that people can trust. This means a monetary standard that keeps its value over time. . . . Let me expand on this.
>
> Consumers make daily decisions based on the prices of the goods and services they want. Businesses make decisions about investment and production based on selling prices and the prices of their inputs. It is a good system, and it defies reason to believe that inflation will make this system work better. Inflation does not just cause difficulties in understanding the meaning of current changes in prices. It compounds the problem by introducing needless uncertainty regarding future price movements. The result is that people make needless errors in their economic decisions. People have to work to shield themselves against inflation — effort that could be used for productive activities. Thus our economies cannot perform as well as we should expect them to.
>
> Inflation carries with it social as well as economic costs. Since some individuals and businesses can protect themselves better than others, inflation reshuffles income and wealth arbitrarily.[7]

Given these undesirable consequences of inflation, should we try to eliminate it altogether?

Eliminating Inflation

Suppose inflation has been running at 5 percent for a number of years. People throughout the economy have come to expect 5 percent inflation

---

7 *Bank of Canada Review*, December 1989, pp. 21–22.

each year. Workers bargain for an extra 5 percent in their wage contracts to protect themselves from expected inflation. Lenders automatically include a 5 percent inflation premium in interest rates to cover the expected inflation over the next year. All economic agents have adjusted their behaviour in anticipation of 5 percent inflation.

If the government decides it wants to eliminate this 5 percent inflation, it will likely have difficulty convincing people to lower their inflation expectations and accept lower wage settlements and lower nominal interest rates. The government has a basic credibility problem: it has to convince everyone that it is no longer willing to let the economic system run at 5 percent inflation. What was acceptable to the government in the past is no longer acceptable. Many people may not believe that the government is now serious about eliminating inflation, or that the government is capable of achieving a lower inflation rate. No one wants to be the first to sign a new contract for a lower wage increase (or purchase a guaranteed investment certificate) without the 5 percent expected inflation premium included in the contract. To overcome this credibility problem, the government must be able to demonstrate that its new anti-inflationary policy will work, that the actual inflation rate will indeed fall below 5 percent.

The only way a government with a credibility problem can achieve a lower inflation rate (short of imposing wage and price controls) is to raise interest rates and slow down total spending in the economy (see Chapter 14). To purge inflation out of the economic system, the government deliberately pushes the economy into a recession. The economy endures "short-term pain" in the form of high interest rates and high unemployment for the "long-term gain" of a lower inflation rate. The early 1980s provides a classic example of the costs of eliminating inflation. Unemployment rates in excess of 12 percent and interest rates in the 17–20 percent range preceded the decline of double-digit inflation to the 4–5 percent range. Ironically, a major cost of inflation appears to be the cost of eliminating inflation.

Living with Inflation

Given the high cost of eliminating inflation, many economists are prepared to live with a modest inflation rate (such as 3 percent). The cure may be more painful than the disease. When looked at closely, the economic costs of inflation (such as resource misallocation attributable to shoe-leather and menu costs) may not be that severe.

As discussed above, *price* inflation must be matched by *nominal income* inflation. Inflation-induced increases in product prices do not disappear from the economic system, but rather reappear on the income side of the national accounts ledger. Second, most forms of wealth increase in value as prices rise. Even financial assets are protected against expected inflation. The interest rate paid on savings accounts and pension funds includes an inflation premium to offset the effects of expected inflation. In short, *aggregate* real wages, real personal income, and real wealth are not eroded by inflation. Only money not held in interest-bearing accounts is diminished in value by inflation.

For economists who advocate living with inflation, the real danger lies in *unstable* inflation, which can play havoc with the economic system. Uncertain or unpredictable inflation transfers purchasing power between different groups in society in disturbing ways and turns economic decision-making into a game of chance. The economic case for a *predictable* inflation rate is exceedingly strong. Given a stable inflation rate, relative price changes can be determined without much difficulty. If we know what the inflation rate is going to be, we can plan accordingly and build the expected inflation rate into our economic decisions, such as wage and mortgage contracts. Although it would be more convenient to have stable prices (as advocated by the Bank of Canada), people appear to adapt to a stable 4 percent inflation rate without much problem.

Inflation can cause distortions throughout the economy if people and institutions do not adapt to it. Prior to 1974 the Canadian income tax system totally ignored the effects of inflation; every year inflation pushed some taxpayers into higher tax brackets, raising the average tax rate and causing distortions in the labour market. At present the Canadian income tax system is partially *indexed* for inflation, but it continues to tax nominal interest income and capital gains, irrespective of the inflation rate (causing additional inflation-induced distortions and resource misallocation problems). Advocates of "living with inflation" argue that the simplest solution may be to adapt or index institutional arrangements (such as tax laws and wage contracts) to inflation, rather than to subject society to a costly recession to purge inflation from the economic system.

The Unemployment Rate

As discussed in Chapter 1, unemployment dominated the Gallup poll as the most important problem facing Canadians during much of the 1980s. In this section we turn to methodological problems in measuring the unemployment rate. For example, who should be counted as an unemployed person? A person casually looking for a "good" job? A worker out on strike? A farmer during the winter months? A university student during the summer months? After briefly reviewing the conceptual problems in measuring the unemployment rate, this chapter concludes with a case study in which we investigate the economic costs of unemployment.

Once a month, interviewers from Statistics Canada question approximately 100,000 Canadians in 48,000 representative households to determine the labour force status of each member of the household. On the basis of this sample, an estimate for the Canadian unemployment rate is obtained. The **unemployment rate** (*UR*) is defined as the number of unemployed persons (*U*) divided by the total size of the **labour force** (*LF*), where the labour force consists of all employed (*E*) and unemployed (*U*) individuals. In addition to this widely cited monthly unemployment rate, the labour force survey also provides information pertaining to the **participation rate** (*PR*), the proportion of the adult population (*APOP*) that is in the labour force.

$$LF = E + U \tag{3.2}$$

$$UR = \frac{U}{LF} \tag{3.3}$$

$$PR = \frac{LF}{APOP} \tag{3.4}$$

The task of the Statistics Canada interviewer is to determine, through a series of questions, whether the respondent and other members of the household are in the adult population, and, if so, whether they are employed, unemployed, or neither employed nor unemployed. Statistics Canada defines each of these three key concepts in the following manner:

1. *Adult population.* All persons in the population 15 years of age and over residing in Canada with the exception of the following: persons living on Indian reserves, inmates of institutions, and full-time members of the armed forces.
2. *Employed.* All persons (a) who did any work at all, or (b) who had a job but were not at work due to illness, personal responsibilities, bad weather, labour disputes (strikes), vacation, or other such reasons.
3. *Unemployed.* All persons (a) who were without work and had actively looked for work during the past four weeks and were available for work,[8] or (b) who had not actively looked for work in the past four weeks but had been on layoff and were available for work, or (c) who had not actively looked for work in the past four weeks but had a new job to start in four weeks or less and were available for work.

Classifying people as "employed" or "unemployed" is not an easy task; there are many shades of grey. For example, should part-time workers be counted as employed? Statistics Canada classifies a person

8 The "available for work" condition disqualifies full-time students from the labour force.

as employed if that person "did any work at all" during the reference week of the sample; the minimum employment requirement is to work more than zero hours. How actively does a person have to look for work to be classified as an unemployed member of the labour force? Not very. If you respond to the question "In the past four weeks what have you done to find work?" with the answer "I looked at job ads in the paper," or "I checked with friends or relatives," Statistics Canada classifies you as an unemployed person (rather than as someone who is not participating in the labour force).

Given the many problems in classifying people as employed, unemployed, or not in the labour force, Statistics Canada's "official" estimate of the unemployment rate may not give a true picture of the actual amount of unemployment in the economy. To the extent that some people are not seriously looking for work (perhaps doing the minimum required to collect unemployment insurance), Statistics Canada will *over*estimate the amount of unemployment. The size of this *over*estimate in the official unemployment rate is difficult to assess. On the other hand, there are three factors that cause Statistics Canada to *under*estimate the actual amount of unemployment, particularly during recessions. To illustrate the potential size of these three errors in the official unemployment rate, Table 3.1 presents relevant characteristics of the Canadian labour market for December 1982 and June 1989, the two months with the highest and lowest unemployment rates during the 1980s.

1. *The "discouraged worker" effect*: Some people may give up actively looking for work because they believe that no jobs are available. Statistics Canada classifies such "discouraged workers" as being outside of the labour force and therefore not part of the unemployed. The proportion of **discouraged workers** varies according to the state of the economy (see the last row of Table 3.1). At the bottom of the recession in December 1982, 156,000 people stopped looking for work believing that no work was available. If Statistics Canada had counted these 156,000 people as unemployed members of the labour force, the December 1982 unemployment rate would have increased by 1.3 percent, and the participation rate would have increased from 62.2 percent to 63.1 percent. When the economy picks up, many of these discouraged workers will re-enter the official labour force as unemployed persons (looking for a job). At the top of the business cycle this "discouraged worker" effect is much smaller (only 22,000 in June 1989, compared to 156,000 in December 1982).
2. *Involuntary part-time employment*: As shown in Table 3.1, during the 1980s almost two million Canadians were employed part-time (working less than 30 hours per week) and the proportion of em-

Table 3.1 Characteristics of the Canadian Labour Market

	Bottom of Recession December 1982	Top of Boom June 1989
Unemployment rate (%)	12.7	6.8
Population, 15 years or older (000s)	18,868	20,127
Total labour force (000s)	11,743	13,801
Participation rate (%)	62.2	68.6
Total employed (000s)	10,249	12,856
Full-time	8,599	11,017
Part-time	(16.1%) 1,650	(14.3%) 1,839
Average hours worked (weeks):		
Full-time	39.4	40.4
Part-time	14.6	15.6
All employed	35.4	36.9
Total unemployment (000s)	1,494	944
Flows into unemployed (000s)		
Job losers	969	454
Job leavers	194	199
Entrants/re-entrants to labour force	330	290
Average duration of unemployment (weeks)	19.6	18.8
Not in labour force, but looked for work during last 6 months (but not during the last 4 weeks) (000s)	156	22

Source: Statistics Canada, *The Labour Force Survey*, December 1982 and June 1989.

ployees working part-time increases during a recession (16.1 percent in December 1982 compared to 14.3 percent in June 1989). Although many people choose not to work full-time, a substantial number of people are forced to take a part-time job because they cannot find a full-time job. In December 1982, 390,000 of the 1,650,000 part-time workers stated that the reason they were working part-time was because they could not find a full-time job. In effect, these 390,000 workers are "involuntarily" unemployed for part of each week. Suppose these 390,000 part-time workers averaged 14.6 hours a week, the average for all part-time workers. Then, 37 percent (14.6 ÷ 39.4) of the work week they would be employed and 63 percent of the work week they would be unemployed (and wanting to have a full-time job). These 390,000 involuntary part-time workers might have been better classified as 144,000 full-time employees (37 percent of the total) and 246,000 unemployed (63 percent of the total). Reclassifying 246,000 part-time employees as unemployed raises the December 1982 unemployment rate by 2.1 percent. Since the remaining 1,260,000 part-time workers chose to work less than full-time, they cannot be regarded as partially unemployed.

3. *Fewer hours per week*: During a recession, many firms reduce the length of the work week and some workers find that they have no choice but to work fewer hours per week. A forced reduction in hours worked per week represents *underemployment* and is a form of hidden unemployment. In December 1982 full-time employees worked an average of 39.4 hours per week, compared to their normal (or usual) average work week of 41.5 hours (as reported by Statistics Canada). On average, full-time employees spent 2.1 hours (or 5 percent) of their usual work week not working. A 5 percent reduction in hours worked by the 8,599,000 full-time employees is equivalent to 430,000 people losing their jobs and the rest of the labour force working their usual hours. Counting the hidden underemployment from a reduction in hours worked per week would add 3.7 percent onto the December 1982 unemployment rate.

Combining the discouraged worker effect (1.3 percent), the involuntary unemployment of part-time workers who cannot find a full-time job (2.1 percent) and the hidden unemployment from a reduction in hours worked per week (3.7 percent) would increase the December 1982 unemployment rate from 12.7 percent to almost 20 percent. Although the official unemployment rate likely understates the degree of unemployment within the economy (as noted above, it is difficult to estimate how many unemployed people are not really "actively looking for work"), Statistics Canada's labour force survey nevertheless provides a consistent measure of the state of the labour market. Even if one does not totally agree with Statistics Canada's exact definitions for employed and unemployed, statistical consistency is an important virtue. By measuring labour force status in the same manner each month, movements in the unemployment rate provide a reasonably good indicator of changes in the state of the labour market and cyclical position of the economy.

The Costs of Unemployment

For both the individual and society as a whole, the costs of unemployment are both immediate and obvious. People who lose their jobs suffer a direct loss in personal income, and the consequent economic pressures often cause unemployed persons to suffer additional social and psychological stress. Economic, social, and psychological stress arising from unemployment can lead to family problems, illness, alcoholism, violence, and crime.

On an aggregate basis, total factor incomes are substantially below what they might have been and the economy's total production of goods and services will fall below its potential level to the extent that unemployment exists. Society as a whole loses the goods and services that the unemployed would have produced if they were employed. To the extent that unemployed people have to be supported by the community from general tax revenues or private charity, there are additional costs to society — funds are diverted from other, more useful, purposes.

Case Study 1: The Cost of Unemployment for the Year 1982

In this case study we examine the economic costs of unemployment by focusing on the year 1982. The economic performance of the Canadian economy in 1982 was the worst since the Great Depression. Real output declined by 3.2 percent in 1982 and the unemployment rate jumped from 7.5 percent in 1981 to 11 percent in 1982, the highest level since the 1930s. More than 1.3 million Canadians were unemployed in the year 1982.

Although it is difficult to assess individual income losses arising from unemployment, an *estimate* of society's aggregate loss of output from the existence of cyclical unemployment can be computed. Jim Brox of the University of Waterloo has estimated the value for Canadian *potential* output, which he defines as the highest level of GDP that is sustainable with given factors of production operating at a 95 percent utilization rate.[9] By subtracting the *actual* level of output from this estimate of *potential* output, one can obtain an estimate for the amount of *additional* output that could have been produced if the economy had been operating at a 95 percent utilization rate. Brox estimates that potential output in 1982 was $422 billion, compared to actual output of only $374.4 billion. Thus, the 11 percent unemployment rate in 1982 translates into a $47.6 billion loss in aggregate output.

Before turning to examine the distributional aspects associated with this output loss, we emphasize the magnitude of this loss in output arising from an 11 percent unemployment rate. To put this eleven-digit number in perspective, $47,600,000,000 would have purchased the following in 1982:

[9] J.A. Brox, "A Note of Capacity Utilization, Productivity, and the Canadian Output Gap," *Empirical Economics*, 1984, pp. 131–38. We would like to thank Jim Brox for providing us with an updated time series for potential output in Canada.

- almost 700,000 new $70,000 homes (more than enough to rehouse the entire Maritime provinces), or
- 6 million new cars (one for every fourth Canadian), or
- 3 billion cases of beer (125 cases of beer per capita).

Alternatively, $47.6 billion in 1982 was equal to the combined incomes of all of the residents of Newfoundland, Nova Scotia, Prince Edward Island, New Brunswick, Manitoba, and Saskatchewan. No matter how you represent it, the aggregate output loss associated with an 11 percent unemployment rate in 1982 was very substantial.

Although society as a whole suffers a substantial output loss from the existence of unemployment, on an individual basis who actually "lost" this output? Put in a slightly different way, who would have received the additional output arising from a lower unemployment rate? For example, would any of this "lost" output have ended up on my kitchen table? To answer this important distributional question, we examine how this $47.6 billion worth of lost 1982 output might have been distributed in income terms had the unemployment rate been 5 percent rather than 11 percent. By identifying the would-be recipients of the income payments associated with the lost output, we describe the distributional losses associated with unemployment.

First and most obvious, there are the previously unemployed people who will now be working and earning an income. By lowering the 1982 unemployment rate from 11 percent to 5 percent, approximately 714,000 previously unemployed people would have had a job.[10] How much of this lost output would have gone to now employed but previously unemployed people in the form of wage payments? In general one would expect that the "potential" wage of an unemployed person would be somewhat less than the wage of the average worker (the unemployed may lack job-specific skills and work experience). Given a 1982 average annual wage of $19,900, we arbitrarily assume that the unemployed might have earned $300 per week, or $15,600 per year. Collectively, the previously unemployed would have received $11.1 billion ($15,60029 × 714,000) in wage income for the year 1982 if they were working.[11] Slightly less than one-

[10] This calculation is based on a 1982 labour force size of 11.9 million workers. We ignore any discouraged worker effects arising from a higher unemployment rate, and assume that the size of the labour force is unaffected by the level of the unemployment rate.

[11] To the extent that the unemployed receive unemployment insurance (UI) or welfare payments, their net gain from being employed would be much lower. For example, if these 714,000 unemployed people had received 44 weeks of UI benefits (at two-thirds of our assumed $300 weekly salary), total UI payments would have been $6.3 billion. On a net basis the 720,000 formerly unemployed individuals would have been only $4.8 billion better off.

quarter of the income associated with the lost output would have gone to unemployed workers who found a job.[12]

Who would have received the remaining three-quarters of the income associated with this lost output? Perhaps surprisingly, most of this extra income would have gone to the factors of production that were already employed when the unemployment rate was 11 percent. The two major recipients of this lost income would have been the *shareholders* of firms (through corporate profits) and the *existing work force*.

To understand where most of the lost income associated with unemployment occurs, we take a brief digression into the realm of managerial economics. For an individual firm, what are the implications of a decline in sales when the economy is in the midst of a recession? First, the firm must still recover its fixed costs such as property taxes and heating costs, but out of a smaller total sales volume. Second, most firms will resist laying off experienced workers when sales decline. Not only are layoffs bad for morale, the firm runs the risk that its experienced workers will find jobs elsewhere. Since the firm has made a substantial investment in recruiting and training its work force, most firms try to hold onto (or *hoard*) their work force when sales decline. If possible, the firm might attempt to reduce the number of hours worked per week, rather than lay off part of its work force. But in many instances, the firm's work force is maintained (and paid) even though production is lower than it would have been if the economy were not in a recession.

As a result, changes in sales will have a dramatic effect on profit levels.[13] When unemployment rates are high and sales are low, fixed expenses and labour hoarding will substantially depress profit levels. Conversely, when the unemployment rate declines and sales increase, profit levels will increase at a very rapid pace (overhead expenses would already be covered and the productivity of hoarded labour increases). Thus, one would expect that a reduction in the unemployment rate from 11 percent to 5 percent would substantially increase corporate profits and greatly benefit the shareholders of corporations.

How much of this $47.6 billion lost income would have gone into corporate profits? To obtain a rough answer to this question, suppose that when output levels are at their potential level, corporate profits are 10.2 percent of total output (the average share of corporate profits in GDP during the 1970s and 1980s). In contrast, the depressed 1982 corpo-

12 Even if the unemployed earned the average annual wage in 1982, the total wage bill for the previously unemployed of $14.2 billion (714,000 × $19,900) would still only represent 30 percent of the lost output.

13 During the period from 1960 through 1989, corporate profits as a share of GDP ranged from a low of 7.2 percent (in 1982) to a high of 13.5 percent (in 1974). On a year-to-year basis, the percentage change in corporate profits ranged from +41 percent (in 1973) to −29 percent (in 1982). Corporate profits movements are clearly much more volatile than changes in nominal GDP.

rate profit share of GDP was only 7.2 percent ($26.8 billion corporate profits divided by actual GDP of $374 billion). Thus, if a 10.2 percent profit rate had been earned on a 1982 potential output level of $422 billion, corporate profits would have been $43.0 billion (0.102 × $422), rather than $26.8 billion. The sharp cyclical downswing in 1982 reduced corporate profits by an estimated $16.2 billion ($43.0 – $26.8).

If our "back of the envelope" calculations are roughly accurate, we still have to account for a large portion of the lost output of $47.6 billion. The now employed but previously unemployed would have earned $11.1 billion in wages and corporate profits would have risen by about $16.2 billion when the unemployment rate declined from 11 percent to 5 percent. Who would have received the remaining $20.3 billion of the $47.6 billion lost output? Since very little of this additional income would likely end up as interest or rent payments (or in capital consumption allowances), most of the remaining income associated with the lost output would have ended up either in indirect (sales) taxes or in the pockets of those who were already employed in 1982. Recall from Chapter 2 that part of GDP is indirect taxes (11.5 percent in 1982). If we apply this average 1982 indirect tax rate to the $47.6 billion of additional output, we estimate that the government's share from indirect taxation would have been $5.5 billion.[14] This leaves almost $15 billion to be shared by currently employed workers.

There are at least three different ways that the already-employed work force might have had their 1982 labour income enlarged if the unemployment rate had been lowered to 5 percent. First, more foremen, supervisors, and managers are required to supervise the larger work force associated with a lower unemployment rate. Since it is unlikely that a firm would hire an unemployed person to be foreman or manager, existing employees will reap the benefits of promotions and job reclassifications that accompany a larger work force. Second and more important, as discussed above, firms will also attempt to vary the number of hours worked per week as demand changes. As sales increase and unemployment declines, the existing work force will likely work more hours per week,[15] and many of these extra hours will command an overtime premium rate of pay. In addition to more paid hours of

[14] Of course, the government would also find direct income tax revenues rising, but these revenues are not a component of GDP.

[15] To illustrate the negative relationship between hours worked per week and the unemployment rate, in 1982 the unemployment rate was 11 percent and the average number of hours worked per week in the manufacturing sector was 37.5 hours. In contrast, when the unemployment rate was much lower in 1980 and 1981 (7.5 percent in both years) average hours worked per week were higher, 38.3 hours in both years. If the unemployment rate in 1982 was reduced to 5 percent and all people worked 2 percent more hours (that is, 38.3 rather than 37.5 hours), total aggregate labour income would have increased by $4.2 billion (0.02 × $19,000 × 10.6 million employees). In other words, about $4 billion of the lost output would have gone to workers who already had jobs in 1982, but who would have worked longer hours if the unemployment rate had been 5 percent rather than 11 percent.

work, an increase in demand accompanying a reduction in the unemployment rate will also increase the productivity of hoarded workers. As a result, some firms will likely reward their employees with bonuses, incentive payments, and additional wage adjustments.

In summary, the income associated with lowering the unemployment rate will be widely dispersed throughout the entire economic system. The lion's share of the additional income would likely be distributed to corporate shareholders and to the existing work force in the form of more paid hours of work, overtime premium pay, promotions, and bonuses. A relatively small share (approximately one-quarter) of this total additional income goes to the previously unemployed people who found jobs. Most of the additional income accrues to the factors of production that are already employed, but are underutilized when the unemployment rate is high.

There is, of course, one other big winner — the government. Much of this additional income would have flowed to the government in the form of income taxes. Even if the government only applied its average 1982 income tax rate of 28 percent to the $42.2 billion additional income (net of indirect taxes), it still would have collected $11.8 billion in additional income tax revenues (in addition to the $5.5 billion of indirect taxes). Considering that the government would have saved several billion dollars in the form of reduced unemployment insurance payments accompanying a lower unemployment rate, the government might well have ended up with an additional $19–20 billion in 1982 (more than enough to pay off the total government deficit of $18 billion).

Although the income associated with the "lost" output would have been widely dispersed throughout the economic system, the *relative* costs of unemployment obviously fall most heavily on the unemployed. The unemployed lose their entire income, which might be offset partially by unemployment insurance, whereas the existing members of the work force lose a relatively small, *marginal* proportion of their income. Not only is the relative cost of unemployment highest for the unemployed, the incidence of unemployment is neither randomly nor evenly shared. As shown in Table 3.2, the odds of being unemployed dramatically increase if you are either young or living in Atlantic Canada, Quebec, or British Columbia. For a young person living in Newfoundland, the unemployment rate in 1982 was almost 30 percent.

In an analysis of the burden of Canadian unemployment (in the years 1980 and 1982), R.P. Shaw offers the following seven labour market generalizations:

1. Workers in primary industries such as fishing, logging, and construction experience more frequent spells (and longer durations) of unemployment than workers with managerial, professional, clerical, sales, or product-fabrication jobs.

Table 3.2 1982 Unemployment Rates By Province and Age (Percent)

	All ages	Ages 15–24	Ages 25 and over
Newfoundland	16.9	28.5	12.5
Prince Edward Island	13.1	n.a.	10.0
Nova Scotia	13.2	23.0	9.7
New Brunswick	14.2	23.3	10.9
Quebec	13.8	23.2	10.9
Ontario	9.8	17.1	7.4
Manitoba	8.5	14.0	6.5
Saskatchewan	6.2	11.4	4.3
Alberta	7.5	12.6	5.6
British Columbia	12.1	21.2	9.2
Canada	11.0	18.8	8.4

Source: Statistics Canada, *The Labour Force Survey*, December 1982.

2. Workers in the Atlantic provinces and Quebec experience the highest incidence of unemployment (and long-term unemployment).
3. Those susceptible to long-term unemployment usually possess skills that earn lower wage rates. Thus during a recession unemployment is likely to exacerbate financial hardship among chronically unemployed individuals on the lower end of the income distribution.
4. Unemployment is particularly high among poorly educated youth.
5. Unemployed women who have dependent children suffer the greatest financial burden of unemployment.
6. The burden of unemployment is not distributed equally among ethnic groups. In particular, Native peoples, French Canadians, and those with multiple ethnic origins are likely to experience the highest unemployment rates.
7. While older workers have relatively low unemployment rates, when they lose their jobs they have much more difficulty finding another job and are more likely to leave the labour force in discouragement.[16]

In conclusion, the relative costs of unemployment are disproportionately large for small, well-defined segments of the labour force. Most of the labour force never experiences unemployment, and suffers relatively small marginal income losses (in foregone overtime pay or bonuses) from higher unemployment rates. To put this key distributional aspect of unemployment into sharper perspective, consider a purely

[16] R. Paul Shaw, "The Burden of Unemployment in Canada," *Canadian Public Policy/Analyse de Politiques*, June 1985, pp. 143–60.

random unemployment-generating mechanism — an unemployment lottery. Suppose that once a month the government conducts a random draw of social insurance numbers to determine who will be the unemployed for the month. If the unemployment rate were 8 percent, then approximately 1,000,000 Canadians would have their social insurance numbers selected each month. Each would receive the following prize: a month off from work without pay. On average, each member of the labour force would be selected once a year and thus experience one month of unemployment in each year. Unemployment would be equally shared by all. Obviously the real world is very different from this hypothetical unemployment lottery. Many workers never have their numbers drawn, while other people continually have their numbers pulled out. Even though the gains from closing the output gap are widely dispersed throughout the economic system, the relative costs of unemployment are disproportionately large for small, well-defined groups of Canadian citizens.

Key Concepts

consumer price index
expected versus unexpected inflation
inflation premium in interest rates
indexation of the income tax system
inflation-induced tax distortions
labour force
unemployment rate
participation rate
discouraged worker effect
involuntary part-time employment effect
lost output from unemployment

Review Questions

1. What are the advantages and disadvantages of a *fixed* weight price index when individual prices change at different rates?
2. Explain why *price* inflation must be matched by *nominal* income inflation.
3. Explain why interest rates will incorporate a premium for the *expected* inflation rate.

4. Explain why foreign exchange rates will reflect differences in domestic versus foreign inflation rates.
5. Describe the debtor–creditor distributional effects arising from an *unexpected* inflation. Explain why there is a transfer of purchasing power from the borrower to the lender when the inflation rate turns out to be lower than expected.
6. What is meant by the "shoe-leather" and "menu" costs of inflation?
7. Explain why the Canadian income tax system "partially" protects labour income from excessive taxation during inflationary periods, but does not protect interest income from inflation.
8. Do you think that a steady 10 percent inflation rate imposes serious economic hardships on society? Why?
9. Why does the unemployment rate likely *underestimate* the degree of unemployed and underutilized labour?
10. Why do corporate profits fluctuate cyclically to a greater degree than the unemployment rate?
11. How would you go about measuring the economic costs of unemployment?
12. Who bears the economic costs of unemployment? Discuss.

Part 2

CHAPTER 4

An Introduction to Macroeconomic Models

To understand my state of mind, however, you have to know that I believe myself to be writing a book on economic theory which will largely revolutionise — not, I suppose, at once but in the course of the next ten years — the way the world thinks about economic problems. When my new theory has been duly assimilated and mixed with politics and feelings and passions, I can't predict what the final upshot will be in its effect on action and affairs. But there will be a great change. . . . I can't expect you, or anyone else, to believe this at the present stage. But for myself I don't merely hope what I say, — in my own mind I'm quite sure.

John Maynard Keynes[1]

The origin of macroeconomics, as a separate field of study within the discipline of economics, dates back to 1936 and the publication of a book entitled *The General Theory of Employment, Interest and Money* by the British economist John Maynard Keynes (pronounced to rhyme with "brains"). In this "revolutionary" book, Keynes presented a set of ideas and theories to explain (1) why an economy might sink into a serious recession (depression) with persistent unemployment and (2) how the government could alleviate such depressed economic conditions. Keynes's analysis of the problem of persistent unemployment, such as existed in the 1930s, provided both a diagnosis of the cause of the problem as well as a policy prescription for this recurring economic disease. Chapters 4 and 5 of this textbook are largely devoted to an analysis of

1 Keynes to George Bernard Shaw, 1 January 1935 in R.F. Harrod, *The Life of John Maynard Keynes* (London: Macmillan, 1963), p. 462.

the basic ideas and theories of John Maynard Keynes, the father of modern-day macroeconomics.

A key assumption in Keynes's analysis is the assumption that prices and wages do not respond to changes in aggregate demand and output levels. As a first-order approximation to reality, Keynes assumed that prices and wages are *fixed*, or given. Even though the assumption of fixed prices and wages is obviously false in a long-run setting, prices and wages tend to be rigid or "sticky" in the short run. Many firms initially respond to a change in demand by altering output, rather than by changing the prices of their products (see Chapter 10 for an explanation of why profit-maximizing firms might not adjust prices). Explicit and implicit contracts in the labour market typically fix the wage rate for one to three years. Given fixed prices and wages, Keynes assumed that firms will produce whatever goods are demanded — output is entirely demand determined. Any decrease (increase) in output and employment can be directly traced to a decline (increase) in aggregate demand.

Although much of this textbook is devoted to an analysis of the joint determination of output and prices (inflation), we retain Keynes's critical fixed price and wage assumption throughout Chapters 4, 5, and 6, and postpone until Chapter 7 a more complete discussion of aggregate supply, the labour market, and flexible wages and prices. Before we start to "run" with a flexible price macroeconomic model, we must first learn to "walk" with a fixed price model.

In this chapter we review the most elementary representation of a fixed price macroeconomic model (the *Keynesian cross* model), the concepts of aggregate expenditure and the multiplier process, and the central message of Keynes's *General Theory*. The next chapter incorporates interest rates and the money supply into the model. The term "model" is used to describe a set of *interrelated* assumptions and theories pertaining to a particular economic phenomenon, such as the problem of chronic unemployment. Throughout this textbook we pay particular attention to how the various individual components of the model "fit together" and to the implications of the set of assumptions and theories when studied together. Subsequent chapters incorporate additional theories and refinements into our model (such as flexible prices, inflation, and expectations) to represent recent developments in macroeconomic thought. As we shall see, macroeconomics has come a long way since 1936. Before commencing our formal analysis of macroeconomics, several observations will help to place Keynesian economics into historical perspective.

Pre-Keynesian Economic Thought

Economics did not, of course, commence in 1936 with Keynes's publication of the *General Theory*. Most economists would at least date the start of their profession back to 1776 and the publication of another book, *The Wealth of Nations* by Adam Smith. Up until Keynes, however, most economists were preoccupied with what we now call *microeconomics*, the study of individual economic agents and the laws of demand and supply. Pre-Keynesian economics was largely devoted to an explanation of how changes in relative prices within a competitive market system allocate resources between competing uses. If, for example, widgets are in short supply, then the excess demand for widgets will force up the price of widgets relative to the price of all other goods. This change in the relative price of widgets will increase the quantity of widgets supplied and decrease the quantity demanded. Relative prices will continue to adjust until the widget market is back in equilibrium with the initial shortage of widgets eradicated. Under competitive market conditions, the "invisible hand" of Adam Smith will see to it that there are just the right number of widgets, hamburgers, barbers, plumbers, and textbook authors to satisfy society's demands.[2]

Prior to Keynes, economists and governments paid very little attention to aggregate output levels and unemployment rates.[3] While not denying the existence of periodic bouts of unemployment and a business cycle, pre-Keynesian or "classical" economists implicitly believed that the natural forces of supply and demand could be relied upon to restore full employment in a relatively short period of time. The labour market was assumed to function just like any other market. If there was an unemployment problem with a "glut" of workers, then the relative price of labour would be bid down to "clear" the labour market and eradicate the unemployment problem. Again, the "invisible hand" of Adam Smith would quickly work its magic and unemployment ought not to be a persistent problem. The competitive market system is fully self-regulating and should maintain an aggregate output level consistent with labour market equilibrium and full employment. Chapter 7 provides a formal analysis of the classical model of macroeconomics and its key assumption of flexible wage rates in a competitive labour market.

The Great Depression

Events of the 1930s shattered economists' rather complacent and fatalistic attitude towards the problem of unemployment. No industrialized

---

2 For a highly entertaining account of the "Wonderful World of Adam Smith," see R.L. Heilbroner, *The Worldly Philosophers* (New York: Simon and Shuster, 1980), Chapter 3.

3 The Canadian government did not start to publish regular data on GDP and the unemployment rate until well after World War II.

country (with the possible exception of the Third Reich) was spared from a decade of economic devastation. As Professor Safarian of the University of Toronto notes in the opening lines of his classic study of the Great Depression in Canada:

> The thirties were quite unlike any other period in the past sixty years. For almost every year of the decade the number of workers unemployed exceeded 10 percent of the labour force, and in 1933 amounted to 20 percent. The decline in activity to 1933 was severe, prolonged and uneven. The recovery after 1933 was also uneven, and it was far from complete when World War II began."[4]

As shown in Figure 4.1, Canadian gross domestic product (measured in 1986 dollars) declined by an incredible 28 percent from 1929 to 1933.[5] For ten years, real output remained below its 1929 level. Between 1929 and 1933, the total Canadian payroll of wages and salaries fell by 39 percent. This tremendous decline in labour income reflects both a decline in the average wage and a decline in the number of workers who were employed. Average *annual* earnings per worker fell from $764 in 1929 to $518 in 1933 (that works out to $9.96 per week).

Despite this 32 percent reduction in annual earnings — the "invisible hand" of Adam Smith — the level of unemployment reached epic proportions. The Canadian unemployment rate climbed from less than 3 percent in the late 1920s to almost 20 percent in 1933 and averaged more than 13 percent for the decade of the 1930s (see Figure 4.1). It was not until Canada was well into World War II that the unemployment rate returned to normal levels. One can only speculate how long the Great Depression would have lasted without the belligerence of Adolf Hitler.

As a final preliminary comment we would note that the 1930s were a very tough time to be an economist, somewhat akin to being a physician during the bubonic plague. According to the conventional wisdom, competitive market forces would quickly correct for any deficiencies in aggregate demand or any increases in unemployment. But in 1936, the year in which Keynes published the *General Theory*, the unemployment rate continued to hover around 13 percent. Despite the fact that wages had fallen by 25 percent in the *seven* years since the Great Crash of 1929, unemployment continued to be a serious problem. Other than advocating even further reductions in wages (perhaps by banning unions), a 1930s classical economist could offer no effective policy prescriptions

---

4 A.E. Safarian, *The Canadian Economy in the Great Depression* (Toronto: University of Toronto Press, 1959), p. 1.

5 The severe 1981–82 recession, the worst in 50 years, pales in significance compared to the early 1930s. During the 1981–82 recession, real output fell by 3 percent for one year, compared to 28 percent over the four years 1929–33.

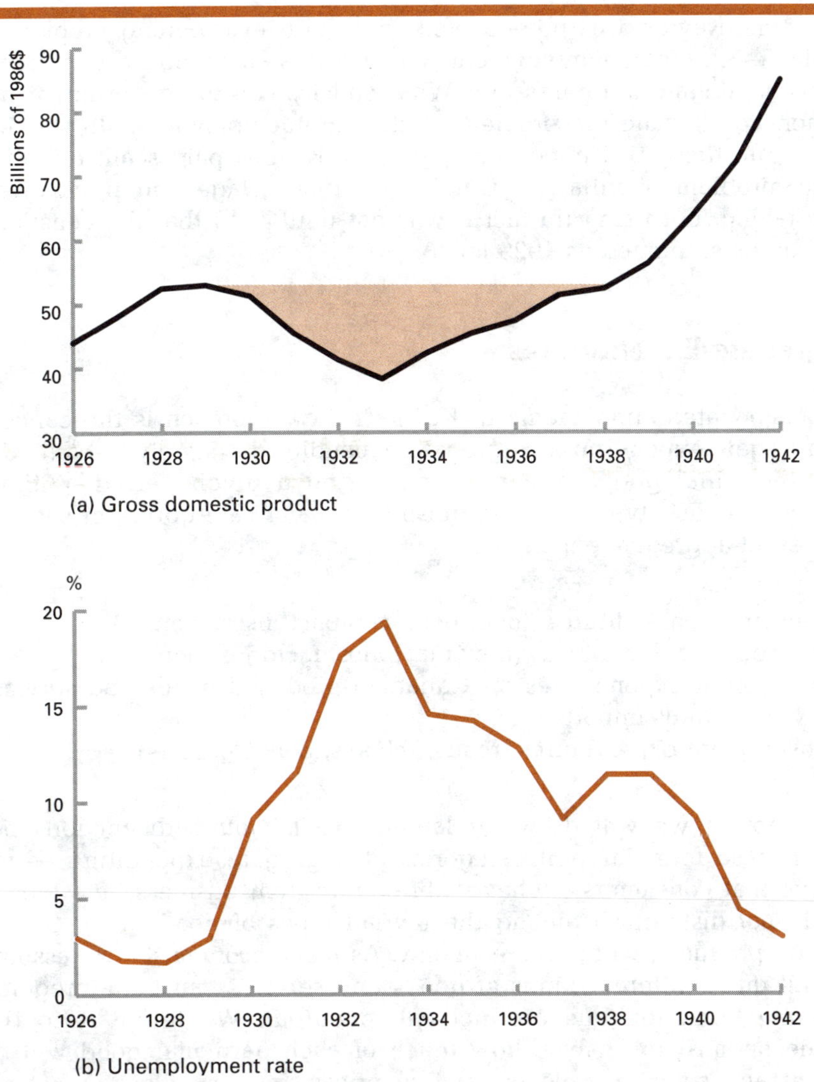

Figure 4.1 The Great Depression

for the problem of chronic unemployment, much like our unfortunate physician during the bubonic plague. According to the conventional economic wisdom, persistent high levels of unemployment could not happen!

Into this intellectual and economic vacuum came John Maynard Keynes. While the *General Theory* did indeed "revolutionize the way the world thinks about economic problems," it is very much a product of its time. Keynes was preoccupied with the overwhelming problem of the day — chronic unemployment. What causes an economy to sink into a prolonged state of depression? What policies can the government implement to alleviate the problem of chronic unemployment? In seeking answers to these two important questions, Keynes paid scant attention to the problem of inflation. During the 1930s wage and price levels were falling, not rising (in fact it was not until 1943 that the consumer price index surpassed its 1929 level).

Aggregate Expenditures

The major integrating theme of Keynes's new approach is the concept of **aggregate expenditure**. Aggregate expenditure is simply the *total* demand for final goods and services during a given period of time. Macroeconomists typically distinguish four major catergories, or sectoral sources, of aggregate expenditure:

1. consumer expenditures (food, beer, compact discs, clothes);
2. investment expenditures (new machines, factories, housing);
3. net foreign expenditures on Canadian-produced goods and services (exports minus imports);
4. government expenditures (roads, schools, police officers).

Even though we will draw fundamental *behavioural* distinctions between these four different categories of aggregate expenditure — we believe that consumers "behave" differently from business investors — we do *not* distinguish among the myriad types of goods and services that are produced within the economy. As macroeconomists, we assume that all these different kinds of goods and services can be aggregated into one homogeneous product called *output*. We leave it to the microeconomist to analyze how much of each particular good will be bought and sold, the role of relative prices and the allocation of resources to different industries. In the macroeconomic arena, output is just output and we focus our attention on *aggregate* issues. What determines the demand for output within the consumer sector of the economy? How does consumer demand differ from business investment demand for output? Is there sufficient planned aggregate expenditure to employ the economy's labour force?

Total aggregate expenditures AE consists of the sum of four sectoral components: consumer expenditures C, business investment expenditures I, exports minus imports $(X - M)$, and government expenditures G.

$$AE = C + I + (X - M) + G \tag{4.1}$$

When Statistics Canada collects data on aggregate expenditures, it does not exclude foreign goods (such as Sony radios, Volkswagen cars, and cognac) from total purchases made by Canadians. Since imports represent a diversion of Canadian aggregate expenditures to foreign production, imports must be subtracted from the other components of aggregate expenditures to obtain a measure of aggregate expenditures on Canadian-produced goods and services.

Having disaggregated aggregate expenditures into four components, we now turn to a brief analysis of each.

Consumer Expenditures — The Consumption Function

On an individual basis, the key determinant of personal consumption expenditures is typically one's income level. The more income one has, the more one likely plans to spend on consumer goods. In the parlance of a microeconomist, the utility-maximizing person's choice of consumer goods is determined by his/her income (budget) constraint. In short, the level of planned consumption expenditures likely depends critically on the level of income.

This assumed relationship between planned consumption expenditures and income levels (the now famous **consumption function**) is the cornerstone of Keynesian economics and represented one of Keynes's more innovative ideas. Unlike his classical contemporaries, who identified the rate of interest as the key determinant of saving and consumption decisions (see below), Keynes hypothesized that the principal determinant of aggregate consumer expenditures is the level of aggregate income. While increased income levels would lead to increased consumer expenditures, Keynes firmly believed that part of any increase in income would be saved:

> . . . men are disposed, as a rule and on the average, to increase their consumption as their income increases, but not by as much as the increase in their income.[6]

Since individuals will not consume the entire increase in income, as income levels increase both consumption and saving will increase. For example, if you receive a $100 raise in your monthly salary, you might increase your monthly purchases of consumer goods by $80, which means that your monthly saving will rise by $20.

The consumption function is conventionally expressed as a simple linear relationship connecting consumer expenditures C to the level of disposable income (total income Y minus taxes T).

---

6 J.M. Keynes, *The General Theory of Employment, Interest and Money* (London: Macmillan, 1936), p. 96.

$$C = C_a + b(Y - T) \tag{4.2}$$

In Figure 4.2(a) this linear (straight line) consumption relationship (Equation 4.2) is drawn with intercept C_a and slope b (recall that the slope is the "rise" over the "run").

A one-unit (marginal) increase in disposable income will result in an increase in planned consumer expenditures equal to b, the slope of the straight line consumption function. As the above quotation indicates, Keynes thought that the slope of the consumption function would be less than unity ("not by as much as the increase in their income") since part of any increase in disposable income would be saved. Given the strategic importance of the slope of the consumption function within his theory (see below), Keynes invented a special title for the slope of the consumption function, the **marginal propensity to consume**, often shortened to the MPC.

The positive intercept C_a of the consumption function represents autonomous consumption expenditures. Even if one has zero disposable income, one must still purchase food and other basic necessities to stay alive (such purchases are presumably financed by drawing down past savings or borrowing against future savings[7]). If for some reason auton-

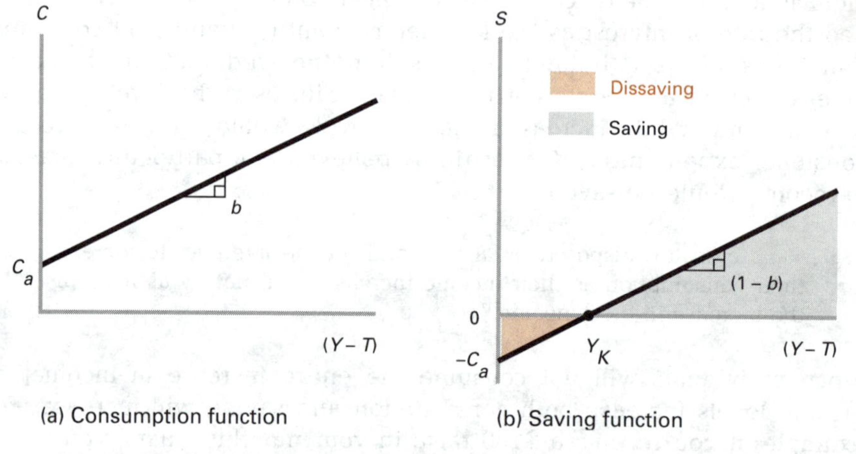

Figure 4.2 Consumption and saving functions

[7] Economists distinguish between *saving* (without an "s"), the amount saved in one particular period (a flow variable) and *savings* (with an "s"), the accumulated stock of past saving. For example, you might save $1,000 during one year (saving) which would bring your total savings up to $5,000 (the accumulated stock of past annual saving).

omous consumption expenditures C_a were to increase, then the intercept of the consumption function would increase and the consumption function would shift vertically upwards.

Since disposable income must be either consumed or saved, saving is simply the difference between disposable income and consumption:

$$S = (Y - T) - C$$

Substituting the consumption function (Equation 4.2), we can derive a linear saving function (Equation 4.3):

$$S = (Y - T) - C_a - b(Y - T)$$

or

$$S = -C_a + (1 - b)(Y - T) \tag{4.3}$$

As long as the MPC b is less than unity, saving will be an increasing function of disposable income (see Figure 4.2(b)). There will be dissaving until disposable income has reached the level Y_K and positive saving for disposable income levels in excess of Y_K. To repeat, the Keynesian consumption function with a marginal propensity to consume less than unity implies that *both* consumption and saving will rise as income levels increase.

Keynes's perception of the consumption/saving decision differed sharply from the prevailing economic thought of the 1930s. Most classical economists thought that interest rates, not income levels, were the prime determinant of saving. Since interest payments are the economic rewards for abstaining from present consumption, classical economists assumed that the higher the interest rate, the greater the incentive to save. Keynes, on the other hand, thought that interest rates would have little effect on the consumption/saving decision:

> The usual type of short-period fluctuation in the rate of interest is not likely, however, to have much *direct* influence on spending either way. There are not many people who will alter their way of living because the rate of interest has fallen from 5 to 4 percent, if their aggregate income is the same as before.[8]

Although classical economists thought that interest rates were the key determinant of saving and consumption, Keynes argued that consumption and saving "mainly depend" on income levels. Which theoretical explanation for consumption/saving behaviour should we believe?

---

8 Keynes, *General Theory*, pp. 93–94.

How do we know when we have discovered the "true" theory? Throughout this textbook we will be presenting different economic theories to "explain" various types of macroeconomic behaviour, such as the aggregate consumption relationship. It is of paramount importance that we establish a general set of procedures and tests to evaluate whether a particular economic theory provides an "acceptable" explanation of macroeconomic behaviour. Case Study 2 explores the methods used by economists to evaluate their theories.

Case Study 2: How Economists Test Their Theories — The Consumption Function as an Illustrative Example

Although there are many different criteria that might be used to evaluate the appropriateness of a particular economic theory (such as simplicity, generality, or mathematical elegance), economists typically judge their theories in terms of empirical accuracy. Is the theory supported by the *facts*? Does the theory generate accurate *predictions* of economic events? The most important test of an economic theory is its ability to explain what is observed in reality, and our confidence in a particular theory increases with each accurate prediction. Using the powerful techniques of mathematical statistics, economists scientifically test their theories for empirical accuracy.

To illustrate how economists test their theories, we return to our two alternative economic theories concerning consumption behaviour. Even though there are undoubtedly many different factors that might influence consumer behaviour (economic, social, religious, geographical), each of these two competing theories abstracts one major determinant of consumption expenditures from the maze of possible influences on consumer behaviour. Keynes hypothesized that aggregate consumption expenditures mainly depend on aggregate disposable income whereas classical economists contended that consumption expenditures vary inversely with the interest rate, that is, an increase in interest rates will prompt more saving and less consumption. In each case, *all other* possible determinants of consumption behaviour are assumed to be relatively unimportant and are ignored in the analysis.

Having advanced two different theories of consumer expenditure behaviour, we must now test whether either theory is empirically accurate. Each theory must be confronted with real world data and subjected to statistical tests. Annual data for aggregate consumer expenditures, disposable income, and interest rates have been collected for the period 1960 to 1990. To prevent any inflation distortions, we have expressed both consumption expenditures and disposable income in constant 1986 dollars. As discussed in the previous chapter, in an inflationary world one must also distinguish between nominal and real interest rates. To correct for the effects of inflation on the return from financial assets, we have subtracted the annual inflation rate from the nominal interest rate. In an inflationary world, borrowing and lending decisions depend on the real rate of interest, the nominal rate of interest corrected for the annual inflation rate (see Chapter 3).

To facilitate our empirical analysis of these two alternative theories of consumption behaviour, we have plotted each year's data in the form of a **scatter diagram** (a scatter of annual data points). In Figure 4.3(a), real consumption expenditures have been plotted against real disposable income, the Keynesian consumption function hypothesis. For example, in 1960 aggregate consumption expenditures were $101.5 billion and aggregate disposable income was $113.2 billion (both measured in 1986 dollars). In Figure 4.3(a) we have located 101.5 on the vertical consumption axis and 113.2 on the horizontal disposable income axis, and have plotted this observation for the year 1960. By 1990 consumption expenditures had increased to $341.0 billion and real disposable income had risen to $385.8 billion (see the 1990 point in Figure 4.3(a)). We have plotted the intervening years of consumption–disposable income data in Figure 4.3; but to keep the diagram as clean as possible, we have only labelled the 1960 and 1990 observations. For the time being, ignore the straight line in Figure 4.3(a).

The empirical evidence presented in Figure 4.3(a) unambiguously favours the Keynesian income hypothesis of consumer expenditures. As real disposable income levels increased during the 1960–90 period, real consumption expenditures rose accordingly. There is a very systematic *upward-sloping* empirical relationship between consumption expenditures and disposable income. Higher disposable income levels (during the 1970s and 1980s) are clearly associated with higher levels of consumption expenditures.

On the other hand, the classical interest rate hypothesis is clearly refuted by the data; Figure 4.3(b) is *all scatter*. To the extent that there is any statistical relationship between real interest rates and consumption expenditures, it is positive (the points have a slight tendency to drift upwards to the right) — the opposite of what classical economists predicted.[9] Higher real interest rates do not lower personal consumption expenditures.

In short, a quick visual inspection of these two scatter diagrams suggests that the Keynesian income hypothesis of consumer expenditures is consistent with the facts whereas the classical interest rate hypothesis of consumer expenditures is contradicted by the facts. As we shall see in Chapter 16, the precise definition of "income" in the consumption func-

9 If one plots the ratio of consumption expenditures to disposable income (C/Y) against the real interest rate, there is a significant positive relationship.

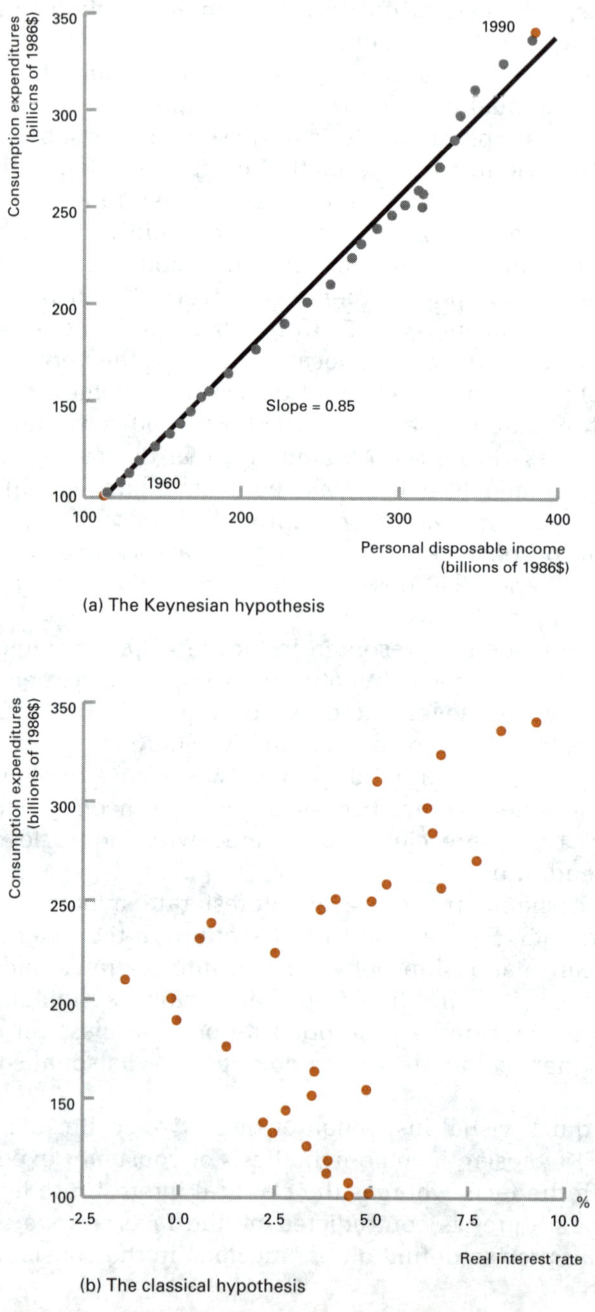

Figure 4.3 Scatter diagrams for consumption expenditures

tion has been a subject of recurring debate in macroeconomics, and there have been several important developments in consumption theory since Keynes.

Rather than relying on visual inspections of scatter diagrams, although that is a useful first step, economists formally test their theories using modern statistical techniques. The application of statistical techniques to economic problems is called *econometrics*. Besides providing formal statistical tests of economic theories by using the laws of probability, econometrics also enables economists to quantify their theoretical relationships. By "fitting" the best straight line through a scatter diagram, an econometrician can provide statistical estimates for the intercept and slope of an economic relationship.

As is evident in Figure 4.3(a), real world data do not lie exactly along a straight line. The major reason that the data points do not lie along a straight line stems from the abstraction process in economic theorizing. All other possible influences on consumption behaviour (except income levels) have been ignored, thus causing our theory to make small errors in prediction. Any particular straight line that one draws through a scatter diagram will miss most of the actual data points. Since there is an infinite number of possible straight lines that can be drawn through a scatter diagram, the econometrician is looking for the straight line that comes as close as possible to the scatter of data points. How does an econometrician decide what is the best straight line through a scatter diagram? Statistical theory suggests that the vertical distances between the data points and the straight line be used as a measure of "closeness" or "goodness of fit," and that the best line is the one that minimizes the *sum of squared* vertical distances. This statistical technique of fitting a line through a scatter of data points by minimizing the sum of squared deviations is called *least squares* (for further details on least squares, see any standard textbook on econometrics).

Returning to Figure 4.3(a), the straight line drawn through this scatter diagram is obtained by the **least squares estimation technique** (using a conventional statistical software package, TSP, on a microcomputer). Based on data from the 1960–90 period, the intercept of the consumption function is estimated to be 0.5 billion 1986 dollars and the slope (the MPC) is estimated to be 0.85, well under unity as Keynes hypothesized. Each additional dollar of disposable income appears to generate an extra 85¢ of consumer spending and an additional 15¢ of saving.

In conclusion, by using conventional statistical and econometric techniques we can test our economic theories as well as quantify economic relationships. These numerical estimates for economic relationships will be important when we come to discuss economic policy. A government must not only decide whether to increase or decrease a particular policy instrument (such as tax rates), it must also decide by exactly how much to increase or decrease this policy instrument. To determine the particular numerical *size* of a tax change, the government must have reliable *quantitative* information on all economic relationships. One needs numerical information to generate numerical answers.

Investment Expenditures

In macroeconomics the term *investment expenditure* does *not* refer to the purchase of corporate shares, mutual funds, bonds, or guaranteed investment certificates. For the most part, such transactions simply reflect the swapping of one financial asset for another (for example, money for stocks). In a macroeconomic context, investment refers to the process by which the economy's stock of *physical* capital is augmented. When a firm purchases new machinery and equipment or constructs a new factory, that's investment. Similarly, the construction of new homes or apartment buildings is considered to be investment expenditure. In each case the country's stock of physical capital has increased. Finally, an increase in the stock of inventories held by firms is also considered to be a form of investment. Given that inventory investment (or disinvestment) is typically not planned by the firm, we defer discussion of inventory investment until later in this chapter and focus our attention on *planned* investment expenditures on machinery, factories, and housing.

Since capital goods such as machines, equipment, factories, and apartment buildings can last for decades, investment decisions depend critically upon the firm's *long-run* appraisal of future profit returns (and risks). The next chapter examines how changes in interest rates affect investment decisions; Chapter 17 provides an extensive review of the different theories of investment (including a discussion of how the firm calculates the rate of return on an investment project).

Given the inherent difficulties in predicting future revenues and profit returns over the next several decades from a new investment project, Keynes placed considerable emphasis on the "state of business psychology and business confidence" as a determinant of planned investment expenditures (what Keynes called the "animal spirits" of investors). If businesspeople are not very confident of the future, they are not likely to invest in new plants and new machinery. Since Keynes thought that the state of business confidence was quite unpredictable and subject to "sudden and violent changes," he considered investment expenditures to be largely **autonomous**, that is, independent of interest rates and income levels. Unlike consumer expenditures, which are a very stable function of income, Keynes felt that investment expenditures were much more unpredictable and volatile, with the source of this instability lying outside the realm of macroeconomics.

Although Keynes undoubtedly overstated the role of business psychology and "animal spirits" in the investment decision, investment expenditures are indeed more unstable and unpredictable than consumer expenditures. Consider, for example, the Great Depression. From 1929 to 1933 real investment spending declined by a staggering 79 percent. Compared to this unprecedented reduction in investment expenditures, real consumer expenditures declined by a much more modest 18 percent over these four years, corresponding to the worst downswing in Canadian history — a 28 percent decline in real output. To survive the Great Depression, consumers spent *more than* their current income by borrowing or by drawing down past savings (the saving rate fell to minus 9 percent in 1933). Businesspeople, on the other hand, simply stopped investing in new machinery, equipment, and factories. The almost complete collapse of business investment, which Keynes attributed to a collapse in business confidence, was a major reason for the depth and length of the Great Depression. Such volatility in investment spending has characterized virtually every decade and has been a recurring source of aggregate demand stimulus (as in 1964–66, 1973–74, 1979–81, and 1987–88) and contraction (as in 1959–62, 1970, and 1982–84). In general, consumer spending has tended to stabilize the economy,[10] whereas investment spending has frequently exerted a destabilizing influence.

For purposes of this initial "model-building" chapter we assume that all planned investment expenditure is autonomous; that is, we assume that the level of planned investment expenditure is given and independent of the level of income. Our concern is with the following types of questions: What is the relationship between aggregate income and a given level of investment expenditure? How will GDP be affected if investment expenditures decline by 13 percent, as occurred in 1982?

Exports Minus Imports

The importance of international trade for the Canadian economy needs little elaboration. Throughout the history of our country, **exports** have played a vital role in developing the economy. Early exports of a few staple commodities, such as cod, fur, timber and later wheat, gradually evolved into a wide variety of export products. In 1989 Canada exported $35 billion in motor vehicles and parts (25 percent of all exports) and another $31 billion in other manufactured goods.

---

10 Modern theories of consumption (discussed in Chapter 16) recognize that consumption expenditures in any particular year are influenced by income levels in other years, particularly expected income levels in the future. Consequently, consumption expenditures may not be very responsive to a change in income if the change in income is not expected to be permanent. Faced with a temporary or transitory decline in income, many people will try to maintain their usual standard of consumption (perhaps by cashing in some stocks or guaranteed investment certificates, or by charging expenditures on their VISA or Mastercard credit card). The peaks and valleys of the business cycle are much more pronounced in investment expenditures than in consumption expenditures.

During the 1960–90 period, exports have risen from less than 15 percent to almost 30 percent of Canadian GDP (see Figure 4.4), with about three-quarters of Canadian exports destined for the U.S. market. The rising importance of exports during the late 1960s is largely attributable to the signing of the Canada–United States Automotive Pact, a 1965 bilateral treaty which permitted "controlled" free trade in automotive products between the two countries. Following the North American rationalization of the automotive industry under the Auto Pact, motor vehicles quickly became Canada's leading export product. Compared to \$5 to \$15 *million* worth of exports of motor vehicle products to the United States in the early 1960s, motor vehicle exports in the latter half of the 1980s were in the \$30 to \$35 *billion* range! Given the signing of the Canada–United States Free Trade Agreement in 1989, Canadian export production of other goods will likely rise and be even more closely linked to economic conditions in the United States.

Imports, while typically less than exports, have followed a similar upward trend during the 1960–90 period (see Figure 4.4). Almost 90 percent of imports consist of fabricated materials and end products; motor vehicle products are the number one imported product. Again the United States is our main trading partner, with over two-thirds of all imports coming from that country. Total imports — and the U.S. share of imports — will undoubtedly rise as the effects of the Canada–U.S. Free Trade Agreement take hold.

Since imports are included in the other components of aggregate expenditures (particularly consumer expenditures), the level of imports ob-

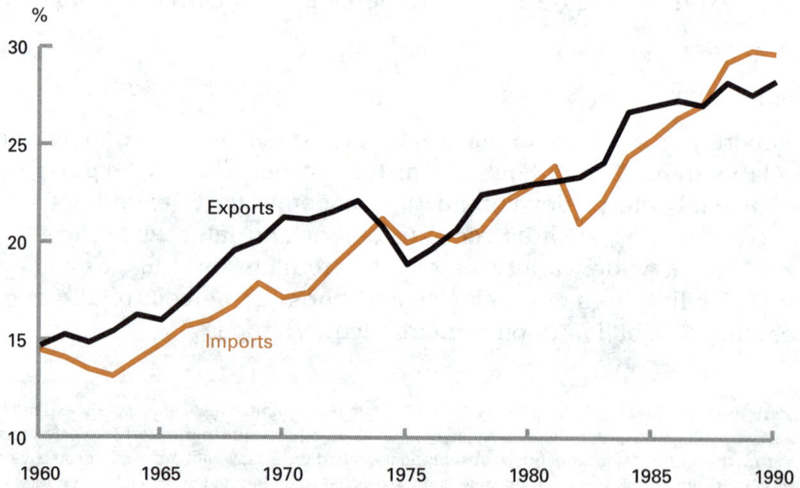

Figure 4.4 Relative importance of exports and imports in GDP

viously depends on total aggregate expenditures and aggregate income (which determines consumption expenditures on domestic and foreign goods). Keeping our model as simple as possible, we assume that Canadian imports M simply depend on Canadian income Y, with the slope m representing the **marginal propensity to import** out of income:

$$M = mY \tag{4.4}$$

Figure 4.5 presents a simple scatter diagram for Canadian imports, using data from the 1960–90 period. As is clear from this scatter diagram, there is indeed a very close *statistical* relationship between imports and income levels. As Canadian income levels have increased, so have imports. Given the slope of the "least squares" line, the marginal propensity to import (MPM) out of income is 0.35. As noted above, the Canada–U.S. Free Trade Agreement will likely increase this marginal propensity to import.

Following the same line of reasoning, if Canadian *imports* are directly related to Canadian income, then Canadian *exports*, which are imports to foreigners, will likely bear a close relationship to foreign income. Since three-quarters of our exports are shipped to the United States, the level of income in the U.S. economy is of vital concern to Canadian exporters. As U.S. income levels rise, Canadian exports rise accordingly. When the United States went into a serious recession in 1974–75 and again in 1982, Canadian exports fell sharply. This cyclical movement in Canadian exports to the United States is particularly acute in the motor vehicle industry. Having integrated our domestic motor vehicle industry to the total North American market (which is dominated by the U.S. market), Canadian exports of motor vehicles are now highly dependent on the U.S. business cycle. With the signing of the Canada–U.S. Free Trade Agreement in 1989, Canadian exports of other goods will be even more closely tied to changes in U.S. income during the 1990s.

In summary, the performance of the U.S. (and world) economy is a key determinant of Canadian exports and the level of aggregate expenditures on Canadian-produced goods. Since our goal is to develop a model of Canadian income determination, not U.S. or world income determination, we take the level of exports as given (exports depend on foreign income, not Canadian income). As we shall see, a change in exports, for example from a change in U.S. or world income levels (the international business cycle), will have important effects on Canadian income levels.

Government Expenditures

The final component of aggregate expenditures is **government expenditures** on goods and services. Consolidating the federal, provincial, and municipal governments into one giant government sector, total govern-

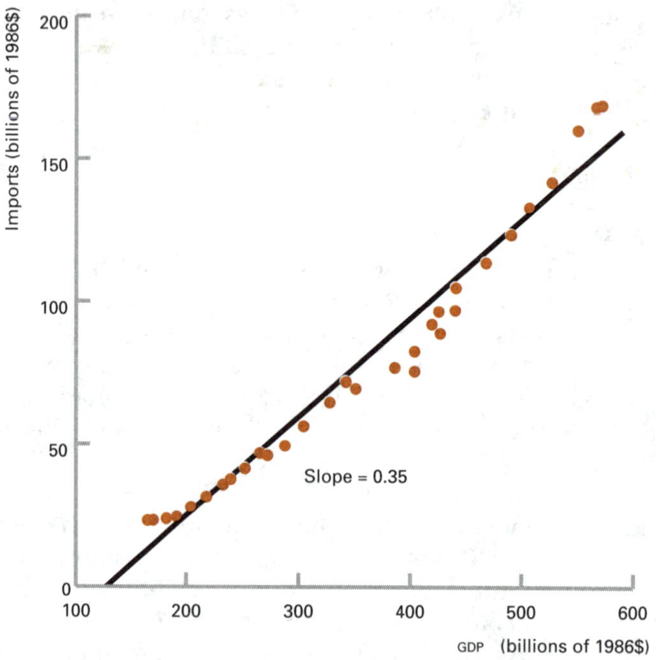

Figure 4.5 Scatter diagram for imports and GDP, 1960–90

ment expenditures G represent about one-fifth of total aggregate expenditures. It is important to note that G only includes government expenditures on goods and services (such as frigates and salaries for civil servants); it does not include "transfers" of money to people and firms (such as welfare payments).

The government can also indirectly affect aggregate consumer expenditures by changing *taxes* or *transfer payments*. To keep our model as simple as possible, we subtract transfer payments from total taxes (transfer payments are like a negative tax in that the recipient receives money from the government rather than paying money to the government). Given the income tax system, tax revenues (net of transfers) are assumed to vary directly with the level of income. Even though the progressivity of the income tax system would suggest a nonlinear relationship between income tax revenues and income levels,[11] to keep the model as simple as possible we assume the following linear **tax function**:

[11] As income rises, taxpayers move into higher tax brackets and pay higher average rates of tax. Therefore government revenues likely increase at an accelerating rate as income levels rise.

$$T = T_a + tY \tag{4.5}$$

In Equation 4.5, t represents the marginal income tax rate for an additional dollar of income. The intercept T_a of the tax function can be thought of as a "lump sum" tax that is levied irrespective of income levels (such as a licence fee or poll tax). By changing T_a or t, the government can change the amount of total tax revenues T and therefore affect the level of disposable income $(Y - T)$, which determines planned consumption expenditures (see Equation 4.2).

The Aggregate Expenditure Curve

In developing a rudimentary macroeconomic model of income determination, we have made the following assumptions:

1. Wage and price levels are fixed and unresponsive to changes in income levels.
2. Aggregate expenditures can be disaggregated into four components: consumption C, business investment I, exports minus imports $X - M$, and government expenditures G (Equation 4.1).
3. Planned consumption expenditures are assumed to depend on the level of disposable income (Equation 4.2).
4. Imports are assumed to depend on the level of income (Equation 4.4).
5. Tax revenues (net of transfer payments) are assumed to depend on the level of income (Equation 4.5).
6. Investment expenditures, exports, and government expenditures are assumed to be given and independent of the level of income (autonomous).

Making use of these assumptions, we can derive the **aggregate expenditure *AE* curve** for the economy. First we substitute the income tax function,

$$T = T_a + tY \tag{4.5}$$

into the consumption function,

$$C = C_a + b(Y - T) \tag{4.2}$$

to obtain

$$C = C_a + b(Y - T_a - tY)$$

and rearrange the terms to produce the following revised consumption function (which is plotted in Figure 4.6(a)):

$$C = C_a - bT_a + b(1 - t)Y \tag{4.2a}$$

The slope of the consumption function plotted in terms of aggregate income Y is $b(1 - t)$: the marginal propensity to consume b multiplied by one minus the income tax rate t. A *decrease* in the income tax rate raises disposable income and increases consumption expenditures — the consumption function rotates upwards. Similarly, a *decrease* in T_a raises disposable income and increases consumption expenditures — in this case, the intercept $(C_a - bT_a)$ increases and the consumption function shifts upwards.

Figure 4.6(b) plots the import function (Equation 4.4). As income levels rise, imports increase. Imports are, of course, a negative item in aggregate expenditures (Equation 4.1).

By summing the various components of aggregate expenditures we can derive the aggregate expenditure AE curve. The bottom "layer" of Figure 4.6(c) consists of autonomous *investment expenditures*. Since we have assumed that planned investment expenditures are autonomous, the same given amount of investment expenditures is associated with each income level. Next we add the given amount of *exports* and *government expenditures*, the next two rectangular "layers" in our diagram. The consumption function plotted against income (Figure 4.6(a)) is placed on top of the G, X, and I layers of autonomous expenditure. Finally, imports, which depend on the level of income, are subtracted from the consumption function to obtain aggregate expenditures on Canadian-produced goods. The shaded area in Figure 4.6(c), corresponding to the import function in Figure 4.6(b), represents imports M. The subtraction of M from the sum of $I + G + X + C$ produces the aggregate expenditure AE curve.

Each point along the aggregate expenditure AE curve represents the total amount of *planned* expenditures that would occur for a given level of income Y. The intercept (height) of the AE curve depends positively on the given amounts of autonomous investment I, exports X, government expenditures G, and autonomous consumption expenditures C_a, and negatively on the T_a intercept in the tax function. If I, X, G, or C_a were to decrease, then the intercept of the AE curve becomes smaller and the AE curve shifts downwards (more on this possibility below).

The slope of the aggregate expenditure curve is determined by the slope of the consumption function $b(1 - t)$ minus the slope of the import function m. Thus, the slope of the AE curve will increase (and the AE curve become steeper) if the marginal propensity to consume b increases, or if the marginal tax rate t decreases, or if the marginal propensity to import m decreases.

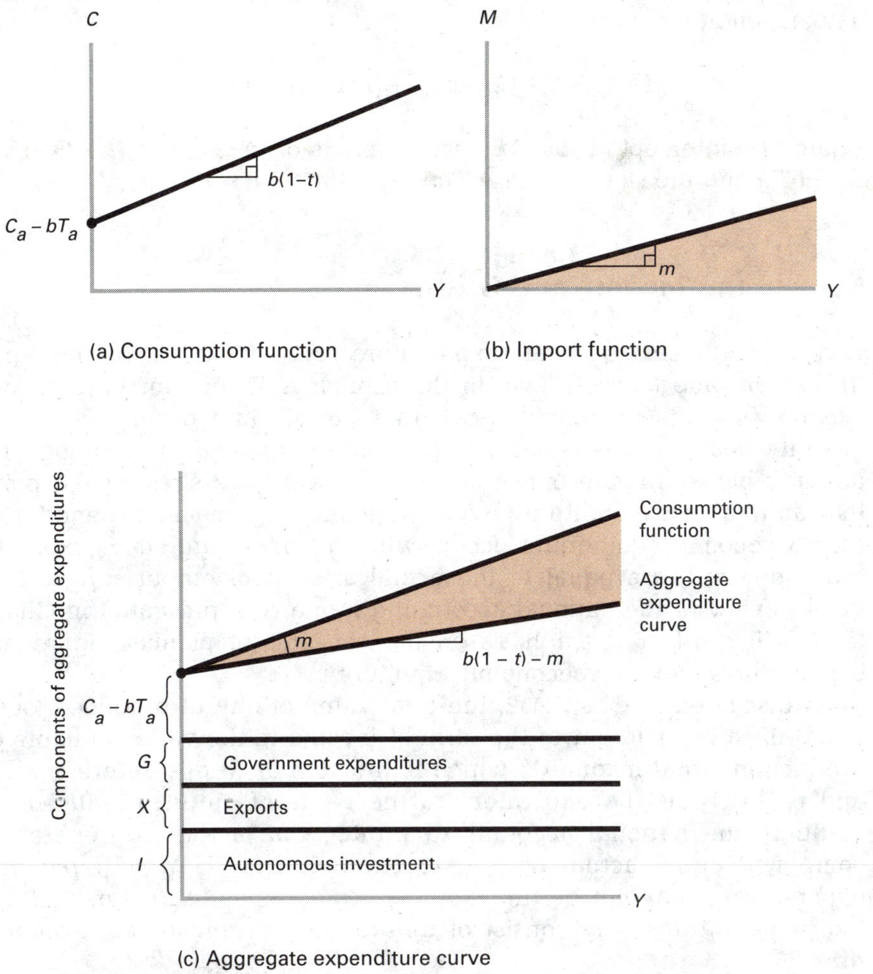

Figure 4.6 Deriving the aggregate expenditure curve

An equation for the aggregate expenditure curve can be readily obtained by substituting the consumption function (Equation 4.2a) and the import function (Equation 4.4) into the aggregate expenditure identity (Equation 4.1).

$$AE = C + I + G + X - M \tag{4.1}$$

$$AE = C_a - bT_a + b(1 - t)Y + I + G + X - mY$$

Rearranging the terms produces the following equation for the aggregate expenditure curve:

$$AE = (I + G + X + C_a - bT_a) + [b(1 - t) - m]Y \tag{4.6}$$

Again, the intercept of the AE curve consists of the sum of $(I + G + X + C_a - bT_a)$ and the slope of the AE curve is $[b(1 - t) - m]$.

Equilibrium Income and Output

Given a particular aggregate expenditure curve, what will be the **equilibrium income** (output) level in the economy? From your introductory economics course you will recall that equilibrium occurs when the quantity *demanded* is equal to the quantity *supplied*. In defining and deriving our aggregate expenditure curve, we have stressed the point that aggregate expenditures refer to *planned* aggregate expenditures. Macroeconomic equilibrium occurs when *planned* aggregate expenditures (demand) are equal to the actual amount of output supplied. A quick review of the national accounting framework presented in Chapter 2 will clarify our emphasis on the concepts of planned aggregate expenditures and macroeconomic equilibrium.

As discussed in Chapter 2, the total value of output produced (supplied) must be paid out in the form of income to the various factors of production. Total income Y, which is the sum of wages, interest, rent, and profits, must be equivalent to the value of output produced. In addition, the national accounts guarantee that actual aggregate income will equal actual aggregate expenditures. However, *planned* expenditures may not be the same as *actual* expenditures; part of actual expenditures may consist of unintended, or *unplanned*, expenditures.

To illustrate, suppose for some reason a store encounters lower sales than anticipated. Under such conditions, inventory stocks will likely pile up. For example, if a store expects to sell an additional 100 units of output in April (and in March orders an extra 100 units of output from factories), April sales of only 50 units would leave the store with an unplanned increase in inventories of 50 units. The national income accountant will classify these 50 extra units of inventories as an investment expenditure by the store. However, such an unplanned increase in (April) inventory stocks will have future ramifications. With inventory stocks piling up, the store will likely cut back on May and June factory orders (to reduce the size of the unexpectedly large April inventory stock), which will lead to reductions in factory production and income. Unexpected or unplanned spending today can lead to a change in income and output tomorrow. Under such circumstances, today's *actual* level of income and expenditure (which includes unintended inventory investment) cannot be the equilibrium level, since forces exist that will lead to a change in future income levels.

The concept of equilibrium implies a state of rest for the macroeconomic system. For an economy to be in equilibrium, no forces or pressures exist that would cause a change in income or production. Aggregate supply — which equals national income — must be in line with *planned* aggregate expenditures, with no **unintended changes in inventory stocks**.

As represented by Equation 4.7, macroeconomic equilibrium requires that aggregate expenditures AE equal aggregate income Y: *demand must equal supply.*

$$AE = Y \tag{4.7}$$

This equilibrium condition is illustrated in Figure 4.7(a). Since both aggregate expenditures AE and aggregate income Y are measured in the same units, the **$AE = Y$ equilibrium condition** is represented by a 45° ray through the origin (all points along this 45° ray are equidistant from both axes). Any point along the $AE = Y$ 45° line is a possible equilibrium position for our hypothetical fixed price economy.

Determining the Unique Equilibrium Position

Having described all possible equilibrium positions for the economy (the $AE = Y$ 45° line), we must now determine at which particular income level the economy will come to rest. To answer this important question, we return to the aggregate expenditure curve which describes total *planned* expenditures in terms of various income levels.

In Figure 4.7(b) we have superimposed the *planned* aggregate expenditure AE curve from Figure 4.6 (without all the layers) on top of the equilibrium condition (the $AE = Y$ 45° line), producing the now famous Keynesian cross diagram. Like most diagrams in economics, the intersection point E is of special significance. When income is at the level Y_E, planned aggregate expenditures are exactly equal to aggregate income. Of all possible equilibrium positions along the $AE = Y$ 45° line, only point E coincides with the *planned* aggregate expenditure curve. Given the aggregate expenditure AE curve in Figure 4.7, point E represents the unique equilibrium position for the economy.

To demonstrate that Y_E represents the unique equilibrium income level, we briefly consider other possible income levels. Suppose that the

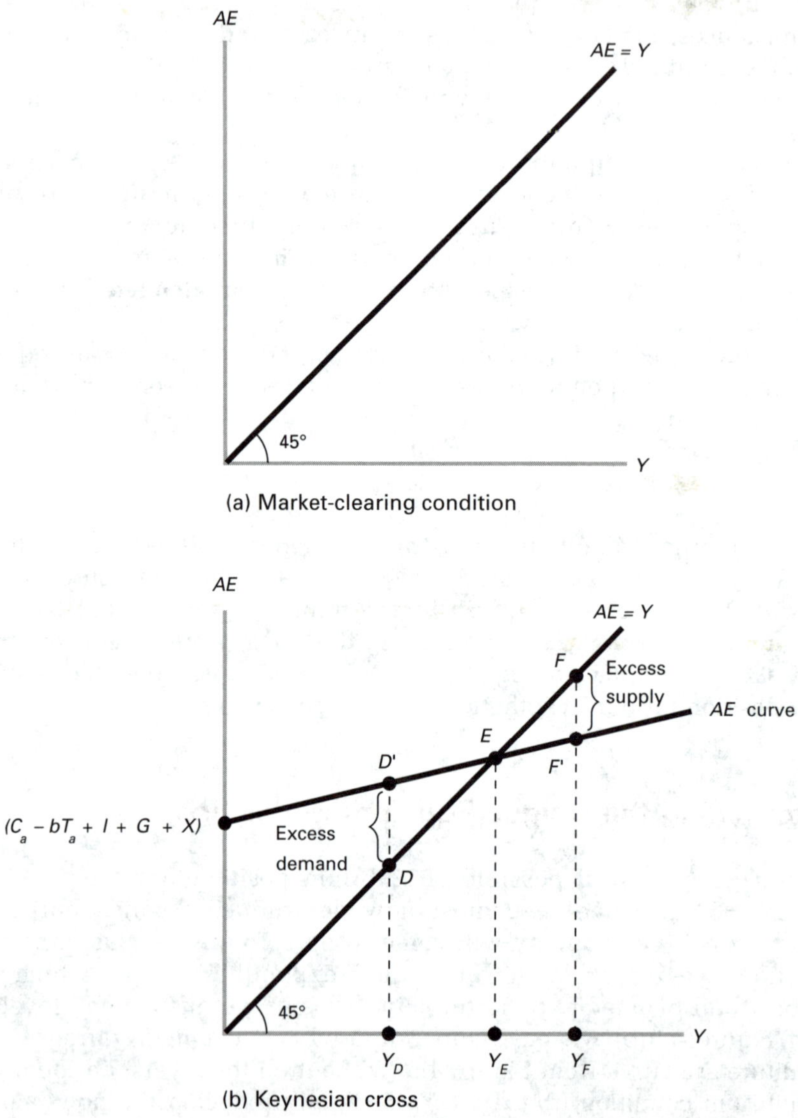

Figure 4.7 Equilibrium in the Keynesian cross model

economy were back at position D, another possible point along the $AE = Y$ 45° line in Figure 4.7(b), with a lower income level Y_D. At this lower income level, planned aggregate expenditures exceed aggregate income (supply) by the vertical distance DD'. Given a state of excess demand in the goods market, firms can sell more goods than are currently being produced. As a consequence of this excess demand, the stock of inventories held by stores will be depleted and new factory orders will be initiated to supply the excess demand and to replenish dwindling inventory stocks. With increased new orders, factories will increase the level of output and generate additional income for the factors of production. The excess demand for goods at Y_D has caused the level of income and output to increase. Our key assumption of inflexible price levels rules out any bidding up of prices under excess demand conditions.

As long as there is *any* excess demand in the goods market, there will be further upward adjustments in income as stores continue to restock dwindling inventories and initiate new factory orders. Once income and output reach Y_E, there will be no excess demand for goods and inventory stocks will remain at their normal levels. With no unintended inventory changes (which would trigger a change in factory orders), output and income levels will stabilize at Y_E, the unique equilibrium income level where *planned* aggregate expenditure equals aggregate income.

A similar set of downward adjustments would occur if the income level happened to exceed Y_E. At point F in Figure 4.7(b), a state of excess supply FF' in the goods market will occur. Since there is insufficient spending to absorb the amount of output being produced, inventory stocks will start to rise, new factory orders will be cut back and production (and income) levels will decline. Given an excess supply of goods, there will be a continual series of downward adjustments in income and output levels until the economy returns to Y_E.

In summary, the intersection point of the *planned* aggregate expenditure curve and the equilibrium $AE = Y$ 45° line represents a unique point of zero excess demand for goods. It is the only point where (1) planned aggregate expenditure is equal to aggregate income and (2) there are no unintended changes in inventory stocks. For any income level other than Y_E, planned aggregate expenditure will not equal income, and inventory stocks will be either accumulating or declining. Changing inventory stocks will lead to changes in factory orders and subsequent adjustments in output and income. Based on this inventory adjustment mechanism, aggregate income will *increase* when the level of income is below Y_E and *decrease* when the level of income is above Y_E. Thus the economy is **stable** in the sense that it will always gravitate back to this unique equilibrium income position if it happens to find itself out of equilibrium. Once the economy reaches point E, where planned aggregate expenditure is equal to aggregate income, there will be no further adjustment pressures. Other things being equal, the economy will perpetually remain at Y_E, the unique equilibrium income position.

The Determinants of Equilibrium Income

In the previous section we defined the equilibrium income position for the economy in terms of planned aggregate expenditures being equal to aggregate income and demonstrated that this unique equilibrium income position is stable. We now wish to explore the fundamental **determinants of equilibrium income** in this simple model. In a superficial sense, equilibrium income is determined by the intersection point of the *planned* aggregate expenditure curve and the $AE = Y$ 45° line. But what determines the exact intersection point in this Keynesian cross diagram? Since the 45° line is inviolate (equilibrium requires the equality of AE and Y), this intersection point depends exclusively on the position (intercept and slope) of the planned aggregate expenditure AE curve. Equilibrium income in the Keynesian cross model is *demand*-determined.

In a fundamental sense, equilibrium income depends on the *behaviour* of consumers and importers (as depicted by the consumption function and the import function) and the level of autonomous expenditure.

A Change in Behaviour

To illustrate the fundamental determinants of equilibrium income, we initially consider the behaviour of consumers. Suppose that people change their consumption behaviour. Rather than spending 85¢ of every *marginal* income dollar (see Figure 4.3), suppose that consumers now spend 90¢ out of every income dollar. Such a change in consumer behaviour increases the marginal propensity to consume from 0.85 to 0.90, causing both the consumption function and the aggregate expenditure curve to become steeper and rotate upwards (in a counter-clockwise direction). For simplicity we assume that the intercept of the consumption function is unaffected by this change in behaviour. As shown in Figure 4.8(a), a *steeper* aggregate expenditure curve will generate a *higher* intersection point in the Keynesian cross diagram (E_1 versus E_0) and a *higher* equilibrium income level (Y_1 versus Y_0).

The explanation for this increase in the equilibrium income level resulting from a higher marginal propensity to consume is straightforward. At the old income level Y_0, the increase in the marginal propensity to consume has created an excess demand for goods (see Figure 4.8) and an unplanned depletion of inventory stocks. As stores restock their inventories, output and income levels will rise. This upward adjustment in income will continue until income has reached the level Y_1, where the excess demand for goods is zero and aggregate

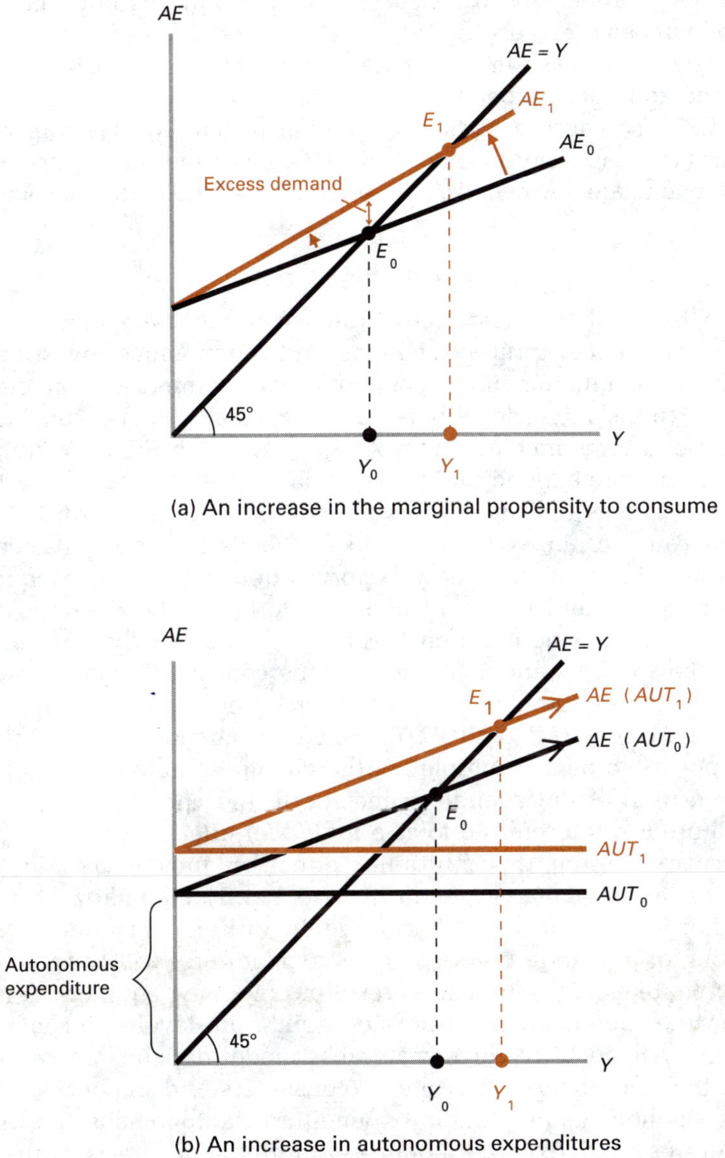

Figure 4.8 Determinants of equilibrium income

income equals the new planned level of aggregate expenditure (based on the new steeper consumption function). An increase (decrease) in the marginal propensity to consume will cause the equilibrium income level to increase (decrease).[12]

Similarly, a decrease in the marginal propensity to import, which also causes the aggregate expenditure curve to become steeper and rotate upwards, will also cause a higher equilibrium income level. An increase in the marginal propensity to import, which causes the aggregate expenditure curve to rotate downwards, will cause a lower equilibrium income level.

A Change in Autonomous Expenditures

Suppose that autonomous expenditures were to change. Perhaps the state of confidence abruptly changes and autonomous investment expenditures (or autonomous consumption expenditures C_a) increase. Or, perhaps exports increase. Whatever the reason, suppose that autonomous expenditures increase from AUT_0 to AUT_1 in Figure 4.8(b), causing the aggregate expenditure curve to shift upwards, from $AE(AUT_0)$ to $AE(AUT_1)$. The equilibrium income level will increase from Y_0 to Y_1 (again because of an excess demand for goods at Y_0, the restocking of inventories, the placing of new factory orders and the consequent increase in output and factor incomes). In terms of the diagram, the resulting increase in equilibrium income, represented by the horizontal distance between Y_0 and Y_1, appears to be considerably larger than the initial increase in autonomous expenditures, represented by the vertical distance between AUT_1 and AUT_0. Since the change in equilibrium income appears to be a "multiple" of the change in autonomous expenditures, the ratio of the change in income to the change in autonomous expenditure is often referred to as a *multiplier effect*.

Before examining this multiplier effect on income arising from a change in autonomous expenditure, we briefly summarize the major conclusions of Figure 4.8. A change in either consumer or import behaviour, or a change in autonomous expenditure, will cause a shift in the aggregate expenditure curve, resulting in a new equilibrium level of income. In a fundamental sense, the equilibrium level of income in our rudimentary fixed price Keynesian cross model depends on two sets of factors: the underlying behaviour of consumers and importers; and the level of autonomous investment expenditures, autonomous consumption expenditures, and exports. Again equilibrium income is entirely demand-determined.

[12] This particular property of the Keynesian cross model is often called the "paradox of thrift." For a given level of autonomous expenditures, the more "thrifty" consumers are (that is, the lower the MPC), the lower will be the equilibrium income level. If everyone decided to save a larger proportion of his/her income, the Keynesian cross model predicts that the equilibrium income level will decline — "thrifty" consumer behaviour is no virtue. However, it should be noted that this striking conclusion depends crucially on the assumption of fixed price levels.

The Multiplier Process

Returning to our analysis of the income effect arising from a change in autonomous expenditures, we now tackle one of the most crucial concepts in Keynesian economics: the multiplier. To illustrate **the multiplier process**, consider the case of a hypothetical fixed price economy represented by the following three equations:

$$C = 10 + 0.8Y$$
$$I = 9$$
$$AE = C + I$$

The marginal propensity to consume is assumed to be 0.8 and autonomous investment expenditure is assumed to be $9 billion per year. For simplicity, we ignore government expenditures, taxes, exports, and imports. Our hypothetical economy will be in equilibrium when aggregate expenditure AE is equal to aggregate income Y.[13]

Now suppose that autonomous investment expenditures increase by $1 billion, to $10 billion per year. By how much will equilibrium income rise? At first glance, the answer would appear to be $1 billion per year since that is the value of the *additional investment* goods that will be produced each year. However, this figure of $1 billion seriously *understates* the income-generating effects of a $1 billion increase in autonomous investment expenditures (assuming fixed price levels). A clue to the problem can be obtained from the equilibrium condition which states that $Y = AE = C + I$. Obviously if investment increases by one unit, income Y must also increase by one unit. But this is not the end of the story. Since consumption depends on income, consumer expenditures will also increase, giving a further boost to income. The final change in equilibrium income will therefore be greater than the initial increase in investment expenditures.

The reason for this larger increase in income following an increase in autonomous investment expenditure is straightforward. The construction workers who are now employed on the *new* investment projects are earning $1 billion in additional income (these construction workers were

---

[13] As computed below, the equilibrium income level is $95 billion per year:

$$Y = AE = C + I = 10 + 0.8Y + 9$$
$$Y = 19 + 0.8Y$$
$$0.2Y = 19$$
$$Y = 95$$

Given an income level of $95 billion, consumers will spend $86 billion [$C = 10 + 0.8(95) = 86$]. Add to this $86 billion of consumption expenditures another $9 billion of autonomous investment expenditures and we have an aggregate expenditure of $95 billion, exactly equal to aggregate income of $95 billion.

unemployed when investment expenditures were $9 billion per year). According to the consumption function, eight-tenths of this extra $1 billion income will be spent on consumer goods and services, representing an increase in induced consumer spending of $0.8 billion per year. Additional factory workers, bartenders, and clerks will have to be employed to produce the goods and services that the *newly* employed construction workers will now demand. But as these extra goods and services are being produced, *additional* incomes of $0.8 billion per year will be paid to the factory workers, bartenders, and clerks. Eight-tenths of this new income will be spent by these factory workers, bartenders, and clerks on new consumer goods, resulting in $0.64 billion *additional* income for another new group of workers. Even though our story is still not over — since 80 percent of the $0.64 billion additional income will be spent on additional consumer goods creating $0.512 billion additional income, etc. — we will spare readers further verses of the "multiplier house that Keynes built."

The total income-generating effects of an increase in autonomous investment expenditure will include the additional $1 billion in investment expenditure *plus* the sum of all of these induced increases in consumer expenditures ($0.8 billion, $0.64 billion, $0.512 billion, and so on). If we represent the marginal propensity to consume out of aggregate income by the symbol z, then the *additional* induced rounds of consumer expenditures following a one-unit increase in autonomous investment expenditure can be represented by the series z, z^2, z^3, z^4, etc. (in the above numerical illustration, the induced rounds of consumer expenditures are 0.8, 0.64, and 0.512, which correspond to 0.8, 0.8^2, and 0.8^3). Including the original one-unit increase in autonomous investment expenditure, the *total* increase in expenditures and income can be represented by the series

$$1 + z + z^2 + z^3 + z^4 + \ldots$$

Assuming that z is less than unity, the sum of this infinite geometric progession can be represented by the expression $1/(1 - z)$. If the marginal propensity to consume out of aggregate income is 0.8, then the multiplier effect is $1/(1 - 0.8)$, or $1/0.2 = 5$. The change in income is five times as large as the original change in autonomous investment expenditures.[14]

14 Thus, the new equilibrium income level will increase from $95 to $100 billion per year, following a $1 billion increase in autonomous investment expenditure. Substituting an income level of $100 billion into the consumption function, consumer expenditures will now be $90 billion per year [$C = 10 + 0.80(100) = 90$]. Adding on the new higher level of autonomous investment expenditure ($10 billion per year), aggregate expenditures will be $100 billion per year, $5 billion higher than when investment expenditures were $9 billion.

The multiplier effect $1/(1 - z)$ depends on z, which is the slope of the *planned* aggregate expenditure curve. The slope of the *AE* curve tells us by how much aggregate expenditures increase or decrease when aggregate income increases or decreases by one unit. As shown in Figure 4.6 (and in Equation 4.6), the slope of the *AE* curve is $[b(1 - t) - m]$. If the marginal propensity to import *m* or the marginal tax rate *t* increases, the slope (z) of the aggregate expenditure curve decreases and the multiplier effect declines (as z decreases, $(1 - z)$ increases and $1/(1 - z)$ decreases). The next section of the chapter presents an algebraic derivation for this multiplier effect.

The above example, with all of its simplifying assumptions (such as the assumption of fixed price levels), illustrates several major macroeconomic propositions. First, a change in the level of autonomous investment expenditures (or autonomous consumption expenditures or exports) will trigger a macroeconomic chain reaction as the economy moves to a new equilibrium position. Second, given the additional induced rounds of consumer expenditures, the change in equilibrium income will exceed the change in autonomous spending expenditures. Thus any instability in autonomous investment expenditures (or exports) will have a magnified (multiplier) effect on income levels, a key Keynesian proposition. Third, the exact value of this multiplier effect depends critically on consumer behaviour. If the marginal propensity to consume were to decline, then the successive rounds of induced consumer expenditures would be lower and the value of the multiplier would decline accordingly. Similarly, if the marginal propensity to import were to increase (or income tax rates were to increase), the successive rounds of induced consumer expenditures on Canadian-produced goods would also be lower and the multiplier would decline.

An Algebraic Representation of a Simple Macroeconomic Model

Our initial analysis of a simple macroeconomic model has relied heavily on the use of graphical techniques, including the now-famous Keynesian cross diagram. In this section of the chapter we retrace our initial steps in macroeconomic model-building by recasting our graphical analysis into algebraic terms. While graphical analysis undoubtedly has intuitive appeal for many readers, there are important advantages to be exploited in an algebraic analysis of macroeconomic models. Recall that a model is simply a set of interrelated theories and assumptions pertaining to a particular economic phenomenon. Since theories can be readily converted into equation form, analysis of economic models implicitly involves "solving" a small system of interrelated equations. The use of a modest amount of high-school algebra not only allows us to solve such macroeconomic models quickly, it also permits us to derive the key properties, characteristics and conclusions of our macroeconomic models in a very succinct, precise manner. In addition, the algebraic mode of analysis has an important advantage in that *qualitative* propositions may be transformed into *quantitative* terms. By combining statistical and algebraic techniques, we can generate numerical answers for key macroeconomic questions, such as determining the actual size of the multiplier effect.

As a means of introducing some necessary "model jargon," we briefly review the basic components of our simple fixed price Keynesian cross macroeconomic model. Five economic relationships comprise this simple model:

The aggregate expenditure identity:	$AE = C + I + (X - M) + G$	(4.1)
The consumption function:	$C = C_a + b(Y - T)$	(4.2)
The import function:	$M = mY$	(4.4)
The tax function:	$T = T_a + tY$	(4.5)
The equilibrium condition:	$AE = Y$	(4.7)

Throughout this textbook, uppercase letters are used to designate economic variables (such as consumption expenditures C and income Y), and lowercase letters are used to designate economic parameters (such as b, the marginal propensity to consume, and t, the income tax rate).

Economic variables

Economic variables within a model can generally be classified into two distinct categories: exogenous and endogenous variables. An **exogenous (or autonomous) variable** is a variable whose value is determined by forces *outside* the economic model; its value does not depend on any other variables that are included in the model, such as income. We take *exogenous* (autonomous) variables as "given." Variables that are explained and determined *within* the model are designated as **endogenous**. In an algebraic sense, the *endogenous* variables are the "unknowns" in the model. The algebraic solution for the model will provide an explanation for each of the endogenous variables. Within our simple fixed price Keynesian cross macroeconomic model, investment expenditure is *assumed* to be independent of income (that is, autonomous) and is therefore classified as an exogenous variable. Exports and government expenditures are also considered to be exogenous. The equilibrium level of income, the key endogenous variable in the Keynesian cross model, is "explained" in terms of the given values for these exogenous variables.

Macroeconomic model-building is very much the art of variable classification. For a particular economic problem, can a particular variable, for example, investment expenditure I, be considered as exogenous — something which we take as given? If not, then variable I must be classified as an endogenous variable and explained within the model. By including an explanation for variable I, the overall model will increase in size by one equation. The more realistic the model, the greater the proliferation of endogenous variables and equations within the model. Unfortunately as economic models get larger and more realistic, our basic understanding of the functioning of the model is quickly impaired. Only computers can sort out the complex interrelationships that exist in large-scale economic models where everything seems to depend on everything else. For pedagogic reasons we start with a very simple, small model in which certain key variables, such as investment and price levels, are *assumed* to be exogenous, or given. As our understanding of macroeconomics increases, more and more variables will be "explained" and incorporated as endogenous variables within our model (for example, investment becomes endogenous in the next chapter and prices become endogenous in Chapter 7).

Parameters

Within an economic model, **parameters** are employed to describe the *stable* features of the economic system. For example, the consumption function states that consumer expenditures depend on income levels. Assuming a linear relationship, the parameters C_a[15] and b depict the consumption function; the slope parameter b indicates the extent to which consumption expenditures change when income changes by one unit. Similarly, the parameter m describes import behaviour and indicates the extent to which imports change when income changes by one unit. The parameters T_a and t represent the income tax system and describe the relationship between income tax revenues and the level of income. As discussed above, statistical and econometric techniques can be used to generate numerical *estimates* for these underlying parameters (see Figures 4.3 and 4.5). As a general rule we will assume that the underlying behavioural parameters (such as b and m) are constant and we will solve our macroeconomic models algebraically in terms of a given set of parameters. As discussed above, if economic behaviour (the parameters) were to change, then a new equilibrium level of income would emerge (see Figure 4.8).

15 Autonomous consumption expenditure C_a (the intercept of the consumption function) might also be thought of as an exogenous variable (like autonomous investment expenditure).

Model Solution

In summary, our simple fixed price Keynesian cross model consists of five equations, five endogenous variables (*AE*, *C*, *M*, *T*, and *Y*), three exogenous variables (*I*, *X*, and *G*), and a set of parameters (C_a, *b*, *m*, T_a, and *t*).

We now wish to solve this five-equation macroeconomic model for the equilibrium income level. Imposing the equilibrium condition for the goods market,

$$Y = AE = C + I + G + (X - M)$$

and then substituting the consumption, tax, and import equations,

$$Y = C_a + bY - b(T_a + tY) + I + G + X - mY$$

produces the following solution equation for the equilibrium income level:

$$Y - bY + btY + mY = C_a - bT_a + I + G + X$$

or

$$Y(1 - b + bt + m) = C_a - bT_a + I + G + X$$

or

$$Y = \frac{(C_a - bT_a + I + G + X)}{(1 - b + bt + m)} \tag{4.8}$$

Equilibrium income, an endogenous variable, has been expressed strictly in terms of the "givens" within the model: autonomous investment expenditure *I*, government expenditures *G*, exports *X*, the tax parameters T_a and *t*, and the behavioural parameters C_a, *b*, and *m*.

This solution equation for *Y* is conventionally known as the **reduced-form** equation for *Y*. Endogenous variables that appear on the right-hand side of the equation have been systematically eliminated by algebraic substitutions; the *endogenous* variable *Y* has been "reduced" to an equation that consists entirely of the "givens" in the model. In fact one can obtain a reduced-form equation for *all* of the endogenous variables within the model.[16] The reduced-form equations of the model express each endogenous variable in terms of the given exogenous variables and parameters.

Once we have obtained the reduced-form equation for income, the underlying determinants of equilibrium income are in full view. If any of the "givens" in the model (C_a, *I*, *G*, *X*, T_a, *t*, *b*, or *m*) were to change,

---

16 For example, substituting our reduced-form income equation (4.8) into the import function produces the following reduced-form equation for *M*:

$$M = mY = m\frac{(C_a - bT_a + I + G + X)}{(1 - b + bt + m)}$$

the equilibrium income level will change in a systematic way. For example, a decline in autonomous investment expenditures I or exports X will cause a lower equilibrium income level (the numerator of Y in Equation 4.8 becomes smaller). Alternatively, if the marginal propensity to import (the parameter m) increases, equilibrium income will also decline (the denominator of Y in Equation 4.8 becomes larger and the ratio declines). In a fundamental sense, the equilibrium income level depends on the values of the exogenous variables and parameters in the model.

The Multiplier Once Again

Earlier we considered the multiplier effect on income that arises during the induced rounds of consumer expenditures following an increase in autonomous investment expenditure. The reduced-form equation for income can be used to determine the precise value of this income multiplier effect.

To illustrate how one can compute this multiplier effect, suppose that the value of autonomous investment expenditure is initially equal to I_0. Given the reduced-form income equation (4.8), the equilibrium income level Y_0 corresponding to I_0 must be the following:

$$Y_0 = \frac{(C_a - bT_a + I_0 + G + X)}{(1 - b + bt + m)} \tag{4.8a}$$

If autonomous investment expenditure increases by one unit (from I_0 to I_1), equilibrium income will rise to Y_1, where

$$Y_1 = \frac{(C_a - bT_a + I_1 + G + X)}{(1 - b + bt + m)} \tag{4.8b}$$

The increase in income arising from this one-unit increase in autonomous investment expenditure can be computed by subtracting Y_0 from Y_1. When Equation 4.8a is subtracted from Equation 4.8b, the C_a, $-bT_a$, G, and X terms will cancel each other out, leaving the following simple expression:

$$Y_1 - Y_0 = \frac{(I_1 - I_0)}{(1 - b + bt + m)}$$

Throughout this textbook the delta symbol Δ will be used to represent a change in a variable, such as $Y_1 - Y_0 = \Delta Y$ and $I_1 - I_0 = \Delta I$. Therefore,

$$\Delta Y = \frac{\Delta I}{(1 - b + bt + m)}$$

or

$$\frac{\Delta Y}{\Delta I} = \frac{1}{(1 - b + bt + m)} \tag{4.9a}$$

A one-unit increase in autonomous investment expenditure results in a $1/(1 - b + bt + m)$ increase in the equilibrium income level.[17] By a similar calculation, it can be shown that a one-unit increase in exports X causes exactly the same multiplier effect on income:

$$\frac{\Delta Y}{\Delta X} = \frac{1}{(1 - b + bt + m)} \tag{4.9b}$$

Note that in the reduced-form income equation (4.8), both I and X appear on the right-hand side of the equation with the same coefficient, $1/(1 - b + bt + m)$. The multiplier effect associated with a change in an exogenous variable (located in the numerator of the reduced-form equation) is simply the coefficient of that exogenous variable in the reduced-form equation.

The size of the multiplier effect on income from a change in I or X depends crucially on the income tax rate t and the underlying behaviour of consumers (the parameter b) and importers (the parameter m). Figure 4.3 provides an estimate of 0.85 for the marginal propensity to consume b and Figure 4.5 provides an estimate of 0.35 for the marginal propensity to import m. Using an estimate of 0.31 for the income tax rate, we can estimate the size of the income multiplier effect in Equations 4.9a and 4.9b.

$$\begin{aligned}\frac{\Delta Y}{\Delta X} = \frac{\Delta Y}{\Delta I} &= \frac{1}{(1 - b + bt + m)} \\ &= \frac{1}{1 - 0.85 + (0.85 \times 0.31) + 0.35} \\ &= \frac{1}{(0.15 + 0.26 + 0.35)} \\ &= \frac{1}{0.76} \\ &= 1.32\end{aligned}$$

In the fixed price Keynesian cross model, the Canadian income multiplier effect is estimated to be only 1.32. A relatively large marginal propensity to import ($m = 0.35$) and a relatively large income tax rate ($t = 0.31$) produce a relatively small income multiplier effect in Canada (if t and m were both zero, the income multiplier effect would be 6.67).

---

[17] Students with an elementary course in calculus will recognize that this multiplier effect is simply the derivative of the reduced-form income equation with respect to autonomous investment.

$$\frac{\Delta Y}{\Delta I} = \frac{dY}{dI} = \frac{1}{(1 - b + bt + m)}$$

Like the elasticity concept in microeconomics, the multiplier concept in macroeconomics is a very general, or generic, concept. The term "multiplier" is used to describe the change in the level of *any endogenous* variable (such as *Y*) given a one-unit change in a *particular exogenous* variable (such as *I* or *X*). Since most macroeconomic models consist of many endogenous and exogenous variables, by definition there are many different multiplier effects that can be computed.[18] The numerical value of a particular multiplier effect depends crucially on the structure of the entire macroeconomic model.

The Central Message of Keynesian Economics

As noted at the beginning of this chapter, the key integrating concept of Keynesian economics is *aggregate expenditure*. Given fixed price levels, income and employment are directly related to the level of *planned* aggregate expenditures. If planned aggregate expenditures decline, because of a decline in autonomous investment or exports, then the equilibrium income level will decrease (by a multiple of the decline in autonomous investment or exports) and the economy will slide into a recession. Given Keynes's critical assumption that wage and price levels are fixed and unresponsive to current economic conditions, the economy will remain trapped in this recessionary state until aggregate expenditure (demand) revives. In his analysis of the Great Depression, Safarian boldly states that the "failure in aggregate demand was at the root of the problem."

Keynes's diagnosis of the cause of persistent recessions and depressions immediately suggested a possible policy prescription. If the problem is insufficient aggregate expenditures, then the government should initiate policies to stimulate aggregate expenditures. In Keynes's view, the government has at its disposal a variety of different policies that are capable of stimulating aggregate expenditures and propelling the economy out of a recession. For example, the government could increase its own spending by building more post offices, buying more flags, pencils, and memo pads, or hiring more government employees to deliver the mail, hoist the flags, and write memos. Alternatively, the government could reduce taxes or increase transfer payments (such as welfare payments) to encourage greater consumer expenditures. In other words, any shortfall in aggregate expenditure could be offset by a government-induced increase in spending. Keynes firmly believed that serious recessions and depressions could be cured by a stimulative fiscal policy.

---

18 For example, the multiplier effect on imports from a one-unit change in autonomous investment expenditure can be calculated directly from the import reduced-form equation (see footnote 16).

$$\frac{\Delta M}{\Delta I} = \frac{m}{(1 - b + bt + m)}$$

The Role of Fiscal Policy in the Keynesian Cross Model

As derived earlier in this chapter, the aggregate expenditure curve is represented by the equation:

$$AE = (I + G + X + C_a - bT_a) + [b(1 - t) - m]Y \tag{4.6}$$

The government can affect the aggregate expenditure curve in two different ways. First, it can increase its own expenditures on goods and services. An increase in G increases the intercept in Equation 4.6, shifting the AE curve upwards. Second, it can lower tax rates, which will increase disposable income ($Y - T$) and increase consumer expenditures. A decrease in T_a, for example, from a decline in licence fees, increases the intercept in Equation 4.6, and shifts the AE curve upwards. A decrease in the marginal tax rate t causes the AE curve to have a larger slope and rotate upwards; for each level of income, a lower tax rate means that consumers will have larger disposable incomes and will therefore spend more on consumption expenditures, thereby raising aggregate expenditures.

The intercept of the aggregate expenditure curve is a very useful expression. It tells us that a \$1 billion increase in either autonomous investment expenditures I, or exports X, or government expenditures G will shift the AE curve upwards by \$1 billion. It also tells us that an increase in T_a of \$1 billion will shift the AE curve downwards by b billion dollars, which is less than \$1 billion (since b, the MPC, is less than unity). This tax-induced downward shift in the AE curve arises because consumers will have \$1 billion less in after-tax disposable income, which will be reflected in a reduction in consumption expenditures of b billion dollars.

As discussed earlier in this chapter, the economy will be in equilibrium when total planned aggregate expenditures AE are equal to aggregate income Y. In Figure 4.9 we lump together the various autonomous expenditure components (such as exports, autonomous investment, and government expenditures) as AUT_0 and draw the corresponding aggregate expenditure $AE(AUT_0)$ curve. Given this AUT_0 level of autonomous expenditures, the $AE(AUT_0)$ curve intersects the $AE = Y$ 45° line at point E_0 and the equilibrium income level is Y_0. For all levels of income below Y_0, aggregate expenditures will exceed aggregate income, inventories will decline and firms will initiate new factory orders which will lead to subsequent increases in output and income. Similarly, for all levels of income above the equilibrium income level Y_0, aggregate expenditures will fall short of aggregate income, and inventories will accumulate, leading to a reduction in factory orders, and a decline in output and income levels. In the face of either excess demand or

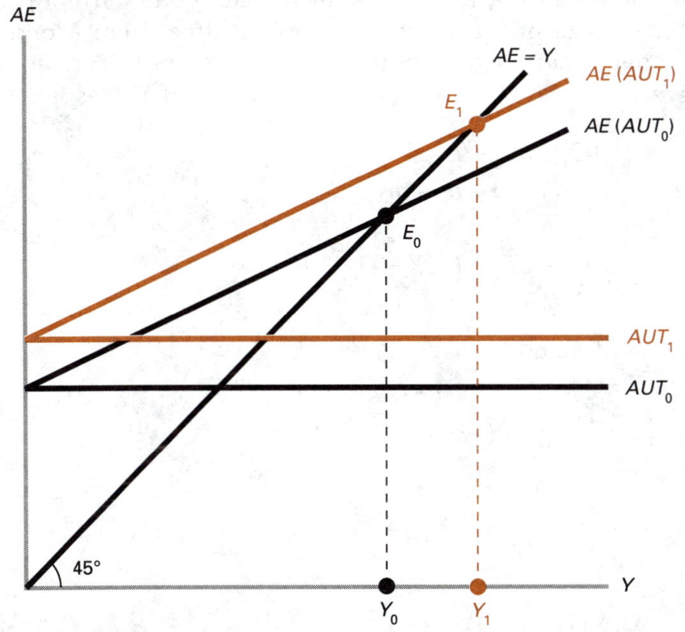

Figure 4.9 The Keynesian multiplier

excess supply in the goods market, income will gravitate back towards Y_0, the unique, stable equilibrium income level.

Now suppose that *either* autonomous investment expenditure *or* government expenditure increases by $1 billion. In either case, the level of autonomous expenditures rises by $1 billion, from AUT_0 to AUT_1, and the aggregate expenditure curve shifts upwards by $1 billion, to $AE(AUT_1)$. The new equilibrium income level will rise to Y_1, corresponding to the new intersection point E_1 of the $AE(AUT_1)$ curve and the $AE = Y$ 45° line. Diagrammatically, it makes absolutely no difference whether autonomous investment expenditure or government expenditure increases by $1 billion. In either case, the shift in the aggregate expenditure curve and the resulting multiplier effect on income $(Y_1 - Y_0)$ is the same.

To illustrate this key proposition, consider the construction of a $1 billion new office building. Irrespective of whether the government or a private sector firm constructs this office building, the subsequent induced rounds of consumer expenditures will be exactly the same. It makes no difference to the construction workers whether the government or the private sector initiated the building project. All paycheques are spent in the same manner.

We can again use the reduced-form income equation (4.8) to determine the exact size of the income multiplier effect from a one-unit increase in government expenditure (from G_0 to G_1). The equilibrium income levels associated with G_0 and G_1 are Y_0 and Y_1, respectively.

$$Y_0 = \frac{(C_a - bT_a + I + X + G_0)}{(1 - b + bt + m)} \tag{4.8c}$$

$$Y_1 = \frac{(C_a - bT_a + I + X + G_1)}{(1 - b + bt + m)} \tag{4.8d}$$

Again, Y_0 is subtracted from Y_1:

$$Y_1 - Y_0 = \frac{(0 + 0 + 0 + 0 + G_1 - G_0)}{(1 - b + bt + m)}$$

or

$$\Delta Y = \frac{\Delta G}{(1 - b + bt + m)}$$

or

$$\frac{\Delta Y}{\Delta G} = \frac{1}{(1 - b + bt + m)} \tag{4.9c}$$

Notice that the income multiplier effect from a change in government expenditure is exactly the same as the income multiplier effect from a change in autonomous investment expenditure (Equation 4.9a) and from a change in exports (Equation 4.9b). The three exogenous variables I, X, and G all appear in the reduced-form income equation (4.8) with the same coefficient and therefore have the same multiplier effect on income (recall our illustration of the construction of a $1 billion new office building).

This key conclusion led Keynes to the following important policy proposition: the macroeconomic effects of a decrease in autonomous investment (or exports) can be offset by an increase in government expenditures exactly equal to the decrease in autonomous investment (or exports). If the private sector is not building sufficient new factories to maintain full employment, the government sector should step in and build some new post offices, or universities, etc., to restore aggregrate expenditures and full employment.

Rather than increasing government expenditures, the government could cut taxes to stimulate expenditures by consumers. Suppose the government lowers the tax parameter T_a by $1 billion by abolishing all licence fees. A $1 billion decrease in T_a causes the aggregate expenditure curve to shift upwards by b billion dollars. Not all of the $1 billion tax cut will be spent, as consumers will save $(1 - b)$ dollars of any increase in disposable income. Unlike the case where the government spends $1 billion, a $1 billion tax cut produces less than $1 billion of first-round consumer expenditures. Subsequent induced rounds of consumer expenditures in the multiplier process will be accordingly smaller and the overall tax cut multiplier effect on income levels will be smaller than that associated with an increase in government expenditures.

The exact size of the income multiplier effects for a change T_a can again be calculated from the reduced-form income equation (4.8).

$$\frac{\Delta Y}{\Delta T_a} = \frac{-b}{(1 - b + bt + m)} \tag{4.9d}$$

This $\Delta Y/\Delta T_a$ multiplier is only b times as large as the $\Delta Y/\Delta G$ multiplier (see Equation 4.9c). Since $(1 - b)$ dollars of this tax cut will be saved (reducing the subsequent induced rounds of consumer expenditures), a \$1 billion cut in T_a generates only b times the income effect as a \$1 billion increase in government expenditures. Based on our statistical estimates for the parameters b, m, and t, the income multiplier effect from a \$1 billion reduction in T_a is estimated to be $0.85 \times 1.32 =$ \$1.12 billion. The fixed price Keynesian cross model suggests that a \$1 billion tax cut results in an increase of income slightly in excess of \$1 billion.

Finally, we consider briefly the government budget and income tax implications associated with these multiplier effects. Since any increase in income will be taxed (at the rate t in Equation 4.5), the size of the government deficit $(G - T)$ will decrease in size following an increase in autonomous investment or exports. Furthermore, when the government spends \$1 billion on new government expenditures, the government deficit will increase by less than \$1 billion because part of the resulting increase in income will flow back to the government in the form of increased income tax revenues. If the income multiplier effect from an increase in government expenditures is 1.32 (as estimated above) and the marginal tax rate is 0.31, a \$1 billion increase in government expenditures will generate an additional \$0.41 billion (0.31×1.32) in income tax revenues. The \$1 billion increase in government expenditures produces an increase in the government deficit of \$0.59 billion (given the induced increase in income tax revenues of \$0.41 billion).

The presence of income taxes also lowers the size of the income multiplier effects associated with a change in exports or autonomous investment expenditure. The higher the income tax rate t, the lower the increase in disposable income, the smaller the subsequent rounds of induced consumer expenditures and the lower the size of the multiplier. Income taxes act as an **automatic stabilizer** by reducing the size of the multiplier effects associated with changes in autonomous expenditures. An economy with high income tax rates will have lower multiplier effects and exhibit greater stability in the face of autonomous changes in aggregate expenditures (compared to an economy with low income tax rates).

Summary

The key integrating concept of Keynesian economics is aggregate expenditures (demand). If aggregate expenditures decline, for example, because of a decline in autonomous investment expenditure or exports, the equilibrium income level will decline and the unemployment rate will rise. There is no reason to believe that the equilibrium level of income (corresponding to the existing level of autonomous investment and exports) is necessarily consistent with full employment. Keynes's assumption of a fixed and unresponsive price level precluded the economy from returning on its own to a position of full employment (see Chapter 7). Faced with insufficient aggregate expenditure to provide full employment, Keynes argued that the government should use fiscal policies to stimulate aggregate demand and alleviate the unemployment problem. A shortfall in aggregate expenditure can be "offset" by an appropriate amount of fiscal stimulus. In Keynes's view, recessions and depressions could be cured by stimulative fiscal policies.

Keynesian economics rationalized a brand new "revolutionary" role for governments. According to Keynes, the government should manage or control aggregate expenditures (demand) to prevent persistent unemployment. The government should be an active player within the macroeconomic system, seeking to stabilize the economy by changing its spending and taxation policies. It is this *activist* or *interventionist* approach to stabilization policy that has attracted a great deal of criticism from monetarist and new classical economists. As we shall see in Chapter 9, there are many difficulties in trying to implement an "appropriate" Keynesian stabilization policy, not to mention the inflation complications arising from pouring on too much aggregate expenditure stimulus.

Key Concepts

aggregate expenditure
consumption (saving) function
the marginal propensity to consume
scatter diagram
least squares estimation technique
autonomous investment expenditure
exports
imports
the marginal propensity to import
government expenditures

income tax function
the aggregate expenditure curve
the equilibrium $AE = Y$ condition in the goods market
equilibrium income
unintended inventory changes
the stability of equilibrium income
the determinants of equilibrium income
the multiplier process
exogenous versus endogenous variables
parameters
the reduced-form equation of a macroeconomic model
the multiplier effect (as derived from the reduced-form equation)
fiscal policy
the effects of fiscal policy on the government deficit
automatic stabilizers

Review Questions

1. Explain how a positively-sloped saving–income relationship can be derived from the consumption function.
2. With respect to the behaviour of consumers, how did Keynes's views differ from the views of classical economists?
3. How do economists test their theories? Explain.
4. Why did Keynes think that most investment expenditures were autonomous?
5. What determines the level of imports?
6. How does a change in the income tax rate affect the consumption function?
7. What are the key assumptions behind the Keynesian cross representation of a simple macroeconomic model?
8. What determines the equilibrium level of income in this Keynesian cross macroeconomic model? Explain.
9. Why is this unique equilibrium income level stable? Explain.
10. Explain why the equilibrium level of income will increase if consumers decrease their marginal propensity to save.
11. What is the effect on equilibrium income when autonomous investment expenditures decline? Explain why the income effect will exceed the decline in autonomous investment expenditures.
12. Explain why the multiplier effect on income from a change in autonomous investment expenditures depends on the marginal propensity to consume, the marginal propensity to import, and the income tax rate.

13. Explain how one can obtain the algebraic reduced-form equation for a macroeconomic model. What are the key characteristics of reduced-form equations? How many reduced-form equations are there in a macroeconomic model?
14. Explain the concept of a multiplier in terms of the reduced form of the model. How many different multipliers are there in a macroeconomic model?
15. How would you go about computing the actual value for the multiplier effects on income associated with a change in autonomous investment expenditures?
16. Given Keynes's diagnosis of the causes of chronic unemployment during the 1930s, what government policies did he recommend? Why?
17. In terms of a simple Keynesian cross model, what are the multiplier effects associated with (a) an increase in government expenditure and (b) a decrease in the intercept of the income tax function?
18. Why are the income effects associated with a one-unit increase in government expenditures identical to those associated with a one-unit increase in autonomous investment expenditures or exports?
19. Why are the income effects associated with a $1 billion increase in government expenditure greater than the income effects associated with a $1 billion tax cut?
20. Explain why the presence of income taxes lowers the size of the income multipliers associated with a change in exports or autonomous investment expenditure.

CHAPTER 5

A Fixed Price Model of Income and Interest Rates: The *IS-LM* Model

> *The* General Theory *was attacked at the time of its publication as a subversive, radical document, but Keynes was in fact a high-caste Establishment figure who condemned Marxists. . . . He saw himself as an economic saviour, providing a way of pulling the world out of the Great Depression without fatally damaging the free enterprise system.*
>
> *Peter C. Newman*[1]

As discussed in the previous chapter, the major integrating theme of Keynesian economics is the concept of aggregate expenditures. Although Keynes assumed that consumer expenditures were a stable function of income levels (the Keynesian consumption function), business investment expenditures were considered to be much less stable and subject to important autonomous shifts. A wave of pessimism in business confidence could cause a serious decline in investment expenditures which would reverberate thoughout the economic system, producing a magnified reduction in income and employment levels. Or, the U.S. economy might enter a recession, causing a sharp reduction in Canadian exports, which would also trigger a negative multiplier effect on Canadian income and employment levels. The equilibrium income level might occur at a relatively low level, too low to ensure full employment. Keynes's assumption of fixed price levels precluded the "invisible hand" of Adam Smith from working its magic and restoring full employment via a reduction in wages and prices (see Chapter 7).

Keynes not only identified insufficient aggregate expenditures as the

1 P.C. Newman, *The Canadian Establishment* (Toronto: McClelland and Stewart, 1975), p. 331.

cause of recessions and depressions, he also suggested a policy prescription. The government has at its disposal a variety of different policies to stimulate aggregate expenditures and propel the economy back to a state of full employment. In Keynes's view, governments had the ability, and therefore the responsibility, to "control" aggregate expenditures and to stabilize output and employment levels. Prolonged bouts of severe unemployment (such as occurred during the 1930s) can be avoided by government policy intervention, although Keynes readily admitted that the "central controls necessary to ensure full employment will, of course, involve a large extension of the traditional functions of government."[2] The management of aggregate expenditures, using various government policies, is the essence of Keynesian economics.

In this chapter we develop a more complete model of Keynesian economics, building upon the Keynesian cross foundations presented in the previous chapter. In particular, we consider the role of interest rates and financial assets (money and bonds) in the macroeconomic system. Interest rates play a pivotal role in our model, affecting both the aggregate demand for goods and the demand for money. The latter part of the chapter reviews the monetary and fiscal policy implications of this more complete Keynesian model. Throughout this chapter we continue to assume that price levels are fixed, the key assumption in Keynesian economics. Chapter 7 permanently relaxes this fixed price assumption and incorporates a theory of price level determination into our macroeconomic model. As we shall see, the supply of money, a new feature of this chapter, has a lot to do with the determination of the price level and the process of inflation.

The basic model that we present in this chapter is the *IS-LM* model. The key to understanding this model is the separation of the economy into two major aggregate markets: the **goods market** (the *IS* part of the model) and the **money market** (the *LM* part of the model). As discussed in the previous chapter, the myriad different kinds of goods and services that are produced are aggregated into one giant goods market in which there are no distinctions drawn between different types of goods and services. As macroeconomists we *assume* that there is only one "good" in the marketplace. Although there are many different forms of financial assets, such as money, savings accounts, guaranteed investment certificates, bonds, and stocks, we *assume* that this set of financial assets can be represented by two assets: money and bonds. In our model, bonds are the representative financial asset that allows people to earn interest on their accumulated savings, rather than having to hold their savings in the form of money.

---

2 J.M. Keynes, *The General Theory of Employment, Interest and Money* (London: Macmillan, 1936), p. 379.

In developing our model, we carefully examine economic behaviour within each of these two large aggregate markets — the goods market and the money market. The various components of our model, such as a new investment function, will be kept as simple as possible in order that the key interactions between these two large aggregate markets can be fully understood. Equilibrium for the economy as a whole can only occur when both of these separate, but interrelated, markets are individually in equilibrium. We begin our analysis by considering the role of interest rates in the investment decision, and then turn to the money market.

Investment Expenditures and the Interest Rate

Suppose that a firm is considering a new investment project, such as the construction of a $10 million factory. The firm must carefully estimate the flow of all future revenues and costs associated with this new factory to determine whether or not it will be profitable. After detailed study of the firm's future demand prospects and costs, suppose that the controller's office of our hypothetical firm estimates that the annual rate of return on this new factory would be 8 percent (Chapter 17 discusses how the controller's office might calculate such a rate of return). Given an 8 percent return, should our hypothetical firm go ahead with its $10 million factory?

Since most firms do not have $10 million in idle cash, our hypothetical firm will probably have to borrow the funds to build the factory. Consequently the decision to invest, or not to invest, depends crucially on the interest rate that the firm must pay to borrow the required funds. If the interest rate exceeds the expected 8 percent rate of return, then a profit-maximizing firm would not want to proceed with this new factory because the cost of borrowing exceeds the estimated return. On the other hand, if the interest rate is less than 8 percent, say 6 percent, the firm would "profit" by building the new factory. After paying the annual interest charges of 6 percent, the firm would still have 2 percent of the estimated 8 percent rate of return left over in profits. Even if the firm had $10 million in idle cash, the same principle still applies. If the interest rate exceeds the return on the new investment project, it would be more profitable for the firm to lend its $10 million at the market interest rate than to undertake a new investment project which has a lower rate of return. The interest rate plays a crucial role in the investment decision. If the interest rate exceeds the estimated return on a proposed new investment project, the profit-maximizing firm will not invest.

Now suppose that the controller's office for our hypothetical firm is considering five mutually independent investment projects. Each investment project is carefully evaluated to determine its expected rate of return. The expected rates of return for these investment projects, ordered from highest return to lowest return, are estimated to be the following:

Investment project	Estimated rate of return
1	18%
2	11%
3	9%
4	7%
5	2%

For the firm to proceed with any particular investment project, the project must pass the profitability test: the estimated rate of return must exceed the interest rate. How many of these investment projects are undertaken depends critically on the level of interest rates.

If the current interest rate is 10 percent, only the first two investment projects pass the profitability test (that is, they have rates of return exceeding the 10 percent interest rate). However, if the interest rate declines from 10 percent to 8 percent, then investment project number 3 would become profitable. A decline in the interest rate increases the amount of investment expenditures. On the other hand, if interest rates were to rise from 10 percent to 12 percent, investment project number 2 would no longer be profitable and the profit-maximizing firm would only invest in project number 1. A rise in interest rates leads to a reduction in investment expenditures.

A similar argument applies to residential construction, another component of total investment expenditures. As interest rates for mortgage loans rise, new home buyers become more reticent. On the other hand, a decline in mortgage rates typically leads to an increase in demand for houses and an increase in residential construction activity.

The cost of borrowing funds is a very important part of the investment decision. A decrease (increase) in interest rates leads to an increase (decrease) in investment expenditures on new factories, machinery, and residential construction. Investment expenditures respond *negatively* to a change in interest rates.

Although Keynes accepted the proposition that investment expenditures tend to be negatively affected by changes in the interest rate, he emphasized the "precarious" process by which expectations of future revenues for an investment project are formulated. Given the difficulty in predicting future economic events and formulating long-term expectations of revenues and profits, Keynes believed that the current state of business confidence was a much more important factor in making investment decisions than was the interest rate. If investors are not very confident about the future, then they are unlikely to invest in new factories and equipment, irrespective of the interest rate. In Keynes's view, the level of investment expenditures depends much more on autonomous forces than on interest rates.

Was Keynes right or wrong? Are investment expenditures largely determined by autonomous forces? Or, are investment expenditures negatively related to interest rates? To examine this important issue we turn to Figure 5.1.

Figure 5.1(a) presents a scatter diagram for *total* investment expenditures on machinery, nonresidential construction (factories), and residential construction for the period 1960–1990. Since investment expenditures trend upwards with the overall growth of the economy, we have divided investment expenditures by GDP. As discussed in Chapter 3, in an *inflationary* world one must distinguish between the *nominal* interest rate and the *real* interest rate (which is the nominal interest rate less the expected inflation rate). In Chapter 17 we demonstrate that investment decisions are based on the real interest rate. To obtain the real interest rate, we subtract the annual percentage change in the consumer price index from the prime lending rate charged by banks. Given the time lags in the construction of new factories and apartment buildings, we plot last year's real interest rate against this year's investment expenditures divided by lagged GDP.

Unlike the statistical evidence presented for the consumption function in Chapter 4, empirical evidence for the **investment function** is not nearly as precise. Figure 5.1(a) appears to be all scatter. For the 30 years from 1960 to 1990, total investment expenditures (divided by GDP) seem to be randomly related to (lagged) real interest rates.[3]

However, this wide scatter of points conceals an important shift in the aggregate investment function in the 1980s. Data points for the 1960s and 1970s reveal a highly significant negative relationship between investment expenditures (divided by lagged GDP) and lagged real interest rates. All of the points for the 1960s and 1970s fall within a fairly narrow downward-sloping band. During the 1960s and 1970s, lower levels of investment expenditures are clearly associated with higher real interest rates. For each one-point increase in the real interest rate, total investment expenditures decreased by about $4 billion (measured in 1986 dollars). On the other hand, the data points for the 1980s form a circular pattern — a "sun" — rising over this downward-sloping band for the 1960s and 1970s. The aggregate investment function of the 1960s and 1970s is no longer applicable in the 1980s.

A skeptic looking at this circle of data points for the 1980s would argue that there is *no* relationship between investment expenditures and interest rates. However, a proponent of the interest rate theory of investment might argue there are at least two downward-sloping sets of points in the 1980s: a lower downward-sloping line for the early 1980s

3 In fact, there is a weak *positive* statistical relationship between investment expenditures (divided by lagged GDP) and lagged real interest rates over the 1960–90 period.

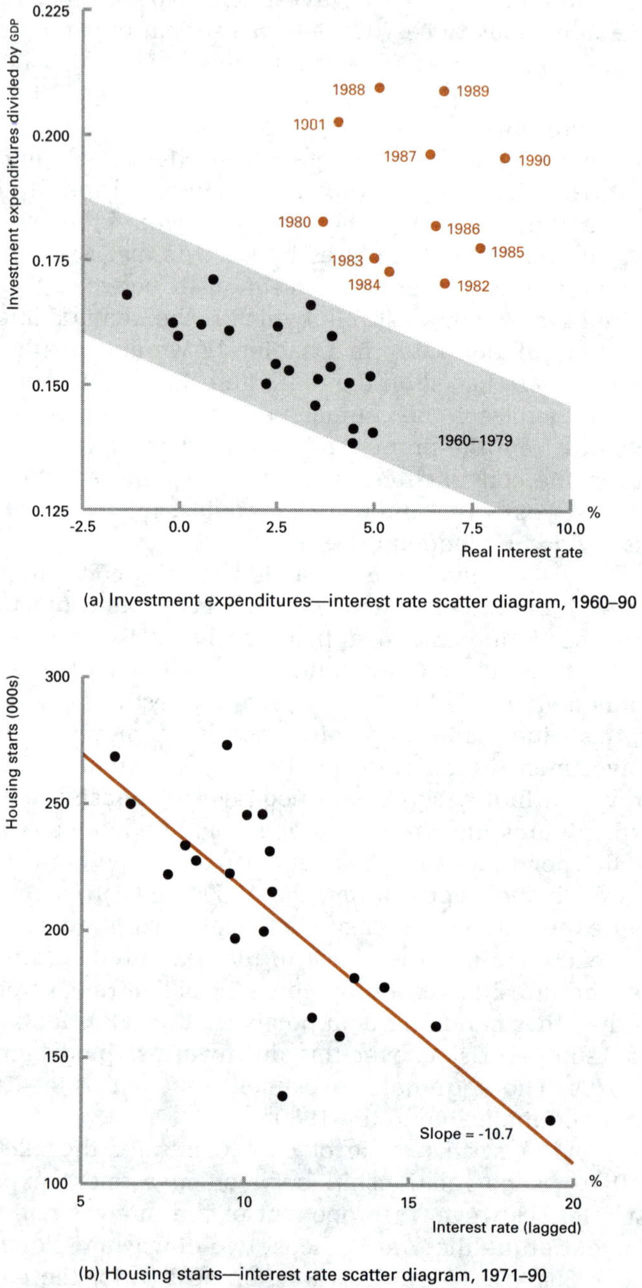

(a) Investment expenditures—interest rate scatter diagram, 1960–90

(b) Housing starts—interest rate scatter diagram, 1971–90

Figure 5.1 Investment expenditures and rate of interest

(1981 is an outlier) and a higher downward-sloping band for the late 1980s (with the mid-1980s caught in the middle). If one splits the 1980s into sub-periods, one can detect a negative relationship between investment expenditures and interest rates. The wide scatter of points in Figure 5.1(a) is attributed to several *autonomous* shifts in the investment function during the 1980s.

Given this wide scatter of points for total investment expenditures, Figure 5.1(b) provides an additional scatter diagram for the number of new housing starts, the key determinant of residential construction expenditures (which accounts for about one-third of total investment expenditures). Since mortgage contracts are specified in terms of the nominal interest rate, the lagged nominal interest rate is plotted on the horizontal axis. There is a very systematic negative relationship between interest rates and housing starts during the 1970s and 1980s; movements in interest rates explain over 60 percent of the variation in housing starts. For each one-point decrease in the interest rate, there are approximately 10,000 additional housing starts. Changes in interest rates clearly have an important influence on housing starts and residential investment expenditures.

Postponing a more complete analysis of investment expenditures until Chapter 17, the following simple linear equation is used to represent the investment function.

$$I = I_a - eR \tag{5.1}$$

Henceforward we will refer to the intercept I_a of the investment function as the **autonomous** (exogenous) element in the investment decision and the interest rate component eR as the **endogenous** element (investment expenditures negatively related to the interest rate). Autonomous investment expenditures I_a are independent of interest rates and income levels. As shown in Figure 5.2, an increase (decrease) in autonomous investment expenditures will cause an upward (downward) shift in the investment function. However, for a given level of autonomous investment expenditures (a given intercept I_a), the level of investment expenditures depends negatively on the rate of interest. A change in autonomous investment expenditures shifts the investment function, whereas a change in interest rates causes a movement along a particular investment function (based on a given amount of autonomous investment).

The *IS* Curve

Having postulated a new investment function in which investment expenditures are negatively related to interest rates, we now must rederive the aggregate expenditure curve. In Chapter 4 we developed the

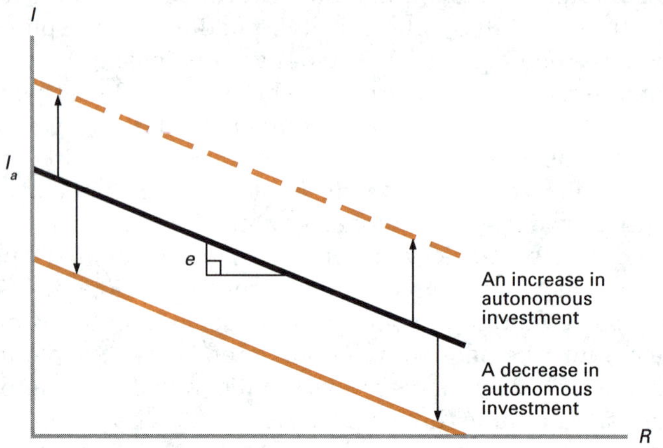

Figure 5.2 The investment function

following four equations to represent a simple (Keynesian cross) macro-economic model:

$$AE = C + I + G + (X - M) \tag{4.1}$$

$$C = C_a - bT_a + b(1 - t)Y \tag{4.2a}$$

$$M = mY \tag{4.4}$$

$$AE = Y \tag{4.7}$$

We now replace our previous assumption that all investment expenditures are autonomous with our new investment function (Equation 5.1). Substituting this new investment function, along with our consumption and import functions, into the aggregate expenditure identity, we obtain the following amended version of the aggregate expenditure curve (Equation 5.2).

$$AE = C + I + G + (X - M)$$

$$AE = [C_a - bT_a + b(1 - t)Y] + (I_a - eR) + G + (X - mY)$$

$$AE = [C_a - bT_a + G + X + (I_a - eR)] + [b(1 - t) - m]Y \tag{5.2}$$

Aggregate expenditures depend not only on the various autonomous or exogenous elements in our model (C_a, I_a, T_a, G, and X) and the level of income (net of income taxes and imports), they also depend on the level of interest rates. A decrease in interest rates causes an increase in investment expenditures which leads to an increase in aggregate expenditures.

Figure 5.3 illustrates our amended model in diagrammatic terms. Panel (a) reproduces the negative relationship between investment expenditures and interest rates (Equation 5.1) presented in Figure 5.2. In panel (b) we have placed the consumption function (Equation 4.2a) net of imports (Equation 4.4) on top of the given amounts of government expenditures and exports (we have labelled the sum of $C_a - bT_a + G + X$ as AUT). Aggregate expenditures AE consists of the sum of $C - M + G + X$ plus I. In our amended model, investment expenditures are no longer a given amount (like G and X) but depend *negatively* on the interest rate. For

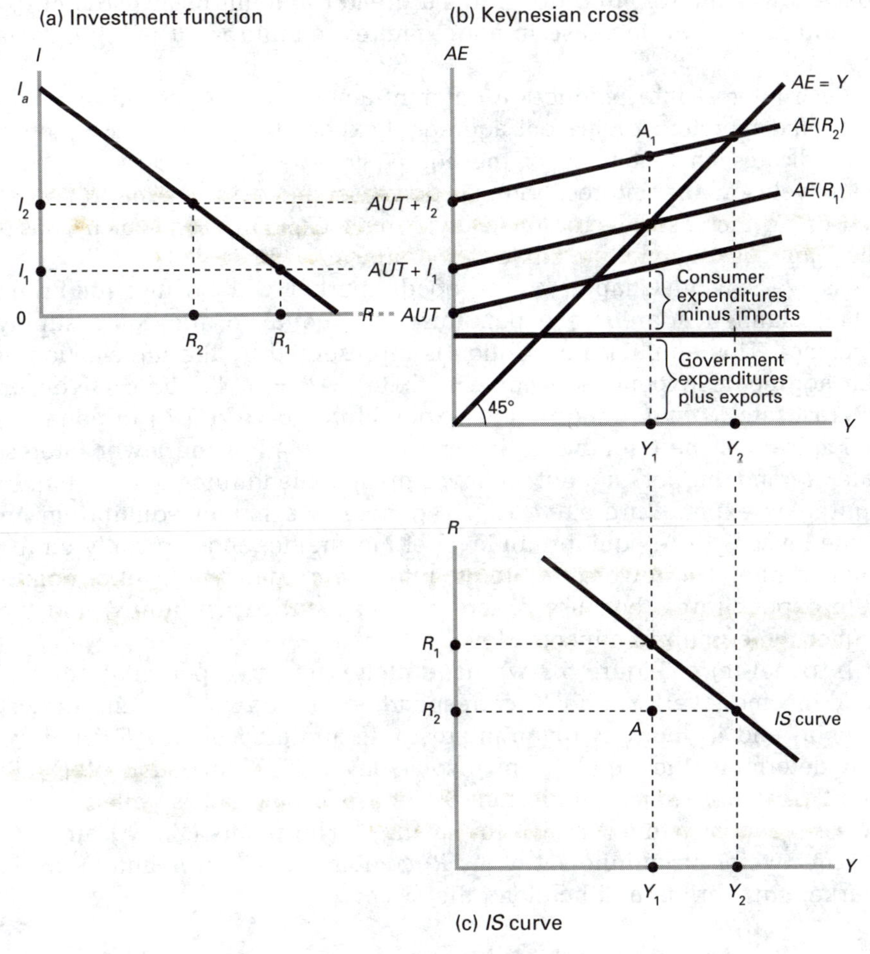

Figure 5.3 Derivation of the *IS* curve

each interest rate there will be a different level of investment expenditures and therefore a different level of aggregate expenditures.

To illustrate how our new aggregate expenditure curve can be constructed, suppose that the interest rate is R_1. From panel (a) of Figure 5.3 an interest rate R_1 generates investment expenditures equal to I_1. By adding this quantity of investment expenditures I_1 to AUT, we obtain the intercept of the aggregate expenditure curve corresponding to an interest rate of R_1. The line $AE(R_1)$ in panel (b) represents the aggregate expenditure AE curve when the interest rate is R_1. If the interest rate declines to R_2, investment expenditures increase to I_2 in panel (a) and the derived aggregate expenditure curve shifts up to $AE(R_2)$ in panel (b). A lower interest rate generates a greater amount of investment expenditures and an increase in aggregate expenditures (at every income level).

Each interest rate produces a different amount of investment expenditures and therefore a different aggregate expenditure curve. As Equation 5.2 indicates, the intercept of the aggregate expenditure curve depends negatively on the interest rate. A decrease (increase) in interest rates causes an increase (decrease) in investment expenditures, which causes the aggregate expenditure curve to shift upwards (downwards).

As we saw in Chapter 4, the goods market will be in equilibrium when planned aggregate expenditures are equal to aggregate supply (income). This equilibrium position is represented by the intersection of the aggregate expenditure curve with the $AE = Y$ 45° line. Given an interest rate R_1 and an aggregate expenditure curve $AE(R_1)$ in panel (b) of Figure 5.3, the equilibrium income level is Y_1. For the lower interest rate R_2 and higher amount of investment expenditures I_2, the higher aggregate expenditure curve $AE(R_2)$ generates a higher equilibrium income level Y_2. The equilibrium level of income depends crucially on the interest rate. The lower the interest rate, the greater the level of aggregate expenditures (because of larger investment expenditures) and the higher the equilibrium income level.

In panel (c) of Figure 5.3 we have plotted our two potential equilibrium income levels Y_1 and Y_2 corresponding to the two different interest rates R_1 and R_2. For any given interest rate and associated AE curve we can determine the equilibrium income level. The collection of (Y, R) points that maintains equilibrium in the goods market is called the ***IS* curve** (*I* for investment and *S* for saving).[4] The points (Y_1, R_1) and (Y_2, R_2) are two of an infinite set of (Y, R) combinations that maintain goods market equilibrium and lie along the *IS* curve.

---

[4] As a historical footnote, Keynes did not invent the *IS* (or *LM*) curve. The *IS-LM* graphical apparatus was first suggested by another British economist, Sir John Hicks, in an article which reviewed and summarized the major features of Keynes's *General Theory* ("Mr. Keynes and the 'Classics': A Suggested Interpretation," *Econometrica*, April 1937, pp. 147–59).

Definition of the *IS* Curve: The *IS* curve is the collection of all possible combinations of income and interest rates that maintain equilibrium in the goods market (assuming a fixed price level).

Any point that is not on the *IS* curve corresponds to a state of disequilibrium in the goods market. Consider an income-interest rate combination that is below the *IS* curve, for example, point A (Y_1, R_2) in panel (c) of Figure 5.3. Based on the $AE(R_2)$ curve corresponding to the (low) interest rate R_2, an income level of Y_1 generates a level of planned aggregate expenditures equal to the vertical distance A_1Y_1 in panel (b) of Figure 5.3. Point A_1 lies above the 45° line, indicating that planned aggregate expenditures, which are measured along the vertical axis, exceed aggregate income (supply), which is measured along the horizontal axis. All points, such as A, that lie below the *IS* curve correspond to a state of excess demand in the goods market, where planned expenditures exceed supply. Similarly, all points above the *IS* curve correspond to a state of excess supply in the goods market. As we saw in the previous chapter, excess demand or supply in the goods market will bring about a change in the level of income (because of an unplanned change in the stock of inventories which leads to a change in factory orders, output, and income). Only points along the *IS* curve represent a state of equilibrium in the goods market — where planned aggregate expenditures equal aggregate income and there are no unexpected changes in inventories.

The *IS* curve has a downward slope because the lower is the interest rate, the greater is the level of investment expenditures, the greater the level of aggregate expenditures, and therefore the larger is the equilibrium level of income.

As illustrated below, the steepness of the *IS* curve depends on the marginal propensity to consume, the income tax rate, the marginal propensity to import, and the slope of the investment function. For example, if investment expenditures are not very sensitive to interest rates (a small value for the parameter e and a relatively flat investment function), a decline in interest rates will produce only a small increase in investment expenditures, a small upward shift in the aggregate expenditure curve and a small increase in equilibrium income. If the equilibrium income level increases by only a small amount when interest rates decline, the *IS* curve will be relatively steep. On the other hand, if investment expenditures are highly responsive to interest rate movements (a large value for the parameter e), a decline in interest rates will lead to a large increase in investment expenditures and equilibrium income, producing a relatively flat *IS* curve.

Shifts in the *IS* Curve

The *IS* curve derived above was constructed by plotting the level of income that maintains equilibrium in the goods market for each interest rate. However, for any given interest rate, the equilibrium income level also depends on the parameters of the consumption, import, and tax functions and the amount of autonomous investment expenditures, government expenditures, and exports. The *IS* curve will shift (in a parallel manner) if any of the following events were to occur:

1. a change in autonomous investment expenditures I_a
2. a change in autonomous consumption expenditures C_a
3. a change in government expenditures G
4. a change in the tax intercept T_a
5. a change in exports X

All of these five changes involve a change in the intercept of the aggregate expenditure curve (see Equation 5.2), which leads to a shift in the *IS* curve.

To illustrate, we begin by considering the effect of a decrease in autonomous investment expenditures on the position of the *IS* curve (Figure 5.4). First, consider the investment function corresponding to I_a units of autonomous investment (see panel (a) of Figure 5.4). As in Figure 5.3, we select two interest rates R_1 and R_2 and then add the corresponding investment expenditures I_1 and I_2 to AUT to produce the two aggregate expenditure curves $AE(R_1)$ and $AE(R_2)$ (see panel (b) of Figure 5.4). Next we locate the two possible equilibrium income levels Y_1 and Y_2 corresponding to R_1 and R_2, respectively. In panel (c) we plot these two possible equilibrium points (Y_1, R_1) and (Y_2, R_2), which are representative of the *IS* curve based on I_a units of autonomous investment expenditures.

Now suppose that autonomous investment expenditures decline, causing the intercept of the investment function to shift downwards to I'_a in panel (a) of Figure 5.4. Along this new (lower) investment function, less investment expenditures will occur at all interest rates, including R_1 and R_2. Thus the two new aggregate expenditure curves $AE'(R_1)$ and $AE'(R_2)$ will lie *below* our original two aggregate expenditure curves $AE(R_1)$ and $AE(R_2)$ in panel (b) of Figure 5.4. Consequently, our two new equilibrium income levels Y'_1 and Y'_2 will have declined relative to our original equilibrium income levels Y_1 and Y_2. In panel (c) of Figure 5.4 we have plotted these two new equilibrium points (Y'_1, R_1) and (Y'_2, R_2), representative of the new *IS'* curve based on I'_a units of autonomous investment expenditures. A decline in autonomous investment expenditures causes the *IS* curve to shift downwards to the left.[5]

---

[5] The exact distance that the *IS* curve shifts leftwards can be computed easily. For any given interest rate, autonomous investment expenditures decline by the amount ΔI_a. As computed in Chapter 4, for a given interest rate the income multiplier effect from a decline in autonomous investment expenditures is $1/(1 - b + bt + m)$. The *IS* curve shifts leftwards by $1/(1 - b + bt + m)$ times the change in autonomous investment expenditures.

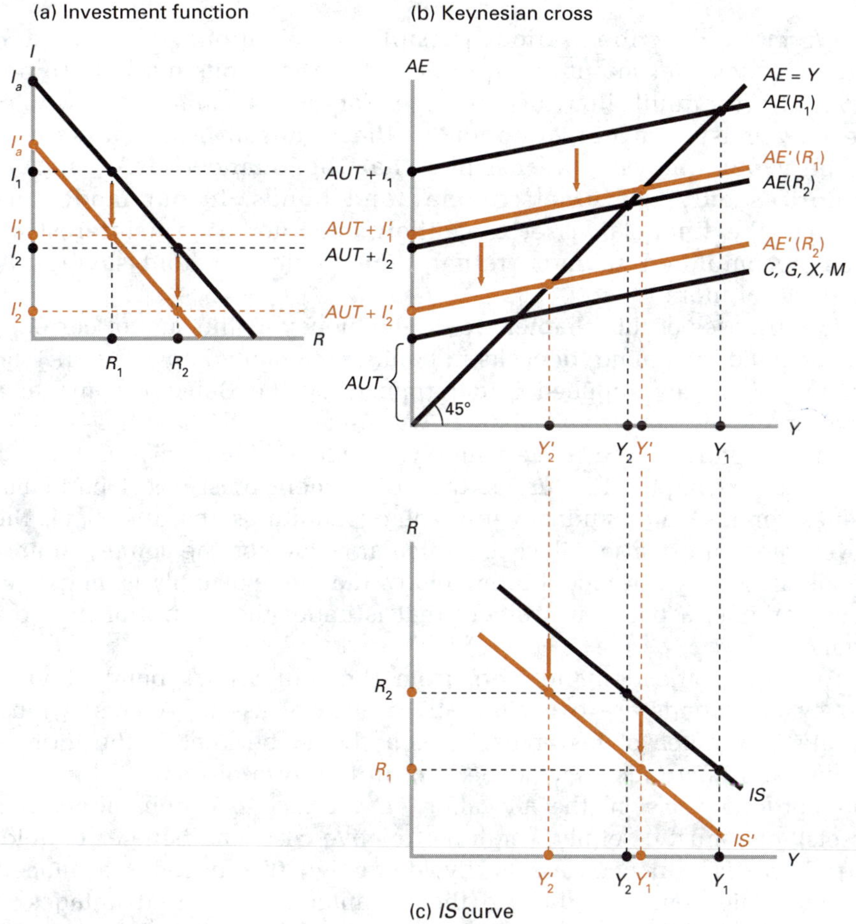

Figure 5.4 Shift in the *IS* curve

In general, any factor that shifts the intercept of the aggregate expenditure curve downwards will shift the *IS* curve downwards to the left. Conversely, any factor that shifts the intercept of the aggregate expenditure curve upwards will shift the *IS* curve upwards to the right. For example, an increase in autonomous consumption expenditures C_a, an increase in government spending G, an increase in exports X, or a decrease in the tax intercept T_a will all lead to an increase in aggregate expenditures, an upward shift in the aggregate expenditure curve and an upward–rightward shift in the *IS* curve.

The Money Market

The *IS* curve describes various possible combinations of income and interest rates that maintain equilibrium in the goods market. To determine *the* equilibrium income level for the economy as a whole, we now must turn our attention to the financial asset market. To simplify our analysis, we assume that the financial asset market comprises only two assets: money and bonds. In our model the bond is the financial asset that allows people to earn interest on their accumulated savings, rather than having to hold savings in the form of money.

For purposes of this chapter we define money as the sum of currency and demand (chequing) deposits in banks, commonly known as M1. The amount of money supplied is determined by the Bank of Canada, a government agency. In this chapter we discuss briefly how the Bank of Canada "controls" the money supply; a full treatment of this topic is provided in Chapter 15. Just as the government must select particular values for tax rates and government expenditures (fiscal policy), the government must also select a particular value for the **money supply** (monetary policy). In model terminology, the money supply is an exogenous variable, a policy instrument that is under the control of the government.

Turning to the demand side, from the individual's point of view money and bonds are two alternative financial assets. A person must decide how much of his or her wealth should be kept in the form of money and how much should be kept in the form of bonds. In making this portfolio decision (the allocation of wealth into various alternative assets), one must carefully weigh the relative costs and benefits of holding alternative financial assets. By identifying the functions of money, we can gain some insight into the advantages and disadvantages of holding wealth in the form of money.

First and foremost, money is the medium of exchange. Rather than having to barter good A for good B, people exchange money when they buy and sell goods, thereby avoiding the "double coincidence" of wants which is required under barter transactions. In a barter transaction not only must I want to exchange good A for good B, someone else must want to exchange good B for good A. Without money as a medium of exchange, a considerable amount of time and effort would be required to find someone who has an "opposite" set of wants. Second, money can serve as a store of value. The existence of money allows people to separate in time the two sides of a transaction. Using money as a medium of exchange and as a store of value, good A can be sold today and the proceeds can be used at some later date to purchase good B. However, the opportunity cost of holding money is the interest rate that could be earned from holding a bond.

The Transactions Demand for Money and the Interest Rate

Given these two major functions of money, we formulate a simple economic theory concerning why people choose to hold or demand money. First, the medium of exchange function of money suggests that people will hold money in order to facilitate economic transactions. Even though most people typically purchase goods and services (such as food and entertainment) on a fairly regular basis, income payments are received relatively infrequently, perhaps once or twice a month. Given that the receipt of income is not perfectly synchronized with expenditure patterns, people find it convenient to hold money to bridge the interval between the receipt and disbursement of income. The greater the level of income, the greater the number of transactions, and the greater the demand for money for transactions purposes.

However, to the extent that money is held to facilitate transactions, the interest payments that could have been earned by holding a bond are foregone. The higher the interest rate, the greater the opportunity cost of holding money for transactions purposes, and therefore the greater the desire to economize on the holding of idle cash by keeping funds invested in interest-earning assets. Although each person will likely differ with respect to the threshold interest rate which prompts him or her to transfer idle cash into interest-earning assets,[6] as the interest rate rises more and more people (and corporations) will manage their holding of money more carefully. Higher interest rates, for a given level of transactions, will lead to a reduction in the quantity of money demanded as people switch idle cash into interest-earning assets. The higher the opportunity cost of holding cash (that is, the higher the interest rate), the less money will be held for transactions purposes.[7]

To keep our theory as simple as possible, we have implicitly assumed that money pays no interest. In recent years the distinction between money and other financial assets has become increasingly blurred (see Chapter 15). For example, people can earn interest on chequing accounts (the major component of M1). However, the interest rate paid on such chequing accounts is typically lower than that paid on bonds and guaranteed investment certificates, and there are often constraints on these chequing accounts (such as a minimum monthly balance to avoid service charges). An increase in the interest rate paid on bonds and guaranteed investment certificates is not likely fully reflected in the in-

---

[6] There are, of course, costs involved in transferring idle cash into interest-earning assets, such as brokerage charges and the time and inconvenience of engaging in financial transactions (see Chapter 15).

[7] As discussed in Chapter 15, Keynes included interest rates as a negative determinant of the demand for money for quite different reasons. Rather than focusing on the cost of holding money when interest rates are high, Keynes suggested the possibility of making a capital gain by holding bonds (the "speculative" motive for demanding less money when interest rates are high).

terest rate paid on chequing accounts, leading people to reallocate money from low-interest chequing accounts into bonds and guaranteed investment certificates. Even with the introduction of interest-bearing chequing accounts, the **demand for money** will still bear a negative relationship to interest rates.

Figure 5.5 presents empirical evidence pertaining to the **demand for money**. Since our theory suggests two determinants of the demand for money, income and interest rates, we have resorted to a "diagrammick" to depict three variables in two dimensions. Along the horizontal axis of Figure 5.5 we have plotted money (as measured by M1) divided by total income (GDP). Our scatter diagram depicts the demand for money (relative to income levels) and interest rates for the years 1960–90.

The evidence presented in Figure 5.5 leaves little doubt that the demand for money varies inversely with the interest rate. With the exception of the year 1981 (when interest rates were at a record high), all of the data points lie quite close to a downward-sloping straight line. As interest rates rise, the quantity of money demanded (relative to income levels) clearly decreases. The empirical evidence presented in Figure 5.5 supports the theoretical concept of a downward-sloping demand for money curve. The demand for money depends negatively on interest rates (the cost of holding money) and positively on income levels (the transactions demand).[8] Collectively Canadians have economized on their holdings of money (relative to income levels) as interest rates have risen.

Equation 5.3 provides a simple linear algebraic formulation of the demand for money ($\$^D$) curve where k and ℓ represent behavioural parameters.

$$\$^D = kY - \ell R \tag{5.3}$$

The parameter k describes the sensitivity of the demand for money to changes in the level of income. Every extra dollar of income raises the transactions demand for money by k dollars. The size of this behavioural parameter k depends on the financial characteristics of the economy. For example, if everyone was paid every day (rather than once or twice a month), the parameter k would have a very low value since there would be a much greater synchronization between the receipt of income and expenditures (that is, there would be no need to hold idle cash for expenditures between pay days). The widespread use of credit cards has likely lowered the value of the parameter k; credit cards better enable one to synchronize the receipt of income with the payment of

---

8 In an inflationary world, the demand for money for transactions purposes obviously depends on nominal income levels. When we relax our assumption of fixed price levels in Chapter 7, we assume that the demand for real money depends on real income levels.

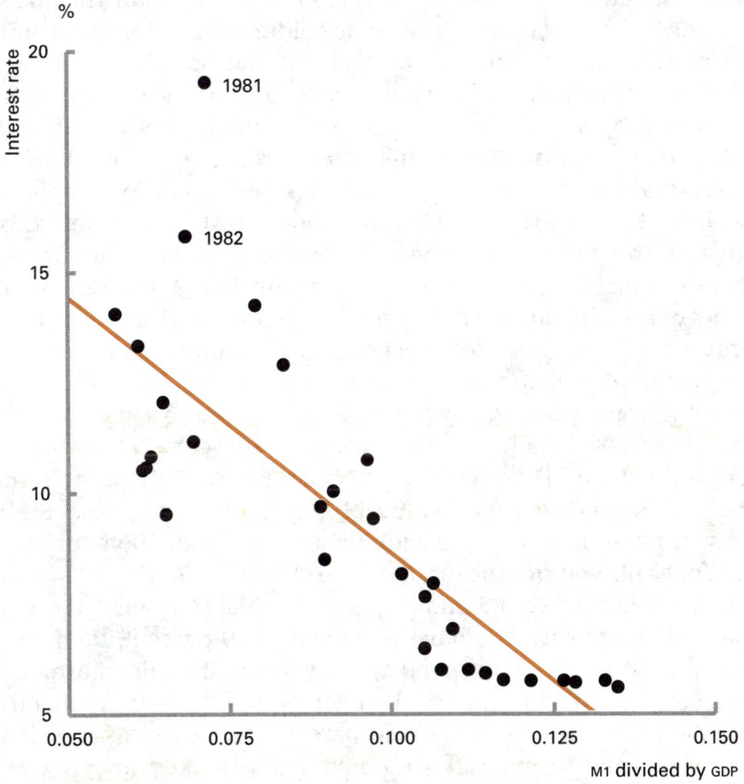

Figure 5.5 Demand for money scatter diagram, 1960–90

purchases. The parameter ℓ describes the sensitivity of the demand for money with respect to changes in the interest rate. Every extra percentage-point increase in the interest rate causes a decline in the demand for money by ℓ dollars. The size of the parameter ℓ is determined by the degree of substitutability between money and bonds. If money and bonds are highly substitutable (with low brokerage costs), the parameter ℓ will likely be very large. Under such circumstances, a one-percentage-point increase in interest rates will cause people to convert large amounts of money into bonds.

Bond Prices and the Interest Rate: A Brief Digression

The most important way in which governments (and many corporations) borrow funds is through the sale of bonds. The purchaser of a new bond lends money to the bond issuer for a given period of time at a *fixed* annual interest rate. For example, a $1,000, 20-year bond that pays 10 percent interest would provide the bondholder with 20 annual interest payments of $100 and at the end of 20 years the bondholder would be repaid the $1,000 principal. However, once a bond is issued, it is unlikely to be shut away in a vault until the maturity (repayment) date of the bond. For a variety of reasons, the purchaser of the bond (the lender) may want to convert the bond back into cash long before the bond matures. The bond market allows people to buy and sell existing bonds. Just as the stock exchange establishes a market price for existing corporate shares, the bond market establishes a market price for outstanding bonds. In this section we demonstrate that bond prices and interest rates move in *opposite* directions. *High* interest rates are associated with *low* bond prices, and vice versa.

Suppose that one year ago you purchased a new bond for $1,000, a bond that pays $100 in interest each year for 20 years. This 10 percent bond yield represented the prevailing market interest rate at the time the new bond was issued at a par value of $1,000. Now suppose that one year later you need money and decide to sell the bond, 19 years before it matures. What will you get for the bond on the bond market?

The market value of your bond depends crucially on what the current interest rate is. If interest rates have remained at 10 percent, then you will receive roughly $1,000 for your bond when you sell it. A purchaser will be indifferent between paying you $1,000 for your one-year-old bond and buying a new bond that also yields 10 percent. However, if interest rates have risen since you purchased your bond, say to 20 percent, you will receive considerably less than $1,000 for your one-year-old bond. Why should a purchaser give you $1,000 for a financial asset that pays only $100 in interest each year when new bonds offer $200 per year? The bond market would set a value for your old bond of approximately $500, because your old bond with its stream of $100 annual interest payments is worth only about one-half as much as a new bond with its stream of $200 annual interest payments. On the other hand, if interest rates have fallen since you purchased your bond, say to 5 percent, then the market price of your bond will have risen well above $1,000, to almost $2,000. Many people would like to purchase old bonds rather than new bonds which have much smaller interest payments. An excess demand for old bonds will push up their price relative to new bonds (issued at $1,000 par value and paying only 5 percent interest). As demonstrated in Chapter 15, there exists a precise mathematical relationship between bond prices and interest rates — they move in *opposite* directions.

Making use of this *negative* relationship between bond prices and interest rates, if bond prices are rising we know that interest rates must be falling. Conversely, if bond prices are falling, interest rates must be rising. For example, if the government wants to raise additional funds in the bond market, the additional supply of government bonds will depress bond prices and raise interest rates. To entice purchasers to buy this new issue (supply) of bonds, the government must offer a higher interest rate. In this chapter we make considerable use of this inverse relationship between bond prices and interest rates.

The *LM* Curve

Having provided a simple economic theory for the demand for money, we now derive a new curve that describes equilibrium in the money market to go along with the *IS* curve, which depicts equilibrium in the goods market. Following the conventions of demand curve analysis in microeconomics, in the left-hand panel of Figure 5.6 we plot the quantity of money on the horizontal axis and the interest rate (cost of holding money) on the vertical axis. As demonstrated empirically in Figure 5.5, the demand for money curve, like the demand curve for all other goods, slopes downwards to the right. A lower interest rate causes an increase in the quantity of money demanded (a downward movement along the demand for money curve). However, an increase in the level of income raises the total number of transactions taking place, which causes a rightward shift in the demand for money curve.[9] At each interest rate, more money will be demanded. In the left-hand panel of Figure 5.6 we

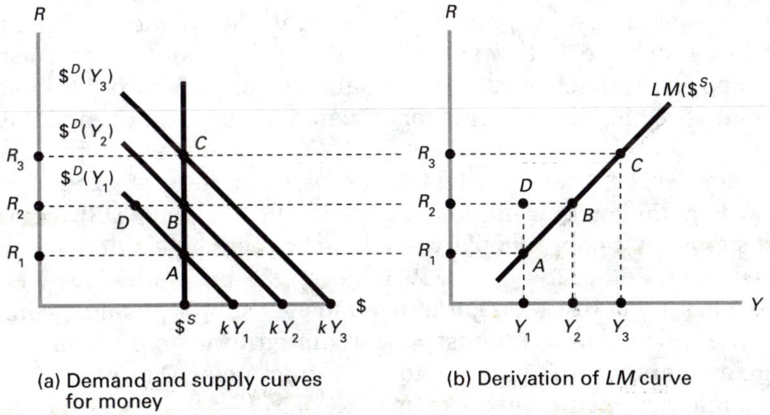

Figure 5.6 Equilibrium in the money and financial asset market

9 The horizontal intercept of the demand for money equation (5.3) is kY (set $R = 0$ and $\$^D = kY$). As income increases, the horizontal intercept shifts to the right and the demand for money curve shifts upwards to the right (see Figure 5.6).

have drawn three representative money demand curves corresponding to three different income levels, where $Y_3 > Y_2 > Y_1$.

On the horizontal axis we locate the particular amount of money that the Bank of Canada has chosen to supply $\$^S$ and have drawn in a vertical money supply curve. We assume that the quantity of money supplied by the Bank of Canada is independent of the prevailing interest rate.

As in all other markets, the money market will be in equilibrium when the demand for money is equal to the supply of money.

$$\$^D = \$^S \tag{5.4}$$

Based on these three hypothetical income levels Y_1, Y_2, and Y_3, points A, B, and C represent three possible equilibrium points where the demand for money is equal to the given supply of money.

The three potential money market equilibrium combinations of income and interest rates, (Y_1, R_1), (Y_2, R_2), and (Y_3, R_3), are plotted in the right-hand panel of Figure 5.6. Connecting these three points, we obtain a new curve which describes all possible combinations of income and interest rates that equate the demand for money to the given supply of money $\$^S$. This new curve is conventionally known as the ***LM* curve**, (L for liquidity and M for money).

Definition of the *LM* curve: The *LM* curve is the collection of all possible combinations of income and interest rates that maintain equilibrium in the money market (assuming a fixed price level).

Only points on the LM curve are compatible with equilibrium in the money market. Consider point D in the right-hand panel of Figure 5.6, which lies above the LM curve. At point D, income and the interest rate are Y_1 and R_2, respectively. The left-hand panel of Figure 5.6 indicates that point D, which lies on the money demand curve associated with an income level of Y_1, is to the left of the given money supply. For an income level of Y_1 and an interest rate of R_2, a state of excess supply will exist in the money market (equal to the distance DB). Given an excess supply of money, people will attempt to buy bonds (the alternative financial asset) and in the process will bid up the price of bonds, which in turn lowers the interest rate. For a given money supply $\$^S$ and an income level Y_1, a lower rate of interest R_1 is required to restore equilibrium in the money market (in Figure 5.6, to move from point D to point A).

To summarize, points that lie above the LM curve represent positions of excess supply in the money market. Conversely, points that lie below the LM curve represent positions of excess demand in the money market. Only points *on* the LM curve represent a state of equilibrium in the money and financial asset markets.

The upward slope of the LM curve can be explained by considering the movement from point A to point B in the right-hand panel of Figure 5.6. At an income level of Y_1, the demand for money curve $\$^D(Y_1)$ intersects the given money supply $\$^S$ at an interest rate of R_1 (point *A* in the left-hand panel). Now suppose that the level of income rises to Y_2. Given this higher income level, the number of transactions increases and the demand for money curve shifts to the right to $\$^D(Y_2)$. Since the supply of money is given at $\$^S$, people will attempt to obtain additional cash to facilitate the increased number of transactions by offering to sell bonds. As bonds are offered for sale in the bond market, the price of bonds declines and the interest rate rises (bond prices and interest rates move in opposite directions). As interest rates rise, people will begin to economize on their holdings of cash because the opportunity cost of holding money has increased. To restore equilibrium in the money market at this higher income level Y_2, the interest rate must rise to R_2. The extra transactions demand for money resulting from an increase in income must be "rationed" by economizing on the holding of cash. Thus, the *LM* curve slopes upwards to the right. To maintain equilibrium in the money market with a given money supply, an increase in income must be accompanied by an increase in interest rates (the upward movement from point *A* to point *B* in Figure 5.6). The actual steepness of the *LM* curve depends on the relative size of the two money demand behavioural parameters k and ℓ (see below).

Shifts in the *LM* Curve

Figure 5.7 illustrates how an increase in the money supply shifts the *LM* curve downwards to the right. The Bank of Canada, on behalf of the federal government, influences financial markets through its control of the money supply. As discussed in Chapter 15, the Bank of Canada can increase or decrease the supply of money in the economy by engaging in open market purchases (or sales) of government bonds. Since banks must maintain a certain fraction of all deposits in the form of cash reserves, the Bank of Canada can control the size of bank deposits (a key component of the money supply) by expanding or contracting the supply of cash reserves. When the Bank of Canada purchases bonds, new money (cash reserves) are injected into the economic system. Conversely, when the Bank of Canada sells bonds, it receives money which will no longer be available for cash reserves and the money supply declines (for further details see Chapter 15).

Turning to Figure 5.7, suppose that initially the money supply is equal to $\$^S_0$. Our three representative combinations of income and interest rates that maintain equilibrium in the money market are given by points A_0, B_0, and C_0, all of which lie along an *LM* curve corresponding to a money supply of $\$^S_0$. Now suppose that the Bank of Canada increases the money supply to $\$^S_1$. Given this larger money supply, our three representative combinations of income and interest rates that maintain equilibrium in the money market will now be given by points

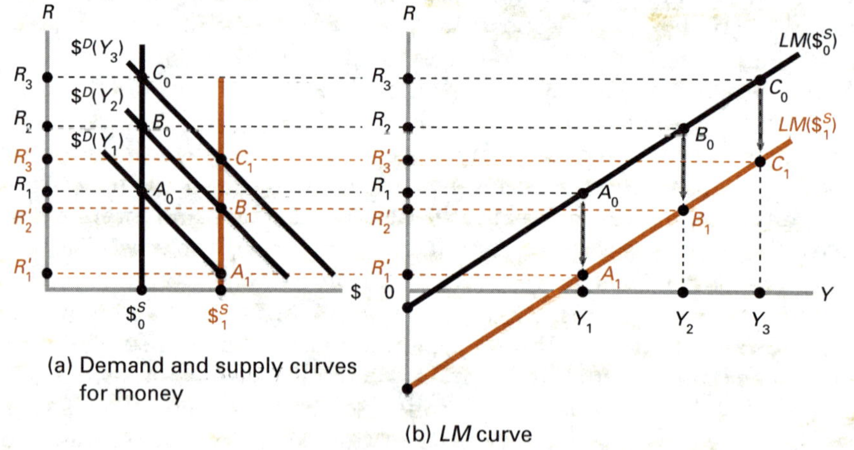

Figure 5.7 Effects of an increase in the money supply on the *LM* curve

A_1, B_1, and C_1. In panel (b) of Figure 5.7 we have again plotted these three new representative points and have drawn the new *LM* curve ($LM(\$^S_1)$) associated with this larger money supply $\$^S_1$. An increase in the money supply has caused the *LM* curve to shift downwards to the right. For a given level of income, say Y_1, the interest rate has declined (to R'_1). This downward shift in the *LM* curve occurs because the increase in the money supply causes an excess supply of money and people will attempt to get rid of the excess money in their portfolios by buying bonds, which lowers interest rates.

Simultaneous Equilibrium in Both the Goods and Money Markets

We now have in place the two major building blocks of a fixed price macroeconomic model: the *IS* curve and the *LM* curve. As shown in Figure 5.8, the downward-sloping *IS* curve describes all possible combinations of income and interest rates that maintain equilibrium in the goods market. The upward-sloping *LM* curve describes all possible combinations of income and interest rates that maintain equilibrium in the money market. There is only one combination of income and interest rates that will simultaneously maintain equilibrium in both the goods and the money market — the intersection point of the *IS* and *LM* curves. As drawn in Figure 5.8, only Y_E and R_E will simultaneously clear both the goods and the money market. By introducing the condition of money market equilibrium, we are now able to determine the unique income level at which the goods market will clear.

For any income level other than that associated with the intersection point of the *IS* and *LM* curves, either the goods market or the money market (or both markets) will be in a state of disequilibrium. Disequilibrium in either, or both, of these key macroeconomic markets will cause a sequence of adjustments which will return the economy to its unique **equilibrium income** level Y_E. In the following description of the disequilibrium adjustment process, we assume that the money market remains in a state of equilibrium. Given the ease of buying and selling bonds, the interest rate likely adjusts very quickly to any disequilibrium situation in the money market and we therefore assume that the economy remains on the *LM* curve. Since firms respond to fluctuating inventory stocks by altering factory orders and production schedules, the goods market likely adjusts more slowly to disequilibrium situations and the economy may spend some time off the *IS* curve.

To illustrate the disequilibrium adjustment process in the goods market, suppose that the economy is at point *A* in Figure 5.8, with an income level Y_A less than the equilibrium income level Y_E (this point would correspond to point *A* in panel (c) of Figure 5.3). While the economy is in money market equilibrium (point *A* is on the *LM* curve), the

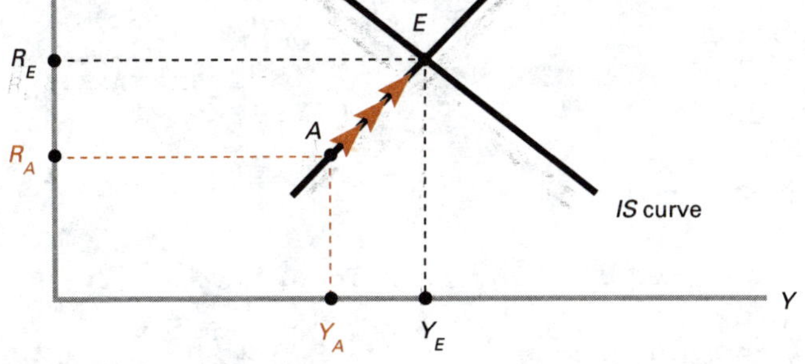

Figure 5.8 Equilibrium in the *IS-LM* model

goods market is out of equilibrium (point A is off the IS curve). As discussed earlier, at point A there will be a state of excess demand in the goods market. At point A planned aggregate expenditures exceed output and inventories will be drawn down. Dwindling inventory stocks will trigger new factory orders and subsequent increases in income. The original income level Y_A will give way to a higher income level, and the economy will begin to move towards the equilibrium income level Y_E. This state of excess demand in the goods market will continue to exist as long as the economy remains below the IS curve. Consequently, a series of inventory adjustments in the goods market will raise income levels and carry the economy from point A back up the LM curve to point E (see arrows in Figure 5.8). As income levels rise, the demand for money for transactions purposes also increases. With no increase in the given money supply, this increased demand for money forces up the interest rate (to R_E).

Similarly, if income levels exceed the equilibrium level, the economic system would undergo a series of downward income adjustments (as inventory stocks pile up and factory orders are cancelled), eventually returning to its unique equilibrium income level Y_E. Only when both the goods market and the money market are simultaneously in a state of equilibrium will the economic system remain at rest. The intersection point of the IS and LM curves represents the unique **stable equilibrium position** for the macroeconomic system.

The *IS-LM* Model in Algebra

Our graphical IS-LM model can also be solved algebraically. For convenience, the eight equations that comprise the model are reproduced below:

Aggregate expenditure identity	$AE = C + I + (X - M) + G$	(4.1)
Consumption function	$C = C_a + b(Y - T)$	(4.2)
Tax function	$T = T_a + tY$	(4.5)
Import function	$M = mY$	(4.4)
Investment function	$I = I_a - eR$	(5.1)
Goods market equilibrium	$AE = Y$	(4.7)
Money demand function	$\$^D = kY - \ell R$	(5.3)
Money market equilibrium	$\$^D = \$^S$	(5.4)

The first six equations describe the goods market and the last two equations describe the money market. The key *exogenous* variables in the model are government expenditures G, the money supply $\$^S$, exports X, and autonomous investment expenditures I_a.

As discussed above, the *IS* curve represents all combinations of income and interest rates that maintain equilibrium in the goods market. Using the goods market equilibrium condition (Equation 4.7) and the definition of aggregate expenditures (Equation 4.1), we obtain:

$$Y = C + I + G + X - M$$

Now substitute the equations for consumption, taxes, investment, and imports,

$$Y = C_a + bY - b(T_a + tY) + I_a - eR + G + X - mY$$

and move the *eR* term to the left-hand side of the equation and the *Y* term to the right-hand side of the equation:

$$eR = -Y + C_a + bY - bT_a - btY + I_a + G + X - mY$$

Grouping all of the *Y* terms together on the right-hand side of the equation and dividing through by the parameter e produces the following equation for the *IS* curve.

$$R = \left[\frac{C_a - bT_a + I_a + G + X}{e}\right] - \left[\frac{1 - b(1 - t) + m}{e}\right] Y \qquad (5.5)$$

Assuming that the marginal propensity to consume *b* and the income tax rate *t* are less than unity, the expression $1 - b(1 - t) + m$ must be positive, as a fraction, $b(1 - t)$, is being subtracted from $(1 + m)$. In the *IS* equation (5.5), *Y* has a negative sign; the *IS* curve slopes downwards. This downward-sloping *IS* curve is shown in Figure 5.9. Both the intercept and the slope of the *IS* curve (see the *IS* equation (5.5)) are labelled.

Earlier we indicated that the less sensitive investment expenditures are to interest rate movements (the smaller the parameter e), the steeper will be the *IS* curve. As the parameter e decreases in size, the absolute size of the slope of the *IS* curve clearly gets larger (since we are dividing by a smaller number) and the *IS* curve becomes steeper. Similarly, a decrease in the marginal propensity to consume *b*, an increase in the income tax rate *t*, or an increase in the marginal propensity to import *m* causes the *IS* curve to become steeper. More important, a change in any of the intercept components of the *IS* curve equation causes the *IS* curve to shift in a parallel manner. An increase in autono-

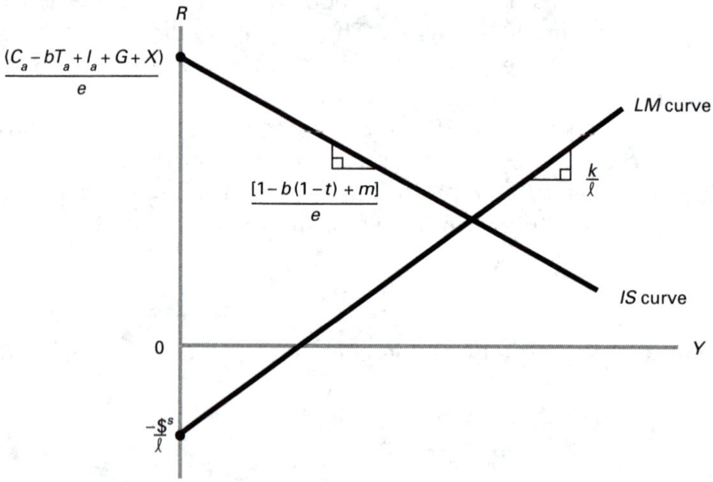

Figure 5.9 Slopes and intercepts of the *IS* and *LM* curves

mous consumption expenditures C_a, an increase in autonomous investment expenditures I_a, an increase in exports X, an increase in government expenditures G, and a decrease in the tax intercept T_a all increase the intercept of the *IS* curve and therefore cause the *IS* curve to shift upwards to the right. Given the algebraic form of the *IS* curve, it is very easy to pinpoint the effects of a change in I_a, X, G, etc., on the position of the *IS* curve.

To derive the *LM* curve equation, we simply substitute the money market equilibrium condition (Equation 5.4) into the demand for money function (Equation 5.3),

$$\$^S = \$^D = kY - \ell R$$

and rearrange terms to produce an upward-sloping *R–Y* relationship:

$$R = \frac{-\$^S}{\ell} + \left(\frac{k}{\ell}\right)Y \qquad (5.6)$$

As shown in Figure 5.9, the slope of the *LM* curve is k/ℓ and the intercept of the *LM* curve is $-\$^S/\ell$. The *LM* curve will become steeper if either the parameter k were to increase or the parameter ℓ were to decrease. An *increase* in the money supply $\$^S$ will not affect the slope of the *LM* curve but will cause the *LM* curve to shift *downwards* to the right (the intercept becomes a larger negative number when $\$^S$ increases in size). A change in the money supply causes a parallel shift in the *LM* curve.

To obtain a reduced-form equation for the equilibrium income level, we again substitute the consumption function, the tax function, the import function, and the investment function directly into the aggregate expenditure identity.

$$Y = AE = C + I + G + X - M$$

$$Y = C_a + bY - b(T_a + tY) + I_a - eR + G + X - mY$$

Next we substitute the *LM* equation for *R*,

$$Y = C_a + bY - bT_a - btY + I_a - e\left[-\frac{\$^S}{\ell} + \left(\frac{k}{\ell}\right)Y\right] + G + X - mY$$

and gather all of the Y terms together on the left-hand side of the equation.

$$Y - bY + btY + \left(\frac{ek}{\ell}\right)Y + mY = C_a - bT_a + I_a + G + X + \left(\frac{e}{\ell}\right)\$^S$$

$$\left(1 - b + bt + \frac{ek}{\ell} + m\right)Y = C_a - bT_a + I_a + G + X + \left(\frac{e}{\ell}\right)\$^S$$

Finally we divide this equation by $(1 - b + bt + ek/\ell + m)$ to produce the following reduced-form equation for the equilibrium income level.[10]

$$Y = \frac{C_a - bT_a + I_a + G + X + \left(\frac{e}{\ell}\right)\$^S}{1 - b + bt + \frac{ek}{\ell} + m} \qquad (5.7)$$

As discussed in Chapter 4, the key characteristic of a reduced-form equation is that an endogenous variable (such as *Y*) is expressed solely in terms of the given parameters and exogenous variables. None of the other endogenous variables in the model (such as *C*, *I*, and *R*) appear in this reduced-form income equation. All of the interaction and feedback effects between the endogenous variables in our macroeconomic model have been allowed for. By making use of this reduced-form *Y* equation (5.7), one can readily obtain reduced-form equations for the remaining endoge-

[10] This equation could also be obtained by equating the *IS* equation (5.5) to the *LM* equation (5.6), and then collecting all *Y* terms together.

nous variables in the model. For example, by substituting the given money supply and the reduced-form Y equation (5.7) into the LM equation (5.6), a reduced-form equation for the interest rate R can be readily derived:

$$R = \frac{-\$^S}{\ell} + \left(\frac{k}{\ell}\right)\left[\frac{C_a - bT_a + I_a + G + X + \left(\frac{e}{\ell}\right)\$^S}{1 - b + bt + \frac{ek}{\ell} + m}\right] \qquad (5.8)$$

The Determinants of Equilibrium Income

On a superficial level, equilibrium income is determined by the intersection point of the IS and LM curves. But what determines the exact location and position of the IS and LM curves? To pinpoint the **determinants of equilibrium income**, we must get behind these two curves and return to the structural components of the IS and LM curves.

The exact location of the IS curve is determined by the consumption, import, and investment functions along with the level of government expenditures, exports, and tax rates. Similarly, the exact location of the LM curve is determined by the demand for money function and the given money supply. The equilibrium level of income, in a fundamental sense, is determined by consumer behaviour, investment behaviour (including autonomous investment expenditures), import behaviour, money demand behaviour, government expenditures and tax rates (fiscal policy), and the money supply (monetary policy).

The reduced-form income equation (5.7) summarizes these factors in a very convenient and precise manner. A change in either a parameter (such as b, m, or T_a) or a change in an exogenous variable (such as I_a, X, G, or $\$^S$) will cause the equilibrium income level to change.

We illustrate the determinants of equilibrium income by considering a decline in exports X (a discussion of monetary and fiscal policy follows in the next section of this chapter). With a smaller amount of exports, the IS curve will shift downwards to the left, bringing about a new lower intersection point with the LM curve (point E_1 in Figure 5.10). A decline in exports causes a reduction in the level of equilibrium income (from Y_0 to Y_1) as well as a decrease in the interest rate (from R_0 to R_1). The downward slide along the LM curve is just the opposite of the case illustrated in Figure 5.8. In the present situation, a decline in exports reduces income levels and the volume of transactions. With a lower transactions demand for money and a given money supply, there will be a state of excess supply in the money market which will force the interest rate down. The interest rate must decline to encourage people to hold the given money supply in the face of declining income transactions, thereby restoring equilibrium in the money market.

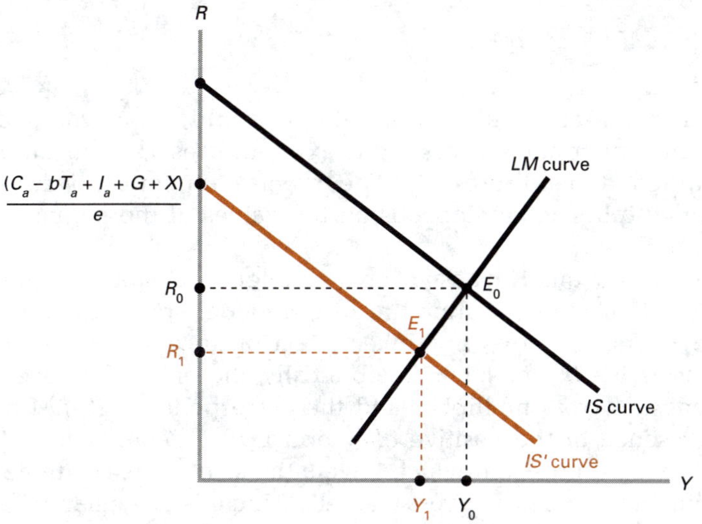

Figure 5.10 Effects of a decline in exports on the equilibrium level of income

To determine the exact magnitude of the decline in income following a change in exports (the distance $Y_0 - Y_1$ in Figure 5.10), we return to our algebraic reduced-form Y equation (5.7).

$$Y = \frac{C_a \quad bT_a \mid I_a \mid G \mid X \mid \left(\frac{e}{\ell}\right)\$^S}{1 - b + bt + \frac{ek}{\ell} + m} \qquad (5.7)$$

The effect of a one-unit change in X on Y is given by the coefficient of X in this reduced-form Y equation:[11]

[11] For students who have taken an elementary course in calculus, the multiplier expression is simply the derivative of Y with respect to X, as computed from the reduced-form equation (5.7). For students who have not taken calculus, we can follow the same steps outlined in Chapter 4 to obtain the change in Y associated with a change in X (from X_1 to X_2):

$$Y_1 = \frac{C_a - bT_a + I_a + G + X_1 + \left(\frac{e}{\ell}\right)\$^S}{1 - b + bt + \frac{ek}{\ell} + m} \qquad Y_2 = \frac{C_a - bT_a + I_a + G + X_2 + \left(\frac{e}{\ell}\right)\$^S}{1 - b + bt + \frac{ek}{\ell} + m}$$

When we subtract Y_1 from Y_2, all the right-hand side numerator terms cancel out except the two terms involving exports.

$$Y_2 - Y_1 = \frac{X_2 - X_1}{1 - b + bt + \frac{ek}{\ell} + m}, \quad \text{or } \Delta Y = \frac{\Delta X}{1 - b + bt + \frac{ek}{\ell} + m}, \quad \text{or } \frac{\Delta Y}{\Delta X} = \frac{1}{1 - b + bt + \frac{ek}{\ell} + m}$$

$$\frac{\Delta Y}{\Delta X} = \frac{1}{1 - b + bt + \frac{ek}{\ell} + m}$$

An identical income multiplier effect would occur for a one-unit change in autonomous investment expenditures I_a or in autonomous consumption expenditures C_a. The precise numerical value for this **income multiplier effect** depends on the values of the parameters b, m, t, e, k, and ℓ.

Compared to our Keynesian cross model in Chapter 4, the income multiplier effects derived from the *IS-LM* model above are lower. Recall that the Keynesian cross multiplier effect on income from a change in exports is $1/(1 - b + bt + m)$. Algebraically, the only difference between the Keynesian cross multiplier and the corresponding *IS-LM* multiplier is the presence of the positive ek/ℓ term in the denominator of the *IS-LM* multiplier expression (which lowers the size of the multiplier effect). Enlarging the Keynesian cross model to include a demand for money function and an interest-sensitive investment function has lowered the multiplier effect on income from a change in exports.

The explanation for the decrease in the income multiplier effect in the *IS-LM* model involves the role of interest rates. A decline in exports of one unit causes a decline in income in the Keynesian cross model of $1/(1 - b + bt + m)$ units. However, in the *IS-LM* model a decline in exports, and the associated downward shift in the *IS* curve, also causes interest rates to decline. With a lower interest rate, firms will increase their endogenous investment expenditures because they can borrow funds at a lower rate. In other words, a decline in exports creates a secondary reaction via the interest rate which will tend to offset part of the initial decline in exports. The extent to which this secondary reaction effect will decrease the Keynesian cross multiplier depends on the size of the parameters in the investment and money demand functions (e, k, and ℓ). For example, the greater the sensitivity of investment expenditures to interest rates, the greater the "offsetting" effect and the less the overall multiplier effect on income levels from a change in exports. As discussed below, an increase in government expenditures will increase interest rates which in turn will reduce (or crowd out) investment expenditures, thus negating part of the stimulative effect on income from the increase in government expenditures.

The Keynesian Diagnosis and Policy Prescription

Although the equilibrium level of income in the *IS-LM* model depends on the underlying parameters within the economy, the key determinants of equilibrium income are the exogenous components of aggregate expenditures. In Keynes's view, investment expenditures are highly susceptible to changes in the state of business confidence and are very unresponsive to interest rate movements. The "delicate balance of spontaneous optimism" within the business community could easily be upset and a loss of business confidence could generate a collapse in autonomous investment expenditures. Even though Keynes undoubtedly overstated the importance of "animal spirits" and "business confidence," investment expenditures have been quite volatile and are the most unstable component of aggregate expenditures. In addition to autonomous changes in investment expenditures, an open economy such as that which exists in Canada is subject to considerable export instability. The level of Canadian exports is highly dependent on U.S. and world economic conditions, and the international business cycle will spread to Canada via changes in world demand for Canadian exports.

Given the instability of various autonomous components of aggregate expenditure, there is no reason to believe that the *IS* curve (which depends crucially on these autonomous factors) will just happen to intersect the *LM* curve at an output level that is compatible with full employment. Autonomous expenditures (of various kinds) may be too low and the *IS* curve may be located too far to the left. For any decline in exports or autonomous investment expenditures, the multiplier process will generate a magnified reduction in income and employment levels and the economy could come to rest in a serious recession. In Keynes's view, the root cause of chronic unemployment was insufficient aggregate expenditures.

Keynes's "revolutionary" new theory of insufficient aggregate expenditures was completely at odds with the prevailing conventional economic wisdom. As discussed in Chapter 7, classical economists firmly believed that the economic system would reach an equilibrium position in which full employment would prevail. Unemployment in a free market system simply could not persist as wages would adjust to clear the labour market. With the Great Depression convincingly proving his case, Keynes argued that wage and price flexibility could not be counted on to lift the economy out of a serious recession.

Deliberate government action must be taken to stimulate aggregate expenditures and propel the economy back to full employment. Keynes advocated that the government should run an expansionary fiscal policy to stimulate aggregate expenditures. A decline in autonomous investment expenditures or exports, and the resulting negative multiplier effects on income and employment, could be offset by an increase in government expenditures or a decrease in tax rates. Keynes argued that governments had the ability, and therefore the responsibility, to manage aggregate expenditures in such a way that serious recessions could be avoided.

We now turn to an analysis of **fiscal and monetary policy** in the context of a fixed price *IS-LM* model. As a starting point for our policy analysis, Figure 5.11 reproduces the basic *IS-LM* diagram, with intercepts and slopes labelled in the appropriate panels. The effect of a change in government expenditures G, tax rates T_a and t, and the money supply $\$^S$ can be determined easily by shifting the appropriate curve in the *IS-LM* diagram (see Figure 5.11, panels (a), (b), and (c), respectively).

A Change in Government Expenditures

An increase in government expenditures G will cause the intercept of the *IS* curve to increase, thereby shifting the *IS* curve upwards to the right. Such a rightward shift in the *IS* curve (from IS_0 to IS_1 in Figure 5.11(a)) generates a higher equilibrium income level (from Y_0 to Y_1) as well as a higher interest rate (from R_0 to R_1).

As discussed in Chapter 4, an increase in government expenditures creates an excess demand for goods within the economy, leading to a decline in inventory stocks and an increase in factory orders. As production increases (to restock inventories), additional factor incomes will be earned generating further rounds of induced consumer expenditures and further increases in production and income. However, this multiplier process will be moderated by a rising interest rate, which reduces investment expenditures. Rising income levels, triggered by the increase in government expenditures, increase the demand for money for transactions purposes. Given a fixed money supply, people will attempt to sell bonds in order to raise sufficient cash to facilitate this increase in transactions. Bond prices will be forced downwards and interest rates will be pushed upwards. This rise in interest rates **crowds out** investment expenditures, which reduces the size of the income multiplier effect associated with an increase in government expenditures.

As noted above, an increase in government expenditures has exactly the same effect on the *IS* curve as an increase in autonomous investment expenditures, or an increase in exports (G, I_a, and X all enter the *IS* curve in an identical manner). It should come as no surprise that Keynesian economists seized upon an increase in government expenditures as the cure for recessions. When autonomous investment expenditures or exports decline, the government could offset (or counter) the inward shift of the *IS* curve with a corresponding increase in government expenditures. Countercyclical fiscal policy is the essence of Keynesian economics.

A Change in Tax Rates

In addition to altering their own expenditures, governments can also affect aggregate expenditures by changing tax rates. A decrease in tax

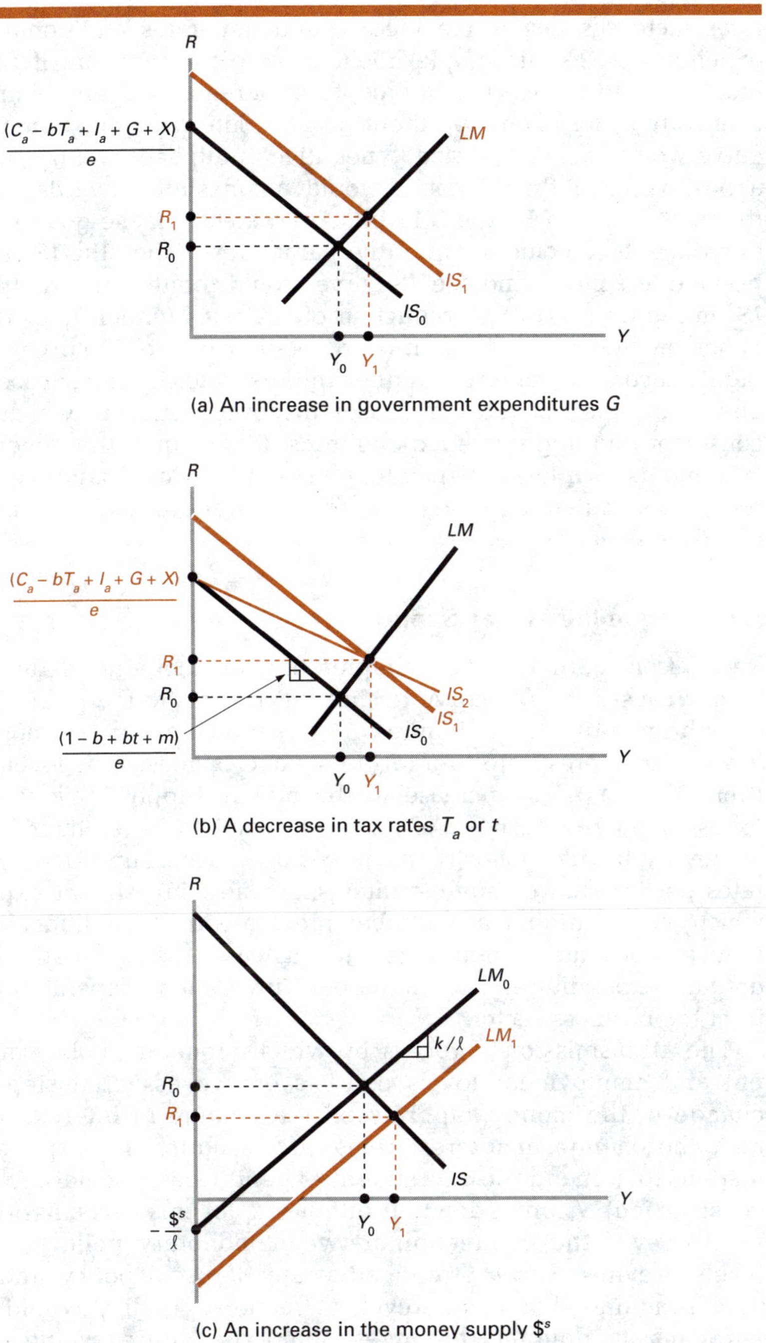

Figure 5.11 Fiscal and monetary policy in the *IS-LM* model

rates increases disposable income and generates additional consumer expenditures. In our simple linear income tax function, if the government were to reduce the intercept tax parameter T_a (by eliminating all licence fees, for example), then the $-bT_a$ intercept component of the *IS* curve would increase in size (a negative multiplied by a negative makes a positive) and the *IS* curve would again shift upwards to the right (from IS_0 to IS_1 in Figure 5.11(b)). Alternatively, if the government were to reduce the income tax rate (the parameter t), then the *IS* curve would become less steep and the *IS* curve would rotate upwards (from IS_0 to IS_2 in Figure 5.11(b)). A reduction of tax rates (either T_a or t) produces either an upward shift or upward rotation of the *IS* curve, creating a higher income level and a higher interest rate. In either case, a reduction of income tax rates increases disposable income which increases consumer and aggregate expenditures. Rather than the government increasing its own level of spending, tax cuts are an alternative Keynesian policy to stimulate aggregate expenditures and propel the economy out of a recessionary state.

A Change in the Money Supply

Recall from earlier in this chapter that an increase in the supply of money causes the *LM* curve to shift downwards to the right. Comparing equilibrium positions in Figure 5.11(c), an increase in the money supply lowers the interest rate (from R_0 to R_1) and increases the level of income (from Y_0 to Y_1). An increase in the money supply initially creates an excess supply of money. As people attempt to lower their holdings of money by buying bonds, bond prices are pushed upwards and interest rates decline. Lower interest rates spark new investment expenditures, which in turn trigger a multiplier process with its additional rounds of induced consumer expenditures. In this case, the initial stimulus to aggregate expenditures (an increase in investment expenditures) comes from the business sector.

The "transmission" process by which monetary policy affects output and employment levels consists of two essential steps. First, a change in the money supply causes a change in interest rates. Second, the change in interest rates affects aggregate expenditures by leading to a change in investment expenditures (including residential construction). A breakdown at either step of this transmission process would sever the connection between monetary policy and income levels. Keynes was a strong advocate of fiscal policy and was not very sanguine that countercyclical monetary policy would work. In particular, he doubted that investment expenditures would respond to lower interest rates in the middle of a recession when business confidence was at a low ebb.

An Algebraic Representation of the Fiscal and Monetary Policy Multiplier Effects

From the reduced-form income equation (5.7), we can determine the exact size of the multiplier effects on Y following a change in G, T_a, and $\$^S$:[12]

$$\frac{\Delta Y}{\Delta G} = \frac{1}{1 - b + bt + \frac{ek}{\ell} + m} = \frac{\Delta Y}{\Delta I_a} = \frac{\Delta Y}{\Delta X}$$

$$\frac{\Delta Y}{\Delta T_a} = \frac{-b}{1 - b + bt + \frac{ek}{\ell} + m}$$

$$\frac{\Delta Y}{\Delta \$^S} = \frac{\frac{e}{\ell}}{1 - b + bt + \frac{ek}{\ell} + m}$$

An increase in G, a reduction in T_a, or an increase in $\$^S$ will each have a positive effect on income levels. We again note that the income effect arising from an increase in government expenditures is exactly the same as the income effect arising from an increase in autonomous investment expenditures and exports. Consequently, the effects of a \$1 billion *decrease* in autonomous investment expenditures or exports can be offset by a \$1 billion *increase* in the level of government expenditures. Alternatively, a tax cut or an increase in the money supply could also be implemented to offset the effects of a decrease in autonomous investment or exports.

As is clear from the preceding multiplier expressions, the precise size of the income multiplier effects associated with monetary and fiscal policy depends on the behavioural parameters (such as b and e). If, for example, investment expenditures are very sensitive to movements in the interest rate (the parameter e is very large), then the reduction in interest rates

---

12 Since the income tax parameter t appears in the denominator (not the numerator) of the reduced-form income equation, obtaining the multiplier effect for a change in t on Y is more complicated. Students with an elementary course in calculus can verify that the income multiplier effect is represented by the following expression:

$$\frac{\Delta Y}{\Delta t} = \frac{-b\left[C_a - bT_a + G + I_a + \left(\frac{e}{\ell}\right)\$^S + X\right]}{\left(1 - b + bt + \frac{ek}{\ell} + m\right)^2} \quad \text{or} \quad \frac{\Delta Y}{\Delta t} = \frac{-bY}{\left(1 - b + bt + \frac{ek}{\ell} + m\right)}$$

created by an increase in the money supply would generate a very large increase in investment expenditures and a very large multiplier effect on income levels. In addition, a high degree of sensitivity of investment expenditures to interest rate movements would negate much of the positive income effects associated with an increase in government expenditures. In this instance, the rise in the interest rate associated with an increase in government expenditures crowds out a large amount of investment expenditures, limiting the size of the income multiplier effects associated with fiscal policy. The larger the parameter e in the denominator of the multiplier expression, the smaller the overall size of the fiscal multipliers. Keynes thought that the parameter *e* was likely relatively small, and therefore that fiscal policy is likely to be more potent than monetary policy.

Since the size of the **government deficit** *D* is equal to the difference between government expenditures G and tax revenues *T* (which depend on income levels), we can use the reduced-form *Y* equation (5.7) to obtain a reduced-form equation for the government deficit:

$$D = G - T_a - tY$$

$$D = G - T_a - \frac{t\left[C_a - bT_a + I_a + G + \left(\frac{e}{\ell}\right)\$^S + X\right]}{1 - b + bt + \frac{ek}{\ell} + m} \qquad (5.9)$$

Using this reduced-form *D* equation (5.9), an increase in government expenditures G has the following effect on the government deficit:

$$\frac{\Delta D}{\Delta G} = \frac{\Delta G}{\Delta G} - \frac{t\Delta Y}{\Delta G}$$

$$= 1 - \frac{t}{1 - b + bt + \frac{ek}{\ell} + m}$$

$$= \frac{\left(1 - b + bt + \frac{ek}{\ell} + m\right) - t}{1 - b + bt + \frac{ek}{\ell} + m} < 1$$

or

$$= \frac{\left[(1 - b)(1 - t) + \frac{ek}{\ell} + m\right]}{1 - b + bt + \frac{ek}{\ell} + m} > 0$$

From the algebra it is clear that the government deficit will increase when government expenditures increase (both b and t are assumed to be less than unity, and therefore both the numerator and denominator of this multiplier expression are positive). Since this multiplier expression is less than unity (the numerator is smaller than the denominator by the factor t), the government deficit increases by a smaller amount than the increase in government expenditures. An increase in government expenditures raises the level of income, which means that the government will collect more income tax revenues, thus limiting the increase in the size of the government deficit to an amount less than the increase in government expenditures.

Financing Fiscal Policy

An increase in government expenditures shifts the IS curve upwards to the right, raising the level of income. As shown above, some (but not all) of the funds required to finance the increase in government expenditures will be generated from the existing income tax system, without raising tax rates (T_a or t). Even though income tax revenues rise, the government deficit will increase when government expenditures increase, thus forcing the government to raise some additional funds to pay for the increase in government expenditures.

This raises an interesting and important question. Where does the government get these additional funds that are required to pay for the increase in government expenditures? We know that the government (the Bank of Canada) does not print more money. If the government were to print the required money to pay for an increase in government expenditures, then both the *IS* curve (from an increase in G) and the *LM* curve (from an increase in $\$^S$) would shift to the right. In our graphical analysis of an increase in government expenditures (see Figure 5.11(a)), only the *IS* curve shifted. The above multiplier expression for a change in government expenditure is calculated on the basis of a given money supply.

If the government does not print more money, how does it finance an increase in its own expenditures? Besides printing money, there are two **alternative sources of funds** that the government can utilize to pay for an increase in government expenditures: funds borrowed in the bond market and funds generated from an increase in tax rates. To pay for an increase in government expenditures, the government has three basic options. It may

1. borrow the necessary funds in the bond market;
2. increase the size of the money supply by printing more money; or

3. raise tax rates (and thereby balance the budget and eliminate any deficit).

Each of these three financing options is discussed in turn.

"Bond-Financed" Government Expenditures

Suppose that the government chooses to finance an increase in government expenditures by borrowing the necessary funds in the bond market (see Figure 5.11(a)). The increase in government expenditures shifts the *IS* curve from IS_0 to IS_1 and raises income levels from Y_0 to Y_1. Financing of the resulting government deficit through the sale of government bonds does not, in itself, cause additional shifts in either the *IS* or *LM* curves derived above.[13] As we shall see below, this is not the case when government expenditures are financed by either an increase in the money supply or an increase in tax rates. Implicitly our earlier analysis assumed that any government deficit must be bond-financed (since we did not alter tax rates or the money supply).

Besides raising the equilibrium income level, an increase in **bond-financed government expenditures** also raises interest rates and alters the composition of aggregate expenditures. In particular, the size of the government sector increases and the size of the private investment sector decreases. In the parlance of a monetarist economist, expansionary fiscal policy "crowds out" new investment expenditures in the private sector. To illustrate this "crowding out" effect, we return to Figure 5.11(a). The increase in government expenditures shifts the *IS* curve from IS_0 to IS_1 and the economy moves up the given *LM* curve to an income level of Y_1. This rising level of income creates an additional demand for money for transactions purposes. Since the government has not supplied any additional money, people will attempt to sell bonds to increase their money holdings to facilitate the increased number of (income) transactions. Bond prices will fall and interest rates will be forced upwards. But rising interest rates cause a reduction in investment expenditures; the extent of that reduction depends upon the sensitivity of investment expenditures to interest rates (the parameter *e*). Although an

[13] The stock of bonds issued by the government is assumed to have no effect on consumer behaviour (the *IS* curve) or on the demand for money (the *LM* curve). In more advanced treatments of the *IS-LM* model, a wealth variable (which could include the stock of government bonds) might be introduced into the *IS* or *LM* curves. Under such circumstances, bond-financed government expenditures would entail additional shifts in the *IS* or *LM* curves, and a different equilibrium income and interest rate would emerge. For example, if the demand for money also depends positively on the stock of government bonds (a wealth effect), then an increase in bond-financed government expenditures would cause both the *IS* and *LM* curves to shift upwards, forcing interest rates even higher and "crowding out" even larger amounts of investment. The role of wealth in the demand for money and the consumption function is discussed in Chapters 15 and 16.

increase in government expenditures increases income levels (and consumer expenditures), the major casualty from an increase in bond-financed government expenditures is in the investment sector.[14] The greater the "crowding-out" effect, the smaller the income multiplier effects associated with an increase in bond-financed goverment expenditures.

Assuming that the money supply and tax rates are held constant, an increase in government expenditures is financed jointly from increased income tax revenues (accruing from higher income levels) and additional borrowing by the government in the bond market. An expansionary bond-financed government expenditure policy will increase the level of income, raise interest rates, "crowd out" investment expenditures and redistribute output *from* the business sector *to* the government sector. Rather than borrowing funds to finance an increase in government expenditures, the government has two other options: increase the money supply or raise tax rates. The multiplier effects for each of these two alternative financing arrangements are quite different and each will be considered in turn.

"Money-Financed" Government Expenditures

Suppose that the government finances the deficit arising from an increase in government expenditures by simply printing the necessary dollar bills. From our previous analysis (see Figure 5.11) we know that when the government increases government expenditures the *IS* curve will shift upwards to the right and when the government increases the money supply the *LM* curve will shift downwards to the right. Consequently, an increase in government expenditures financed by an expansion of the money supply will produce a *double*-whammy effect on income levels, as both the *IS* and *LM* curves shift to the right (see Figure 5.12). Since this double-whammy effect on income levels will also have a double-whammy effect on income tax revenues, *only a portion* of the cost of the new government expenditures will have to be "printed" in the form of new money.

Clearly, financing government expenditures by printing money will have a much larger multiplier effect on income than financing government expenditures through the bond market. By supplying additional dollars, the increased transactions demand for money that accompanies rising income levels can be accommodated without

[14] We would also point out that if exports (or any other autonomous aggregate expenditure component) were to rise, crowding-out of investment expenditures would also take place. This crowding-out effect arises because the *IS* curve has shifted upwards and interest rates have risen, irrespective of the reason for the *IS* curve shift.

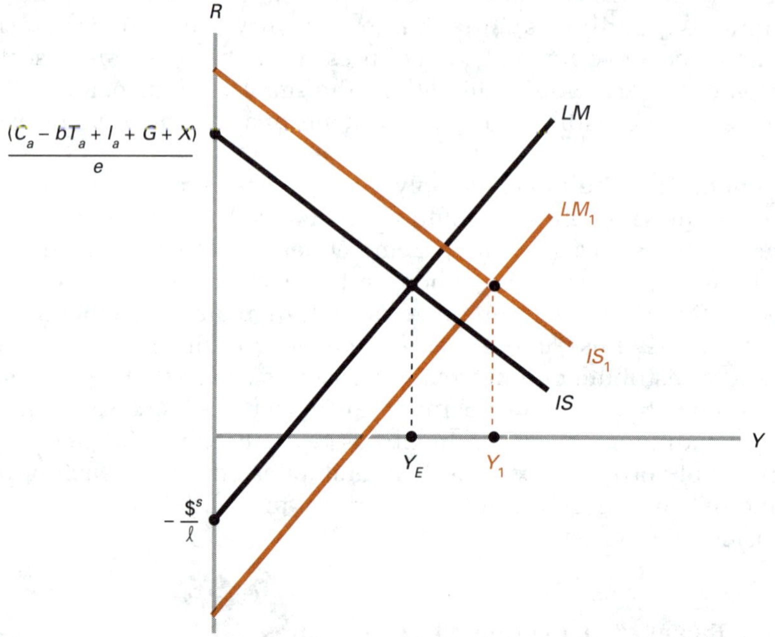

Figure 5.12 An increase in government expenditures financed by an increase in the money supply

pushing interest rates up (which would crowd out investment expenditures and limit the income-generating effects of the expansionary fiscal policy). Whether interest rates rise or fall following an increase in **money-financed government expenditures** is indeterminate in Figure 5.12. To determine whether interest rates rise or fall, we would have to know how much *additional* money was printed (that is, how far the *LM* curve shifted to the right). As discussed above, the increase in the money supply required to finance additional government expenditures depends on the marginal income tax rate and on the size of the change in income.

The above analysis only considers the money financing of government expenditures in the *initial* time period. In the second and subsequent time periods, additional increases in the money supply will be required to finance any government deficit that still exists, leading to *further* shifts in the *LM* curve (not shown in Figure 5.12). These subsequent increases in the money supply and rightward shifts of the *LM* curve will only come to a halt when income levels have sufficiently increased to generate *additional* income tax revenues ($t\Delta Y$) *exactly* equal to the increase in government expenditures (ΔG), that is, when there is no government deficit to be money-financed. For ΔG to equal $t\Delta Y$, income levels must increase by $\Delta Y = \Delta G/t$. A dynamic analysis of our *IS-LM* model suggests that the full income multiplier effects of money-financed government expenditures will be equal to the reciprocal of the marginal tax rate t, a much larger income multiplier effect than that found for bond-financed government expenditures.

"Tax-Financed" Government Expenditures

The final option available to the government to finance an increase in government expenditures is to raise tax rates. The government can increase its expenditures and at the same time increase tax rates by an appropriate amount to maintain a *balanced budget.* From our earlier analysis we know that an increase in tax rates will have a negative effect on income. Consequently a tax increase financing arrangement will tend to *offset* at least part of the positive income effect from an increase in government expenditures. Will the negative income effect from an increase in tax rates totally offset the positive income effect from an increase in government expenditures? Does an increase in government expenditures totally paid for by higher tax rates have any effect on income levels? To answer this important policy question concerning balanced government budgets, we return to the algebraic formulation of our model.

If the government maintains a *balanced* budget, then total tax revenues T must equal government expenditures G:

$$T = G$$

This new balanced-budget constraint will now override our original income tax function in the model. The government must change either tax parameter, T_a or t, to maintain a balanced budget. Which particular tax parameter the government chooses to vary to keep $T = G$ has no effect on the analysis below.

Given this balanced-budget constraint, the reduced-form income equation must be recomputed. Substituting our new balanced-budget constraint ($T = G$) directly into the consumption function,

$$C = C_a + b(Y - T) = C_a + b(Y - G)$$

the *IS-LM* model can be re-solved to produce a new reduced-form income equation for a *balanced-budget* economy:

$$Y = AE = C + I + G + X - M$$

$$Y = (C_a + bY - bG) + (I_a - eR) + G + X - mY$$

$$Y = C_a + bY - bG + I_a - e\left(\frac{-\$^S}{\ell} + \frac{k}{\ell}Y\right) + G + X - mY$$

$$(1 - b + \frac{ek}{\ell} + m)Y = C_a + (1 - b)G + I_a + \left(\frac{e}{\ell}\right)\$^S + X$$

$$Y\Big|_{G=T} = \frac{C_a + (1 - b)G + I_a + \left(\frac{e}{\ell}\right)\$^S + X}{(1 - b + \frac{ek}{\ell} + m)} \qquad (5.10)$$

The key distinguishing feature of this *new* reduced-form income equation is that it imposes the constraint that the government always maintains a balanced budget, hence our subscript notation that $G = T$. Our *previous* reduced-form income equation (5.7) did not force the government to balance its budget and maintain equality between total tax revenues and government expenditures.

From this new "balanced-budget" reduced-form income equation (5.10) we can readily obtain the effect on income for a one-unit increase in government expenditures that is financed by raising tax rates:

$$\frac{\Delta Y}{\Delta G}\Bigg|_{G=T} = \frac{1 - b}{1 - b + \frac{ek}{\ell} + m}$$

As long as the marginal propensity to consume b is less than unity, the balanced-budget multiplier effect on income from an increase in government expenditures must be positive (both the numerator and denominator will be positive). However, this **balanced budget multiplier effect** will be *less than unity* since the denominator of this balanced-budget multiplier expression exceeds the numerator by $ek/\ell + m$. Given our Chapter 4 estimates for $b = 0.85$ and $m = 0.35$, the balanced-budget income multiplier effect from an increase in government expenditures is less than 0.30 (that is, $0.15/(0.15 + ek/\ell + 0.35)$). Thus, a growing government sector which is financed by increased tax rates will exert a very modest expansionary effect on aggregate expenditures.

In addition, the presence of a balanced-budget constraint alters the value of all of the other multiplier effects within the *IS-LM* model. For example, under balanced-budget conditions, a one-unit change in exports will have an income multiplier effect equal to the following expression (based on the new reduced-form Y equation (5.10)):

$$\left.\frac{\Delta Y}{\Delta X}\right|_{G=T} = \frac{1}{1 - b + \dfrac{ek}{\ell} + m}$$

Compared to our *previously* computed multiplier effect, which did not constrain the government to maintain a balanced-budget,

$$\frac{\Delta Y}{\Delta X} = \frac{1}{1 - b + bt + \dfrac{ek}{\ell} + m}$$

this *new* balanced-budget income multiplier effect from a change in exports *must be larger*. The only difference between these two algebraic expressions is the absence of $+bt$ in the denominator of the balanced-budget multiplier expression — the smaller the denominator, the larger the multiplier value.

The reason for the additional income-generating effects arising from an increase in exports under balanced-budget conditions is straightforward. When exports increase, both income and income tax revenues increase and the government budget is pushed towards a *surplus* position. To restore balance within the government budget, the government must either reduce tax rates or increase government expenditures. Either fiscal action will increase income levels and *reinforce* the original income multiplier effects from the increase in exports. Thus, an economy that always maintains a balanced government budget will be subject to larger swings in output arising from changes in exports and other exogenous components of aggregate expenditures.

Given that tax revenues are very closely tied to income levels via the income tax system, the *absence* of a balanced-budget constraint provides a very important "automatic stabilizing" influence on the macroeconomic system. If the economy starts to slide into a recession, say from a decline in exports, income tax revenues will decline and the government budget will automatically move towards a deficit position (in addition, rising transfer payments for unemployment insurance and welfare will further reinforce the movement towards a deficit position). The *stimulative* effects arising from an excess of government expenditures over tax revenues (the deficit) will somewhat offset the *negative* effects triggered by the decline in exports. On the other hand, if the government always balances its budget, then when exports decline (causing income levels and income tax revenues to decline) the government would be forced to either cut government expenditures or raise tax rates to maintain a balanced budget. Either balanced-budget policy option would further depress income levels and reinforce the original negative effects arising from the decline in exports. An unbalanced government budget is the essence of Keynesian countercyclical fiscal policy.[15]

In summary, the financing arrangements for government fiscal policy are of crucial importance and have important economic ramifications. Depending on whether the government finances increased government expenditures by borrowing funds in the bond market, printing money, or raising tax rates, the income multiplier (and interest rate) effects will be very different. The largest income multiplier effects arise when government expenditures are money-financed, in which case fiscal policy is reinforced by an increase in the money supply. The least expansionary effects of increased government expenditures occur when the government increases tax rates to pay for the extra government expenditures. In this case, the negative effects of the tax rate increase reduce the positive effects from the increased government expenditures to a "fractional" income multiplier effect. In addition, the maintenance of a balanced government budget increases the income multiplier effects associated with a change in exports or autonomous investment expenditures. The economic system will be more unstable under balanced-budget conditions as it will exhibit larger changes in income for a given change in exports or autonomous investment expenditures.

Concluding Comments on Keynesian Policy

By employing appropriate fiscal policies, Keynes believed that output and employment levels could be stabilized. The Marxist prediction that the capitalist system would eventually collapse, a prediction that looked very good in the 1930s, need not become a reality. Rather than overthrowing the free enterprise system, as many socialist and communist parties were advocating throughout the world during the 1930s, Keynes argued that all that was required was for the government to manage the economy. By direct government intervention, which was also a radical and revolutionary thought in the 1930s, aggregate expenditures would be stimulated and chronic unemployment could be cured. Writing dur-

[15] A Keynesian economist might well argue that the length of the business cycle is the appropriate time interval to maintain budgetary balance. Fiscal surpluses in boom years would be used to pay for deficits in recessionary years.

ing the worst depression in history, Keynes saw himself as the economic saviour of the free enterprise system.

Although direct government intervention to stimulate or manage aggregate expenditures is the essence of Keynesian economics, it is important to point out that there is no unique Keynesian policy prescription. A wide variety of alternative policy options are available to the government to stimulate or manage aggregate expenditures. In terms of our simple *IS-LM* model, the government could increase its own expenditures, cut tax rates, increase transfer payments, or increase the money supply. Either the *IS* or the *LM* curve can be shifted by the government to bring about a desired level of income. As a consequence, Keynesian economics quickly became a popular rationalization for many different types of policies, ranging from improved transfer payments for the poor to investment incentives for corporations. As long as the policy affected aggregate expenditures, it could be defended in Keynesian terms.

Which particular policy option should the government choose to manage aggregate expenditures? Unfortunately there is no simple answer to this important policy question and "political economy" considerations may well dominate. The choice of which particular group of citizens will receive the direct benefits from a stimulative fiscal policy (such as an increase in government expenditures on universities or a selective tax cut) is, at heart, a political decision. However, two basic economic principles apply to the selection of an "appropriate" instrument for aggregate expenditure management policy.

First, a very important characteristic of Keynesian policy is that it is only a *temporary* policy. Consequently, the policy selected must be capable of being stopped or reversed at a later date. For example, if the United States were to enter a serious recession leading to a decline in Canadian exports, a Keynesian-oriented government might attempt to stimulate the economy by implementing an expansionary policy. However, once the U.S. economy recovered from its recession and Canadian exports returned to their "normal" level, this stimulative policy would no longer be needed. The stimulative Keynesian policy (say an increase in G) must be reversed (G must be decreased back to its original level). As we shall see in subsequent chapters, if the government continues with its stimulative policies when they are no longer required, the economy will experience serious inflationary problems.

Keynesian countercyclical policies are, by definition, temporary policies that must be stopped or reversed at a later stage in the business cycle. Thus the government's choice of a particular Keynesian policy instrument should not include permanent changes in the fiscal system, such as hiring government workers who cannot be released at a later date, raising transfer payments which cannot be lowered at a later date, or cutting taxes which cannot be raised at a later date. A "good" Keynesian policy instrument is one that can be changed quickly in either direction, without political or bureaucratic resistance. Unfortunately, the fiscal tap is much easier to turn on than to turn off. Governments are typically very reluctant to raise tax rates or to cut back on services provided, and risk antagonizing particular political constituencies. On a political level, fiscal policy often tends to be a "one-way street" and is not easily reversed or made more restrictive.

In addition to the reversibility problem, the government must also carefully consider the effects of alternative policies on a wide range of other key macroeconomic variables. Besides a stable level of income and full employment, governments seek to obtain other desirable objectives or targets (such as stable price levels and low interest rates). As the full reduced-form of the *IS-LM* model indicates, a change in a particular policy instrument (such as G or $\$^S$) will affect the values of all endogenous variables within the model. For example, interest rates, often an additional target variable of government policy, will increase with a stimulative fiscal policy but will decrease with a stimulative monetary policy. As we shall see in subsequent chapters, however, a stimulative monetary policy may lead to a higher price level or higher inflation rate. It is exceedingly unlikely that any policy alternative will affect all target variables in a desirable manner. Consequently, government policymakers must carefully weigh the various costs and benefits of different policy alternatives and select that particular policy option that has the most desirable "net" effect on the set of target variables. Since each policy alternative will likely involve a different set of winners and losers, the choice of an appropriate Keynesian policy instrument is likely to be dominated by considerations of political economy.

Unfortunately, the world in which the policymaker lives is not nearly as clean and clear-cut as the exposition in this chapter suggests. It is much easier to shift *IS* and *LM* curves on a textbook page, or blackboard, to achieve a target income level than it is to turn "real world" monetary and fiscal policy levers. As we shall see in Chapter 9, the Keynesian policy analysis presented in this chapter is subject to a number of important theoretical and practical limitations and qualifications.

Key Concepts

goods market
money market
investment function

autonomous investment versus endogenous investment
IS curve (definition, derivation, slope, and intercept)
money supply
demand for money
LM curve (definition, derivation, slope, and intercept)
equilibrium income
stability of equilibrium income
determinants of equilibrium income
income multiplier effects of fiscal and monetary policy
crowding-out effect
government deficit
alternative financing arrangements for fiscal policy
multiplier effects of bond-financed government expenditures
multiplier effects of money-financed government expenditures
multiplier effects of tax-financed government expenditures
multiplier effects under a government balanced-budget policy

Review Questions

1. Explain why investment expenditures depend negatively on the interest rate.
2. Using the Keynesian cross diagram, derive a set of aggregate expenditures curves corresponding to different interest rates. Does an increase in the interest rate cause the aggregate expenditure curve to shift up or down? Explain.
3. Define and derive the *IS* curve. How would you categorize all points that lie below the *IS* curve? Why does the *IS* curve slope downwards to the right?
4. How would the *IS* curve be affected by each of the following events:
   (a) an increase in autonomous investment expenditures?
   (b) an increase in the marginal propensity to consume?
   (c) a decrease in exports?
   (d) a decrease in the marginal propensity to import?
   (e) an increase in the marginal income tax rate?
   (f) a decrease in the sensitivity of investment spending with respect to interest rate movements?
   (g) a decrease in the interest rate?
5. Why do people hold money? What are the economic determinants of the demand for money?
6. Define and derive the *LM* curve. How would you categorize all

points that lie below the *LM* curve? Why does the *LM* curve slope upwards to the right?

7. What effect does an increase in the money supply have on the *LM* curve? Explain.
8. What determines the equilibrium income level and interest rate in the *IS-LM* model? Carefully explain.
9. What would happen if the income level exceeds the equilibrium income level? Explain.
10. How would the equilibrium level of income and interest rates be affected by the following events:
    (a) a decrease in autonomous investment expenditures?
    (b) an increase in autonomous consumption expenditures?
    (c) a decrease in the marginal propensity to consume?
    (d) a decrease in the marginal income tax rate?
    (e) an increase in the marginal propensity to import?
    (f) a decrease in the money supply?
11. If the United States goes into a serious recession, what will be the effect on the equilibrium income level and interest rates in Canada? What would be the effect on income levels if the Canadian government restricts imports and effectively lowers the marginal propensity to import?
12. Compare the multiplier effects on income of a $1 billion increase in exports with a $1 billion increase in autonomous investment expenditures.
13. Carefully explain why the income multiplier effects from a change in government expenditures in the *IS-LM* model is smaller than that found in the Keynesian cross model.
14. Explain in words why the level of income rises when the money supply is increased. What are the various factors that determine the size of the multiplier effects on income arising from an increase in the money supply?
15. In 1982 the level of real GDP declined by $14 billion (measured in 1986 dollars). Suppose that the government wanted to increase 1982 income levels by $14 billion. What alternative policies are available? What factors would you consider important in choosing a particular policy?
16. Suppose that the government decides to increase government expenditures but refuses to raise tax rates or to print more money to pay for these extra government expenditures. How much funds will have to be borrowed in the bond market?
17. Compare and contrast the income and interest rate effects of an increase in government expenditures that are financed by:
    (a) borrowing funds in the bond market
    (b) printing money
    (c) raising tax rates.

18. Why does a balanced-budget policy increase the multiplier effects from a change in exports? Explain.
19. Explain how the values for the interest rate parameters in the investment function and the money demand function affect:
    (a) the slope of the *IS* and *LM* curves
    (b) the potency of fiscal and monetary policy.
20. If the government wishes to achieve both a target income level and a target interest rate, what are the implications for fiscal and monetary policy? Explain either diagrammatically or algebraically.

CHAPTER 6

The Balance of Payments and the Foreign Exchange Rate

The exchange rate is a very important price in a country that trades with the outside world on a scale that Canada does. . . . It is not therefore possible to ignore it, even when it floats.[1]

Every year Canadian residents make millions of financial transactions with Americans, Japanese, and other nonresidents. A large number of these transactions are the result of Canada's trade with other countries, but others arise because Canadians travel abroad, send gifts abroad, buy property in foreign countries, and invest in foreign assets such as U.S., German, or Japanese stocks, bonds, and bank accounts. And of course, nonresidents come to Canada for vacations and business trips and they invest in Canada by purchasing Canadian companies and property and by lending to Canadian institutions such as the federal and provincial governments, Hydro Quebec and Stelco.

These international transactions play an extremely important role in the Canadian economy. For example, in 1990 Canada exported goods and services worth about $187 billion, representing about 25 percent of GDP. But in addition to the flow of goods and services there are enormous flows of a purely financial nature, such as transactions involving stocks and bonds. In 1990 nonresidents made net purchases of $11.7 billion worth of Canadian stocks and bonds. Economic linkages to the rest of the world (especially to the United States, which typically purchases over half of Canada's exports and about two-thirds of all Canadian stocks and bonds purchased by foreigners) make the Canadian economy particularly vulnerable to events in foreign countries.

Economies that are influenced by events that take place outside their

1 Bank of Canada, *Annual Report, 1970*, p. 9.

borders are often described as "open." Frequently, the source of economic problems in open economies lies abroad and policymakers must deal with disequilibria in both their domestic goods and financial markets as well as in their balance of international payments. As the name suggests, **balance of payments** problems involve imbalances between the outflow of payments made by Canadian residents to nonresidents and the inflow of payments made by nonresidents to Canadians. The 1974–75 recession in the United States is an example of an external shock to the Canadian economy. U.S. recessions not only cause disequilibrium in the domestic goods market (export industries are depressed and unemployment increases) but also a disequilibrium in the balance of international payments because the immediate effect of a foreign recession is to reduce the value of Canadian sales to nonresidents but not the value of purchases by Canadians from nonresidents. In short, a balance of payments deficit emerges.

As in all free markets, there are natural forces that tend to restore equilibrium to the balance of payments. From the Canadian point of view, a balance of payments deficit is reflected in a shortage of foreign exchange. Exports are not earning enough to pay for imports. The excess demand for foreign exchange tends to raise the value of foreign currencies in terms of the Canadian dollar, and the dollar falls in value or depreciates. As we shall see, this adjustment in the foreign exchange value of the Canadian dollar is part of the natural mechanism that restores equilibrium to the balance of payments. However, governments are not always prepared to accept equilibrium prices in important markets. The price of the Canadian dollar (the foreign exchange rate) is an example. In the early 1970s the Canadian government did not want to allow the exchange rate to appreciate to the extent that market forces dictated. Reflecting on monetary policy at the time, G.K. Bouey, then Senior Deputy Governor of the Bank of Canada and later Governor, said:

> The primary objective of monetary policy over the past two years has been to encourage economic expansion; a related objective has been to moderate the upward pressure on the Canadian dollar in foreign exchange markets. An unduly strong Canadian dollar hampers both our export industries and those domestic industries that must compete with imports.[2]

But the story was quite different in the second half of the 1970s when market forces were pushing the dollar in the downward direction. Mr. Bouey, then Governor of the Bank of Canada, answered his own rhetorical question this way:

---

[2] Extract of remarks by G.K. Bouey at the annual meeting of the Canadian Mutual Funds Association, Toronto, 25 May 1972, reprinted in *Bank of Canada Review*, June 1972, p. 8.

> How should a problem of this kind, basically a problem of confidence, be dealt with? Not, I believe, by standing completely aside and letting the Canadian dollar fall as far as it might on the basis of market forces. . . . The trouble with standing aside was that the greater the fall in the exchange rate the greater the impact on our prices and costs. . . . We do not want to see a situation where exchange rate depreciation produces more inflation which, in turn, results in further depreciation — a vicious circle.[3]

Clearly one can list disadvantages to both a rise and fall in the exchange value of the Canadian dollar! The conclusion that most central bankers appear to draw is that the exchange rate should be stabilized at whatever the existing level happens to be. The Governor of the Bank of Canada admitted as much in 1985, when he said:

> The Bank of Canada is almost a daily participant in the exchange market, resisting sharp fluctuations in the exchange rate in either direction in as evenhanded a manner as the particular circumstances permit. Our objective is to have a steadying influence on the market forces, lending a measure of stability to the exchange rate and at the same time contributing to a sound and viable exchange market in Canada. We are very conscious, however, that strong and persistent moves in the exchange rate cannot be countered through intervention alone, and reinforcing domestic actions are typically required as well.[4]

In 1986, John Crow became Governor of the Bank of Canada. Although the Bank of Canada's chief focus has been on the long-term problem of inflation in Canada for nearly two decades, since the arrival of John Crow at the helm of the Bank of Canada, controlling inflation seems to have become the only target. While speaking in Paris, Mr. Crow had this to say about monetary policy and exchange rates:

> . . . it is vital to retain one central point . . . focussing monetary policy on exchange rates and hoping that inflation will take care of itself is not, at the most general level, the place to start — not even for exchange rate stability. Indeed for stability in exchange markets experience indicates that monetary authorities cannot provide a better basis than . . . limiting monetary expansion to a non-inflationary pace.[5]

Much of the remainder of Mr. Crow's speech stressed the importance of

---

3 Statement by G.K. Bouey before the House of Commons Standing Committee on Finance, Trade and Economic Affairs, 16 May 1978, reprinted in *Bank of Canada Review*, June 1978, p. 4.

4 Remarks by G.K. Bouey, Governor of the Bank of Canada, to the 27th Annual Congress of the Association Cambiste Internationale, Toronto, Ontario, 1 June 1985.

5 Remarks by John W. Crow, Governor of the Bank of Canada to the Chamber of Commerce France–Canada, Paris, France, 13 November 1990. Reprinted in *Bank of Canada Review*, November 1990, p. 23.

price stability. Yet despite this single-minded emphasis in speeches to the public, the Bank of Canada is still an active participant in the foreign exchange markets.

For much of the period after World War II, many countries have followed a fixed exchange rate policy. From time to time Canada has fixed the exchange value of the Canadian dollar in terms of the U.S. dollar. For example, from May 1962 to May 1970 the Canadian dollar was pegged at $0.925 in U.S. funds. Just as fixing the price of, say, bread will prevent the laws of supply and demand from restoring equilibrium in the market for bread, fixing the exchange value of the Canadian dollar suppresses an important mechanism through which equilibrium in the balance of international payments is restored following a disturbance. As we shall see, the effectiveness of monetary and fiscal policies is not independent of the government's exchange rate policy.

Specifically, the multiplier effects within our macroeconomic model depend on whether the government intervenes to fix the foreign exchange rate or allows it to be determined by market forces. The purpose of this chapter is to introduce the balance of payments into our macroeconomic model. Essentially we are adding one more market, the foreign exchange market, to our model to go along with the goods and money markets that have already been introduced. Full equilibrium in our expanded "open economy" model will be achieved only when all three markets are simultaneously in equilibrium. Throughout the analysis in this chapter we will continue to assume that the aggregate price level is fixed. In Chapter 7 and all subsequent chapters, this assumption is permanently dropped. In Chapter 12 we will examine the balance of payments adjustment process in an inflationary world.

Canada's Balance of International Payments

Four times a year Statistics Canada publishes details of Canada's international transactions.[6] Table 6.1 shows a summary of these accounts for 1990. As in all accounting systems, transactions are recorded as either current or capital items. The current account records all the payments that are made for current items, such as the importing of stereos or the exporting of wheat. The capital account records the transactions in financial assets, such as the sale of BC Tel bonds to a U.S. pension fund or the purchase of building land by the Cadillac Fairview Corporation.

---

6 See Statistics Canada, *Canada's Balance of International Payments*.

Table 6.1 Canada's Balance of International Payments, 1990 (Millions of Dollars)

Current Account			
Merchandise exports	146,057	Merchandise imports	135,259
Service receipts		Service payments	
Travel	7,437	Travel	11,961
Freight and shipping	5,332	Freight and shipping	5,370
Business services	7,976	Business services	10,888
Other	1,632	Other	1,987
Investment income	8,701	Investment income	32,923
Transfers	10,613	Transfers	5,350
Total receipts	187,748	Total payments	203,738
NET CURRENT BALANCE			−15,990

Capital Account	
Direct investment	
Foreign direct investment in Canada	5,729
Canadian direct investment abroad	−1,422
Portfolio investment, long-term	
Canadian securities	11,698
Foreign securities	−1,150
Other net capital flows	6,574
NET BALANCE ON CAPITAL ACCOUNT	21,609
Reconciliation	
Net balance on current account	−15,990
Net balance on capital account	21,609
Statistical discrepancy	−4,970
CHANGE IN OFFICIAL RESERVES	649

The Current Account

Canadian residents sell both goods and services to nonresidents. The value of goods that are sold to nonresidents is recorded under the heading "Merchandise exports," which amounted to just over $146 billion in 1990. Under the heading "Service receipts" are recorded such items as travel, transport, and business services. Travel refers to the payments made by foreigners travelling in Canada for such things as hotel accommodation and restaurant meals. Another major item refers to the investment income received by Canadian residents on their holdings of foreign assets (interest on U.S. government or corporate bonds, dividends paid on U.S. stocks, and rental income on Canadian-owned condominiums in Florida) which also enters as a positive item on the current account. One further item in the accounts, listed as "Transfers," completes the total of current receipts. Included in this final item are gifts and inheritances received by Canadian residents from nonresidents and the funds that immigrants bring with them. Since all of these items generate receipts for Canadians they are entered as positive items in the balance of payments. Table 6.1 shows that total current receipts, which represent the value of all goods and services sold to nonresidents, amounted to almost $190 billion in 1990.

On the other side of the ledger there is a corresponding list of payments (negative items) that Canadians make to nonresidents for merchandise imports and services. Again services include such things as foreign travel by Canadians and the interest and dividend payments made by Canadians to nonresidents. Such interest payments are made by Canadian governments and corporations that have borrowed funds abroad sometime in the past. The dividend payments that flow out of Canada go to the foreign owners of Canadian firms. Notice that investment income paid to foreigners is about four times larger than the investment income Canadians receive from abroad. This imbalance reflects the fact that over the years Canada has imported much more foreign capital than Canadians have invested abroad.

Two frequently quoted indicators of the state of the balance of payments are the merchandise trade balance and the current account balance. The first is the difference between the value of merchandise exports and merchandise imports. As Figure 6.1 shows, Canada rarely experiences a payments deficit on the trade account. In 1990 the surplus amounted to $10.9 billion. The current account surplus or deficit is a broader measure since it includes services as well as merchandise trade. A deficit on the current account as a whole implies that the value of goods and services that Canadians are buying from abroad exceeds the value of goods and services that are being sold to nonresidents. Just as an individual must either sell some of his assets or borrow from someone else if he wishes to spend more in a year than he receives, so too must a country. Consequently, whenever a country runs a deficit on the current account of its balance of international payments the residents of that country are, in one way or another, reducing their assets or borrowing from nonresidents. This process can take many forms. Suppose, for example, that a Canadian firm that wants to expand its operations borrows from U.S. residents by selling bonds in the United States. The proceeds of this borrowing might be used to import capital equipment, steel, and other supplies into the country. As long as the firm's investment projects yield a return that is greater than the cost of the borrowed funds, the foreign loan can be repaid out of the income generated by the new physical investment.

In other words, it can make good economic sense for a growing economy to run a current account deficit and borrow from abroad. However, if the borrowing is not used to finance new physical investment but is simply used to maintain a high level of consumption, then the country is

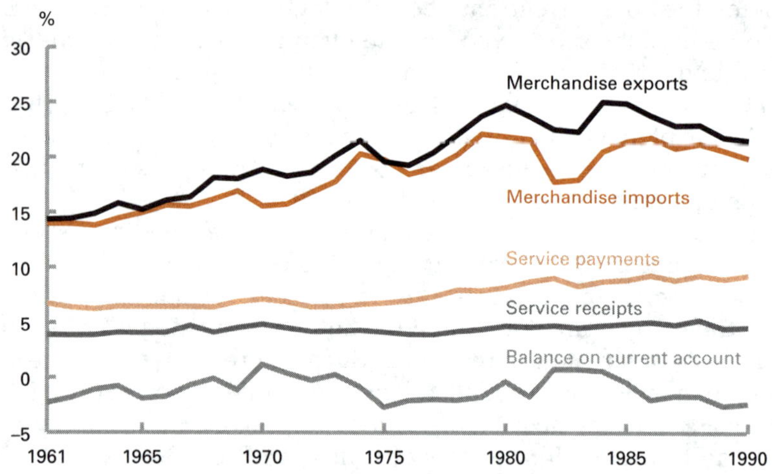

Figure 6.1 Balance of payments components as a percentage of GDP, 1961–90

in some sense living beyond its means. The foreign loans will eventually have to be paid back and, since the loans have not been used to create physical capital and therefore future income, the debt will be paid off at the expense of future consumption, and the country will be heading towards an inevitable period of "belt tightening."

The Capital Account

In our discussion of the current account we pointed out that any shortfall between total current receipts and total current payments must be reflected in either net foreign borrowing or an increase in foreign ownership of Canadian assets. That is to say, if Canadians pay out more than they receive in any given period, then Canadians must have financed this deficit by either borrowing abroad or selling off Canadian assets such as land, buildings, or stocks. It is the capital account that records the flow of assets between countries. Table 6.1 shows the net flow of the major items for the year 1990.

The capital account distinguishes between several kinds of capital flows. Portfolio investment includes investments in both stocks and bonds.[7] When foreigners buy Canadian bonds, foreign ownership is unchanged, but Canadian indebtedness to foreigners increases. When foreigners purchase Canadian stocks, foreign ownership of Canadian

7 In this context the term investment does not refer only to the accumulation of physical capital goods but rather to the wider concept of the acquisition of income-earning assets.

assets increases. Direct investment into Canada also implies ownership, since it refers to investments made by foreign firms in Canada. An example of direct investment would be the physical expansion of a foreign-owned plant, such as an automobile assembly line. In all capital transactions that result in the export of Canadian assets (stocks or bonds), the corresponding capital inflow (a receipt to some Canadian) is recorded as a *positive* item in the balance of payments accounts. Notice that both the export of goods and services (current account) and the export of Canadian assets (capital account) are recorded as positive items in the Canadian balance of payments.

Similarly, when Canadian residents buy condominiums in Florida or when Canadian companies take over U.S. companies they become owners of U.S. assets. These transactions are recorded in the capital account as a *negative* item under the heading "Canadian direct investment abroad." Essentially, Canadians are importing the assets or the title to the assets — recall that imports are included as negative items in the current account because these international transactions involve payments by Canadians.

A large part of short-term capital flows involves bank deposits. Nonresidents' holdings of Canadian bank deposits may change simply as a result of other international transactions. If a U.S. exporter leaves the payment he received for his exported goods at a Canadian bank, then this transaction will appear as an import item on the current account (negative) and as an increase in nonresident holdings of Canadian bank deposits on the capital account (a short-term capital inflow, a positive item). These and other transactions have been collected under the heading "Other net captial flows" in Table 6.1.

In the last few paragraphs we have made the point that any deficit (surplus) on the current account must be matched by a surplus (deficit) on the capital account. If Canadians import more than they export, then nonresidents must finance this by buying title to Canada's physical assets (an inflow of direct investment), by lending to Canadians (an inflow of portfolio investment) or by holding Canadian-dollar bank deposits (an inflow of short-term portfolio investment).

However, as Table 6.1 indicates, the deficit on the current account is not matched exactly by the surplus on capital account. Canadians can import more than they export to the extent that Canada's **official foreign exchange reserves** are run down. Alternatively, if high domestic interest rates draw in large capital inflows, then the Bank of Canada may offset the upward pressure on the exchange rate by purchasing foreign exchange, thereby adding to Canada's foreign exchange reserves. In 1990, for example, Canadian foreign exchange reserves were increased by about $0.6 billion. In other words, the sum of the net balances on current and capital accounts equals the net change in Canada's official foreign exchange reserves (plus the inevitable accounting errors and omissions). The Bank of Canada manages Canada's foreign exchange reserves and it is through sales from (or additions to) this foreign exchange fund that the Bank of Canada is able to influence the exchange rate of the Canadian dollar. We turn now to consider the sources of the demand for and supply of foreign exchange, and how these demand and supply forces interact to determine the equilibrium value of the exchange rate.

The Foreign Exchange Market

In this section we will derive the supply and demand curves for foreign exchange from the Canadian perspective. Since each of the many countries in the world has its own currency, there are, of course, many exchange rates for the Canadian dollar (*The Globe and Mail* lists about 60 every day), but we will confine our analysis to a two-country world made up of Canada and the rest of the world, where the rest of the world will be represented by the United Kingdom for expositional convenience.

Table 6.2 illustrates three hypothetical balance of payments accounts for Canada. We will look at each in turn and discuss the supply and demand for Canadian dollars in the foreign exchange market which each set of transactions implies. In column A, Canada's international transactions consist of only current transactions. Exports of $100 are balanced by imports of $100. However, foreign trade is not typically barter,

Table 6.2 Three Illustrations of Canada's Balance of Payments

	A	B	C
Current account			
Exports	+$100	0	0
Imports	–$100	–$100	–$100
Current balance	0	–$100	–$100
Capital account			
Net investment flows into Canada:			
Direct	0	+$ 50	0
Portfolio	0	+$ 50	0
Capital balance	0	+$100	0
Reconciliation			
Current balance	0	–$100	–$100
Capital balance	0	+$100	0
Net change in official reserves	0	0	–$100

but involves the exchange of national currencies. Normally a British importer will need to obtain Canadian dollars in order to pay for the goods. If the British importer does pay in pounds sterling, then the Canadian exporter will have to exchange the pounds for Canadian dollars since he can pay his domestic expenses only in Canadian dollars. Either way, the export of Canadian goods to the United Kingdom ultimately gives rise to a demand for Canadian dollars in the foreign exchange market. Similarly, the Canadian importer of goods from the United Kingdom will need to pay the British exporter in British pounds. In order to obtain the required pounds, the Canadian importer will have to go to a bank and offer Canadian dollars in exchange for pounds sterling. Since we are focusing on the supply and demand for Canadian dollars in the foreign exchange market, this example illustrates that imports into Canada give rise to a supply of Canadian dollars in the foreign exchange market.

Our second example, illustrated in column B of Table 6.2, assumes that imports into Canada are valued at $100 but exports are zero. The net balance on current account is therefore $100, which on its own implies a supply of $100 to the foreign exchange market. However, the capital account shows a net inflow of foreign investment totalling $100. This capital inflow is a receipt and therefore a positive item in the balance of payments. It may be that British residents have purchased $50 of Stelco stock and $50 of Quebec government bonds. In order to make these financial investments, British residents will need to obtain Canadian dollars. Again a positive item in the balance of payments corresponds to a demand for Canadian dollars in the foreign exchange market. In this example Canadian importers supply $100 to the foreign exchange market and British investors demand $100 in the foreign exchange market. Canadian and/or British banks reconcile the amount of currency demanded and supplied.

In the final column of Table 6.2 we illustrate the case where Canadian imports are financed not by exports, nor by net capital inflows, but by a reduction in Canada's official foreign exchange reserves. Again the deficit of $100 on the current account implies a supply of Canadian dollars in the foreign exchange market. If British residents do not want Canadian exports (suppose there is a recession in the United Kingdom) and British investors do not want to invest in Canada (suppose high interest rates in the United Kingdom are more attractive), where will Canadians get the foreign exchange (British pounds) to pay for Canada's imports? We have a disequilibrium in the foreign exchange market that will set up forces which, left to themselves, would push the foreign exchange market towards equilibrium. However, in the present example this adjustment mechanism is short-circuited by government action. The Bank of Canada intervenes by selling foreign exchange (pounds) from its holdings of foreign exchange and buys up Canadian dollars. In other words, it is the Bank of Canada that supplies the needed pounds. Through the banking system the Canadian importer is therefore able to get the foreign exchange required to pay for the imports.

To summarize, the supply of Canadian dollars in the foreign exchange market derives from international payments that Canadian residents want to make, payments which typically cannot be made in Canadian dollars. These international payments consist of the negative items in Canada's balance of payments accounts and include such things as merchandise imports, foreign travel, outflows of interest and dividends, and outflows of capital, both of the direct and portfolio type. All such payments give rise to a demand for foreign currencies and a supply of Canadian dollars in the foreign exchange market. Conversely, the demand for Canadian dollars in the foreign exchange market is derived from Canada's international receipts because Canadians need to receive payment in their own currency. These international receipts, which are entered in the balance of payments as positive items, are in turn the result of merchandise exports, inflows of interest and dividends, and inflows of foreign investment. In addition to these private supplies and demands there is the possibility that the Bank of Canada will supply (demand) Canadian dollars in the foreign exchange market by purchasing (selling) foreign exchange, thus adding to (reducing) Canada's official foreign exchange reserves. In Figure 6.2 we have drawn supply and demand curves for the Canadian dollar in the foreign exchange market. As usual, along the horizontal axis we measure the quantity per time period — in this case the quantity of Canadian dollars offered or demanded per period of time. Along the vertical axis is measured the unit price of the Canadian dollar. In the foreign exchange

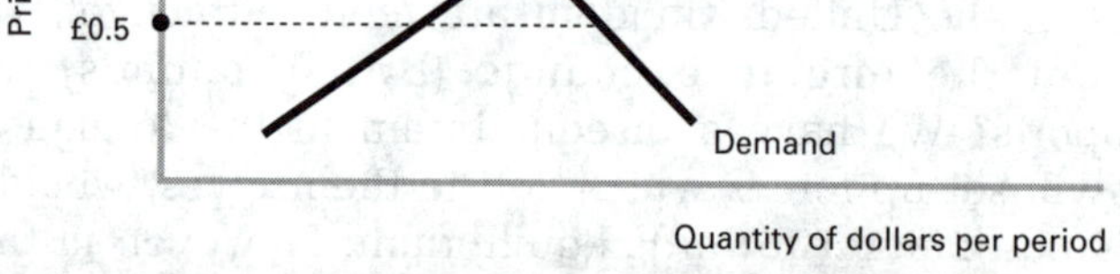

Figure 6.2 The demand and supply of Canadian dollars in the foreign exchange market

market the price of the dollar is measured in terms of foreign currency (such as the pound) since it is foreign currency that must be given up in order to obtain dollars. Notice that as the price of one dollar in terms of pounds rises (movement up the axis), the dollar is rising in value (one dollar buys more pounds), just as when the price of gold rises we can say the value of gold has risen. In other words, movement up the vertical axis implies that the Canadian dollar is rising in value or appreciating.

The Demand Curve

As with all demand curves, the demand curve for Canadian dollars slopes downwards to the right. When the Canadian dollar depreciates, the dollar value of Canada's exports increases. Nonresidents require more dollars to purchase Canada's exports. Table 6.3 illustrates the case of Canadian cheese exports to Britain.

In the first row of the table we assume that the price of the dollar is £1 so that a package of cheese that sells for $2 in Canada will sell for £2 in Britain (we are ignoring transportation charges and any tariff that might apply). Suppose that at this price British demand for Canadian cheese is ten packages per month. The British value of this Canadian cheese is 10 × £2 = £20, which at the exchange rate of $1 = £1 amounts to $20. In order to import the ten packages of Canadian cheese, a British importer must obtain $20 in the foreign exchange market. Now suppose the Canadian dollar depreciates to £0.5. We will assume that the Canadian-dollar price of cheese is not affected by the value of the exchange rate so that the price in Britain falls to £1 per package.[8] As long as the British demand curve for Canadian cheese is downward-sloping, the fall in the price of cheese will lead to an increase in quantity de-

Table 6.3 Canadian Cheese Exports and the Quantity of Canadian Dollars Demanded in the Foreign Exchange Market

Exchange	Price of Cheese/Package		Amount of Cheese Sold in Britain		
Rate	In Canada	In Britain	No. of Pkgs.	Value in £	Value in $
$1 = £1	$2	£2	10	£20	$20
$1 = £0.5	$2	£1	25	£25	$50

8 An alternative assumption is that the price of Canadian cheese is determined by the world price of cheese so that changes in the exchange rate of the Canadian dollar have no effect on the world price of cheese but do affect the domestic price of cheese. This assumption also leads to the conclusion that the demand for Canadian dollars in the foreign exchange market increases as the Canadian dollar depreciates.

manded, say to 25 packages. The change in the British value of cheese sales when expressed in terms of pounds depends in general on the price elasticity of demand for Canadian cheese in Britain. In our example the value of cheese sales in Britain rises from £20 to £25 (the demand for Canadian cheese in Britain is price elastic). In terms of the foreign exchange market, the important point is that an increase in the quantity of cheese sold in Britain together with a fixed Canadian price of $2 per package means that the value of export sales in Canadian dollars must rise. Table 6.3 shows that the demand for Canadian dollars jumps from $20 to $50 per month. A depreciation of the Canadian dollar lowers the price in pounds of Canadian exports, which in turn makes Canadian goods more competitive.

As a result both the volume and the value of exports in Canadian dollars increases, which implies an increase in the quantity of Canadian dollars demanded in the foreign exchange market. The demand curve for Canadian dollars in the foreign exchange market slopes downwards to the right, as shown in Figure 6.2.

The Supply Curve

We turn now to the slope of the supply curve for Canadian dollars. Table 6.4 illustrates the case of imports of British cars. The first row of the table shows the situation when the price of a Canadian dollar is £1. At this exchange rate a British car that costs £9,000 to produce in Britain will sell for $9,000 in Canada. At this price we assume that sales will be ten cars per month. In the second row the Canadian dollar is assumed to have depreciated to £0.9, which implies that the £9,000 car now sells for $10,000 in Canada.

A 10 percent depreciation of the Canadian dollar raises the price of imports by 10 percent. The higher price of British cars in Canada will mean that fewer are purchased. However, the change in the supply of dollars to the foreign exchange market depends on the change in expenditure in Canadian dollars on British cars. In general, the price elasticity of demand for a product determines whether total expenditure will

Table 6.4 Imports of British Cars and the Quantity of Canadian Dollars Supplied in the Foreign Exchange Market

Exchange	Price of British Car		Cars Sold in Canada		
Rate	In Britain	In Canada	No. of Cars	Value in £	Value in $
$1 = £1	£9,000	$ 9,000	10	£90,000	$90,000
$1 = £0.9	£9,000	$10,000	8	£72,000	$80,000

rise or fall in response to an increase in price. A price-elastic demand curve implies total expenditure falls when price rises. The figures shown in Table 6.4 imply that the demand for British cars in Canada is elastic.[9] The increase in price leads to a fall in expenditure from $90,000 to $80,000. Notice that if the demand for British cars had been perfectly inelastic at ten cars per month, then the rise in British car prices would have implied an increase in total expenditure to $100,000. Clearly the slope of the supply curve of Canadian dollars in the foreign exchange market depends on the price elasticity of demand for imports. Since traded goods generally have close domestic substitutes (for example, domestic cars versus British cars) it seems reasonable to assume that the demand for imports as a whole is price-elastic. In conclusion, a depreciation of the Canadian dollar raises the price of imports, reduces the volume of imports, and will reduce total expenditure on imports if the demand for imports is price-elastic. Given a price-elastic demand for imports, a depreciation leads to a reduction in the quantity of dollars supplied to the foreign exchange market. The supply curve slopes upwards to the right.

Equilibrium in the Foreign Exchange Market

The equilibrium point in the foreign exchange market, as shown in Figure 6.3, occurs where the supply and demand curves for Canadian dollars intersect. At the equilibrium price, the demand for Canadian dollars by nonresidents who want to buy Canadian goods and services or invest in Canada is exactly equal to the supply of Canadian dollars offered by Canadians who want to buy foreign goods and services or invest abroad. When the foreign exchange market is in equilibrium, Canada's balance of international payments must also be in equilibrium as the net balances on the current and capital accounts will sum to zero. There are no changes in official reserves when the balance of payments is in equilibrium.

To illustrate how the foreign exchange market adjusts to a disturbance, consider the effect of a recession in the United Kingdom. This will have a direct effect in the foreign exchange market because Canada's exports to the United Kingdom will decline as part of the overall decline in aggregate demand in the U.K. economy. This initial fall in exports implies that the demand curve for Canadian dollars in the foreign exchange market will shift to the left. Figure 6.3(a) illustrates the situation. The excess supply of Canadian dollars causes the price of

---

9 Notice that the percentage change in quantity (20 percent) is greater than the percentage change in price (10 percent).

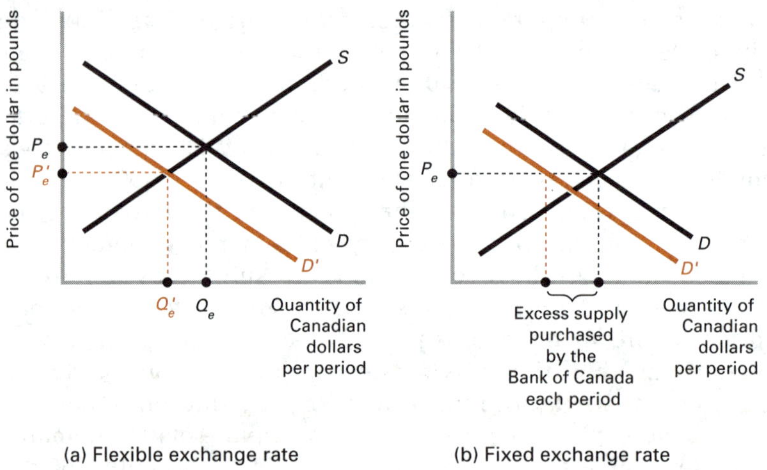

Figure 6.3 Effect of a decline in Canadian exports in the foreign exchange market

dollars to decline in terms of foreign exchange. The depreciation of the Canadian dollar makes Canada's exports cheaper from the point of view of foreign buyers and makes imports into Canada more expensive. As the Canadian dollar depreciates, Canada also becomes an inexpensive place to visit while at the same time foreign vacations become more expensive for Canadians. The effect of these relative price changes is to increase exports from their depressed level and to decrease imports. The effects of the depreciation of the Canadian dollar are reflected in movements along the supply and demand curves (*S* and *D*′). At the new equilibrium point the dollar has depreciated sufficiently to restore the balance between imports and exports that was disturbed by the recession in the United Kingdom.

In the above illustration it is adjustments in the **foreign exchange rate** that restore equilibrium in the foreign exchange market and in the balance of payments. However, suppose the government is following a fixed exchange rate policy at the time of the decline in Canada's exports. As Figure 6.3(b) shows, the exchange rate P_e can be maintained only if the government, through the Bank of Canada, buys up the excess supply of dollars. The Canadian dollars are purchased by the Bank of Canada with foreign exchange reserves. In effect the Bank of Canada is supplying part of the foreign exchange that is needed to finance the current level of imports, which now exceed exports. By doing so the foreign exchange rate is maintained but the equilibrating mechanism is suppressed and the balance of payments will remain in disequilibrium.[10] In addition there is an important side effect to this policy. As the excess supply of dollars in the foreign exchange market is mopped up by the Bank of Canada, the stock of money in Canada is reduced. Again one can think of Canadian importers as buying their foreign exchange from the Bank of Canada. As they do so the quantity of Canadian dollars in the Canadian economy is reduced. Similarly, when there is an excess demand for dollars in the foreign exchange market, the Bank of Canada can prevent the exchange rate from rising by selling Canadian dollars for foreign exchange. In the process foreign exchange reserves are accumulated by the Bank of Canada and the stock of dollars — the Canadian money supply — is increased.

In summary, a **flexible exchange rate** ensures that imports and exports will always adjust so that the balance of payments is either in equilibrium or moving towards equilibrium. On the other hand, a **fixed exchange rate** regime that maintains the existing import and export levels requires that the government intervene in the foreign exchange market by either buying or selling Canadian dollars in exchange for foreign currencies depending on the state of the foreign exchange market. An important corollary of a fixed exchange rate policy is that the domestic money supply responds to conditions in the foreign exchange market. Essentially, the government gives up control of the domestic money supply when it chooses to stabilize the exchange rate.

The analysis in this section has been partial in that we have looked at the foreign exchange market in isolation from the rest of the economy. In our illustration we ignored the effect of the drop in Canadian exports on the level of domestic income. The decline in income associated with the drop in exports will have repercussions on the demand for imports in Canada and on domestic interest rates, both of which have an impact on the balance of payments. In the next section we integrate the balance of payments into our *IS*-*LM* model so that we can discuss the full general equilibrium effects throughout the economy that result from both exogenous events and policy changes.

Balance of Payments Equilibrium: The *BP* Curve

In Chapter 5 we introduced the *IS* and *LM* curves. The *IS* curve describes all combinations of the interest rate and level of income that are consistent with equilibrium in the goods market. The *LM* curve de-

[10] Since foreign exchange reserves are finite, this balance of payments disequilibrium cannot be maintained indefinitely. Either the exchange rate must be allowed to fall or other policies aimed specifically at the balance of payments problem must be followed. One possibility is to engineer a recession so that the demand for imports will be reduced. Alternatively, import quotas or restrictions on capital outflows may be used to reduce the supply of dollars to the foreign exchange market.

scribes all income–interest rate combinations that are consistent with equilibrium in the money market. Full equilibrium in our expanded open economy model also requires that the balance of payments be in equilibrium. In order that we can represent all three markets in one diagram it is useful to develop a new curve, the *BP* curve, which describes all the combinations of income and the interest rate that are consistent with balance of payments equilibrium.

As we discussed above, balance of payments equilibrium requires that:

$$\text{Exports} + \text{Capital Inflows} = \text{Imports} + \text{Capital Outflows}$$

This balance of payments equilibrium condition can be rearranged in the following way:

$$\text{Net Capital Inflows} + \text{Net Exports} = 0 \qquad (6.1)$$

The combinations of income and the interest rate that are consistent with Equation 6.1, and therefore ensure **balance of payments equilibrium**, will define a curve that we will refer to as the ***BP* curve**.

Definition of the *BP* Curve: The *BP* curve is the collection of all interest rate and income combinations that are compatible with balance of payments equilibrium, given that all other factors that affect the balance of payments are held fixed.

But how do the level of interest rates and the level of income affect the balance of payments? One of the major factors that influences where investors place their money is the rate of return that the funds will earn. If interest rates are high in Canada, then not only will Canadians find it attractive to invest in Canada but so too will Americans, Germans, and Japanese. Do firms actually invest funds in foreign countries on the basis of interest rate differentials? Figure 6.4 shows the scatter diagram for net capital flows into Canada and the interest rate differential for three- to five-year government bonds. The least squares line has a positive slope,[11] which means that the data support the hypothesis that the greater is the interest differential, the greater are net capital inflows into Canada. In other words, higher Canadian interest rates, other things being equal, will generate greater net capital inflows into Canada. The linear relationship between net capital inflows, NCI, and the Canada–U.S. interest rate differential, $R - R^{US}$, that is shown in Figure 6.4 can be represented algebraically as:

[11] The slope coefficient is statistically significantly different from zero (with a *t*-statistic of 6.0). It is interesting that the unrestricted regression of NCI on the Canadian and U.S. interest rates produced coefficient estimates of 6364.4 and –6373.1, that is, the unrestricted estimates are almost identical, except for sign. Hence, the unrestricted model confirms that it is the interest differential that determines total net capital flows.

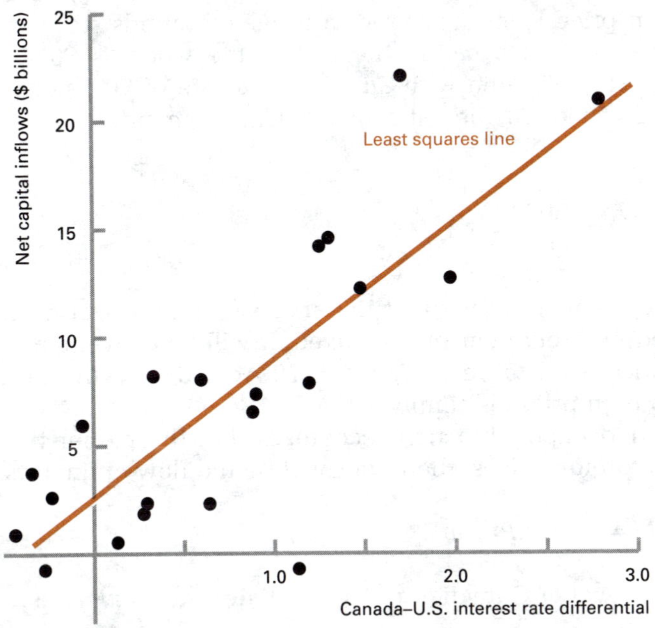

Figure 6.4 Net capital inflows into Canada and the Canada–U.S. interest rate differential, 1970–90

$$\text{NCI} = p + q(R - R^{US}) \tag{6.2}$$

We turn now to the question of how the level of income affects the balance of payments. Figure 4.5 demonstrates clearly that imports depend directly on domestic income levels. We have represented this relationship in the form of a linear equation:

$$M = n + mY \tag{4.4}$$

However, the level of income is not the only variable that determines the level of imports. The ratio of the Canadian price level to the foreign price level will influence the volume of imports into Canada and the volume of Canada's exports. The higher the ratio of Canadian prices to foreign prices, the larger will be the flow of imports into Canada and the smaller will be the level of exports from Canada. The ratio of Canadian to foreign prices can be represented by the quantity $\pi P/P^w$, where P is the Canadian price level (measured in dollars), P^w is the price level in the rest of the world (measured in, say, pounds sterling), and π is the Canadian foreign exchange rate (the price of one Canadian dollar in pounds sterling). The product πP is therefore the Canadian price level measured in terms of pounds sterling. For example, if the price of a car in the rest of the world is £5,000 and in Canada it is \$11,000, then with an exchange rate of £0.5 per Canadian dollar (π = £0.5 per \$) the ratio of the Canadian price to the foreign price is:

$$\frac{0.5 \times 11{,}000}{5{,}000} = 1.1$$

Since we will assume throughout the analysis that the world price level P^w expressed in foreign currency is fixed, it will be convenient to define the world price level to be unity ($P^w = 1$). Accordingly, the ratio of Canadian to foreign prices is simply πP.

The modified import function recognizes that the higher the ratio of Canadian to foreign prices, the larger will be the flow of imports:

$$M = n + s'(\pi P) + mY \tag{6.3}$$

Similarly, the level of Canadian exports will decline as πP rises:

$$X = X_0 - s''(\pi P) \tag{6.4}$$

By subtracting imports from exports we obtain an expression for net exports:

$$X - M = (X_0 - n) - s(\pi P) - mY \tag{6.5}$$

where $s = s' + s''$.

The quantity $(X_0 - n) - s(\pi P)$ is the intercept in this equation. In order to find the combinations of the level of income and the rate of interest that are consistent with balance of payments equilibrium — the equation of the *BP* curve — we substitute Equations 6.2 and 6.5 into the equilibrium condition (Equation 6.1). This gives:

$$(X_0 - n) - s(\pi P) - mY + p + q(R - R^{US}) = 0$$

A more convenient form for this *BP* equation is obtained by expressing the Canadian interest rate R in terms of the other components of the model.

$$R = R^{US} + \frac{s\pi P + n - X_0 - p}{q} + \left(\frac{m}{q}\right)Y \qquad (BP\ \text{Curve}) \tag{6.6}$$

The Slope of the *BP* Curve

Figure 6.5(a) illustrates the *BP* Curve. The *BP* curve slopes upwards to the right because the slope coefficient m/q is the ratio of two positive parameters. To see why this must be so from a more intuitive point of view, suppose that the economy is initially in balance of payments equilibrium at point *A* in Figure 6.5(a). Now suppose that the level of income rises from Y_1 to Y_2 but that the Canadian interest rate remains at R_1. The economy will move to point *B*. But because *net* exports decline as income rises, the balance of payments will be in a *deficit* position at point *B*. Equilibrium can be restored to the balance of payments at income level Y_2 only if net capital inflows increase sufficiently to offset exactly the decline in net exports. This will require an increase in domestic interest rates in order to attract foreign funds into Canada. In Figure 6.5 this higher interest rate is labelled R_2. At point *C* the balance of payments is back in equilibrium. It follows that the *BP* curve passes through the points *A* and *C* and that the *BP* curve slopes upwards to the right. We have also shown that all points *below* the *BP* curve, such as point *B* in Figure 6.5(a), correspond to situations in which the balance of payments is in a *deficit* position. This is because a movement to a point below the *BP* curve involves a drop in the domestic interest rate at a given level of income and this in turn leads to a reduction in net capital inflows. A similar argument shows that points *above* the *BP* curve correspond to situations in which the balance of payments is in a *surplus* position.

Equation 6.6 shows that the precise value of the slope of the *BP* curve is the ratio m/q, where m is the marginal propensity to import and q is a measure of the sensitivity of net capital inflows to changes in

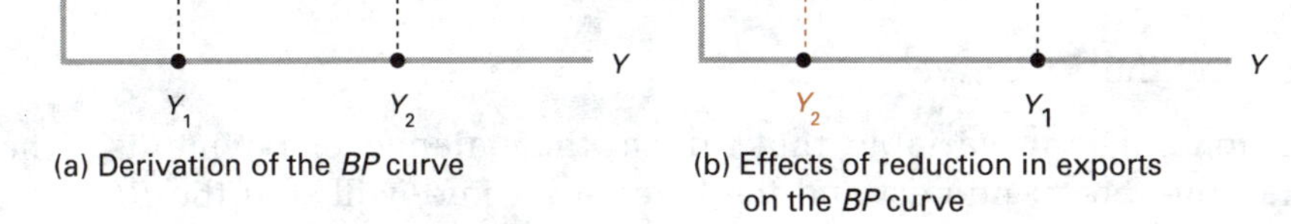

Figure 6.5 The balance of payments curve

the level of Canadian interest rates. Referring to Figure 6.5(a), we see that if the marginal propensity to import m is low, then the increase in income from Y_1 to Y_2 implies that only a small current account deficit will emerge at point B and therefore only a small increase in the interest rate is required to restore balance of payments equilibrium. A low marginal propensity to import implies a rather flat BP curve. In addition, the more sensitive capital flows are to interest rate differentials (the larger the parameter q), the smaller is the rise in the interest rate (to R_2 from R_1) that is needed to restore balance of payments equilibrium and therefore the flatter is the BP curve. The algebraic form of the BP curve confirms that the smaller is m and the larger is q, the smaller will be the slope of the BP curve, m/q.

In a world of perfect capital mobility between countries, Canada's interest rate could not deviate from the world interest rate, because any difference would result in massive capital flows. Higher interest rates in Canada would simply attract funds from other countries that would reduce the cost of borrowing in Canada. In terms of the net capital inflows equation, the slope coefficient q would tend to infinity. In this extreme case, the slope of the BP curve m/q will be zero, and the BP curve will be perfectly horizontal at the world interest rate.

Figure 6.4 presents some Canadian evidence on the sensitivity of capital flows to interest rate differentials. The scatter diagram plots annual net capital flows into Canada on the vertical axis and the Canada–U.S. interest rate differential on the horizontal axis. The data span the period from 1970 to 1990. We would expect short-term capital flows to be influenced by the difference between short-term interest rates, and long-term capital flows to be influenced by long-term interest rates. Since the net capital flows plotted in Figure 6.4 include both short-term and long-term financial assets, the interest differential is calculated using a medium term interest rate (in particular, the difference in the yields of Canadian and U.S. five-year government bonds). The upward sloping least squares line summarizes the positive relationship between international capital flows. The slope of the line indicates that a one-percentage-point increase in Canadian interest rates relative to U.S. interest rates increases the flow of capital into Canada by approximately \$6 billion per year.[12]

Shifting the *BP* Curve

In general, any variable that affects the balance of payments, other than the rate of interest and the level of income, will shift the BP curve.

[12] From a statistical point of view the relationship between interest rate differentials and capital flows is strongly significant. In other words, we can be fairly confident that the slope of the least squares line is a reliable estimate.

In Figure 6.5, the intercept of the *BP* curve on the vertical axis is labelled:

$$R^{US} + \frac{s\pi P + n - X_0 - p}{q}$$

This expression is found by setting the level of income equal to zero in the *BP* curve (Equation 6.6). By examining this intercept term we can see how different events affect the position of the *BP* curve. For example, a sudden decline in Canada's exports in the wake of a U.S. recession can be represented by a decline in the intercept X_0 in the export function (Equation 6.4). The vertical intercept of the *BP* curve indicates that a decline in X_0, which has a negative sign attached to it, shifts the *BP* curve upwards through a distance $\Delta X_0/q$, where ΔX_0 is the change in exports. This example is illustrated in Figure 6.5(b).

The initial position of the economy is at point *A*, but the decline in exports creates a balance of payments deficit at the initial income level Y_1 and at the initial rate of interest R_1. To restore balance of payments equilibrium, either net capital inflows must increase, which can be generated only by a rise in the rate of interest, say to R_2 (point *B*) or imports must decrease, which can be brought about only by a reduction in income, say to Y_2 (point *C*). The new *BP* curve corresponding to the lower level of exports passes through the points *B* and *C*, which are above and to the left of the original *BP* curve. Another way to look at this shift in the *BP* curve is to notice that point *A*, which initially corresponded to a position of balance of payments equilibrium, represents a position of balance of payments deficit as soon as exports decline. It follows that after exports have dropped, *A* must be below and to the right of the *new BP* curve, and so the *BP* curve must have shifted upwards and to the left.

Indeed *any* event that creates an initial balance of payments deficit will shift the *BP* curve upwards and to the left. Examples of such events are a reduction in net capital inflows to Canada in response to fears of impending depreciation of the Canadian dollar, which would reduce the value of Canadian assets and create capital losses (p of Equation 6.2 falls and the vertical intercept of the *BP* curve rises); the threat of foreign exchange controls or government plans to nationalize some Canadian industries (again p falls); or an appreciation of the dollar (π rises), which reduces Canada's exports, increases imports and therefore reduces net capital exports. On the other hand, events that cause an initial balance of payments surplus will shift the *BP* curve downwards and to the right. Examples of such events are a depreciation of the dollar (π falls — this encourages exports and reduces imports) or a surge in net capital inflows due, perhaps, to the discovery of new natural resources (p rises).

General Macroeconomic Equilibrium: Fixed Exchange Rates

Full equilibrium in our open economy macro model requires that the goods market, the money market, and the balance of payments (the foreign exchange market) all be in equilibrium simultaneously. In diagrammatic terms, the equilibrium level of income and interest rate must lie on the *IS* curve, the *LM* curve, and the *BP* curve. The immediate question is what are the forces that guarantee that these three curves will intersect at a single point; if they do not intersect at a single point, then the prevailing interest rate and income level will not correspond to equilibrium in all three markets. The answer to this question depends crucially on the government's exchange rate policy. In this section we deal with the case in which the exchange rate is fixed through government intervention in the foreign exchange market. The key proposition that emerges from the analysis is that the *LM* curve adjusts passively: wherever the *IS* and *BP* curves intersect, the *LM* curve will shift so that it too passes through this point.

Figure 6.6(a) illustrates this fixed exchange rate adjustment process. Suppose, for example, that the economy is initially at point *B* where the *IS* curve intersects LM_1. At this point both the goods and the money markets are in equilibrium, but the balance of payments is in disequilibrium. Because point *B* lies below the *BP* curve, the balance of payments is in a deficit position. This means that Canada's international receipts fall short of international payments and there is an *excess supply of Canadian dollars* in the foreign exchange market. Market forces put downward pressure on the Canadian dollar, but because the government is maintaining a fixed exchange rate policy the Bank of Canada intervenes, using existing foreign exchange reserves to buy up the excess Canadian dollars. As noted earlier, the Bank of Canada's purchase of Canadian dollars in the foreign exchange market causes a reduction in the stock of money as Canadians purchase some of their required foreign exchange from the Bank of Canada. This reduction in the money supply has the effect of shifting the *LM* curve to the left. One can think of the economy sliding up the *IS* curve as the *LM* curve shifts left. However, the balance of payments will remain in a deficit position as long as the economy is below the *BP* curve. Consequently, as long as the *IS* and *LM* curves intersect at a point that is below the *BP* curve, the Bank of Canada must continue to purchase Canadian dollars in the foreign exchange market and therefore the *LM* curve will continue to shift leftwards. This adjustment process will come to a halt when the *LM* curve is at LM_0, where the *IS*, *LM*, and *BP* curves all intersect at the single point *A*. At this point, the balance of payments is in equilibrium, along with the goods and money markets, and there is no need for further intervention in the foreign exchange market.

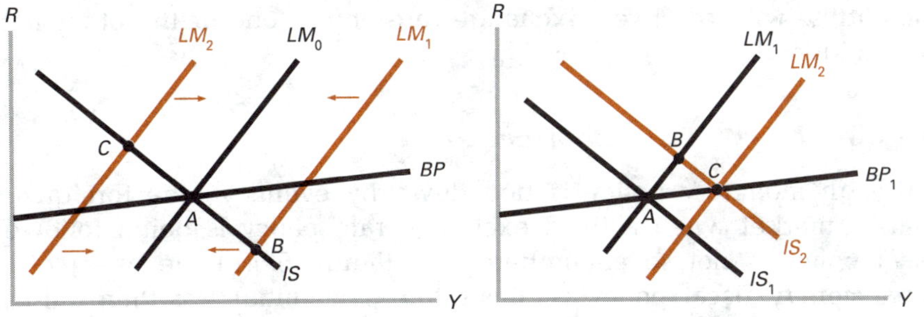

(a) Balance of payments adjustment (b) Expansionary fiscal policy

Figure 6.6 General macroeconomic equilibrium under fixed exchange rates

A similar sequence of events will occur if the economy is initially at point *C* where the goods and money markets are in equilibrium, but there is a balance of payments surplus. In the foreign exchange market there is an excess demand for Canadian dollars — foreigners need more Canadian dollars to buy Canada's exports and to invest in Canada than Canadians are offering in the foreign exchange market. To avoid the appreciation of the dollar that would otherwise result, the Bank of Canada supplies additional dollars to the foreign exchange market. Canada's official reserves are built up and the money supply increases. The increase in the stock of money pushes the *LM* curve to the right. The need for intervention by the Bank of Canada in the foreign exchange market will come to an end only when the *LM* curve has shifted down to LM_0. Again the economy is in full macroeconomic equilibrium at point *A*.

By following a fixed exchange rate policy, the government gives up its control of the domestic money supply. Monetary policy becomes a by-product of exchange rate policy, and the government cannot use monetary policy for domestic stabilization purposes as long as a fixed exchange rate policy is maintained. For example, suppose that at point *A* in Figure 6.6(a) the level of income is well below the full-employment level. If the government attempts to stimulate investment spending by increasing the stock of money and lowering the rate of interest, the result is a balance of payments deficit and downward pressure on the dollar. This is because lower interest rates imply reduced net capital inflows and an increase in income leads to greater imports. Attempts to stabilize the foreign exchange rate by buying up the excess supply of Canadian dollars will simply reverse the original expansionary monetary policy. Expansionary monetary policy is incompatible with the fixed exchange rate policy; one or the other must be abandoned.

Fiscal Policy with Fixed Exchange Rates

Although monetary policy is tied down by events in the foreign exchange market when a fixed exchange rate policy is being followed, fiscal policy is not so encumbered. In Figure 6.6(b) the effect of an expansionary fiscal policy is illustrated. The initial less-than-full-employment position is assumed to be at point *A*, where IS_1, BP_1, and LM_1 all intersect. In order to stimulate demand in the economy, the government can either cut taxes or increase spending. The effect of each of these policy measures is to shift the *IS* curve to the right, say to IS_2. We know from our previous discussion that the result of the fixed exchange rate policy will be that the *LM* curve will adjust passively to the new intersection point of IS_2 and BP_1. The expansionary fiscal policy, which is financed in the bond market, will push up interest rates which in turn will cause an increase in net capital inflows so that at point *B* there is balance of payments surplus. To prevent the dollar from appreciating, the Bank of Canada must supply additional dollars to the foreign exchange market, buying up foreign exchange in the process. The effect of the increase in the stock of money is to shift the *LM* curve to the right. Ultimately balance of payments equilibrium will be restored when the *LM* curve comes to rest at LM_2 and the new equilibrium position for the economy will be at point *C*. Compared to our closed economy analysis of Chapter 5, fiscal policy has a much larger multiplier effect on income when the government is pursuing a fixed exchange rate policy.

What determines the size of the fiscal policy multiplier when the government is maintaining a fixed exchange rate? The answer essentially boils down to the flatness of the *BP* curve. A flat *BP* curve means that an increase in government spending, which shifts the *IS* curve to the right, has a relatively large effect on the level of income and only a small effect on the interest rate. The reason for this is that under a *fixed* exchange rate policy the government expands the domestic money supply at the same time that the expansionary fiscal measures are put into effect. In our open economy model, any increase in the interest rate attracts foreign funds into the country and causes the Canadian dollar to appreciate. In order to maintain the fixed exchange rate, the Bank of Canada has to sell Canadian dollars in the foreign exchange market, buying up foreign exchange in the process. But as more Canadian dollars are printed to buy up foreign exchange, the money supply is increased. This helps to keep down the interest rate and private investment is not crowded out by expansionary fiscal policy.[13]

Although the fiscal policy multipliers are relatively large under a fixed exchange rate policy when the *BP* curve is relatively flat, there is an important side effect to expansionary fiscal policy. In Figure 6.6(b) the effect of the expansionary fiscal policy was to move the economy along the *BP* curve from point *A* to point *C*. By definition all points along the *BP* curve correspond to equilibrium points in the balance of international payments, but the composition of the balance of payments changes as the economy moves along the *BP* curve. At point *C* the interest rate is higher than at *A* so net capital inflows are greater at point *C* than at *A*. But the higher level of income at *C* implies that imports are greater than at *A*, and consequently the current account deficit is larger at *C* than at *A*. Notice that exports will be the same at points *A* and *C*. This structural change in the balance of payments — a larger capital account surplus coupled with a larger current account deficit — may cause some political concern because the larger current account deficit must be financed either through foreign borrowing (Canada's indebtedness to foreigners is increasing) or through foreign direct investment (foreign ownership in Canada is rising). The political ramifications of these shifts within the balance of payments may put constraints on the government's use of fiscal policy for internal stabilization purposes under a fixed exchange rate policy.

An External Shock Under Fixed Exchange Rates

Suppose the Federal Reserve Board (the U.S. central bank) decides to impose a tight monetary policy that raises interest rates and reduces aggregate demand in the U.S. economy. How does this external shock impinge on the Canadian economy and what will be its ramifications? There are two routes through which the tight-money policy in the United States will affect Canada. The most immediate effect will be seen in the capital account of Canada's balance of payments as funds of Canadian and U.S. investors will be drawn from Canada to the United States by the higher U.S. interest rates. The second effect will be felt somewhat later. As the level of aggregate demand in the United States declines in response to higher interest rates, the demand for Canada's exports will also decline. An early casualty is typically the Canadian

---

13 If the *BP* curve is steeper than the *LM* curve, an expansionary fiscal policy will create a balance of payments deficit. The exchange rate will tend to depreciate. To avoid this, the Bank of Canada must buy up Canadian dollars thereby reducing the Canadian money supply and causing the *LM* curve to shift leftwards. In this case the "openness" of the economy reduces the effect of fiscal policy on the level of income because the maintenance of the fixed exchange rate requires a reduction in the money supply.

lumber industry because it is tied to the U.S. housing market, which is particularly sensitive to swings in interest rates.

These two effects are analyzed in Figure 6.7. The initial position is described by IS_1, LM_1, and BP_1, which intersect at point A. The immediate effect of the higher interest rates in the United States is to reduce Canada's net capital inflows as funds are attracted to the U.S. capital market. The *BP* curve therefore shifts upwards through a vertical distance equal to the size of the increase in the U.S. interest rate. Notice that in Equation 6.6 (the equation of the *BP* curve) the intercept of the *BP* curve on the vertical axis is:

$$R^{US} + \frac{s\pi P + n - X_0 - p}{q}$$

Consequently, the vertical intercept increases point for point with the U.S. interest rate, R^{US}.[14] The original equilibrium position, point A, will now lie below the new *BP* curve and therefore the balance of payments is in a deficit position since net capital inflows have declined. Market forces would normally cause the Canadian dollar to depreciate, but be-

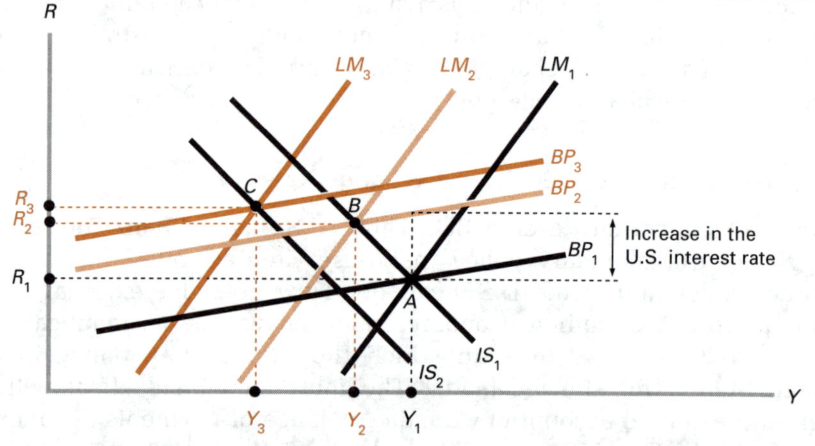

Figure 6.7 The effect on the Canadian economy of monetary restraint in the United States (Canada is assumed to be following a fixed exchange rate policy)

---

14 Notice that at any given level of Canadian income, Canada's imports and exports are also given. But because the interest rate rises in the United States, a difference emerges between Canadian and U.S. interest rates that causes Canada's net capital inflow to decline. The interest rate differential can be restored to its previous level only if the Canadian interest rate rises by the same amount as the U.S. interest rate. This would also restore Canada's net capital inflow to its previous level and so the balance of payments would again be in equilibrium. In other words, the *BP* curve shifts upwards through a vertical distance equal to the rise in the U.S. interest rate.

cause the government is following a fixed exchange rate policy the Bank of Canada uses foreign exchange reserves to buy up the excess supply of Canadian dollars in the foreign exchange market. By taking Canadian dollars out of circulation the Bank of Canada reduces the Canadian money supply and the *LM* curve shifts to the left. The economy moves up the *IS* curve until it finally reaches point *B* where the balance of payments is again in equilibrium and no further Bank of Canada intervention is required in the foreign exchange market.

This analysis has demonstrated how a *fixed* exchange rate policy forces Canadian monetary policy into lock step with U.S. monetary policy. As we have seen, a tight-money policy in the United States will inevitably lead to a tight-money policy in Canada if the exchange rate is to be maintained at its original level. The consequences of an increase in U.S. interest rates under a fixed foreign exchange rate policy are that the Canadian interest rate rises and the level of Canadian income falls (compare points *A* and *B*). Of course, the drop in the level of Canadian income can be linked to the higher Canadian interest rate that discourages investment in plant and equipment. But the original cause was a restrictive U.S. monetary policy coupled with a Canadian fixed exchange rate policy. One final point is that the rise in the interest rate in Canada is not as large as in the United States. The reason is that by the time the economy reaches point *B* the balance of payments deficit that emerged at point *A* is partially offset by a decline in imports into Canada due to the decline in Canadian income. Consequently, net capital inflows at point *B* do not have to be restored to their original level at point *A*, and the required rise in the Canadian interest rate is not as large as the vertical shift in the *BP* curve.[15]

We turn now to the second-round effects of the U.S. tight-money policy which are also illustrated in Figure 6.7. Higher interest rates in the United States will eventually cause a drop in U.S. aggregate demand that will ultimately be felt by Canada's export industries. A drop in exports shifts the *IS* curve downwards and to the left, but it also causes a further deterioration in the balance of payments deficit. The *BP* curve will again shift upwards because of the fall in exports. Point *B* will lie below the new *BP* curve BP_3 and above the new *IS* curve IS_2. In the domestic goods market there is an excess supply of goods — inventories build up when export markets are depressed — and the balance of payments is again in a deficit position. The result is that the level of income declines and there is downward pressure on the dollar. In order to maintain the exchange value of the dollar the Bank of Canada intervenes, buying up more Canadian dollars and causing the *LM* curve to shift further to the left. As we have argued above, the final equilibrium

[15] None of these conclusions is altered if the *BP* curve is assumed to be steeper than the *LM* curve.

position is at the point where the *IS* and *BP* curves intersect, point *C*. The *LM* curve responds passively; the fixed exchange rate policy ensures that the domestic money supply will change and the *LM* curve will also pass through the point *C*. By comparing point *C* with point *B* we can see that the decline in exports has had a relatively large effect on the level of income. Again monetary policy has been handcuffed to the fixed exchange rate policy. Had the money supply been kept constant, the domestic recession would have caused the Canadian interest rate to drop, which would have stimulated physical investment and partly offset the effects of declining exports. In addition, without the support of the Bank of Canada, our dollar would depreciate, which would improve the competitive position of Canadian industry and soften the impact of the U.S. recession. Consequently, the maintenance of the fixed exchange rate increases the vulnerability of the Canadian economy to external shocks, such as a decline in exports. This conclusion is not contingent on the *BP* curve being flatter than the *LM* curve.[16]

The major conclusions of our analysis of an open economy under a fixed exchange rate policy regime can be summarized as follows. First, by choosing to maintain a fixed exchange rate the government effectively ties monetary policy to the foreign exchange market. It is impossible for Canada to follow a monetary policy that is independent of U.S. monetary policy. We have illustrated this proposition with an example in which the United States follows a tight-money policy. However, it is equally true that if the Federal Reserve Board decides to increase the money supply, then Canada will have to follow suit with an ultimately inflationary expansionary monetary policy if the exchange value of the dollar is to be maintained. In short, the Canadian economy is more vulnerable to external disturbances when the Canadian government follows a fixed exchange rate policy. A second example was provided by the case of a drop in exports from Canada, which has a greater impact on Canadian income under a fixed exchange rate policy than under a flexible exchange rate policy. These conclusions do not depend on the relative slopes of the *BP* and *LM* curves. Turning to fiscal policy, given that the *BP* curve is flatter than the *LM* curve, the multiplier effect of fiscal policy on income is greater in the open economy under a fixed exchange rate than in a closed economy. This larger fiscal multiplier effect under a fixed exchange rate is due to the fact that the money supply increases passively as the Bank of Canada maintains the fixed exchange rate and this reinforces the

---

[16] A decline in exports will tend to cause a depreciation of the Canadian dollar, whichever of the *LM* and *BP* curves is steeper. This is because a drop in exports causes a leftward shift of the *BP* curve ($\Delta X/m$) that is larger than the leftward shift of the *IS* curve [$\Delta X/(1 - b + bt + m)$]. This implies that the intersection point of the new *IS* curve and the original *LM* curve will be below the new *BP* curve. Thus, after the decline in exports, the point where the goods and money markets are in equilibrium corresponds to a balance of payments deficit.

rightward shift of the *IS* curve. However, when the *BP* curve is steeper than the *LM* curve, an expansionary fiscal policy causes the Canadian dollar to depreciate. A by-product of the Bank of Canada's support of the Canadian dollar in the foreign exchange market is a reduction in the Canadian money supply. This in turn causes a leftward shift of the *LM* curve and limits the multiplier effect of fiscal policy.

General Macroeconomic Equilibrium: Flexible Exchange Rates

When the exchange rate is allowed to find its own level according to the supply and demand conditions in the foreign exchange market, the achievement of balance of payments equilibrium ceases to be a policy concern. Monetary policy is no longer preoccupied with exchange rate considerations, and the *LM* curve no longer moves passively to the point where the *IS* and *BP* curves intersect. On the contrary, now that the exchange rate is flexible, it is the *IS* and *BP* curves that shift as conditions in the foreign exchange market change. Consider, for example, the effect of a depreciation of the Canadian dollar on the position of the *IS* and *BP* curves. Since a depreciation of the Canadian dollar tends to make imports more expensive for Canadians and exports from Canada less expensive for foreigners, the effect of a depreciation is to give a boost to exports but to reduce the flow of imports. As we saw in Chapter 5, an increase in exports will shift the *IS* curve to the right. This effect is compounded by the reduced flow of imports. Not only are export industries given a boost by the depreciation of the dollar, but so too are import-competing industries.

The effect of a depreciation of the Canadian dollar on the *BP* curve is to shift the *BP* curve downwards and to the right. At any given level of income and the interest rate, a depreciation results in an increase in *net* exports, and a movement towards a balance of payments surplus. As discussed above, any event that causes a balance of payments surplus to arise shifts the *BP* curve down and to the right. From an algebraic point of view, a decline in the value of π, which appears in the vertical intercept term of the *BP* curve (Equation 6.6) with a *positive* sign, causes the vertical intercept of the *BP* curve to decline.

The process of adjustment to a point of overall macroeconomic equilibrium is illustrated in Figure 6.8. The initial disequilibrium state is described by the curves IS_1, LM_1, and BP_1. These curves do not intersect at a single point and so there is no interest rate–income combination that is consistent with simultaneous equilibrium in all three markets. Suppose the economy is initially at point *A*, which lies on IS_1 and LM_1 but is below BP_1. Points below BP_1 are characterized by an excess supply of Canadian dollars in the foreign exchange market. In the absence of Bank of Canada intervention, the Canadian dollar will depreciate. As the Canadian dollar depreciates (and exports rise and imports fall), the *IS* curve shifts up and to the right and the *BP* curve shifts down and to the right. It is useful to think of the economy as sliding up the *LM* curve as the *IS* curve shifts upwards. At the same time, the downward-moving *BP* curve will also be sliding down LM_1. This process continues as long as the balance of payments deficit persists and the Canadian dollar continues to depreciate. Eventually the *IS* and *BP* curves cross the stationary LM_1 at the same point (point *B* in Figure 6.8). Once the economy is at point *B*, all three markets are simultaneously in equilibrium and the exchange rate stabilizes at its new equilibrium level.

Monetary Policy Under Flexible Exchange Rates

Figure 6.9(a) illustrates the effect of an increase in the supply of money under a flexible exchange rate policy. Initially, the economy is at point *A*, where IS_1, LM_1, and BP_1 intersect. When the Bank of Canada increases the stock of money, the *LM* curve shifts rightwards to LM_2. The immediate effect of the expansion of the stock of money is to reduce the interest rate. This encourages business investment in plant and equipment and gives the economy a boost. In the absence of balance of payments considerations the new equilibrium would be at point *B* where LM_2 cuts IS_1. But point *B* lies below the *BP* curve BP_1, meaning that the balance of payments is in a deficit position. This is due to the fact that the lower interest rate discourages capital inflows into Canada and the higher income raises imports. There is an excess supply of Canadian dollars in the foreign exchange market and the dollar depreciates. It is this depreciation of the Canadian dollar that restores overall macroeco-

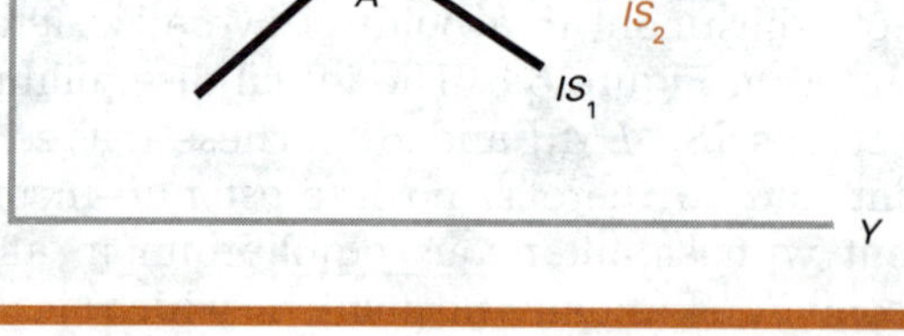

Figure 6.8 Balance of payments adjustment under flexible exchange rates

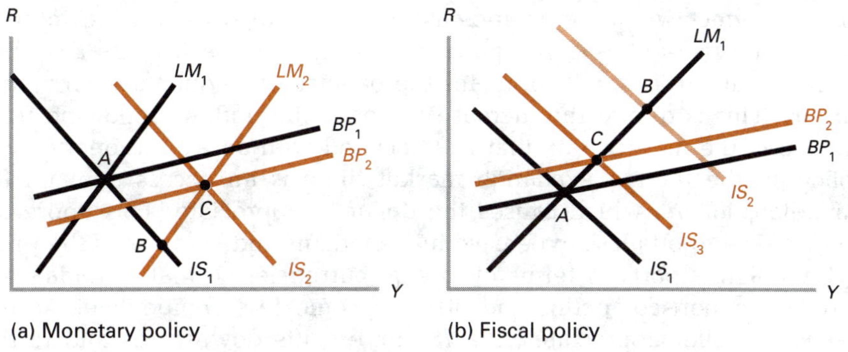

Figure 6.9 Monetary and fiscal policy under flexible exchange rates

nomic equilibrium. The analysis is exactly as we described in the last section. As the Canadian dollar depreciates, exports increase and imports decrease in response to the relative price changes of Canadian and foreign goods and services. In the diagram the *IS* curve shifts upwards and to the right while the *BP* curve shifts downwards and to the right until eventually they both intersect LM_2 at the same point, *C*. At this point all three markets are again back in equilibrium.

By comparing point *C* with point *A* we can see that the effect of the increase in the money supply is to increase the level of income. Furthermore, since point *C* is to the right of point *B*, the effect on income is greater than it would have been in a closed economy. The reason for this larger multiplier effect on income is that the drop in the interest rate associated with an expansionary monetary policy causes a depreciation of the dollar because net capital inflows decline, and this in turn gives the economy a boost by making both export and import-competing industries more competitive. In other words the foreign-exchange-rate effects of the monetary expansion reinforce the direct interest-rate effects and make monetary policy a potentially more potent policy tool when the exchange rate is flexible.[17]

Fiscal Policy Under Flexible Exchange Rates

Figure 6.9(b) illustrates the effect of fiscal policy. Again at the initial point *A*, IS_1, LM_1, and BP_1 intersect. An increase in government spend-

[17] The conclusions of this section are not altered when the *BP* curve is assumed to be steeper than the *LM* curve.

ing (or a tax cut) shifts the *IS* curve rightwards to IS_2. In a closed economy the effect would be to increase income and drive up the interest rate, giving rise to the new equilibrium point *B* where IS_2 cuts LM_1. But point *B* is above BP_1, which means the balance of payments is running a surplus. This is due to the increase in net capital inflows following from the rise in the interest rate that is associated with an expansionary fiscal policy. In the foreign exchange market there is an excess demand for Canadian dollars, which causes the dollar to appreciate. This appreciation makes imports less expensive in Canadian funds but raises the price of Canadian exports in terms of foreign currencies so that Canada's export and import-competing industries become less competitive. As the Canadian dollar appreciates, the *IS* curve shifts downwards and to the left while the *BP* curve shifts upwards and to the left. This process continues until both curves intersect LM_1 at the same point. This occurs at the intersection point of IS_3, BP_2, and LM_1, which is labelled *C*.

Notice that point *C* lies between *A* and *B* on LM_1. An expansionary fiscal policy has a smaller effect on income in a flexible exchange rate, open economy than in a closed economy. In an open economy, the higher interest rates associated with an expansionary fiscal policy cause the exchange rate to appreciate, which puts export and import-competing industries at a disadvantage compared to their foreign competitors. In other words, the indirect balance of payments effects of fiscal policy work against the direct expansionary effect.[18] This is quite the opposite to the fixed exchange rate case where fiscal policy multipliers were found to be relatively large because the monetary adjustments prevent domestic interest rates from rising and the Canadian dollar from appreciating.

Money and Fiscal Multipliers: A Summary

Table 6.5 summarizes the comparisons we have made between the money and fiscal policy multiplier effects on income in an open economy framework and the closed economy multipliers that were obtained in Chapter 5. Clearly in an open economy the size of money and fiscal policy multipliers depends crucially on the nature of the government's foreign exchange rate policy. For example, under a fixed exchange rate regime the money supply is endogenous within the model; it simply adjusts to the prevailing conditions in the foreign exchange market. Consequently, unlike the closed economy model, in the open economy model with a fixed exchange rate there is no possibility of an independent monetary policy and the money multipliers do not exist. The effec-

[18] The conclusions are reversed when the *BP* curve is steeper than the *LM* curve, in which case the multiplier effects of the fiscal policy are enhanced by the balance of payments effects because the exchange rate depreciates.

tiveness of fiscal policy under a fixed exchange rate policy depends on the slope of the *BP* and *LM* curves. If the *BP* curve is flatter than the *LM* curve, fiscal policy has a large multiplier effect because the money supply expands as the Bank of Canada intervenes in the foreign exchange market to prevent the exchange rate from appreciating. On the other hand, if the *BP* curve is steeper than the *LM* curve, then the fiscal multipliers are relatively small. An expansionary fiscal policy is accompanied by a decrease in the money supply as the Bank of Canada intervenes to support the foreign exchange value of the Canadian dollar, which would otherwise depreciate.

Under a flexible exchange rate policy the government is able to follow an independent monetary policy. Compared to the closed economy model, the money multiplier effect on income is relatively large because as the economy expands imports increase and a merchandise trade deficit emerges. Moreover, as domestic interest rates fall, net capital inflows also decline. The effect of the deficits on both the current and capital accounts is to cause a depreciation of the Canadian dollar. It is this depreciation that gives monetary policy its extra punch in the flexible-exchange-rate open-economy case because exports increase and imports decline in response to the changes in relative international prices. Unlike the case of fiscal mul-

Table 6.5 Comparison of Money and Fiscal Policy Multipliers in Closed and Open Economy Models*

Endogenous Variable	Fiscal Multipliers†	Money Multipliers
	Fixed Exchange Rate Regime	
Income *Y*	$\left\|\frac{\Delta Y}{\Delta G}\right\|_O > \left\|\frac{\Delta Y}{\Delta G}\right\|_C$	$\left\|\frac{\Delta Y}{\Delta \$^S}\right\|_O = 0 < \left\|\frac{\Delta Y}{\Delta \$^S}\right\|_C$
Rate of Interest *R*	$\left\|\frac{\Delta R}{\Delta G}\right\|_O < \left\|\frac{\Delta R}{\Delta G}\right\|_C$	$\left\|\frac{\Delta R}{\Delta \$^S}\right\|_O = 0 < \left\|\frac{\Delta R}{\Delta \$^S}\right\|_C$
	Flexible Exchange Rate Regime	
Income *Y*	$\left\|\frac{\Delta Y}{\Delta G}\right\|_O < \left\|\frac{\Delta Y}{\Delta G}\right\|_C$	$\left\|\frac{\Delta Y}{\Delta \$^S}\right\|_O > \left\|\frac{\Delta Y}{\Delta \$^S}\right\|_C$
Rate of Interest *R*	$\left\|\frac{\Delta R}{\Delta G}\right\|_O < \left\|\frac{\Delta R}{\Delta G}\right\|_C$	$\left\|\frac{\Delta R}{\Delta \$^S}\right\|_O < \left\|\frac{\Delta R}{\Delta \$}\right\|_C$

*The open economy multipliers are subscripted with an *O* and the closed economy multipliers are subscripted with a *C*. The absolute values of the multipliers are compared.

†These inequalities, which are based on the assumption that the *BP* curve is flatter than the *LM* curve, are reversed when the *BP* curve is steeper than the *LM* curve.

tipliers, these conclusions do not depend on the relative slopes of the *BP* and the *LM* curves.

Finally, the effectiveness of fiscal policy in the open economy model with flexible exchange rates depends on the relative slopes of the *BP* and *LM* curves. If the *BP* curve is flatter than the *LM* curve, then an expansionary fiscal policy has a limited multiplier effect on income because the expansion leads to an appreciation of the Canadian dollar due to large capital inflows and this hampers Canada's import-competing and export industries. On the other hand, if the *BP* curve is steeper than the *LM* curve the expansionary fiscal policy leads to a depreciation of the Canadian dollar because the large import flows that accompany the rise in income levels create a balance of payments deficit. The depreciation gives a competitive advantage to Canada's import-competing and export industries, which consequently expand production. This effect reinforces the initial effect of the expansionary fiscal policy.

Flexible Prices and the Foreign Exchange Rate

Throughout our discussion we have assumed that the price level is fixed. In Chapter 9 this assumption will be dropped so that the problems of inflation and unemployment can be dealt with in one consistent model. In this section we consider briefly how the flexibility of prices affects the analysis of the foreign exchange market. Although most countries have experienced chronic inflation since the end of World War II, rates of inflation have differed greatly from country to country. Such differences in national rates of inflation initially tend to give a competitive advantage to the country that has a relatively low rate of inflation. If the inflation rate in country A is *lower* than the inflation rate of country B, the relatively inexpensive exports from country A will expand while at the same time high-priced imports into country A will be squeezed out of domestic markets by country A's low-cost producers. Consequently, country A will find that its balance of payments will move towards a surplus position. In the foreign exchange market there will be an excess demand for country A's currency. But country B, which has a relatively high rate of inflation, will experience a decline in export sales and a rise in imports. Country B will move towards a balance of payments deficit position and in the foreign exchange market there will be an excess supply of country B's currency. Market forces will cause an appreciation of country A's currency vis-à-vis country B's currency. Over the long term the required adjustment in exchange rates due to differences in national inflation rates may be so large that the adjustment cannot be prevented by central bank intervention or by other kinds of intervention such as restrictions on trade and capital flows. Indeed, over the long term the major determinant of exchange rate movements is the difference in the rates of inflation between trading countries. This proposition is referred to as the **Purchasing Power Parity (PPP) theorem**.

The central idea of the PPP theorem is that foreign exchange rates must be at levels that ensure that the prices of traded goods are identical in all markets throughout the trading world (apart from transportation costs and customs duties). Take, for example, the case of Canada and Britain. Let the prices of traded goods in these two countries be P^C and P^B, respectively. These prices are expressed in terms of the appropriate *domestic* currency — P^C in dollars and P^B in pounds sterling. The PPP theorem states that the exchange rate π between dollars and pounds sterling — the price of one dollar in pounds — must be such that the prices of traded goods are the same in Canada and Britain whether these prices are quoted either in dollars or pounds sterling. Converting Canadian-dollar prices to pounds sterling, the following relationship must hold for traded goods:

$$\pi P^C = P^B$$

The accuracy with which differences in national rates of inflation predict exchange rate movements has recently been examined by Professor L.H. Officer.[19] Using data from 14 countries over periods as long as 125 years, Officer finds that there is substantial support for the PPP theorem. For example, Officer calculates that from Canada's perspective, the ratio of the foreign price level to the Canadian price level rose by 18.1 percent over the period 1910 to 1975. The PPP theorem predicts that the Canadian dollar would appreciate against a suitable average of other currencies by 18.1 percent. In fact, the Canadian dollar appreciated by 22 percent over this 65-year period, implying that the forecast error of the PPP theorem was less than 4 percent over a 65-year period. The PPP forecast error can be interpreted as meaning that on the basis of price-level movements alone, the Canadian dollar was overvalued in 1975 by 4 percent.[20] Given the subsequent behaviour of the Canadian dollar, few will disagree with that assessment.

Canada's Recent Exchange Rate Policy

From May 1962 to May 1970, Canada followed a fixed exchange rate policy which pegged the Canadian dollar at the value of $0.925 U.S. Since May 1970, the value of the Canadian dollar has been determined

19 L.H. Officer, "Effective exchange rates and price ratios over the long run: A test of the purchasing-power-parity theory," *Canadian Journal of Economics*, May 1980, pp. 206–30.

20 This presumes the Canadian balance of payments was in equilibrium in 1910 and ignores the fact that factors other than relative rates of inflation affect exchange rates. The discovery of new resources, for example, could raise the exchange value of a nation's currency.

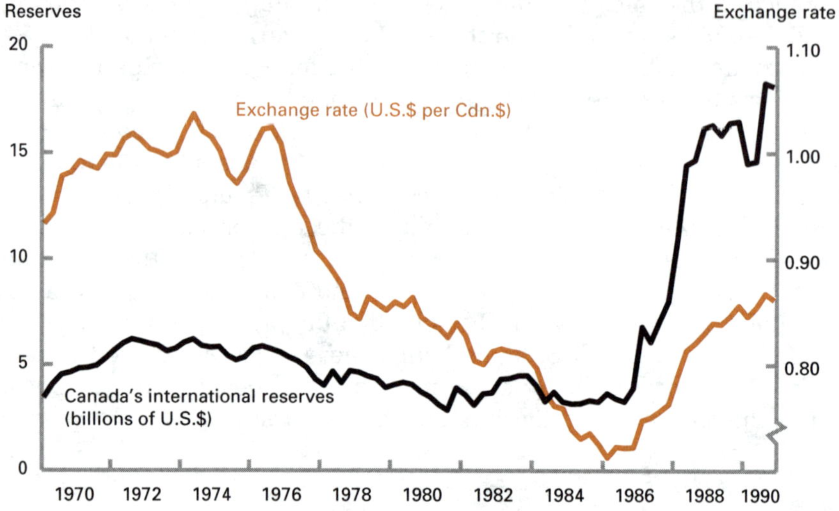

Figure 6.10 Canada's international foreign reserves and foreign exchange rate, 1970–90

largely by market forces, although the Bank of Canada has intervened regularly to moderate the dollar's movement. This is illustrated in Figure 6.10, where the value of the Canadian dollar in U.S. funds is plotted, along with the quantity of Canada's international reserves. The fact that these two series have such similar paths is evidence that the Bank of Canada has attempted to offset market forces. During periods when the Canadian dollar was falling in value, the quantity of foreign exchange reserves has also fallen, indicating that reserves have been used to buy up Canadian dollars, thereby slowing the depreciation. Conversely, when the dollar has appreciated, foreign exchange reserves have been accumulated. For example, immediately after the freeing of the Canadian dollar in May 1970, strong upward pressure on the exchange rate was resisted by the Bank of Canada. Purchases of foreign exchange (sales of Canadian dollars which were in strong demand) throughout the 1970–72 period are reflected in the rising quantity of international reserves. Despite the Bank of Canada's interventions, the dollar continued to rise towards par with the American dollar, and even exceeded it at times.

The reasoning behind this exchange rate policy was a belief that the Canadian economy needed stimulation as it recovered from the 1969–70 recession. A rising Canadian dollar could have hindered that recovery by making imports more competitive and raising the price of Canadian exports in foreign currencies. The Bank of Canada therefore resisted the appreciation of the dollar to protect the economic expansion. As it turned out, the expansion continued in very strong fashion both here and abroad. By the mid-1970s the world-wide growth of economic activity led to the highest peace-time rates of inflation in living memory in many Western countries. Because Canada's inflation rate had been generally higher than in the United States, by 1976 the Canadian dollar was overvalued (the purchasing power parity theorem). In late 1976 the Canadian dollar began a slide that was not reversed until 1986.

The ten years between 1976 and 1986 saw the Canadian dollar depreciate approximately 42 percent. Throughout the decline the Bank of Canada defended the dollar whenever it came under severe pressure. The quotation on page 166 makes it very clear that throughout this period the Governor of the Bank of Canada feared speculative overshooting in the downward direction at a time when inflation was the primary policy issue. Since a depreciating dollar raises import prices, it aggravates the inflation problem. Moreover, inflation itself leads to downward pressure on the exchange rate. The Bank of Canada wanted to avoid this "vicious circle" of inflation and depreciation.

The unusually deep recession of 1982 saw the inflation problem diminish, yet the downward pressure on the Canadian dollar continued. The major reason was the high level of U.S. interest rates, which attracted heavy flows of foreign capital, including Canadian capital, into the United States. Although high domestic interest rates inhibit economic expansion at a time when unemployment is high, unfortunately Canada's interest rates cannot be set independently of world levels given the integration of Canada's financial market with the world market. Only to a very limited extent can Canadian interest rates take an independent course when world interest rates rise and then only to the degree that we accept a depreciating dollar. In his annual report of 1984, the Governor of the Bank of Canada noted that Canada's response to high U.S. interest rates had been to "allow some of the resulting impact to be taken on Canadian interest rates and some of it on our exchange rate."[21] That is, Canadian interest rates have gone up with U.S. rates, but not enough to avoid a declining exchange rate. However, the Governor warned that we should not attempt to keep domestic interest rates low by allowing the dollar to depreciate substantially because this "carries the risk of disrupting the progress we have made on inflation."[22] Again, exchange rate policy has focused primarily on maintaining an orderly market rather than fixing the exchange rate at a particular level.

The present Governor of the Bank of Canada, John Crow, has continued the Bank's policy of focusing monetary policy on long-term inflation targets. In Mr. Crow's view, the appropriate inflation target is zero.

---

21 Bank of Canada, *Annual Report, 1984*, p. 8.

22 Ibid., p. 10.

Throughout the late 1980s and early 1990s Canada consistently maintained a tight rein on monetary growth. This has been reflected in the historically large differences between Canadian and U.S. interest rates. For example, during the five years 1986–90, the yield on Canadian government bonds (with maturities between three and five years) exceeded the corresponding U.S. yields by an average of 1.9 percentage points. In the first half of the 1980s the difference averaged only 0.4 percentage points, just slightly higher than the average differential during the 1970s. As Figure 6.4 illustrates, the high interest differential leads to larger capital inflows and upward pressure on the value of the Canadian dollar. Figure 6.10 indicates that between the first quarter of 1986 and the last quarter of 1990, the Canadian dollar appreciated by 21 percent. At the same time, the rise in the Canadian dollar was resisted by the Bank of Canada. Official exchange reserves grew very rapidly throughout this period. Clearly the Bank of Canada wanted to keep monetary policy tight to fight inflation, but tried to prevent the exchange rate from rising too sharply, since that would have made Canadian exports and import-competing industries less competitive. Canada's high interest rate policy has been extremely unpopular in many quarters of Canadian society. The Governor of the Bank of Canada has tried to put some distance between his tight monetary policy and the rising value of the Canadian dollar.

> While Canadian monetary policy has no exchange rate objective as such, this widening of spreads at the short end of the market did provide, as a by-product, a measure of support for the Canadian dollar. But it is worth noting that the bulk of the appreciation of the Canadian dollar took place between 1987 and the spring of 1989, that is before the widening of interest differentials. This earlier appreciation cannot therefore be directly attributed to monetary policy, but must rather have stemmed from such non-monetary factors as the extraordinary boom in our commodity exports.[23]

We can summarize the Bank of Canada's exchange rate policy since 1970 as one of leaning against the wind. The Bank has attempted to moderate exchange rate movements to avoid speculative overshooting, but has not tried to maintain a fixed exchange rate. Such a policy of stabilizing a floating exchange rate is sometimes rather ungraciously referred to as a "dirty float."

Apart from this last section where we have discussed how flexible prices affect the analysis of the foreign exchange market, we have assumed that the aggregate price level is fixed; our analysis has been

---

23 Remarks by John W. Crow, Governor of the Bank of Canada, to the Chamber of Commerce France–Canada, Paris, France, 13 November 1990. Reprinted in *Bank of Canada Review*, November 1990, p.26.

confined to a non-inflationary world. In the following chapter we will discuss how the aggregate price level is determined and then we will be concerned with the causes of inflation and the role of monetary and fiscal policies in economies that face the two major problems of unemployment and inflation. In order to keep the analysis of this expanded model manageable, the balance of payments repercussions are deferred until Chapter 12. In Chapter 12 the *BP* curve will be integrated into the expanded model to demonstrate how an inflationary open economy responds to shocks under fixed or inflexible exchange rates. It will also be shown that the expanded model is consistent with the purchasing power parity theorem.

Key Concepts

current and capital accounts of the balance of payments
official foreign exchange reserves
foreign exchange rate
fixed and flexible exchange rates
balance of payments equilibrium and the *BP* curve
purchasing power parity (PPP) theorem

Review Questions

1. What is meant by balance of payments equilibrium?
2. Which international transactions give rise to a demand for (supply of) Canadian dollars in the foreign exchange market?
3. How does a depreciation of the dollar affect Canada's export and import-competing industries?
4. Distinguish between portfolio and direct investment.
5. What is meant by the *BP* curve? Explain why it slopes upwards to the right.
6. How does the structure of the balance of payments change as the economy moves up a stationary *BP* curve?
7. In general, what kind of events cause the *BP* curve to shift downwards and to the right (upwards and to the left)?
8. Do points above the *BP* curve correspond to balance of payments deficits or surpluses? Explain.
9. Full equilibrium requires that equilibrium be attained in the goods market, the money market, and the balance of payments, that is,

that the *IS*, *LM*, and *BP* curves all intersect at a single point. If these curves do not intersect at a single point, which curve(s) adjust(s) when the exchange rate is (a) fixed and (b) flexible? Explain the adjustment mechanism in each case.

10. If the government is following a fixed exchange rate policy at a time when foreigners suddenly find Canada a very attractive place to invest their funds, what will happen to Canada's foreign exchange reserves and money supply?
11. To what extent is the Canadian economy insulated from events in the rest of the world when the foreign exchange rate is flexible?
12. What is meant by the term "perfect capital mobility"? What does the *BP* curve look like in such a case? Examine the effects of fiscal and monetary policy when the exchange rate is flexible and capital is perfectly mobile.

Part 3

CHAPTER 7

Aggregate Demand, Aggregate Supply, and the Determination of the Price Level

If I were writing again, I should feel disposed to define full employment as being reached at the same moment at which the supply of output in general becomes (price) inelastic.

John Maynard Keynes[1]

Throughout the last three chapters we have assumed that wage and price levels are fixed and do not respond to changing economic conditions. As we have seen, the fixed price *IS-LM* and *IS-LM-BP* models are useful for exploring a number of macroeconomic issues. But clearly, the model must be extended if we are to understand other important macroeconomic problems, such as inflation. Canada's rate of inflation during the late 1980s and early 1990s has not approached the double-digit levels seen in the previous decade. Nevertheless, throughout the past 20 years, the ever-present threat of accelerating inflation has kept the inflation problem at or near the top of Canada's macroeconomic policy agenda. Before we can understand the process of inflation, we need to understand how the equilibrium price level is determined. As in microeconomics, the fundamental tools in analyzing equilibrium prices are supply and demand curves. The purpose of this chapter is to derive specifically *aggregate* supply and demand curves that can be used to determine the *aggregate* price level.

The nature of the aggregate demand curve is relatively straightforward and uncontroversial. It is based on the *IS-LM* model that we have

---

1 J.M. Keynes, *The General Theory and After: A Supplement.* Volume 29 of *The Collected Writings*, D. Moggridge, ed. (New York: Cambridge University Press, 1979), p. 235.

already examined in some detail. Although the *IS-LM* model has a richly developed demand side, it gives very little attention to the supply side of the economy. Much of this chapter will be devoted to a discussion of the factors that determine the aggregate supply of goods. As we shall see in this and later chapters, this is a much more controversial issue.

The Aggregate Demand Curve

The **aggregate demand curve** represents the physical quantity of goods and services demanded at various price levels. To derive the aggregate demand curve, we must return to the *IS-LM* model, which contains the key demand relationships within the goods and financial asset markets. Our development of the *IS-LM* model in Chapter 5 was premised on *inflexible* prices and all changes in output, consumption, investment, government expenditures, exports, and imports were changes in real physical quantities. In that model, the intersection of the *IS* and *LM* curves determine the demand for aggregate output. If we can now identify how the *IS* and *LM* curves will be affected by a change in the aggregate price level, we can plot the aggregate demand for goods and services (based on the intersection of the *IS* and *LM* curves) against the changing price level. In this way we will uncover the aggregate demand curve.

Effects of a Change in Price Levels on the *IS* and *LM* Curves

In this and all subsequent chapters we will assume that the position of the *IS* curve is independent of the aggregate price level, so that variations in the price level will not affect the position of the *IS* curve. The fundamental reason for this is that the underlying theories behind the *IS* curve describe real macroeconomic behaviour. For example, the consumption function describes the real quantity of goods and services consumed in terms of real disposable income levels. While a change in the price level will increase the nominal level of both consumption expenditures and income, the underlying consumption function continues to hold in real terms. Subject to a minor qualification discussed in Chapter 16, a change in the price level will have no effect on *real* consumption. Similarly, all the other components of aggregate expenditure (C, I, G, X, and \$) that are incorporated in the *IS* curve are real variables. If we wish to write the nominal value of a variable, such as income, it will be expressed as the real variable multiplied by the price level — that is, PY. Notice that in none of the equations used to derive the algebraic *IS* curve does the price level appear.

It is therefore not surprising that changes in the price level have no effect on the position of the *IS* curve.[2]

A change in the price level will, however, have a direct effect on the money market and the position of the *LM* curve. Since the supply of money is obviously a nominal quantity, changing price levels will directly affect the real purchasing power of the nominal money supply and will result in a shift of the *LM* curve. To understand how a change in price levels affects the *LM* curve, we return to a discussion of the demand for money. In Chapter 5, we discussed two major determinants of the demand for money: income and interest rates. The inclusion of income in the demand for money function reflects a transactions demand for cash balances. Transactions balances are needed because income is received regularly, but infrequently, say only once or twice a month. But purchases of goods and services are made on a daily basis, so individuals must hold money between paycheques in order to cover daily expenses. Obviously the transactions demand for money balances depends on the *nominal* value of expenditures, that is, the real quantity of purchases multiplied by the prevailing price level. If, for example, the price level were to double, one would expect that the transactions demand for cash balances would also double, since the same real quantity of goods would now cost twice as much as before.[3]

An equation for the demand for nominal money balances that incorporates all of these properties is given in Equation 7.1. In parentheses, on the right-hand side, the level of real income has a positive sign while the interest rate has a negative sign. The entire expression is multiplied by *P*, the aggregate price level. This ensures that the demand for nominal money balances is proportional to the price level. Notice that if the price level is fixed, as we have assumed in earlier chapters, then we may as well set $P = 1$. In this case, Equation 7.1 collapses to the demand for money equation used in Chapters 5 and 6.

$$\$^D = P(kY - \ell R) \qquad (7.1)$$

Recall that the *LM* curve shows all combinations of the interest rate and income level that guarantee equilibrium in the money market. Thus to derive the *LM* curve, we must set the supply of money, \$, equal to the demand for money, $\$^D$, by substituting the supply of money balances for the demand for money balances in Equation 7.1. Notice that

---

2 The exception is the effect of the Canadian price level on the relative price of Canadian and world goods. This ratio does affect the flow of trade between Canada and the rest of the world. However, we assume here that a change in Canada's aggregate price level will be offset by an appropriate change in the exchange rate. This will leave the ratio of Canadian to world prices unchanged and trade flows will be unaffected. This offsetting effect is discussed more fully in Chapter 12.

3 This is discussed more fully in Chapter 15.

this substitution, which equates supply with demand, directly imposes money market equilibrium. In the *IS-LM* diagram, the interest rate appears on the vertical axis. To write the equation of the *LM* curve so that it corresponds to the diagram, after the substitution of \$ for $\$^D$, the interest rate *R* must be brought to the left-hand side. The resulting form of the *LM* curve equation is:

$$R = \frac{-\$}{\ell P} + \frac{k}{\ell}Y \tag{7.2}$$

The equation of the *LM* curve shows clearly that the price level *P* and the nominal money supply \$ have exactly opposite effects on the intercept of the *LM* curve. In fact, the vertical (*R*-axis) intercept of the *LM* curve is proportional to the *real* money supply, \$/*P*. An increase in the nominal money supply, given a fixed price level *P*, will increase the real money supply and the negative vertical intercept ($-\$/\ell P$) will become larger in the negative direction. The result is to shift the *LM* curve down, in the direction of lower interest rates. This movement agrees with our intuition — an increase in the money supply shifts the *LM* curve in the direction of lower interest rates. Another way that the real money supply can increase is if the price level falls while the nominal money supply remains constant. In this case, the real money supply increases because the denominator of \$/*P* is reduced. The effect on the *LM* curve is again to shift it downwards in the direction of lower interest rates. The important point to notice is that the position of the *LM* curve depends on the *real* money supply. An increase in the real money supply, whether caused by an increase in \$ or a decrease in *P*, will shift the *LM* curve downwards.

Conversely, a decrease in the real money supply will shift the *LM* curve upwards, in the direction of higher interest rates. One way that the real money supply can fall is if the Bank of Canada reduces the nominal money supply at a time when the price level is constant (zero inflation). Alternatively, the real money supply will fall if the Bank of Canada holds the nominal money supply constant at a time when the price level is rising, that is, when inflation is positive. Regardless of how the decline in the real money supply comes about, it will cause the *LM* curve to shift upwards.

An important special case occurs when the nominal money supply and the price level increase at the same percentage rate. For example, inflation may be running at 5 percent per year and the Bank of Canada may be expanding the nominal stock of money at 5 percent per year. In this case, the real money supply \$/*P* is held constant because the increases in \$ and *P* exactly offset each other. The result is that the *LM* curve remains stationary. Most of the time the economy experiences rising prices and a growing nominal money supply. The effect on the position of the *LM* curve depends on which is rising faster. As long as \$ is rising faster than *P*, the real money supply continues to rise and the *LM* curve continues to shift downwards. But whenever P is rising faster than \$, \$/P is falling and the LM curve is shifting upwards.

The Derivation of the Aggregate Demand Curve

The aggregate demand (AD) curve shows the level of aggregate demand for Canadian-produced goods and services at each price level. To derive the aggregate demand curve we will determine the intersection point (Y, R) of the IS and LM curves at every possible price level P. This is done in Figure 7.1, where the IS and LM curves are illustrated in the upper panel. The initial position is at point A, where the IS and LM(\$/P_0) curves intersect. The initial price level is P_0 and the levels of aggregate demand and the interest rate are Y_0 and R_0, respectively. In the lower panel of Figure 7.1, the combination of P_0 and Y_0 defines one point on the aggregate demand curve. This point is also labelled A.

Now consider what happens to aggregate demand when the price level rises to P_1. With a fixed nominal money supply, the real money supply falls to \$/P_1 and the LM curve shifts upwards. Recall that the IS curve remains fixed when the price level changes, so the new intersection point is at B on the original IS curve. Notice that the higher price level P_1 is associated with a lower level of aggregate demand Y_1. The new combination (Y_1, P_1) defines a second point on the aggregate demand curve, which is labelled B in the lower panel of Figure 7.1. Obviously, there are an infinite number of price levels that could be considered. Each price level P defines a unique LM curve that cuts the given IS curve at a certain value of Y. By varying the price level in a continuous fashion, the entire aggregate demand curve can be sketched out.

Let us consider in more detail what changes have taken place in the economy during the movement from point A to point B in Figure 7.1. The immediate cause of the movement is a decline in the real money supply which raises the interest rate. Because investment spending depends on the interest rate, investment demand declines (fewer new houses are built). Through the familiar multiplier effect on income, consumer spending also declines. Thus the higher price level P_1 is associated with a lower level of aggregate demand. At point B, both investment and consumption are lower than at point A. The exogenous components of demand (government expenditures and exports) have not changed. However, other endogenous variables will be affected by the move from point A to point B. In particular, all the variables that depend on income will fall. This includes tax revenues and imports. Since government expenditures are fixed along a given aggregate demand curve, but tax revenues fall as the economy moves up the demand curve, clearly the government budget deficit ($G - T$) increases as the economy moves from point A to point B. Although the decline in

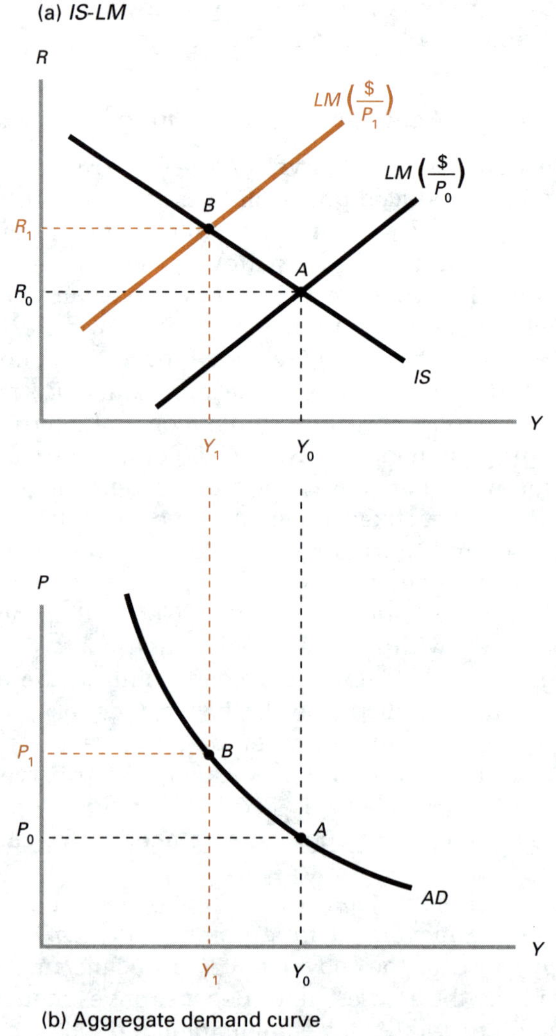

Figure 7.1 The derivation of the aggregate demand curve

aggregate demand increases the government's budgetary deficit, the trade balance ($X - M$) improves, that is, it increases. This follows from the negative effect of falling income on the demand for imports while (exogenous) exports remain at a fixed level along a given *AD* curve.

In summary, there are several important features of the aggregate demand curve that should be noted. First, at all points along the *AD* curve the *IS* and *LM* curves intersect. Since the economy is on an *LM* curve, the money market is in equilibrium. Second, all the variables that were considered exogenous in the *IS*-*LM* model (the exogenous components of demand and the nominal money supply) are held fixed along a given aggregate demand curve. Third, the *AD* curve slopes downwards to the right because a lower aggregate price level means a higher real stock of money, which in turn implies lower interest rates. It is the lower interest rates that are responsible for the increase in demand through their effect on investment expenditures. Finally, all income-responsive variables, including consumption, tax revenues, and imports, increase as the economy moves down a given *AD* curve in the direction of increasing *Y*.

Shifts in the Aggregate Demand Curve

The aggregate demand curve in the lower panel of Figure 7.1 illustrates the relationship between the price level and aggregate demand. Remember the rule that in any diagram whenever one of the variables labelled on an axis changes, the result can only be a movement *along* the curve; these "axis" variables cannot shift the curve. Thus, it is changes in the price level that cause movements along a given aggregate demand curve. But there are many exogenous variables in the model that have a direct effect on aggregate demand and it is these variables that shift the *AD* curve. In general, any exogenous variable or parameter that can shift either the *IS* curve or the *LM* curve (other than *P*) will cause a shift in *AD*. As we shall see, demand factors that tend to stimulate the economy will shift the *AD* curve to the right, in the direction of higher income and higher prices. Figure 7.2(a) illustrates how an *IS* shift factor, namely an increase in government expenditures, shifts the *AD* curve to the right. Figure 7.2(b) shows how an increase in the money supply (an *LM* curve shift factor) also shifts the *AD* curve to the right. Let us consider these effects in more detail.

At the top of Figure 7.2(a), we focus on a change in government spending. The initial position is at point *A*, where the *LM* curve intersects $IS(G_0)$. The corresponding level of aggregate demand is Y_0. The position of the *LM* curve is determined by the real money supply $\$/P_0$. Consequently, the point (Y_0, P_0) is the initial position on the aggregate demand curve $AD(G_0)$. Now suppose that government spending increases to G_1, which shifts the *IS* curve out to $IS(G_1)$. Given a fixed money supply \$ and the initial price level P_0, the new intersection point is at *B*, where aggregate demand is Y_1. In the lower panel of Figure 7.2(a), the point (Y_1, P_0) lies on the new aggregate demand curve, which is labelled $AD(G_1)$. An outward shift of the *IS* curve causes an outward shift of the aggregate demand curve. It makes sense intuitively that an increase in government spending shifts the aggregate demand curve outwards in the direction of greater output.

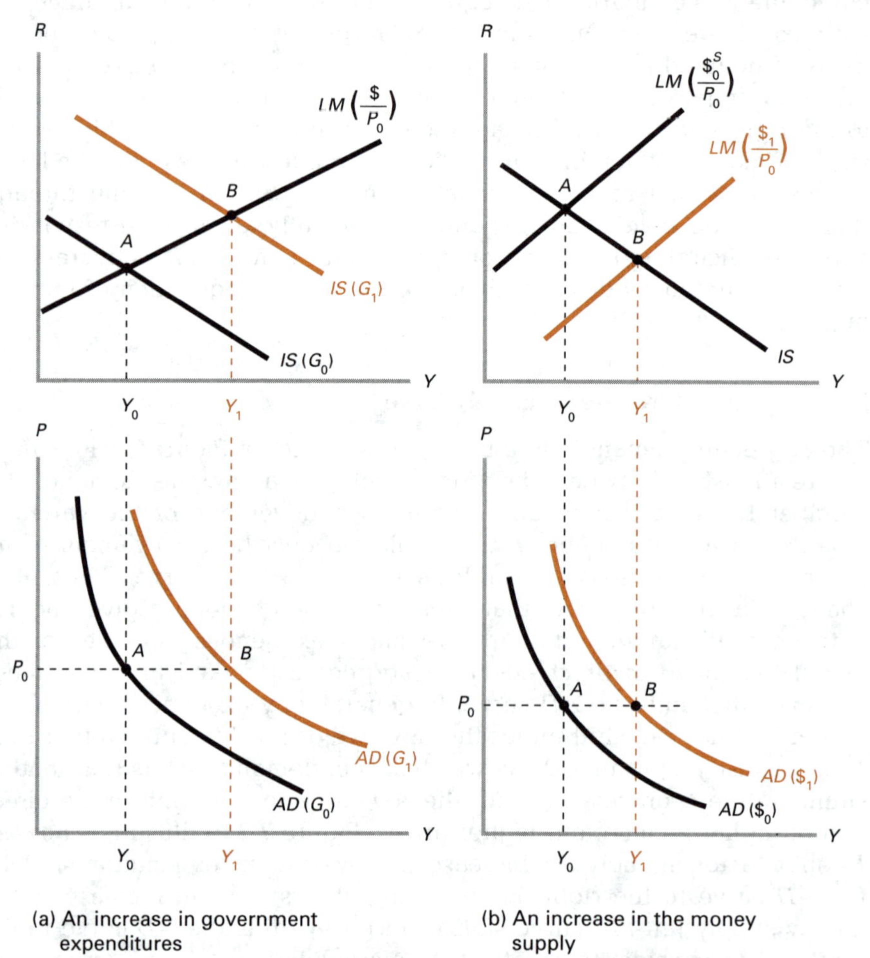

Figure 7.2 Shifts of the aggregate demand curve

Next consider an increase in the nominal money supply. This is illustrated in Figure 7.2(b). In the upper panel the initial position is at point *A*, where the fixed *IS* curve cuts $LM(\$_0/P_0)$. In the lower panel, the point (Y_0, P_0) lies on the initial aggregate demand curve $AD(\$_0)$. Recall that the *AD* curve is sketched out by varying the price level, that is, changes in the price level cause movements along $AD(\$_0)$. In this exercise we will hold the price level fixed at P_0 and increase the nominal money supply to $\$_1$. In the upper panel the *LM* curve shifts to $LM(\$_1/P_0)$, which cuts the *IS* curve at point *B*. The new level of aggregate demand increases to Y_1 because the higher real money supply $\$_1/P_0$ causes interest rates to drop and investment expenditures to increase. In the lower panel (Y_1, P_0), labelled as point B, lies on a new aggregate demand curve $AD(\$_1)$. Again, it makes sense that when the Bank of Canada increases the money supply, the aggregate demand curve shifts out in the direction of greater output and higher prices.

In summary, any exogenous variable that shifts either the *IS* or the *LM* curve (other than the price level, which is an endogenous variable in the full model) can also shift the aggregate demand curve. Changes in an exogenous variable that stimulate aggregate demand will shift the aggregate demand curve in the direction of greater output and higher prices. Remember that when the nominal money supply is fixed, a change in the price level will shift the *LM* curve, but this shift causes a movement *along* a given aggregate demand curve.

Aggregate Supply

In this section we will be concerned with the relationship between the aggregate price level and the aggregate supply of goods — the aggregate supply curve. Later we will be able to combine the demand and supply components of our model to determine the equilibrium price and output levels for the economy as a whole, much in the same way that the supply and demand curves for bread determine the equilibrium price and quantity of bread.

In the short run, the quantity of output depends fundamentally on the amount of labour that is employed. Since the amount of labour employed is determined by the market for labour, much of our discussion will focus on this market. Indeed, the critical factor that determines the nature of the aggregate supply curve depends on how the labour market responds to changes in the price level. We begin our analysis of aggregate supply with a discussion of the aggregate production function and its relationship to the demand for labour.

The Aggregate Production Function

The upper panel of Figure 7.3 shows the relationship between the amount of labour employed and the quantity of output produced. It is drawn on the assumption that the quantity of capital used in production is fixed. This is reasonable because we are concerned with the relatively short period of time required to complete a business cycle. Clearly the level of employment varies during the business cycle, but the amount of investment made in new plant and equipment is relatively small in relation to the total quantity of plant and equipment al-

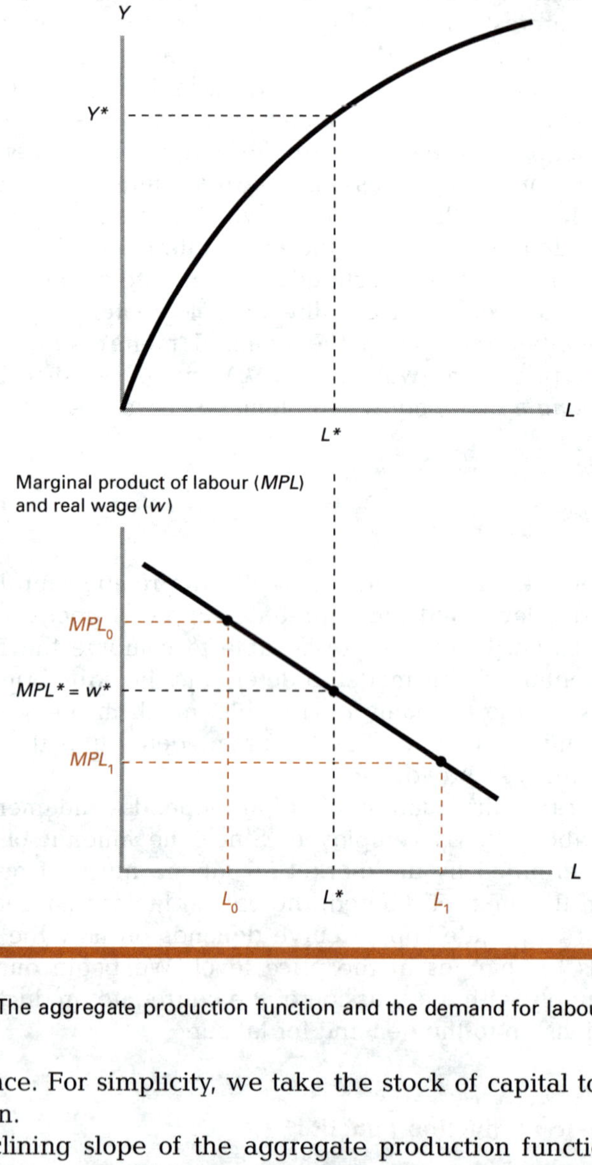

Figure 7.3 The aggregate production function and the demand for labour

ready in place. For simplicity, we take the stock of capital to be fixed in the short run.

The declining slope of the aggregate production function indicates that additional units of labour add positive, but ever decreasing, increments to total output as more labour is added. The increase in total output when one extra unit of labour is hired is called the **marginal product of labour**. The declining slope of the aggregate production function implies that the marginal product of labour, or *MPL*, declines as the amount of labour employed increases. This inverse relationship between the *MPL* and employment is illustrated in the lower panel of Figure 7.3. Given a level of labour input, say L_0, the *MPL* schedule indicates that the amount of extra output produced by one or more unit of labour is MPL_0. At a greater level of labour input, such as L_1, one extra unit of labour will still raise output, but by only MPL_1 units.

When markets are competitive, the marginal product of labour schedule is also the demand for labour schedule. Notice that both *MPL* and the **real wage** paid to workers are measured in units of output per period, say pizzas per hour. Of course, workers are not literally paid in pizzas, but in a pizza economy, the hourly real wage is precisely the number of pizzas that one hour's labour will purchase. Since the real wage and the *MPL* are measured in the same units, these two quantities can be plotted along the same vertical axis, as in the lower panel of Figure 7.3. The *MPL* schedule is the demand for labour schedule in the sense that when the vertical axis measures the real wage, the *MPL* schedule shows (on the horizontal axis) precisely how much labour is demanded at any real wage. Now consider why this is so.

Profit-maximizing firms are prepared to hire one extra unit of labour provided the extra revenue exceeds the increase in costs. As long as revenue increases more than costs, total profits rise. Consider the effect on profits of hiring one more unit of labour — say one more person for one more hour. Taking the price of output to be fixed at P, and noting that an extra unit of labour produces *MPL* units of output per hour, we find that the increase in revenue is $P \times MPL$. At the same time, costs rise by W (the nominal wage rate) when one extra unit of labour is hired. The change in profits is $(P \times MPL - W)$. Clearly profits rise if $P \times MPL$ is greater than W and the firm will hire the extra labour. However, as more labour is hired, *MPL* declines and at some level of labour input, the point is reached where

$$P \times MPL = W$$

This is the point where profits are maximized because if more labour is hired, *MPL* will continue to decline and contributions to revenue will fall short of the rise in costs — that is, $P \times MPL$ will be less than W.

An alternative way of writing the profit-maximizing conditions is

$$MPL = \frac{W}{P} = w$$

That is, the marginal product of labour equals the *real wage*, w, which is the ratio of the nominal wage to the price level: W/P.

Firms that operate in competitive output and input markets take the price of output, P, and the wage rate, W, as given. Hence, such firms take the real wage, W/P, as given to them by the marketplace. Firms must decide how much labour to hire given the real wage, W/P. The demand for labour is precisely the amount of labour that ensures profits are maximized — that is, the level of labour input that equates the marginal product of labour to the real wage.

Figure 7.3 illustrates this point. Suppose the real wage is w^*. Firms would like to hire more labour than L_0 because at this level of labour input $MPL_0 > w^*$. Starting at L_0, profits rise as more labour is hired. Conversely, at L_1, too much labour has been hired, and with $MPL_1 < w^*$ profits rise as *less* labour is hired. At L^*, $MPL^* = w^*$ and profits are maximized. We conclude that given the real wage w^*, profit-maximizing firms will hire L^*. In the upper panel of Figure 7.3 the production function determines that the employment level L^* produces output Y^*.

We could repeat this argument for any real wage. We would find that the (profit-maximizing) quantity of labour demanded is read off the *MPL* schedule. In other words, in a diagram with the real wage on the vertical axis and the quantity of labour on the horizontal axis, the *MPL* curve is the demand for labour schedule.

The Supply of Labour

The theory of labour supply is based on the utility-maximizing behaviour of individuals. It is supposed that individuals enjoy both their leisure or spare time, S, and their level of goods consumption, C. Utility is therefore a function of these two enjoyable items:

$$U = f(S, C)$$

In order to pay for consumption, individuals need to work for wages. However, the more time that is spent working, the less spare time the individual has. The utility maximization problem therefore becomes a problem of how to allocate time between work and spare time.

Let us consider the opportunity cost to a worker of giving up one more hour of spare time. This opportunity cost must be measured in terms of the quantity of consumption goods forgone, since spare time S and consumption C are the two variables in the utility function. A one-hour increase in spare time requires a one-hour reduction in work time. This entails a drop in earnings of W, the hourly wage rate. The price of the consumption good is P, so the drop in earnings of W implies that consumption falls by (W/P). For example, if W is \$10 per hour and P is \$2 per unit, then the cost of taking one more hour of spare time is a drop in consumption of $10/2 = 5$ units. This argument demonstrates that the opportunity cost of an hour of spare time is the real wage, W/P. This means that the demand for spare time is a function of the real wage. An increase in the real wage is likely to reduce the amount of spare time an individual chooses to take because spare time has become more costly in terms of consumption good. But choosing to take less spare time is the same thing as choosing to work more hours. Hence this argument suggests the supply of labour is an increasing function of the real wage.[4]

Equilibrium in the Labour Market

The equilibrium position in the labour market is illustrated in Figure 7.4. The real wage, w, is recorded on the vertical axis. The intersection of the labour supply and demand curves $S(L)$ and $D(L)$ is at the equilib-

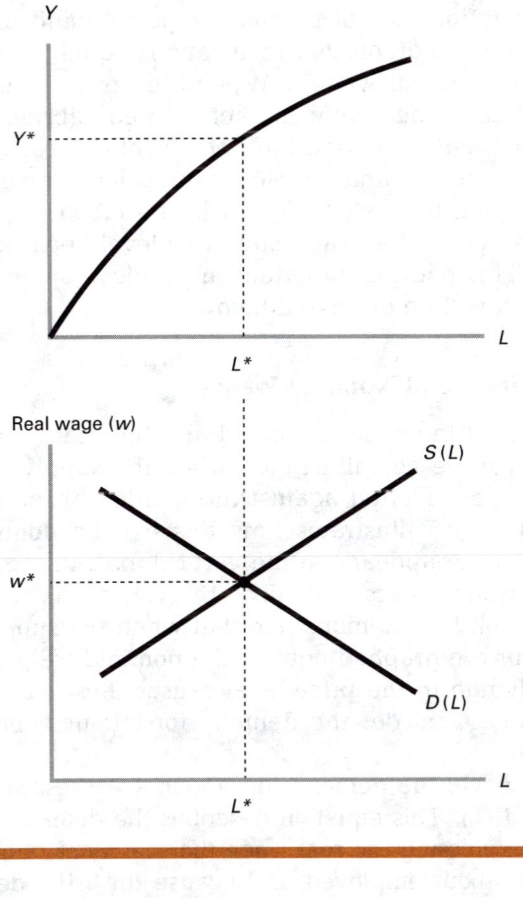

Figure 7.4 Equilibrium in the labour market

4 It is theoretically possible for an increase in the real wage to lead to a reduction in the hours of labour supplied. This occurs if the income effect of an increase in the real wage outweighs the substitution effect, resulting in an increase in the demand for spare time. A good deal of empirical evidence has been reviewed by Mark Killingsworth in *Labour Supply*, Cambridge Surveys of Economic Literature (New York: Cambridge University Press, 1983). The results are ambiguous, but on balance suggest that labour supply is an upward-sloping function of the real wage.

rium real wage, w^*, and the equilibrium employment level, L^*. At this real wage, competitive firms maximize profits by hiring the amount of labour L^*. At the same time, individuals, who treat the real wage w^* as given by the labour market, maximize their utility by supplying the amount of labour L^*. The aggregate production function determines the quantity of output, Y^*, that this level of employment produces.

It is important to note that while the equilibrium real wage is determined in the labour market, the nominal wage and the price level can be determined only when the complete macroeconomic model is specified, and this we have not yet done. The equilibrium wage w^* can be achieved by an infinite set of nominal wage rate and price level pairs, subject only to the condition that their ratio is equal to w^*. For example, suppose that the nominal wage is W_0 and the price level is P_0 and that $(W_0/P_0) = w^*$. Clearly the labour market is in equilibrium. Now suppose that both the nominal wage and the price level rise by, say, 5 percent to W_1 and P_1. Since both P and W rise by the same proportion, their ratio remains unchanged, that is $(W_1/P_1) = w^*$. The labour market is in equilibrium at the new nominal wage and price level because the real wage is unchanged. This point is important in the development of the classical model, which will be discussed below.

The Labour Market and Nominal Wages

The implications of the classical model and the other models discussed in this chapter can be best illustrated when the supply and demand for labour schedules are plotted against the *nominal* wage rather than the *real* wage. Figure 7.5 illustrates how this can be done. In the upper panels the real wage appears on the vertical axis; in the lower panels it is the nominal wage that is plotted on the vertical axis. The major purpose of this section is to demonstrate that when the supply and demand curves for labour are graphed against the nominal wage rather than the real wage, a change in the price level causes these curves to shift in a very specific way. Consider the demand for labour which is illustrated in Figure 7.5(a).

In the upper panel the demand for labour is expressed in terms of the real wage: $w = D(L)$. This equation describes the demand side of the labour market by expressing the real wage that firms are prepared to pay, w, as a function of labour employed, L. Because the *MPL* declines as more labour is hired, the wage rate firms are prepared to pay decreases as L increases. In the lower panel of Figure 7.5(a) the demand for labour is drawn in terms of the *nominal* wage, W, that firms are prepared to pay at each level of employment. But the nominal wage firms are prepared to pay also depends on the price of the output that firms sell, P. The precise way that the nominal wage offer depends on P can be seen by simply rewriting $w = D(L)$ as $W/P = D(L)$. Now multiply through

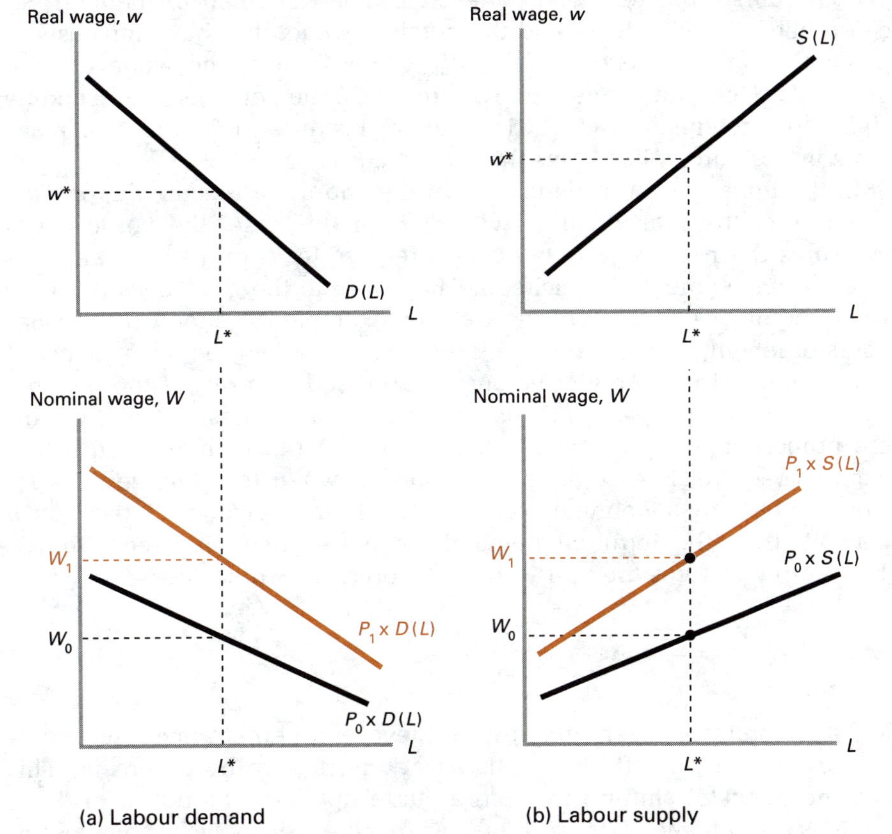

Figure 7.5 The labour market and nominal wages

by P: the nominal wage offered by firms at each level of employment is $W = P \times D(L)$. This shows that the nominal wage offer is proportional to the price level P. For example, if the output price rises 5 percent, the wage offer *at each level of employment* will be increased by 5 percent.

This important point is illustrated in Figure 7.5. If the price level is P_0, the nominal wage offer at L^* is W_0. Of course, there is only one possible real wage offer at L^*, so it must be the case that $W_0/P_0 = w^*$. Now suppose that the price level increases to P_1 (to be specific, let this be a 5 percent increase). As discussed above, when output prices increase, firms are prepared to raise their nominal wage offer. In the lower panel, this is shown as an upward shift of the demand for labour schedule. More precisely, every point on the labour demand schedule moves up by the same multiplicative factor. For example, at L^* the 5 percent increase in the price level raises the wage offer by 5 percent from W_0 to

W_1. Of course, the real wage offer at L^* has remained unchanged because both the price level and the nominal wage offer have increased 5 percent. That is to say, $W_1/P_1 = W_0/P_0 = w^*$. Since the wage offer at every level of employment moves up by 5 percent, as the schedule shifts up it rotates in a clockwise manner because high wages increase more in absolute dollar terms than low wages.

In the upper panel of Figure 7.5(b) the supply of labour is expressed in terms of the real wage — $w = S(L)$. In this case, the vertical axis measures the real wage that workers require for supplying a particular level of employment. The schedule slopes up to the right because more work requires a higher real wage. For example, to supply L^* person-hours of labour, workers require the real wage w^*. In the lower panel of Figure 7.5(b), the supply of labour is expressed in terms of the nominal wage, namely, $W = P \times S(L)$. Just as the nominal wages offered by firms are proportional to the price level, so too are the nominal wages that workers require. For example, to supply L^* when the price level is P_0, workers require a nominal wage of W_0. If the price level rises by 5 percent, then the required nominal wage also rises 5 percent to W_1. This simply restores the real wage to its original value, since

$$\frac{W_1}{P_1} = \frac{W_0}{P_0} = w^*$$

More generally, at every employment level a 5 percent increase in output prices will raise the wage that workers require by 5 percent. This has the effect of shifting the entire curve upwards through a distance equal to 5 percent of the original wage rate. Since higher wages increase more in absolute dollar terms than lower wages, the supply curve rotates counter-clockwise as it moves upwards.

In this section we have redrawn the supply and demand schedules for labour by measuring the nominal wage on the vertical axis. We have seen that the nominal wage offered by firms and the nominal wage required by workers depends on the level of employment and on the price of output. Specifically, the nominal wage is proportional to the price level. This fact means that when the price of output increases by x percent, both the nominal-wage supply and demand for labour schedules shift upwards by x percent. In the remainder of this chapter, supply and demand curves for labour will always be represented in diagrams with the nominal wage on the vertical axis.

The Classical Model

In this section we will show that the classical aggregate supply curve is vertical at the output level Y^* (see Figure 7.4). The critical assumption behind this conclusion is that nominal wages are completely flexible and adjust fast enough for the labour market to be considered in equilibrium at all times. The role of this assumption is illustrated in Figure 7.6. Note that the nominal wage rate appears on the vertical axis in the diagram of the labour market. The supply and demand for labour are shown to be functions of the wage rate and the price level. In Figure 7.6, the price level is taken as given by firms and workers.

At the price level P_0, the supply and demand curves for labour inter-

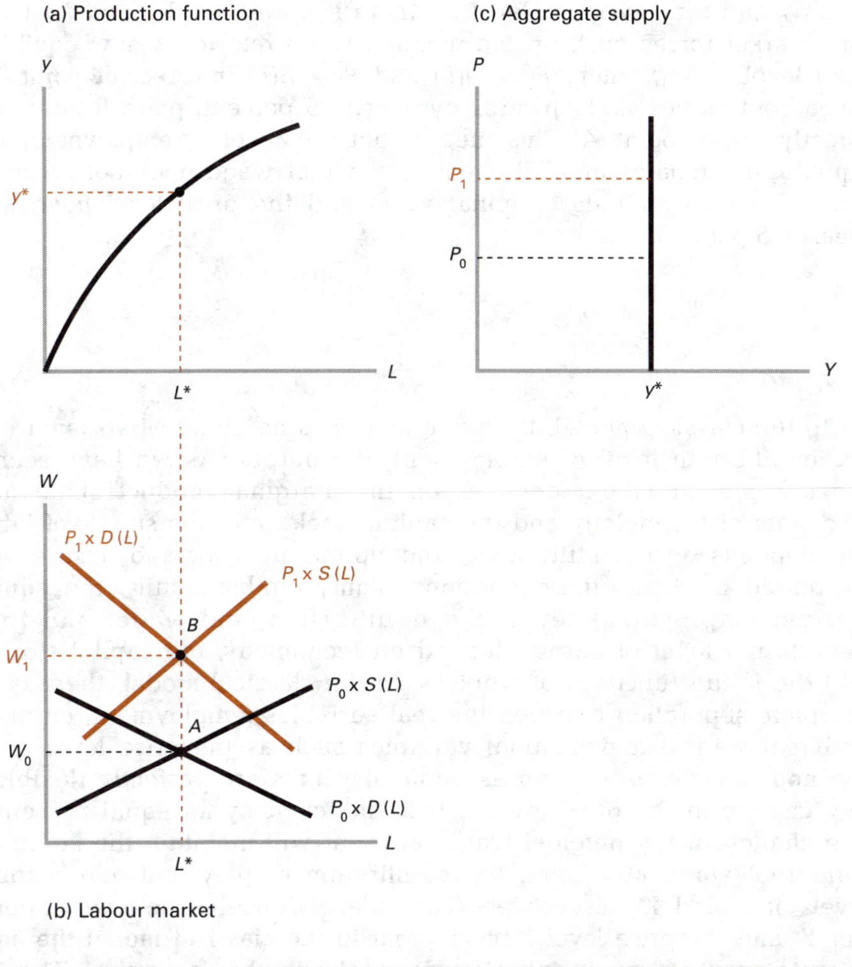

Figure 7.6 The classical aggregate supply curve

sect at point *A* to determine the equilibrium nominal wage rate W_0 and equilibrium employment L^*. This is precisely the same point as in Figure 7.4. The key difference is that in Figure 7.4 only the equilibrium real wage w^* is determined. In Figure 7.6 we have assumed the price level is P_0, and this extra information allows us to determine the equilibrium nominal wage rate W_0 as well. The real wage implied by Figure 7.6 is (W_0/P_0) and this is equal to the equilibrium real wage w^*. The equilibrium employment level is L^*, and given the current capital stock and state of technology, the supply of output is Y^*.

Now suppose that the price level rises by 5 percent from P_0 to P_1. In Figure 7.6 the effect of raising P from P_0 to P_1 is to shift the supply and demand curves upwards by 5 percent. At the original nominal wage rate W_0 and the new price level P_1, there is an excess demand for labour. Market forces push up the nominal wage rate to its new equilibrium level of W_1, where $P_1 \times D(L)$ and $P_1 \times S(L)$ intersect at point *B*. Since both curves shift upwards by exactly 5 percent, point *B* must be directly above point *A*. This means that the level of employment in equilibrium remains at L^*. Moreover, the real wage does not change either because both the nominal wage and the price level have increased 5 percent; that is,

$$\frac{W_0}{P_0} = \frac{W_1}{P_1} = w^*$$

In the classical model, the price level has no effect whatsoever on the equilibrium level of employment and output. As we have seen, the *demand* for labour depends on the marginal product of labour (the state of technology and the capital stock), and the *supply* of labour depends on the attitudes of individuals to work and leisure, as expressed in their utility functions. Thus, fundamentally, the equilibrium employment level, the equilibrium real wage, and the equilibrium level of output depend on technology, the capital stock, and the utility functions of workers. In the classical model, there is a complete separation between the real variables (employment, output, and real wages) and nominal variables such as the price level and the nominal wage. As long as nominal wages are perfectly flexible, any change in the price level will be matched by an equal percentage change in the nominal wage rate that will maintain the equilibrium real wage at w^* and the equilibrium employment and output levels of L^* and Y^*, respectively. The independence of the level of output Y^* and the price level P means that **in the classical model the aggregate supply curve is entirely price-inelastic**, that is, vertical. This is illustrated in Figure 7.6(c).

Macroeconomic Equilibrium in the Classical Model

Having developed the price-inelastic classical aggregate supply curve in the previous section, we can now complete the classical model by adding the aggregate demand curve. This is done diagrammatically in Figure 7.7.

The initial equilibrium point is labelled *A*. The analysis begins in the product market, which is illustrated in Figure 7.7(b). As we have seen,

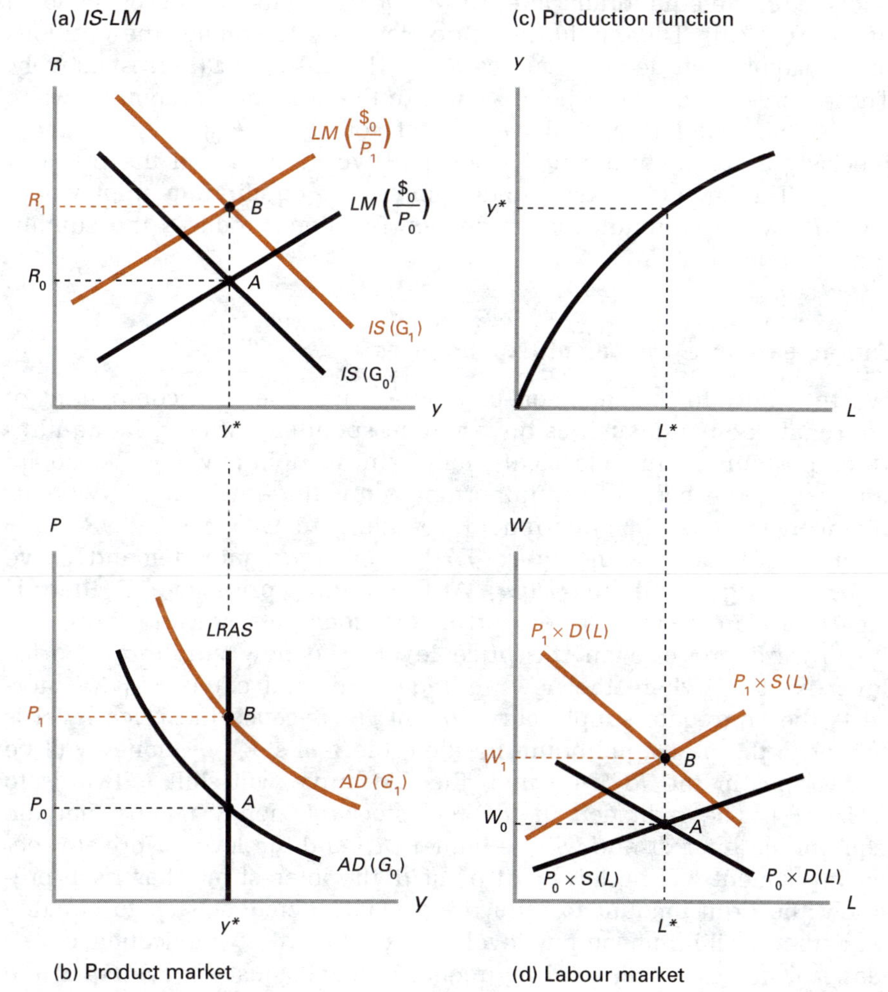

Figure 7.7 An increase in government expenditures in the classical model

the position of the aggregate demand curve is determined by all exogenous components of aggregate expenditure and by the nominal stock of money. The initial aggregate demand curve is labelled $AD(G_0)$. The only shift-variable shown explicitly is the level of government spending G_0, because in a moment we will analyze the effect of an increase in government spending in the classical model. The inelastic classical supply curve intersects $AD(G_0)$ at P_0. Thus, in the product market the equilibrium price level is P_0 and the equilibrium output level is Y^*.

Moving to Figure 7.7(a), the $IS(G_0)$ curve and the $LM(\$_0/P_0)$ curve intersect at the equilibrium interest rate R_0. The labour market is shown in Figure 7.7(d). The equilibrium price level P_0 determines the positions of the supply and demand curves $P_0 \times S(L)$ and $P_0 \times D(L)$, respectively. These curves intersect at point A, where the equilibrium nominal wage is W_0. The equilibrium real wage is of course $(W_0/P_0) = w^*$, which is precisely the equilibrium real wage that we described in the previous section. The labour market also determines the equilibrium employment level L^*, which, through the production function, produces the equilibrium output level Y^*.

An Increase in Government Expenditures

We turn now to the question of how an increase in a component of aggregate demand, such as government spending, affects the equilibrium position in the classical model. In so doing, we will also be illustrating the basis of the important "crowding-out" effect. A bond-financed increase in government spending to G_1 shifts the IS curve rightwards to $IS(G_1)$. In Figure 7.7(b), the aggregate demand curve also shifts rightwards to $AD(G_1)$. At the original price level P_0 there is clearly a state of excess demand in the goods market and there will be upward pressure on the price level. The new equilibrium price level is at P_1, where the new aggregate demand curve $AD(G_1)$ intersects the aggregate supply curve (point B). Because the price level is higher in the new equilibrium position, the real stock of money will be lower and, in the IS-LM panel, the LM curve will shift leftwards to $LM(\$_0/P_1)$. The reduction in the real stock of money means that the equilibrium interest rate will be higher (R_1) and the level of private sector investment will be lower. At point B, the interest rate has risen precisely the right amount to reduce aggregate demand back to equality with the equilibrium output level Y^*. An important implication of the classical model is that total aggregate demand must always equal the supply-determined equilibrium level of output Y^*. A permanent increase in one component of demand must crowd out other components. In this case, the increase in government spending has caused an equal decline in private investment.[5] The mechanism that guarantees this complete crowding-out is a rising price level that reduces the real stock of money, which in turn drives up the rate of interest.

The increase in government spending also has an effect in the labour market. The excess demand for goods causes the price level to rise. As we saw in the previous section, this results in a leftward shift in the supply of labour and a rightward shift in the demand for labour schedules, because at the original nominal wage W_0 the real wage is reduced by the rising price level. The resulting excess demand for labour forces up the nominal wage rate to W_1. However, the real wage at point B is precisely the same as the real wage at point A. Both firms and households are satisfied with the equilibrium level of employment L^* at this unique equilibrium real wage. The total volume of output remains unchanged between points A and B, although the *product mix* does shift in favour of government goods and services at the expense of private investment expenditures.

An example of the crowding-out phenomenon could result from a government decision to increase public housing. To undertake this new public investment, resources (labour, land, and materials) have to be bid away from the private sector. In addition, if funds are borrowed then the government must compete with the private sector for loans. The additional demand created by the government puts upward pressure on the interest rate and on the price level. This has the effect of displacing some private sector investment, such as housing. The assumptions underlying the classical model lead to the conclusion that the crowding-out effect is one-for-one; every unit increase in government spending ultimately leads to a one-unit decrease in private sector investment.

An Increase in the Money Supply

The classical model provides a very precise prediction concerning the effect of changes in the nominal stock of money. An increase of, say, 10 percent in the nominal stock of money will raise both the price level and the nominal wage by 10 percent, but the equilibrium levels of employment and output will be unaffected. And, unlike the case of an increase in government spending, the composition of aggregate demand

---

5 The other components of aggregate demand are consumption and exports. Exports are assumed to be exogenous and consumption depends only on disposable income. Since income returns to its original level, so too does consumption. Consequently, the only component of aggregate demand that can offset the increased government spending is investment. However, if the increased government spending were financed in whole or in part by increased taxes rather than through bond sales, consumption would also be displaced.

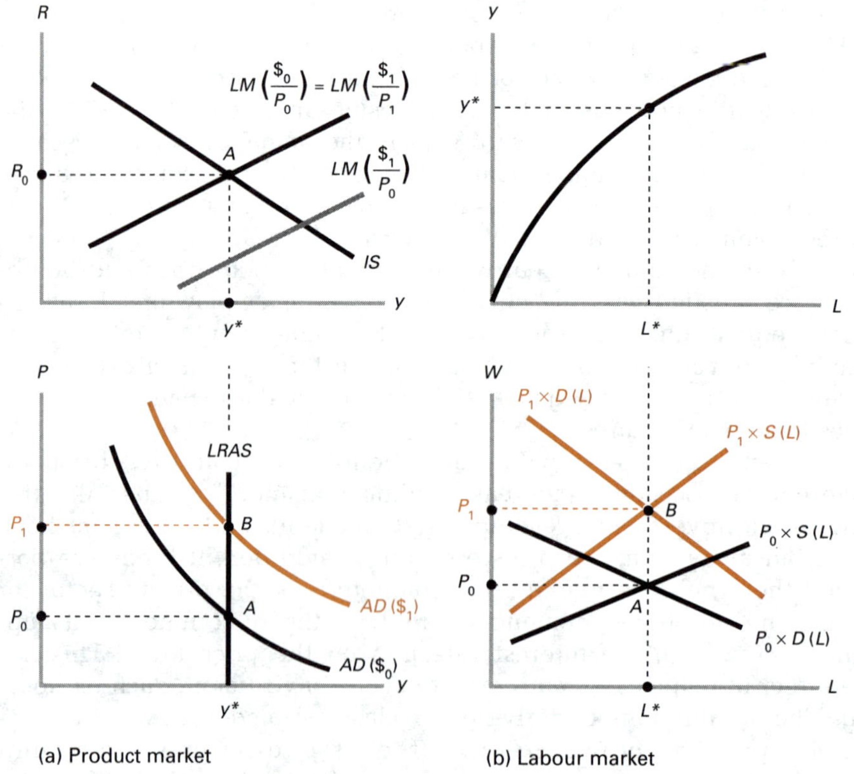

Figure 7.8 An increase in the money supply in the classical model

will be unchanged by movements in the stock of money. Because changes in the stock of money affect no real variables (only nominal ones), the stock of money is said to be neutral in the classical model. The **neutrality of money** is illustrated in Figure 7.8.

The initial equilibrium is again described by point *A* in all panels. Suppose this equilibrium is disturbed by a 10 percent increase in the nominal stock of money from $\$_0$ to $\$_1$. The immediate effect is to shift the *LM* and *AD* curves rightwards to $LM(\$_1/P_0)$ and $AD(\$_1)$, respectively. Notice that at the initial price level P_0, there is now a state of excess demand in the product market. The price level will rise to its new equilibrium level, P_1, where the new aggregate demand curve $AD(\$_1)$ intersects the aggregate supply curve. This higher price level causes a reduction in the real stock of money to $\$_1/P_1$ which will shift the *LM* curve leftwards. Since the equilibrium output level Y^* is supply-determined, the demand for output must equal Y^*. This means the *LM* curve must return to its original position, where it once again intersects the *IS* curve at the equilibrium level of output Y^*.

The fact that the *LM* curve returns exactly to its original position has an important implication. We have already seen that the position of the *LM* curve depends on the real stock of money $\$/P$. Since the *LM* curve returns to its original position, the real stock of money must also be restored to its original level, that is,

$$\frac{\$_0}{P_0} = \frac{\$_1}{P_1}$$

But this means that the percentage change in the price level from P_0 to P_1 must be exactly the same as the percentage increase in the nominal money stock that started the whole process. The classical model therefore predicts that a 10 percent rise in the nominal stock of money will raise the equilibrium price level by exactly 10 percent.

Of course, the inelastic supply curve of the classical model means that the equilibrium output level in the product market remains at Y^*. In the labour market, the higher price level shifts the supply and demand curves for labour, creating a state of excess demand for labour. This is removed as nominal wages rise and the real wage is restored to its original level. In our example, a 10 percent increase in the nominal stock of money raises both the price level and the nominal wage by 10 percent, leaving the equilibrium real wage unchanged.

Now let's turn to the question of the composition of demand. In fact, the components of aggregate demand are no different in the new equilibrium from what they were originally. The *IS* and *LM* curves are exactly where they were, so that the interest rate and the level of investment are also unchanged. The increase in the stock of money affects only the *nominal* variables *P* and *W*. All *real* variables, such as the level of employment, output, and the components of aggregate demand, are unaffected. In this sense, money is *neutral* in the classical model.

While the neutrality of money proposition is the most important single feature of the classical model, this model also has very definite implications for fiscal policy. As we have seen, the level of government expenditure has no role in determining the equilibrium level of output. Fiscal multipliers are zero. This is because output in the flexible-price and flexible-wage classical model is determined exclusively by *supply-side* factors, namely, the state of technology, the size of the capital stock, and the supply of labour. This is quite the opposite to the fixed price *IS-LM* model of Chapters 5 and 6, where equilibrium output is demand-determined. In that Keynesian fixed price model, equilibrium output can fall short of the economy's potential capacity to produce goods and services. But in the Keynesian model, fiscal and monetary policies do have real effects. In the next section we will return to the Keynesian view that wages are not perfectly flexible in the short run because of institutional rigidities in the labour market. We will derive the Keynesian short-run supply curve and examine the role of fiscal and monetary policy in this alternative model.

The Keynesian Inflexible-Wage Model

The modern interpretation of the Keynesian inflexible-wage model focuses on the role played by labour contracts. It is a matter of fact that nominal wage rates are not determined on a daily basis according to the forces of supply and demand. For a large part of the work force, wage rates are negotiated and then fixed for a definite period of time. The explicit terms of **wage contracts** set down the wage rates to be paid during the life of the contract. It has been argued that wage contracts also have an unwritten or implicit component. For example, firms may implicitly agree not to treat employees as casual labour that can be hired or fired according to daily needs. Rather, there is an implicit agreement that minor variations in demand will not lead to changes in employment. This does not rule out the possibility of layoffs when demand declines substantially and for sustained periods of time, but it does imply a degree of employment stability in normal times. For their part, employees agree to work additional hours in the event that demand is temporarily high, without demanding a new wage contract.

In Canada wage contracts are typically in force for up to three years. For many workers, wages are fixed in nominal terms for long periods of time. Only for that small part of the labour force currently renegotiating its contract is the wage rate flexible; over the economy as a whole, wages are essentially contractually fixed in the short run. As inflation accelerated during the 1970s, the average length of wage contracts declined and cost-of-living clauses became more common. Both of these innovations tend to make wages more flexible in the short run, at least in the upward direction. For example, if all wage contracts last three years, then in any given year only one-third of workers will be renegotiating their wages. In this case, wage levels in the economy as a whole are only partially flexible in the short-run period of one year. But if wage contracts last only two years on average, then in any given year one-half of contracts will be renegotiated, making the economy-wide average wage somewhat more flexible in the short run.

Although average contract length is the major determinant of wage flexibility in the upward direction, other factors limit the degree of downward flexibility of wages. Industry-wide unions often take the view that hard-won wage levels and benefit packages should not be given up lightly. In some cases this pits local workers against their own union. The union may take the view that if the weakest firms succeeded in getting wage concessions in order to maintain employment, then all firms would demand the same concessions and all workers would suffer. Moreover, the union would have to fight battles already won in order to restore wage and benefit levels once market conditions improved. Consequently, unions seem to be prepared to see a small part of their membership lose their jobs before agreeing to industry-wide wage cuts. In the deep recession of the early 1980s some unions, such as the United Auto Workers, did agree to wage concessions. Thus, even in unionized industries, when economic conditions are sufficiently bad, wage rates do occasionally fall. The point being made here is not that wages never fall, but that wages are more flexible in the upward direction than in the downward direction.

Aggregate Supply With Wage Inflexibility

In this section we will develop an aggregate supply curve that recognizes the short-run inflexibility of wages. As we will see, this leads to a **positively sloped short-run aggregate supply curve**. Over a period of time long enough for the renegotiation of wage contracts, wages are flexible in the upward direction and the long-run aggregate supply curve is vertical, as it is in the classical model. However, in the downward direction the supply curve is vertical only after a much longer period of time, because even when contracts come up for renewal, employees may stoically resist wage cuts.

Figure 7.9 illustrates the **inflexible-wage model**. Figure 7.9(a) illustrates the labour market with the nominal wage on the vertical axis. Figure 7.9(b) shows the marginal product of labour schedule, which represents the demand for labour as a function of the real wage. The aggregate supply curve is depicted in Figure 7.9(c). In all three panels, the initial position is at a point *A*.

In the labour market, point *A* is determined by the intersection of the labour supply curve $P_0^e \times S(L)$ and the labour demand curve $P_0^e \times D(L)$. The nominal wage rate $\overline{W}$ represents the negotiated wage rate that will be in force during the life of the contract. The symbol P_0^e stands for the price level that is expected to hold, on average, during the life of the contract. At the time of wage negotiations, firms and employees do not know what the actual price level will be. That is, the *real* wage during the contract is unknown. But it is the real wage that determines the demand for and supply of labour. Consequently, firms and employees must make an estimate of what the price level will be. The supply and demand curves are drawn on the basis of the price expectations that are held at the time of negotiations. Given the negotiated equilibrium nomi-

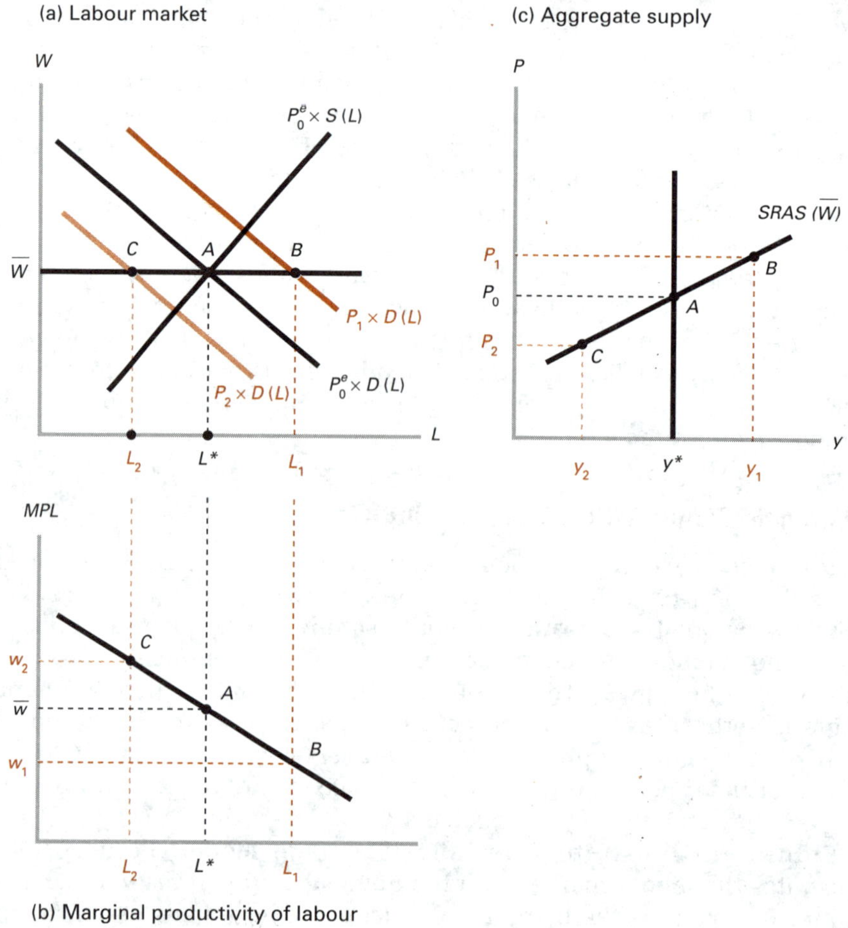

Figure 7.9 Short-run aggregate supply with contractually fixed wages

nal wage $\overline{W}$, the expected real wage is $\overline{W}/P_0^e$ and the anticipated level of employment is L^*. In Figure 7.9(b), point *A* marks the position on the marginal productivity of labour schedule where the equilibrium real wage is w^* and the equilibrium employment level is L^*. If expectations turn out to be correct, then the actual price level during the contract period, say P_0, will be equal to P_0^e. In this case, the actual real wage and the actual employment level will be at their equilibrium levels (w^* and L^*) and output will equal Y^*. In Figure 7.9(c), when price expectations are correct, the economy will be at position *A*, which lies on the inelastic aggregate supply curve where the price level is P_0 and output is Y^*.

Now suppose that during the contract period the actual price level turns out to be P_1, which is above the expected price level P^e_0. Unlike the classical model, in which nominal wages are perfectly flexible, this model assumes that the nominal wage $\overline{W}$ is contractually fixed in the short run. Hence, when the price level is higher than expected the real wage turns out to be lower than expected. At the lower real wage $w_1 = \overline{W}/P_1$, profit-maximizing firms would like to hire more labour than previously planned. In particular, the marginal product of labour schedule shows that firms would like to hire labour L_1, (see point B on the MPL schedule). Similarly, in Figure 7.9(a), the (nominal-wage) demand for labour schedule shifts upwards to $P_1 \times D(L)$. Given the contractually fixed nominal wage $\overline{W}$, the demand for labour is at point B, where employment is L_1.

Since we assume that under the implicit terms of the wage contract, employees will work all the hours demanded at the negotiated wage $\overline{W}$, the short-run supply curve of labour is effectively, perfectly horizontal (infinitely elastic) at the nominal wage $\overline{W}$. In other words, firms that are bound to a fixed nominal wage during the life of a wage contract have the advantage of choosing the level of employment once the product price has been determined. The supply of labour simply matches demand.[6] Given that firms determine employment, the actual price level P_1 leads to an actual employment level of L_1 during the current contract. This level of employment produces the output level Y_1 (production function is not illustrated in Figure 7.9). Hence, under the terms of the current wage contract, the higher than expected price level P_1 results in an actual output level of Y_1. The new price-output pair is plotted in the aggregate supply diagram. The short-run positive relationship between prices and output is labelled $SRAS(\overline{W})$ to indicate that this supply curve is based on the contractually fixed nominal wage $\overline{W}$, which in turn depends on the expected price level P^e_0. Recall that the movement along $SRAS(\overline{W})$ from point A to point B is due to a decline in the real wage below the equilibrium level. It is this decline in the real wage that makes it profitable for firms to raise employment and output.

Now consider what happens if the price level turns out to be P_2, which is lower than the expected level P^e_0. When prices are lower than expected, the real wage is higher than expected and firms want to hire less labour than previously anticipated. In Figure 7.9(b) firms find themselves higher up the marginal productivity of labour schedule at point

6 The insider–outsider model of the labour market assumes that there is always a pool of workers who are willing and able to work at the current market wage. But due to agreements between firms and the current workers or "insiders," the unemployed "outsiders" cannot bid away the jobs of employed workers by offering to work for lower wages. However, if firms want to expand employment they can hire workers from the pool of unemployed. Hence, in the insider–outsider model, employment is demand-determined. The insider–outsider model is described more fully in Chapter 10.

C, where the real wage is $w_2 = \overline{W}/P_2$ and the demand for labour is L_2. In Figure 7.9(a), the lower than expected price level causes the demand for labour curve to shift down below its expected position. Although firms have agreed to guarantee the fixed nominal wage $\overline{W}$, when the price of goods turns out to be lower than expected, firms have the right to lay off workers. In the present case, the price level P_2 leads to a reduced employment level L_2. Some workers who expected to be employed will be involuntarily laid off. Hence, at point C there is involuntary unemployment in the sense that unemployed workers would like to work at the going wage rate. However, since the wage rate is fixed by the contract, unemployed workers cannot bid away the jobs of the employed by offering to work at a lower wage.

Since employment is lower than expected at the price level P_2, so too is the level of output. In the aggregate supply diagram, the lower price level P_2 is associated with the output level Y_2, which is below Y^*. The point (Y_2, P_2), which is labelled C, defines one more point on the short-run aggregate supply curve.

The slope of the short-run aggregate supply curve has important implications for the reactions of output and prices to macroeconomic disturbances. Given a typical shift in the aggregate demand curve, the flatter is the short-run aggregate supply curve (*SRAS* curve), the greater is the change in output and the smaller is the change in the price level. The key factor that determines the slope of the *SRAS* curve is the slope of the marginal productivity of labour schedule. In Figure 7.9(b), the movement from point A to point B along the marginal productivity schedule is traced out by raising the price level from P_0 to P_1, while the nominal wage is held fixed. This reduces the real wage from its expected value of w^* to w_1 and provides firms with an incentive to hire more labour. If the *MPL* is relatively flat, firms find it profitable to substantially increase the level of employment, with a correspondingly large increase in output. A flat *MPL* schedule means that a significant amount of additional labour can be hired before the *MPL* declines to the new real wage. Thus, given a certain price increase, the flatter the *MPL* schedule, the greater is the increase in output and the more elastic is the short-run aggregate supply curve.

An Increase in the Money Supply

Figure 7.10 illustrates the effects of an unexpected increase in the money supply when nominal wages are contractually fixed in the short run. We will assume that the money supply increases in period one and that in all subsequent periods, the money supply remains fixed at its new level. Just before period one, firms and workers have expectations about what the price level will be. We will denote period one's expected price level to be P_1^e. In Figure 7.10(a), the supply and demand for labour

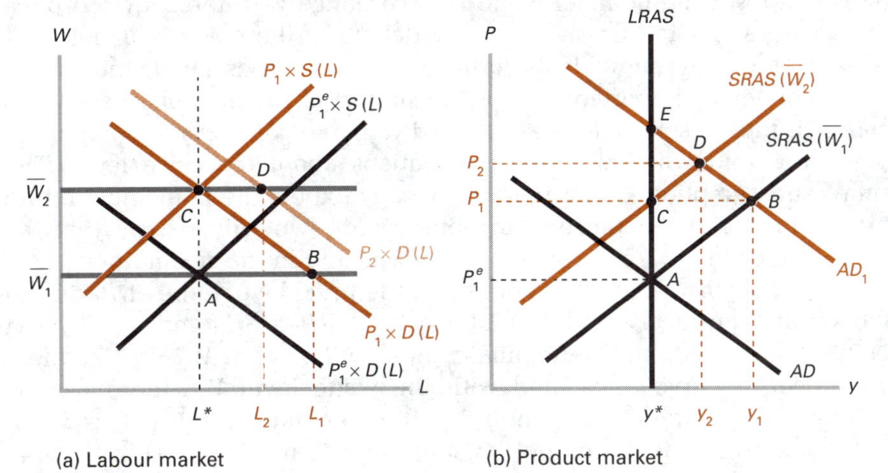

Figure 7.10 An increase in the money supply with contractually fixed wages

schedules intersect at point A where employment is L^*. Given the price expectations P_1^e, the wage contract for period one sets the nominal wage at $\overline{W}_1$. The product market is illustrated in Figure 7.10(b). Given the current wage contract, there is a $SRAS$ curve labelled $SRAS(\overline{W}_1)$, which passes through point A on the long-run supply curve. If the price level turns out to be exactly as expected, employment and output will be at their natural levels.

However, suppose that during the period one contract there is an unexpected increase in the money supply which shifts the aggregate demand curve to AD_1. As a result, the economy moves to point B where AD_1 intersects $SRAS(\overline{W}_1)$. At point B, the price level is P_1 (higher than expected) and the level of output is Y_1. Back in the labour market panel, the higher price level shifts the demand for labour up to $P_1 \times D(L)$. Given that the nominal wage is fixed at $\overline{W}_1$, the real wage is lower than expected and firms increase employment to L_1. The increased employment is responsible for the higher output level Y_1.

Clearly the assumption that wages are inflexible in the short run has important implications for the impact of monetary policy. Recall that the classical model predicts that an increase in the money supply has no effect on output — just a price effect. But when wages are inflexible in the short run, the real wage is not free to adjust instantaneously to the long-run equilibrium value that is consistent with the natural levels of employment and output. The inflexible-wage model is therefore able to explain how output can deviate from its natural level, Y^*.

Of course, when contracts come up for renegotiation, workers and firms can reset the nominal wage in accordance with their revised price expectations. There has been a lively debate in the macroeconomics literature as to how individuals form their expectations about the future. This enormously important area is the subject of the next chapter. But to continue the present analysis, we need to make some assumption about how firms and workers make expectations about the price level. The simplest assumption is that people typically expect the immediate future to be much like the present. In other words, we will assume that the current price level P_1 is expected to be repeated in the second period.[7]

Given that firms and workers expect the price level to be at P_1 during the second contract period, the intersection of $P_1 \times S(L)$ and $P_1 \times D(L)$ at point *C* indicates that the nominal wage will be set at $\overline{W}_2$. Just as there was a *SRAS* curve associated with the wage level $\overline{W}_1$, there will be another *SRAS* curve corresponding to the nominal wage $\overline{W}_2$. This *SRAS* curve relates the actual output level to the actual price level in the second contract period. In the product market panel, the new *SRAS* curve, $SRAS(\overline{W}_2)$ passes through point *C*, which is determined by the output level Y^* and the expected price level P_1. Notice that firms and workers have not made the correct prediction about the second period's output price. The aggregate demand curve, AD_1, intersects $SRAS(\overline{W}_2)$ at point *D*, where output is Y_2 and the price level is P_2, which is higher than P_1.[8] In the labour market panel, the demand for labour schedule $P_2 \times D(L)$ depends on the actual price, P_2. The supply of labour $P_1 \times S(L)$ depends on the expected price, P_1. These two curves intersect at the employment level L_2, which produces output Y_2.

So far we have looked at what happens in the inflexible-wage model in the first two periods after an unexpected increase in the money supply. Where the economy goes in subsequent periods depends on two things: (1) how expectations are formed and (2) what exogenous shocks hit the economy. If there are no further changes in the exogenous variables and if expectations about the price level continue to based on the "no-change" principle that the current price level is the best guess for next period's price level, then the economy will gradually converge on point *E* in Figure 7.10(b). The aggregate demand curve will remain at AD_1 and the short-run aggregate supply curve will steadily shift up-

---

7 There is no ongoing inflation in the present model, so there is no particular reason for anyone to expect prices to rise on that account.

8 If firms and workers were able to predict the exact effects of the increase on the money supply, they would know where the equilibrium price level would be; namely, where AD_1 intersects the vertical supply curve above Y^*. Then, provided the *AD* curve remained in its new position during the second contract period, price expectations would be correct and output and employment would return to Y^* and L^*, respectively. In general, expectations are almost certain to be wrong. First, individuals do not know what the exact effects of past changes will be on the future values of endogenous variables. Second, there is no way to guarantee accurate forecasts of future exogenous variables, such as the money supply, government spending, and exports.

wards until it passes through point *E*. In other words, in the long run, the inflexible-wage model will reach the same conclusion as the classical model.[9] In the long run, an increase in the money supply only has effects on nominal variables such as wages and prices. Output, employment, and real expenditures will return to their original values. But unlike the classical model, the inflexible-wage model predicts that output will deviate from the natural level. As we have seen, an increase in the money supply leads to a temporary increase in employment and output. In the longer term, output and employment return to their natural levels. The important distinction is that, unlike the classical model, the inflexible-wage model is capable of explaining business cycle variations in output and employment.

Our analysis of the effects of an increase in the money supply makes it abundantly clear that expectations have enormous influence on actual events. In the preceding paragraph, the levels of output, employment, and prices that materialized in the second contract period depended crucially on the expectations assumption. We assumed that in the second contract period, firms and employees expected the price level to be P_1, as it was in the first contract period. If we had used some other expectations assumption, the market outcome in the second period would have been quite different. Since the predictions generated by an economic model are sensitive to the expectations assumption it is not surprising that expectations modelling has been a controversial area in macroeconomics. In the next chapter we will examine the two major approaches to expectations modelling, namely, the rational expectations hypothesis and adaptive expectations. These competing models yield very different macroeconomic implications.

Unemployment

In this chapter we have discussed two models of aggregate supply: the classical model and the inflexible-wage model. In both cases we have examined the effect of a change in aggregate demand on prices and output. In the classical model, output is always equal to its supply-determined equilibrium level, so cyclical unemployment does not arise. On the other hand, the rigid-wage theory does provide an explanation for the cyclical behaviour of prices, output, and unemployment. There is considerable controversy surrounding the nature and causes of unemployment. In this last section we will use the classical and Keynesian rigid-wage models to guide our discussion of this important topic.

---

9 This process of adjustment is explained more fully in the next chapter. In particular, see Figure 8.2 and the related discussion of adaptive expectations.

In the classical model, output is always equal to its supply-determined equilibrium level and the labour market is always in equilibrium. Yet the unemployment rate is not zero in this model. For a variety of reasons there will be unemployed people and unfilled job vacancies existing simultaneously even when the labour market is, in some sense, in equilibrium. For our purposes we can define labour market equilibrium to mean that the number of unemployed persons equals the number of job vacancies. Under this definition, we consider the labour market to be in equilibrium if, somewhere, there is a job vacancy that would be acceptable to each unemployed person. Unemployment exists because the unemployed are not yet matched with the vacancies. This **equilibrium unemployment** has two components: frictional and structural.

Frictional unemployment exists because the Canadian labour market is always in a state of flux: graduating students join the labour force and retirees leave; employed people quit to take jobs elsewhere or to leave the labour force altogether, while others who have previously dropped out re-enter the labour force. Since it takes time for job seekers to find suitable jobs and for employers to fill vacancies with suitable employees, it follows that even in equilibrium there will always be frictional unemployment.

The second component of equilibrium unemployment is due to *structural* factors: a mismatching of the characteristics of the unemployed and the job vacancies. For example, at any given time, some industries are in a state of relative decline, while others are experiencing rapid growth. This may lead to a mismatch between the skills of the unemployed and the skills demanded by the growing industries. Alternatively, the declining and expanding sectors may be in different locations and, given the cost of moving, unemployment and job vacancies may well exist simultaneously.

From this brief discussion of the nature of the equilibrium unemployment rate it is clear that the equilibrium unemployment rate is not necessarily fixed through time. Frictional unemployment will be low if job seekers find jobs after brief searches. For example, in a hypothetical case, job search would take no time at all if all job applicants could be matched instantaneously with suitable employers. In this ideal world, there would be a zero rate of frictional unemployment. In practice, people spend time searching for a job. How long people search depends on such factors as the generosity of unemployment benefits. Two important components of the Canadian unemployment scheme are the benefit period and the replacement ratio. The benefit period refers to the time that unemployment benefits can be drawn. The replacement ratio refers to the proportion of the unemployed person's previous wage covered by unemployment benefits. Although the primary purpose of the Canadian unemployment scheme is to provide a financial safety net to unemployed Canadians, the terms of the scheme also have an effect on the efficiency of the labour market. Liberal benefits tend to encourage long searches. This probably leads to better labour market matches between workers and firms, but it also raises the equilibrium unemployment rate.

Structural unemployment can also vary over time. During periods of rapidly changing patterns of demand or rapid technological change, the structural unemployment rate will rise. Over several decades, workers in Western countries have been leaving the agricultural sector to work in cities. The proportion of the working population employed on farms has steadily declined. More recently, the importance of the service sector, for example, banking, insurance, retailing, and tourism, has increased at the expense of manufacturing and mining. These ever-changing patterns of employment give rise to structural unemployment as workers are displaced from one industry or region to another. In Chapter 10 we will present estimates of the Canadian equilibrium unemployment rate and discuss some important features that have caused it to change over time.

As we will see in the next chapter, the Keynesian and new classical theories have very different interpretations of *cyclical unemployment.* Models in the Keynesian tradition take the nominal wage rate to be contractually fixed in the short run. When aggregate demand is less than expected, the price level falls below the level that was anticipated by firms and workers. As a result, the real wage is higher than anticipated. Since firms have the last say on employment levels, the higher than expected real wage causes layoffs. Clearly the laid-off workers are involuntarily unemployed. They had expected to work and are willing to work at the currently available wage rate, yet they cannot find work. The important point is that the inflexible-wage model is consistent with the view that **cyclical unemployment is involuntary** and that it may well persist for long periods of time.

In the next chapter we will see that the new classical economics maintains that it is methodologically incorrect to model the business cycle as a disequilibrium phenomenon. The new classical economics maintains that the economy is always in equilibrium. This view puts cyclical unemployment in a very different light.

Key Concepts

aggregate demand curve
marginal product of labour
real wage

price-inelastic classical supply curve
neutrality of money
wage contracts
positively sloped short-run aggregate supply curve
inflexible-wage model
equilibrium unemployment
cyclical unemployment

Review Questions

1. Suppose points *A* and *B* lie on a particular aggregate demand curve and that point *B* corresponds to a lower price level and higher output than point *A*. Compare the levels of consumption, investment, and the rates of interest at points *A* and *B*. Explain the differences.
2. Explain the factors that determine the size of the horizontal shift in the aggregate demand curve when the level of government spending rises by $1 billion.
3. What is meant by the "neutrality of money" in the classical model?
4. In the classical model, analyze the effects of an autonomous decline in investment expenditure on the price level, the interest rate, and the level of consumption.
5. Explain how the existence of wage contracts leads to a positively sloped short-run aggregate supply curve.
6. What factors influence the size of the equilibrium unemployment rate?

CHAPTER 8

The New Classical Model and the Expectations Revolution

All these circumstances, however, had sent up the price of corn, as tends to happen not merely because of present shortage, but also because of fears for the future.

Julius Caesar[1]

The above words, written by Julius Caesar in the first century B.C., show that for at least two thousand years people have been well aware of the importance of expectations for the determination of current prices. But it is only in very recent times that economists have seriously attempted to model the manner in which the public forms its expectations about future economic variables. This chapter is about this important topic, which has had an enormous influence on the way in which macroeconomic models are constructed.

Beginning with Jan Tinbergen in the 1930s, economists have spent considerable effort on building macroeconomic models that can be used for policy analysis and forecasting. In almost all models, expectations variables play an important role, but in most cases direct observations of people's expectations are simply not available. Economists have therefore had to make assumptions about the way the public forms its expectations or forecasts. Two important hypotheses are: the **adaptive** expectations model and the **rational** expectations model. The adaptive expectations model was first introduced by Phillip Cagan in the mid-1950s[2] and has been widely used ever since. Although the concept of rational expectations can be traced back to an article by John Muth in

1 Julius Caesar, *The Civil War*, translated by Jane F. Gardner, (Penguin Classics, 1967), p. 62.

2 Phillip Cagan, "The Monetary Dynamics of Hyperinflation," in Milton Friedman, ed., *Studies in the Quantity Theory of Money* (Chicago: University of Chicago Press, 1956).

1961,[3] it did not become incorporated into macroeconomic modelling until the mid-1970s. However, the idea that optimizing economic agents should formulate expectations using rational calculations rather than *ad hoc* rules was so overwhelmingly appealing to many theorists that a whole new school of macroeconomic thought emerged. The "new classical macroeconomics" was led by Robert Lucas at the University of Chicago and Thomas Sargent at the University of Minnesota. Much of this chapter is devoted to an analysis of the key assumptions (including rational expectations) of the new classical school and to an evaluation of some striking predictions, such as the idea that anticipated changes in policy variables have no effect on output — the so-called Policy Ineffectiveness Proposition (PIP).

New Classical Macroeconomics

The new classical economists have strong views on how macroeconomic theory should be developed. They believe that the methodologically correct approach to macroeconomics is to build models on the principles that individuals maximize utility, firms maximize profits, and markets reach equilibrium instantaneously. Macroeconomic predictions should then be based on the comparison of one market equilibrium with another. These ideas are familiar from microeconomics, but they have proved to be controversial in macroeconomics. One contentious issue is the proposition that markets reach equilibrium instantaneously. To do so, all prices, including wages, must adjust freely and quickly to any market disturbance. This is in direct conflict with the Keynesian tradition, which sees ample empirical evidence for wage and price stickiness. Since different assumptions about the speed of price adjustment lead to very different predictions about how the macroeconomy behaves, it is not surprising that this has been a hotly debated issue.

Another controversial issue is the notion of rational expectations. The very name suggests reasoned calculations and the concept fits neatly into the new classical approach. But the combined assumptions of rational expectations and instantaneous market-clearing produce some remarkable conclusions, including the radical proposition that anticipated government policies have no effect on real variables such as output and employment. In this section we will derive a new aggregate supply curve that stresses the role of price expectations. In the new classical economics, the supply of output depends on *price surprises*, not on the price level itself. This means that increases in the supply of output are

3 John Muth, "Rational Expectations and the Theory of Price Movements," *Econometrica*, July 1961, pp. 315–35.

associated with increases in the price level only if the price increase is unexpected. Price increases that are fully anticipated will have no effect on output. The **Price Surprise Supply Function** (*PSSF*) is the cornerstone of the new classical macroeconomics and is associated with the work of Robert Lucas.

The Price Surprise Supply Function

As we saw in the previous chapter, the key elements in the supply side of the economy are the aggregate production function and the labour market. For convenience, where algebra is used in this chapter these relationships will be expressed in purely linear terms. Consider first, the supply of labour L, which is assumed to be an increasing function of the real wage. In the new classical model, great emphasis is placed on the information that is available to economic agents at the time they make decisions. As far as workers are concerned, they will obviously be aware of their own nominal wage as soon as the market clears. But it is assumed that workers cannot possibly know immediately the prices of all the numerous individual items that they buy. Even though all equilibrium prices are determined at the same moment in time, workers become aware of the general price index some time later when all the necessary information has been compiled. This means that at the time market equilibrium is determined, labour supply decisions must be based on the expected general price level P^e. Labour supply therefore depends on the expected real wage, not on the actual real wage, since the actual real wage is not immediately observable. In linear terms, the real wage is simply $(W - P)$ and the supply of labour can be written as[4]

$$L = a(W - P^e) \tag{8.1}$$

To keep the algebra as simple as possible, no intercept is included in the linear labour supply equation (8.1).

Now consider the demand side of the labour market. The production function indicates how much output, Y, is produced by labour input, L. The linearized production function in which the level of output is proportional to the level of employment can be written as

$$Y = bL \tag{8.2}$$

[4] When the real wage is written as $(W - P)$, W and P are usually taken to represent the logarithms of the wage rate w and the price level p. Then $W = \log(w)$ and $P = \log(p)$. The difference of logarithms, $(W - P)$ is $\log(w) - \log(p) = \log(w/p)$; that is, $W - P$ represents the logarithm of the real wage. Also, if L is the logarithm of labour supply, then Equation 8.1 indicates that the log of labour supply is an increasing function of the log of the real wage.

Notice that when labour input is zero, no output is produced. The demand for labour is determined by the profit-maximizing condition that equates the real wage to the marginal product of labour. In linear terms the real wage is $(W - P)$ and the marginal product of labour is the slope of the linear production function, which is simply the constant b.[5] The demand for labour equation simply defines the real wage that firms are prepared to offer:

$$W - P = b \tag{8.3}$$

A key distinction between the demand and the supply side of the market is that we assume firms make their decisions based on the *actual* price level and not on the *expected* price level. This can be justified by the following argument. The profits of the ith firm depend on the nominal wage W and the price of its own product P_i. Hence, the real wage that is relevant to the ith firm is $W - P_i$. Furthermore, firms will know their own output prices without delay, so at no time will firms have to base their decisions on expected prices. The key difference between firms and workers is that firms always have all the information they need to make decisions, but workers, who buy hundreds of different products, do not know all the equilibrium prices at the time their labour supply decisions are made.

New classical economists have made an important refinement to this argument, which is to consider what happens when all economic agents observe the current prices in their own local market. Based on this limited information, agents then estimate what must be happening in the economy as a whole. For example, workers who see an increase in the price of the product they make would like to know if this price increase is purely local or symptomatic of price increases throughout the economy. In the first case, their real wage is virtually unaffected by an increase in a single product price. But in the second case, their real wage will fall because the prices of all the things they buy increase. The task of inferring what is happening in the wider world when only partial information is available is known as the *signal extraction problem*. It is the basic argument used by new classical economists to derive the price surprise supply function. The details of this approach are described more fully in an appendix to this chapter.

Figure 8.1 illustrates the labour market, production function, and the

---

5 Again, if Y and L are the logarithms of output y and labour input l, then the production function (Equation 8.2) is linear in the logarithms. In terms of output y and labour l, the production function looks just like the one in Figure 7.3, which has a decreasing marginal product of labour. To avoid the formal mathematics of logarithms, in the text we assume the marginal product of labour (and the real wage offer) is constant, rather than declining linearly with labour input. This approximation in no way alters the substantive conclusions.

price surprise supply function. The simple linear production function technology is illustrated by a ray through the origin. The slope is equal to b. The demand for labour is given by the marginal product of labour, which is simply the constant b. Since the marginal product of labour is constant, firms offer a fixed real wage that is independent of the level of employment. (In this version of the model, employment is determined by the supply of labour.) In the labour market diagram, the nominal wage is represented on the vertical axis. The demand for labour is therefore shown as a horizontal line: $W = P + b$. The horizontal demand line means that the nominal wage offered by firms is the same at all levels of output. However, a one-unit increase in the price level will shift the nominal wage offer line upwards by exactly one unit.

The supply of labour is also drawn with the nominal wage on the vertical axis. To find the nominal wage workers must be paid for supplying a given level of labour, we must invert the labour supply equa-

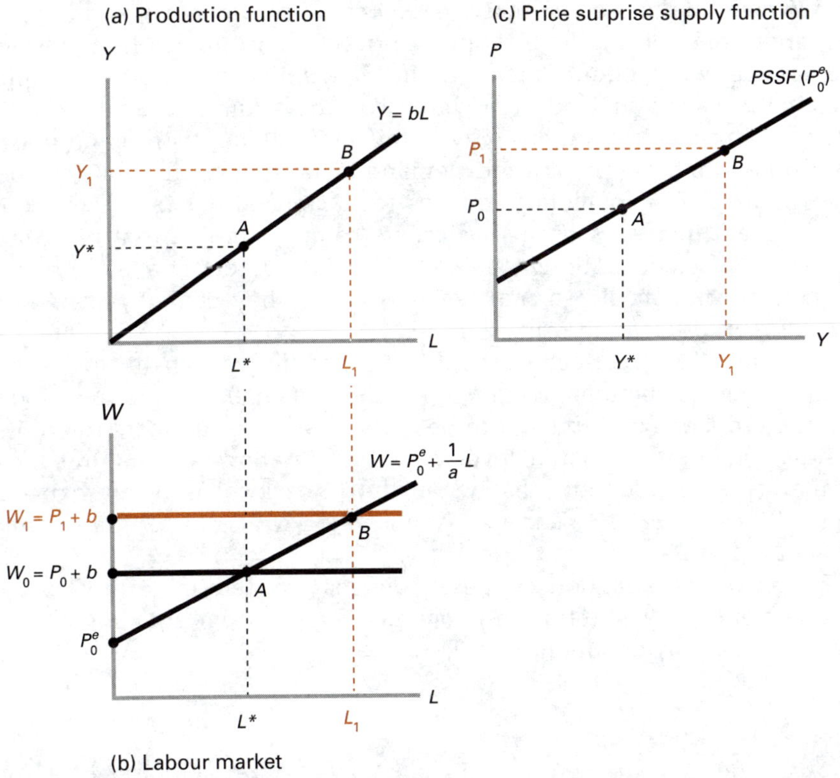

Figure 8.1 Derivation of the price surprise supply function

tion (8.1). When the nominal wage is brought to the left-hand side, the supply of labour equation becomes: $W = P_0^e + (1/a)L$. The linear labour supply schedule has a positive slope equal to $(1/a)$. The intercept on the vertical axis is the expected price level P_0^e. Since the intercept P_0^e has a coefficient of unity, a one-unit increase in the expected price level will shift the labour supply curve upwards by exactly one unit.

The intersection of the supply and demand curves for labour determine the level of employment. In the initial situation we assume that expectations are correct; that is, we assume that $P_0 = P_0^e$. When price expectations are correct, supply and demand intersect at point A and employment is at the natural level L^*. Output, which is determined by the production function, is also at its natural level Y^*. We have now determined one point on the aggregate supply curve. At this particular point, labelled A, expectations about the price level are perfectly correct and output is at the natural level.

To find a second point on the aggregate supply curve, where expectations are not fulfilled, suppose that the actual price level increases to P_1. We continue to assume that the expected price level is fixed at P_0^e. In the labour market, the higher output price P_1, encourages firms to raise the nominal wage offer. The wage-offer line shifts up. But labour supply remains in its original position since we are assuming that there is no change in price expectations. Given this assumption, there is no reason for workers to raise their wage demand. The new equilibrium position is at point B. Employment increases to L_1 and output increases to Y_1. Employment increases because workers estimate the current real wage to be W_1/P_0^e, which is higher than W_0/P_0^e. Workers cannot avoid the error in their estimation of the real wage because they cannot observe the current market-clearing price, P_1.

In Figure 8.1(c), a second point has been derived on the price surprise supply function; namely (Y_1, P_1), which is labelled B. In this model, when the price level turns out to be above the expected level (there is a positive price surprise) the level of output is above the natural level. Similarly, we could show that when the price level is below expectations, the negative price surprise is associated with a lower than normal level of output.

To derive the equation of the *PSSF*, first we determine the level of employment by substituting the nominal wage W from Equation 8.3 into the labour supply equation (8.1):

$$L = a(b + P - P^e) \tag{8.4}$$

Now substitute the level of employment given by Equation 8.4 into the production function (8.2) to determine aggregate supply:

$$Y = ab(b + P - P^e) \tag{8.5}$$

Clearly the level of output depends on the difference between the actual price and the expected price. As we saw in Figure 8.1, when the equilibrium price level P equals the expected price level P^e, output is at its natural level Y^*. From Equation 8.5, the natural level of output is

$$Y^* = ab^2$$

The aggregate supply curve is most conveniently represented by substituting Y^* back into Equation 8.5:

$$Y = Y^* + ab(P - P^e) \qquad \text{(aggregate supply)} \qquad (8.6)$$

This form of the aggregate supply curve shows that output Y will be above the natural level Y^* when the actual price level is above the expected price level. Hence, positive price surprises lead to increases in output above the natural level. On the other hand, recessions are associated with negative price surprises which occur when the actual price level is below the expected price level.

In Figure 8.1 the *PSSF* is shown with the price level on the vertical axis. The equation of the *PSSF* can be rearranged to agree with the diagram by bringing the price level to the left-hand side. A few simple manipulations give an alternative expression for the *PSSF*:

$$P = P^e + \frac{1}{ab}(Y - Y^*) \qquad (8.7)$$

An important point to notice about this form of the *PSSF* is that the vertical intercept includes the expected price level P^e with a coefficient of unity. Changes in the expected price level therefore cause shifts in the *PSSF*. For example, a one-unit increase in the expected price level will shift the *PSSF* upwards by precisely one unit.

Before we look at the implications of the *PSSF* for the behaviour of the macroeconomic policy analysis, two other important components of the model must be discussed. In particular, the aggregate demand equation must be specified and specific assumptions must be made about the way expectations are formed.

Aggregate Demand

As mentioned at the beginning of Chapter 7, the demand curve is not particularly controversial and the following equation is almost identical to the one derived in that chapter:

$$P = (\$ + F) - cY \qquad (8.8)$$

Unlike previous demand equations, Equation 8.8 is entirely linear. On the left-hand side is the aggregate price level. On the right-hand side, the intercept term is written ($ + *F*). $ and *F* represent, respectively, the influence of monetary and fiscal policy on aggregate demand. An increase in either will shift aggregate demand upwards and outwards in the direction of increased output and higher prices.[6] The slope of the aggregate demand curve is negative and equal to $-c$.

Modelling Expectations

As we have seen, price expectations play the crucial role of determining the positions of both the labour supply and the aggregate supply schedules. But we have not yet discussed how price expectations are formed. The issue of price expectations modelling has been the subject of an enormous amount of research and debate. The traditional model of adaptive expectations has been used by monetarists and Keynesians alike. As we shall see, when expectations are formed in an adaptive way, the economy reacts to disturbances by following a path of gradual adjustment towards the new equilibrium. During the adjustment phase, output and employment deviate from their natural levels. While monetarists stressed the potent effect of monetary policy, Keynesians downplayed the importance of the money supply and emphasized the impact of fiscal policy on aggregate demand. Although monetarists and Keynesians disagreed on the major causes of business cycles and the value of countercyclical policies, there was no disagreement over the basic point that government policies can have a substantial effect on output and employment in the short run.

The rational expectations revolution dramatically shifted the emphasis away from the monetary/fiscal policy debate. The important distinction became one of anticipated versus unanticipated policies. Like the classical economists of an earlier generation, the new classical school initially focused on variations in the money supply as the major cause of macroeconomic fluctuations. But it is only the unexpected component of changes in the money supply that affect real variables such as employment and output. The proposition that fully anticipated government policies will have no effect at all on output (the famous policy ineffectiveness proposition) is the most controversial of the new classical predictions.

To demonstrate just how important expectations assumptions are, we will first examine the concept of the adaptive expectations model. As

---

6 It is usual to interpret Equation 8.8 as being linear in the logarithms of the variable. If *P*, *M*, *F*, and *Y* are the logarithms of the price level *p*, the money supply *m*, the fiscal variable *f*, and real output y, then Equation 8.8 is equivalent to $p = mfy^{-c}$. The important points about this multiplicative aggregate demand curve are that the price level *p* is still proportional to the money supply *m*; the fiscal variable shifts demand to the right and the *p*–*y* curve slopes downwards to the right.

we will see, this assumption has important implications for the way the economy reacts to macroeconomic policies, such as restrictive anti-inflation monetary policy. We will then turn to the criticisms of the rational expectationists and examine why rational expectations leads to such different conclusions about the way the economy functions, including the controversial policy ineffectiveness proposition.

Adaptive Expectations

The essential feature of the adaptive expectations model is that individuals are assumed to adjust their future expectations in light of past forecast errors. Consider the situation of a person who, every year, needs to forecast the following year's price level. Since the same forecasting problem is faced annually, the individual is likely to try to learn from past mistakes. One way to do this is to construct the current forecast by revising the previous forecast up or down, depending on the sign and size of the previous forecast error. This is precisely what the adaptive expectations model does. Let P^e_t be the expected price level in period t. This forecast is made at the beginning of period t. At this time, the forecast error in the most recent period $t-1$ is known to be $(P_{t-1} - P^e_{t-1})$. This error is simply the difference between the actual price level in $t-1$ and the expected price level in $t-1$. The adaptive expectations model specifies that the current forecast is the previous forecast plus a fraction, δ, of the previous forecast error:

$$P^e_t = P^e_{t-1} + \delta(P_{t-1} - P^e_{t-1})$$

where typically, $0 \leq \delta \leq 1$. Notice that if the forecast was too low in period $(t - 1)$, the forecast error would be positive. To "correct" the current forecast, a fraction, δ, of this positive error is added to the previous forecast.

To see how this adaptive expectations model works, suppose that unknown to the price level forecaster, the actual price level will hold steady at 100 for several periods. Assume that the first forecast is 92, so that in the first period, the error is $100 - 92 = 8$. Now suppose that the forecaster sets $\delta = 0.5$. In the second period, the price level forecast is adjusted by adding half the previous error to the first period forecast: $92 + 0.5 \times 8 = 96$. The modified forecast for period two generates a second period forecast error of $100 - 96 = 4$. In the third period the forecast is again modified in the same way: $96 + 0.5 \times 4 = 98$. Using the same scheme, the forecast in the fourth period is 99. In this example, the sequence of adaptive forecasts: 92, 96, 98, 99, . . . is converging to the actual price level of 100. Generally, adaptive expectations forecasts will ultimately converge onto the target, *provided the target is stationary.*

The speed of convergence depends on the error correction parameter, δ. In the example we have just considered, it seems that the forecaster could converge on the actual price level faster by using a much higher value of δ. In fact, setting $\delta = 1$ in this particular case will ensure that whatever the first forecast is, all subsequent forecasts will be exactly right. The problem is that this only works when the target is constant in every period. In practice, the forecast target rarely remains stationary and it is unlikely that the optimal value of δ will be unity.

The adaptive expectations model can be expressed in a different way:

$$P_t^e = \delta P_{t-1} + (1 - \delta)P_{t-1}^e \tag{8.9}$$

This form of the model shows that the current forecast is a weighted average of the previous actual price level and the previous forecast price level. Larger values of δ attach a greater weight to the latest piece of information (last period's actual price level) and downplay the importance of the previous forecast.[7] Finally, the forecast can be expressed as a weighted average of all previous actual values. This is done by repeatedly substituting for the expectation on the right-hand side of Equation 8.9. The expected price level for earlier periods can be written in a way similar to Equation 8.9:

$$P_{t-1}^e = \delta P_{t-2} + (1 - \delta)P_{t-2}^e \tag{8.10}$$

$$P_{t-2}^e = \delta P_{t-3} + (1 - \delta)P_{t-3}^e \tag{8.11}$$

The sequential substitution of Equation 8.11 into Equation 8.10 and then Equation 8.10 into Equation 8.9 gives

$$P_t^e = \delta P_{t-1} + \delta(1 - \delta)P_{t-2} + \delta(1 - \delta)^2 P_{t-3} + (1 - \delta)^3 P_{t-3}^e \tag{8.12}$$

By repeatedly substituting for the expectation on the right-hand side, the current forecast can be expressed as a weighted sum of all previous actual values. Notice that if $0 < \delta < 1$, the weights decline geometrically and larger values of δ cause the weights to die out faster. In the special case $\delta = 1$, the weights die immediately after period $t - 1$. Equation 8.12 demonstrates that the adaptive expectations model not only assumes that the target variable can be forecast from knowledge of its past history, but adaptive expectations also assumes that the weights attached to all the previous values decline geometrically.

---

[7] If $\delta = 1$, then the forecast is simply the previous value of the variable. This works really well if the variable is actually constant! It is also the best you can do if the variable to be forecast is a constant plus or minus an (unforecastable) random component that has a mean or average value of zero.

Adaptive Expectations and Macroeconomic Adjustment

To illustrate the implications of adaptive expectations for the behaviour of the macroeconomy, consider the effect of a decrease in the money supply. In Figure 8.2 the economy is initially in equilibrium at point *A*. We assume that this equilibrium has been maintained for a sufficiently long period of time that the price level P_0 is fully anticipated: $P_0^e = P_0$. The labour market is in equilibrium in that firms are maximizing profits and workers' real wage expectations are always realized. Remember that in the new classical model, workers know their current nominal wage, but are not immediately aware of the general price level the instant that all markets clear. At the moment markets clear and labour supply decisions have to be made, workers can only deflate their observable nominal wage by the expected market-clearing price level in order to estimate the real wage. Based on the expected real wage, workers make their labour supply decisions. When the actual price level becomes known, workers will know whether their expectations were correct. Point *A* describes a continuing situation in which price expectations are correct period after period.

Now suppose that the government decides to reduce the money supply from $\$_0$ to $\overline{\$}$. In recent times, Canadians have associated tight monetary policy with the government's goal of reducing inflation. In later chapters, a model will be developed specifically for the purpose of analyzing an economy that experiences a varying rate of inflation. For the

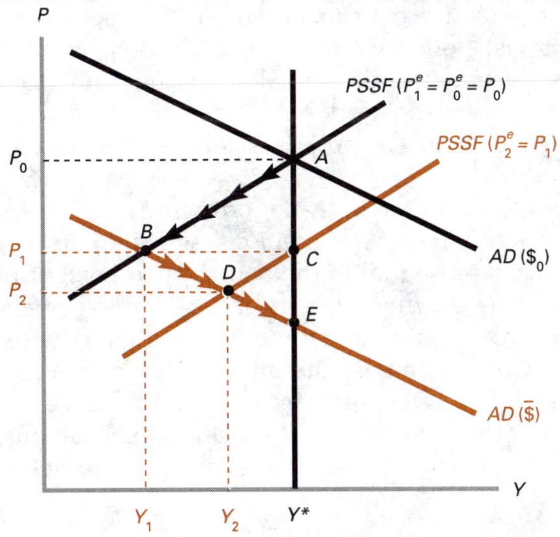

Figure 8.2 A decrease in the money supply — adjustment under adaptive expectations

time being, we will consider the goal of reducing the price level rather than the rate of inflation.

To trace out the path the economy will follow after the money supply is reduced to a new lower level, we need to specify the exact nature of the adaptive expectations scheme. The simplest to illustrate in a diagram is the case of static expectations in which workers expect the current price level P_t to be identical to the previous price level P_{t-1}. In terms of Equation 8.12 the adjustment parameter δ is set to unity.[8] In all periods prior to the cut in the money supply, we assume that price expectations are constant and identical to the unchanging price level P_0, that is, $P^e_0 = P_0$.

As soon as the money supply is cut, the aggregate demand curve shifts down to its new permanent position, labelled $AD(\bar{\$})$. The position of the price surprise supply function depends on the expected price level in the first period. Given the static expectations model, the expected price level in period one is identical to the actual price level in period zero (before the change in the money supply): $P^e_1 = P_0$. Hence in period one, the aggregate supply curve $PSSF(P^e_1 = P_0)$ remains in the same position as the original supply curve $PSSF(P^e_0 = P_0)$. The equilibrium position in period one is at point B, where output has fallen to Y_1 and the price level has fallen to P_1.

The reason for the drop in output is that firms, which are aware of the current market-clearing price for their product (which is all they need to know), reduce the nominal wage offer. Workers do not have the benefit of observing all market prices immediately and evaluate the real wage on the basis of price expectations. In period one, the expected price level P^e_1 is last period's price level P_0, which is above P_1. Hence workers see the decline in the nominal wage, but anticipate no changes in the price level. From the workers' perspective, the real wage in period one declines and they supply less labour. The result is a drop in output to Y_1.

In period two, workers have an opportunity to revise their price expectations. Given the static expectations scheme, the expected price level in period two is set equal to the actual price level of period one. In symbols, $P^e_2 = P_1$. The downward revision in price expectations causes a downward shift of the aggregate supply curve. Since the expected price level has a coefficient of unity in the intercept of the supply curve equation (8.7), the supply curve drops by exactly the same amount as the decline in the expected price level. With static expectations, the change in price expectations is the same as the drop in the actual price level

---

8 Many economists believe that daily and weekly changes in stock market prices can be forecast just as well with static expectations as they can with any other forecast, including those based on so-called "technical analysis." This view of the stock market is explained in an entertaining style by Burton Malkiel, *A Random Walk Down Wall Street*, 4th ed., (Norton, 1985).

one period ago; that is, $P_2^e - P_1^e = P_1 - P_0$. Between period one and two, the *PSSF* drops through a distance $P_1 - P_0$. To find the position of the supply curve in period two, extend a horizontal line from P_1 to point *C*, which lies vertically below the original position at point *A*. The distance between *A* and *C* is the same as the drop in the price level from P_1 to P_0. Hence the new supply curve passes through point *C*.

The equilibrium position in period two is at point *D*, which is determined by the intersection of $AD(\overline{\$})$ and $PSSF(P_2^e = P_1)$. The price level falls again to P_2, but the level of output rises somewhat to Y_2. The second successive decline in the price level causes firms to lower the nominal wage offer once again. However, workers also lower their price expectations and by a larger amount than the drop in the nominal wage offer. Hence workers expect the real wage to be higher in period two than in period one, so there is an increase in the level of employment and output.

The process of adjustment following the one-time cut in the money supply continues in this way until the new long-run equilibrium position is reached at point *E*. During the transition, price expectations continue to chase the falling price level and the aggregate supply curve gradually drops down in a sequence of ever smaller steps. The net effect of the restrictive monetary policy is to reduce the aggregate price level, but in the meantime, the economy is dragged into a recession during which output declines and unemployment increases. When the aggregate supply curve finally passes through point *E*, the adjustment process comes to an end: the expected price level equals the actual price level and employment and output are restored to their natural levels.

This example of static expectations illustrates the general point that under any adaptive expectations scheme, the process of macroeconomic adjustment takes time. When aggregate demand changes for whatever reason, the new long-run equilibrium is not reached instantaneously, rather output and employment deviate from their natural levels for extended periods. The adaptive expectations model is therefore consistent with the fact that booms and recessions persist for months and even years at a time. There are numerous examples: the depression of the 1930s accounted for most of that decade, while the recovery from the 1982–83 recession turned into several years of uninterrupted economic growth that did not end until 1990. The concept of adaptive expectations also explains why, in the late 1970s and in 1980, so many economists were worried about the severe unemployment effects that they felt were bound to follow the Bank of Canada's extremely tight monetary policy. History has shown that it took the deepest recession since the 1930s to get the Canadian inflation rate down from 12 percent to between 4 and 5 percent (see Chapter 14 for a full discussion).

Despite the ability of the adaptive expectations model to explain persistent periods of recession and economic expansion, macroeconomic theorists of the 1970s became increasingly dissatisfied with this model of expectations formation. In the next section we will look at the main limitations of the adaptive expectations approach and explain why the idea of rational expectations was so quickly adopted by the new classical school and by others.

A Critique of the Adaptive Expectations Model

The popularity of the adaptive expectations model up until the 1970s was due largely to its simplicity and intuitive plausibility. But a number of conceptual problems with the adaptive expectations model led many economists to reject it in favour of formulations based on rational expectations.

1. The fundamental difficulty with the adaptive expectations model is that it is not based on any optimization principle. First, adaptive expectations are based exclusively on the past values of the series in question; no other information that might be available is used. But in most forecasting situations, other information will be helpful in generating more accurate forecasts. For example, it is widely accepted that inflation is significantly affected by the growth of the money supply. Why then, would individuals try to forecast inflation by using only past inflation data when information on past monetary growth is freely available? More precisely, if individuals believe in a certain theory of inflation, then to act consistently with their beliefs, they should use this theory for forecasting. But the criticism of adaptive expectations goes beyond this. Even if we assume people use only past values of inflation to forecast inflation, then in general, the adaptive expectations model will not make the best use of this limited information. The geometrically declining weights we derived earlier typically will not be the optimal weights.
2. An implication of the first point is that forecasts generated by adaptive expectations will typically exhibit systematic forecasting errors. The reason is simply that the "wrong" model is being used to make forecasts. Systematic forecasting errors are unsatisfactory from a theoretical point of view because, with enough experience, people should be able to detect systematic errors and correct them; that is, discover a forecasting model that does not generate systematic errors.
3. The adaptive expectations model is entirely "backward-looking" in that only past information is used. In reality, announcements about future events can influence expectations. A clear example was the introduction of the Goods and Services Tax (GST) in January 1991. This well-publicized tax increase was bound to raise the rate of inflation in January 1991. Most Canadians took this into account well be-

fore the event, yet the adaptive expectations model has no way to incorporate this significant information.

Rational Expectations

The rational expectations approach overcomes the basic problems inherent in the adaptive expectations model. The fundamental principle of rational expectations is that individuals who need to make forecasts should do so in an efficient manner. First, this means that economic principles should apply to the gathering of information. The more information one has, the better one's forecasts are likely to be. However, additional information should be collected only if the expected benefits exceed the acquisition costs. It is important to note that the information set does not refer just to historical data. While this is clearly very important, individuals also possess valuable information about the structure of the economy. As discussed above, it is widely accepted that *monetary growth* is the most important single factor in determining the rate of inflation. If individuals know the precise relationship between monetary growth and inflation, then this structural information is obviously very useful to anyone who needs to forecast inflation. In Muth's words, "I would like to suggest that expectations, since they are informed predictions of future events, are essentially the same as the predictions of the relevant economic theory. . . . We shall call such expectations 'rational'."[9]

The second element of rational expectations is that the available information should be used in an efficient way, that is, the best possible forecast should be extracted from the available set of information.[10] In many cases, the optimal forecast of a random variable P_t is the so-called *conditional expectation*, which is written $E[P_t|I_{t-1}]$. In this expression, I_{t-1} refers to all the information available at the time the forecast is made, namely, period $(t - 1)$. The entire term refers to the value of P that can be expected in period t given that the expectation or forecast is based on the available information I_{t-1}. The value of P that actually materializes in period t will differ from the forecast value by a random term, v_t.

$$P_t = E[P_t|I_{t-1}] + v_t$$

We can be sure that the random term v_t will have a zero mean and

9 J. Muth, "Rational Expectations and the Theory of Price Movements," *Econometrica*, July 1961, p. 316.

10 In general terms, the "best possible forecast" cannot be defined independently of the loss function that tells us how forecast errors are translated into economic costs.

be entirely unforecastable, given the information set I_{t-1}. If some part of v_t were forecastable, it would have been incorporated into the forecast, thereby reducing the size of the forecast error. This important observation means that the sequence of forecast errors generated by rational forecasts should have no systematic component; rather the sequence should be consistent with a purely random process. In a case study presented later in this chapter we will examine whether Canadian forecasting firms produce rational forecasts. But first, consider Figure 8.3, which illustrates some of the shortcomings of adaptive expectations.

Adaptive and Rational Forecasts Compared

Figure 8.3 presents two time series. The black graph represents the price level, which is denoted by P_t. The coloured graph represents forecasts of P_t that have been generated by an adaptive expectations model. As we saw in an earlier section, adaptive price expectations can be expressed as a weighted average of past price levels. Equation 8.13 approximates the adaptive forecast scheme:

$$F_t = 0.7 \times P_{t-1} + 0.3 \times P_{t-2} \tag{8.13}$$

where F_t is the forecast of P_t. The value of P was assumed to be 10 in the two periods before the graph begins, so the first forecast is also 10. From then on, the forecasts depend on the actual values of P that appear in Figure 8.3.

At first glance, the forecasts seem to track the actual series quite

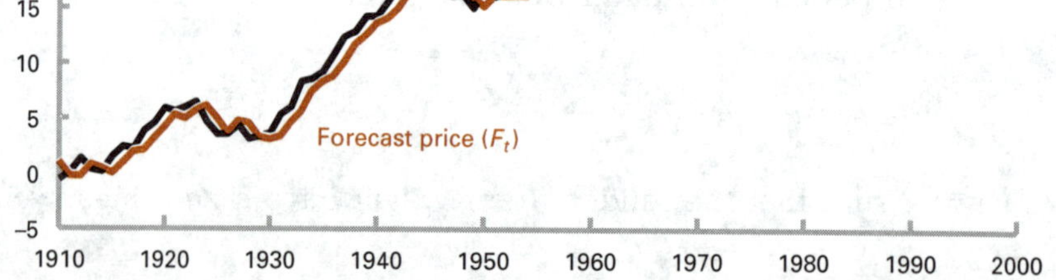

Figure 8.3 An example of adaptive forecasts

closely, but a closer look reveals patterns in the forecast errors. The most obvious one is that when the black line rises steadily for several periods, the coloured line is always below the black line. In other words, whenever the price level experiences a sustained increase, the forecast errors ($P_t - F_t$) are systematically positive. Another systematic feature is that the only time the coloured line rises above the black line is when the black line is falling: forecast errors are negative only when the price level is falling. Finally, by quickly scanning the plots from left to right, it is clear that the black line is predominantly above the coloured line. This implies that over the entire sequence, the forecasts tend to fall short of the actual price level: the forecasts exhibit a downward bias. Another way to express this bias is in terms of the average forecast error, which is 0.53, rather than zero.

The presence of systematic patterns in the forecast errors indicates that the adaptive forecasts are not optimal. The reason becomes clear when we examine the equation that was used to prepare the computer-generated artificial prices graphed in Figure 8.3:

$$P_t = P_{t-1} + 0.5 + v_t \tag{8.14}$$

where v_t is an unforecastable random term.[11] Equation 8.14 can be thought of as the mysterious truth that lies hidden from ordinary mortals. At time $(t - 1)$ the potentially knowable part of P_t is $(P_{t-1} + 0.5)$, because v_t has not yet been drawn. The part of P_t that is determined in period $(t - 1)$ is the conditional expectation of P_t at time $(t - 1)$ and it represents the optimal or rational forecast of P_t. The forecast error associated with the rational forecast, $E[P_t|P_{t-1}]$, can be obtained by subtracting the conditional expectation from the actual value:

$$P_t - E[P_t|P_{t-1}] = v_t$$

In the present case, the forecast error is

$$P_t - (P_{t-1} + 0.5) = v_t$$

The rational expectation error is simply v_t, which is completely unforecastable.

Given the true model (Equation 8.14), we can compute the adaptive forecast errors by subtracting Equation 8.13 from Equation 8.14:

---

11 This process is known as a "random walk with drift." Notice that P equals its previous value plus two other terms. Just like someone walking, P takes a step from its previous position P_{t-1}. The step is partly random (v_t), hence the term "random walk." But there is also a constant, 0.5, that is added to P every period. This is the drift part; it ensures that P drifts upwards through time.

$$(P_t - F_t) = (P_{t-1} + 0.5 + v_t) - (0.7 \times P_{t-1} + 0.3 \times P_{t-2})$$

$$= v_t + [0.5 + 0.3(P_{t-1} - P_{t-2})]$$

The adaptive forecast error has two components. The first is the unforecastable random term v_t. The second, in square brackets, varies systematically. It is this second term that accounts for the patterns we detected in Figure 8.3. With enough forecasting experience, this part of the forecast error could be uncovered by the forecaster and used to improve the forecasts. By making the proper correction we would arrive at the rational forecasts discussed above.

The great significance of Muth's contribution to modelling expectations was not to improve forecasting techniques, which have been well developed in the statistical literature, but rather to dramatically change the way macroeconomists construct their economic models. The key to his contribution was to force economists to introduce expectations into their models in a coherent and logical way. The assumption of rational expectations ensures that the expectations of individuals are consistent with the theoretical model that explains their economic behaviour. Almost immediately, a startling policy implication became associated with rational expectations modelling. This is the hypothesis that if changes in government policy are fully anticipated, they have no effect on output and unemployment. The so-called policy ineffectiveness proposition (PIP) is a controversial implication of the new classical economics of Lucas, Sargent, and Barro. In the next section we will develop a simple version of this model that highlights the main features and predictions of the new classical economics.

The Policy Ineffectiveness Proposition

For convenience, the equations of the aggregate demand and aggregate supply curves are reproduced here:

$$P = (\$ + F) - cY \qquad \text{(aggregate demand)} \qquad (8.8)$$

$$P = P^e + \frac{1}{ab}(Y - Y^*) \qquad \text{(aggregate supply)} \qquad (8.7)$$

Figures 8.4(a) and (b) illustrate goods market and labour market equilibrium. In the goods market, the initial *PSSF* has an intercept equal to $P^e - (Y^*/ab)$ and a positive slope. An important point is that P^e appears in the intercept with a coefficient of unity.

In the labour market, the demand side of the market is described by the nominal wage offer which is derived from Equation 8.3:

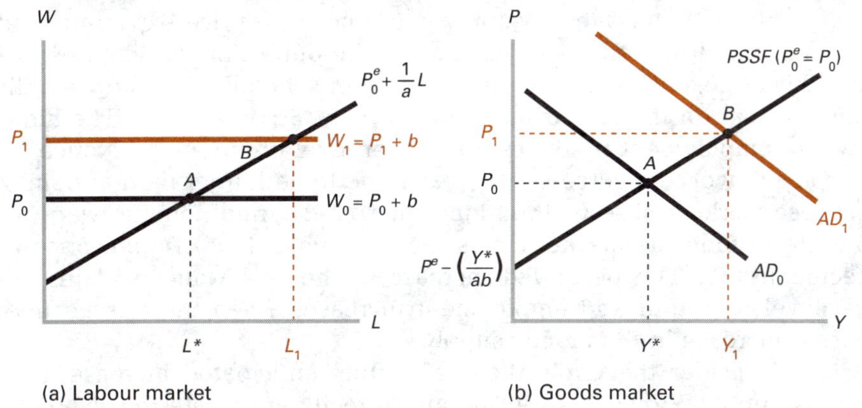

Figure 8.4 An unexpected increase in the money supply

$$W - P = b \tag{8.3}$$

It is represented in Figure 8.4(a) as a horizontal line. The supply of labour is given by Equation 8.1, rewritten here with W on the left:

$$W = P^e + \frac{L}{a}$$

The labour supply curve has a positive slope, $1/a$. The intercept is P^e. In both markets the initial positions are at point A. In the goods market, the output level is Y^* and the price level is P_0. In the labour market, the level of employment is L^* and the nominal wage is W_0.[12]

Now suppose that the money supply is increased and that the increase is *unexpected*. The aggregate demand curve shifts upwards to AD_1 in Figure 8.4(b). The position of the *PSSF* depends crucially on price expectations. The *PSSF* will remain fixed in position as long as price expectations remain unchanged; that is, as long as workers expect the price level to stay at P_0. Since expectations are formed rationally, the only way expectations can be wrong is if the shift in the aggregate demand curve is completely unexpected, which it is in this example. Hence, the new equilibrium position is at point B: the unexpected increase in the money supply causes output to increase to Y_1 and the price level to increase to P_1.

12 L^* is the natural employment level, which can be determined from the labour market equations by setting $P = P^e$. The result is $L^* = ab$. When this is substituted into the production function (Equation 8.2), the output level is precisely $Y^* = ab^2$.

In the labour market, the unanticipated increase in the money supply has no effect on the labour supply curve because price expectations do not change. However, as we have seen, the output price increases to P_1 and this causes firms to raise the wage-offer schedule. The new equilibrium position in the labour market is at point B (W_1 and L_1). The higher level of employment produces the higher level of output Y_1. Notice that at point B, workers perceive the real wage to be higher than at point A, because workers observe the higher market-clearing nominal wage W_1, but at the time the market clears they still hold their original price expectations, P_0^e. The perceived increase in the real wage explains why the level of output and employment increases when there is an *unexpected* increase in the money supply.

Now consider the implications of a fully anticipated increase in the money supply. Provided expectations correctly anticipate the size of the increase in the money supply, there will be no change in output. Since everyone knows that upward movements in aggregate demand cause the price level to rise, people will anticipate the price increase. But to ensure that economic agents can predict exactly how much the price level will increase, the new classical economists endow the inhabitants of their models with precise knowledge of the economic structure. Armed with the equations of the model and correct expectations concerning the increase in the money supply, it is possible to predict exactly what the new price level will be.

The effects of a fully anticipated increase in the money supply are illustrated in Figures 8.5(a) and (b). In Figure 8.5(b), the aggregate demand curve shifts upwards to AD_1 as before, but this time the aggregate supply curve also shifts up to $PSSF(P_1^e = P_1)$ due to the upward

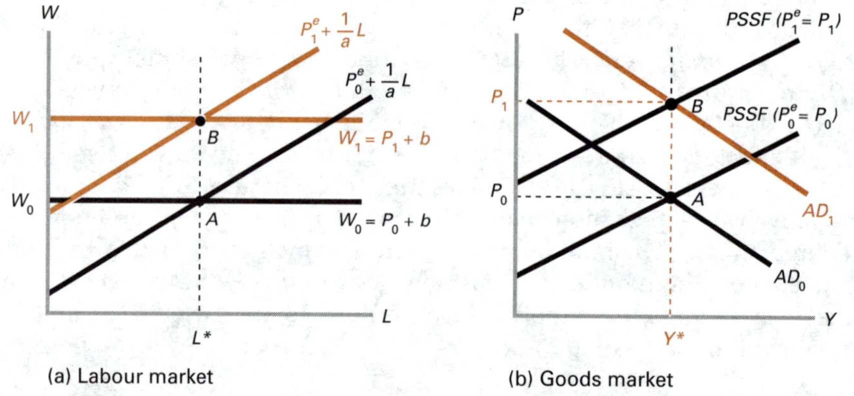

Figure 8.5 An expected increase in the money supply

revision of expected price level. The new equilibrium position is at point *B*. Given that expectations are rational and the increase in the money supply is correctly anticipated, the expected price level is identical to the actual price level P_1. Moreover, the level of output is Y^*, the natural level of output. The net result of the fully anticipated increase in the money supply is to instantaneously move the economy from point *A* to point *B*. The price level immediately jumps to its new equilibrium level, but output does not deviate from Y^*.

In the labour market (Figure 8.5(a)), the results are similar in that employment never deviates from L^*. The labour supply schedule shifts upwards due to the upward revision of price expectations to P_1^e. The nominal wage-offer curve also shifts and the new equilibrium is at point *C*, directly above point *A*. The nominal wage is higher, but the employment level and the real wage are unchanged. Moreover, workers correctly anticipate the market-clearing real wage.

Rational expectations analysis has some remarkable implications. For example, it suggests that if the Bank of Canada wants to reduce the price level (or more likely the rate of inflation), then the decision to decrease the money supply should be announced well in advance. If the public (a) believes the Bank's announcement, and (b) understands how the economy will ultimately react to the tight monetary policy, then it will make the correct predictions about the future price level. Under these ideal conditions, as soon as the policy is implemented on the preannounced date, the targeted reduction in the price level will be achieved instantaneously. There will be no period of high interest rates, rising unemployment, and business failures. The level of output and employment will simply remain at their natural levels.[13]

The Algebra of the Policy Ineffectiveness Proposition

The equations of the aggregate supply and demand curves were reproduced at the beginning of the previous section. There are three endogenous variables contained in these two equations: *P*, *Y*, and P^e. The solution to the system can be found only when we have derived one more equation; one that captures the rational expectations assumption.

Under the rational expectations hypothesis (REH), the expected price level must be identical to the price level that would be predicted by the model given the anticipated values of the exogenous variables. In short, P^e, must be consistent with Equations 8.7 and 8.8. Since under the REH it must be that $P = P^e$, then it follows from the supply equation (8.7) that $Y = Y^*$. The expected price level must also be consistent with aggregate demand (Equation 8.8) once we have substituted Y^* for *Y* and inserted

13 The dynamics of anti-inflation monetary policy is described fully in Chapter 14.

the expected values of \$ and F, which we will label $\$^e$ and F^e. The missing price expectations equation is therefore

$$P^e = \$^e + F^e - cY^* \tag{8.15}$$

Equation 8.15 expresses the rational expectations hypothesis in algebraic form. Combined with the supply and demand equations (8.7 and 8.8), the three equations determine Y, P, and P^e. We will confine the analysis to deriving and interpreting the reduced-form equation for Y. Start by multiplying Equation 8.7 throughout by ab, so $Y - Y^*$ can be written as

$$Y - Y^* = ab(P - P^e)$$

By subtracting Equation 8.15 from Equation 8.8, and multiplying the result by ab, we obtain

$$ab(P - P^e) = ab[(\$ - \$^e) + (F - F^e)] - abc(Y - Y^*)$$

The last two equations can be used to find the reduced-form equation for Y:

$$Y = Y^* + k[(\$ - \$^e) + (F - F^e)] \tag{8.16}$$

where $k = ab/(1 + abc)$.

The most important implications of the new classical model can be seen in Equation 8.16. First, if monetary policy is correctly anticipated, then $(\$ - \$^e)$ is zero and the monetary variables play no role in determining output Y. A correctly anticipated monetary policy will change the price level, but no real variables such as output and employment will be affected. Second, an identical argument applies to the fiscal variable F. A fully anticipated increase in government spending, or a fully anticipated cut in taxes means that $F = F^e$ in Equation 8.16 and the fiscal variables drop out of the equation. Hence, any changes in fiscal policy that are fully expected will have absolutely no effect on output and employment. This observation has a further remarkable implication. If the government adopts consistent policy rules aimed at influencing the business cycle, before long the public will learn what the rules are. Hence, the government's demand management policies will become fully anticipated and under the REH, totally ineffective!

The third message of the new classical model concerns the causes of business cycle fluctuations. It is *unanticipated* changes in the money supply and/or the government's fiscal position that catch people off guard. Expectations about the future will turn out to be wrong when the government's behaviour is erratic and output and employment will deviate from the natural levels. In general, output and employment will be above the natural levels when prices exceed their expected values — positive price surprises are associated with increased output. It is difficult to see how repeatedly successful demand management policies can be based on totally unexpected shifts in government behaviour. Consequently, the new classical model leaves no room for such interventionist policies. Indeed, new classical economists would go further and argue that it is unstable and unpredictable government behaviour, particularly monetary policy, that is the fundamental cause of instability in the private sector. The prescription is clear: the government should get out of the macroeconomic stabilization game and concentrate on acting in a predictable and consistent fashion. This would not directly offset the effect of unavoidable random shocks that emanate from nongovernment sectors, but it would reduce the amount of uncertainty faced by the private sector and lead to a reduction in the volatility of output and employment.

A Critique of the Policy Ineffectiveness Proposition

Given the striking conclusions of the new classical macroeconomic model, which deny even a short-run effect from anticipated government policy, it should come as no surprise that the assumptions and conclusions of new classical economists have been strongly challenged. The two key assumptions that generate the policy ineffectiveness proposition are (1) the rational expectations hypothesis and (2) prices and wages are sufficiently flexible that markets always clear.

Bennett McCallum has described why he thinks the REH has been so influential:

> After a slow start, the rational expectations hypothesis moved forward strongly during the 1970s into its current position as the dominant hypothesis concerning expectation formulation. One reason for its success, I believe, was the dawning realization that it is the "natural" hypothesis to use in neoclassical economic analysis. More specifically, the basic idea of the hypothesis is simply that economic agents behave purposefully in collecting and using information, just as they do in other activities, an idea that is hard for an economist to reject without considerable embarrassment.[14]

Despite the almost "natural" appeal of the rational expectations hypothesis, even some of the most enthusiastic supporters have recognized its major weakness: it assumes that economic agents possess an enormous

---

14 Bennett T. McCallum, "Rational Expectations and Macroeconomic Policy," *Journal of Money, Credit and Banking*, November 1980 (Part 2), p. 717.

amount of detailed information concerning the structure of the economy. For example, in the simple economic model considered in this chapter, we derived the PIP by assuming that all economic agents knew the precise equations that describe the economic system. As McCallum, an economist usually associated with the new classical school, has noted,

> In practice, of course, this compelling idea [the REH] usually gets translated into the requirement that expectations are . . . formed in a way that is stochastically consistent with the behaviour of the realized values of the variables in question. This is clearly a much stronger hypothesis, one that an economist can reasonably dispute.[15]

M.H. Pesaran makes the same point more bluntly:

> What seems to be completely unacceptable about the Muthian notion of rational expectations is the amount of information that individuals are assumed to command. It is not explained how individuals are supposed to acquire the amount of information that underlies the REH. Nor is it made clear whether the individual could ever obtain the required information.[16]

These criticisms point to the virtual impossibility of individuals knowing the true structure of the economy. The mere fact that there is so much disagreement over macroeconomic theory implies that not even the most prominent economists can, as a group, satisfy the assumptions required by the REH. One only has to look at the debate over the fundamental causes of the business cycle. Traditional Keynesians focus on the instability of demand, particularly investment; monetarists emphasize the money supply; new classical economists claim the major force is due to unanticipated fluctuations in monetary growth; and real business cycle theorists argue that money is irrelevant, and that productivity shocks are the root cause of macroeconomic fluctuations. After years of theoretical and statistical research, economists cannot agree on the main driving force behind business cycles. When economists believe in different models, given the same information, economists will construct different forecasts of the future. Two recent examples concern (1) the effects of the Canada–U.S. Free Trade Agreement on job creation versus job losses and (2) the effect of the GST on price inflation.

The new classical economists and monetarists have argued that theories should be judged on the basis of their predictions, not on their assumptions. Obviously, if a set of plausible assumptions lead to false

---

15 McCallum, "Rational Expectations," p. 717.

16 M.H. Pesaran, "A Critique of the Proposed Tests of the Natural Rate-Rational Expectations Hypothesis," *Economic Journal*, September 1982, p. 534.

predictions, then the theory must be rejected. But whether a theory should be rejected because the assumptions are strictly known to be false is a moot point. In physical science it is recognized that many assumptions are, strictly speaking, false, yet the theories they support are extremely useful. (Einstein's theories of relativity have replaced Newtonian mechanics, but Newtonian mechanics was good enough to get astronauts to the moon and back.) Assumptions may be false, yet contain enough truth to yield correct predictions within our range of experience.

Many economists have argued that the second assumption required by the PIP, namely, that all markets clear instantaneously, is so far off the mark as to be completely misleading. Market equilibrium is constantly being disturbed by a stream of events that shift supply and demand curves. In the labour market, if wages and prices are not free to adjust as frequently as new disturbances impinge on the market, then the real wage cannot adjust fast enough to ensure market-clearing at every moment.

Critics argue that the widespread use of wage and price contracts inevitably impedes the adjustment of wages and prices. Over 40 percent of the Canadian labour force is unionized and signs wage contracts that typically run for one to three years. Generally, multi-year contracts specify precisely how wages will be incremented during the contract. In most cases the increments are preset; they are not triggered by changing circumstances, such as an increase in the unemployment rate or firms' profit performance. One exception to this is a cost-of-living allowance (COLA) clause which compensates workers for a rise in the general price level. Typically, the COLA clause gives only limited protection from unexpected inflation. For example, firms may agree to automatically increment wages to cover only 50 percent of inflation during the contract. Firms can also limit their COLA clause payments by covering inflation up to some preset maximum, say 10 percent. Inflation beyond the capped limit generates no automatic wage increment. Finally, the COLA clause may not cover, for example, the first 3 percent of inflation; this limit is called a *trigger*, since inflation must exceed 3 percent to trigger the COLA clause.

The important point about wage contracts is that they essentially prevent wages from being adjusted during the term of the contract. Even when events occur that would otherwise cause the nominal wage to change, the contract "protects" the negotiated wage.

Turning to the product market, the assumption of instantaneous market-clearing does apply to commodities traded in the international spot markets. Prices in these markets vary moment by moment and adjust virtually immediately to shifts in supply and demand. But these so-called spot markets are not typical of most transactions and account for only a fraction of all raw commodity trades. The iron ore, coal, and electricity needed by steel-makers are frequently supplied under long-term contracts with fixed prices. In some cases the quantities of coal are so huge that new mines are devoted to a single purchaser. The risks faced by both the mining company and the coal user can be reduced through long-term contracts.[17]

The contractual stability of input prices, including wages, is not the only reason that the prices of manufactured goods adjust less than instantaneously. This is especially true of high-priced products, such as cars, houses, and major appliances. Because the products are high-priced and heterogenous, potential buyers do a good deal of searching before making a purchase. Sellers understand that if the first potential customer walks away, this does not mean that the product price is too high and should be lowered immediately. Rather, prices are maintained even in the face of variations in demand. In the housing market for example, the effect of a drop in demand is likely to be seen first in the time it takes to sell houses and only later in the price of houses.

In addition, high-priced products are often associated with a reputation for quality that is signalled to the market through a steadily maintained high price. The reputations of Cadillac, Jaguar, and BMW cars would not be enhanced if dealers sold cars at fire-sale prices at the first sign of a recession. The long-term reputation of the product is enhanced by its high and stable price tag.

Clearly there are a number of institutional arrangements that reduce the flexibility of both wages and prices. Some of these are formalized in legal contracts and others reflect profit-maximizing pricing practices of firms. But whatever the cause of wage and price stickiness,[18] the inescapable conclusion is that instantaneous market-clearing is more fiction than fact. If wages and prices are slow to adjust to fluctations in supply and demand, then inevitably the real wage will deviate from its market-clearing level, regardless of whether the disturbance was anticipated or not. When this happens, employment and output must deviate from their natural levels. In short, wage and price stickiness makes it impossible for wages and prices to react to even anticipated events. Hence, even anticipated events can have output and employment effects.

It is always possible to raise the defense that predictions, not assumptions, should be tested. So how has the new classical policy ineffectiveness proposition done in practice? As Benjamin Friedman has pointed out, the new classical PIP has failed a most decisive empirical test. Well-

---

[17] But it is possible to get stung by a long-term contract. Newfoundland is still smarting over an agreement to sell huge amounts of hydroelectricity to Quebec for what is now a bargain price.

[18] For economists in the Keynesian tradition, the great challenge has been to develop persuasive economic explanations for wage and price stickiness. For example, considerable progress has been made in contract theory, which explores the economic basis of long-term contracts between two parties. These issues will be taken up in more detail in Chapter 10.

publicized policies of monetary disinflation dragged both the U.S. and Canadian economies through deep and protracted recessions on the way to reducing the rate of inflation.

> Experience has belied the most significant policy implication of the new classical macroeconomics. . . . The tight monetary policy during this period [1980–82] was probably as well anticipated as such a policy is ever likely to be. . . . Economic events suggest anything but costless disinflation.[19]

Case Study 3: Are Canadian Inflation Expectations Formed Rationally?

In this case study we look at some evidence as to whether Canadian inflation expectations are formed in a rational manner. By necessity, the rational expectations hypothesis (REH) can be tested only indirectly. To carry out direct tests one would need to see if expectations are consistent with the correct model that generates inflation. But what model is that? As soon as we purported to write down the "correct" model, someone would provide a good argument as to why it is wrong! Another difficulty is that there is little data on the price expectations that Canadians have about the future — no-one has surveyed the Canadian population on a regular basis to ascertain the average inflation forecast.

However, with the limited data that are available, it is possible to test some of the implications of rational expectations. If expectations are rational, then actual inflation will be equal to the forecast of inflation plus or minus a random error term. We can use a simple equation that includes, as a special case, this specific prediction of rational expectations theory:

$$\pi_t = a + b\pi_t^e + v_t$$

where π_t is the actual inflation rate, π_t^e is the expected inflation rate, and v_t is the random prediction error. Rational expectations theory implies three testable hypotheses concerning this equation:

1. The intercept a is equal to zero.
2. The slope coefficient b is unity.
3. The random errors do not portray any systematic patterns.

19 Benjamin M. Friedman, "Recent Perspectives in and on Macroeconomics," National Bureau of Economic Research Working Paper #1208, September 1983.

If either one or both of the first two points are incorrect, then the inflation forecasts cannot be unbiased. Failure of these two hypotheses means that all rates of inflation (except one) are consistently overpredicted or underpredicted. Figure 8.6 shows why this is so. On the vertical axis, the actual inflation rate is plotted. Predicted inflation is plotted on the horizontal axis. The line along which actual and predicted inflation are equal passes through the origin and has a slope of unity — it is the 45° line, shown in black. Any other line could not possibly maintain equality between predicted and actual inflation at every point.

To test these two hypotheses, we have plotted annual inflation forecasts together with the actual rate of inflation for the years 1980 to 1990. The inflation forecasts for a particular year represent the average of 15 to 17 forecasts made by Canadian organizations in the fourth quarter of the previous year. The individual forecasts included in this average have been made by Canadian banks, leading investment companies, and economic forecasting firms. Fortunately, the Conference

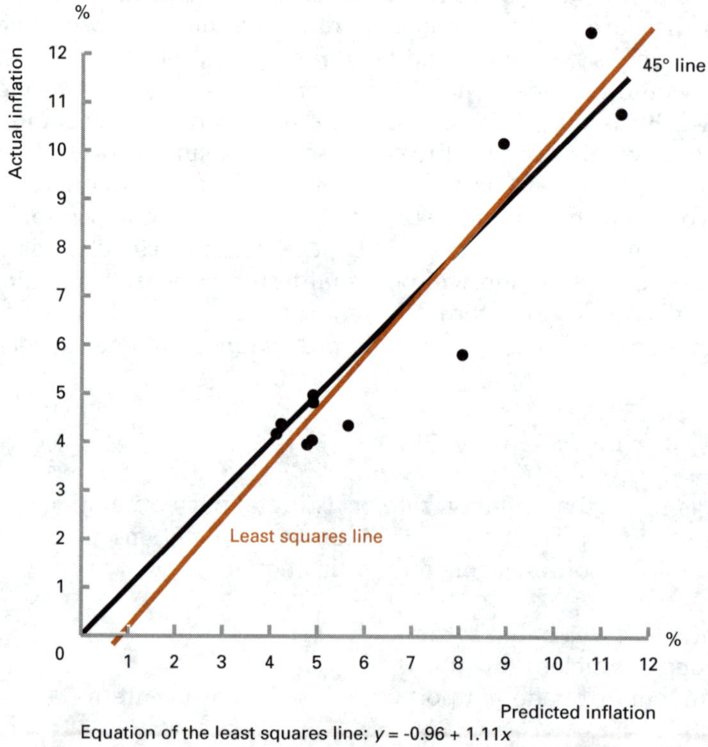

Figure 8.6 A least squares test of the rational expectations hypothesis

Board in Canada has collected these forecasts on a regular basis since the late 1970s. We have restricted ourselves to the data from the 1980s to avoid the aftermath of Canada's three-year experiment with wage and price controls, which ended in 1978.

In Figure 8.6, the line that best fits the actual and predicted inflation is plotted in colour.[20] The equation of the fitted line is given below the graph. Notice that the intercept is –0.96 and the slope is 1.11. It must be remembered that these parameter estimates are just that, estimates; they are not the "true" parameters. After all, they are bound to be revised when more observations become available. However, the estimates are close enough to the values predicted by the rational expectations hypothesis that we have to conclude there is no evidence here against rational expectations.

The third hypothesis implied by rational expectations theory is that the forecast errors should display no systematic patterns that could be used to improve inflation forecasts. To examine this hypothesis, Figure 8.7 plots actual and predicted inflation through time. Here we do find some weak evidence against rational expectations. Notice that inflation peaked in 1981, but predicted inflation peaked one year later in 1982. Prior to the peak, actual inflation was rising while predicted inflation lagged behind. Also, as inflation dropped steadily for five years in suc-

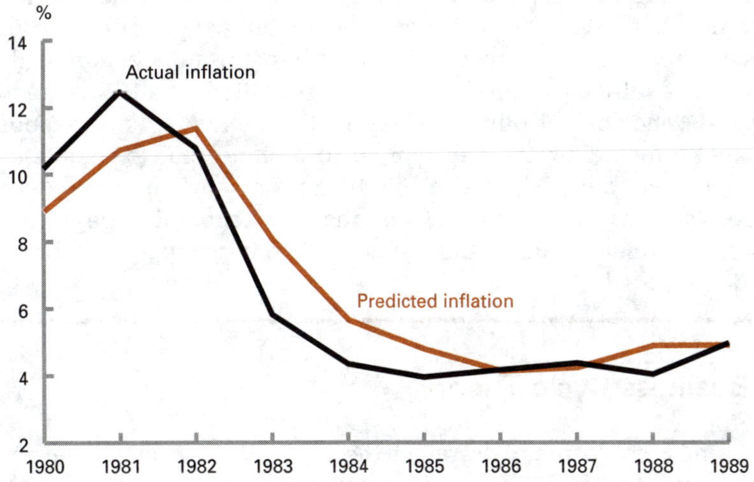

Figure 8.7 Actual and predicted inflation, 1980–89

[20] The best fit is defined in terms of the vertical distances (errors) from the line to the data points. Once a line has been drawn, it is possible to calculate the total value of all the squared errors. No other straight line has a smaller total sum of squared errors than the coloured "least squares" line.

cession, the forecasts continued to lag behind actual inflation. As we saw earlier in this chapter, this pattern is exactly what we would observe if inflation forecasts were formed adaptively. Unfortunately, there are simply insufficient observations in our sample to draw clear conclusions and we cannot argue convincingly that this evidence rejects rational expectations in favour of adaptive expectations. When someone offers you a bet on a coin toss and then proceeds to toss five tails in succession you may be convinced there is some chicanery going on. But on purely statistical grounds you would need more evidence than five tosses to convince a disinterested observer that you are playing with a cheat. On the other hand, if you have other reasons for believing the coin tosser is a cheat, five tails in a row could be very convincing.

Interestingly, researchers who have investigated the inflation expectations formation process in a more rigorous fashion have found similar results. For example, Figlewski and Wachtel found that "inflation expectations in the post-war period were formed in a manner that is inconsistent with rational expectations. . . . The adaptive expectations model is the one which best describes inflation expectations."[21] After reviewing the published evidence, Carter and Maddock conclude that "taken as a whole, the literature . . . cannot be regarded as favourable to the rational expectations hypothesis."[22]

Even though empirical studies of survey data suggest that the assumption of rational expectations perhaps should be viewed with some skepticism, it is likely that rational expectations will continue to play a significant role in macroeconomic modelling. From a theoretical perspective, it is difficult to justify *ad hoc* expectations models. When analyzing the behaviour of otherwise rational economic agents, economists are virtually forced by their discipline to assume that expectations are also formed rationally. However, this is not the same thing as assuming all markets clear instantaneously or that all economic agents possess complete information about the structure of the economy in which they make decisions.

Real Business Cycle Theory

Real business cycle theorists reject the new classical view that macroeconomic fluctuations are caused primarily by unanticipated movements in the stock of money. In many real business cycle models, the money supply plays no role whatsoever, so the distinction between anticipated

---

21 Stephen Figlewski and Paul Wachtel, "The Formation of Inflationary Expectations," *The Review of Economics and Statistics*, February 1981, p. 1.

22 M. Carter and R. Maddock, *Rational Expectations, Macroeconomics for the 1980s* (London: Macmillan, 1984), p. 126.

and unanticipated changes in the money supply cannot even arise. Rather than focusing on aggregate demand, real business cycle models see productivity shocks and shifts in aggregate supply as the root cause of business cycles. But, like the new classical model, real business cycle models maintain the assumption of continuous market-clearing and they explicitly recognize that individuals make decisions in a multi-period setting — that is, individuals make decisions in the *present* based on their current resources, information, and expectations about the *future*.

One of the major implications of this idea is that labour supply is thought to be substitutable over time. In other words, it is assumed that workers will readily work long hours when the current wage is high in relation to what it is expected to be in the future. Similarly, when the current real wage opportunities are poor in relation to what they are expected to be in the future, workers are assumed to want to work less today and consume relatively more leisure. In this way, the intertemporal substitution of labour effort explains how employment can vary so much during the business cycle, yet workers remain on their supply curves of labour. According to this view, cyclical unemployment is costly to the individual, but nevertheless voluntary.

But the most prominent aspect of real business cycle theory is the central role played by **productivity shocks**. The most frequently cited examples of productivity shocks are the dramatic oil price increases of 1973 and 1978. These price increases were engineered by the 13 member-nations of the oil cartel known as OPEC (Organization of Petroleum Exporting Countries). The price increases were enforced through production cutbacks, which looked just like productivity shocks to the rest of the world. It was as if oil wells had been lost (Kuwaiti oil wells were quite literally destroyed in 1991, but the effect of this productivity shock was offset by Saudi Arabia's increased oil production). In 1974, with less oil available, labour and capital in the importing countries became less productive. In terms of an economic model this can be depicted by downward shifts in both the aggregate production function and in the marginal productivity of labour.

The effect of a negative productivity shock on aggregate output is illustrated in Figure 8.8. The initial position is point A in all three panels. When the productivity shock strikes, the aggregate production function shifts downwards from $F_1(L)$ to $F_2(L)$. Notice that at every level of labour input, output is lower. This reflects the lower average productivity of labour. A downward shift of the production function is enough to shift the aggregate supply curve to the left. But, it is also likely that the marginal productivity of labour will decline as well. A drop in the marginal productivity of labour (MPL) is shown in the labour market by a downward shift from MPL_1 to MPL_2. Notice that in this labour market diagram, the vertical axis measures the *real* wage, not the usual nominal wage. The decline in demand for labour causes both the real wage

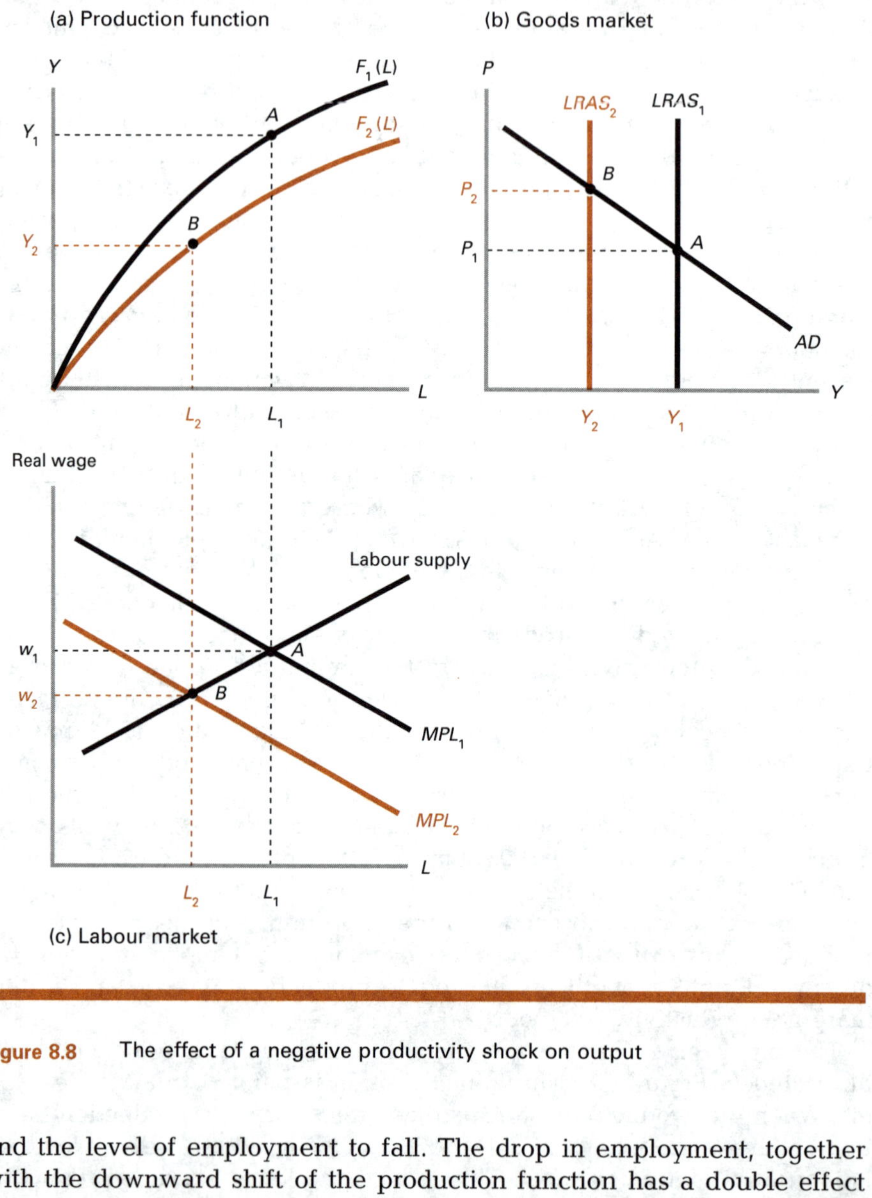

Figure 8.8 The effect of a negative productivity shock on output

and the level of employment to fall. The drop in employment, together with the downward shift of the production function has a double effect on the supply of output, which falls from Y_1 to Y_2. In the goods market, aggregate supply shifts left to $LRAS_2$, causing a decrease in output but an increase in the price level.

Unlike a negative demand shock, which reduces employment, output, and the price level, a negative supply shock is doubly unpleasant: not only is there a recession, but prices increase also. In the 1970s, when supply shocks hit massively for the first time in living memory, a new term was invented to describe the malaise: *stagflation* is the combination of economic stagnation together with inflation.

Proponents of real business cycle theory argue that productivity shocks, both large and small, positive and negative, arrive in a steady stream. It is these shocks that are primarily responsible for macroeconomic fluctuations in employment and output; not the vagaries of the money supply or random variations in the exogenous components of aggregate demand. But in a recent review article, Charles Plosser pointed out that real business cycle theory is in its infancy and will likely incorporate other influences as the literature develops:

> While real technology shocks have occupied the central focus in the literature, other shocks arising from preferences, government, terms of trade and eventually money can be included. Thus real business cycle models do not have to be confined to analyzing technological or productivity shocks. Nevertheless, real technological disturbances generate rich and neglected dynamics in the basic neoclassical model that appear to account for a substantial portion of observed fluctuations.[23]

Critics of real business cycle theory naturally attack the literature as it stands. They accept that supply shocks do occur, but reject the idea that technical reversals and advances are responsible for cyclical fluctuations; there simply are not enough examples of technical reversals to explain all of the recent economic downturns. Just as controversial is the assumption that labour supply is highly substitutable over time. To explain the substantial changes in employment during downturns in economic activity, real business cycle models assume that people are prepared to make significant voluntary adjustments to the hours they work. The motive is assumed to be driven by a willingness to work hard when the real wage is unusually high and to work much less when the real wage is unusually low. All of this adjustment is assumed to be part of ordinary optimizing behaviour. So in a recession, many people voluntarily choose to take more leisure than usual because the lower than usual real wage makes it sensible to do so.

Most Keynesians and new Keynesians reject this view of cyclical unemployment. They point to the fact that most job losses during a recession are not voluntary, but forced on workers unilaterally by firms that impose layoffs and plant closings. Gregory Mankiw summarized his recent review of real business cycle theory with these words: "My own forecast is that real business cycle advocates will not manage to produce convincing evidence that there are substantial shocks to technol-

---

23 Charles I. Plosser, "Understanding Real Business Cycles," *The Journal of Economic Perspectives*, Summer 1989, pp. 51–77.

ogy and that leisure is highly substitutable over time. Without such evidence their theories will be judged as not persuasive. . . . I predict [real business cycle theory] will ultimately be discarded as an explanation of observed fluctuations."[24]

Case Study 4: Some Evidence on Canadian Business Cycles

The quest to find the fundamental causes of business cycles has preoccupied economists for well over a hundred years. In this case study we will take a look at the Canadian evidence to see what kind of statistical support there is for the leading challengers in this fascinating competition of ideas.

In the years immediately after World War II, the memory of the "ten lost years" of the Great Depression of the 1930s was still fresh. At that time, the most persuasive and influential explanation of the depression was the *Keynesian view* of insufficient aggregate demand. As we have seen in earlier chapters, in the fixed price Keynesian model, variations in the exogenous components of aggregate demand such as investment and exports are the root cause of economic fluctuations.

The Keynesian model had its greatest influence on macroeconomic policy in the 1950s and 1960s, although even today many of the most sophisticated econometric models show considerable Keynesian influence. But in the 1970s, the simultaneous appearance of high inflation and high unemployment gave a boost to the *monetarist* argument that placed the major blame for macroeconomic fluctuations at the door of central banks: variations in the money supply are the source of the problem. Traditional monetarists, such as Milton Friedman, recognized the importance of expectations, but they took for granted that there are long reaction lags in economic affairs. Hence, even anticipated changes in the money supply would have real effects. The monetarists, as the name suggests, looked at variations in the money supply to find the cause of output fluctuations.

It was the *new classical* school that came up with the intriguing hypothesis that *fully anticipated changes* in economic policy variables would have no effect at all on output and employment. It is no surprise to new classical aficionados that this theory had such a large impact on the profession; after all, the theory itself was entirely unexpected! According to the new classical school, fluctuations in output are associated with price surprises, which are primarily due to unanticipated changes

---

[24] Gregory Mankiw, "Real Business Cycles: a New Keynesian Perspective," *Journal of Economic Perspectives*, Summer 1989, pp. 79–89.

in the money supply. Exogenous demand factors are considered to be of minor importance.

Finally, the great supply shocks of the 1970s inspired the fourth school of thought: *real business cycle* enthusiasts see a steady stream of random technological shocks hitting the economy like meteorites hitting the Earth (cynics might prefer a UFO analogy, since few people admit to seeing them). These technological shocks buffet the aggregate supply curve up and down. A straightforward implication of this view is that the price level and real output should move in opposite directions as the shifting supply curve slides up and down a stationary demand curve.

Figure 8.9 presents some evidence on each of these four contending

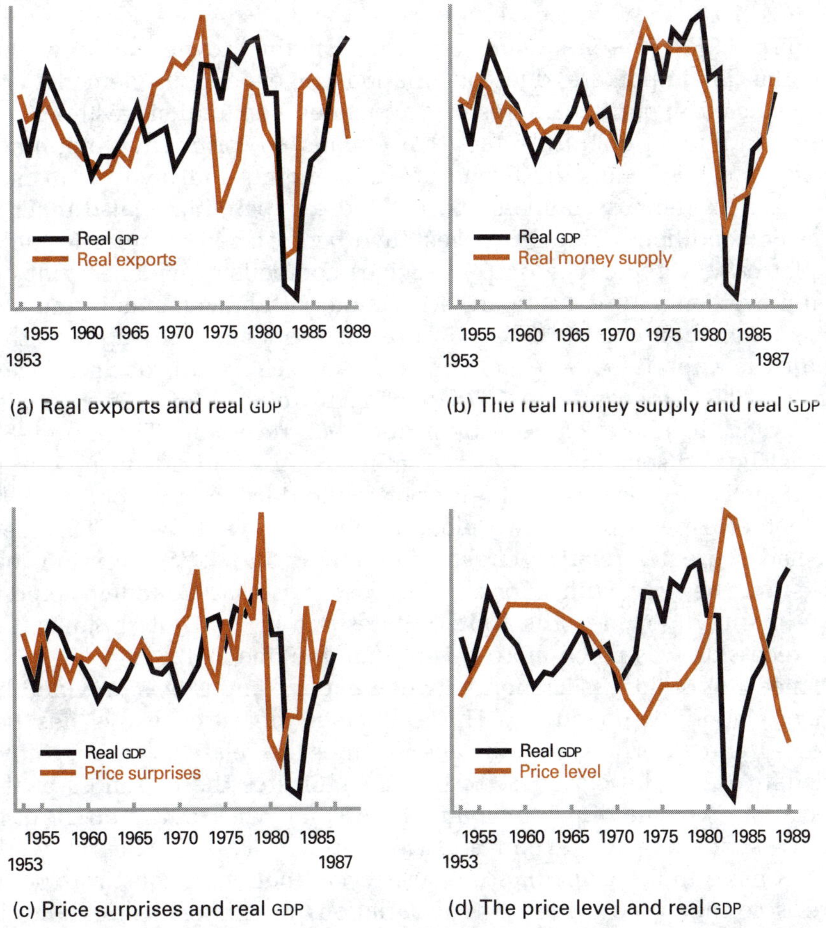

Figure 8.9 Canadian evidence on the business cycle

explanations of macroeconomic fluctuations. In each graph, the black line plots the cyclical movements in real Canadian GDP since 1953. The cyclical variations in real GDP have been isolated by subtracting the trend component of GDP from actual GDP. The major recessions are clearly visible. For example, the recession of 1970 was followed by strong growth for several years until the recession of 1974–75. There was modest growth during the remainder of the 1970s, but the collapse in 1982–83 was the deepest recession in Canada since the 1930s. From 1983 to 1990, Canadian real GDP grew strongly. Notice that the highest point on the GDP plot occurs in 1979. This simply means that GDP was further above the trend line in 1979 than it was in, say, 1989. It does not mean that GDP was higher in 1979 than in 1989. When the trend is taken into account, real GDP was actually 35 percent higher in 1989 than in 1979.

Figure 8.9(a) presents some evidence on the Keynesian view that variations in output are due to variations in exogenous demand. We have selected exports to represent exogenous demand, since there can be little argument about the fact that exports are primarily determined by factors outside Canada. Government spending and investment may well have exogenous components, but these expenditures also react to domestic conditions. The two series have been scaled in order to make the plot easy to read. The graph provides compelling evidence that cyclical movements in real GDP are associated with movements in the volume of Canadian exports. The more recent evidence also suggests that changes in exports have led changes in GDP. The sharp decline in exports in 1974 preceded the 1975 decline in total output. Exports also began their decline ahead of GDP in the 1982 recession. Then, in 1983, exports showed something of a cyclical recovery while GDP turned up in 1984. Finally, in 1989, exports fell prior to the decline in output in 1990. Some other aspects of the two plots do not fit so well. The 1982 recession had a greater relative effect on GDP than the 1975 recession, but this is not the case with exports. The reason is that Canadian exports are primarily directed to the United States and in the United States, the 1975 recession was much more severe than the one in 1982.

A measure of the association between exports and GDP is provided by the correlation coefficient, ρ. This particular measure always lies between -1 and $+1$. The sign indicates whether the relationship is positive or negative and the closeness of ρ to ± 1 indicates the closeness of the association. A value of $\rho = 0$ means there is no synchronization at all in the two series. For the export and GDP series, ρ is 0.43. Clearly, while there is more to the Canadian business cycle than variations in exports, there is considerable evidence that variations in exogenous demand do play a part.

Figure 8.9(b) turns the spotlight onto the traditional monetarist position. Along with the cyclical component of GDP, the cyclical movements of the real money supply have been plotted (the real money supply is Bank of Canada's M1 divided by the CPI). Again, to make the graphs easy to read, the two series have been scaled accordingly. In anyone's eyes this has to be an impressive plot. The patterns in the two series are very close. This is confirmed by the high positive correlation coefficient of 0.82. The issue of causality can be examined by asking which series leads the other. A careful look at the turning points provides strong evidence that changes in the real money supply precede movements in real GDP. Traditional monetarists seem to have a good case.

How do the new classical economists fair? Figure 8.9(c) presents a series that is intended to represent price surprises. There is no obviously unique way to determine what the price surprise was in 1988, or any other year. We have not tried to find out what the error is in the forecast generated by the "correct" model of the Canadian economy because we do not know what that is. Instead we have used a technique known as *time series analysis* to try to find the patterns in the Canadian CPI. These identifiable patterns can then be used to forecast the price level. The difference between the predictable component of the price series (the systematic pattern) and the actual price level, we have called the "price surprise." It must be admitted that new classical economists may disagree with the method used here because there are so many ways to estimate price surprises. In any case, the new classical theory has not been left out in the cold by our interpretation of the theory. There is a weak positive correlation between price surprises and changes in output. The correlation coefficient is a modest 0.28, which lags behind the strong performance of the real money supply and the creditable job done by exports.

Finally, we turn to the real business cycle theory. Real business cycle theorists have gone to great lengths to see how well their models can account for the co-movements of actual macroeconomic time series. We cannot possibly reproduce such efforts here. However, we can ask the simple question: Is there any evidence that macroeconomic fluctuations are due mainly to shifts in the supply curve along a (fixed) demand curve? If this is the main reason for business cycles, then the cyclical movement in the price level should be opposite to the cyclical movement in output — the economy is simply moving up and down the aggregate demand curve.

Figure 8.9(d) shows the graph of cyclical movements in GDP together with the cyclical movements in the price level. The graph is immediately striking in its support for the real business cycle theory. The cyclical components of the price level and real GDP are indeed negatively related, just as a supply-side theory would suggest. The correlation coefficient is –0.69. In absolute terms, this measure ranks second only to the correlation coefficient between the cyclical component of real money supply and the cyclical component of real output.

What we have presented here is little more than casual evidence. The academic journals present much more sophisticated analyses of these important questions. But our findings do illustrate an important lesson. Despite the very different predictions that are implied by the alternative theories, it is not as easy as one might expect to sort them out by an appeal to the facts. In a simple way, we have found some degree of support for all four theories. Just think how much better each would look in the hands of its supporters! Armed with their own theories, a common set of facts and a battery of fancy statistical methods, the combatants are sure to continue the debate over what really causes business cycles.

Summary

The main focus of this chapter has been on the important role played by expectations in macroeconomic modelling. Since the decisions that firms and workers take in the present depend crucially on the the current information they possess and their expectations about the future, it is not surprising that macroeconomists have devoted so much attention to modelling expectations.

We began this chapter by developing the price surprise supply function (*PSSF*), which shows explicitly how last period's expectations about the current price level affect aggregate supply in the current period. In this development, the way in which firms and workers form their price expectations was left open (price expectations were simply taken to be exogenous). The main contribution of this section was to explain why the short-run aggregate supply curve is upward-sloping, that is, why more output is produced the higher is the current price level.

Since it is not at all satisfactory to assume price expectations are exogenous, we then considered the two major models that explain how expectations are formed, namely the adaptive and rational expectations schemes. An impressive feature of the adaptive expectations model is that it can explain why macroeconomic disturbances frequently have persistent effects. The key is that under adaptive expectations, economic agents learn to adapt to new circumstances slowly. However, adaptive expectations suffer from some conceptual difficulties. The main point is that economic agents who are assumed to act rationally when making economic choices should also act rationally when they form expectations about the future. In other words, expectations should be based on all the relevant information that is available to economic agents. An important piece of information that is ignored by adaptive expectations but is incorporated into rational expectations is the structure of the economy. To the extent that workers and firms understand how the economy functions, this knowledge is useful in forming economic predictions (expectations).

Within a theoretical model, explicit assumptions must be made about what information economic agents have at their disposal. In rational expectations modelling, firms and workers are assumed to know how the economy functions (they are aware of the equations that describe the economy). In such a world, we have seen that all anticipated changes in government policy variables have no effect on output and employment. This is the famous policy ineffectiveness proposition (PIP), which has been so controversial. After discussing some criticisms of the rational expectations hypothesis, we examined some evidence on Canadian expectations of future inflation. A least squares test indicated that we could not reject the rational expectations hypothesis. However, the pattern of forecast errors looked very much like the patterns that are typical of adaptive expectations. Unfortunately, the data were too few to yield firm conclusions.

Finally, we discussed real business cycle theory, which suggests that the main cause of business cycles is a steady stream of productivity shocks that shift aggregate supply. In a case study we found evidence to support four alternative theories of the business cycle and concluded that it is not as straightforward as we might hope to distinguish between sharply different theories of the macroeconomy.

Appendix: The Signal Extraction Problem and The New Classical Theory of Aggregate Supply

In the new classical model, product and labour markets are disaggregated into local markets. Aggregate supply response is the sum of the supply responses in individual local markets. As in the classical model, all markets are assumed to clear at all times. But unlike the classical model, the new classical model allows for a positively sloped short-run aggregate supply curve. This important difference rests on two elements of the new classical model. The first is that firms and workers calculate the real wage in different ways. This allows for a spread between the real wage paid by firms and the real wage that workers estimate they are getting. Whenever this spread exits, employment deviates from the natural level. The second feature is the role of information. Participants in a given local market are assumed to have current information on local conditions only. On the other hand, economy-wide information is revealed with a one-period lag. Since workers are assumed to purchase goods from all markets, workers are concerned about the aggregate price level. But given the above assumption concerning the availability of information, they are not aware of the current aggregate price level when labour supply decisions are made and therefore they must settle for the best estimate they can make.

Firm and Worker Behaviour

Firms in the ith market sell their product for p_i. Given the local nominal wage w_i, firms maximize profits by hiring labour up to the point where the marginal product of labour equals the real wage w_i/p_i. Workers in the ith market receive the nominal wage w_i, but they purchase goods from all markets. Consequently, a worker's real wage is w_i/P, where P is the aggregate price level.

The Information Set

At time t, the information available to agents in the ith market consists of w_i and p_i plus all variables realized in period $t - 1$ and earlier. The key problem facing workers is to make the best possible estimate of the general price level P, given the information available. We will focus on the information embodied in the currently observable local price p_i. To see how the local price contains information about the general price level P, consider how prices are determined in the local market.

Price Determination in the ith Market

Figure 8.10(a) illustrates supply and demand schedules in the ith market. The equilibrium price is random because demand is random. The randomness has both a local and a global (economy-wide) component. Local shocks u affect only the local demand curve and only the local price p_i. Global shocks v affect prices in all markets equally. The local price p_i can be expressed as

$$p_i = p^* + u + v \tag{8A.1}$$

where u is a local shock and v is a global shock. We assume that through time the average values of u and v are both zero. In statistics, the average is referred to as the expected value, so we are assuming that $Eu = Ev = 0$, where E stands for the "expected value of." These assumptions imply that through time, the average price in the ith market is simply p^*. Before the random disturbances are drawn, the expected price in the ith market is therefore p^*, that is, $Ep_i = p^*$. This prediction is hardly ever correct, but because there is no more reason to expect prices will be above average than to expect they will be below average, one assumes they will be average. The "average situation" is

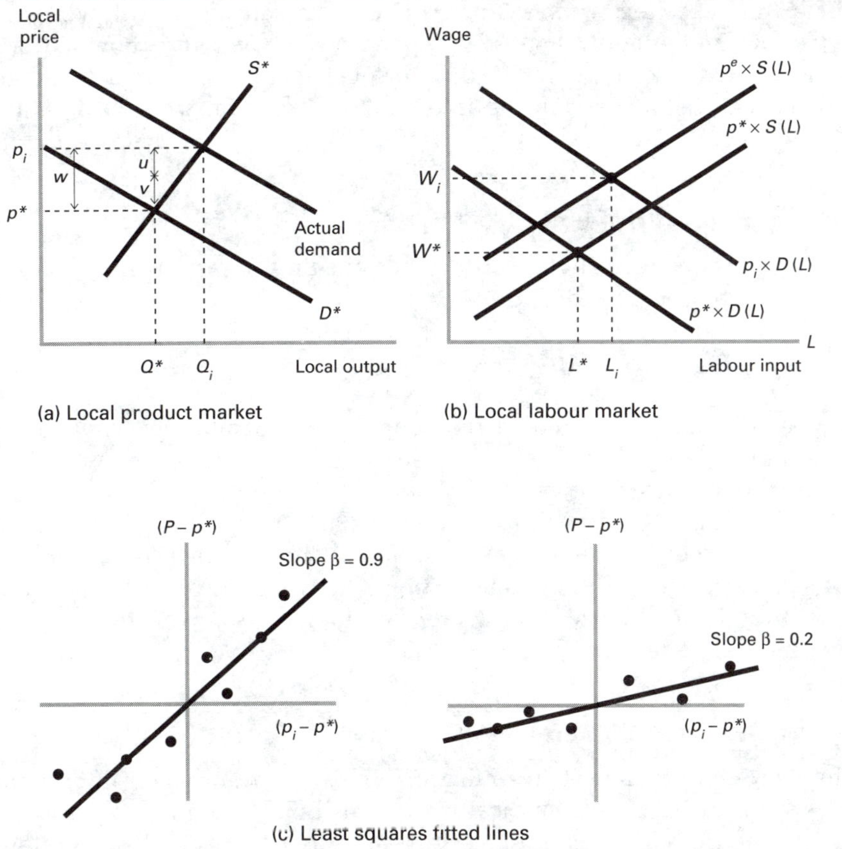

Figure 8.10 The signal extraction problem and the new classical theory of aggregate supply

depicted by the expected demand and supply curves, D^* and S^* in Figure 8.10(a). The actual demand curve for a particular period is also shown. It is displaced above the expected demand curve as a result of the two random disturbances.

It is important to be clear about what people can observe in the *i*th market. p^* is known from experience, since p^* is the average price over time. In the current period p_i is also known. From these data, the *sum* of the random disturbances, say *w*, can be deduced: $w = u + v = p^* - p_i$. But there is no way to know with certainty the individual values of *u* and *v*. In practical terms, workers who observe an increase in the price of the product they make do not know whether this is due to an increase in the demand for that product alone (a local shock) or whether there has been a general increase in demand (due to a global shock).

For example, when we see house prices rising in our own town, we do not know immediately if this is happening all over the province or all over the country. It might be due to local factors or global (economy-wide) factors. Later, when the information comes in, we will be able to distinguish these influences.

The Aggregate Price Level

The aggregate price level P in the current time period is defined to be the average of all the local price levels:

$$P = E(p_i) = E(p^* + u + v) = p^* + v \tag{8A.2}$$

Notice that when we take the average over all markets at a point in time, only the local shocks cancel out. This is because there will be as many negative as positive local shocks throughout the economy. But at any given time, there is only one global shock v and this affects all local prices in exactly the same way. The global shock, which is embodied in every local price, therefore shows up in the general price level P. Over time, the global shocks also average out to zero. So, over time the average general price level is p^*.

The Signal Extraction Problem

The workers' problem is to estimate P based on the known information, p_i and p^*. Equation 8A.2 indicates that this boils down to estimating the size of the global shock v, since this alone is responsible for the deviation of the current general price level from its average value of p^*. A naive approach would be for a worker in the ith market to simply assume that the local shock in his market u is zero. After all, the average value of u over time is zero. Under this assumption, the worker would simply argue that the deviation of the general price level P from p^* is the same as the deviation of p_i from p^*. The expected general price level would simply equal the observed local price level: $P^e = p_i$.

But the worker can do much better than this naive approach. The reason is that whenever the local price is above average, the chances are greater than 50 percent that the local shock is positive. Hence, it does not make sense to assume that u is zero when it is known that $p_i > p^*$. But whenever $p_i > p^*$, the chances are that the global shock is positive too. (Who would systematically bet on a negative shock every time $p_i > p^*$ is observed?) In other words, when one observes $p_i > p^*$, the best guess is that both P and p_i are greater than p^*. Since it is likely that both u and v are positive (when $p_i > p^*$), then $P - p^* = u$ is probably only a fraction of $p_i - p^* = u + v$. Suppose this fraction is β, where $0 < \beta < 1$, then we can write

$$P - p^* = \beta(p_i - p^*) \tag{8A.3}$$

Once β is known or estimated, Equation 8A.3 can be used to generate the rational expectations price forecast by substituting P^e for P and taking p^* to the right-hand side:[25]

$$P^e = p^* + \beta(p_i - p^*) \tag{8A.4}$$

The remaining issue is the estimation of β. This can be done with historical data on P and p_i. One simply plots the deviations $(P - p^*)$ and $(p_i - p^*)$ as illustrated in Figure 8.10(c). The slope of the least squares line is an estimate of β, which reveals the historical relationship between the global and local price deviations around p^*. The fitted line can be used to generate predictions. Given an observed $(p_i - p^*)$ on the horizontal axis, the fitted line defines a corresponding predicted point on the vertical axis, which we would label $(P^e - p^*)$. The predictions generated this way are consistent with Equations 8A.3 and 8A.4.

One last point concerns the factors that determine the value of β. In the left-hand panel of Figure 8.10(c), β is close to unity. This situation comes about when most of the variations of local prices around p^* are due to *global* shocks, that is, local shocks are typically very small. In this case, the deviation of P about p^* will be very close to the deviation of p_i about p^*. The right-hand panel of Figure 8.10(c) illustrates the case in which *local* shocks play a big role in local price movements. In this second case, a positive local price deviation is not very informative about global shocks; the typically smaller global shocks are hard to pick out of local price movements. Consequently, even large positive local price deviations lead to expectations of only small global deviations — β is small.

Implications for Aggregate Supply

In this appendix we have presented an alternative model of expectations formation at the microeconomic level that implies a positively sloped price surprise supply function at the aggregate level. Figure 8.10(b) illustrates the *i*th local labour market. The typical situation is described by variables marked with an asterisk. Consider the effect of an increase in the money supply. This positive global shock will increase product demand in every local market. But in the current period, assume that the money supply is not observable, nor is the complete set

[25] If the random shocks u and v are normally distributed, then it can be shown formally that Equation 8A.4 does give the best unbiased predictor of the price level. The best unbiased predictor is generally given by the conditional mean or the regression function. The importance of the normal distribution is that it results in a linear regression function; that is, the prediction equation is linear.

of market prices. Workers and firms see only that the local market price has increased. This encourages firms to increase the nominal wage offer in proportion to the increase in the local price — the demand for labour schedule shifts upwards. As we have seen, the position of the labour supply schedule depends on the general price level, which is assumed to increase as well, but only by a fraction, β, of the increase in the local price. Hence, labour supply shifts upwards less than demand. The smaller is β, the smaller is the upward shift in labour supply. Workers perceive the real wage they receive W_i/P^e to be higher than the real wage firms are paying W_i/p_i, and employment increases to L_i.

Clearly the increase in employment and output in the *i*th market depends on β. If there were never any local shocks, β would be unity because everyone would know that all local price movements are due to global shocks that produce identical changes in the general price level. In this case, labour demand and supply shift upwards through the same distance and there would be no effect on output when the money supply increases. But if local shocks mask the influence of global shocks, β is less than one and there are positive effects on employment and output in every local market. In the aggregate, there is an upward-sloping price surprise supply curve. Its slope depends on the relative importance of global and local shocks as summarized by the parameter β.

Key Concepts

price surprise supply function
adaptive expectations
rational expectations
policy ineffectiveness proposition
real business cycle theory
productivity shocks
signal extraction problem

Review Questions

1. Explain how the price surprise supply function is derived. How does this framework account for the positive relationship between the current price level and the current supply of output?
2. Explain the idea of adaptive expectations and write down an equation that describes this concept. Show that an adaptive expectation

can be expressed as a weighted average of the previous expectation and the previous actual value. Finally, show how an adaptive forecast can be expressed in terms of the entire past history of the series in question.

3. Use a diagram to show how a permanent macroeconomic shock (such as an increase in the money supply) leads to a gradual process of adjustment when expectations are formed adaptively.
4. Outline the main conceptual difficulties that economists have with the concept of adaptive expectations.
5. Describe the concept of rational expectations. What is its relationship to the policy ineffectiveness proposition?
6. Outline the assumptions the rational expectations model makes about the information economic agents possess. Critically evaluate these assumptions.
7. Describe some implications of the rational expectations hypothesis that could be used to test this hypothesis.
8. Outline the basic features of the real business cycle theory.
9. Describe some predictions that follow from these theories of the business cycle: the traditional Keynesian theory, the monetarist theory, the new classical theory, and the real business cycle theory. How would you analyze macroeconomic data in an attempt to distinguish between these theories?

CHAPTER 9

Policy Options for Supply and Demand Shocks

> *Most economists now more or less agree that aggregate demand policies should not permit the unemployment rate to fall below its natural, or its nonaccelerating, inflation rate for any length of time. But whether unemployment should be allowed to rise above its natural rate in the presence of a price shock from the supply side — and by how much and for how long — is a much more difficult question.*
>
> *Edward M. Gramlich*[1]

Sources of Instability Within the Economy

The most convenient way to categorize the numerous economic disturbances that strike the economy is to distinguish between **demand shocks** and **supply shocks**. As we have seen in earlier chapters, the demand side of the model is derived from the *IS-LM* diagram, which synthesizes the money market and the expenditure decisions of firms, households, government, and foreigners. Any macroeconomic disturbance that impacts in the *IS-LM* diagram is classified as a demand shock because such disturbances cause shifts in the aggregate demand curve. Demand shocks can be further categorized depending on whether the disturbance is due to a change in an *exogenous variable* in one of the *IS-LM* equations or whether the shock is due to a change in one of the *behavioural parameters*. For example, the level of exports and autonomous investment are two *exogenous* variables that shift the *IS* curve. If either of these were to increase, the *IS* and aggregate de-

---

1 Edward M. Gramlich, "Macro Policy Responses to Price Supply Shocks," *Brookings Papers on Economic Activity*, vol. 1, 1979, pp. 125–66.

mand curves would shift to the right and the repercussions would involve changes in all of the endogenous variables within the model. Similarly, the effect of an increase in the money supply (an exogenous variable under the control of the Bank of Canada) would be to shift the aggregate demand curve to the right, although the reaction results from a shift of the *LM* curve rather than the *IS* curve.

The second type of demand shock results from changes in *behavioural* parameters. For example, if consumers were to become more thrifty, the marginal propensity to consume declines and the aggregate demand curve shifts to the left. Alternatively, if the income elasticity of the demand for money balances were to decrease, the *LM* curve would shift downwards (while rotating counter-clockwise) and the aggregate demand curve would shift out to the right.

Since demand shocks shift the aggregate demand curve, naturally, all disturbances that cause shifts in the aggregate supply curve are categorized as **supply shocks**. In the last two chapters, we have seen that aggregate supply has its foundations in the labour market and the aggregate production function. Consequently, supply shocks can be traced back to shifts in the supply or demand for labour or to shifts in the aggregate production function. For example, if attitudes towards work and leisure change, then the supply of labour schedule will shift. This will have an effect on employment, the real wage, and aggregate supply. As discussed in the previous chapter, real business cycle theorists emphasize the importance of technological shocks that shift the aggregate production function up or down. Such shocks obviously have a direct effect on labour productivity and the aggregate supply curve. (Evidence on the cyclical behaviour of Canadian labour productivity will be presented below.) Another important source of supply shocks are the international commodity markets. In previous chapters we have assumed that firms produce output by employing labour and capital. In practice, firms also use material inputs. When the prices of imported raw materials rise, this adds to the costs of production for Canadian firms and causes the aggregate supply curve to shift. The troubling experiences of the 1970s demonstrated that the unemployment and inflation consequences of supply-price shocks are very difficult for policymakers to deal with.

The main purpose of this chapter is to use the aggregate supply and demand framework that has been developed in the two previous chapters to analyze how supply and demand shocks affect the Canadian economy. The model will also be used to examine the alternative stabilization policies that can be used to counteract supply and demand shocks. Traditional Keynesian analysis focused on the problems of demand shocks and much of the early debates were concerned with the issue of whether the government could or should try to achieve low rates of unemployment by controlling aggregate demand. In the past two decades, the more difficult problems associated with supply shocks have gained greater recognition. Before launching into the theory of macroeconomic policy, let us first look at the empirical evidence on macroeconomic shocks.

Illustrations of Demand Shocks

To give some idea of the importance of demand shocks for the Canadian economy, Figures 9.1 and 9.2 show the real rates of growth of the major components of aggregate demand between 1960 and 1990. The growth of the real money supply is also depicted. Summary statistics for the annual percentage changes in these demand variables are presented in Table 9.1.

Figure 9.1 illustrates the behaviour of three components of business investment, as well as total investment. Figure 9.2 presents the same kind of information for other important macroeconomic variables. By comparing the graphs and examining Table 9.1, it is clear that investment expenditures exhibit by far and away the greatest instability of all the components of aggregate demand. A measure of the instability of investment is provided by the range covered by the annual percentage changes. For example, changes in residential construction activity fall within the bounds of –16.3 to 18 percent — a range of 34.3 percentage points. Changes in total investment activity fall within a span of 29.3 percentage points. Not only is the range of fluctuations wide, but changes in investment expenditures frequently come close to the limits of the range. For example, there was a strong surge of investment expenditures in the mid-1960s — the time when baby boom children placed great demands on housing and schools. In the four-year period from 1963 to 1966, total business investment grew at an average rate of 9.75 percent, which is well above the economy's long-term capacity for growth. But the instability of investment is not just a feature of the distant past. Some of the wildest fluctuations have occurred in the 1980s. In 1982 real spending on residential construction fell a whopping 16.3 percent, while investment in machinery and equipment fell 14 percent. Then in 1983, there was a tremendous rebound in residential construction activity which pushed this component of demand up by over 16 percent.

Investment is not the only component of aggregate demand that shows great volatility. International trade is an extremely important component of the Canadian economy which makes the instability of exports especially important to Canadian aggregate demand. Between 1960 and 1990, annual changes in Canadian exports varied over the range from –6.8 to 17.7 percent. The instability shown by investment and exports is in dramatic contrast to the other components of demand, such as the expenditures of households and gov-

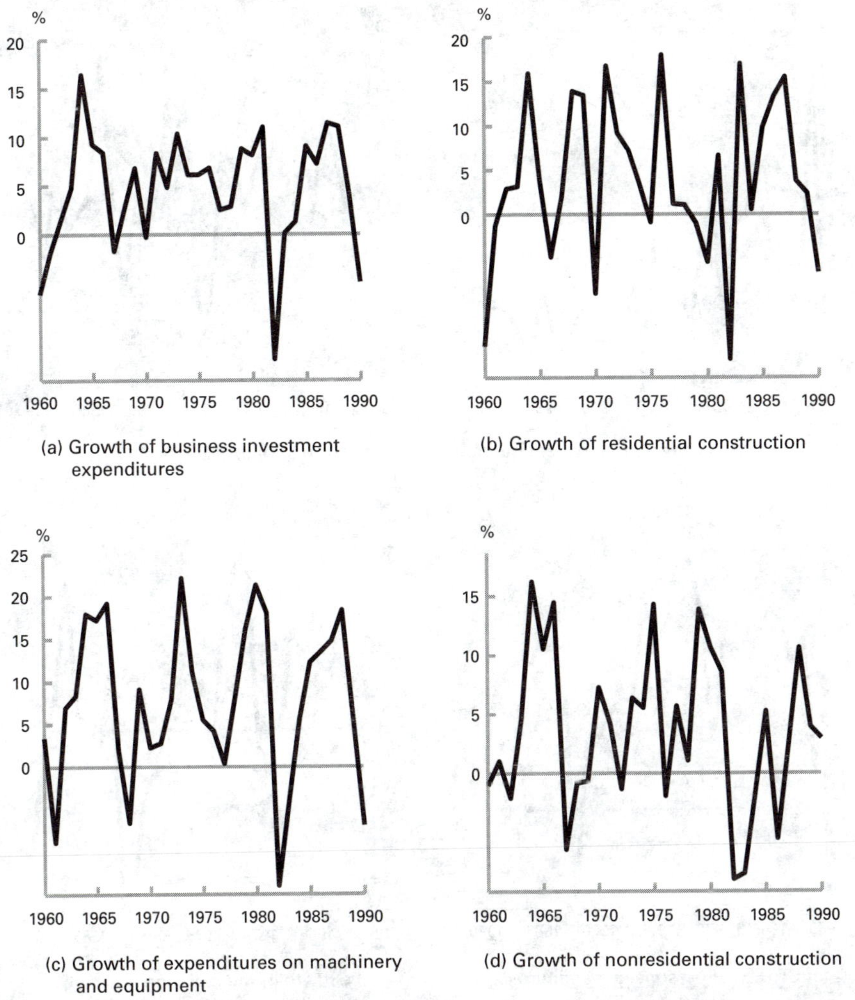

Figure 9.1 Fluctuations in the components of investment

ernment. Personal expenditure (consumption) is the largest component of demand. Since 1960, annual changes in real consumption spending have been confined to the narrow range of –2.7 to 7.5 percent. Indeed one could argue that consumption spending acts as a stabilizer since it varies less than real GDP. Consumption tends to smooth out the business cycle. During a recession when aggregate demand is low, con-

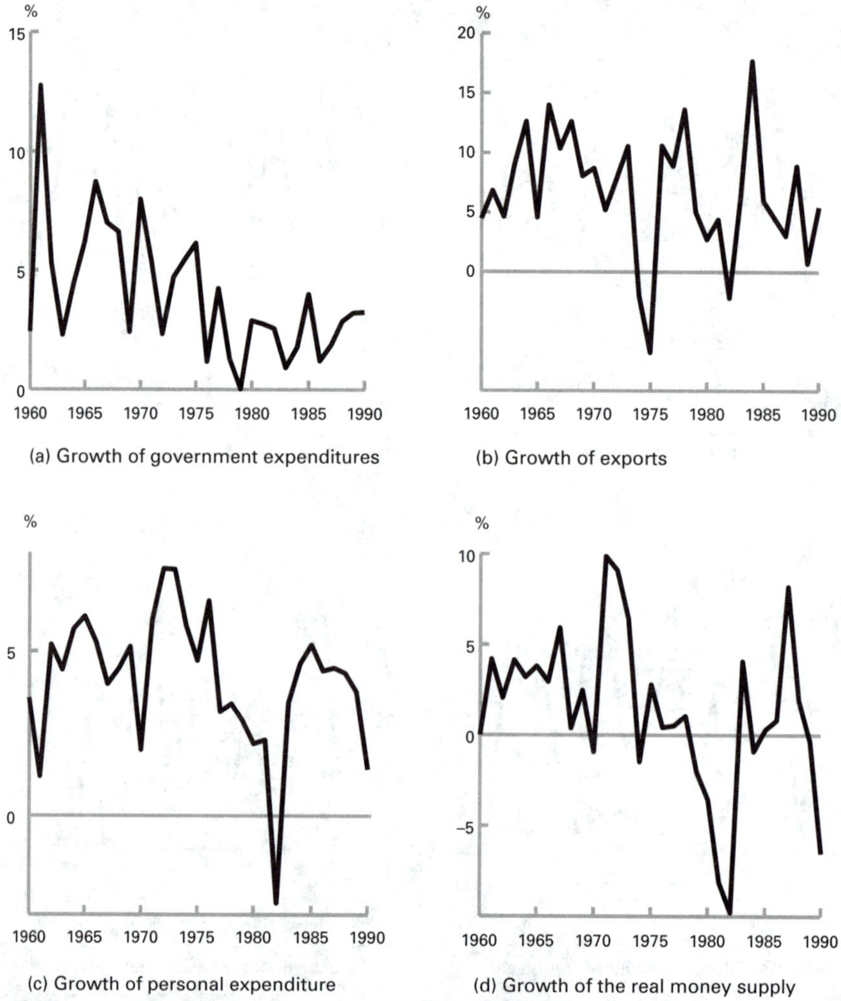

Figure 9.2 Fluctuations in demand variables

sumption accounts for a larger share of total demand than normal.[2] Conversely, at the peak of the business cycle, when most components of demand are at unusually high levels, consumption accounts for a smaller than average share of total expenditure. Government spending

2 A complete discussion of consumption is presented in Chapter 16.

has also been fairly stable. One of the more interesting features of Figure 9.2 is that the growth of government spending has been both reduced and stabilized during the past 30 years.

The other variable that is controlled by government (through the Bank of Canada) is the money supply. Figure 9.2 shows how the real money supply (M1 divided by the consumer price index) has changed on an annual basis. Of course, the Bank of Canada has direct control of the *nominal* money supply, not the *real* money supply. However, by making forecasts of the price level, the Bank of Canada can try to predict what the real money supply will be. Since it is the real stock of money that determines the position of the *LM* curve, our attention will focus on the real rather than the nominal stock of money. As Figure 9.2 and Table 9.1 indicate, the real money supply has grown rapidly in some years, thereby shifting the *LM* curve to the right, and declined in others, shifting the *LM* curve to the left.

With annual data it is difficult to be precise about the actual timing of events during business cycles. However, it seems that changes in the real money supply do precede changes in real GDP. For example, the rapid growth of real GDP in the early 1970s, which began in 1971 and peaked in 1973, was accompanied by an extraordinary surge in the real money supply in 1971. This was followed by two more years of strong, but somewhat slower monetary expansion. Similarly, the real money supply fell in 1974 and one year later, the growth of output was at its cyclical low point. The 1982 recession provides a more dramatic example. The real money supply fell four years in succession (1979, 1980, 1981, and 1982) before rebounding in 1983. The growth of real GDP fluctuated in the years 1979 to 1981, but collapsed in 1982.

Table 9.1 Percent Changes in Demand Variables, 1960-90

	Average Annual Change	Minimum Annual Change	Maximum Annual Change	Range of Annual Changes
	%	%	%	%
Business investment	4.6	–12.8	16.5	29.3
Residential construction	3.9	–16.3	18.0	34.3
Nonresidential construction	3.6	– 9.0	16.2	25.2
Machinery & equipment	7.5	– 9.3	14.0	23.3
Exports	6.6	– 6.8	17.7	24.5
Government expenditures	4.0	0.0	12.8	12.8
Personal consumption	4.1	– 2.7	7.5	10.2
Real money supply	1.2	– 9.8	9.9	19.7

Of course, changes in the real stock of money are the result of two factors, namely the change in the nominal stock of money and the change in the price level. The Bank of Canada does not have direct control over the price level, so it may be that some declines in the real stock of money are not fully anticipated by the Bank of Canada. At other times, the Bank of Canada may consciously reduce the real stock of money in order to fight inflation. But whether declines in the real stock of money are planned or unplanned, such declines do shift the *LM* curve leftwards, giving the economy a negative demand shock.

In summary, the Canadian economy has experienced considerable instability in aggregate demand and the *IS* and *LM* curves have been buffeted about by substantial and frequent demand shocks. Figures 9.1 and 9.2 show that the variations in investment expenditures and exports are primarily responsible for the shifts in the *IS* curve. There is no evidence to suggest that these shocks are getting any smaller through time. However, the growth of government spending has become slower and more stable. The same cannot be said about monetary policy. Despite all the rhetoric about the importance of monetary stability, the real money supply (as measured by M1) has demonstrated greater instability in the last 15 years compared to the period between 1960 and 1975.

From the Great Depression of the 1930s (see Chapter 4) to the boom and bust cycles of the 1970s and 1980s, the Canadian economy has been subjected to strong negative and positive demand shocks. Since the adverse unemployment effects of a temporary negative demand shock are much more obvious than the inflationary effects of a temporary positive demand shock, we will focus our policy analysis on negative demand shocks. After considering the effects of both Keynesian and monetarist policy approaches for negative demand shocks, we then turn to the difficulties posed by supply shocks. First, we look at some empirical evidence on supply shocks.

Illustrations of Supply Shocks

Shocks or disturbances that enter our model via the labour market, the production function, or the price of material inputs all affect Canadian costs of production and hence cause shifts in the aggregate supply curve. At critical times in the 1970s, price changes in internationally traded commodities and raw materials had a major effect on the Canadian economy. Professor Alan Blinder[3] has called the years 1973 and 1974 "the years of the great exogenous price shocks." The trouble started in 1972 with a rash of poor harvests throughout the world. The

3 Alan S. Blinder, *Economic Policy and the Great Stagflation* (Academic Press, 1979), p. 36.

price of wheat in the international commodity markets jumped 9.5 percent; rice, sugar, and cocoa prices rose even more sharply, posting increases that averaged over 20 percent. With the world economy booming, there were widespread fears that resources in general would soon be in short supply. The world economic expansion continued in 1973, and brought with it an unprecedented price explosion that affected almost all commodities and raw materials. In 1973 the world prices of wheat, rice, cocoa, rubber, logs, and zinc more than doubled on average over 1972 price levels. Copper and cotton prices rose 65 percent. In 1974 the recessionary effects of the price shocks were being felt and this had a dampening influence on the commodity price explosion. Nevertheless, some prices continued to soar well into 1974. World sugar prices almost tripled that year and the price of tin shot up 70 percent.

The most infamous price shock of all was the explosion of world oil prices. In the fall of 1973, 13 oil exporting nations, known collectively as the Organization of Petroleum Exporting Countries — OPEC, took advantage of the Arab oil embargo that was imposed during the Arab–Israeli war. OPEC flexed its monopoly muscles and quadrupled the world price of oil. In the United States the effect was muted somewhat because the overall oil price is a blend of world and domestic prices. But the impact was still substantial. Blinder reports that in the four months between October 1973 and February 1974, the price of crude oil rose about $1.00 U.S. per month, from about $4.50 per barrel to $8.50 per barrel.[4] The increase in oil prices quickly spilled over into other fuel prices, raising the price of energy in general.

Figure 9.3(a) illustrates the annual rate of change in the price of Canadian imports. The effects of the commodity price explosions of the early 1970s are clearly visible: in 1974 import prices rose 20 percent and climbed a further 14.6 percent in 1975. The effect of such dramatic price increases is to raise the costs of Canadian firms. Whenever costs increase, profit-maximizing firms must raise the price at which they sell goods and services. As we will see later, the effect of increased material prices is to shift the inelastic long-run aggregate supply curve to the left while short-run elastic supply curves shift upwards.

Figure 9.3(b) illustrates the annual percentage change in labour productivity, as measured by the ratio of real GDP to the number of employed persons. Real business cycle theorists such as Edward Prescott claim that variations in productivity are the result of exogenous advances and setbacks in technology.[5] The Canadian data reveal substantial variations in labour productivity and these variations are *procyclical.*

---

4 Ibid., p. 78.

5 Edward Prescott, "Theory Ahead of Business Cycle Measurement," *Carnegie-Rochester Conference on Public Policy*, Autumn 1986, 25, pp. 11–44.

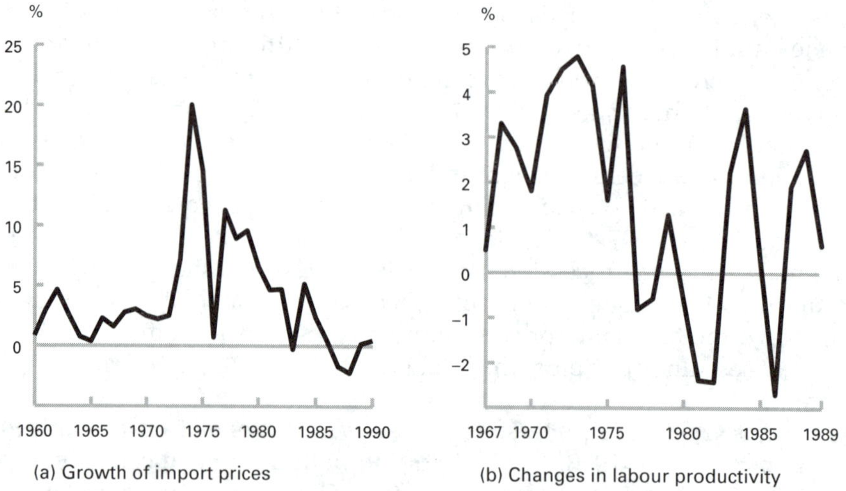

Figure 9.3 Illustrations of supply shocks

For example, labour productivity grew rapidly in the economic expansion of the early 1970s and fell just as sharply in the 1974–75 recession. In the recession of the early 1980s, labour productivity continued to decline three years in a row (1980–82) before rebounding during the subsequent economic expansion. But whether these variations in labour productivity are due to exogenous technological shocks is a moot point. Mankiw argues that the procyclical behaviour of productivity can be more reasonably explained as observations that are "off the production function."[6] He suggests that "productivity appears to fall in recession because firms keep unnecessary and underutilized labor. In a boom the hoarded laborers begin to put out greater effort; output increases without a large increase in measured labour input." In other words, a cyclical decline in labour productivity does not mean the economy has suffered an exogenous technological reversal; more likely firms have cut output because demand has declined. Further, it may be profitable to "hoard" skilled labour rather than let people go when demand falls. As a result, labour productivity declines during recessions and expands rapidly during economic recovery. If Edward Prescott is correct, the variations in labour productivity are exogenous and should be classified as supply shocks. If Mankiw is right, cyclical changes in labour produc-

---

[6] N. Gregory Mankiw, "Real Business Cycles: A New Keynesian Perspective," *Journal of Economic Perspectives*, Summer 1989, pp. 79–90.

tivity are endogenous responses to some other kind of exogenous shock, such as a decline in demand.

Stabilization Policy Options for a Negative Demand Shock

In this section we will examine the policy options that are available to the government when the economy is hit by a negative demand shock. Essentially, there are two alternatives. The traditional Keynesian position has been that demand shocks are often severe enough to warrant intervention in the business cycle to offset the negative demand shock, thereby mitigating the unemployment effects. Critics in the monetarist and new classical camps have argued that trying to smooth out the business cycle is a fool's game that typically ends up making things worse. The government simply cannot know enough and act quickly enough to steer the economy along a smooth path. The consequences of these two alternative policies will be examined in the context of the wage–contract model that was developed in Chapter 7. The wage–contract model explicitly recognizes that nominal wages are typically fixed in the short run under the terms of a labour contract. As discussed in Chapter 7, some wage contracts allow for limited cost-of-living adjustments during the contract. In the last part of this section, we will examine how these so-called COLA contracts affect the economy's response to a demand shock.

Keynesian Countercyclical Policies

The case for **Keynesian countercyclical policy** intervention is illustrated in Figure 9.4. Before the first period opens, firms and workers have expectations about the state of aggregate demand and the price level. In Figure 9.4(b), the expected position of the *AD* curve is at AD_1^e, which intersects the inelastic long-run aggregate supply curve at point *A*. Both firms and workers expect the price level to be P_1^e in the first period. The labour market is shown in Figure 9.4(a). Given the expected price level P_1^e, the nominal wage is set at $\overline{W}_1$ for the duration of the first-period contract. As we discussed in Chapter 7, there is a short-run aggregate supply (*SRAS*) curve passing through point *A* in the product market diagram. The *SRAS* curve is labelled $SRAS(\overline{W}_1)$ to indicate that its position is conditional on the fixed wage $\overline{W}_1$.

Now consider what happens when there is a negative demand shock in the first period. Instead of being at AD_1^e, the actual aggregate demand curve shifts leftwards to AD_1. There are many possible explanations for the unexpectedly low level of aggregate demand. Some discouraging news may have caused firms to invest less than expected, or foreign markets may have weakened, causing exports to fall. What-

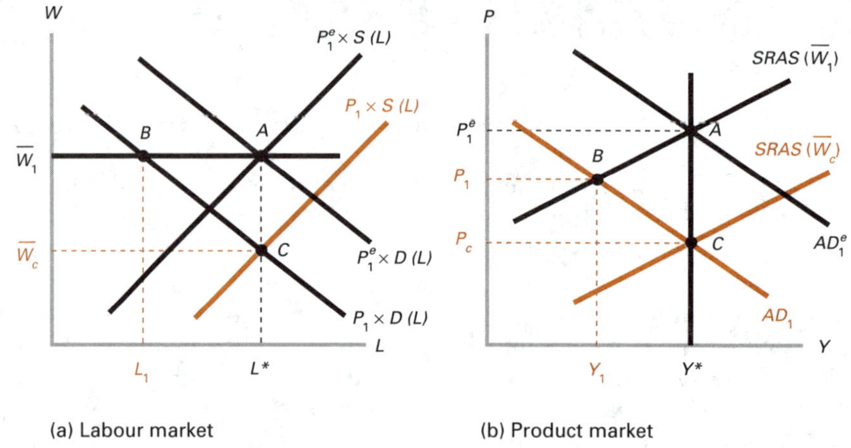

Figure 9.4 Policy options for demand shocks

ever the cause, the equilibrium position during the first period is at point B. The price level is P_1 and the level of output is Y_1, which is below the natural level of Y^*.

The implications for the labour market are shown in Figure 9.4(a). The lower price level P_1 causes the demand for labour schedule to shift down to $P_1 \times D(L)$. During the first period, nominal wages are fixed at $\overline{W}_1$, and since firms determine the level of employment, employment falls to L_1. The decline in employment is responsible for the decline in output to Y_1 (see Figure 9.4(b)). At point B there are a number of workers who are unexpectedly and involuntarily unemployed. The wage contract had been signed with the expectation that employment would be maintained at the natural level L^*, but events have not turned out as well as expected. There are hundreds of thousands of newly unemployed people who are willing and able to work at the going wage rate. In all democratic societies, the economic performance of the government depends to a large extent on its unemployment record. Consequently, governments come under considerable pressure to take active measures to increase economic activity and reduce unemployment.

Keynesian economists have traditionally had considerable sympathy with this argument. Since the lost output and the social costs of unemployment (increased family tensions and crime) are so great, many people believe the government should do what it can to alleviate the consequences of a recession and even take action to avoid or end a recession. The most obvious tactic is to try to shift the aggregate demand curve back to the right. This could be achieved by a number of measures. For example, the government could urge the Bank of Canada to adopt an expansionary monetary policy that would lower interest rates and stimulate interest-sensitive components of aggregate demand, such as business investment and consumer expenditures on durable goods. Within the *IS-LM* model, this policy would shift the *LM* and aggregate demand curves to the right. Traditional Keynesians have generally not supported this kind of demand management policy because it was felt that monetary policy would not be effective in stimulating demand. If expenditures are not interest-sensitive, then monetary policy has little effect. This view is not nearly so popular today partly because interest rates are much higher and more variable than they were in the early post-war period. It is now generally accepted that monetary policy and the level of interest rates have a significant effect on aggregate expenditures.

An alternative way to stimulate aggregate demand in a recession is to temporarily cut income taxes and hope that consumers will use the extra disposable income to increase personal spending. This would shift the *AD* curve to the right. As discussed in Chapter 16, it is highly debatable whether such policies can have much stimulative effect. Economic theory and empirical evidence suggest that temporary income tax cuts tend to increase saving rather than spending. In other words, this policy is likely to simply increase the government deficit and increase personal saving, with little effect on total expenditures. Keynes himself was skeptical of consumption-based stabilization policies. He recommended direct intervention in the form of increased government expenditures. Keynes was actually rather conservative and did not support reckless growth of government expenditures. But he did think the government could arrange its capital expenditures on roads, airports, hospitals, etc., to coincide with slumps rather than with booms. By managing aggregate demand in this way, the government could help to smooth out the business cycle and avoid competing with the private sector for resources when they are most in demand.

The ideal countercyclical demand management policy is illustrated in Figure 9.4. The basic goal is to maintain the levels of output and employment at their natural levels. When aggregate demand declines, the ideal policy would increase demand by exactly the same amount as the unexpected shortfall. If this could be done quickly, then the *AD* curve would essentially remain at AD_1^e and output and employment would be stabilized at their natural levels.

The Non-Interventionist Approach

For macroeconomic stabilization policies to be effective, clearly the government must either anticipate the negative demand shock, or be able to respond very quickly after the demand shock has struck. Monetarist and new classical critics of macro-demand management policies have argued that neither of these is possible. Obviously if the government could anticipate negative demand shocks, then the government might have time to take perfectly synchronized offsetting actions. But critics argue that this is an illogical position to take. If the government could anticipate negative demand shocks surely the private sector would be able to do the same thing. In our model of wage contracts, if firms and workers could anticipate where the aggregate demand curve would be throughout the current wage contract, they would also know what the average price level would be and the nominal wage would be set accordingly. Since there is no reason to believe that the government can forecast events any better than the private sector, there is no presumption that the government can initiate perfectly synchronized policies that essentially try to correct the forecasting mistakes of the private sector.

This leaves us with the question of whether the government can react quickly enough after a negative demand shock to successfully offset the unemployment effects. Skeptics in the monetarist and new classical camps reject this possibility as well. The first argument is that the government simply cannot react fast enough. Given the political nature of government spending decisions, it is simply impossible to pass the appropriate tax or expenditure legislation in time for the expansionary effects to coincide with the recession. Second, there are other delays in the system. Once the legislation is passed, it takes more time to get the policies initiated and more time still for the multiplier effects to ripple through the economy. By the time all these stages have been completed, it is likely that the economy will be on the road to recovery. Then, instead of offsetting a decline in demand, the new government spending is likely to contribute to an already expanding economy. Given the enormous timing problems, critics argue that demand management is just as likely to contribute to cyclical swings as it is to stabilize the business cycle. Instead, the government should simply let the natural recuperative mechanisms do the job of restoring the economy to the natural levels of employment and output.

There are several other arguments against demand management policies. For example, demand shocks tend to strike particular sectors of the economy and they do not hit the same sectors every time. One reason why government fiscal policies are ineffective is that they are not precise enough to target specific sectors or regions of the country. Increasing demand generally may cause excess demand in some sectors or regions, but fail to increase demand enough where the demand shock is centred. This may lead to a bias in favour of overstimulating the economy during a recession.

Finally, there is the danger that trying to prevent unemployment from rising above some target figure will ultimately result in an expanding government sector at the expense of the private sector. Since negative demand shocks are usually temporary, the offsetting increases in government spending should also be temporary. Thus, when private sector investment picks up and foreign markets improve, the government should cut its expenditures and/or raise taxes back to the original levels. Given the political nature of these decisions, it is often easier to justify expenditure increases than to impose expenditure cuts. Usually, the beneficiaries of government spending programs are easily identifiable, vocal groups. They include farmers, pensioners, university professors, the members of the Canadian Armed Forces, artists and writers, and an almost endless list of other formal and informal coalitions. Invariably, the beneficiaries of government expenditures support the spending but resist the cuts that have a direct bearing on their own economic position. Since spending can be financed by borrowing, which will only later be repaid through tax revenues, there is a clear temptation for the government to satisfy the current demands of identifiable voters at the expense of anonymous future taxpayers. Both monetarists and new classical economists prefer less government to more, so they argue against any institutional arrangements that encourage the growth of government. Active demand management is just one example of institutional arrangements that have a bias in favour of government growth.

The implications of the **non-interventionist approach** can be illustrated in Figure 9.4. As discussed above, the unexpected leftward shift in the aggregate demand curve puts the economy at point *B*. Despite the fact that there is considerable unemployment at point *B*, the non-interventionist approach recommends that the government take no specific countercyclical fiscal or monetary measures. If the temporary negative demand shock is short-lived, the aggregate demand curve will soon shift back to its normal position and the recession will quickly come to an end.

But if the aggregate demand curve remains at AD_1 for an extended period of time, the natural rates of output, employment, and unemployment will be restored only when wages and prices adjust downwards. If wages and prices were perfectly flexible, the economy would move to point *C* in the product market panel, where output is once again equal to Y^* and the price level is P_C. In order to get to point *C*, the nominal wage must be flexible enough to fall to $\overline{W}_C$. The labour market panel shows the new equilibrium position in the labour market. But when wages are contractually fixed it will take time for nominal wages to be reduced to $\overline{W}_C$. In most cases, wages are adjusted only when current contracts expire. If there is no resistance to lower nominal wages, then the adjustment towards point *C* will be completed as soon as all contracts have been renegotiated. In Canada, this could take several years because wage contracts are typically signed for one to three years.

But it is possible that even three years will not be long enough. Currently employed workers may resist nominal wage cuts for a number of reasons. First, although employment is lower at point B than at point C, the real wage of employed workers is higher during the recession because prices are lower. Those who are fortunate enough to keep their jobs during a recession benefit from discounted prices on durable goods, plane tickets, house renovations, and a number of other goods and services. It may not be easy for firms to persuade workers that wages should be cut in nominal and real terms so that employment (and profits) can be increased. Second, even if workers would be prepared to take wage cuts if more jobs would be created, it may be difficult to make the case when the linkage between wage cuts and more jobs is indirect. Workers at a tire plant may take a wage cut in exchange for a guaranteed job at that particular plant. But how many tire plant employees will volunteer to accept wage cuts because this may help to increase employment in the tire retailing sector? The favourable employment effects of lower tire prices in tire-using industries, such as truck transportation and taxicab services, are even more remote and tenuous. Experience suggests that existing workers do resist cuts in their own wages, so even when contracts are renegotiated, it is possible that the economy will either stay at point B or make only partial headway towards point C. Of course, if wages are completely inflexible downwards, then it is impossible to reach point C. The only way for output and employment to return to Y^* and L^* is for aggregate demand to pick up again.

COLA Clauses and Demand Shocks

There are a number of reasons why firms and workers agree to fix wages over a definite period of time. First, most people prefer to minimize financial risk whenever possible and by fixing wages at a satisfactory level, workers are protected from potential adverse shocks that might otherwise reduce their wages. Firms also benefit from wage contracts because contracts limit the frequency of wage negotiations, which can be very costly. A considerable amount of research has to be done prior to the wage negotiations and a team of high-priced negotiators may have to work several weeks or months before a settlement is reached. In addition, the firm has to be prepared for the eventuality of a strike. These preparations may take the form of stockpiling output, hiring security firms, and hiring alternative labour to maintain equipment and/or production. Strikes can also result in the permanent loss of customers. For example, in 1990 steelworkers at Stelco fought a long and bitter strike. When the strike was settled, Stelco discovered that many customers had found alternative sources of supply.[7] Since the chances of

[7] *The Globe and Mail*, "Stelco Sales Dive," 26 April 1991, p. B1.

strike action are much lower during a contract than during negotiations, firms have an interest in signing long-term contracts.

The main problem with long-term contracts from the worker's point of view is that inflation gradually reduces the real value of fixed nominal wages unless a **cost of living adjustment (COLA) clause** is built into the contract. The longer the wage contract, the greater is the risk that real wages will be substantially reduced by inflation. In many Canadian industries, firms and workers incorporate COLA clauses into wage contracts. This allows firms to negotiate contracts for a longer term while protecting employees from the uncertainties of inflation.

COLA clauses have important macroeconomic implications and in this section we will analyze the effects of demand shocks when wages are indexed to the general price level through COLA clauses. Figure 9.5 illustrates the product market. To capture the effects of uncertainty, we assume that aggregate demand can be either high or low. These alternative states are labelled AD_H and AD_L in Figure 9.5. Let us consider the consequences of the two wage contracts that are based on these two states of aggregate demand. First, if firms and workers act on the assumption that demand will be low, the nominal wage will be set at a low level, say $\overline{W}_L$. The corresponding *SRAS* curve is labelled $SRAS(\overline{W}_L)$, which intersects AD_L at point *A*. If expectations are fulfilled, the economy will be at point *A* throughout the wage contract and output and employment will be at their natural levels. But if demand turns out to be high, the aggregate demand curve will be at AD_H, which intersects

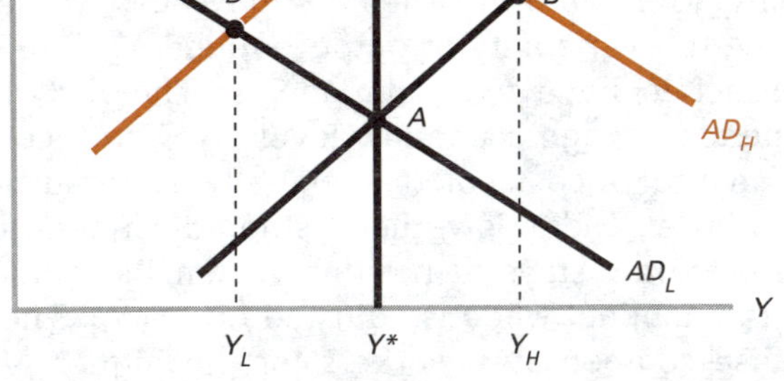

Figure 9.5 Demand shocks and COLA clauses

$SRAS(\overline{W}_H)$ at point *B*. At point *B* output and employment is higher than at point *A*. But the workers who signed the wage contract are actually earning lower real wages than they expected. This is due to the fact that workers settled for a low nominal wage, but the price level is higher than expected. Of course, it is the reduction in the real wage that allows firms to hire more labour inputs (person-hours) than was originally anticipated.

Now consider what happens when workers and firms act on the assumption that demand will be at AD_H. In this second case, negotiations lead to the higher nominal wage $\overline{W}_H$, which guarantees a higher real wage during the contract. Provided that the high level of demand actually materializes, the economy will be at point *C*. At point *C* the real wage is higher than it is at point *B* (but the same as at point *A*), which explains why firms hire less labour input at point *C* compared to point *B*. Of course, there are risks to assuming that demand will be high. If workers negotiate the high nominal wage $\overline{W}_H$, but aggregate demand turns out to be low, the economy ends up at point *D*. With high wages and low prices, the real wage is higher than expected and firms reduce employment and output. Hundreds of thousands of workers who expected to be gainfully employed find themselves out of work.

The dilemma that faces workers at the time of wage negotiations is this: if nominal wages are set low, but demand is high, workers will end up with a real wage lower than they would get if they could predict demand with certainty. But, if workers settle for a high nominal wage and demand turns out to be low, then a significant number of employees will not have jobs at all. If firms and workers guess right as often as they guess wrong, then the economy will spend about half the time at points *A* and *C* (where output is Y^*) and half the time in boom (point *B*) or bust (point *D*). Given the unpredictability of aggregate demand, output would vary between the extremes of Y_L and Y_H. The uncertainty of aggregate demand means that workers and firms have to try to guess what actual demand will be.

When the source of the uncertainty is unstable demand, a COLA clause can easily get around the dilemma that faces workers and simultaneously reduce the variability of output around Y^*. The solution is for the wage contract to have two components. The first, noncontingent part, sets the nominal wage at the low level $\overline{W}_L$. The second component is contingent on the price level that actually materializes during the contract period. If demand is low, there is no adjustment to the nominal wage and the economy stays at position *A*. On the other hand, if demand is high, the nominal wage is adjusted up to $\overline{W}_H$. The price-contingent COLA clause compensates workers for the higher price level and the economy moves to point *C*. With a COLA clause in the wage contract, the real wage is guaranteed and is completely independent of the level of aggregate demand. In addition, the economy always moves to point *A* or to point *C*. With a 100 percent COLA clause, the economy never reaches the extremes at points *B* and *D*.

In practice, very few contracts protect wages from 100 percent of changes in the price level. Many firms are simply unable to underwrite the inflation risks that workers face. The firms that are likely to be able to include COLA clauses in their wage contracts tend to be large, diversified firms that produce finished goods for the consumer market. The revenues of such firms are highly correlated with the general price level. In other words, when the general price level is high, the revenues of these firms are high. Consequently, they have the financial resources to compensate workers for the higher price level. But less diversified firms, and firms that produce raw materials or intermediate goods and services are likely to find that, too often, movements in their own revenues do not match the movements in the general price level. Such firms may not have the resources to compensate their workers for unexpected increases in the general price level so they will be reluctant to include 100 percent COLA clauses.

A second reason for firms to resist 100 percent COLA clauses is that firms are clearly better off if workers can be persuaded to settle for low wages with no inflation protection. In this case, firms benefit from unexpectedly higher profits when demand is higher than expected. In any negotiation, it is likely that both workers and firms will simply have to settle for less than they would ideally like: the COLA clause will either be absent from the contract or guarantee only partial protection from price increases. However, even a partial COLA clause will reduce the uncertainty faced by workers and lessen the variability of output.

Policy Options for Negative Supply Shocks

The two major macroeconomic problems of the post-war period have been unemployment and inflation. In the previous section we saw that negative demand shocks lead to increases in unemployment, but lower prices (or inflation) and lower interest rates. Weak aggregate demand tends to make the unemployment problem worse, but it eases any inflation difficulties the economy may have. But if demand shocks present policymakers with difficult choices, then supply shocks seem to leave policymakers with no choices at all. As discussed in the previous chapter, negative supply shocks have the effect of worsening both the unemployment problem and the inflation problem simultaneously. In this section, we will analyze the effects of a negative demand shock on output, employment, and the price level when nominal wages are contractually fixed. Then, we will examine why the traditional tools of demand management are inadequate for dealing with the unemployment consequences of supply shocks. Finally, COLA clauses will be reintroduced into the analysis. In the previous section, it was argued that COLA clauses can help to stabilize output. But when the macroeconomic shocks emanate from the supply side, COLA clauses can actually amplify the unemployment effects.

Supply Shocks With Fixed Wages

Figure 8.8 in the previous chapter illustrated the effects of a negative supply shock when wages are flexible. It will be useful to briefly review the conclusions of that analysis in the context of contractually fixed nominal wages.[8] The main point to be made here concerns the location of the short-run aggregate supply curve after a negative productivity shock has hit the economy. Rather than plotting the real wage on the vertical axis, as is done in Figure 8.8, Figure 9.6(a) plots the nominal wage on the vertical axis. We will maintain the assumption that the negative supply shock has two components; namely, that both the aggregate production function and the marginal productivity of labour schedule shift down. The initial position in the product and labour markets is denoted by point *A*. Firms and workers expect the price level to be P^e. Given this assumption and the expectation that the marginal productivity of labour will be determined by $D^e(L)$, the nominal wage is set at $\overline{W}$ in the current contract.

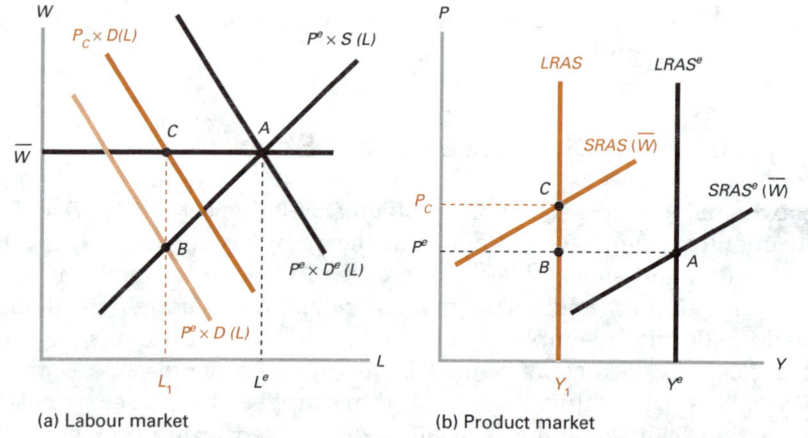

Figure 9.6 The effect of a negative productivity shock on aggregate supply

8 Students are advised that a careful study of Figure 8.8 and the associated text is essential preparation for the analysis contained in this section.

The negative productivity shock unexpectedly shifts the marginal productivity of labour schedule down to $D(L)$. As Figure 8.8 demonstrates, the effect in the labour market is to reduce both the real wage and the level of employment. In Figure 9.6, the employment effect can be determined by the intersection of the labour demand schedule $P^e \times D(L)$ and the labour supply schedule $P^e \times S(L)$. The intersection point is labelled B. Even though this intersection point is based on the expected price level rather than the actual price level, it nevertheless shows what the level of employment will be if nominal wages are flexible rather than fixed. The reason employment can be determined without knowing the actual price level is simply that changes in the price level shift both the supply and demand curves through the same *vertical* distance. So whatever the price level turns out to be, if wages are flexible, the productivity shock results in an intersection point that lies vertically above or below L_1. Since employment is L_1, output can be determined by the aggregate production function (not shown) to be Y_1. In the product market, the new inelastic long-run aggregate supply curve lies above the output level Y_1.

The main issue we are concerned with here is the location of the new short-run aggregate supply curve which is based on the contractually fixed nominal wage $\overline{W}$. What we need to determine is the price level where $SRAS(\overline{W})$ intersects $LRAS$. In the labour market panel, there will be some price level P_C, which is certainly above P^e, that locates the new labour demand curve $P_C \times D(L)$ through point C, where employment is L_1. In fact, given the fixed nominal wage $\overline{W}$, the price level P_C is the unique higher price level that immediately reduces the real wage to its new long-run equilibrium value following the productivity shock (see Figure 8.8) without requiring any change in the nominal wage. In the product market, the $SRAS(\overline{W})$ curve intersects $LRAS$ at the price level P_C.

Given the location of the new vertical $LRAS$ curve, the long-run employment and output effects of a negative productivity shock are determined exclusively by the location of $LRAS$. In the long run, the nature of the aggregate demand curve only influences the price level (and the nominal wage rate when wages are flexible). But since the $SRAS$ curve is not inelastic, when the nominal wage is fixed, the short-run effect of a negative productivity shock on employment and output does depend on the slope of the aggregate demand curve. The issue we turn to now is what effect does a contractually fixed wage have on the short-run employment effects of a negative productivity shock? In particular, are these short-run employment effects larger or smaller when nominal wages are fixed rather than flexible?

The key to this question is the slope of the aggregate demand curve. This is illustrated in Figure 9.7, which is similar in construction to Figure 9.6, with the addition of an aggregate demand curve. As before, the expected position is at point A, where the price level is P^e and output is

Y^e. Given these expectations, the nominal wage is set at $\overline{W}$. Obviously, the demand curve is expected to pass through point A. The main issue concerning the short-run employment effect of a negative productivity shock is the elasticity of aggregate demand. Suppose that by chance the demand curve coincides with the line AD', which passes through point C (the same point C we derived in Figure 9.6). Since aggregate demand is at AD', the new equilibrium position in the product market is at point C. The price level rises to P_C. Given the contractually fixed nominal wage $\overline{W}$, this increase in the price level reduces the real wage to the long-run equilibrium value without requiring any change in the nominal wage. Clearly this is a very special case. In general, a negative productivity shock will put market pressure on the nominal wage to change. Whether the nominal wage has to rise or fall depends on the elasticity of the aggregate demand schedule. Let us consider the case when aggregate demand is price-elastic.

Figure 9.7 illustrates the situation in which aggregate demand is more elastic (flatter) than AD'. The aggregate demand schedule AD also passes through point A, but it is flatter than the AD' schedule. Consequently, the short-run effect of the negative productivity shock is to move the economy to point D, where AD intersects $SRAS(\overline{W})$. Since the price level is lower at point D than at point C, clearly, when nominal wages are fixed, the real wage is higher at point D than at point C. This explains why employment and output are lower at point D than at point C. In the labour market panel, the demand for labour $P_D \times D(L)$, intersects the fixed nominal wage schedule, $\overline{W}$, at point D, where the level of employment is L_D.

Since point D is not on the $LRAS$ line, it does not represent a long-run equilibrium position. The new long-run position is at point E, which is where the economy will move when nominal wages are free to adjust. Since the demand curve is fairly elastic, the negative productivity shock does not raise the market price a great deal. Hence, the necessary decline in the real wage must be achieved by a combination of a small rise in the price level together with a decline in the nominal wage. This is seen in the labour market, where the price level P_E (which is below P_D) implies the lower nominal wage $\overline{W}_E$. When wages are fixed in the short run, the downward adjustment in the nominal wage is not possible. Hence, the nominal wage contract means the real wage is kept temporarily high and output and employment decline more than they would if nominal wages were free to adjust. Hence, when aggregate demand is elastic, nominal wage contracts tend to amplify the unemployment effects of a negative demand shock by preventing the real wage from falling.

The analysis of the fixed-wage case has so far been premised on the assumption that the aggregate demand curve is elastic (relatively flat). Given this assumption, we conclude that fixed-wage contracts amplify

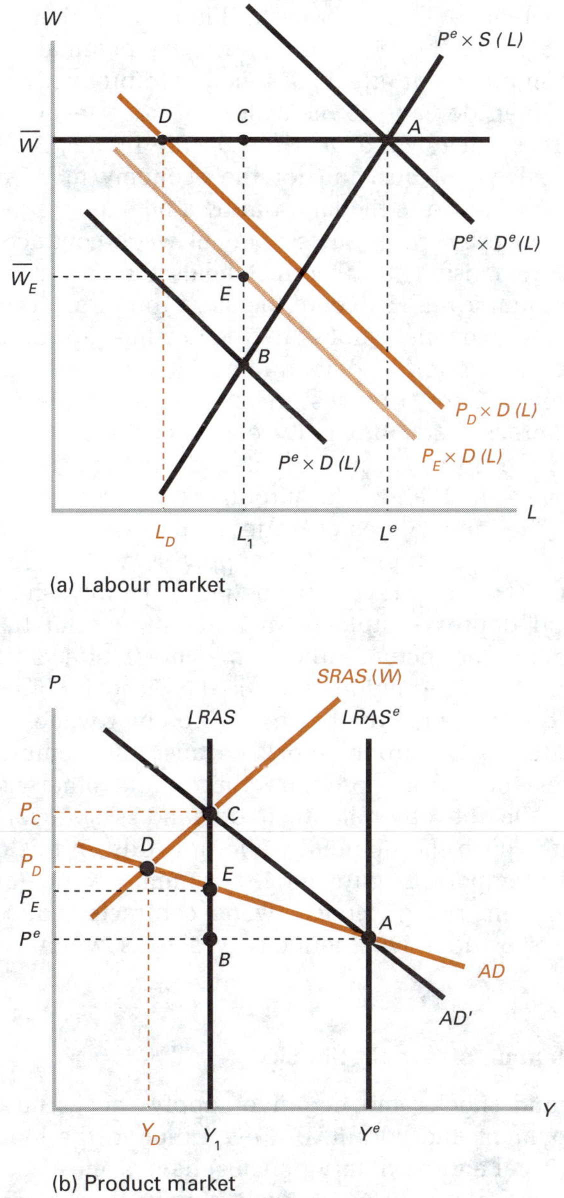

Figure 9.7 A productivity shock when nominal wages are contractually fixed

the negative output and employment effects of a negative supply shock. The story is quite different if demand is inelastic and the negative supply shock shifts the price level up a great deal. If the aggregate demand curve is steeper than *AD′* (not shown in Figure 9.7), then the *AD* curve intersects $SRAS(\overline{W})$ to the right of Y_B and the nominal wage contract reduces the unemployment effects of a negative productivity shock. The reason is that when demand is inelastic, the price level rises so much, and market forces put *upward* pressure on the nominal wage. It is still true that the real wage must fall for the economy to be on the *LRAS* curve. But this is achieved in the long run by a nominal wage increase and an even larger price increase. Since nominal wage contracts prevent the nominal wage from rising, the contract holds the real wage below the long-run equilibrium level. Hence, in the short run, firms hire more labour than they will when nominal wages are free to adjust upwards.

In the earlier discussion of demand shocks we saw that the effect of fixing wages in the short run has an unambiguous effect on the business cycle. Whereas wage flexibility ensures that variations in aggregate demand have no effect on output and employment, contractually fixed wages cause fluctuations in output and employment around their natural levels. The implications of wage contracts are not so clear when disturbances have their origin in the supply side. First, in the market-clearing model of wage flexibility, negative supply shocks certainly raise prices and depress employment and output. But fixing nominal wages may reduce or increase the employment effects of a negative demand shock. The determining factor is the elasticity of aggregate demand. Elastic demand implies that fixing nominal wages increases the employment effects of a supply shock because the nominal wage contract suppresses the market pressure that would otherwise lower the nominal wage. On the other hand, if demand is sufficiently inelastic, market pressures push the nominal wage upwards. In this case nominal wage contracts temporarily prevent the nominal wage (and therefore the real wage) from rising. Hence, wage contracts reduce the unemployment effects of negative productivity shocks when demand is inelastic.

The Policy Dilemma of Supply Shocks

Negative demand shocks and negative supply shocks have similar effects on employment and output. But even though the tools of demand management (fiscal and monetary policies) have some hope of offsetting the effects of a negative demand shock, supply shocks are much more troublesome. Figure 9.8 illustrates the basic limitations of demand management policies when disturbances emanate from the *supply side*. In the previous section we discussed the effects of a decline in the average and marginal productivities of labour. Given the size of the productivity shocks, the leftward shifts of the long- and short-run aggregate supply curves are straightforward to determine. In Figure

9.8, this type of negative shock shifts the long-run aggregate supply curve leftwards from its expected position, $LRAS^e$, to the actual posi-

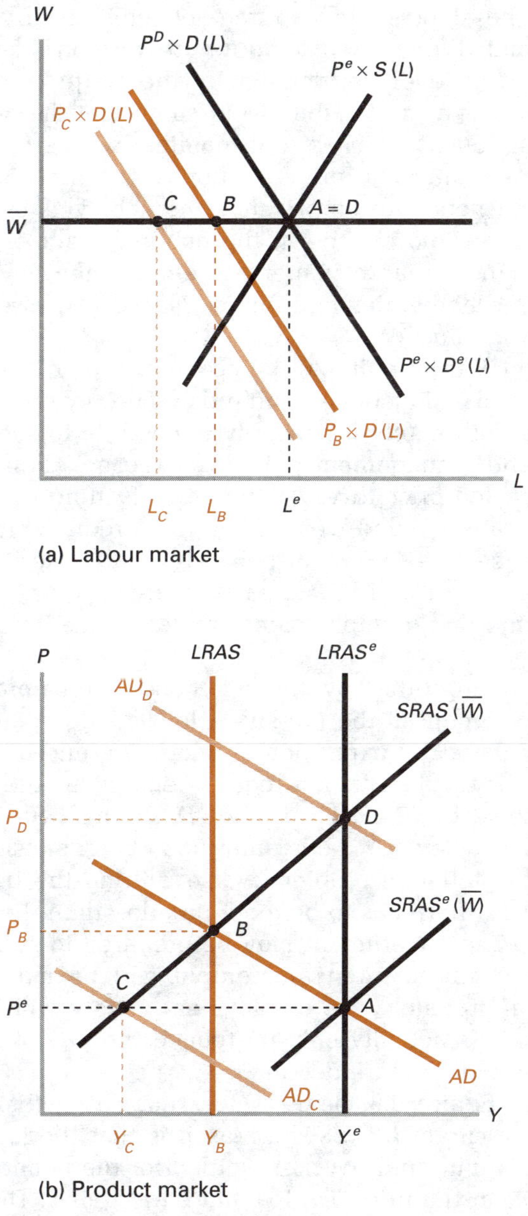

Figure 9.8 The policy dilemma of a negative productivity shock

tion, *LRAS*. The short-run supply curve shifts left to $SRAS(\overline{W})$ from the expected position $SRAS^e(\overline{W})$. Point *B* is determined by the intersection of *LRAS* and $SRAS(\overline{W})$.

In this section we will make the diagram as simple as possible by assuming that the slope of the aggregate demand curve causes it to pass through point *B*, thereby placing no pressure on the nominal wage to change from the level determined by the wage contract. In other words, even if wages were flexible, we assume that the negative supply shock would not cause any change in nominal wages from the original level $\overline{W}$. In this special case, the reduction in the real wage that is necessitated by the negative supply shock is achieved by a rise in the price level alone and no change in the nominal wage is required. Notice that in the labour market panel, the employment level L_B is determined where the labour demand curve $P_B \times D(L)$ passes through the fixed nominal wage line $\overline{W}$.

To get to point *B* from point *A*, the economy would experience rising unemployment and rising prices (inflation). The government faces two problems and unfortunately it is simply impossible to solve both by resorting to demand management policies. If the government chooses to achieve the expected price level P^e (thereby offsetting the unanticipated inflation), aggregate demand would have to be reduced to the low state AD_C, which intersects $SRAS(\overline{W})$ at point *C*. Clearly the negative supply shock together with an anti-inflationary fiscal–monetary policy mix will greatly exacerbate the unemployment problem since the level of output declines to Y_C.

On the other hand, if the government chooses to maintain the level of output and employment at the pre-shock levels, aggregate demand will have to be stimulated by expansionary monetary and/or fiscal policies. This type of policy will shift aggregate demand to the high position AD_D, which intersects $SRAS(\overline{W})$ at point *D*. Output will be held at the previously expected level Y^e, but unfortunately, expansionary demand policies make the inflation problem worse. During the transition to the high price level P_D there has to be more inflation than there would have been otherwise. The government may be prepared to suffer some additional inflation if employment and output can be maintained at the higher level. Unfortunately, the employment victory will be short-lived. The government has actually only postponed the day of reckoning. Let us consider this point in more detail.

Notice that in Figure 9.8, point *D* does not lie on the new long-run aggregate supply curve, *LRAS*. The reason is that the labour market is not in long-run equilibrium. Workers settled for the nominal wage $\overline{W}$ on the assumption that the price level would be P^e, but at *D* the price level is very much higher than expected. Two factors have led to the higher price level. The first is the negative productivity shock, which raises costs. The second is the inflationary effect of the government's expansionary policies, which were implemented in order to stabilize employment and output. When wage contracts come up for renegotiation, workers will want higher nominal wage settlements. Given the current state of technology and the preferences of workers, the free market equilibrium inevitably calls for output to decline to Y_B, with a concomitant decline in employment. If the government chooses to resist the impending declines in employment and output, another round of expansionary policies will be necessary, with further inflationary consequences. The government will soon find itself on an accelerating inflationary path and with a ballooning budget deficit. At some point, inflation and the government deficit will become *the* overriding economic problem and the government will be forced to abandon the high employment policy. At long last, the inevitable negative employment and output effects of the negative supply shock will be realized.

If the government had been able to recognize the negative supply shock in the first place and foresee the consequences of trying to prevent output and employment from falling, then it is possible that the government would not have embarked on the expansionary demand policy. But this requires the government to be able to distinguish supply and demand shocks and to resist the enormous political pressure that comes to bear when negative shocks hit the economy. The fact the federal and provincial debt has risen so dramatically since the late 1970s seems to indicate that governments have yet to find a way to bear the political heat generated by fiscal responsibility. In the last section of this chapter, we will examine the problems associated with the government's burgeoning debt. First, we will briefly explore the macroeconomic implications of a negative productivity shock when wage contracts include cost-of-living adjustment (COLA) clauses.

COLA Clauses and Supply Shocks

In the earlier section on demand shocks, we saw that COLA clauses can remove some of the real wage uncertainty faced by workers who sign long-term wage contracts. A COLA clause not only maintains the real wage when prices are higher than expected, but aggregate employment and output will be stabilized when the price surprises are generated by demand shocks. In this section we will demonstrate that COLA clauses can protect the real wage even when the price shock emanates from the *supply side* of the economy. However, the unfortunate consequences of maintaining the real wage include greater unemployment. Hence, COLA contracts actually amplify the unemployment effects of a negative productivity shock.

Figure 9.9 illustrates a situation in which firms and workers sign a wage contract that includes a COLA clause. For simplicity, we will assume that the COLA clause completely protects the real wage from any price rises that occur during the contract. The wage contracts considered so far have fixed the nominal wage rather than the real wage. With a 100 percent COLA clause, it is the *real* wage that is fixed at, say, $\overline{w}$ for the duration of the contract. Since the focus of attention is now the real wage, the labour market panel of Figure 9.9(a), plots the real wage along the vertical axis.

In the absence of any unexpected supply (or demand) shock, the product market settles at point A where the aggregate demand curve intersects the inelastic $LRAS$ schedule above Y^e, the expected level of output. In the labour market, the supply and expected demand for labour schedules $S(L)$ and $D^e(L)$ also intersect at point A. Given expectations, the equilibrium level of employment is at L^e. During the contract period, the negative productivity shock shifts the marginal productivity of labour schedule (the demand for labour) down to $D(L)$. In a market-clearing, flexible-wage model, the supply shock results in the equilibrium position marked by point B. Employment falls to L_B and the real wage declines to w_B. In the product market, the market-clearing model leads to a leftward shift of the $LRAS$ schedule to $LRAS_B$. The equilibrium price rises and output declines.

However, in the wage-contract model with 100 percent real wage protection, the negative productivity shock is not allowed to reduce real wages. But firms determine employment, which means that actual employment lies on the demand for labour schedule $D(L)$ at the original real wage $\overline{w}$. Despite the decline in productivity, under the COLA con-

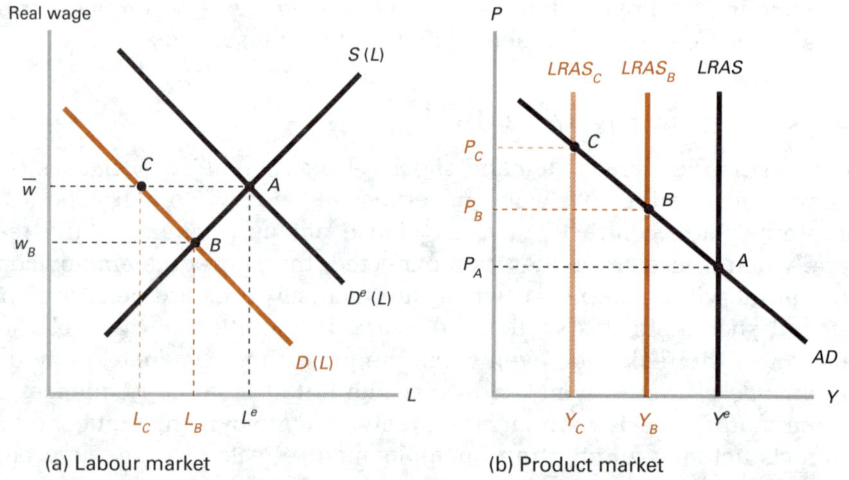

Figure 9.9 COLA clauses and negative productivity shocks

tract firms must pay workers the original real wage $\overline{w}$. Firms will therefore reduce employment until the marginal productivity of labour rises to its pre-shock level. This position is labelled C in the labour market. The new level of employment is L_C, which produces output Y_C. Since output does *not* depend on the price level, there is an inelastic aggregate supply curve $LRAS_C$ vertically above Y_C. The equilibrium price level, P_C, is determined by the intersection of AD with $LRAS_C$. Clearly the COLA clause has increased the negative effect of the productivity shock on employment. Although workers have protected their real wage, some workers have paid the price by losing their jobs.

Supply and Demand Shocks: A Summary

Before going on to examine the important issue of the government's rising debt, it is convenient to summarize our analysis of demand and supply shocks. The economy is exposed to a constant stream of shocks that can be conveniently categorized into supply shocks and demand shocks. Supply shocks originate in the supply side of the model and directly affect firms' costs. The initial disturbance can enter the model through the labour market, the production function, or material costs. Demand shocks originate in the *IS-LM* quadrant of the model and shift the aggregate demand curve.

When wages and prices are perfectly flexible, demand shocks have no effect on output and employment. But when nominal wages are fixed by wage contracts, demand shocks cause variations in output and employment. Positive shocks raise the price level and reduce the real wage, which encourages firms to increase employment and output. Negative demand shocks do the opposite and in particular, lead to unemployment. The government can try to offset the unemployment consequences of a negative demand shock by increasing aggregate demand. At least in theory, fiscal policy can maintain the aggregate demand curve in a fixed position. In practice, it is difficult to synchronize the fiscal stimulus with the negative demand shock and critics have argued that fiscal demand management policies are just as likely to destabilize the economy as to stabilize it. Critics also claim that demand management is biased towards increasing the role of government because it is politically easier to expand government spending than to reduce it.

When labour signs long-term wage contracts, demand shocks create uncertainty about what the real wage will be during the contract. A cost-of-living adjustment (COLA) clause can remove some or all of this uncertainty, depending on the degree of inflation protection. In addition, COLA clauses tend to reduce the variability of output and employment that is caused by demand instability.

Supply shocks have similar output and employment effects to demand shocks but the price effect moves in the opposite direction: a negative supply shock reduces employment, but raises the price level. Even when wages are perfectly flexible, a negative productivity shock reduces employment and the real wage. Although non-COLA nominal wage contracts definitely increase the amplitude of output swings after a demand shock, the effect of a supply shock may be weakened or strengthened by nominal wage rigidities. The issue hinges on the slope of the aggregate demand curve. An elastic (flat) demand curve means that a negative productivity shock puts downward pressure on the nominal wage. Since the wage is fixed by a contract, firms lay off more workers than they would if the wage could be reduced. In this case, nominal wage rigidities increase the employment effects of negative productivity shocks. But, if demand is inelastic, a negative productivity shock puts upward pressure on the nominal wage. Since the wage is held down by the contract, firms do not reduce employment so drastically: the wage contract reduces the employment effect of a negative productivity shock.

When wage contracts include a COLA clause, nominal wages are not necessarily fixed throughout the contract. In fact, a 100 percent COLA actually fixes the real wage. This type of COLA clause can completely insulate employment from demand shocks, but unfortunately it exacerbates the negative employment effects of a negative supply shock. Hence, if workers try to protect their standard of living when it is threatened by a negative supply shock, the net result is a greater loss of jobs and output.

The policy options for combatting negative supply shocks are limited. Traditional demand management policies can only temporarily avoid rising unemployment when this is caused by a supply shock. The cost of delaying the inevitable unemployment is to create increasing inflation and a rising government debt. Ultimately, the policy must be abandoned.

The Problem of the Government Deficit

In the 1980s and 1990s the problem of Canada's growing national debt muscled its way to the top of the federal government's list of economic concerns. Unemployment, inflation, regional economic disparities, child care, and poverty are still very important issues that need to be dealt with, but any measures the federal government takes in these areas must be tempered by the overriding concern for their effect on Canada's total indebtedness. Every year, the government must borrow to cover the gap between its expenditures and tax revenues. This gap is known as the **federal government deficit**. So every year there is a deficit, the government must make additional borrowing and the total indebtedness grows. After years of consuming more government services than we have been paying for, the debt has grown at a remarkably fast rate. Now the annual interest payment on the debt itself has become the biggest contributor to the annual deficit.

By the end of the 1984–85 fiscal year, the national debt reached $206 billion. In that single year, another $38 billion had been added to the total debt, which represents an increase of over 20 percent. Clearly such a rapid rate of growth is not sustainable and in the following years, debt growth slowed somewhat. Nevertheless, in the late 1980s the debt became so large and interest rates so high that the government had to borrow just to pay the interest on the existing debt. For example, by 1990, the government was spending more on interest than it was on old age security, family allowances, veterans' pensions, and unemployment insurance *combined*. By mid-1990 the total debt reached $400 billion, which amounts to about $15,000 for every man, woman, and child in Canada — a staggering $60,000 for a family of four. The annual interest on this debt comes to $6,400 for a four-person family.

In order to get the debt problem under control, federal government budgets have taken painful steps towards cutting government services and raising taxes. These actions had to be taken even in the face of weak economic conditions. For example, the unpopular Goods and Services Tax (GST) was introduced in January 1991, just as the economy was sliding deeper into recession. The federal budget of February 1991 went further by cutting federal transfer payments to the provinces, forcing the provinces to either cut expenditures, raise their own taxes, or borrow funds in the capital markets. Clearly the belt-tightening that must follow a spending binge is likely to be both unpleasant and unpopular. We begin our discussion of the deficit–debt problem by considering how the deficit is measured. Then we will consider the alternative means of financing the deficit and their economic consequences.

Measuring the Deficit

Although the figures reported in newspapers for the federal deficit get the most public attention, they are not necessarily the most useful numbers for analyzing trends in the annual deficit or for assessing its economic consequences. Two important adjustments give a clearer picture: first, the deficit should be adjusted for the current phase of the business cycle and second, a correction should be made for inflation.

When the economy slides into a recession tax revenues fall. In a recession, workers work fewer hours, some people lose their jobs, and business profits decline. Consequently, income tax collections on wages and profits are reduced. In addition, declines in sales mean that sales tax revenues fall. But not only do revenues fall in a recession, many components of government expenditures increase. In particular, unemployment insurance and welfare payments rise. The deficit, D, is the difference between government expenditures G and net tax revenues T, so recessions have a double effect on $D = G - T$. This is illustrated in Figure 9.10, which plots the annual deficit and the unemployment rate, which we use here to measure the business cycle. Clearly the deficit is countercyclical; it falls in economic expansions and rises in recessions. To correct the deficit for the economy's position in the business cycle, it is necessary to estimate what revenues and expenditures would be if the economy were at some fixed level of unemployment.

A cyclically adjusted series for the federal deficit is also plotted in Figure 9.10. Notice that the **cyclically adjusted deficit** varies less around the trend. The trend in the deficit depends on the basic structure of tax rates and government's expenditure commitments and not on the cyclical position of the economy. Hence the adjusted series reveals the underlying, long-run, deficit position. A cyclically adjusted series can also offer greater insight into the degree of fiscal stimulus of current tax and expenditure policies. For example, if the government has a plan to balance its budget, the plan presumably means that the budget should be balanced at some natural rate of unemployment, not at every possible unemployment rate. The cyclically adjusted data give an indication of how closely the goal of the plan is being achieved.

The second major adjustment that should be made to the annual def-

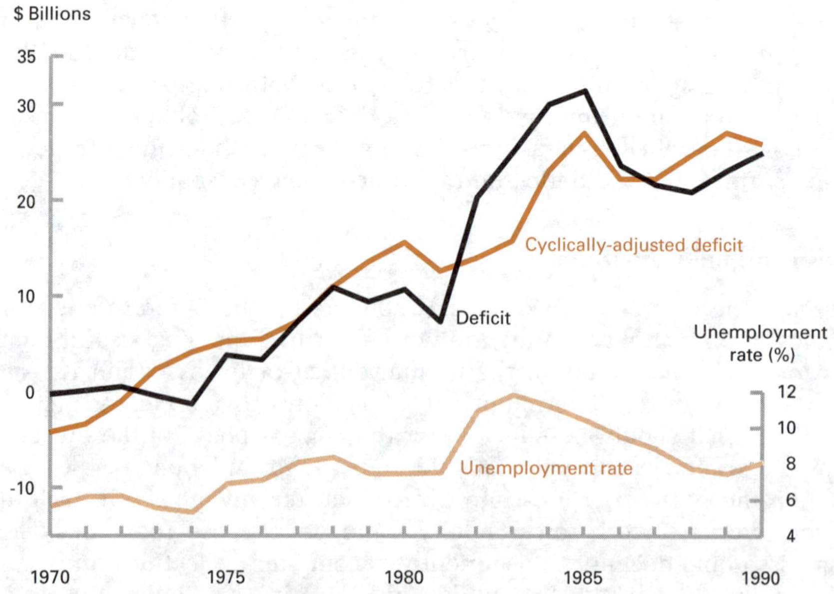

Figure 9.10 The cyclically adjusted federal deficit, 1970–90

icit depends on the rate of inflation. The issue is best illustrated with a simple example. Table 9.2 reports data from economies A and B. The two economies are identical in all real measures, but while economy A has no inflation, in economy B prices are expected to rise by 6 percent in the future. However, we assume that in the year under consideration, the price *levels* are identical in the two economies. By assuming price levels in economies A and B are both unity, all data are automatically expressed in real terms. Consider economy A first. In economy A, where inflation is zero, the real and nominal interest rates are both 4 percent. The government's budget position is as follows. Operating expenditures, that is, the part of spending exclusive of interest payments, are $96. The interest rate of 4 percent generates total interest payments of $4. Hence, total expenditures are $100. Since total government revenue is also $100, the government of economy A has a balanced budget.

Now consider economy B. The government of economy B also has an outstanding debt of $100, which in real terms, is the same as the debt of government A. In addition, the real operating expenditures of government B are $96. However, government B must pay a nominal interest rate of (4 + 6) = 10 percent because inflation is expected to be 6 percent in economy B. Hence, in the current year, government B pays interest payments of $10. Notice that all of this represents real purchasing power, that is, total government spending in economy B is $106 in real terms. Tax revenues are the same as in economy A; namely, $100 in real terms. Hence, government B has an annual deficit of $6 in real terms.

Table 9.2 Adjusting Deficits for Inflation

	Economy A	Economy B
Assumptions:		
Inflation	0%	6%
Nominal interest rate	4%	10%
Real interest rate	4%	4%
National debt outstanding	$100	$100
Government budgets:		
Operating expenditures	$ 96	$ 96
Interest payments	4	10
Total government spending	100	106
Total government revenue	100	100
Government deficit	0	6
Subtract inflation adjustment:		
Inflation × Debt	0	6
Equals:		
Inflation-adjusted deficit	0	0

Since government B has a real deficit, why should we be interested in making an adjustment for inflation? Well, consider the size of the real debt in the two economies at the end of the year. In economy A, where inflation is zero and the budget is balanced, the real value of the debt will remain at $100 in constant purchasing power. But in economy B, the debt at the end of the year will be increased to $106 in current dollars. Since inflation will raise prices 6 percent, the real value of the debt at the end of the year will be $100. Consequently, in both economies the real value of the outstanding government debt after one year will be $100 in constant dollars. In the non-inflationary economy A, this is achieved by balancing the budget (no new bonds are sold). In economy B, there is a deficit every year. The new bonds that are sold to the public simply maintain the real value of the total stock of bonds. Interestingly, if the government of economy B balanced its budget, inflation would erode the real stock of government bonds outstanding: the government of economy B would be reducing the size of its debt in real terms. If one wants to compare two economies on the basis of what is happening to their national debts in real terms, then it is necessary to adjust the current deficit by subtracting an amount equal to the current debt multiplied by the current inflation rate. This adjustment factor equals the decline in the purchasing power of the debt. By subtracting this quantity from the current deficit, we are left with an inflation-adjusted deficit. Only the inflation-adjusted deficit actually adds to the real value of the national debt.

In our example, the inflation adjustment for economy B's deficit is 6 percent of the outstanding debt, which is 6 percent of $100 or $6. Notice that if this is subtracted from the reported deficit, the inflation-adjusted deficit is zero, just as it is in economy A. In practice, the size of the inflation adjustment is enormous. By mid-1990, Canada's total debt reached $400 billion. With inflation running at 5 percent per year, the inflation adjustment is a massive $20 billion. In his budget of February 1991, Finance Minister Michael Wilson projected that the federal deficit would be $30.5 billion. Hence, the inflation-adjusted deficit was $10.5 billion. In other words, Canada's national debt was expected to rise by $10.5 billion in real terms between April 1991 and the end of May 1992. Clearly by the early 1990s, after several years of trying to control the growth of government spending, the government of Canada still had much to do to halt the growth of the public debt.

Financing the Deficit

When the government fails to raise sufficient revenue to cover its expenditures it has two other alternative means of financing the deficit. By far and away the most important of these is to borrow from the private sector. Governments can typically borrow at lower rates than the private sector because the government has the legislative right to raise tax revenues to pay its debts. Unlike firms that must persuade people through reputation and advertising to buy their products or services, the government can simply expropriate the funds it needs to pay its bills. Of course, there are limits to this expropriation. In a democratic society, the government must face periodic re-election. Where democracy breaks down, governments may be overthrown. Consequently, investors who purchase government debt must weigh the risks that governments will default on their bonds. Professional rating services continuously monitor the fiscal position of the federal and provincial governments. A high rating is rewarded in the marketplace. High quality (low risk) bonds pay a lower interest rate than higher risk bonds. Immediately after the Ontario NDP government's spring budget in 1991, which tripled Ontario's projected deficit to $9.7 billion, the Dominion Bond Rating Service Ltd. and the Canadian Bond Rating Service Ltd. both placed Ontario on *rating alert*.[9] The influential American bond rating service, Moody's of New York, quickly lowered its assessment of Ontario's debt to AA2, below the AA1 ratings that Moody's assigns to Alberta and British Columbia.[10] A lowering of a province's credit rating typically raises the costs of borrowing.

Money Financing

Another, more cynical way for governments to raise revenue is through inflation. The government is usually the sole issuer of a country's currency (although in extreme cases of abuse the domestic currency becomes worthless and only foreign exchange has value in private markets). To issue new currency, the central bank buys government bonds and credits the government's account with spendable cash. These balances are then transferred to the private banking system and spent like any other kind of money. Essentially, the government prints money and spends it in the open market. In this way, the government obtains resources (labour, materials, capital) from the private sector.

Notice that the economy's real resources are not bid away through taxing citizens or through people volunteering their savings by buying government bonds. The government gains control of the resources by creating an inflation that reduces the purchasing power of the general public's money balances. The public's loss to inflation is the government's gain. Of course, this can only work if the government can

9 In May 1991 only three provinces were rated AA by DBRS (Ontario, British Columbia, and Alberta). Only the federal government has the top rating of AAA. Most other provinces were rated as A or low A at that time. Newfoundland had the lowest rating, at BBB. See, "Ontario Government Debt Placed on Rating Alert," *The Globe and Mail*, 1 May 1991, p. B1, and *The Globe and Mail*, 6 May 1991, p. B1.

10 "Ontario Credit Rating Lowered," *The Globe and Mail*, 17 May 1991, p. B1.

spend the domestic currency, that is, if the public is prepared to accept domestic money in exchange. Hence, it is not surprising that the revenue the government can raise through this means is determined by the money demand function. In most modern economies we take for granted that the government can spend its own currency, but this is only true because these governments have not abused this method of financing expenditures.

Let us consider how much the government can gain by increasing the money supply. Suppose that the government suddenly increases the nominal money supply to M_{t+1} from M_t in a short period of time. The period is so short that the price level is considered to be fixed at P_t. The real value to the government of the increase in the money supply is $(M_{t+1} - M_t)/P_t$. If the numerator and denominator are multiplied by M_t, the real revenue that accrues to the government from monetary growth is $m(M_t/P_t)$, where $m = (M_{t+1} - M_t)/M_t$ is the rate of growth of the money supply. In the long run, the rate of inflation equals the rate of monetary expansion, m. Consequently, the real revenue gained by the inflation tax is the product of the money-induced inflation rate m and the quantity of real money balances willingly held by the public. Unfortunately for the government, the demand for real money balances is a decreasing function of the rate of price inflation (who wants to hold money that is depreciating in value?). So a policy of increasing monetary expansion m in an attempt to increase the real revenue from the inflation tax (mM/P) will only increase m. The public will react by reducing real money balances M/P. Eventually, increasing inflation will only lead to lower real revenues for the government as citizens manage with smaller and smaller real cash balances.

In principle, the government could choose the rate of inflation that maximizes the revenue earned by the inflation tax.[11] But the purpose here is not to design the optimal inflation tax. Rather, we want to stress that there are limits to the resources that the government can seize through monetary expansion. The limits are imposed by the money demand function, which dictates the terms on which the public will hold the government's money.

Bond-Financed Expenditures

The basic method of financing government deficits is through bond sales to the public. Since these sales are made in a free and open mar-

---

[11] For example, suppose the demand for real money balances is linearly decreasing in the rate of inflation: $M/P = a - bp$, where p is the rate of inflation. To maximize inflation-tax revenue, the government must choose inflation so as to maximize $p(M/P) = ap - bp^2$. The appropriate rate of inflation is $a/2b$. Notice that a and b are parameters in the demand for money equation. This reinforces the idea that the potential revenues from an inflation tax depend on the characteristics of the demand for money function.

ket, the interest rates that governments must pay are market-determined. As we discussed earlier, governments have the great advantage of being able to raise taxes to pay the interest on their debts. For this reason, governments rarely go bankrupt and the interest paid by governments is typically less than that paid by corporations.

However, as with the inflation tax, there are limits to how much borrowing a government can undertake. When a government spends so much that it needs to borrow just to pay the interest on the existing public debt, then the bond markets are likely to get skittish about absorbing ever more debt. One way to put the question of whether an annual government deficit can be sustained is to consider the conditions under which the ratio of the deficit to GDP can be maintained at a constant level. As discussed above, the Canadian government separates its expenditures into the interest payments on the existing debt and the operating budget, which is exclusive of all interest payments. Let $d = D/Y$ be the ratio of the total deficit, D, to GDP, Y, and let d^* be the ratio of the operating deficit to GDP. Some simple calculations show that when the operating deficit ratio d^* is held constant, the rate of change in the deficit/GDP ratio, $\hat{d}$, is determined by:

$$\hat{d} = d^*g + (R - g)d$$

where g is the annual growth rate of nominal GDP, R is the nominal interest rate, and d^* is the constant operating deficit/GDP ratio.[12] In order for the deficit/GDP ratio to stabilize at a constant value, it must be that the change in this ratio, $\hat{d}$, is zero. By imposing this condition and solving for d, we find that $d = gd^*/(g - R)$. This solution can be reached only if $g > R$, that is, if the rate of growth of nominal GDP exceeds the nominal interest rate. If the nominal interest rate exceeds the rate of growth of nominal GDP, the deficit/GDP ratio explodes because interest payments grow too fast.

To illustrate the formula, suppose that the ratio of the federal government's operating deficit to nominal GDP is maintained at 0.01. In terms of 1990 data, this would mean that the government's operating expenditures (which exclude interest payments) would exceed revenues by \$6.8 billion, since GDP in 1990 was approximately \$680 billion. We will suppose that as the economy grows, so too does the operating deficit, but

12 The total deficit is $D = D^* + RB$, where D^* is the operating deficit and B is the outstanding government debt. RB is the interest payment on the debt B. Now define the deficit ratios $d = D/Y$ and $d^* = D^*/Y$, where Y is nominal income. The total deficit equation can be written $dY = d^*Y + RB$. Now differentiate both sides with respect to time, treating the operating deficit and the nominal interest rate as fixed: $Y\hat{d} + \hat{Y}d = d^*\hat{Y} + R\hat{B}$, where $\hat{}$ indicates the derivative with respect to time. The change in the size of the national debt B is equal to the annual deficit D. By making this substitution and dividing through by the level of nominal GDP, Y we get $\hat{d} + gd = d^*g + Rd$, where g is the percentage rate of growth of nominal GDP, $g = \hat{Y}/Y$.

in such a way that the ratio is always 0.01. The total deficit includes the operating deficit and interest payments on the rising debt. Since the government borrows more every year, the question becomes: will the ratio of the full deficit to GDP stabilize at some constant level, or will it explode to infinity? The analysis in the previous paragraph indicates that the deficit/GDP ratio will stabilize provided the growth of nominal GDP is greater than the nominal interest rate. To continue the numerical example, suppose nominal GDP increases by 10 percent per year and nominal interest rates average 9 percent per year. Under these conditions, an operating deficit ratio of 0.01 would ultimately create a full deficit ratio of $0.01 \times 0.1/(0.1 - 0.09) = 0.1$. In 1990 dollars, an operating deficit of $6.8 billion would ultimately lead to a full deficit of $68 billion.

Between 1970 and 1990, Canadian nominal GDP grew at an average annual rate of 10.6 percent. Over the same period, the average yield on one- to three-year government bonds was 9.5 percent. These data suggest that Canada would be able to sustain a consistent federal government operating deficit. If the 20-year period covering the 1970s and 1980s is a guide to the future, then Canada's GDP growth is sufficiently high to cover the rising interest costs generated by a sequence of deficits. However, a weakness in this argument is that interest rates may rise to higher levels as a result of chronic deficits which increase the competition for the pool of annual savings. Nor can we be sure that Canada's real economic growth will be as rapid in the future as it has been in the past. In part this depends on what the government's deficit is used for. If it is ploughed into productive social capital rather than used simply to finance consumption (through personal transfer payments), then there is a better chance that real growth will be maintained at a high rate. Regrettably, there is no evidence that the deficit is being used to finance investment and we should not assume that any federal deficit can be sustained indefinitely.

Consequences of Bond-Financed Deficits

The popular wisdom amongst the business community and a substantial number of economists is that government deficits crowd out private sector investment by increasing the competition for private sector saving, thereby raising interest rates. However, some economists do not subscribe to this view because the empirical evidence linking deficits to higher interest rates is rather weak. One of the key problems in estimating the relationship between deficits and interest rates is that changes in these variables are often influenced by another set of common factors. For example, a recession caused by an autonomous decline in investment increases the deficit and lowers interest rates. In this case, the evidence is apparently against the crowding-out argument. Any statistical study must allow for events that obscure the independent and causal relationship between deficits and interest rates.

Paul Evans recently examined the history of U.S. deficits. The largest deficits in relation to GDP occurred during the Civil War and the two world wars. Interest rates did not rise significantly during any of these periods. Evans also looked at the more recent monthly movements of the deficit and interest rates and found little connection. One difficulty with the interpretation of wartime experiences is that during war private sector saving is unusually high. Certainly governments exhort citizens to be patriotic by investing in government bonds. In addition, direct intervention of government in investment decisions lowers private sector investment (tanks are made instead of cars). Moreover, the temporary lack of consumer goods tends to encourage saving. In many countries during World War II, goods were rationed, so money alone is not enough to buy goods. In such circumstances, saving increases. For all these reasons, interest rates are kept lower during wartime than they would be otherwise.

An influential minority of economists argue that government deficits do not raise interest rates because they automatically cause private sector saving to increase. The argument is that everyone knows the interest on the public debt must be paid. Hence, when government spending increases, households and firms anticipate that taxes must rise in the future in order to pay the interest charges on the debt. Knowing that tax obligations will increase, consumers and firms reduce spending (increase saving) to cover the future tax burden. A deficit caused by lower taxes will therefore lead to increased saving to match the deficit. The net result is that there is no change in aggregate demand. The deficit has no effect on output, employment, or interest rates. This view is known as *Ricardian Equivalence*, after the economist, David Ricardo, who first mentioned it as a theoretical possibility. More recent economists, such as Robert Barro of Harvard, have taken it as a serious empirical phenomenon.[13]

Most economists reject the extreme position of Ricardian Equivalence and believe that deficits have some real effects in the short run. For Ricardian Equivalence to hold, households must take a very long view of events and even treat the tax liabilities of their descendants as equivalent to their own. But how many parents increase their saving to help their children (or children's children) to pay the tax burden that may come due?

In an open economy, domestic saving can be augmented by foreign saving. Whenever a country runs a balance of payments deficit, this must be financed somehow. One possibility is that foreigners buy domestic bonds. Essentially, foreigners save in order to finance domestic spending. In this international context, a government deficit that would

---

[13] Robert J. Barro, *Macroeconomics* (New York: John Wiley & Sons, Inc., 1990).

raise domestic interest rates will tend to draw in foreign capital. The extra source of funds will prevent interest rates from rising as much as they would otherwise. Consequently, there is also less crowding-out of investment spending. However, inflows of foreign capital tend to increase the demand for domestic currency in the international foreign exchange markets. The result is an appreciation of the domestic currency. Exports decline and import-competing industries shrink. Hence, in an open economy context, the crowding-out effect of government deficits is not limited to private investment; it also affects the output of export and import-competing industries.

As economists continue to debate the economic consequences of government deficits, the political pressure in Canada to reduce annual deficits and the total size of the public debt is at least having an effect on federal budgets. The first budget of Ontario's first ever NDP government showed little concern for the economic consequences of government deficits. But at the federal level, the size of the deficit and the public debt dominated Michael Wilson's budget speech of February 1991. Mr. Wilson listed the following measures in his budget:

1. We will put government finances firmly on course to a balanced budget.
2. The government will legislate mandatory program spending limits.
3. By law, all revenues from the Goods and Services Tax and from privatization will go into a Debt Servicing and Reduction Fund.
4. Operating budgets will be frozen at current levels and the wages and salaries of public servants will be tightly restrained.

These actions are expected to:

1. Eliminate new federal borrowing after 1993–94.
2. Limit program spending growth to 3 percent per year after 1991–92.
3. In 1992–93 reduce the deficit to below $25 billion for the first time in a decade.[14]

With the Bank of Canada preoccupied with low inflation targets (2 percent by 1995 and lower thereafter) and the government committed to fiscal restraint, the focus of monetary and fiscal policy seems to be sharper than at any time in the past 20 years. It remains to be seen how successful the government will be in achieving its inflation and deficit targets.

---

[14] Department of Finance. *The Budget Speech in Brief*, 26 February 1991, p. 3.

Key Concepts

demand shocks
supply shocks
Keynesian countercyclical policies
non-interventionist approach to shocks
COLA clauses
the government's deficit
the cyclically adjusted deficit
adjusting deficits for inflation
the structural deficit
money-financed deficits
bond-financed deficits

Review Questions

1. On what basis are macroeconomic disturbances categorized as demand shocks or supply shocks? Give examples of each.
2. Describe the objectives of Keynesian demand management policies and explain how these objectives are achieved when the economy suffers a negative demand shock.
3. Discuss the criticisms of Keynesian demand management policies. What are the implications of a non-interventionist approach when the economy suffers a negative demand shock?
4. Can demand management policies be effective against supply shocks?
5. Explain the macroeconomic implications of COLA clauses. Distinguish between the effects of supply shocks and demand shocks.
6. Explain why it is useful to adjust the government's fiscal position for (a) the phase of the business cycle and (b) inflation. Create a numerical example to illustrate the inflation adjustment.
7. The government can finance a deficit by borrowing or by printing money. Explain how the demand for money function places limits on the scope for raising revenue through inflation. Explain why there are limits to bond-financing also.

Part 4

CHAPTER 10

Inflation and the Rise of the Phillips Curve

> *On the usual time scale of the dissemination of ideas in economics, the Phillips curve and the associated "Dilemma" problem achieved a prominent place in under-graduate textbooks almost instantly. . . . the déjà vu reaction was so strong that the Phillips curve immediately achieved a life of its own in professional discussion.*
>
> *Axel Leijonhufvud*[1]

In this part of the text we turn our attention to the problem of inflation. What causes inflation? What determines the rate of inflation? Why did the inflation rate average almost 10 percent per year during the ten years from 1973 to 1982 (compared to only 1 to 4 percent during the 1950s and 1960s)? How do we stop inflation once it gets started? Is there a trade-off between inflation and unemployment? Can inflation be brought under control without having to endure a serious recession, with high interest rates and high unemployment?

In this chapter we develop the price-expectations Phillips (*PEP*) curve, a relationship connecting the rate of inflation to the unemployment rate and the expected rate of inflation. Chapter 11 integrates this *PEP* curve with the *IS-LM* model and Chapter 12 extends the *IS-LM-PEP* model to an open economy setting (by including a *BP* curve). The controversial issue of a trade-off between inflation and unemployment is examined in Chapter 13 and policy options to eliminate inflation are analyzed in Chapter 14.

In the previous three chapters we used aggregate demand and sup-

---

1 A. Leijonhufvud, "Comment: Is there a Meaningful Trade-Off Between Inflation and Unemployment," *Journal of Political Economy*, July 1968, p. 738.

ply curves to determine the equilibrium price and output level. Under classical and new classical wage flexibility assumptions, the equilibrium price level corresponds to equilibrium in the labour market and a state of "full" employment (at the natural rate of output). In contrast, Keynesian models assume that wages are fixed or inflexible and thus the labour market can experience successive periods of disequilibrium unemployment.

The price-expectations Phillips (*PEP*) curve provides a bridge between the classical assumption of highly flexible wages (labour market equilibrium) and the Keynesian assumption of fixed wages (labour market disequilibrium). The *PEP* curve assumes that wages respond to demand and supply conditions in the labour market, but wages do not instantaneously adjust to their new equilibrium level. Following a change in demand or supply, the labour market will undergo a disequilibrium adjustment period as wages gradually return to equilibrium. If wages are very flexible, then this disequilibrium adjustment period will be very short and the labour market will typically be in a state of equilibrium (as classical and new classical economists believe). However, if wages adjust quite slowly to changing economic conditions, then the labour market will be subject to lengthy periods of disequilibrium unemployment (as Keynesians believe). A key question in macroeconomics concerns the length of time required for the labour market to return to equilibrium. To answer this important question, we must analyze the process by which prices and wages adjust to their new equilibrium levels.

Unlike the comparative static equilibrium analysis in the previous three chapters, we now focus on the disequilibrium dynamics of wage and price adjustments. Rather than using an aggregate supply function, we provide a *direct* explanation for wages and prices. Given a downward-sloping aggregate demand curve, a macroeconomic model can be completed with either an aggregate supply function or a price determination relationship — they represent opposite sides of the same coin. Once a firm determines the profit-maximizing price to charge for its output, the firm knows exactly how much output to supply. The firm's pricing decision represents the firm's supply function.

We begin this chapter with an analysis of the determinants of the firm's profit-maximizing price level. Having identified wage costs as a key determinant of prices, we turn to the determinants of wage changes and a discussion of the now-famous Phillips curve, a negative relationship between wage changes and the unemployment rate. Based on an important subsequent contribution by Milton Friedman, we next examine the role of price inflation expectations as an additional determinant of wage changes. Using empirical estimates for the price-expectations Phillips curve, we are able to estimate the size of the natural rate of unemployment in Canada. We conclude the chapter with a review of some of the more recent (new Keynesian) ideas concerning why prices and wages might not adjust to their new equilibrium levels (even when firms and workers behave rationally) and why the unemployment rate might not revert to a given natural rate.

Determinants of Price Movements

As a starting point for our analysis, we briefly review the firm's **pricing decision**. Suppose a profit-maximizing firm faces a downward-sloping demand (average revenue) curve. To increase sales, the firm must lower the price that it charges for its product. Unfortunately, a "new" lower price will apply to all sales, including sales which previously would have been sold at a higher price level. Thus, the marginal revenue from selling one more unit of output will be less than the "new" lower price: the revenue loss from cutting the price on all sales must be subtracted from the revenue gain obtained by selling one more unit of output. As shown in Figure 10.1, the downward-sloping *marginal* revenue MR curve lies below the downward-sloping *average* revenue AR curve.

The firm's cost structure is represented by an upward-sloping marginal cost MC curve. The MC_0 curve represents the additional cost of producing one more unit of output, assuming a given set of factor input prices. The marginal cost curve slopes upward because of diminishing returns due to hiring additional labour. As the marginal product of lab-

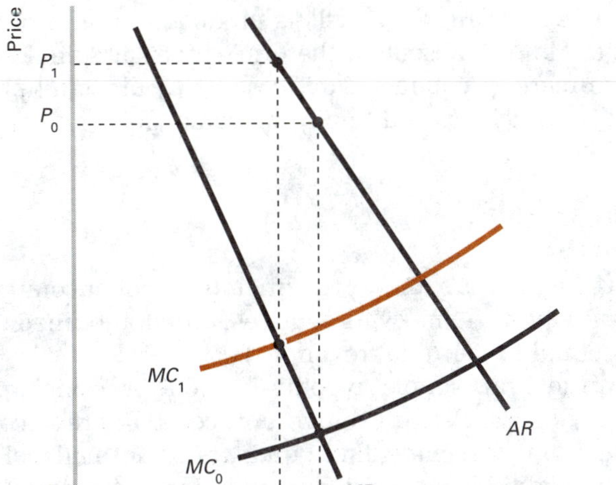

Figure 10.1 The profit-maximizing firm's pricing decision

our declines when more labour is hired, marginal costs rise; an additional worker is paid the same wage rate as existing workers but produces less output, thereby raising the costs of production. If wages or other input prices were to rise, marginal costs would increase and the MC_0 curve would shift upwards (to MC_1).

Recall from your introductory economics course that a profit-maximizing firm will continue to increase production until marginal costs equal marginal revenues. For a given set of factor input prices (the MC_0 curve), the profit-maximizing firm will set a price P_0 and supply Q_0 units of output. The firm's pricing decision depends crucially on the costs of producing output. If wage rates increase, the marginal cost curve will shift up to MC_1 and the profit-maximizing firm will now charge a higher price P_1. The price level varies directly with wages and the prices paid for other factor inputs.

Although it is true that a shift in demand (the *AR* and *MR* curves) will also affect the price set by the profit-maximizing firm, changes in marginal costs arising from changes in wages have proven to be *quantitatively* very important. For example, the average annual wage in Canada (total wages, salaries, and supplementary income divided by total employment) has increased from $6,066 in 1970 to $30,484 in 1990! This *quintupling* of the average wage has obviously shifted marginal cost curves substantially upwards, leading to higher prices.

Given that the profit-maximizing price level depends on the costs of producing output, many economists use a simple price *markup* model to describe the firm's pricing decision. For example, if it costs $1.00 to produce a unit of output, a firm might sell its product at a price of $1.10, with the 10 percent markup representing the firm's profit margin. In the following simple price markup equation, unit costs (*UC*) are multiplied by the markup factor *k*, which exceeds unity in value ($k = 1.1$ in the above illustration):

$$P = k \times UC \tag{10.1}$$

As noted above, a markup theory of pricing is not incompatible with profit-maximizing behaviour (where prices are determined by setting marginal costs equal to marginal revenues).

Before we can test this simple hypothesis about firm pricing behaviour (Equation 10.1), we must define average unit costs. For the economy as a whole, wages account for almost three-quarters of net national income at factor cost. We begin by focusing our attention on **unit labour costs** (*ULC*), the largest component of the economy's cost structure. Unit labour costs are the wage payments to labour for producing one unit of output. Since most workers are paid on an hourly or weekly basis (not on a "piece rate" basis), wage rates must be converted into unit labour costs. Unit labour costs depend not only on the wage rate (*W*) but also on the productivity (*PROD*) of workers. If a worker can produce two widgets per hour and the wage rate is \$5.00 per hour, then the *ULC* of one widget is \$2.50:

$$P = k \times ULC \tag{10.1a}$$

$$ULC = W/PROD \tag{10.2}$$

Either an increase in the wage rate (say to \$10.00 per hour) *or* a decrease in labour productivity (say to one widget produced per hour) will increase unit labour costs (to \$5.00 per widget) and result in a higher price for widgets. It is important to note that if wage rates and labour productivity *both* increase by the *same* percentage, then unit labour costs will *not* change. Only wage increases in excess of labour productivity increases result in higher unit labour costs and higher prices.

Up to this point we have only considered unit labour costs as a determinant of prices. At the individual firm level, the cost of producing a particular good depends not only on unit labour costs but also on the price of material inputs that are necessary to produce the good. For example, General Motors must hire not only labour to produce an automobile, it must also purchase large quantities of steel, glass, rubber, and other materials. In establishing a price for an automobile, General Motors must recover material costs as well as labour costs.

Although this argument is undoubtedly important at the level of the individual firm, it loses much of its relevance for the economy as a whole. To produce the necessary material inputs for an automobile, other firms producing "intermediate" goods must hire labour. Intermediate goods (such as steel and glass) can be traced back to another firm in which labour is the principal factor input (if one goes back far enough, one will find a worker). For the economy as a whole, average unit labour costs should also reflect the price level of most intermediate goods that are used in the production process.[2]

To test this simple pricing model ($P = k \times ULC$) at the aggregate level, Figure 10.2 presents a scatter diagram in which the level of the consumer price index (CPI) is plotted against labour income per unit of output. As is obvious from Figure 10.2, the level of the consumer price index is closely related to average unit labour costs in Canada. There is

---

2 For an open economy, such as Canada's, changes in foreign prices and changes in the value of the foreign exchange rate will have some effect on domestic prices. Canadians must pay the world price for imported goods, be they imported Japanese consumer goods or imported raw materials used in Canadian production. For example, if a Middle East crisis triggers an increase in oil prices, there will be a direct effect on Canadian consumer prices (at the gas pump) and energy costs in the production process. If the value of the Canadian dollar declines in international currency markets, the price of imported goods will increase, putting upward pressure on production costs and on domestic prices. The previous chapter considered the effects of supply shocks on the macroeconomy. In this chapter we abstract from such supply shocks.

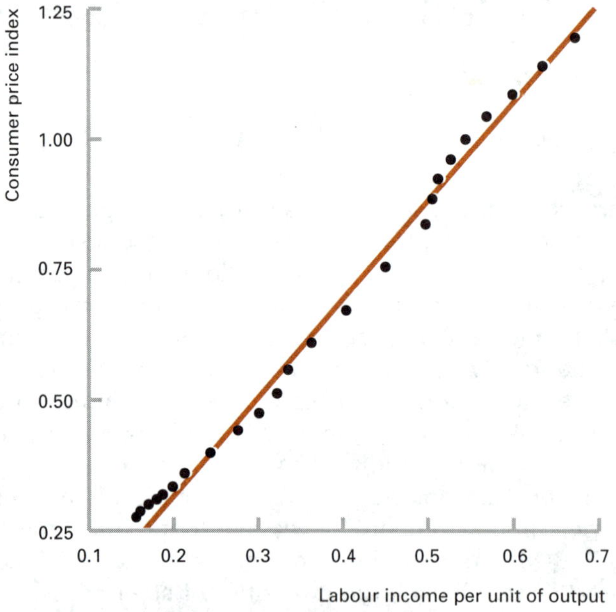

Figure 10.2 Price–unit labour cost scatter diagram, 1967–90

very little scatter to the diagram. Most of the data points lie quite close to an upward-sloping straight line.[3]

Throughout this part of the book we are primarily interested in the *rate* of price changes (the process of inflation), rather than the *level* of prices. Since the percentage change in the product of two numbers can be approximated by the sum of the percentage changes in the two individual components of the product, our price level model can be expressed in percentage change form:[4]

---

3 The slight deviations of the data points from the straight line in Figure 10.2 can be attributed to factors that we have ignored, such as foreign price movements (for example, oil prices), changes in the value of the foreign exchange rate, any changes in sales tax rates, and cyclical changes in labour productivity (see below).

4 To illustrate this general concept, consider the gate receipts *R* of two football games, where *R* is equal to attendance *A* multiplied by the average ticket price *P*:

	A	P	$R = A \times P$
Game 1	20,000	\$5.00	\$100,000
Game 2	20,400	\$5.25	\$107,100

The total gate receipts of the second game are 7.1 percent higher than the gate receipts for the first game, which is approximately equal to the 2 percent increase in attendance plus the 5 percent increase in average ticket prices.

Level of prices: $P = k \times ULC$ (10.1a)

Percentage change of prices: $\dot{P} = \dot{k} + U\dot{L}C$ (10.3)

Assuming that *k*, the markup factor, is constant, the percentage change in the price level will equal the percentage change in unit labour costs. In terms of our previous widget example, if unit labour costs increase by 100 percent (from \$2.50 to \$5.00), the price of widgets also increases by 100 percent (if *k* equals 1.1, the price of widgets increases from \$2.75 to \$5.50).

Since the percentage change in unit labour costs can be approximated by the percentage change in wage rates ($\dot{W}$) minus the percentage change in labour productivity growth ($PR\dot{O}D$),[5] the rate of price inflation depends on the rate of change in wages minus the rate of change in labour productivity (assuming a constant markup factor, that is, $\dot{k} = 0$):

$$\dot{P} = U\dot{L}C = \dot{W} - PR\dot{O}D \qquad (10.4)$$

Most price analysts relate price changes to changes in *normal* unit labour costs, where the average (or trend) growth rate of labour productivity ($PR\dot{O}DT$) is subtracted from the change in wage rates:

$$\dot{P} = \dot{W} - PR\dot{O}DT \qquad (10.4a)$$

Labour productivity tends to vary cyclically. Given the use of overtime labour in booms, labour productivity substantially increases in "good times." In recessions, many firms hoard labour which lowers the productivity of labour. Since most firms wish to minimize transitory movements in price levels (because of the costs of adjusting prices), firms typically price their products in terms of *normal* unit labour costs, costs that would occur under *average cyclical* conditions.

The rate of price inflation depends on the rate of change in wages minus the average growth rate of labour productivity (Equation 10.4a). We now turn our attention to an analysis of changes in wages.

---

5 For example, if wage rates rise from \$5.00 to \$5.50 per hour (a 10 percent increase) and productivity levels rise from 5 to 5.15 widgets per hour (a 3 percent increase), unit labour costs will rise from \$1.00 to \$1.068 per widget (\$5.50 ÷ 5.15). The percentage change in unit labour costs (6.8 percent) is approximately equal to the percentage change in wage rates (10 percent) minus the percentage change in labour productivity (3 percent).

The Determinants of Wage Changes

Research on the wage determination process has identified the following three factors as key determinants of the size of wage changes:

1. The state of the labour market (usually represented by the unemployment rate).
2. The expected rate of price inflation.
3. The growth rate of labour productivity.

Each of these three factors will be discussed in turn, beginning with the effects of unemployment on the rate of wage inflation.

The Rise of the Phillips Curve

In 1958 A.W. Phillips of the London School of Economics published a paper demonstrating that British wage changes during the previous 95 years were systematically related to the level of unemployment. As the opening lines of this now-famous study reveal, Phillips was simply applying a basic economic principle to the labour market:

> When the demand for a commodity or service is high relative to the supply of it we expect the price to rise, the rate of rise being greater the greater the excess demand. . . . It seems plausible that this principle should operate as one of the factors determining the rate of change of money wage rates, which are the price of labour services. When the demand for labour is high and there are very few unemployed we should expect employers to bid wage rates up quite rapidly, each firm and each industry being continually tempted to offer a little above the prevailing rates to attract the most suitable labour from other firms and industries.[6]

When unemployment rates were low, Phillips found that the rate of British wage inflation was relatively high; and conversely when unemployment rates were high, British wage inflation was low (or negative).

Phillips's paper provided economists and policymakers with an important "new" relationship connecting wage inflation to the level of unemployment — the now-famous **Phillips curve**. Even though a great deal of controversy has subsequently engulfed the Phillips curve, it is important to re-emphasize the simple and straightforward economic

---

6 A.W. Phillips, "The Relation Between Unemployment and the Rate of Change of Money Wage Rates in the United Kingdom, 1861–1957," *Economica*, November 1958, p. 283.

principle behind the Phillips curve. The wage rate, the price of labour, responds to demand and supply conditions within the labour market.[7]

Wage Changes and the State of the Labour Market

Phillips's 1958 paper was quickly followed by a study by Canadian-born economist Richard Lipsey. Lipsey's contribution was twofold. First, Lipsey used more conventional econometric techniques in his analysis of the same 95 years of British data and reconfirmed Phillips's basic empirical findings: "The data are shown to support Phillips' main contention that there is a significant relation between the rate of change of money wage rates and the level . . . of unemployment."[8] Second, and perhaps more important, Lipsey recast Phillips's verbal rationale for a relationship between wage changes and unemployment into an explicit wage adjustment function based on the existence of disequilibrium in a competitive labour market. A brief review of Lipsey's reformulation of the Phillips curve is useful to highlight the key assumptions implicit in the Phillips curve model.

To illustrate the mechanics of Lipsey's disequilibrium model, Figure 10.3(a) depicts conventional labour demand and supply curves, with the nominal money wage rate plotted on the vertical axis. The market-clearing wage rate is W^* and L^* represents the equilibrium (full employment) level of employment (see Chapter 7). A wage rate of W_A would give rise to a state of excess labour demand (*XLD*), while a wage rate of W_B would result in a state of excess labour supply (*XLS*). In each case, excess labour demand or supply is represented by the horizontal distance between the labour demand and supply curves for the particular disequilibrium wage rate, W_A and W_B, respectively. Elementary economics argues that the wage rate will be bid up in the event of excess labour demand and will be bid down in the event of excess labour supply. In either case, market forces will (eventually) return the wage rate to its equilibrium level, W^*.

Although virtually all economists accept the proposition that eventually the labour market will clear,[9] the key area of dispute concerns the

---

7 Given the simplicity of the essential idea behind the Phillips curve, it should come as no surprise that other economists before Phillips had considered the possibility of a "Phillips curve" effect. For example, the very first equation in Jan Tinbergen's 1936 econometric model of the Dutch economy was a Phillips curve. Tinbergen states: "It is assumed that the change in the wage level from year to year is influenced by changes in the cost of living and by the state of employment . . . [W]hen employment exceeds the value which is considered normal wages will rise, while a subnormal level of employment leads to wage decreases." (Jan Tinbergen, "An Economic Policy for 1936," in L.H. Klassen et al., eds., *Jan Tinbergen: Selected Papers* (North-Holland, Amsterdam, 1959), pp. 51–52).

8 R.G. Lipsey, "The Relation Between Unemployment and the Rate of Change of Money Wage Rates in the United Kingdom, 1862–1957: A Further Analysis," *Economica*, February 1960, p. 2.

9 For a dissenting view, see J. Cornwall, "Do We Need Separate Theories of Inflation and Unemployment," *Canadian Public Policy — Analyse de politiques*, Supplement, April 1981, pp. 165–78.

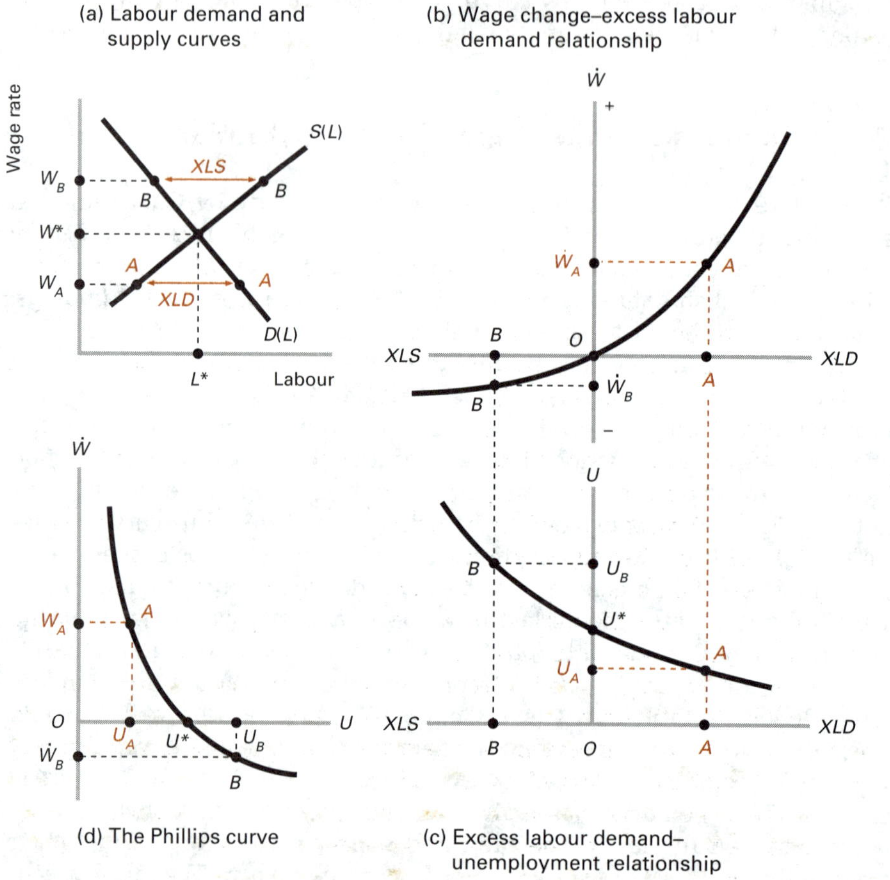

Figure 10.3 Derivation of the Phillips curve

length of time required to achieve labour market equilibrium. How quickly do wage rates change? Even though price theory has very little to say about how fast prices and wages adjust to a new equilibrium level, the general presumption is that the speed of price adjustment is proportional to the amount of excess demand. In a competitive market setting, prices likely rise more quickly when there is a large amount of excess demand. The Phillips curve model not only assumes that wage rates respond to excess labour demand (an elementary economic principle), but it goes one step further and assumes that the *speed* of the wage adjustment is directly related to the *amount* of excess demand (disequilibrium pressure) in the labour market. The greater the amount of excess labour demand (supply), the larger the upward (downward) adjustment in wage rates in a given interval of time. Because there is a lack of a solid theoretical basis for this latter assumption relating the speed of wage adjustments to the amount of excess labour demand, many economists have charged that the Phillips curve is simply an *ad hoc* empirical relationship in search of an economic theory.

In Figure 10.3(b) amounts of excess labour demand (positive values) and excess labour supply (negative values) are plotted on the horizontal axis and the wage adjustment per unit of time is plotted on the vertical axis. When the labour market is in equilibrium (zero excess labour demand), there will be no change in the wage rate. Thus, point *O* in Figure 10.3(b) corresponds to labour market equilibrium. The second, and more controversial, assumption of the Phillips curve model is represented in panel (b) by the upward-sloping curve (which goes through point *O*). Larger amounts of excess labour demand (supply) are assumed to generate larger wage increases (decreases) during a given interval of time. This hypothesized wage change–excess labour demand function probably is curved (or kinked at the origin). Wages tend to be much less flexible in a downward direction than in an upward direction, as workers (and their unions) strongly resist wage decreases. A given amount of excess labour demand (the horizontal distance *OA* in Figure 10.3(b)) will likely generate a larger wage increase than the wage decrease associated with a corresponding amount of excess labour supply (the horizontal distance *OB* in Figure 10.3(b)). The Phillips curve *curves.*

The classical and Keynesian models presented in Chapter 7 can be identified as polar opposites in terms of this wage change–excess labour demand diagram. Classical (and new classical) economists assume that wages adjust very quickly given any change in demand or supply. Under classical assumptions, very large wage adjustments would quickly restore a state of labour market equilibrium. The *classical* wage change–excess labour demand relationship would be represented, in the limit, by the *vertical* axis in Figure 10.3(b). The Keynesian assumption of inflexible wages implies a zero wage change whenever there is any amount of excess labour supply. Thus, the *Keynesian* wage change–excess labour supply relationship corresponds to the *horizontal* axis (to the left of the origin). The Phillips curve model represents an intermediate position between the polar classical and Keynesian assumptions. When excess labour supply conditions prevail, the wage rate is assumed to decline through time, but not instantaneously to its new equilibrium level. When excess labour demand conditions prevail, wage rates are assumed to rise, but again not instantaneously to their new equilibrium level. The greater the amount of excess labour demand, the larger the hypothesized wage change per unit of time.

To make the Phillips curve model operational, *excess labour demand*, an unobservable theoretical concept, must be approximated by an existing data series. Most wage analysts have assumed that the unemployment rate can be used to approximate demand and supply conditions in the labour market. As the amount of excess demand in the labour market increases, it is assumed that the level of unemployment systematically decreases: workers are more in demand and it is therefore easier for the unemployed to find jobs. Since the unemployment rate cannot fall below zero, this hypothesized relationship between unemployment and excess labour demand is not likely to be linear. As excess labour demand increases, unemployment will likely decline at a decreasing rate as the economy approaches some minimum level of unemployment (see Figure 10.3(c)).

As discussed in Chapter 7, even when the labour market is in equilibrium, some unemployment will always exist. *Frictional* unemployment occurs because an unemployed worker typically requires time to locate a job that "matches" his or her set of skills, education, and work experience. *Structural* unemployment occurs when there is a "mismatch" between the unemployed and the available jobs, that is, the unemployed do not have the necessary skills or experience to fill the vacant jobs in their local labour market. Since frictional and structural unemployment will occur even when the labour market is in equilibrium, we can locate the equilibrium level of unemployment (U^*) in Figure 10.3(c). U^* must be the point at which the unemployment–excess labour demand relationship crosses the vertical unemployment axis (where excess labour demand is zero).

Given a wage change–excess labour demand relationship (Figure 10.3(b)) and an unemployment–excess labour demand relationship (Figure 10.3(c)), the Phillips curve can be derived easily. For a given level of excess labour demand (say distance *AA* in Figure 10.3(a)), the corresponding change in the wage rate ($\dot{W}_A$ from Figure 10.3(b)) and the corresponding unemployment level (U_A from Figure 10.3(c)) can be plotted as point *A* in Figure 10.3(d). Point *A* represents one point on the derived Phillips curve. Similarly, *B* represents a second point on the derived Phillips curve, depicting a level of excess labour supply equal to *BB* in Figure 10.3(a). Taking all possible levels of excess labour demand and supply, we can trace out a smooth Phillips curve that relates wage changes to the level of unemployment. Again we can easily locate the equilibrium unemployment level in Figure 10.3(d). U^* occurs when excess labour demand is zero and there is a zero wage change. Thus, the point at which the Phillips curve crosses the horizontal axis must be U^*.

In Figure 10.3 we have graphically derived a *negative* relationship between wage changes and the level of unemployment (a proxy for excess labour demand). To facilitate subsequent algebraic derivations, we use the following equation to convert the Phillips *curve* into a *linear* expression:

$$\dot{W} = j(U^* - U)$$

or

$$\dot{W} = jU^* - jU \tag{10.5}$$

where $\dot{W}$ denotes the percentage change in the wage rate and U^* is the equilibrium level of unemployment. If the actual level of unemployment U is equal to the equilibrium unemployment level U^*, then the wage rate will not change ($\dot{W} = 0$). For unemployment levels below (above) the equilibrium unemployment level, wage changes will be positive (negative). The greater the **gap between actual unemployment and equilibrium unemployment**, the larger the wage change (be it positive or negative). The parameter j indicates the effect on the size of wage changes for a one-unit change in unemployment (given U^*). The greater the responsiveness of wages to labour market conditions, the larger will be the parameter j and the steeper the Phillips curve. Finally, if the equilibrium unemployment level were to increase for any reason, the Phillips curve would shift upwards (the vertical intercept jU^* would increase).

Even though the Phillips curve is based on the assumption of a competitive labour market, the general state of the labour market will also influence wage changes in less competitive settings, such as collective bargaining between unions and oligopolies. When aggregate demand is strong and unemployment is low, labour typically holds the upper hand in collective bargaining and can reinforce its wage demands by threatening to go on strike. Firms are particularly anxious to avoid the costs of a lengthy strike during periods of strong demand and are often willing to grant larger wage increases. In addition, with strong demand conditions prevailing throughout the economy, some firms will be attempting to increase their work forces by bidding labour away from other employers. As a consequence, firms may have to raise wage rates simply to retain their own workers (or to avoid a strike). In general, labour is in a better position to negotiate large wage increases when the unemployment rate is low (relative to U^*). Conversely, when the unemployment rate is relatively high (and jobs are scarce), workers may have to accept very low, or even negative, wage changes. With depressed economic conditions, the threat of a strike is very hollow: going on strike may simply give the firm the opportunity to get rid of unwanted inventory stocks. Depressed economic conditions and high unemployment rates exert a negative effect on the size of wage increases.

The Role of Inflation Expectations

As Milton Friedman noted in his presidential address to the American Economics Association in December 1967,

> Phillips' analysis of the relation between unemployment and wage change is deservedly celebrated as an important and original contribution. But, unfortunately, it contains a basic defect — the failure to distinguish between *nominal* wages and *real* wages.[10]

Friedman argued that the Phillips curve must be restated in terms of the **real wage**, not the **nominal wage**:

> A lower level of unemployment is an indication that there is an excess demand for labor that will produce upward pressure on real wage rates. A higher level of unemployment is an indication that there is an excess supply of labor that will produce downward pressure on real wage rates.[11]

Even though wage rates are typically set in *nominal* terms, Friedman argued that both firms and workers make labour market decisions in terms of the *real* wage rate. As discussed in Chapter 7, labour is interested in the *real* value of its *nominal* wage, that is, the nominal wage adjusted to reflect its real purchasing power. Labour will demand wage increases to offset increases in prices and will strongly resist any wage settlement that does not keep pace with the cost of living. As discussed in Chapter 7, an increase in the price level (from P_0 to P_1) will shift the labour supply curve upwards to the left (from $P_0S(L)$ to P_1S(L) in Figure 10.4). Without any compensating increase in the nominal wage rate, workers will reduce their

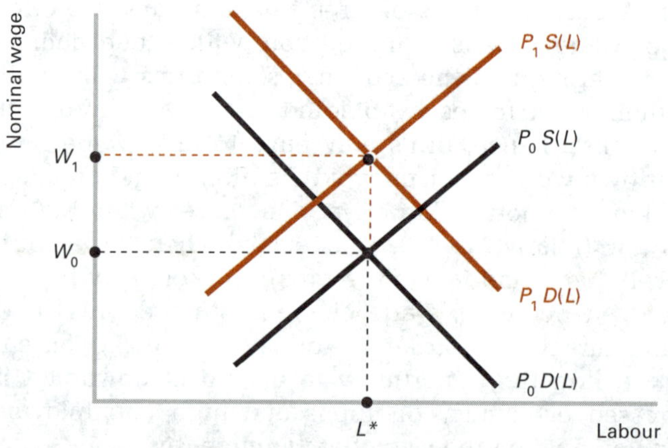

Figure 10.4 Demand and supply of labour under different price levels

[10] Milton Friedman, "The Role of Monetary Policy," *American Economic Review*, March 1968, p. 8.
[11] *Ibid.*

supply of labour when the price level increases. Labour supply decisions are based on the *real* wage rate, not the *nominal* wage rate.

The firm's demand for labour also depends on the nominal wage rate adjusted for the price level. Figure 10.4 presents a conventional downward-sloping labour demand curve. As discussed in Chapter 7, if all prices throughout the economy increase (including the price of the firm's output), the labour demand curve will shift upwards to the right. Given that the firm can now sell its products at a higher price (P_1), the firm will want to expand production and hire more labour at the given nominal wage. Without a compensating increase in the nominal wage, an increase in the price level produces an increase in the firm's demand for labour (from $P_0D(L)$ to $P_1D(L)$ in Figure 10.4).

Thus, if all prices throughout the economy rise from P_0 to P_1, as shown in Figure 10.4, the labour supply curve shifts upwards to the left and the labour demand curve shifts upwards to the right. At the existing wage rate W_0, a state of excess labour demand arises and the nominal wage will eventually be bid up to its new equilibrium value, W_1. Once the labour market has returned to equilibrium, the quantity of labour demanded and supplied (L^*) will be exactly the same as before prices increased. The nominal wage will have increased in direct proportion to the increase in prices. As discussed in Chapter 7, an increase in the price level has no effect on the real wage or on the equilibrium quantity of labour. Labour demand and supply decisions depend on the *real* wage, not the *nominal* wage.

It is important to recognize that the labour market differs from many other markets in one important respect. Unlike auction markets, such as the stock exchange, the price of labour does not typically change hourly, or daily, or even monthly. Approximately 40 percent of the work force belongs to unions or employee associations, and typically signs wage contracts that fix the wage schedule for one to three years. Non-unionized employees usually have their wages reviewed once a year (in an annual performance review), with an appropriate annual adjustment made to the wage. The transactions and negotiating costs are simply too large to permit firms to renegotiate (or reset) wages each day, week, or month. By fixing wage rates for periods of time, explicit or implicit contracts in the labour market severely limit the short-run flexibility of wages.

Given such contractual rigidities in the labour market, the relevant price consideration in setting the real wage is the *expected* value of future prices. In bargaining for a new contract, workers compare a prospective wage rate for the next contract period with the *expected* price level of goods that will be purchased during this period of time. If workers *expect* prices to rise, they will demand higher wages to compensate them for this expected future inflation. Firms will be willing to pay higher wages because they also expect their product prices, and therefore their total revenues, to rise.

Returning to Figure 10.4, suppose that a firm and a group of workers are about to negotiate a new wage contract. Let us assume that the labour market is currently in equilibrium, with a nominal wage of W_0 and a price level of P_0. Now if the labour demand and supply curves are *expected* to remain stable over the next contractual period, no wage adjustment will be required; the labour market is expected to remain in equilibrium throughout the contract period at the existing W_0 nominal wage.

However, if price levels are expected to rise from P_0 to P_1, the labour demand and supply curves will not be expected to remain stable but rather will be expected to shift upwards during the course of the contract. If *no* nominal wage adjustment is included in the new contract, the expected price increase (to the extent that it materializes) will create excess labour demand during the next contractual period. Such labour market disequilibrium imposes costs on both workers and the firm. Workers obviously suffer a real wage loss if prices increase but nominal wages do not increase. If the real wage falls below its equilibrium level (because the nominal wage has not been increased), the firm will find it difficult to hire new workers to satisfy its additional demand for labour and to replace disgruntled workers who have quit because of the decline in the real wage.

If the nominal wage is not increased to offset the effects of this expected increase in prices, a substantial amount of excess labour demand will build up over the course of the wage contract. While this build-up of excess labour demand will trigger a "Phillips curve" wage adjustment at the time of the next contract negotiation (perhaps several years later), during the upcoming contract period both labour and the firm will experience disequilibrium costs arising from a decline in the real wage. To avoid these disequilibrium costs, the nominal wage should be increased to offset the effects of *expected* price inflation. If the nominal wage increases in direct proportion to any price increase, the real wage will remain constant and the labour market will remain in a state of equilibrium (at L^* in Figure 10.4) throughout the contract period.

Thus, the basic Phillips curve should be augmented to include the *expected* price inflation rate (over the next contract period). Denoting the expected price inflation rate by $\dot{P}^e$, Equation 10.5 presents a linear version of the **price-expectations Phillips (*PEP*) curve**:

$$\dot{W} = \dot{P}^e + j(U^* - U) \tag{10.5}$$

The size of wage changes now depends on two factors: excess demand in the labour market (which is represented by the difference between the equilibrium unemployment level U^* and the actual unemployment level U) and the expected inflation rate ($\dot{P}^e$). Either a decrease in unemployment (for a given U^*) or an increase in the expected inflation rate will lead to larger wage increases.

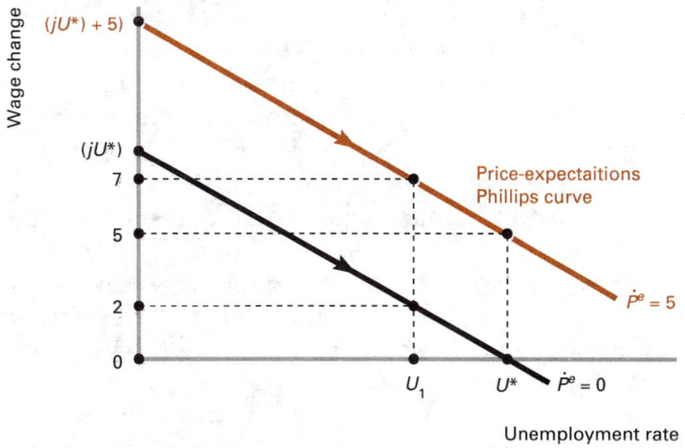

Figure 10.5 The effects of a change in inflation expectations on wage adjustments and the Phillips curve

Note in Equation 10.5 we have assumed that the nominal wage will increase by the expected increase in the price level, that is, the coefficient on $\dot{P}^e$ is implicitly unity. Each extra percentage point of expected inflation increases the intercept of the (linear) Phillips curve by exactly one point. As shown in Figure 10.5, an increase in the expected inflation rate from 0 percent to 5 percent will cause a 5 percent upward shift in the underlying Phillips curve and result in wage increases that are 5 percent higher, irrespective of the level of unemployment.

Although many early Phillips curve studies included a price inflation variable in the wage change equation, Friedman's contribution to the Phillips curve literature is twofold. First, Friedman stressed that it is the *expected* inflation rate that is relevant: labour market participants are *forward-looking*, not *backward-looking*. Second, on the basis of labour market theory, Friedman argued that the coefficient on inflation expectations in the price-expectations Phillips curve should be exactly equal to unity, to preserve the real wage rate. Early Phillips curve studies frequently reported estimated inflation coefficients that were substantially less than unity. For *theoretical* reasons Friedman rejected the *empirical* possibility that the inflation coefficient could be less than unity.

Wage Adjustments and the Role of Productivity Growth

Conventional microeconomic theory suggests that workers will be paid their marginal product. Thus an increase in labour productivity ought to be reflected in an increase in wage rates. For example, if workers increase their productivity by 2 percent annually, then wages should increase by 2 percent each year, *ceteris paribus*. In terms of our standard labour demand and supply diagram, an increase in labour productivity shifts the demand for labour curve to the right: profit-maximizing firms will want to hire additional "more productive" workers, whatever the prevailing wage rate. For a given labour supply curve, an increase in labour demand will cause an increase in the equilibrium wage rate.

Using the same argument as outlined above, if workers are expected to increase their productivity during the next contract period, new wage contracts will likely include an additional wage adjustment to reflect the expected increase in labour productivity. Without such a wage adjustment, excess labour demand will arise during the next contract period (because the demand for labour curve shifts to the right but the wage rate has not been adjusted). To avoid the costs of disequilibrium, new wage contracts will include a provision for the *expected* growth in productivity. We assume that firms and workers base their expectations of future labour productivity growth on the average productivity growth rate during the recent past, which we have represented by $PR\dot{O}DT$.

Expanding our price-expectations Phillips curve to include the effects of **labour productivity growth**, our linear *PEP* equation can be represented in the following manner:

$$\dot{W} = PR\dot{O}DT + \dot{P}^e + j(U^* - U) \tag{10.6}$$

Each extra point of labour productivity growth is assumed to increase the size of the wage change by one point. Even when the labour market is in equilibrium, the *real* wage rate increases one-for-one with (expected) labour productivity growth. The presence of the unemployment rate in Equation 10.6 continues to give the Phillips curve its essential disequilibrium characteristics. Whenever the labour market is in disequilibrium (U does not equal U^*), nominal wages will be changing and the labour market will be heading back towards equilibrium. Labour productivity growth and/or expected inflation represent additional determinants of the size of wage changes, and affect nominal wages whether or not the labour market is in equilibrium.

The Empirical Evidence for a Price-Expectations Phillips Curve

The Phillips, Lipsey, and Friedman papers provided the stimulus for a great outpouring of empirical research on wage changes and a number of early Canadian studies played a prominent role in the international acceptance of the Phillips curve concept.[12]

In Figure 10.6(a) we present a scatter diagram for average annual wage settlements, based on new wage contracts (without a COLA clause) signed each year, and the Canadian unemployment rate. Since Labour Canada did not publish data on the size of new wage settlements until 1967, our scatter diagram is based on the years 1967 through 1990. In two dimensions this scatter diagram is rather discouraging; the points appear to be almost randomly scattered throughout the diagram. However, our theoretical *PEP* curve model asserts that wage settlements depend on three factors:

1. the gap between the equilibrium unemployment rate and the actual unemployment rate,
2. the expected inflation rate, and
3. the average labour productivity growth rate.

Assuming that the average productivity growth rate and the equilibrium unemployment rate remained relatively constant over this time period, the *PEP* curve model predicts that the size of wage settlements will depend on the unemployment rate and the expected inflation rate. A two-dimensional diagram (for wage changes and the unemployment rate) may easily produce a wide scatter of points if the missing factor (expected inflation) is not constant over the time period.

The Canadian inflation rate and the expected inflation rate clearly were not constant over the 1967–90 period. For the years 1967 through 1972, the Canadian inflation rate fluctuated in the narrow interval between 2.9 and 4.8 percent, averaging less than 4 percent. For the next ten years the Canadian inflation rate ranged from 7.5 to 12.5 percent, with an average value of 9.6 percent. Finally, in 1983 the inflation rate receded to 5.7 percent and remained between 4 and 5 percent for the next seven years (1984–90).

To bring a little order to this scatter diagram, we have plotted the first six years (1967–72) and last seven years (1984–90) of relatively low inflation in colour. These 13 low inflation observations are scattered very close to a "low" *PEP* curve, reflecting a low expected inflation rate. The remaining observations for the high inflation years, 1973–83, plotted in black, are more widely scattered about a "high" *PEP* curve. The 1972 and 1973 observations, as well as the 1983 and 1984 observations, straddle the low and high *PEP* curves. The most obvious outlier is the

12 Most notably the papers by S.F. Kaliski, "The Relation Between Unemployment and the Rate of Change of Money Wages in Canada," *International Economic Review*, January 1964, pp. 1–33; and J. Vanderkamp, "Wage and Price Level Determination: An Empirical Model for Canada," *Economica*, May 1966, pp. 194–218.

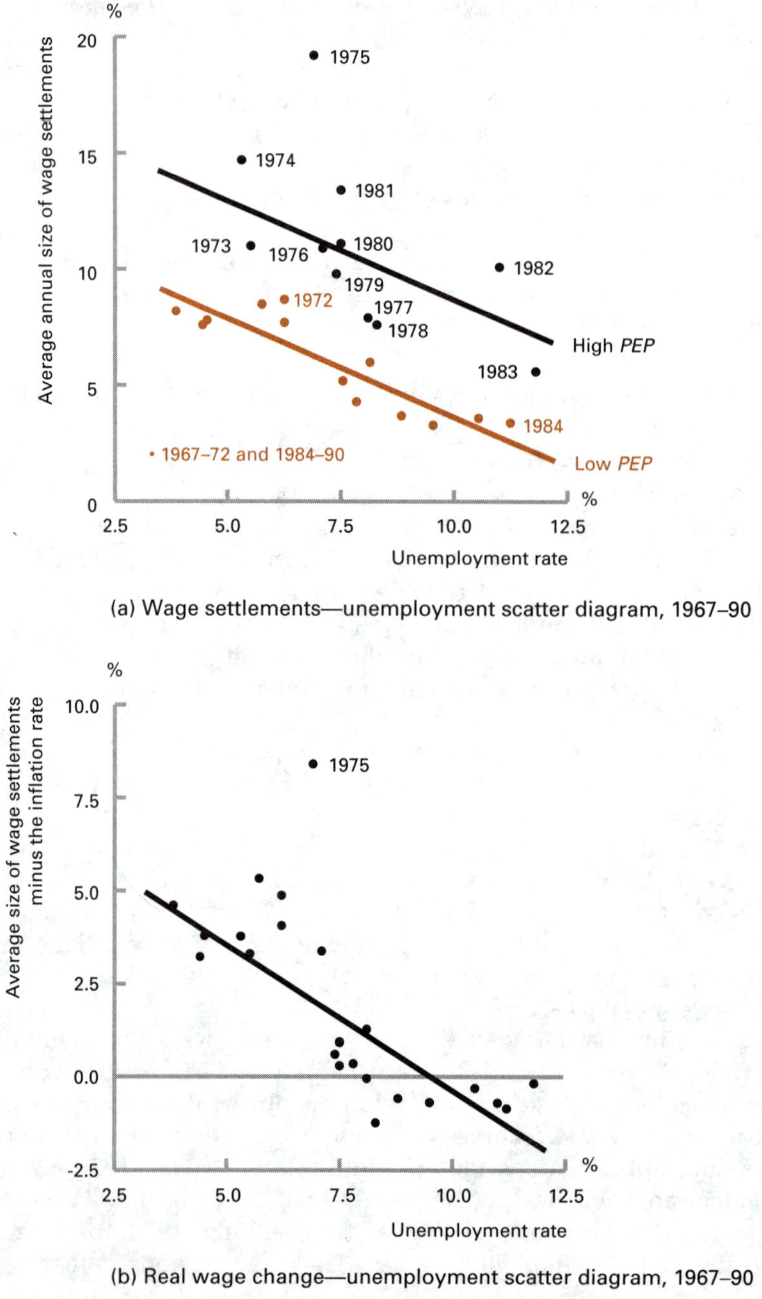

Figure 10.6 Price-expectations Phillips curves in Canada, 1967–90

1975 observation. The extremely high average wage settlement of 19.2 percent in 1975 reflected a substantial amount of wage catch-up for the unexpected double-digit inflation of 1974 and 1975.[13] The other three highest points (1974, 1981, and 1982) all correspond to years in which the inflation rate was at its highest point (10.9, 12.5, and 10.8 percent, respectively).

Thus the scatter of data points in Figure 10.6(a) is consistent with a price-expectations Phillips curve. As the (expected) inflation rate increased during the 1970s, the size of wage changes rose accordingly. When inflation is relatively constant, wage changes decrease in size as the unemployment rate rises (the data points drift downwards to the right).

A more direct test of the price-expectations Phillips curve hypothesis would be to plot the change in the *expected real* wage against the unemployment rate. However, before we can perform such a test, we must first quantify inflation expectations, another unobservable theoretical construct to go along with excess labour demand. By their very nature, price expectations are highly subjective and difficult to quantify. There is a world of difference between obtaining a measure of today's price of X and providing an estimate of what people *think* next year's price of X will be. The Conference Board in Canada only began to publish private forecasts of the change in the consumer price index in the 1970s (see Case Study 3 in Chapter 8); no continuous inflation expectations data exist back to 1967 (the start of our time series on wage settlements). As a proxy for inflation expectations we use the actual inflation rate during the year.[14] The *expected real* wage change is approximated by the average size of wage settlements minus the actual inflation rate.

Figure 10.6(b) presents a scatter diagram for the *expected real* wage change and the unemployment rate. Unlike the wide scatter of points in panel (a), most of the *expected real* wage change points are quite close to a downward-sloping line. The estimated slope of the least squares regression line is –0.8;[15] each additional point of unemployment lowers the *expected real* wage increase by 0.8 percent. Holding inflation expectations constant, a 2.5 percentage-point increase in the unemploy-

---

13 Multi-year wage contracts signed before the unexpected outbreak of double-digit inflation in 1973–74 were based on inflation expectations estimates that were far too low, and large "catch-up" wage increases were required to restore the *real* wage rate. For example, if a three-year wage contract signed in late 1972 was based on an expected inflation rate of 4 percent, the cumulative 1973–1975 inflation rate of over 29 percent would have produced an unexpected real wage decline of over 17 percent.

14 In Case Study 3 in Chapter 8 we showed that the average inflation forecasts published by the Conference Board of Canada during the 1980s were *rational*. The actual inflation rate deviated from the forecast inflation rate only by a small error.

15 Since the 1975 "catch-up" observation is an obvious outlier, we have omitted it from the calculation of the least squares line.

ment rate (say from 7.5 to 10 percent) is required to lower the rate of wage inflation by 2 percent. In statististical terms, about 80 percent of the variation in nominal wage changes is explained by movements in the inflation rate and in the unemployment rate.

The empirical evidence presented in Figure 10.6 clearly demonstrates that nominal wage changes in Canada are strongly influenced by the unemployment rate and the expected inflation rate. The *PEP* curve is alive and well in Canada. In Case Study 5 we use estimates of the Canadian *PEP* curve drawn through this scatter of points in Figure 10.6(b) to obtain an estimate for the Canadian natural rate of unemployment U^*.

Case Study 5: The Canadian *Natural* Rate of Unemployment (NAIRU)

The purpose of this case study is to provide an estimate for the *natural* rate of unemployment (or NAIRU) in Canada during the 1970s and 1980s, based on econometric estimates for the *PEP* equation (10.6):

$$\dot{W} = \dot{P}^e + PR\dot{O}DT + j(U^* - U) \qquad (10.6)$$

or

$$\dot{W} - \dot{P}^e = (PR\dot{O}DT + jU^*) - jU$$

Figure 10.6(b) presents a scatter diagram for the *expected real* wage change and the unemployment rate. The least squares estimates for the line drawn through this scatter diagram are given below (with standard errors for the two coefficients given in parentheses below the respective coefficients):

$$\dot{W} - \dot{P}^e = \underset{(0.93)}{7.66} - \underset{(0.12)}{0.806}U \qquad R^2 = 0.68$$

Comparing the parameters in the theoretical *PEP* equation (10.6) with the above statistical estimates, the sum ($PR\dot{O}DT + jU^*$) is estimated to be 7.66 and the parameter j is estimated to be 0.806. To determine the value of jU^* we must subtract the trend productivity growth rate $PR\dot{O}DT$ from 7.66. From 1967 through 1990 the average growth rate of labour productivity, as measured by real GDP per employee, was 1.48 percent per annum. Subtracting 1.48 (for $PR\dot{O}DT$) from 7.66, the estimated value of jU^* is 6.18. Dividing 6.18 (jU^*) by 0.806 (j), the natural rate of unemployment U^* in Canada is estimated to be 7.67 percent.

Our econometric results for the price-expectations Phillips curve suggest that during the 1970s and 1980s the equilibrium unemployment rate in Canada was slightly in excess of 7.5 percent. In calculating this estimate for U^* we have made a number of important assumptions, which we briefly enumerate. First, we have linearized the Phillips curve. Second, we have assumed inflation expectations can be proxied by the actual inflation rate and have assumed that the coefficient on inflation expectations in the Phillips curve equation is exactly one. Third, we have assumed a constant labour productivity growth rate of 1.48 percent over the entire 1967 to 1990 period. Fourth we have ignored all other factors that might have influenced wage settlements, such as the Anti-Inflation Board during the period 1975–1978 (see Chapter 14). Finally, we have assumed that the equilibrium unemployment rate has remained constant over this entire 24-year period.

The *equilibrium* or *natural* rate of unemployment depends on specific features of the labour market that determine the amount of frictional and structural unemployment. A general consensus exists that the Canadian *natural* rate of unemployment increased in the early 1970s. In retrospect, most economists believe that the Canadian economy was very buoyant in the early 1970s, and that the 1971 and 1972 unemployment rates of 6.2 percent (the highest unemployment rate since 1961) represented a very misleading picture of the state of the Canadian labour market. The Economic Council of Canada concluded in its 1976 study of the Canadian labour market that "basic changes in the labour market have rendered the message of the unemployment rate today rather different from that of a decade ago."[16] In other words, unemployment rates for the 1970s and 1980s cannot be directly compared to unemployment rates for the 1950s and 1960s. A 6 percent unemployment rate is *high* in the 1960s but *low* in the 1980s, because the *equilibrium* unemployment rate increased from about 5 percent to over 7 percent during the early 1970s.

Two possible explanations have been suggested to account for this increase in the natural rate of unemployment around 1970. The first explanation focuses on demographic changes in the Canadian labour force. During the 1960s and 1970s the age, sex, and family status characteristics of the Canadian labour force changed dramatically. The participation rate of females aged 25 to 54 doubled, rising from 28.9 percent in 1960 to 57.8 percent in 1979. In addition, the under-25 age component of the labour force substantially increased during this same time period. The composition of the labour force and the unemployed clearly shifted towards younger people and secondary earners in the family. The traditional stereotype of the unemployed worker as a prime-age male with a family to support became less and less typical. This trend towards multiple-earner family units may have alleviated some of

---

16 Economic Council of Canada, *People and Jobs: A Study of the Canadian Labour Market* (Ottawa, 1976), p. 211.

the economic hardship associated with unemployment and may have reduced the urgency for some secondary workers to obtain a job (that is, secondary earners may be able to spend longer periods of time searching for a "suitable" job). In addition, the changing demographic composition of the labour force likely heightened structural unemployment problems, as the skills and experience levels of the large number of new entrants into the labour force may not have matched the existing set of job vacancies. For a variety of reasons, the changing demographic structure of the the Canadian labour force during the 1960s and early 1970s may have resulted in a higher natural rate of unemployment.

An alternative explanation for an increase in the *natural* rate of unemployment focuses upon revisions to the Unemployment Insurance Act in 1971, revisions that may have exacerbated demographic effects. The 1971 Unemployment Insurance Act revisions increased unemployment insurance benefits, extended benefit periods, and decreased qualification time periods. After reviewing unemployment insurance programs in the United States and Europe, the Economic Council of Canada concluded that "Canada's unemployment [insurance] program is among the most generous."[17] The improvements in the unemployment insurance program in 1971 significantly altered the incentive structure within the labour market, particularly for secondary workers. It would be very surprising if some workers did not respond to this new, enriched unemployment insurance *dis*incentive structure and change their labour supply behaviour. As the Department of Finance acknowledged:

> Other things being equal, such changes [in unemployment insurance] would be expected to increase the attractiveness of labour force participation, increase the rate at which people tend to quit existing jobs and lengthen the duration of time unemployed people tend to spend unemployed. Each of these effects would tend to increase the measured unemployment rate associated with each rate of inflation. The available evidence suggests that in varying degrees all three effects could very well have been operating after 1971.[18]

To the extent that people responded to the 1971 improvements in the unemployment insurance program and exercised more discretion over the choice of jobs that they would accept, the natural rate of unemployment would have increased. A number of studies have examined the effect of the 1971 unemployment revisions and have concluded that the level of unemployment in Canada was significantly higher than it would

[17] *Ibid.*, p. 271.

[18] Department of Finance, *Canada's Recent Inflation Experience* (Ottawa, November 1978), p. 36.

have been in the absence of any changes to the Unemployment Insurance Act.[19]

These two factors may be operating in reverse fashion during the 1990s to lower the natural rate of unemployment. With the baby boomers now fully absorbed into the labour force, the growth rate of the labour force has slowed down considerably (averaging only 1.25 percent per year in 1989–90, compared to 3 percent average annual increases in the late 1960s and early 1970s). With fewer new entrants to the labour force, frictional and structural unemployment problems should be less severe. In addition, the Conservative government has instituted measures to tighten up the unemployment insurance system, which should exert downward pressure on the equilibrium unemployment rate.

Summary of the *PEP* Curve

Our structural explanation for inflation is based on two interrelated theories of wage and price behaviour. Given profit-maximizing behaviour (or a *markup* pricing model), prices will vary directly with changes in unit labour costs. Approximating the percentage change in unit labour costs by the percentage change in wage rates ($\dot{W}$) minus the percentage change in average labour productivity growth ($PR\dot{O}DT$), the following equation for the rate of price inflation is obtained:

$$\dot{P} = \dot{W} - PR\dot{O}DT \qquad (10.4a)$$

Although we assume that the average growth rate of labour productivity is *exogenously* determined, the rate of wage change is a key *endogenous* variable within our model.

Following the important research of Phillips, Lipsey, and Friedman, the rate of wage change is assumed to depend on three factors: the *expected* rate of price inflation ($\dot{P}^e$), the average growth rate of labour productivity ($PR\dot{O}DT$), and excess labour demand, which is represented by the gap between equilibrium unemployment U^* and actual unemployment U. A decrease in unemployment (for a given U^*) will cause an increase in the rate of wage change:

$$\dot{W} = \dot{P}^e + PR\dot{O}DT + j(U^* - U) \qquad (10.6)$$

Substituting this wage change equation (10.6) into the price change

19 See, for example, C. Green and J.-M. Cousineau, *Unemployment in Canada: The Impact of the Unemployment Insurance* (Ottawa: Economic Council of Canada, 1976).

equation (10.4a) produces the following combined relationship (the $PR\dot{O}DT$ terms cancel out each other):

$$\dot{P} = \dot{P}^e + j(U^* - U) \tag{10.7}$$

The rate of price inflation depends on the expected inflation rate ($\dot{P}^e$) and the level of unemployment (for a given equilibrium level of unemployment) — the price-expectations Phillips curve.

As noted at the beginning of the chapter, the Phillips curve can be thought of as a bridge between the *classical* assumption of highly flexible wages with continual labour-market clearing and the *Keynesian* assumption of wage rigidity with persistent disequilibrium unemployment. Under the Phillips curve hypothesis, wage and price inflation will occur whenever the unemployment rate is below the equilibrium unemployment rate. By expanding the simple Phillips curve model to include the role of inflation expectations, the simultaneous occurrence of both high inflation (because of high inflation expectations) and high unemployment can be explained. The price-expectations Phillips curve provides a possible explanation, absent from both classical and Keynesian models, of how an economic system can simultaneously experience both inflation and unemployment.

Simple variants of the Phillips curve (without price inflation expectations) were quickly assimilated into the conventional economic wisdom and almost immediately the Phillips curve took on "a life of its own."[20] The rapid acceptance of the Phillips curve concept by both economists and policymakers can largely be attributed to two factors. First, the Phillips curve describes an economic system in which both inflation and unemployment can exist simultaneously. Macroeconomics was no longer confined to the straight jacket of either *zero* inflation or *full* employment. Second, the policy ramifications of a negative relationship between inflation and unemployment were ominous and could not be overlooked. The Phillips curve introduced an important new constraint into macroeconomic policy formulation. If the government pursues an expansionary fiscal or monetary policy to reduce unemployment, wages and prices will start to rise. The desirable goals of low unemployment and low inflation may not be mutually obtainable: the Phillips curve *suggested* that low rates of unemployment may have to be *traded off* against higher rates of inflation (or vice versa). In this context, the rapid conversion of policymakers to the Phillips curve concept was perhaps understandable. A government should not be expected to lower both inflation and unemployment *simultaneously*: the best that policymakers

[20] To illustrate the speed with which the Phillips curve was assimilated into economics, the 1961 revision of P.A. Samuelson's widely used introductory economics textbook included a section on Phillips's 1958 paper.

may be able do is to *trade off* one problem for the other. The notion of a *trade-off* between unemployment and inflation was quickly incorporated into the politician's lexicon, and the Phillips curve became a popular explanation or rationalization for the existence of either unemployment or inflation.

As we shall see in subsequent chapters, the inflationary process runs much deeper than the price-expectations Phillips curve. If the government (unexpectedly) pursues a more expansionary monetary or fiscal policy, unemployment declines and the inflation rate rises (via the Phillips curve). However, people will adjust their inflation expectations upwards, thus causing the price-expectations Phillips curve to shift upwards. An (unexpected) expansionary policy produces both a movement along and a shift in the price-expectations Phillips curve. Thus, the Phillips curve does not represent a *stable* inflation–unemployment trade-off curve that policymakers can exploit. The inclusion of inflation expectations within the Phillips curve eliminates the possibility of a permanent trade-off between inflation and unemployment. Attempts by the government to lower the actual level of unemployment below the natural rate will lead to repeated upward shifts in the price-expectations Phillips curve (as inflation expectations are continually adjusted upwards), triggering a wage–price spiral and an accelerating inflation rate.

Recent Developments in Keynesian Theory to Explain Price and Wage Rigidities

The three key assumptions of new classical macroeconomics (discussed in Chapter 8) are: (1) optimizing behaviour on the part of economic agents, (2) rational expectations, and (3) continual market-clearing. Most economists find it difficult to argue that people and firms do not act in their own best interests, that is, that they do not optimize. Although some economists have criticized the assumption of rational expectations on the grounds that people may not be this rational, most economic theorists accept the assumption of rational expectations. Most new Keynesian macroeconomists are willing to accept the first two assumptions of new classical macroeconomics (optimizing behaviour and rational expectations) but not the third assumption (continual market-clearing). New Keynesian macroeconomists find it hard to believe that the goods and labour markets were in equilibrium during the 1930s (or 1981–82 and 1990–91) and are unimpressed with new classical explanations for equilibrium output and employment during depressions and recessions (see Chapter 8). Did 15 to 20 percent of the labour force *voluntarily* opt for leisure during the decade of the 1930s (and 12 percent of the labour force in 1982–83)?

New Keynesian macroeconomists believe that cyclical movements in output, employment, and unemployment can be explained by various price and wage rigidities that prevent the goods and labour markets from clearing continually (even when people optimize and form their expectations rationally). In the final section of this chapter we review several new Keynesian theories concerning the existence of price and wage rigidities.

Price Rigidities in the Goods Market

Even though there are many commodities (such as oil and copper) that are bought and sold in *auction* markets where prices quickly adjust to changing demand and supply conditions, many goods are sold in *price tag* markets where the price on the tag remains fixed for a period of time. Unlike auction markets where goods tend to be standardized and homogeneous (such as a litre of gasoline), price tag markets typically consist of heterogeneous, nonstandardized commodities (such as "brand name" goods found in most stores). In price tag markets customers typically shop around before they purchase, comparing the price tags (say on VCRs) in different stores. To promote a continuing relationship with their customers, most stores try to maintain stable prices. Regular shoppers can become very irritated if prices are constantly changing: you will not be very happy if the VCR you looked at last week has a higher price this week, or if the VCR you purchased last week has a lower price this week. Besides the risk of alienating regular customers, changing price tags, catalogues, and menus involves obvious printing and labour costs.

Given the **costs of adjusting prices**, profit-maximizing firms may not immediately change prices to a new equilibrium price level. Suppose that the marketplace is characterized by imperfect competition and the typical firm faces a downward-sloping demand (average revenue AR) curve. To maximize profits, the firm sets prices so that marginal costs equal marginal revenues. Figure 10.7(a) presents the firm's *expected* average revenue (AR^E), marginal revenue (MR^E), and marginal cost (MC^E) curves. The firm *sets* its price tags at the *expected* profit-maximizing price level P_0, based on the intersection point of the MR^E and MC^E curves; the firm expects to sell Q_0^E units of output (point E on the AR^E curve).

But suppose there is an *unexpected* decrease in aggregate demand; the firm's *actual* average revenue AR^A curve turns out to be to the left of the *expected* AR^E curve (see Figure 10.7(b)). With price tags already set at P_0, the firm finds itself at point A on the *actual* AR^A curve (rather than point E on the *expected* AR^E curve). Actual sales (Q_0) are lower than expected sales (Q_0^E), because of the unexpected decrease in aggregate demand.

Assuming that actual marginal costs are the same as expected mar-

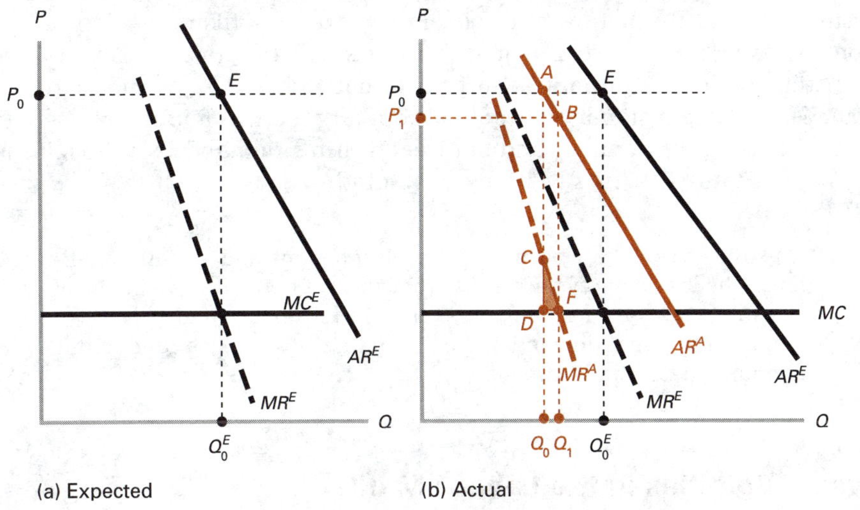

Figure 10.7 Price setting behaviour

ginal costs, the *new* profit-maximizing price level is now P_1, based on the intersection point F of the MC curve and the *actual* MR^A curve in Figure 10.7(b). Given an unexpected decline in demand, the profit-maximizing firm should cut prices from P_0 to P_1 and increase output from Q_0 to Q_1; it should move down its *actual* AR^A demand curve from point A to point B.

However, the costs of changing price tags and reprinting catalogues may prevent the profit-maximizing firm from lowering prices to this *new* equilibrium price level P_1. The marginal profit from lowering prices from P_0 to P_1 and raising output from Q_0 to Q_1 is represented by the triangular area CDF between the *actual* marginal revenue MR^A curve and the marginal cost MC curve. Lowering prices to their new equilibrium level may raise profits by a relatively small amount. If the costs of changing price tags and reprinting catalogues exceeds the additional profit from lowering prices to the new equilibrium level P_1, the profit-maximizing firm will maintain its existing *disequilibrium* price level P_0. Price inflexibility can arise, even when firms maximize profits and form their expectations rationally.

If all firms find that the costs of changing price tags and reprinting catalogues exceed the additional profits from lowering prices, then the aggregate price level will not decline following an unexpected decline in aggregate demand. The economy will remain trapped in a recession, because of rigid prices. Although there may be large benefits to society from all firms lowering their prices (which would move the economic system back to the natural rate of output), the benefits of a price reduction for each individual firm may be too small (relative to the costs of adjusting prices) to prompt each firm to cut prices. Under such circumstances, an expansionary fiscal or monetary policy might be used to restore aggregate demand and shift each firm's demand curve back out to AR^E in Figure 10.7. As Mankiw has noted,

> . . . sticky prices can be both privately efficient and socially inefficient. The business cycle results from the suboptimal adjustment of prices in response to a demand shock. To the extent that policy can stabilize aggregate demand, it can mitigate the social loss due to this suboptimal (price) adjustment.[21]

Wage Rigidities in the Labour Market

Efficiency Wage Theories

Efficiency wage theories have been proposed to explain wage rigidities in the labour market and the possible existence of permanent excess labour supply (unemployment). The key element of an **efficiency wage theory** is the assumption that worker effort (productivity) depends on the level of the wage. Higher wages are assumed to increase worker productivity and efficiency. If the increase in productivity exceeds the increase in wages, firms' profits will increase. If profits increase, the profit-maximizing firm will choose to pay higher wages, for *efficiency* reasons.

Figure 10.8 presents a standard labour demand and supply diagram. A profit-maximizing firm may choose to pay a wage above the market-clearing wage W^*, for *efficiency* reasons. At a higher wage, such as W_{EFF}, workers may put out more effort (increasing their productivity), which would result in higher profits for the firm. But at this higher *efficiency* wage W_{EFF}, the supply of labour exceeds the demand for labour. There will be $L_S - L_D$ people who want to work at W_{EFF} but who receive no offers of employment. Even though there may be unemployed workers competing for jobs, firms may refuse to lower the wage because they fear that a reduction in wages for existing workers will reduce their productivity by more than the gain from lowering wage costs. Efficiency wage theories provide a possible explanation for why profit-maximizing firms may be unwilling to reduce wages in periods of

---

[21] N.G. Mankiw, "Small Menu Costs and Large Business Cycles: A Macroeconomic Model of Monopoly," *Quarterly Journal of Economics*, May 1985, p. 529.

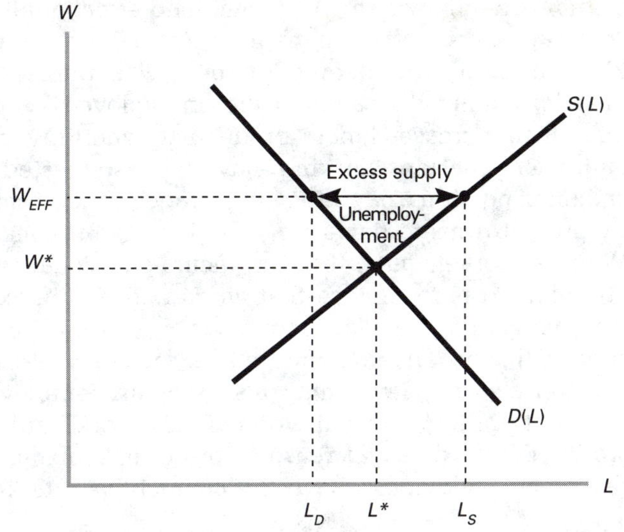

Figure 10.8 Efficiency wages and unemployment

unemployment; to do so may lower the productivity of existing workers by more than the cut in wages, and hence reduce firms' profits.

Carl Shapiro and Joseph Stiglitz[22] of Princeton University have suggested that paying a wage higher than the market-clearing wage may reduce shirking (slacking off) on the job and thus increase labour productivity and efficiency. If all workers are paid the market-clearing wage, there would be no unemployment. A worker can shirk on the job without any penalty. If a shirker is caught and fired, he can easily find another job at the market-clearing wage. To reduce shirking on the job (and increase labour productivity), a firm may decide to raise the wage above the market-clearing wage. If a worker is now caught shirking and fired, that worker will face the penalty of receiving the lower market-clearing wage at another firm. Raising the wage rate above the market-clearing level increases the cost of shirking and provides an incentive for employees to work harder to keep their *high* paying jobs.

But what is good for the goose is good for the gander. All firms may decide to raise their wage rates to eliminate shirking on the job. But if all firms pay workers a wage higher than the market-clearing wage (to eliminate shirking), then the supply of labour will exceed the demand for labour at this higher efficiency wage. If a shirker is caught and fired,

---

22 C. Shapiro and J.E. Stiglitz, "Equilibrium Unemployment as a Worker Discipline Device," *American Economic Review*, June 1984, pp. 433–44.

the penalty is now unemployment. The combined effect of all firms paying efficiency wages creates permanent excess labour supply, a "reserve army" of unemployed people (to borrow a phrase from Karl Marx). The fear of joining the ranks of the unemployed keeps workers from shirking, which increases labour productivity and firms' profits.

Other explanations (besides shirking) have been suggested to explain why profit-maximizing firms pay efficiency wages. The costs of labour turnover may prompt firms to pay a wage higher than the market-clearing wage. When a worker quits, the firm incurs additional recruitment, hiring, and training costs to replace that worker. To retain existing employees and minimize the costs of labour turnover, a profit-maximizing firm may choose to pay an efficiency wage premium. Paying wages above the market-clearing level may also increase employee morale and loyalty to the firm; happy, loyal workers may work harder, increasing firms' profits. For a variety of reasons, profit-maximizing firms may choose to pay efficiency wages above the competitive, market-clearing level.

Efficiency wage theories provide a possible explanation for the existence of wage rigidities in the labour market (why profit-maximizing firms may be unwilling to lower wages) and for the phenomenon of permanent excess labour supply (unemployment).

The Insider–Outsider Model

Some new Keynesians, such as Olivier Blanchard of MIT and Lawrence Summers of Harvard University,[23] view the labour market as being divided into two groups: those with jobs (insiders) and those without jobs (outsiders). Insiders are assumed to be able to negotiate a wage that is in the best interests of the insiders; they do not concern themselves with the economic plight of the outsiders (the unemployed). Given the wage negotiated by the insiders, the outsiders remain unemployed.

To illustrate the **insider–outsider** model, suppose that there are L_0 insiders (see Figure 10.9) and these insiders expect the labour demand curve to be located at position $D_0(L)$ next year. The L_0 insiders are assumed to have sufficient bargaining power to negotiate a wage of W_0, the maximum wage that insiders can receive and still expect to keep their jobs. If actual labour demand turns out to be the same as expected labour demand $D_0(L)$, profit-maximizing firms will employ all L_0 insiders at the negotiated wage W_0. The insiders stay insiders and any outsiders remain on the outside. Given no unexpected shocks to the economy, any unemployment that happened to exist will continue to exist.

[23] O.J. Blanchard and L.H. Summers, "Hysteresis and the European Unemployment Problem," in Stanley Fischer, ed., *Macroeconomics Annual 1986* (National Bureau of Economic Research, The M.I.T. Press, Cambridge, Mass., 1986), pp. 15–78.

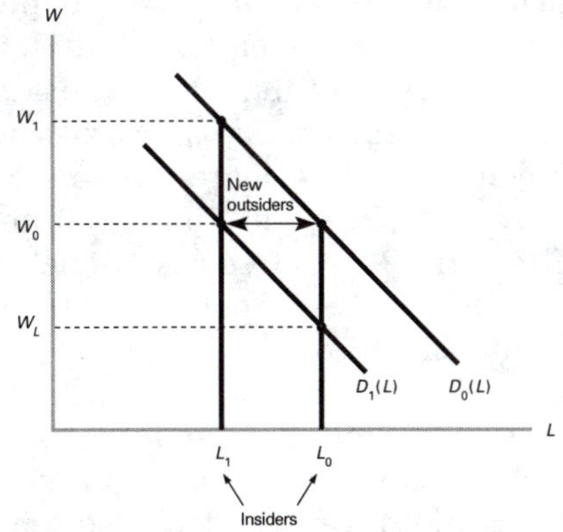

Figure 10.9 Insider–outsider model

Suppose that aggregate demand turns out to be lower than expected and the actual labour demand curve turns out to be $D_1(L)$, to the left of the expected $D_0(L)$. At the negotiated wage W_0 (which is already set), profit-maximizing firms will reduce employment to L_1 and $L_0 - L_1$ insiders will lose their jobs. These former insiders are now on the outside, with the rest of the unemployed. An unexpected decline in demand creates additional unemployment.

If this decline in aggregate demand and lower $D_1(L)$ labour demand persists into subsequent periods, the new smaller group of insiders L_1 will want to keep the wage set at W_0. Insiders are assumed to be unwilling to take a wage cut (say to W_L) so that outsiders (even if they were former insiders) can be hired. The additional amount of unemployment $(L_0 - L_1)$ will persist into subsequent periods.

Suppose that several years later aggregate demand and the labour demand curve $D_1(L)$ *unexpectedly* shifts back to $D_0(L)$. The existing L_1 group of insiders have already negotiated a wage of W_0, based on the expected $D_1(L)$ labour demand curve. Given the higher $D_0(L)$ labour demand curve and the negotiated wage of W_0, the firm will increase employment to L_0. An *unexpected* positive demand shock will increase employment and decrease unemployment.

However, if this shift in the labour demand curve to $D_1(L)$ was *expected*, then the existing group of insiders L_1 will try to negotiate a wage of W_1, the maximum possible wage that keeps all the L_1 insiders employed (given expected demand conditions). An *expected* increase in demand may have *no* effect on employment or unemployment. Again, the key assumption in the insider–outsider model is that outsiders (even if they are former insiders) have no influence on wage negotiations between the current insiders and the firm. The unemployed have no effect on wages.

In the insider–outsider model, an *unexpected* decrease in demand creates more outsiders and more unemployment, which will persist into subsequent periods. The only way that these outsiders may be able to get back on the inside is if demand *unexpectedly* increases, which will lead profit-maximizing firms to hire more workers at the wage negotiated by the current group of insiders. Thus, a large negative demand shock (such as occurred in 1929–32) can continue to affect unemployment for many years, until a large positive demand shock (such as World War II) reverses the situation.

In a world of rational expectations, it is not obvious how the government can generate an *unexpected* increase in demand when unemployment is high. The public is bound to catch on to the fact that whenever unemployment increases the government will step in and stimulate aggregate demand (say by increasing the money supply). Insiders will expect this government-induced increase in demand and set the wage at a higher level (the maximum wage that is expected to keep all insiders employed), thereby preventing the outsiders from getting jobs (even though the government has stimulated aggregate demand). Rational expectations rule out the use of government policy to lower the unemployment rate in an insider–outsider model. New Keynesians who subscribe to the rational expectations hypothesis tend to be much less optimistic than "old" Keynesians about the prospects of finding government policies that will lower the unemployment rate.

If insiders are considered to be union members and outsiders are considered to be non-unionized, the insider–outsider model suggests that governments should try to weaken unions in order to give outsiders access to jobs. This would move labour markets in the direction of free competition and remove the obstacle to higher employment. Blanchard and Summers, however, do not make a connection between unions and the insider–outsider distinction. They argue that their theory applies to the U.S. experience in the 1930s when unions were weak but high unemployment persisted.

Many economists disagree with the labour supply assumptions of an insider–outsider model. The key assumptions are that insiders have monopoly power in setting the wage but are powerless to prevent the firm from hiring more workers when an unexpected positive demand shock occurs. To maximize their wage at the time of negotiations, the insiders are able to impose a vertical labour supply curve on the firm. However, if there is an unexpected positive demand shock, the insiders passively let the firm hire more workers, which is not in the best interests of the current group of insiders. As Robert Hall of Stanford University has noted,

> . . . the only serious weakness in Blanchard and Summers's model is the willingness of the incumbent workers to allow a favorable de-

> mand surprise to dilute their [bargaining strength]. Why don't they impose a rule against hiring, so that every demand surprise can be translated into further wage increases? The all-powerful union in the model slips in only one respect, but it is a terribly important respect. The sensible union would pursue a policy described by Lloyd Ullman as the "Cheshire Cat" theory of unionism — union membership gradually declines through retirement and attrition, and wages rise along the demand curve for labor. Ultimately all that is left is the smile of the last member, who is paid an astronomical wage.[24]

Hysteresis

A key feature of an insider-outsider model is the phenomenon of **hysteresis**. Hysteresis occurs when a *temporary* shock has a *permanent* effect; the effects of the *temporary* shock do not disappear when the shock ends. For example, a large negative demand shock may result in a permanently higher level of unemployment (until a large positive demand shock brings the unemployment rate back down). This new higher unemployment rate becomes the equilibrium unemployment rate. *Hysteresis* implies that the current equilibrium position is determined by the history of all past shocks (and past periods of disequilibrium). We believe that the possibility of hysteresis in the labour market was first suggested by Edmund Phelps in 1972. In Phelps's words, "The *live* hand of history produces a hysteresis effect: The time path to equilibrium partially shapes that equilibrium."[25]

Phelps suggested that on-the-job training and job experience may give rise to a "hysteresis effect." Although Phelps considered the possibility that a booming labour market might reduce the equilibrium unemployment rate, we consider the reverse situation of a prolonged recession. When workers are unemployed for long periods of time, they are unable to acquire the necessary labour market skills (such as demonstrating that they can get to work every day on time), on-the-job training, and work experience that employers seek. By failing to get this on-the-job training and work experience (human capital), the unemployed may permanently reduce their job prospects and a pool of "hard to employ" individuals may be created.

To illustrate, suppose a serious recession lasts for three years. Let us consider the fate of the three classes of students who graduate during the recession. Even though some graduating students will always be able to find a "good" job, many will be unable to find suitable jobs during a recession (in a "normal" labour market they would have found

---

[24] R.E. Hall, "Comment," in Stanley Fischer, ed., *Macroeconomics Annual 1986* (National Bureau of Economic Research, The M.I.T. Press, Cambridge, Mass., 1986), p. 87.

[25] E.S. Phelps, *Inflation Policy and Unemployment Theory* (New York: W.W. Norton & Company, Inc., 1972), pp. 77–80.

suitable jobs). Some graduating students will take whatever job they can get (perhaps working in the food service industry at the minimum wage), some may stay a few extra years in university or college, and others will join the ranks of the unemployed.

When the economy recovers after this three-year recession, these three groups of graduating students who were unable to find suitable jobs will have to compete against a new group of graduating students. Employers may regard the older unemployed graduates as being less desirable than the new graduates; the "good" prospects from the older graduating classes have already found suitable jobs and only the "not-so-good" prospects (those who couldn't find a job) are still available. Employers may choose to hire the "fresh" new graduates, rather than the older (passed over) graduates who have been unemployed, or underemployed. Some of the graduating students who enter the labour force during a recession may never fit properly into the work force because they never get a chance to develop job skills, on-the-job training, and work experience in their formative years. They may end up spending most of their life alternating dead-end jobs with unemployment insurance. Some of the additional unemployment during the recession may become permanent. The failure to develop human capital through on-the-job training and work experience may lead to unemployment hysteresis.[26]

The possibility of hysteresis is particularly troubling for economists. As noted above, hysteresis implies that temporary shocks can permanently affect the equilibrium position of the economy. Equilibrium is no longer a unique position; the economy no longer reverts to a unique natural rate of output and unemployment. The disequilibrium path that an economy follows after an unexpected disturbance can affect the new equilibrium position. Temporary cyclical unemployment can become permanent equilibrium unemployment.

Many economists reject the possibility of hysteresis on theoretical grounds. The current equilibrium position for a market does not depend on past disequilibrium. To generate hysteresis one has to suspend market forces, for example, give insiders the power to set the wage irrespective of the number of unemployed people wishing to supply labour.

---

[26] An alternative explanation for unemployment hysteresis focuses on the effect of negative shocks to investment, which result in a permanently smaller physical capital stock. If labour and capital are employed in relatively fixed proportions, a smaller capital stock reduces the demand for labour. A series of recessionary years of weak investment could therefore permanently reduce employment and permanently increase unemployment. The major objection to this "physical capital" explanation for unemployment hysteresis is that labour and capital are not used in fixed proportions; firms can substitute one factor input for another. A decline in the capital stock may lead to a decline in real wages and an increase in the ratio of labour to capital, leaving employment and unemployment essentially unchanged. For example, the destruction of much of the European capital stock during World War II did not prevent full employment in the years immediately after the war.

If the labour market functions as a competitive market, hysteresis should not exist. The equilibrium employment level will depend on the forces of demand and supply, not on past values of excess labour demand or excess labour supply (unemployment).

Key Concepts

the profit-maximizing firm's pricing decision
unit labour costs as a determinant of the price level
the Phillips curve
the gap between actual unemployment and equilibrium unemployment
nominal versus real wages
price inflation expectations as a determinant of wage changes
the price-expectations Phillips curve
labour productivity growth as a determinant of wage changes
the costs of adjusting prices
efficiency wage theory
insider–outsider distinction
hysteresis

Review Questions

1. What determines the price that a profit-maximizing firm will charge for its products?
2. What will be the effect on the price charged by a profit-maximizing firm if the wage rate increases by 5 percent and labour productivity increases by 2 percent?
3. Contrast the views of Keynes and classical economists concerning the nature of wage adjustments.
4. Outline and explain the key assumptions in the theoretical derivation of a wage adjustment function for a competitive labour market.
5. Explain why an increase in the level of equilibrium unemployment will cause the Phillips curve to shift upwards to the right.
6. Why does Friedman argue that 100 percent of inflation expectations will be incorporated into wage settlements? Do data support Friedman's inflation expectations hypothesis?
7. Explain why wage settlements (and the wage-change Phillips curve) will reflect an increase in labour productivity.

8. What will be the net effect on the rate of price inflation if labour productivity increases by 2 percent per year?
9. Explain why the costs of adjusting prices may lead to price inflexibility.
10. What is the key assumption of an efficiency wage theory? Explain how an efficiency wage theory accounts for wage inflexibilities and persistent unemployment.
11. What are the key assumptions of an insider–outsider model? Explain how an insider–outsider model accounts for persistent unemployment. Why is it difficult for government policy to reduce unemployment in an insider–outsider model?
12. What is meant by the term "hysteresis"? Explain. Outline a "human capital" explanation for unemployment hysteresis.

CHAPTER 11

The *IS-LM* Model with a *PEP* Curve

The following sketchy account of the "prospecting" ceremony among the Macro brings out several of the riddles that currently perplex Econologists. . . . The elder grasps the LM *with his left hand and the* IS *with his right and, holding the totem out in front of himself with elbows slightly bent, proceeds in a straight line — "gazing neither left nor right" in the words of their ritual — out over the chosen terrain. The grads of the village skip gaily around him at first, falling silent as the trek grows longer and more wearisome. On this occasion, it was long indeed and the terrain difficult . . . the grads were strung out in a long, morose and bedraggled chain behind their leader who, sweat pearling his brow, face cast in grim determination, stumbled onward over the obstacles in his path. . . . At long last, the totem vibrates, then oscillates more and more; finally, it points, quivering, straight down. The elder waits for the grads to gather around and then pronounces with great solemnity: "Behold, the Truth, and Power of the Macro."*

Axel Leijonhufvud[1]

The objective of this chapter is to combine the price-expectations Phillips *PEP* curve of Chapter 10 with the *IS-LM* model developed in Chapter 5 to form an integrated macroeconomic model of inflation, interest rates, output, and unemployment. The inclusion of a *PEP* curve within the *IS-LM* model allows us to reconsider the determination of output and interest rates in a world in which prices are flexible but do not adjust instantaneously to their equilibrium level. In the course of analyzing the

---

1 A. Leijonhufvud, "Life Among the Econ," *Economic Inquiry*, September 1973, pp. 331–32.

properties of the *IS-LM-PEP* model we will be able to shed considerable light on some of the key differences between classical–monetarist economists and Keynesian economists. Perhaps surprisingly, the *IS-LM-PEP* model is consistent with both Keynesian and classical–monetarist beliefs about the effects of fiscal and monetary policy on output and unemployment. Even though fiscal and monetary policy can have important *short-run* effects on output (a Keynesian proposition), there are no *long-run* multiplier effects (a classical–monetarist proposition).

Before providing a more formal analysis of the effects of monetary and fiscal policy in an inflationary economy, we must first demonstrate that our *IS-LM-PEP* model has a unique, stable equilibrium solution. Only one missing link must be discussed prior to solving the complete *IS-LM-PEP* model. The unemployment rate (from the *PEP* diagram) must be linked up with the level of income/output (in the *IS-LM* diagram).

The *PEP* Curve Expressed in Output Terms

We have frequently referred to an increase in the level of output as being synonymous with a lower level of unemployment. If output increases, then more labour will be required to produce this additional output and, *ceteris paribus*, unemployment should decline. In this section we review and formalize this negative relationship between movements in the level of output and movements in the unemployment rate.

Figure 11.1(a) presents the economy's aggregate production function, which describes the various amounts of output Y that can be produced given different quantities of employed labour L. The size of the existing labour force LF is also identified in Figure 11.1(a). The horizontal distance between this given labour force LF and the quantity of labour employed L represents the level of unemployment U. Given the equilibrium quantity of labour L^* (the intersection point of the labour demand and supply curves), the level of output will be Y^*. As discussed in previous chapters, even when the labour market is in equilibrium, some frictional and structural unemployment will still exist. The equilibrium unemployment rate is simply the equilibrium level of unemployment U^* in Figure 11.1(a) divided by the size of the given labour force LF. In Figure 11.1(b), point A represents this combination of output Y^* (produced by the equilibrium quantity of labour L^*) and the equilibrium unemployment rate U^*.

If employment decreases from L^* to L_1, the level of output produced will decline from Y^* to Y_1 and a number of previously employed people will now find themselves out of work; the level of unemployment rises from U^* to U_1 in Figure 11.1(a). In panel (b) the higher unemployment rate U_1 (the level of unemployment U_1 in panel (a) divided by the size of the labour force LF) is also plotted with the lower level of output Y_1

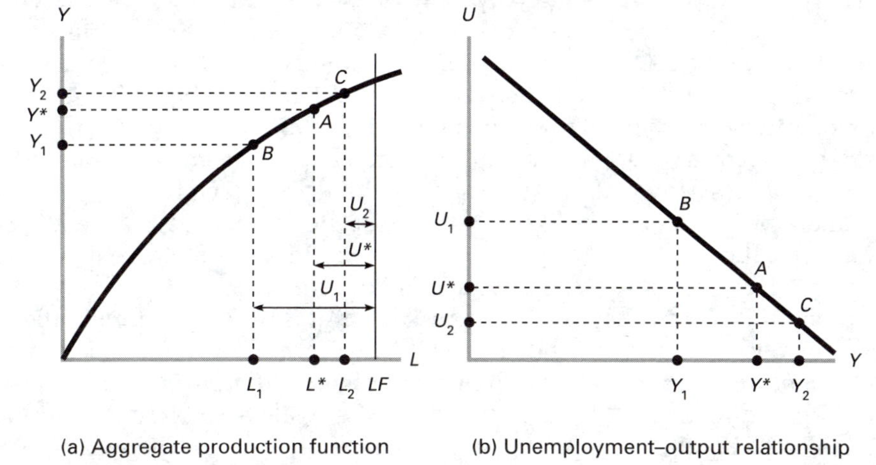

Figure 11.1 The output–employment relationship

(point *B*). Similarly, if employment rises to L_2, the amount of output produced increases to Y_2 and the unemployment rate falls to U_2 (point *C*). Connecting points *B*, *A*, and *C* in Figure 11.1(b) produces a downward-sloping line; an increase in the level of output is accompanied by a decrease in the unemployment rate.

This downward-sloping *U Y* line can be represented by the following equation, which links deviations in the actual unemployment rate *U* from the equilibrium unemployment rate U^* to deviations in output *Y* from Y^* (the amount of output produced when the labour market is in equilibrium):

$$(U^* - U) = -v(Y^* - Y) \qquad (11.1)$$

or

$$U = U^* + v(Y^* - Y) = U^* + vY^* - vY$$

When the labour market is in equilibrium, *Y* equals Y^* and *U* equals U^*. However, if *Y* declines below Y^* (that is, $Y^* - Y$ is positive), then *U* will rise above U^* ($U^* - U$ is negative). A decrease in output *Y* will be accompanied by an increase in the unemployment rate *U*, assuming U^* and Y^* remain constant. Conversely, an increase in output is associated with a decrease in the unemployment rate.

In Equation 11.1 the slope parameter *v* indicates the magnitude of the change in the unemployment rate associated with a one-unit change in output (relative to Y^*). The larger the parameter *v*, the greater the decline in the unemployment rate for a one-unit increase in output. The pioneering empirical research on the relationship between changes in output and unemployment rates was carried out by the late Arthur Okun, an American economist. Okun found that during the 1950s and early 1960s a decrease in the unemployment rate of one percentage point required an increase in output of 2.5 percent (over the trend growth rate in output), an empirical relationship which became widely known as "Okun's law." Equation 11.1 represents a simple version of Okun's law, with the parameter v being the reciprocal of Okun's estimate of 2.5 (that is, $v = 1/2.5 = 0.4$). The slope v of this U–Y relationship (Equation 11.1) is of critical importance in translating real output changes into changes in the unemployment rate.

Since the *IS-LM* diagram is expressed in income/output terms, there are obvious diagrammatic advantages in converting our inflation–*unemployment PEP* curve relationship into an inflation–*output PEP* curve relationship. If the *IS*, *LM*, and *PEP* curves are all expressed in output terms, we can then employ a common horizontal output axis for both the *IS-LM* diagram and the *PEP* curve diagram. The unemployment rate axis in the *PEP* curve diagram can be readily converted to an output axis by substituting Equation 11.1 into the price-expectations Phillips curve:

$$\dot{P} = \dot{P}^e + j(U^* - U) \qquad (10.7)$$

$$\dot{P} = \dot{P}^e - jv(Y^* - Y) \qquad (11.2)$$

or

$$\dot{P} = \dot{P}^e - jvY^* + jvY$$

Assuming a constant value for Y^*, a higher level of output is associated with a lower unemployment rate, and therefore a higher rate of wage and price inflation. In output terms, the price-expectations Phillips curve slopes upwards.

Figure 11.2 presents this upward-sloping inflation–output *PEP* curve. This *upward*-sloping inflation–*output PEP* curve is simply a backwards version of the *downward*-sloping inflation–*unemployment PEP* curve of Chapter 10.[2] If one views the inflation–output diagram from right to left (*backwards*), then the inflation–output *PEP* curve slopes downwards. Lower rates of wage and price inflation are associated with lower output levels and higher unemployment rates. Since it will frequently be useful to switch back to an inflation–unemployment context, Figure 11.2 includes a lower horizontal axis running from right to left. This backward-facing axis denotes the implicit unemployment rate associated with a particular output level. As described by Equation 11.1, the unem-

---

[2] As a historical footnote, Phillips first suggested such an upward-sloping inflation–output relationship in 1954, four years prior to his now-famous 1958 paper (see A.W. Phillips, "Stabilisation Policy in a Closed Economy," *Economic Journal*, June 1954, pp. 290–323). In a sense, this upward-sloping inflation–output curve is a 1954-vintage Phillips curve.

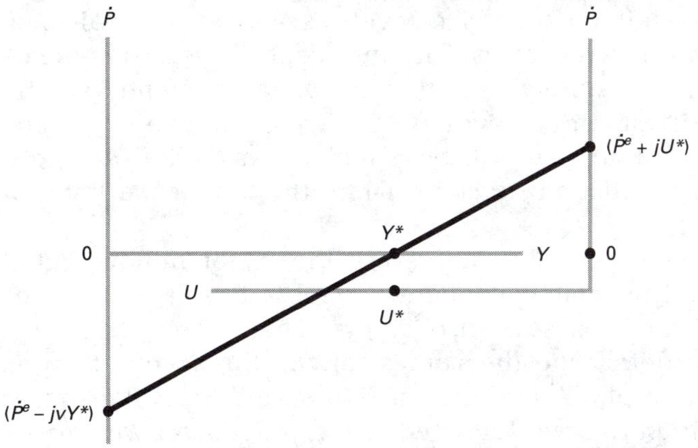

Figure 11.2 The *PEP* curve

ployment rate is a *negative* function of the level of real output (for a given U^* and Y^*). Throughout the next three chapters, this backward-facing unemployment axis will often be included in our *PEP* diagram to allow us to translate output levels into unemployment rates.[3]

A Brief Summary of the Major Components of the *IS-LM-PEP* Model

Having analyzed the relationship between the level of output and the unemployment rate, we can now bring together the *IS* and *LM* curves developed in Chapter 5 to form an integrated model to determine the inflation rate, the level of output, the interest rate, and the unemployment rate. Our macroeconomic model consists of the following three major composite relationships:

IS Curve: $$R = \frac{C_a - bT_a + I_a + G + X}{e} - \left[\frac{1 - b(1 - t) + m}{e}\right]Y \quad (5.5)$$

LM Curve: $$R = -\frac{\$}{\ell P} + \frac{k}{\ell}Y \quad (5.6)$$

PEP Curve: $$\dot{P} = \dot{P}^e - jvY^* + jvY \quad (11.2)$$

3 Since the slope of the $\dot{P}$–U relationship is $-j$ (not jv, the slope of the $\dot{P}$–Y relationship), the scaling of the $\dot{P}$ axis on the right-hand side of the diagram will differ (by the factor $1/v$) from the scaling of the $\dot{P}$ axis on the left-hand side of the diagram.

Recall from Chapter 7 that in an inflationary world the demand for money depends on the price level, as well as on real income levels and nominal interest rates. The intercept of the *LM* curve depends on the *real* money supply, which is the *nominal* money supply deflated by the existing price level. As indicated above, Y^* represents the amount of output that can be produced, according to the economy's aggregate production function, when the labour market is in equilibrium.

The *IS*, *LM*, and *PEP* curves are the major building blocks of our inflation–output macroeconomic model and will be used extensively thoughout the next several chapters. These three macroeconomic relationships determine the values for the three key endogenous variables: real output Y, the interest rate R, and the inflation rate $\dot{P}$. Since in any time period we know what the price level was in the previous period, once we determine the inflation rate $\dot{P}$ we will have also determined the value of the current price level P. The major exogenous variables in our model can be divided into two categories: (1) policy instruments that are under the direct control of the government (G, T_a, t, and \$) and (2) uncontrollable autonomous factors (such as I_a and X). If an exogenous variable were to change, either the *IS* or *LM* curve would shift and output would deviate from Y^*. Much of this chapter is devoted to an analysis of the macroeconomic disequilibrium that arises following a change in the value of various exogenous variables.

Before "solving" our macroeconomic model, the status of one particular variable, the expected inflation rate $\dot{P}^e$, must be clarified. In the preceding paragraph we did not classify $\dot{P}^e$ as an exogenous variable, nor have we provided a structural equation to "explain" inflation expectations. It would be very hard to argue that the expected inflation rate is exogenous and independent of macroeconomic phenomena. Expectations concerning future inflation rates are undoubtedly shaped by recent inflation experience and the government's choice of policies to "fight" (or not fight) inflation. As discussed in Chapter 8, the precise process by which people form their inflation expectations has been the subject of much debate in macroeconomics.

Rather than adopting a particular assumption about the manner in which people *might* form their expectations about future inflation, we introduce the concept of inflation expectations into our model in stages. We begin our analysis by assuming that the expected inflation rate is fixed at zero ($\dot{P}^e = 0$). Having solved our model under this admittedly unrealistic assumption, in Chapter 13 we allow inflation expectations to be non-zero and to adjust (in a single step) to past inflation rates. Finally, in Chapter 14 we examine the macroeconomic implications of adaptive and rational inflation expectations models. By "staging" the entry of inflation expectations into our macroeconomic story we not only simplify the early analysis of our *IS-LM-PEP* model, but we also highlight the key role that inflation expectations have played in the development of macroeconomic thought and in the debate between Keynesian, monetarist, and new classical economists.

Equilibrium in the *IS-LM-PEP* Macroeconomic Model

As summarized above, our integrated output–inflation model consists of three composite relationships or equations (the *IS*, *LM*, and *PEP* equations) that determine the values for our three key endogenous variables: real output Y, the interest rate R, and the inflation rate $\dot{P}$ (or price level P). Unfortunately a complete algebraic solution to our model is no longer possible. The inclusion of changing price levels (inflation) within the model has introduced both a dynamic element ($\dot{P}$) and a nonlinear element ($\$/P$). A full algebraic solution to our *IS-LM-PEP* model would require the use of *nonlinear difference* equation techniques, a subject that is best left to mathematicians. In practice, economists rarely solve such nonlinear dynamic models, but rather rely on computers to provide numerical solutions to such complicated models. Although we no longer provide algebraic solutions to our macroeconomic models, we can obtain a solution to our *IS-LM-PEP* model using diagrammatic techniques.

Figure 11.3 presents our basic two-panel diagram, which will be used extensively throughout the next several chapters. The upper panel depicts the *IS* and *LM* curves; the lower panel presents our derived inflation–output *PEP* curve.[4] Both panels share a common horizontal axis, the level of output Y. We have identified the level of output Y^* associated with labour market equilibrium and have added a backward-facing unemployment rate axis in the lower panel. For our initial analysis of the *IS-LM-PEP* model we assume that the expected inflation rate is zero, and have labelled the *PEP* curve accordingly. Unlike the aggregate demand and supply model presented in Chapter 7, the *IS-LM-PEP* model permits us to determine the inflation rate and the interest rate directly from the diagram, as well as providing a convenient analytical tool to describe disequilibrium adjustments in the economy.

Suppose that the labour market is in equilibrium and the economy is producing an aggregate output level of Y^*. Given the existing positions of the *IS* and *LM* curves in Figure 11.3, Y^* also represents the only income level that is consistent with both goods market and money market equilibrium (Y^* coincides with the intersection point A of the *IS* and

4 To our knowledge, this two-panel *IS-LM*-Phillips curve diagram was first suggested by Richard Lipsey (see R.G. Lipsey, "The Place of the Phillips Curve in Macroeconomic Models," in A.R. Bergstrom, et al., eds., *Stability and Inflation* (Chichester, England: John Wiley & Sons, 1978), pp. 49–75).

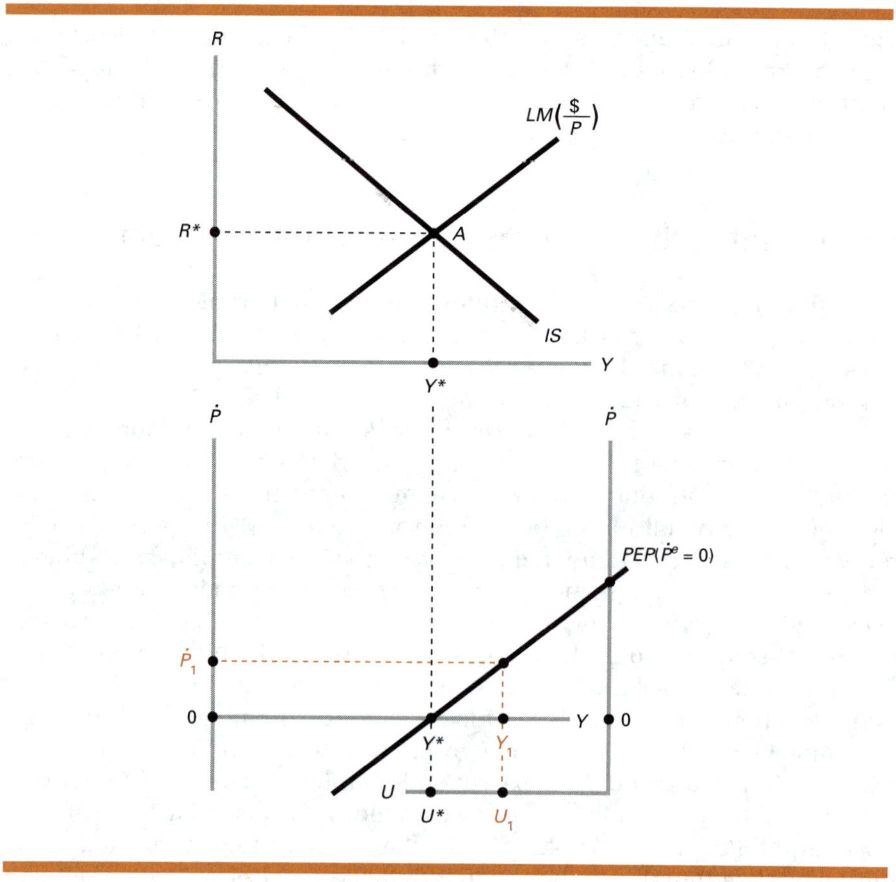

Figure 11.3 Equilibrium in the basic *IS-LM-PEP* model

LM curves). As long as the *IS* and *LM* curves do not shift, point *A* in Figure 11.3 represents the equilibrium position for this economy; all three major macroeconomic markets (goods, money, and labour) are simultaneously in equilibrium.

Assuming a given set of *exogenous* variables (G, T_a, t, \$, I_a, and X), the only variable that could prevent point *A* from being the equilibrium solution to our model is the *endogenous* price level, an intercept shift variable in the *LM* curve. As discussed in Chapter 7, if the price level changes, the *real* money supply \$/P will change and the *LM* curve will shift. If the *LM* curve shifts, Y^* and R^* (point *A*) will no longer correspond to the intersection point of the *IS* and (new) *LM* curves. Under such circumstances, the goods and/or money market would no longer be in equilibrium at an income level Y^* and an interest rate R^*. For Y^* and R^* (point *A*) to be the equilibrium position for the economy it must be demonstrated that the *LM* curve will not shift (that is, the price level will not change).

As drawn in the lower panel of Figure 11.3, an income level Y^* generates a *zero* inflation rate along the *PEP* ($\dot{P}^e = 0$) curve. Provided that the *PEP* curve does not shift (Y^*, U^*, and $\dot{P}^e$ do not change), when income is equal to Y^* price levels will remain constant and the *LM* curve will remain stationary. For the given set of exogenous variables, the economic system will remain at Y^* and R^*, the equilibrium solution to our *IS-LM-PEP* model. Notice that in equilibrium the inflation rate is zero and people's inflation expectations (which we assume to be zero) are correct.

It can easily be demonstrated that this equilibrium income level (Y^*) is unique. For all income levels other than Y^*, the inflation rate generated by the *PEP* ($\dot{P}^e = 0$) curve will *not* be zero and price levels will be changing. For example, when income is equal to Y_1 in Figure 11.3, price levels will rise by $\dot{P}_1$ during each time period. As discussed in Chapter 7, an increase in price levels will reduce the real money supply, causing the *LM* curve to shift upwards to the left. For all income levels other than Y^*, price levels will be changing and the *LM* curve will be shifting. Each time the *LM* curve shifts, a new *IS-LM* intersection point will emerge and a new level of income will arise. The economy clearly cannot be at rest in an equilibrium position if income levels are constantly changing. Since Y^* represents the unique income level for which price levels are constant and the *LM* curve remains stationary, it is the only income level that will sustain itself. All other income levels will lead to inflation or deflation, shifts in the *LM* curve, and a changing output level.

Although we have demonstrated that Y^* represents the unique income level in our model for which the goods, money, and labour markets are all simultaneously in equilibrium, we have not yet proved that this is a *stable* equilibrium position. What would happen if the economic system experiences a level of income that is different from the equilibrium value Y^*? Will the economic system remain out of equilibrium or will it tend to gravitate back towards the equilibrium income level Y^*? With all economic models it is important to demonstrate that the equilibrium position is stable, that is, that the economic system will move from any disequilibrium position back to the equilibrium position. In demonstrating the **stability of the Y^* equilibrium income position** in our model, we also obtain a preview of the key dynamic features of the *IS-LM-PEP* model.

Figure 11.4 replicates the basic two-panel diagram presented in Figure 11.3 with one crucial difference: the solid coloured *LM* curve associated with a real money stock of $\$/P_1$ does not intersect the *IS* curve at the equilibrium income level Y^*. At point *A* in Figure 11.4, the economic system has an income level Y_1 that is considerably larger than the equilibrium income level Y^*. The key question is whether the economic system can sustain this higher income level Y_1, or whether the system will gravitate back to the equilibrium income level Y^*.

Tracing this higher Y_1 income level down to the lower panel, we observe that the economy is experiencing a considerable amount of infla-

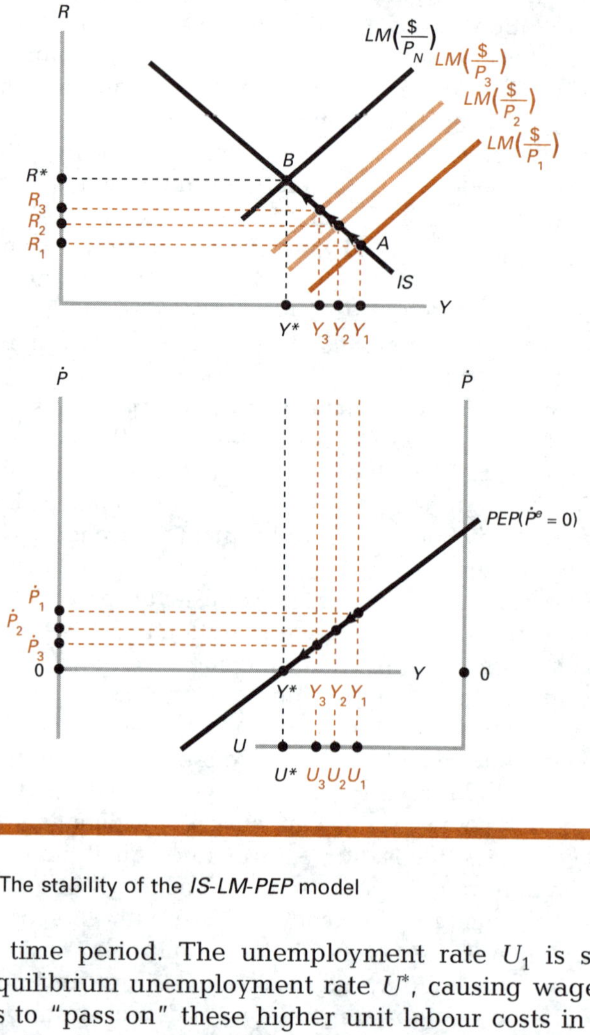

Figure 11.4 The stability of the *IS-LM-PEP* model

tion, $\dot{P}_1$ per time period. The unemployment rate U_1 is substantially below the equilibrium unemployment rate U^*, causing wages to be bid up and firms to "pass on" these higher unit labour costs in the form of higher prices. By the end of the first time interval, the price level rises from its initial value of P_1 to P_2 (reflecting the inflation rate of $\dot{P}_1$). This rising price level will trigger the key feedback effect within the money market. For a given nominal money supply, a rise in the price level will diminish the real money supply causing the *LM* curve to shift upwards to the left (from $LM(\$/P_1)$ to $LM(\$/P_2)$ in Figure 11.4). This upward shift in the *LM* curve will raise the interest rate from R_1 to R_2, which in turn will bring about a reduction in investment expenditures and a downward (multiplier) adjustment in real income to Y_2.

Having shown that an income level of Y_1 will trigger an inflationary chain reaction leading to a lower income level of Y_2, we must now consider the viability of Y_2. Will the income level Y_2 sustain itself, or will Y_2

(like Y_1) give way to a further downward adjustment in income? Using the same argument as above, it can be demonstrated that Y_2 will set off an inflationary chain reaction that will produce a new lower income level Y_3. Along the *PEP* curve, Y_2 also generates a positive inflation rate $\dot{P}_2$, although slightly lower than the previous inflation rate $\dot{P}_1$ at Y_1. Again the price level will rise to P_3, eroding the real money supply $\$/P_3$ and causing the *LM* curve to shift upwards again. The interest rate is forced up another notch, to R_3, further reducing investment spending and leading to a further decline in real income to Y_3.

In a similar fashion, Y_3 will give way to a lower income level Y_4, which will give way to a lower income level Y_5, and so on. This disequilibrium adjustment process will continue to lower the level of income as long as the inflation rate is greater than zero. Given a constant nominal money supply, any positive inflation rate reduces the real money supply causing the *LM* curve to shift upwards to the left. Only when the inflation rate reaches zero (and the real money supply remains constant) will this adjustment process come to a halt. This, of course, corresponds to our unique equilibrium income position, Y^*. A salient characteristic of equilibrium within the *IS-LM-PEP* model is a *stationary LM* curve. Given a constant nominal money supply \$, the *LM* curve will only be stationary under conditions of zero price inflation (a constant value for *P*). In the *PEP* curve panel, Y^* must occur at the point where the $PEP(\dot{P}^e = 0)$ curve crosses the output axis, that is, where the inflation rate is zero. As demonstrated in Chapter 13, if we allow the nominal money supply to change each period, then the equilibrium solution to our *IS-LM-PEP* model will no longer exhibit this unrealistic property of zero inflation.

In summary, any income level greater than Y^* will generate a sufficient amount of inflation to return the economy to the equilibrium income level Y^*, the amount of output that can be produced by the equilibrium quantity of labour. In a diagrammatic sense, the economic system is simultaneously sliding down the *PEP* curve and climbing up the *IS* curve (see arrows in Figure 11.4). Each step down the *PEP* curve produces a further increase in the price level (and a consequent reduction in the real money supply), thereby causing the *LM* curve to climb one step further up the *IS* curve. The economic system will eventually return to the equilibrium income level Y^*, the unique income level that is consistent with labour market equilibrium. A similar argument can be advanced to explain how the economic system will converge to Y^* from an income level below the equilibrium income level (see the next section of this chapter). In short, no matter what level of income happens to exist, the economic system will automatically gravitate back towards Y^*, the unique equilibrium income level in our *IS-LM-PEP* model. Once the economic system is at Y^*, the labour, goods, and money markets will all simultaneously be in equilibrium and the economy will be at rest (no pressures will exist to cause the *LM*, *IS*, or *PEP* curves to shift).

Our emphasis on the **stability of the equilibrium level of income**

within the *IS-LM-PEP* model is not meant to imply that the economy must necessarily return *quickly* to its equilibrium position. Although the structure and logic of the *IS-LM-PEP* model ensures that the economy will always gravitate towards its equilibrium position, we have not yet discussed how long it will take the economy to get back to Y^*. The length of the disequilibrium adjustment process is one of the most controversial issues in macroeconomics. Classical and monetarist economists argue that the economy will quickly return to its "natural" equilibrium position (with the labour market in equilibrium), whereas Keynesian economists emphasize the slowness of the macroeconomic adjustment process (and the likelihood of prolonged cyclical unemployment). Before formally analyzing the length of the adjustment period, we first reconsider the determinants of the equilibrium income level Y^* and then re-examine the nature of the multiplier process within an inflationary macroeconomic model.

The Determinants of Y^*

In a fundamental structural sense, the equilibrium level of income Y^* is determined in the labour market and production (supply) sector of the economy. Y^* is simply the amount of output that can be produced when the labour market is in equilibrium. If either the aggregate production function, the demand for labour, or the supply of labour were to shift, then the equilibrium quantities of labour and output would change. In this section we demonstrate how (and why) the equilibrium output level will be affected by an increase in labour supply.

Panels (a) and (c) of Figure 11.5 reproduce our standard labour market and aggregate production function diagrams. Given the labour demand L^D curve and labour supply L_0^S curve, the equilibrium quantity of labour L_0^* produces the equilibrium quantity of output Y_0^*. In panels (b) and (d) of Figure 11.5, this equilibrium level of output Y_0^* corresponds to a zero inflation rate, the point at which the $PEP_0(\dot{P}^e = 0)$ curve crosses the output axis in Figure 11.5(d), and is characterized by a stationary *LM* curve in Figure 11.5(b).

Now suppose that the economy's labour supply increases from L_0^S to L_1^S, say because of a greater number of graduates than retirees. At the previous equilibrium *real* wage $(W/P)_0^*$, an excess supply of labour will now exert downward pressure on wages within the labour market. Given sufficient time, this excess supply of labour will force the real wage down to its new equilibrium level $(W/P)_1^*$. At this new lower equilibrium real wage, a larger number of people will now be employed $(L_1^* > L_0^*)$ and the economy's aggregate production will increase from Y_0^* to Y_1^*.

In Figure 11.5(d), this increase in the equilibrium level of output from Y_0^* to Y_1^*, arising from an increase in the supply of labour, will cause the *PEP* curve to shift downwards to the right (recall that the intercept of

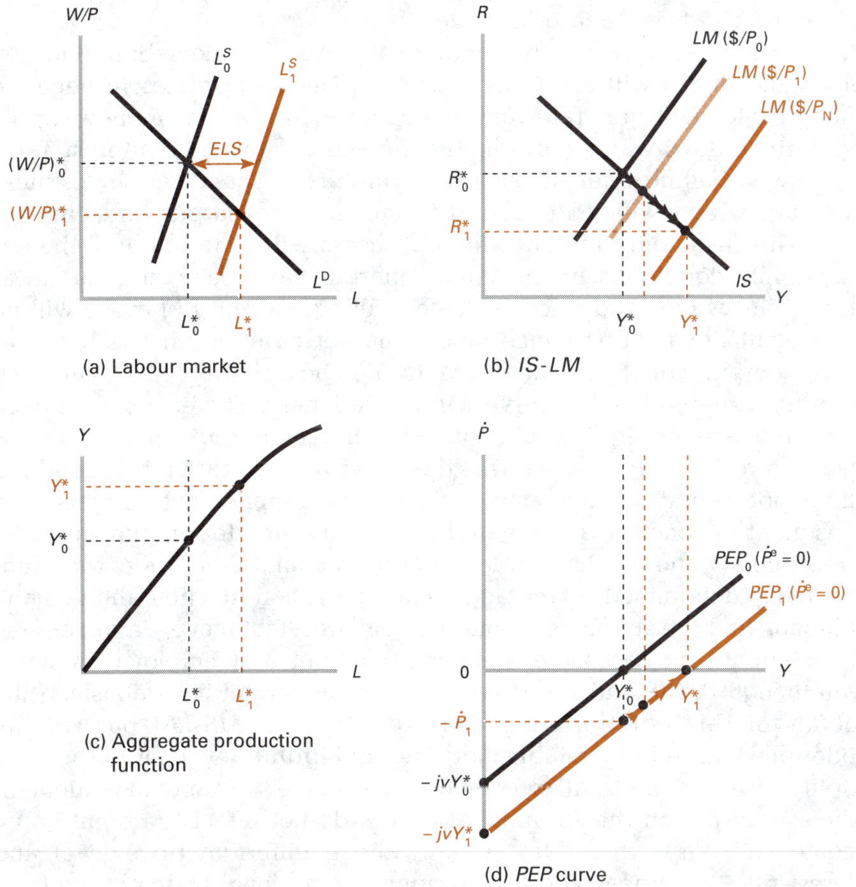

Figure 11.5 The effect of an increase in labour supply on the equilibrium output level

the *PEP* curve contains the term $-jvY^*$). At the original equilibrium income position Y_0^*, the new lower coloured PEP_1 curve will cause the inflation rate to decline to a negative number $-\dot{P}_1$. The increased supply of labour puts downward pressure on nominal wages in the labour market. As nominal wages decline, firms face lower unit labour costs and are thus able to lower prices.[5] As the price level declines (from P_0 to P_1), the real money supply increases (from $\$/P_0$ to $\$/P_1$) and the *LM* curve shifts downwards, causing interest rates to decline. Lower interest rates will lead to an increase in investment expenditures and an increase in

5 Since the real wage rate is falling in the labour market, the decline in prices will not be as large as the decline in nominal wages.

output. The additional labour force participants will begin to find jobs as Y and L rise from their original levels.

As long as excess supply conditions prevail in the labour market, wages and prices will continue to decline. Declining prices (a negative inflation rate) will generate further increases in the real money supply and further downward shifts in the *LM* curve, pushing interest rates even lower. Falling interest rates will continue to spark new investment spending, which will lead to further increases in output and employment. This disequilibrium adjustment process will continue until the excess supply conditions in the labour market have been eliminated, at which point wages and prices will stop falling and the *LM* curve will no longer shift downwards. Once labour market equilibrium has been restored, output will have increased to Y_1^*, the inflation rate will once again be zero and the *LM* curve will be stationary. The economy is back in macroeconomic equilibrium, but at a higher output level Y_1^* and a lower interest rate R_1^*. In fact, it is the lower interest rate (attributable to falling prices and an increasing real money supply) that triggers new investment expenditures, increased output, and greater employment.

In summary, the equilibrium levels of income and employment are fundamentally determined by the aggregate production function, the demand for labour, and the supply of labour. As demonstrated above, an increase in labour supply increases the equilibrium output and employment level. Even though the *IS* and *LM* curves are very important in establishing the *stability* of this equilibrium income position, the *IS-LM* part of the model plays no role in establishing the equilibrium levels of output and employment. As we shall see below, aggregate demand management policies that act on the *IS* and *LM* curves do not affect the equilibrium income and employment levels, only the equilibrium price level and interest rate. To repeat, the equilibrium income level is determined exclusively in the labour market and production sector of the economy.

A Reappraisal of the Keynesian Multiplier Process

In Chapter 5 the multiplier effects on income arising from a shift in the *IS* and *LM* curves were analyzed under the assumption of inflexible price levels. In this section we analyze the multiplier process for an economy in which prices are flexible but do not adjust instantaneously to their new equilibrium level. To keep our analysis as simple as possible, the assumption that inflation expectations are fixed at zero is retained. We first examine the output and inflation effects arising from a shift in the *IS* curve, followed by a similar analysis of the effects associated with an increase in the nominal money supply. Incorporating inflation (a *PEP* curve) into the *IS-LM* model substantially alters our earlier conclusions (in Chapter 5) concerning the nature of the multiplier process. Perhaps surprisingly, our *IS-LM-PEP* model is consistent with both

Keynesian and classical–monetarist conclusions, depending upon one's perception of the length of the disequilibrium adjustment period.

The Inflation and Output Effects Associated with a Shift in the *IS* Curve

Figure 11.6 reproduces our standard two-panel *IS-LM-PEP* diagram. Our hypothetical economy is assumed to be initially in equilibrium at Y^* with a zero inflation rate, an interest rate of R_0^* and a price level of P_0 (point *A* in Figure 11.6). Now suppose that the IS_0 curve shifts rightwards to IS_1, say because of an increase in exports or government expenditures. Since the nominal money supply has not changed, this increase in aggregate demand and rightward shift in the *IS* curve will initially push the economy up the given $LM(\$/P_0)$ curve to a new higher income level Y_1 and a higher interest rate R_1 (point *B* in Figure 11.6). However, in the *PEP* curve panel of Figure 11.6, this higher income level Y_1 (and lower unemployment rate U_1) will generate a substantial amount of wage and price inflation ($\dot{P}_1$). As price levels increase, the real money supply will decrease and the *LM* curve will start to shift upwards. As the *LM* curve shifts upwards, interest rates increase further, leading to a decline in investment expenditures, income, and employment. In the initial time period following the outward shift in the IS_0 curve, the inflation rate $\dot{P}_1$ will have increased the price level to P_1, shifted the *LM* curve up to $LM(\$/P_1)$, raised the interest rate to R_2, and lowered the income level from Y_1 to Y_2.

However our story is by no means over. An income level of Y_2 will still generate inflation in the *PEP* curve panel. Even though the inflation rate $\dot{P}_2$ in the second time period is less than the previous inflation rate $\dot{P}_1$, price levels are still rising. During this second time period after the outward shift in the IS_0 curve, the price level will rise again, to P_2, the real money supply will decline accordingly, to $\$/P_2$, the *LM* curve will again shift upwards, to $LM(\$/P_2)$, the interest rate will be pushed up another notch, to R_3, investment expenditures will decline further, and the level of income will decline again, to Y_3. But an income level of Y_3 still generates a positive inflation rate $\dot{P}_3$ in the *PEP* curve panel. Again the real money supply will decline, the *LM* curve will shift upwards, interest rates will rise, investment expenditures and income levels will decline. As discussed earlier in this chapter, this inflation-induced erosion in the real money supply, and consequent reductions in investment expenditures and output, will only come to a halt when the economy has moved all the way back to Y^*, where the inflation rate is zero and the *LM* curve remains stationary. The economic system will climb up the new higher IS_1 curve (to point *C* in Figure 11.6) and slide down the *PEP* ($\dot{P}^e = 0$) curve until it returns to its original equilibrium position Y^*.

In summary, an increase in exports or an increase in government expenditures has no lasting income and employment effects. An outward shift in the *IS* curve will initially produce a Keynesian multiplier effect on

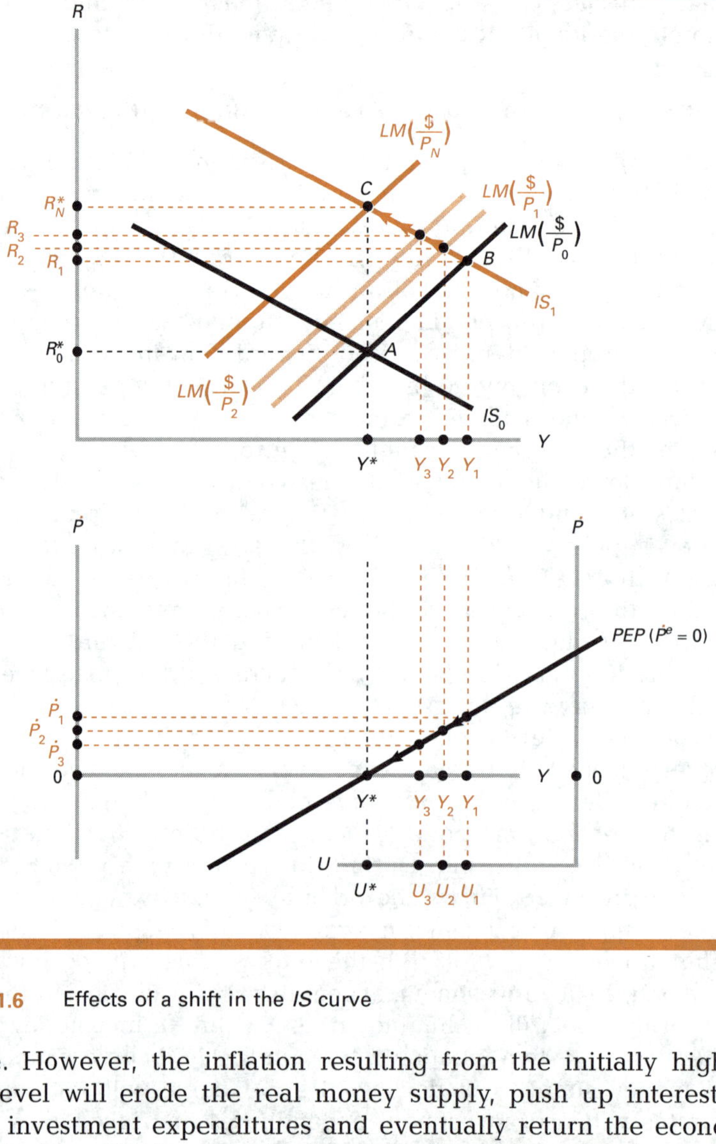

Figure 11.6 Effects of a shift in the *IS* curve

income. However, the inflation resulting from the initially higher income level will erode the real money supply, push up interest rates, reduce investment expenditures and eventually return the economy to its original equilibrium income position. Thus, the only lasting (long-run) effects from an increase in government expenditures are a higher price level, a higher interest rate, and a redistribution of output from the business sector to the government sector (since there has been no permanent increase in income/output levels, the decline in investment expenditures associated with an increase in the interest rate must be equal to the increase in government expenditures). To repeat, an outward shift of the *IS* curve in the *IS-LM-PEP* model does not produce a permanently higher income level or a permanently lower unemployment rate: the equilibrium level of income and employment in the *IS*-

LM-PEP model do not depend on aggregate demand and the position of the *IS* curve.

The Inflation and Output Effects Arising from a Change in the Nominal Money Supply

The macroeconomic effects associated with an increase in the nominal money supply are very similar to the macroeconomic effects arising from a shift in the *IS* curve. As demonstrated in Figure 11.7, an increase in the nominal money supply from $\$_0$ to $\$_1$ will initially cause the *LM* curve to shift downwards, bringing about a lower interest rate R_1, an increase in investment spending, and a higher income level Y_1 (movement from point *A* to point *B*). However, this increase in income following an increase in the nominal money supply will trigger the same inflationary chain reaction process described above. The inflation rate $\dot{P}_1$ associated

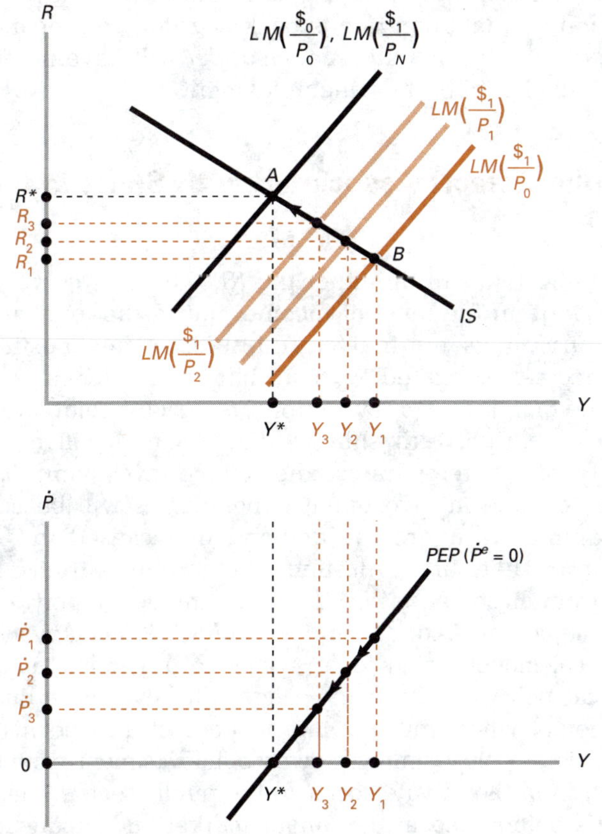

Figure 11.7 Effects of an increase in the nominal money supply

with the increased income level Y_1 will erode the real value of the increased nominal money supply and the *LM* curve will begin to shift back up. Each round of inflation ($\dot{P}_1$, $\dot{P}_2$, $\dot{P}_3$ in Figure 11.7) will erode the real money supply (to $\$_1/P_1$, $\$_1/P_2$, $\$_1/P_3$) and continually push the *LM* curve back upwards. These upward shifts in the *LM* curve lead to higher and higher interest rates, and lower and lower income levels.

As in the previous case of an outward shift in the *IS* curve, the adjustment process following an increase in the nominal money supply will only come to a halt when the inflation rate is back to zero and the economy has returned to its original equilibrium income level Y^*. The *LM* curve will have shifted back up to its original position (at point *A*), with $\$_1/P_N$ equal to $\$_0/P_0$. The only difference from the shift in the *IS* curve described above concerns the interest rate. An increase in the nominal money supply will temporarily depress the interest rate below its equilibrium level, but once the adjustment process has concluded the interest rate will return to its original equilibrium level R^*. The only permanent effect from an increase in the nominal money supply is a higher price level P_N, but not lasting inflation (the inflation rate is back to zero). To repeat, in the long run an increase in the nominal money supply will have no effect on the (equilibrium) level of output or unemployment.

The Multiplier Effects Associated with Shifts in the *IS* and *LM* Curves

As described above, a shift in either the *IS* or the *LM* curve will initially produce a change in the level of income, but in the long run the economy will return to its original equilibrium income position Y^*. The change in income associated with a shift in the *IS* curve, or from a change in the nominal money supply, is strictly temporary. Inflation generated from a rightward shift in the *IS* curve will erode the real money supply, raise interest rates, and reduce investment expenditures. The resulting decline in investment expenditures will be equivalent to the initial stimulus in aggregate demand that caused the *IS* curve to shift rightwards. There are no lasting income effects from a shift in the *IS* curve, or from an increase in the nominal money supply.

Thus, the major conclusions from our *IS-LM-PEP* model would appear to be very classical–monetarist in tone. A change in exports, autonomous investment, fiscal policy, or monetary policy will have *no* lasting effects on income or unemployment rates. In the parlance of a monetarist economist, expansionary fiscal policy simply crowds out investment expenditures and diverts output from the private sector to the public sector. The equilibrium output level is determined in the labour market and production sector of the economy, and is unaffected by fiscal and/or monetary policy.

Although the basic conclusions from our *IS-LM-PEP* model appear to be very damning for Keynesian economists, one should not lose sight of the fact that during the disequilibrium adjustment period following a shift in the *IS* or *LM* curve, the economy experiences income levels that differ from the equilibrium income level Y^*. There are *temporary* increases or decreases in income and unemployment during the adjustment period following a shift in the *IS* or *LM* curve. For example, a leftward shift of the *IS* curve, say from a decline in exports, will generate a temporary reduction in output levels. Even though in the *long run* the economy will return to its equilibrium income Y^* position (but with a lower interest rate), in the *short run* the economy will experience a recession with unemployment rates in excess of the equilibrium unemployment rate U^*.[6]

Consequently, an assessment of the income and unemployment effects associated with a shift in either the *IS* or the *LM* curve depends critically on the time period considered. If one adopts a *long-run* perspective and focuses on the effects after all the inflation feedback effects have worked their way throughout the economy, then the Keynesian income multiplier effects are zero. Under such a *long-run equilibrium* perspective, a change in government expenditures (or exports) has no permanent effect on the level of output or on the unemployment rate; the only *long-run* effects are on the price level, the interest rate, and the distribution of output between the investment and government (export) sectors. On the other hand, if one focuses on the ***short-run disequilibrium* adjustment** phase, then a change in exports or government expenditures will affect output and the unemployment rate, although these effects will diminish through time.

In a temporal sense the *IS-LM-PEP* model is consistent with both classical–monetarist and Keynesian conclusions. Classical and monetarist economists look to the *long-run equilibrium* properties of the *IS-LM-PEP* model, whereas Keynesian economists are much more interested in the *short-run disequilibrium* properties of the model. A key area of dispute between Keynesian and classical–monetarist economists concerns the length of the short-run adjustment period. How long does it take the economy to return to its long-run equilibrium position?

To illustrate, suppose that the *IS* curve shifts to the left, say because of a decline in exports. If the short-run adjustment period is in fact quite long, then the economy will experience a lengthy recession (with $U > U^*$) before returning to its long-run equilibrium position. To avoid this lengthy short-run recession, an expansionary Keynesian policy could be used to hasten the economy back to its long-run equilibrium position. On the other hand, if the short-run disequilibrium adjustment period is very short, then the

6 The leftward shift in the *IS* curve will produce a lower level of output and deflation. Falling price levels increase the real money supply, causing the *LM* curve to shift downwards to the right. The resulting lower interest rates stimulate investment expenditures and eventually return the economy to its equilibrium income position (the opposite case to that illustrated in Figure 11.6).

economy will quickly return to its long-run equilibrium position and there is no need for Keynesian policy intervention. Classical and monetarist economists tend to think that the long run is "just around the corner," whereas Keynesian economists are more apt to respond with Keynes's now famous dictum, "In the long run we're all dead!" In the next section we examine the major determinants of the length of the short-run disequilibrium adjustment phase in the *IS-LM-PEP* model.

Determinants of the Length of the Short-Run Adjustment Period

As described above, the adjustment mechanism that returns the economy to its equilibrium income level Y^* is a sequence of inflation-induced shifts in the *LM* curve arising from repeated changes in the real money supply. For any level of output greater than Y^*, a positive inflation rate erodes the real money supply and causes the *LM* curve to shift upwards. These upward shifts in the *LM* curve will only come to a halt when the inflation rate is back to zero, at which point the real money supply is constant. The adjustment process must increase the price level sufficiently so that the *LM* curve intersects the *IS* curve at the equilibrium income level Y^*. The short-run adjustment period can therefore be defined as the length of time required to move the existing disequilibrium price level to the new equilibrium price level. In terms of Figure 11.6, how long does it take to increase the price level from P_0 to P_N? Alternatively, how long does it take for the $LM(\$/P_0)$ curve to shift up to the new equilibrium position $LM(\$/P_N)$?

Within the *IS-LM-PEP* model, the price-expectations Phillips curve determines the speed with which prices adjust during the short-run disequilibrium adjustment process. Both the slope of the underlying Phillips curve and the manner in which inflation expectations are formed will affect the duration of the short-run adjustment period. In addition, the existence of contracts within the labour market impedes the adjustment of wages (and consequently prices) to changing economic conditions.[7] Much of the macroeconomic controversy between Keynesian, monetarist, and new classical economists has concerned the properties of the Phillips curve, the nature of inflationary expectations, and the role of labour market contracts. We consider briefly how the slope and the inflation expectations component of the Phillips curve will affect the length of the short-run adjustment period.

---

[7] Such contracts may be explicit, such as legal collective agreements in the union sector that fix wage rates for up to three years, or implicit understandings between employers and employees in the non-union sector regarding how frequently the wage rate will be adjusted (typically once a year). Given the long-term attachment between most employees and their employers, such contracts or implicit understandings are an efficient way to deal with changing economic circumstances.

The Slope of the Underlying Phillips Curve

To illustrate the key role which the slope of the underlying Phillips curve plays in the macroeconomic adjustment process, Figure 11.8 pres-

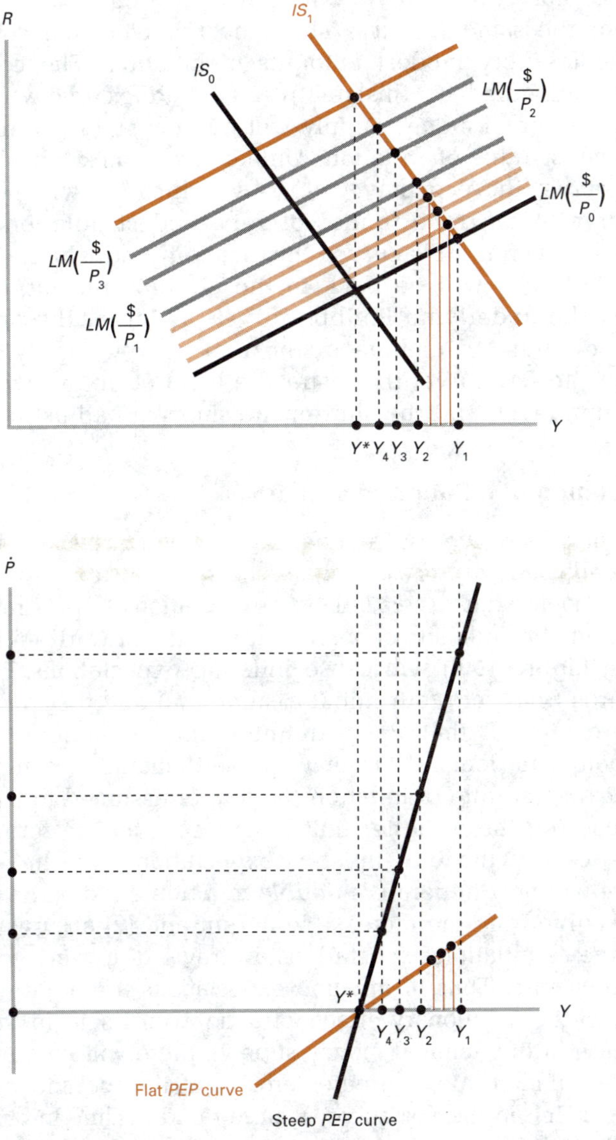

Figure 11.8 The slope of the Phillips curve and the length of the short-run adjustment process

ents our standard *IS-LM-PEP* diagram with two very differently sloped *PEP* curves passing through the equilibrium income point Y^*. Following a shift in the *IS* curve from IS_0 to IS_1, the *steep* black *PEP* curve generates very high rates of inflation and consequently very sizeable shifts in the *LM* curve. After three rounds of substantial inflation associated with the steep *PEP* curve, the level of output is almost back to its equilibrium level Y^*. For the same *IS* curve shift, the relatively *flat* coloured *PEP* curve generates very modest amounts of inflation. The coloured *LM* curve shifts generated by this relatively flat *PEP* curve will be much smaller since the real money supply will be only slightly diminished by the very modest rates of inflation. Unlike the "quick slide" down the steep *PEP* curve, the economy will "slowly inch" down the relatively flat *PEP* curve. After three rounds of very modest inflation generated by the relatively flat *PEP* curve, the economy still has a very long way to go before it will be back to the equilibrium output level Y^*. The steeper the underlying Phillips curve, the larger the price adjustments, the greater the change in the real money supply, the larger the shifts in the *LM* curve, the faster the level of output will return to its equilibrium level, and the shorter the short-run adjustment period.

The Formulation of Inflation Expectations

If we relax our restrictive assumption that inflation expectations are fixed at zero, the adjustment process will also be speeded up. Suppose, for example, that people adjust their inflation expectations to past rates of price inflation. Then the inflation generated from an outward shift in the *IS* curve ($\dot{P}_1$ in Figure 11.6) will cause inflation expectations $\dot{P}^e$ to be revised upwards from zero (our initial assumption) and the *PEP* curve will shift upwards (recall that $\dot{P}^e$ is an intercept component of the *PEP* curve). Labour will demand larger wage settlements to compensate for the higher expected rate of inflation (no longer assumed to be zero) and firms will pass on these higher unit labour costs in the form of higher price levels. Given "flexible" inflation expectations, a rightward shift in the *IS* curve will now generate a *double* inflation effect: (1) a movement up the *PEP* curve from the increase in output and (2) an upward shift in the *PEP* curve as inflation expectations are revised upwards to reflect the higher inflation rate. Thus, if inflation expectations are adjusted upwards in response to the inflationary effects of a rightward shift in the *IS* curve (or an increase in the nominal money supply), there will be a much larger effect on the inflation rate, a greater erosion of the real money supply, a larger upward shift in the *LM* curve, a more rapid decline in output levels, and a "shorter" short-run adjustment period.

As discussed in Chapter 8, monetarists have argued that inflation expectations will *adapt* to current and past inflation rates, thus speeding up the short-run adjustment period. New classical economists have taken this expectational argument one step further, by assuming *rational* expectations and instantaneous wage and price adjustments. Under new classical assumptions, an anticipated monetary or fiscal policy will have absolutely no short-run effects on output or employment, as instantaneous adjustments in expectations, wages, and prices will maintain the economy at its natural (equilibrium) output level (see Chapter 8). Having established the proposition that the length of the short-run adjustment period depends on the nature of the inflation expectations assumption, we defer further analysis of the macroeconomic implications of different inflation expectations assumptions until Chapter 14.

Summary

Inflation (or deflation) generated during the short-run disequilibrium adjustment period is the self-correcting mechanism that returns the economy to its equilibrium income/output level (which is determined by the aggregate production function and equilibrium in the labour market). Given a rightward shift in the *IS* or *LM* curve, the higher the inflation rate during the adjustment period, the faster the return trip to the equilibrium income position and the shorter the short-run adjustment period. As discussed above, the magnitude of the inflation rate during the short-run adjustment period depends on the slope of the underlying Phillips curve and the nature of the inflation expectations formation process.

By emphasizing the price flexibility of the free enterprise system, classical, monetarist, and new classical economists implicitly believe that the underlying Phillips curve must be quite steep. If the government would only leave the economic system alone, wages and prices would quickly adjust to changing market conditions. Furthermore, economic agents will adjust their inflation expectations in light of current (and expected) economic circumstances. Given competitive market forces, the free market system will be inherently stable in output and employment terms. Any shift in the *IS* curve, say from a change in exports or fiscal policy, will produce a substantial price effect that will quickly move the economy back to its equilibrium income position. The *LM* curve shifts rapidly to offset any shift in the *IS* curve. From a classical–monetarist perspective, there is a great deal of *PEP* in the *IS-LM-PEP* model. The long-run equilibrium properties of the *IS-LM-PEP* model quickly materialize and the Keynesian short-run income multiplier effects are negligible.

As discussed in Chapter 10, Keynesians emphasize the inflexibility or rigidity of wages and prices. Given a flat underlying Phillips curve (wages and prices are unaffected by changing economic conditions), the short-run adjustment period would persist indefinitely and in the long run we would be dead! Most Keynesians do not deny the existence of a Phillips curve, but rather argue that

1. "wages, and perhaps prices, do not adjust quickly to eliminate excess supplies and demands, especially excess supplies"[8] (that is, the underlying Phillips curve is *relatively* flat),
2. inflation expectations tend to adjust quite slowly, and
3. the existence of implicit and explicit (multi-year) wage contracts in the labour market impedes the adjustment of wages to changing economic conditions.

As discussed at the end of the previous chapter, new Keynesians have offered a number of theoretical explanations for rigid prices and wages, even when agents optimize and form their expectations rationally. From a Keynesian perspective, there is very little *PEP* in the *IS-LM-PEP* model. Given rigid wages and prices, the short-run output effects associated with a shift in the *IS* curve are likely to persist for a number of years.

Although Keynesian and classical–monetarist arguments are frequently stated in polar terms (a model with either no *PEP* or an infinite amount of *PEP*), reality probably lies somewhere between these two extremes. Unlike Keynes's crucial *inflexibility* assumptions, wages and prices do respond to changing economic conditions, but not as fast as classical, monetarist, and new classical economists think. Inflation expectations are adjusted to reflect changing economic circumstances, but not instantaneously. Long-term labour contracts fix the wage rate for millions of workers for up to three years at a time and non-union workers rarely receive a wage adjustment more frequently than once a year. Thus, the length of the short-run adjustment phase likely lies somewhere between the "ephemeral" short run of a hard core monetarist, new classical economist, and the "permanent" short run of Keynes. Consequently we cannot dismiss important short-run output effects (as many monetarist and new classical economists are prone to do), nor can we dismiss long-run inflationary considerations (as Keynes did). Both the short-run disequilibrium adjustment phase and the long-run equilibrium properties of our *IS-LM-PEP* model must be studied carefully. As we shall see, the nature of the *PEP* curve is often the crucial factor in our analysis. One-half century after the publication of Keynes's *General Theory*, economists continue to debate the degree of wage and price flexibility in the macroeconomic system.

---

[8] R.M. Solow, "Alternative approaches to macroeconomic theory: a partial view," *Canadian Journal of Economics*, August 1979, p. 343.

Key Concepts

determinants of equilibrium income in the *IS-LM-PEP* model
stability of equilibrium income in the *IS-LM-PEP* model
short-run disequilibrium adjustment period
the short-run versus the long-run

Review Questions

1. What is the relationship between the unemployment rate and the level of output? How can this relationship be used to translate a downward-sloping inflation–unemployment *PEP* curve into an upward-sloping inflation–output *PEP* curve?
2. How does the level of prices affect the demand for money and the position of the *LM* curve? For a given nominal money supply, what effect does inflation have on the *LM* curve?
3. What determines the equilibrium output level, unemployment rate, and interest rate? Demonstrate that the equilibrium income level is both unique and stable.
4. In determining the equilibrium level of output and interest rates, what role does the *IS-LM* part of the model play?
5. Carefully examine the short-run and long-run effects on output, unemployment, interest rates, and inflation of the following events:
   (a) a decrease in the supply of labour
   (b) a decrease in exports
   (c) an increase in government expenditures
   (d) an increase in the nominal money supply
   (e) an increase in the demand for labour.
6. Explain in a temporal sense how the *IS-LM-PEP* model is consistent with both Keynesian and classical–monetarist conclusions.
7. What factors determine the length of the short-run adjustment period?
8. How do you assess the debate between Keynesian and monetarist economists over the length of the short-run adjustment period?

CHAPTER 12

Inflation, Unemployment, and Output in an Open Economy

The recent gyrations of the dollars have looked more to me like a gold standard on the booze than the ideal managed currency which I hope for.

John Maynard Keynes[1]

Half a century has passed since Keynes made the above comment and we have yet to see the "ideal managed currency" that Keynes hoped for. In recent years the international economy has been buffeted by a number of disturbances (oil price shocks and large differences between national rates of inflation to name two significant ones) that have caused large swings in exchange rates. The Canadian dollar declined approximately 30 percent against the U.S. dollar over the period from 1976 to 1986. Now that we have introduced inflation and the *PEP* curve into our *IS-LM* model, we can consider the balance of payments adjustment process in an inflationary economy by incorporating into the *IS-LM-PEP* model the *BP* curve that was introduced in Chapter 6. First we will examine the effects of disturbances in **domestic demand** (consumption, investment, and government spending) under both **fixed and flexible exchange rate** regimes and then we will consider the effects of an increase in the Canadian money supply on the price level and the exchange rate. In a case study we tackle the question of whether Canada should follow a fixed or flexible exchange rate policy in the face of a tight U.S. monetary policy that maintains U.S. interest rates at very high levels. In the final section we examine the adjustment that follows a decline in Canadian exports. This is an example of an *external* shock

1 J.M. Keynes in 1933, quoted in "Sayings of our Times," *Observer*, 31 May 1953.

that disturbs both the Canadian balance of payments and the domestic goods market.

Domestic Disturbances Under Flexible Exchange Rates

Figure 12.1 shows our standard two-panel diagram with the economy initially described by IS_0, LM_0, and BP_0.[2] The initial equilibrium income level and interest rate are Y^* and R^*, respectively (point *A*). In the upper panel, R^* and Y^* lie on all three of the curves IS_0, LM_0, and BP_0, so that at this income level and interest rate the goods market, the money market, and the balance of payments are all in equilibrium. The economy is simultaneously in both internal and external balance. Recall that at all points along the *BP* curve, any surplus or deficit on the current account of the balance of payments is exactly matched by a deficit or surplus on the capital account. Consequently, in the absence of any intervention by the Bank of Canada, the demand for and supply of Canadian dollars in the foreign exchange market are equal at the initial equilibrium exchange rate.

As the lower panel of Figure 12.1 shows, at the income level Y^* the rate of inflation is zero. Indeed, as long as the government maintains a fixed *nominal* money supply, a zero rate of inflation is necessarily a characteristic of the equilibrium position. If the rate of inflation is not zero, then with a fixed *nominal* stock of money the *real* stock of money will be changing. For example, a positive rate of inflation will cause the real stock of money to decline and the *LM* curve will shift leftwards. Since in equilibrium all curves must be stable, it follows that the rate of inflation must be zero in equilibrium. The lower panel of Figure 12.1 shows that the *only* income level that is consistent with zero inflation is Y^*, where *PEP* cuts the horizontal axis. In all of the exercises that we do in this chapter, both the initial and final equilibrium output levels will be at Y^*. To a considerable extent our attention will be focused on the behaviour of the economy during the disequilibrium period as the economy moves from one equilibrium position to another.

Returning to Figure 12.1, suppose that there is an increase in one component of domestic demand, such as business investment or government spending, which causes the *IS* curve to shift rightwards from IS_0

[2] The figures in this section show the *BP* curve to be flatter than the *LM* curve. However, unlike the fixed price model of Chapter 6, none of the conclusions discussed here is *necessarily* changed when the *LM* curve is assumed to be flatter than the *BP* curve. Although the exchange rate may tend to appreciate or depreciate in response to an increase in domestic demand depending on the sizes of certain parameters in the model, the relevant parameters include more than the slopes of the *BP* and *LM* curves. This point is developed later in this section and is treated formally in the appendix to this chapter.

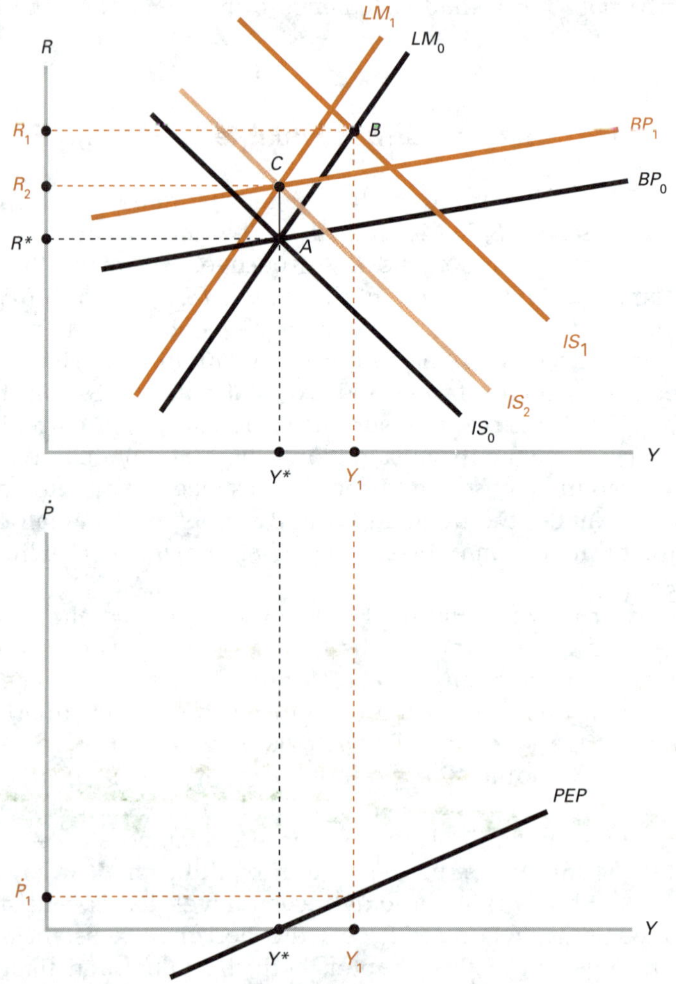

Figure 12.1 The effects of an increase in domestic demand under flexible exchange rates

to IS_1.[3] The curves IS_1 and LM_0 intersect at point B, which lies *above* BP_0. At the income level Y_1 and the interest rate R_1, while the goods and money markets are in equilibrium, there is a balance of payments surplus. (Recall from Chapter 6 that all points above the BP curve are characterized by balance of payments surpluses.) This surplus arises de-

[3] If the disturbance in aggregate demand involves either imports or exports, both the *IS* and *BP* curves will shift. We will consider an example of such an *external* shock at the end of the chapter.

spite the fact that the current account of the balance of payments deteriorates as the level of income rises from Y^* to Y_1. While the level of imports increases with the level of income, the higher rate of interest stimulates additional net capital inflows. The net effect is that the overall balance of payments is in a surplus position. Consequently, at the point (Y_1, R_1) there is an excess demand for Canadian dollars in the foreign exchange market which results in an appreciation of the Canadian dollar. The lower panel of Figure 12.1 shows that at the new income level Y_1 the rate of inflation has risen to $\dot{P}_1$ from the initial position of zero inflation at Y^*. In summary, the effect of the increase in domestic demand is to shift the *IS* curve from IS_0 to IS_1. At the intersection point of IS_1 and LM_0 the exchange rate is appreciating and the price level is rising at the rate $\dot{P}_1$.

Let us now determine how the appreciation of the Canadian dollar and the positive rate of inflation $\dot{P}_1$ affect the positions of the *IS*, *LM*, and *BP* curves which are presently at IS_1, LM_0, and BP_0. Since the price level is rising and the *nominal* money supply is given, the *real* stock of money is falling. As a result, the LM_0 curve will shift leftwards. The fact that the Canadian dollar is appreciating in value does not affect the position of the *LM* curve. However, as the dollar appreciates, the price of Canadian goods rises *relative* to the price of foreign goods, causing imports into Canada to become cheaper and Canadian exports to become more expensive for foreigners. The effect of the appreciation of the Canadian dollar on relative international prices is reinforced by the higher Canadian inflation rate. Both the appreciation of the Canadian dollar and the higher rate of inflation cause the price of Canadian goods and services to rise *relative* to prices in the rest of the world, assuming as we do throughout that the rate of inflation in the rest of the world remains at zero. As a result, Canadian exports decline and imports into Canada rise. This decrease in exports and increase in imports will cause the *IS* curve to shift to the left. In addition, because the trade balance deteriorates as a result of the change in relative international prices, the *BP* curve also shifts to the left (see Chapter 6). Consequently, at point *B*, where IS_1 intersects LM_0, the disequilibria in the labour market and the balance of payments set up the forces of price inflation and currency appreciation that push all three curves (*IS*, *LM*, and *BP*) to the left.[4]

To establish where the new equilibrium position will be following a permanent increase in domestic demand, consider the properties of

---

[4] Strictly speaking, the *PEP* curve shifts downwards to the right when the Canadian dollar appreciates because import prices are falling. However, in the new equilibrium the foreign exchange rate will be stable and *PEP* will return to its original position. Thus, this effect does not change the final equilibrium position although it does affect the dynamic path that the economy follows to get to the new equilibrium. To simplify the diagrammatic analysis we suppress this temporary shift in the *PEP* curve that accompanies the changing foreign exchange rate.

macroeconomic equilibrium. As we discussed earlier, when the government maintains a fixed nominal money supply the *LM* curve will be stationary only when the price level is stable. Consequently, in the final equilibrium position the rate of inflation must be zero. The lower panel of Figure 12.1 shows that the only income level that is consistent with a zero rate of inflation is Y^*. Given that the economy will converge back to Y^*, the intersection point of the leftward shifting *IS*, *LM*, and *BP* curves must be at Y^*. In Figure 12.1 the new equilibrium is at point *C* where the three curves IS_2, LM_1, and BP_1 intersect. The level of income is Y^* and the interest rate R_2. At this point the rate of inflation is once again zero and, because the balance of payments is in equilibrium, the foreign exchange rate is again stable.

It is instructive to compare this new equilibrium position with the original equilibrium position that existed prior to the increase in domestic demand. First, note that a shift in the *IS* curve has no lasting effect on the level of real income. During the adjustment phase the level of income rises above Y^*, but ultimately returns to this level once again. During the disequilibrium period the rate of inflation is positive so that the domestic price level is higher in the new equilibrium position than initially. It is this rise in the price level that causes the real stock of money to decline and the *LM* curve to shift to the left. And, because the real money supply is lower in the final equilibrium compared to the initial position, the rate of interest must be higher. During the adjustment phase the exchange rate appreciates so that in the new equilibrium the foreign exchange value of the Canadian dollar is greater than initially. This, together with the fact that the Canadian price level rises during the adjustment phase, means that the price of Canadian goods rises relative to foreign prices. Thus, in the new equilibrium the merchandise trade surplus (deficit) is smaller (larger) compared to the initial position. However, the overall balance of payments is once again in equilibrium because the higher Canadian interest rate results in larger net capital inflows — the deterioration on the current account is exactly matched by an improvement on the capital account.

The introduction of the balance of payments into the analysis does not change the conclusion that a shift in the *IS* curve has no lasting effect on the equilibrium level of income. The equilibrium income level is Y^* both before and after the *IS* curve shift. However, the adjustment mechanism for an open economy with a flexible exchange rate is more complex. In our previous analysis (Figure 11.6) the adjustment to a rightward shift of the *IS* curve comes about because the price level rises, the real stock of money falls, and the rate of interest rises. It is the rise in the rate of interest that crowds out private investment expenditures. This adjustment mechanism is reinforced by the balance of payments effects in the open economy model. Both the rise in the domestic price level and the appreciation of the Canadian dollar depress

Canada's export and import-competing industries. Excess aggregate demand in the Canadian economy is reduced both because investment expenditures fall in response to higher interest rates and because exports fall and imports rise as Canadian prices rise relative to foreign prices. An open economy with a flexible exchange rate should adjust more quickly to a shift in domestic demand than a closed economy, because the balance of payments repercussions push the economy back towards the equilibrium income level.

Domestic Disturbances Under a Fixed Exchange Rate

Figure 12.2 illustrates the adjustment of an open economy to a rightward shift in the *IS* curve when the government has a fixed exchange rate policy. The initial situation is described by the three curves IS_0, LM_0, and BP_0, which intersect at point *A*. Initially the economy is in equilibrium with a zero rate of inflation. Now suppose the *IS* curve shifts to the right to IS_1 because of an increase in government expenditures. The effect of the increase in demand is to raise income and domestic interest rates (compare point *B* with point *A* in Figure 12.2). As we saw in the previous section, the rise in domestic interest rates puts upward pressure on the value of the Canadian dollar in the foreign exchange market because higher Canadian interest rates attract larger inflows of foreign capital. In order to maintain a fixed exchange rate, the Bank of Canada must purchase foreign currency and supply Canadian dollars. The expansion of the domestic money supply will moderate the rise in domestic interest rates. As discussed in Chapter 6, under a fixed exchange rate policy, monetary policy is concerned exclusively with maintaining a fixed exchange rate. Consequently, under a fixed exchange rate policy the *rightward* shift of the *IS* curve is accompanied by a *rightward* shift of the *LM* curve to LM_1 as the Bank of Canada increases the money supply to prevent the exchange rate from appreciating. The comparison of points *B* and *C* in Figure 12.2 shows that the rightward shift of the *LM* curve accentuates the effect on income of the rightward shift of the *IS* curve. At point *C* in Figure 12.2, where IS_1, LM_1, and BP_0 intersect, the balance of payments is in equilibrium, but the rightward shifts of the *IS* and *LM* curves have caused a positive rate of inflation $\dot{P}_1$ to emerge. It is the positive rate of domestic inflation that pushes the economy back to its final equilibrium position.

Since the Canadian rate of inflation $\dot{P}_1$ exceeds the rate of inflation in the rest of the world, which we assume throughout to be zero, the prices of Canadian goods will rise relative to prices in the rest of the world. This will put Canadian industries at a steadily worsening disadvantage that will eventually cause exports to drop and imports to rise. Both of these factors cause the *IS* and *BP* curves to shift to the left. The

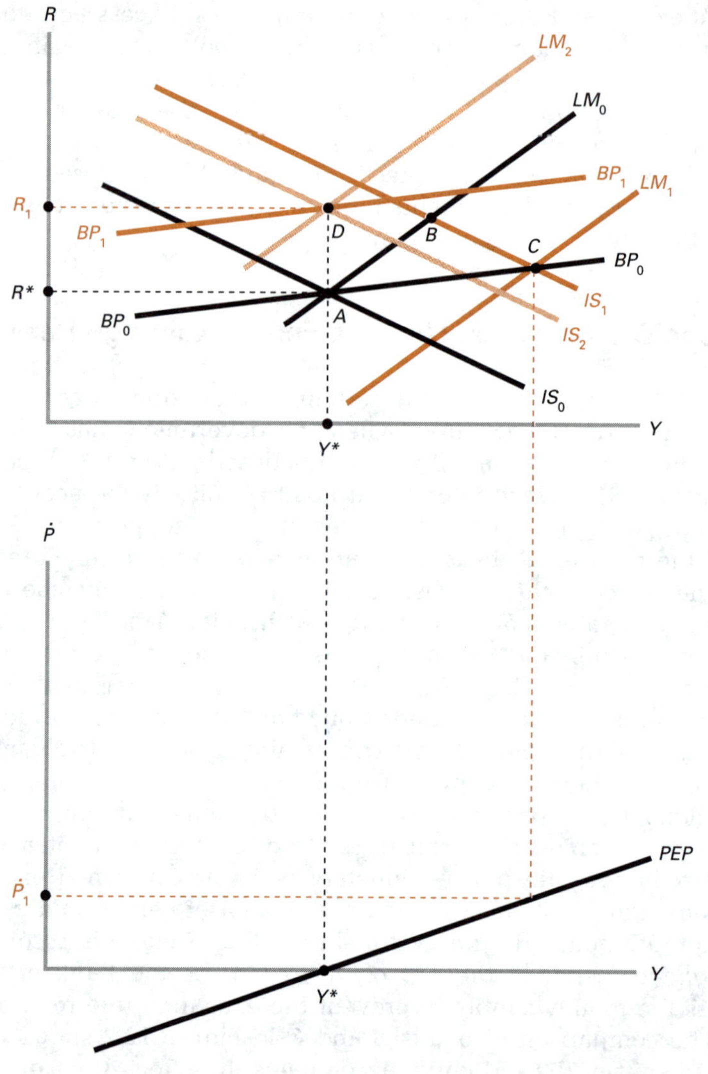

Figure 12.2 The effects of an increase in domestic demand under fixed exchange rates

intersection point of the *IS* and *BP* curves will therefore shift leftwards. Because monetary policy is devoted to the task of maintaining balance of payments equilibrium at the original exchange rate, the *LM* curve will adjust passively so that it too passes through the intersection point of the *BP* and *IS* curves. As the intersection point of the *BP* and *IS* curves drifts leftwards, the level of income and the rate of inflation both decline until ultimately the level of income returns to Y^* and the rate of inflation returns to zero. Once again, only at the income level Y^* is the rate of inflation zero. The final equilibrium position is at point D, where IS_2, LM_2, and BP_1 intersect. At point D the nominal money supply, the price level, and the foreign exchange rate are all stable.

Nothing we have said so far tells us whether the new equilibrium interest rate will be equal to, below, or above the initial interest rate R^*. In fact, the final equilibrium interest rate R_1 must be above R^*. The reason is that throughout the inflationary adjustment phase the current account of the balance of payments steadily deteriorates as exports decline and imports increase. In order for the balance of payments to return to equilibrium, the worsening current account must be matched by an equal improvement on the capital account; net capital inflows must increase. This can be achieved only if domestic interest rates rise to attract additional capital inflows. Consequently, in the new equilibrium the current account of the balance of payments has a smaller surplus (larger deficit) than initially while the capital account has a larger surplus (smaller deficit) than initially.

Again we find that a shift in the *IS* curve has no permanent effect on the level of income. An autonomous boom in one sector of the economy, whether due to an increase in government spending or some other component of domestic demand, leads to higher interest rates and a positive rate of inflation. The higher interest rates cause a decline in investment expenditures on plant and equipment while the rate of inflation causes a reduction in exports and an increase in imports. In the final equilibrium these two negative effects exactly offset the positive effect of the initial increase in spending so that ultimately the overall level of aggregate demand and the level of income are unchanged. This can be represented conveniently in symbols. The equation that represents the initial equilibrium position is

$$Y^* = C_0 + I_0 + G_0 + (X - M)_0 \tag{12.1}$$

If, for example, government expenditures are increased to G_1, the equilibrium income level is once again equal to Y^*. Although the level of investment expenditure I and net exports $X - M$ will change as a result of the increase in government spending, the level of consumption will not. This is because consumption depends only on the level of income, which is once again equal to Y^*. The equation that describes the *new* equilibrium position is

$$Y^* = C_0 + I_1 + G_1 + (X - M)_1 \tag{12.2}$$

Subtracting Equation 12.1 from Equation 12.2 gives

$$0 = 0 + (I_1 - I_0) + (G_1 - G_0) + (X - M)_1 - (X - M)_0$$

or

$$0 = \Delta I + \Delta G + \Delta(X - M)$$

To reveal more clearly the fact that the increase in government spending crowds out an equal amount of investment spending and net exports, this last equation can be rewritten:

$$\Delta G = -\Delta I - \Delta(X - M)$$

An interesting conclusion (which is demonstrated in the appendix) is that the final equilibrium interest rate, level of income, and the ratio of domestic prices to foreign prices are all independent of which exchange rate policy the government adopts. Given the size of the initial increase in government spending ΔG, the same quantity of investment I and net exports $X - M$ has to be crowded out. The rise in the interest rate R crowds out investment and the rise in the ratio of the domestic price level to the foreign price level crowds out net exports. Whether the government follows a fixed exchange rate policy or a flexible exchange rate policy does not change this fact; nor does it change the share of the crowding-out burden that is borne by the two expenditure components (investment and net exports). Consequently, the increase in the interest rate, which crowds out investment, and the increase in the ratio of domestic to foreign prices, which crowds out net exports, following a rightward shift of the *IS* curve is exactly the same whether the government adopts either a floating or a fixed exchange rate policy. What is different between the two exchange rate policy regimes is the way in which the increase in the ratio of domestic to foreign prices is achieved.

The ratio of Canadian to foreign prices can be written as:

$$\frac{\pi P}{P^W}$$

where P is the Canadian price level in Canadian dollars and π is the exchange rate. The product πP is therefore the price of Canadian goods expressed, for example, in pounds sterling. The price of foreign goods in the rest of the world in pounds sterling is P^W. Suppose the price ratio $\pi P/P^W$ rises 10 percent from one equilibrium position to another. Under the fixed exchange rate regime π is fixed so that the domestic price level must rise by the full 10 percent. In the flexible exchange rate case, the total change in the ratio of domestic to foreign prices is broken down into an exchange rate movement and a domestic price level movement. For example, the 10 percent rise in the overall ratio may be achieved by a 5 percent appreciation of the Canadian dollar and a 5 percent rise in the Canadian price level P. It would appear that in the flexible exchange rate case the domestic price level rises less than under a fixed exchange rate policy when the economy is subject to an increase in exogenous spending. This is because the flexible exchange rate policy allows the exchange rate to appreciate. This rise in the value of the Canadian dollar contributes to the increase in the ratio of domestic to foreign prices, which is necessary for the crowding out of net exports. In the fixed exchange rate case the upward pressure on the exchange rate is removed by an expansion of the nominal money supply. It is this expansion in the nominal money supply that fuels the extra inflation when a fixed exchange rate policy is followed.

This argument suggests that when a domestic demand shock hits the economy, a flexible exchange rate regime will allow the economy to recover more quickly than if a fixed exchange rate is maintained. Following an increase in demand, the period of excess demand will be shorter under a flexible exchange rate policy than under a fixed exchange rate policy because the amount by which domestic prices must rise to restore equilibrium is less in the former case. This argument is put into sharper focus when we consider a decline in autonomous domestic demand. For example, if autonomous investment is reduced, the price level must fall for equilibrium to be restored. If the exchange rate is flexible and if a depreciation follows the decline in demand, then the required reduction in the domestic price level is less than if the exchange rate is fixed because the depreciation stimulates net exports, which bolsters aggregate demand. Under a fixed exchange rate policy the only force pushing the economy back to Y^* is the declining price level. With a fixed exchange rate, the economy will languish for a longer period of time in a state of high unemployment. Output will be below Y^* until the domestic price level has fallen sufficiently.

The above argument is based on the assumption that an *appreciation* of the Canadian dollar accompanies an *increase in domestic demand* and a *depreciation* accompanies a *decrease in domestic demand*. Unfortunately, we cannot say that this will always be the case. In the flexible exchange rate case the actual breakdown of the total change in the ratio of domestic to foreign prices between an exchange rate movement and an increase in domestic prices depends on a number of parameters in the model. It is demonstrated in the appendix to this chapter that it is possible that a rightward shift of the *IS* curve will actually cause a depreciation of the foreign exchange rate.[5] In terms of our previous numerical example it may be, for example, that the 10 percent rise in the ratio of domestic to foreign prices is achieved by a 15 percent rise in domestic prices and a 5 percent *depreciation* of the Canadian dollar. In this situation an increase in exogenous domestic spending leads to a

5 Whether the exchange rate appreciates or depreciates following a rightward shift of the *IS* curve does not depend uniquely on the slopes of the *LM* and *BP* curves. The exchange rate may appreciate (depreciate) even if the *BP* curve is steeper (flatter) than the *LM* curve.

more severe inflation under a flexible exchange rate regime than under a fixed exchange rate regime. This situation will occur if, for example, net exports are very sensitive to changes in the ratio of domestic to foreign prices. As the domestic price level rises following the increase in domestic spending, net exports are crowded out to such a large degree that a depreciation is necessary in order to limit the crowding out of net exports. A second factor is the sensitivity of net capital inflows to interest rate differentials. If net capital inflows are unresponsive to interest rate differentials between Canada and the rest of the world — the *BP* curve is very steep — then the rising interest rate that follows an increase in domestic demand draws in only a small amount of additional net capital inflows. Consequently, only a small decline in net exports is required to restore balance of payments equilibrium. In this case the rise in the domestic price level that is needed to raise the interest rate and displace investment spending may cause too large a decline in net exports. A depreciation will be required so that there is only a modest rise in the ratio of domestic to foreign prices.

If the structure of the economy is such that an *increase* in autonomous domestic demand leads to a *depreciation* under a flexible exchange rate policy, then such a policy leads to a prolonged period of disequilibrium compared with a fixed exchange rate policy. In the case of an increase in domestic demand the maintenance of a fixed exchange rate will force the Bank of Canada to buy Canadian dollars and sell foreign exchange. The reduction in the money supply exerts a dampening influence on the excess demand and equilibrium is restored more quickly with less inflation than if the exchange rate were flexible. Similarly, in the case of a decline in domestic demand the maintenance of a fixed exchange rate policy will require the Bank of Canada to sell Canadian dollars in the foreign exchange market, thereby expanding the domestic money supply. This stimulus helps to push the economy back to the equilibrium level of output Y^*. The amount by which the domestic price level must fall is less than if the exchange rate were flexible and so the economy languishes in an underemployed state for a shorter period of time.

In summary, *in an open economy a permanent change in one component of domestic demand will have no lasting effect on the level of real income*. For example, in the case of an increase in domestic demand, during the adjustment phase the price level rises, the real stock of money declines, and the interest rate rises. It is the increases in the rate of interest and the ratio of domestic to foreign prices that crowd out investment and net exports, respectively. The sum of the declines in investment and net exports is exactly equal to the size of the stimulus that shifted the *IS* curve and disturbed the initial equilibrium. The effect of the exogenous stimulus on the exchange rate is ambiguous — it may appreciate or it may depreciate depending on the size of certain parameters in the model. If net capital flows are very sensitive to interest rate differentials between Canada and the rest of the world and net exports are insensitive to changes in the ratio of Canadian to foreign price levels, then an increase in domestic demand will tend to cause an appreciation of the Canadian dollar while a decrease in domestic demand will tend to cause a depreciation of the Canadian dollar. In these circumstances a flexible exchange rate policy allows the economy to adjust quickly to the disturbance with a relatively small change in the domestic price level compared with the situation in which a fixed exchange rate is maintained. This means that a decline in domestic demand leads to less unemployment for a shorter period of time if the exchange rate is flexible.

However, if net capital inflows are unresponsive to interest rate differentials and net exports are very sensitive to the ratio of the Canadian price level to the foreign price level, then the government may follow a fixed exchange rate policy in the face of a decline in domestic demand. Such a policy will minimize the unemployment problem during the recession. In the case of an increase in domestic demand the government can shorten the period of excess demand and inflation by following a fixed exchange rate policy. Of course the government may prefer to bathe in the euphoria of excess demand and have few concerns about a prolonged bout of inflation, in which case it might allow the exchange rate to depreciate. Output will be above Y^* for a longer period of time, but the resulting inflation will be greater.

An Increase in the Stock of Money Under Flexible Exchange Rates

In this section we analyze the effects of an increase in the nominal stock of money within the *IS-LM-BP-PEP* model under the assumption of a flexible foreign exchange rate. The major conclusion is that an increase in the nominal money supply of, say, 10 percent will lead to a period of inflation that will raise the price level 10 percent and cause the currency to depreciate 10 percent in the foreign exchange market. The model is therefore consistent with the purchasing power parity theorem, which was discussed in Chapter 6.

Figure 12.3 illustrates the analysis. The economy is initially in equilibrium at the point where IS_0, LM_0, and BP_0 intersect. The inflation rate is initially equal to zero. Now suppose the monetary authority increases the nominal stock of money so that the *LM* curve shifts rightwards to LM_1. The increase in the nominal stock of money lowers domestic interest rates, stimulates investment expenditures, and raises the level of income to Y_1. Both the drop in the rate of interest and the increase in the level of income tend to cause a balance of payments deficit to emerge;

lower interest rates discourage net capital inflows while a higher level of income reduces net exports. Consequently, at the point where LM_1 cuts IS_0 there is a positive rate of inflation equal to $\dot{P}_1$ and the exchange rate is depreciating in the foreign exchange market.

One effect of this domestic inflation is to raise domestic prices relative to foreign prices (which are assumed to be fixed in foreign currency). This would tend to reduce net exports and cause both the *BP* and *IS* curves to shift *leftwards*. However, the Canadian dollar is depreciating and this reduces domestic prices relative to foreign prices. For example, Canadian exports become cheaper in terms of British pounds. The effect of the depreciation is therefore to push both the *IS* and *BP* curves *rightwards*. In other words, the domestic inflation and the depreciation of the exchange rate shift the *IS* and *BP* curves in opposite directions. Let us assume that these countervailing forces exactly balance one another so that the *IS* and *BP* curves remain stationary.

The *LM* curve, however, cannot remain stationary. The new inflation

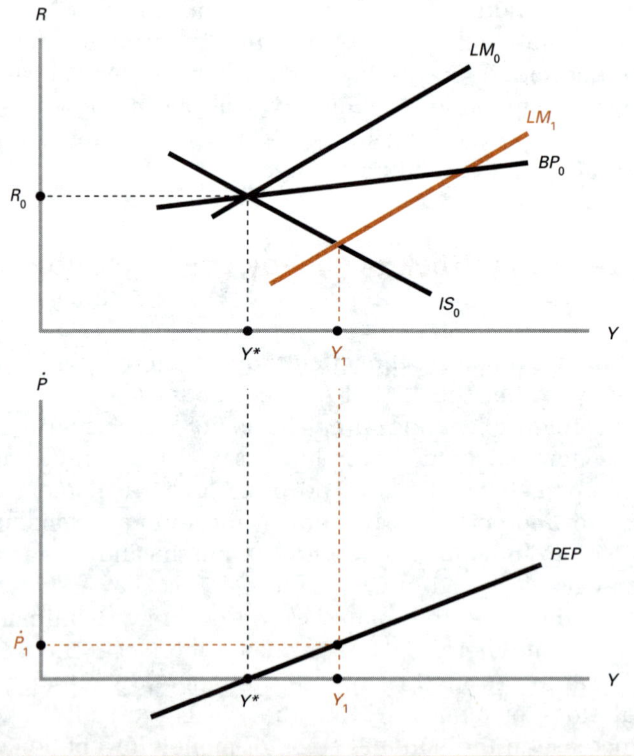

Figure 12.3 The effect of an increase in the nominal stock of money in an open economy

rate of $\dot{P}_1$ reduces the real stock of money and shifts the *LM* curve back to the left. It is convenient to think of the economy sliding up the stationary *IS* curve as the *LM* curve shifts leftwards. As the economy moves up the *IS* curve, the level of income falls towards Y^* and the rate of inflation diminishes towards zero. At the same time the economy moves closer to the *BP* curve so that the balance of payments deficit is gradually removed.

Ultimately, the *LM* curve will return to LM_0, the interest rate will again be R^* and the level of income will once more be at Y^*. Since the *LM* curve has returned to its original position, the *real* stock of money in the final equilibrium position must be exactly equal to the initial *real* stock of money. That is, the percentage increase in the price level during the adjustment period is exactly equal to the percentage increase in the nominal stock of money so that the real stock of money remains unchanged. Since the *IS* and *BP* curves have not shifted during the adjustment period, the ratio of domestic to foreign prices is exactly the same in the final equilibrium as it was initially. In other words, the foreign exchange value of the Canadian dollar depreciates by exactly the same percentage as the Canadian price level rises. This leaves the foreign price of Canadian goods and services unchanged. This result is exactly what the purchasing power parity theorem predicts (see Chapter 6).

The results we have obtained do not depend on the fact that the *IS* and *BP* curves were assumed to be stationary throughout the analysis. Even if these curves do shift during the disequilibrium period, they must eventually return to their original positions. Moreover, the fact that the *BP* curve is drawn flatter than the *LM* curve does not in any way influence the conclusions that the percentage changes in the price level and the exchange rate are equal (in absolute value) to the percentage change in the nominal stock of money that disturbs the initial equilibrium. These points are developed formally in the appendix to this chapter.

Case Study 6: Should the Canadian Dollar Float When the United States Adopts a Restrictive Monetary Policy?

We have already seen that the government's exchange rate policy has an important bearing on the path that the economy follows as it moves from one equilibrium position to another. Choosing the wrong exchange rate policy can lead to more unemployment than necessary when there is a decline in domestic demand, or more inflation than necessary when there is an increase in domestic demand. However, we found that choosing the correct exchange rate policy in the face of disturbances in domestic demand requires knowledge of key structural parameters within the model. Economists who disagree about the size of these parameters will disagree about which exchange rate policy is appropriate.

However, we will see in this case study and in the following section that when the disturbances that rock the Canadian economy are external in source, the predictions of our model are unambiguous. This conclusion will be illustrated in this case study by considering the effect of a tight U.S. monetary policy on the Canadian economy under alternative exchange rate regimes. As we saw in Chapter 6, a tight U.S. monetary policy affects Canada through the capital account of the balance of payments. High U.S. interest rates change the Canada–U.S. interest rate differential and therefore the flow of capital.

High U.S. Interest Rates: Flexible Exchange Rate

Figure 12.4 illustrates the effect of an increase in U.S. interest rates when the Canadian government is following a flexible exchange rate policy. The initial position is described by the curves IS_0, LM_0, and BP_0, which intersect at point *A*. Notice that in the initial equilibrium the level of output is at Y^* where the *PEP* curve cuts the horizontal axis, indicating that the price level is stable.

In Chapter 6 we developed the equation of the *BP* curve, which we reproduce here for convenience:

$$R = R^{US} + \frac{s\pi P + n - X_0 - p}{q} + \left(\frac{m}{q}\right)Y \tag{6.6}$$

It is clear from Equation 6.6 that an increase in the U.S. interest rate R^{US} will shift the *BP* curve upwards through a distance that is exactly equal to the increase in the U.S. interest rate. In Figure 12.4 the new "high U.S. interest rate" *BP* curve is labelled BP_1. At the initial equilibrium position (point *A*), which is below BP_1, the balance of payments is in deficit because the increase in the U.S. interest rate reduces the net flow of capital into Canada. In the foreign exchange market there is an excess supply of Canadian dollars, and the Canadian dollar begins to depreciate. This depreciation reduces the ratio of the Canadian price level to the foreign price level $\pi P/P^W$ and net exports increase. The economy is given a boost and output increases beyond the non-inflationary output level Y^*.

During the disequilibrium phase, the economy will pass through a point such as *B*. Let us consider what is happening to each of the three curves in the upper panel while the economy is temporarily at point *B*. First, the output level is above the non-inflationary output level Y^* and, as the lower panel shows, there is a positive rate of inflation equal to $\dot{P}_B$. Because the price level is rising, the real stock of money is falling and the *LM* curve is shifting upwards and to the

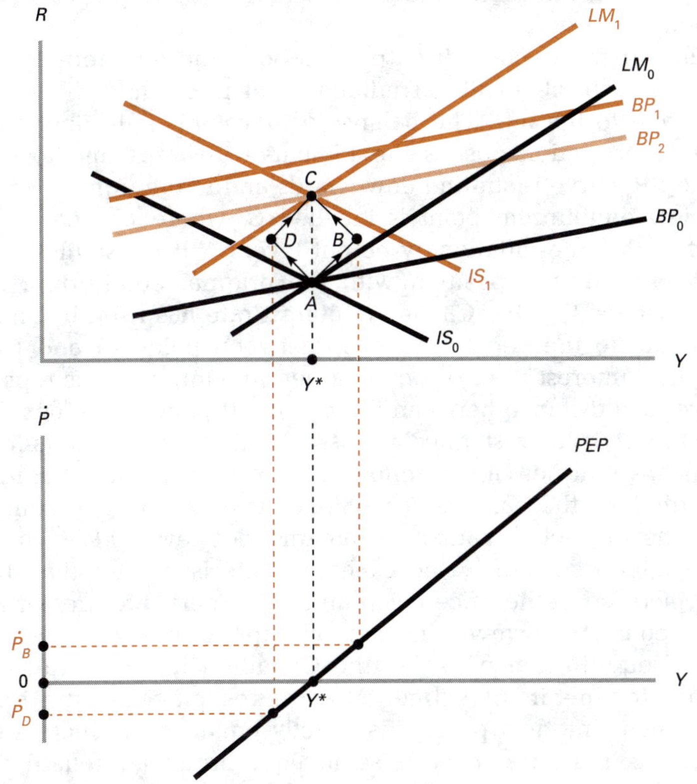

Figure 12.4 The effects of an increase in U.S. interest rates on the Canadian economy

left. We turn now to the *IS* and *BP* curves. At point *B*, which is below BP_1, the balance of payments is in deficit because of the reduction in net capital inflows that was caused by the increase in R^{US}. To restore balance of payments equilibrium, net exports must rise. This can happen only if the ratio of the Canadian price level to the foreign price level falls. The balance of payments deficit implies there is an excess supply of Canadian dollars in the foreign exchange market. The excess supply precipitates a rapid deterioration of the Canadian dollar, which ensures that the international price ratio $\pi P/P^W$ falls despite the fact that the Canadian price level P is rising at the rate $\dot{P}_B$. This is no accident: the higher the Canadian inflation rate, the more expensive will be Canadian exports, the larger will be the balance of payments deficit and the faster will be the depreciation of the Canadian dollar. Because the ratio of Canadian to foreign price levels $\pi P/P^W$ is declining, the *IS* curve is shifting upwards and to the right as net exports expand. At the same time the BP curve is shifting from BP_1 downwards and to the right.[6]

To summarize, at point B output is above the equilibrium level Y^*, and there is a positive rate of inflation that is pushing the LM_0 curve upwards and to the left. The balance of payments is in deficit and the resulting depreciation pushes the IS_0 curve upwards and to the right while the BP_1 curve is shifting downwards and to the right.

The new equilibrium point is labelled C, where IS_1, LM_1, and BP_2 intersect at the non-inflationary output level Y^*. It is useful to compare this new equilibrium position with the original equilibrium position (point A). Notice that the Canadian interest rate has risen by an amount that is equal to the vertical distance between points A and C. Recall that the U.S. interest rate rose by a larger amount, which is represented by the vertical distance between the curves BP_0 and BP_1. Consequently, overall, the U.S. interest rate has risen relative to the Canadian rate, which means that net capital inflows are lower at point C than at point A. Nevertheless, the balance of payments is once again in equilibrium, because the ratio of Canadian to foreign price levels $\pi P/P^W$ has fallen (the percentage decline in the exchange rate is greater than the percentage increase in the price level) and net exports are greater at point C than at point A. However, investment expenditures decline throughout the disequilibrium phase as the Canadian interest rate rises. Indeed the decline in investment that takes place as the economy moves from point A to point C is exactly equal to the increase in net exports. This must be so because in equilibrium aggregate demand must again be equal to the output level Y^*. An increase in one or more components of aggregate demand must be offset by an equal decline in other components. In this case only two components change: net exports increase and business investment declines, leaving total aggregate demand unchanged.

An important prediction of our *IS-LM-PEP-BP* model is that the adoption of a flexible exchange rate policy in the face of a tight U.S. monetary policy that raises U.S. interest rates will result in a period of excess demand during which output will be above its long-run level and there will be a positive rate of inflation. At the same time, the *Canadian dollar will depreciate* and Canadian interest rates will rise, but by less than U.S. interest rates.

---

6 As we pointed out earlier in this chapter, while the Canadian dollar is depreciating, the *PEP* curve will be in a higher position because a depreciating dollar raises the price of imports and therefore the overall rate of inflation at every given level of output. In equilibrium the exchange rate is stable and the *PEP* curve will return to its original position. In the text we ignore this temporary effect, which does not alter the final equilibrium position, in order to keep the analysis as straightforward as possible.

High U.S. Interest Rates: Fixed Exchange Rate

Figure 12.4 can also be used to illustrate the effects of an increase in the U.S. interest rate when the Canadian government adopts a fixed exchange rate policy. Initially, the economy is at point A, where the curves IS_0, LM_0, and BP_0 intersect. The immediate effect of the increase in the U.S. interest rate is to shift the BP curve upwards to BP_1 and to create a balance of payments deficit as net capital imports decline. The excess supply of Canadian dollars in the foreign exchange market puts downward pressure on the Canadian dollar. Under a fixed exchange rate regime the government does not allow the dollar to depreciate. The Bank of Canada's response to the "balance of payments crisis" is to enter the foreign exchange market and buy up Canadian dollars with Canada's foreign exchange reserves. This supports the value of the dollar, but also reduces the domestic money supply. At the current level of income Y^* the transactions demand for money exceeds the diminishing supply of money and interest rates are bid up. As Canadian interest rates rise, the volume of investment spending declines and the Canadian economy is dragged into a recession. The level of output declines below Y^* and during the disequilibrium phase the economy passes through a point such as D in Figure 12.3. Unlike the flexible exchange rate case there is no offsetting stimulus to net exports from a depreciating Canadian dollar.

Consider now the forces that are acting on the curves IS_0, LM_0, and BP_1 while the economy is at point D. From the lower panel it is clear that the Canadian price level is falling at the rate $\dot{P}_D$. With a fixed exchange rate, the decline in the Canadian price level reduces the ratio of Canadian to foreign prices. This gives an increasing advantage to Canadian import-competing and export industries, which expand their output. The effect on the IS curve is a shift up and to the right, while the BP curve shifts downwards and to the right. While the economy is at a point such as D, there are two opposing forces influencing the position of the LM curve. First, because the economy is in a depressed state the price level is falling at the rate $\dot{P}_D$. The effect of the falling price level is to raise the real stock of money which, by itself, would push the LM curve downwards and to the right. However, the second and more powerful influence on the real stock of money is due to the Bank of Canada's purchases of Canadian dollars in the foreign exchange market which reduce the nominal stock of money. How do we know that the nominal money stock is falling faster than the price level so that the real money stock is falling? As long as the economy is below the BP_1 curve, the balance of payments crisis persists and the Canadian dollar will be subject to downward pressure. The only way to restore equilibrium to the balance of payments is to create a domestic recession by reducing the *real* stock of money. A reduction in the real stock of money will do two things: the domestic price level will fall, allowing net exports to increase; and second, domestic interest rates will rise, which will raise net capital inflows from their depressed level. The cost of maintaining a fixed exchange rate when U.S. interest rates are increased is that the government must engineer a domestic recession in order to restore equilibrium to the balance of payments. This is done by reducing the real stock of money and shifting the *LM* curve upwards and to the left.

The final equilibrium point is labelled *C*, where the curves IS_1, LM_1, and BP_2 intersect. This is exactly the same position that the economy would reach if the government had allowed the exchange rate to depreciate. As we discussed earlier, the final values of the real endogenous variables in the model following any disturbance are independent of the particular exchange rate policy that the government follows. In the present case the disturbance is a sudden increase in the U.S. interest rate. Regardless of the Canadian government's exchange rate policy, the economy will move from its initial position at point *A* to a new equilibrium position at point *C*. However, the paths that the economy takes under the alternative exchange rate regimes are entirely different. Under a flexible exchange rate policy the economy experiences an inflationary boom with output temporarily rising above its equilibrium level. Under the fixed exchange rate policy the level of output declines and the unemployment rate rises during the disequilibrium period.

The following example illustrates how these two very different paths can lead to the same final equilibrium position, at least as far as the real variables are concerned. Consider the flexible exchange rate case first. Suppose that during the disequilibrium period the Canadian price level rises 10 percent. This means that the real stock of money declines 10 percent and it is this decline that pushes the *LM* curve from LM_0 to LM_1. In addition, suppose that the Canadian dollar depreciates by 15 percent. This means that the ratio of the Canadian price level to the foreign price level $\pi P/P^W$ declines by 5 percent. It is this reduction in relative prices that allows Canadian net exports to increase and to help restore equilibrium to the balance of payments. In the fixed exchange rate case, the ratio of the Canadian price level to foreign price level must also decline by 5 percent. This is achieved by a 5 percent decline in the Canadian price level itself. Since the real stock of money must decline by 10 percent in order to shift the *LM* curve from LM_0 to LM_1, it follows that the Bank of Canada must reduce the *nominal* stock of money by 15 percent.

The options that face the Canadian government at the time that the U.S. interest rate rises are therefore twofold. First, to continue with our numerical example, the government can allow the exchange rate to depreciate by 15 percent and experience a temporary inflationary boom that will raise the price level by 10 percent. Alternatively, the government can maintain a fixed exchange rate by reducing the nominal stock of money by 15 percent and drag the economy through a recession that will cut the price level by 5 percent.[7] In 1981, when U.S. interest rates soared above 20 percent, the federal government came much closer to following the second alternative than the first. It would appear that the government's fears of inflation were much greater at that time than its fears of unemployment and recession. As we will see in later chapters, from the mid-1970s the main preoccupation of macroeconomic policy was to reduce the rate of inflation. When the United States adopted an extremely tight monetary policy in 1981, the Canadian government was faced with the choice of either supporting the Canadian dollar and maintaining its tight-money, anti-inflationary stance, or allowing the dollar to depreciate and suffering additional inflationary pressures. The fact that the Canadian inflation rate had been accelerating upwards during the previous several years was no doubt an important factor in the government's decision to support the value of the Canadian dollar by reducing the growth rate of the money supply and living with the recessionary effects. However, it is doubtful that the government anticipated the severity of the 1982 recession, which turned out to be the most severe economic decline since the Great Depression of the 1930s.

An External Disturbance: A Decline in Exports

In this final section we examine the effects of an *external* shock that disturbs both the Canadian balance of payments and the Canadian goods market. In particular, we will look at the adjustment that follows a decline in exports. Throughout the analysis we will assume that the government takes no *internal* policy initiatives, such as changes in tax rates or changes in government spending. However, at the end of the section we will comment briefly on what fiscal policies might be adopted to speed up the adjustment towards the new equilibrium position. Rather than trying to describe the dynamic path that the economy embarks on when exports decline, we will first establish some properties of the new equilibrium position. We will then go back and consider the paths the economy might follow as it moves between the initial and final equilibrium positions. As we shall see, the government's exchange rate policy has an important bearing on this question.

---

[7] Of course the government could choose any number of intermediate courses. For example, the government could reduce the nominal money supply by 10 percent and watch the exchange rate depreciate by 5 percent. In this case the price level would not change between one equilibrium and another. The rate of inflation would average out to zero and the level of output would be, on average, equal to Y^*.

A decline in net exports immediately disturbs two markets: the balance of payments will be in deficit and there will be excess supply in the domestic goods market as unsold exports accumulate. The size of the balance of payments deficit and the amount by which aggregate demand is deficient are identical, and in the following discussion we will use the symbol *D* to denote this quantity. To restore equilibrium to the balance of payments, net exports and/or net capital inflows must increase. To restore equilibrium to the domestic goods market, aggregate demand must increase. This could be achieved by an increase in net exports and/or an increase in investment expenditures. Note that an increase in net exports helps to restore equilibrium to both markets. Suppose, for example, that net exports increase by *D* so that net exports return to their original level. Clearly both markets will be back in equilibrium and neither net capital inflows nor investment expenditures will have changed between the original and final equilibrium positions. In fact this is precisely what must happen. Suppose, for example, that net exports increase during the adjustment period but by less than *D*. Balance of payments equilibrium will be restored only if there is an increase in the Canadian interest rate that stimulates additional capital inflows. While this will restore balance of payments equilibrium, it is not consistent with equilibrium in the goods market. Because net exports increase by less than *D*, aggregate demand is still deficient. The gap can be removed only if the interest rate falls and investment is stimulated. If net exports increase by less than *D*, the rate of interest must rise to restore equilibrium to the balance of payments, but the rate of interest must fall to restore equilibrium to the domestic goods market! The inescapable conclusion is that net exports will, in fact, increase by *D*, and net exports will return to the original level.

Whether the government follows a fixed or flexible exchange rate policy, the fact remains that a sudden decline in net exports that creates a balance of payments deficit and an excess supply in the domestic goods market must be followed by a process of adjustment that restores net exports to their former level. In comparing the original and final equilibrium position no other *real* variables will change — the interest rate, the level of investment expenditures, net capital inflows, and the *real* money supply will all show no net change. The increase in net exports is realized through a decline in the ratio of the Canadian price level to the foreign price level. Under a flexible exchange rate policy, the exchange rate will depreciate sufficiently to restore net exports to their former level. In the fixed exchange rate case, it is through a decline in the domestic price level itself that the required drop in the ratio of the Canadian price level to the foreign price level is achieved. Let us now look at the dynamic adjustment process under alternative exchange rate policies.

Flexible Exchange Rate

Figure 12.5 illustrates the adjustment process that follows a decline in Canadian exports. The initial position is at point *A*, where the curves IS_0, LM_0, and BP_0 intersect. The immediate effect of the drop in export sales is that the *IS* curve shifts downwards and to the left to IS_1, and the *BP* curve shifts upwards and to the left to BP_1. At the initial position two markets are out of equilibrium. Because of the drop in exports the balance of payments is in deficit (point *A* is below BP_1) so that there is an excess supply of Canadian dollars in the foreign exchange market which puts downward pressure on the value of the Canadian dollar. Also, in the domestic goods market there is an excess supply of goods (point *A* is above IS_1) because export sales have declined. As we have seen, the final equilibrium position is also at point *A*.

In the flexible exchange rate case, one version of the dynamic story is that the economy never leaves point *A*. The exchange rate adjusts so

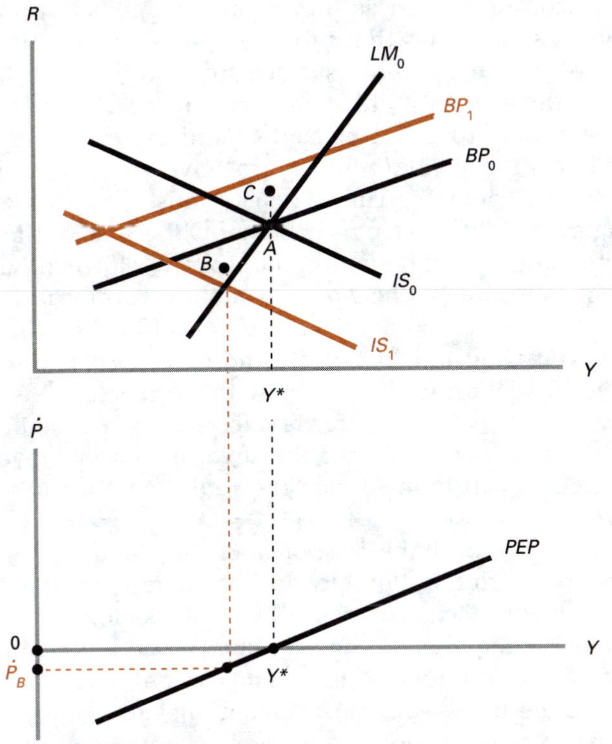

Figure 12.5 An example of an external shock: a decline in exports

quickly that as one component of exports declines with the falling U.S. income, the exchange rate depreciates and another component of Canadian exports increases because of the relative price advantage that is created by the depreciation of the Canadian dollar. In this version, the *IS* and *BP* curves, strictly speaking, never deviate from the original positions IS_0 and BP_0. They remain quite stationary as the simultaneous declines in U.S. real income and the value of the Canadian dollar have instantaneous offsetting effects that leave net exports at a constant level. The balance of payments never experiences a deficit and the Canadian economy suffers no excess supply of goods even for a moment. Left to itself, the free enterprise price system works its marvellous magic: the flexible exchange rate so perfectly insulates the Canadian economy from the external shock that it is not even noticed, even for a moment.

A somewhat more realistic possibility is that when the level of U.S. income declines, Canadian exports to the U.S. will also decline, and that there will indeed be a balance of payments deficit and a state of excess supply in the Canadian goods market. The economy will soon find itself at a position such as *B* in Figure 12.5, where output is below Y^*. The lower panel shows that in this depressed state the price level is declining at a rate $\dot{P}_B$. Interestingly, this implies that the dynamic adjustment path back to point *A* involves a cyclical approach during which the level of output will exceed Y^* and the economy will experience a positive rate of inflation. As we have seen, the final equilibrium position is at point *A*. The *LM* curve must come back to LM_0 and the *real* money supply must be the same at the end of the adjustment process as it is in the initial equilibrium position. However, under a flexible exchange rate policy, the *nominal* money supply is fixed so that the price level must also remain unchanged after the adjustment process has worked itself out. If the decline in exports pushes the economy to point *B* in Figure 12.5, where the price level is falling, the *real* money supply will temporarily increase, which will eventually stimulate the economy and push the level of output beyond Y^*. The resulting inflation will then reduce the *real* money supply back to its original level.

In conclusion, the probable response of the Canadian economy to a drop in exports under a flexible exchange rate regime is that the level of output will oscillate around Y^*, first declining as the drop in exports creates unemployment and a falling price level and then rising beyond Y^* to create a period of high employment and a positive rate of inflation. Since the price level must remain unchanged overall, the price inflation must exactly offset the initial price deflation. For example, if the price level initially falls by 10 percent when output is below Y^*, the level of output will rebound above Y^* until the price level has risen by 10 percent.

Fixed Exchange Rate

When the government maintains a fixed exchange rate policy there is no doubt that in the absence of fiscal policies the economy will go through a recession that will not be offset by a period of high employment. Indeed, it is through the effects of the recession on the Canadian price level that net exports are stimulated and the disequilibria in the balance of payments and the goods market are removed. Figure 12.5 illustrates the story.

Again the initial equilibrium position is at point *A*. As we have seen, the drop in exports shifts the *IS* and *BP* curves to IS_1 and BP_1, respectively. The decline in exports creates an excess supply of goods which leads to a decline in output below the equilibrium level Y^*. The economy therefore moves to a position such as *B*, which is above IS_1 — there is an excess supply of goods — and below BP_1 — there is a balance of payments deficit and an excess supply of Canadian dollars in the foreign exchange market. The lower panel of Figure 12.5 shows that the price level is falling at a rate equal to $\dot{P}_B$. This tends to increase the real stock of money. However, since there is an excess supply of Canadian dollars in the foreign exchange market, the Bank of Canada must use foreign exchange reserves to buy up Canadian dollars. These purchases of Canadian dollars reduce the nominal stock of money. For simplicity, let us assume that the rate of decline of the price level $\dot{P}_B$ is exactly equal to rate of decline of the nominal money stock at point *B*. Given this assumption, the real money stock remains constant and the *LM* curve remains stationary at LM_0.

However, the *IS* and *BP* curves will not remain at IS_1 and BP_1. As the Canadian price level declines, the ratio of the Canadian price level to the foreign price level also declines. This stimulates net exports and shifts the *IS* curve upwards and to the right while the *BP* curve shifts downwards and to the right. This process will continue until net exports have been restored to their original level. At this point the *IS* and *BP* curves will be back at IS_0 and BP_0, respectively. The level of output will once more be at Y^* and the price level will be constant.

It is interesting to compare the adjustment paths following a drop in Canadian exports under alternative exchange rate policies. Whether the exchange rate is flexible or fixed, the adjustment involves a reduction in the ratio of the Canadian price level to the foreign price level which is just sufficient to restore exports to their original level. In the *flexible exchange rate case* this is achieved through a depreciation of the Canadian dollar. As we have seen, it is likely that during the depreciation the level of output will oscillate around the equilibrium value. An initial and relatively mild recession will later give way to a period of higher employment and inflation. However, when the dust finally settles and the level of output returns to its unique equilibrium level, the recession and boom cycle will have cancelled out each other in the sense that the Canadian price level will end up at exactly the point where it started. The decline in the price level during the recession is exactly offset by an equal rise in the price level during the boom phase.

The adjustment under a *fixed exchange rate* is quite different. Since the exchange rate is prevented from falling, the price level itself must decline. If the adjustment requires a 10 percent decline in the value of the Canadian dollar under a flexible exchange rate policy, then a fixed exchange rate policy will drag the economy into a recession and hold it there until the domestic price level has fallen by 10 percent. This is an example of how an external shock can create a "balance of payments crisis" under a fixed exchange rate policy and force the government to take harsh restrictive domestic policies to correct the situation. Advocates of flexible exchange rates argue that such harsh policies are unnecessary since a flexible exchange rate will insulate the domestic economy from external shocks.

Our analysis of the adjustment process under a fixed exchange rate regime following a decline in Canadian exports has assumed that the government simply allows the adjustment process to work itself out and that the government does not intervene with offsetting fiscal policies. As we have seen, the decline in exports immediately disturbs two markets. The balance of payments is in a deficit position and there is an excess supply of goods in the domestic goods market. One way to remove this state of excess supply is to increase government spending by an amount exactly equal to the decline in exports. In Figure 12.5 the leftward shift of IS_0 to IS_1 due to the decline in exports is immediately offset by the increase in government spending, and the *IS* curve returns to IS_0. The state of the economy is now described by IS_0, LM_0, and BP_1. Assuming that the expansionary fiscal policy occurs simultaneously with the decline in exports so that the economy remains at the initial position at point *A*, only the balance of payments will be in disequilibrium on account of the decline in exports.

The arrangement of the *IS*, *LM*, and *BP* curves is now exactly the same as in Figure 12.4, when the increase in U.S. interest rates shifted the *BP* curve upwards to BP_1. Consequently, the adjustment process that the economy follows after the simultaneous drop in exports and the exactly offsetting increase in government spending is just as we described in the case study. Balance of payments equilibrium will be restored through a combination of an increase in the Canadian interest rate, which will raise net capital inflows, and a decline in the Canadian price level, which will raise Canadian exports. In Figure 12.5 the final equilibrium position with fiscal policy will be at a point such as *C* rather than at *A*. Because the Canadian price level must decline under a fixed exchange rate policy, the Canadian economy will not be spared from a recession as it moves from point *A* to point *C*. However, the interesting point is that since capital inflows will be higher at point *C* than at point *A*, net exports do not have to be restored to the original level for balance of payments equilibrium. The expansionary fiscal policy that immediately restores equilibrium in the domestic goods market leaves the economy with a *smaller* price level adjustment and consequently a less severe recession. In other words, the fixed exchange rate adjustment process in the absence of any offsetting fiscal policy takes the economy from point *A* through a recession and back to point *A*. This recession is deeper than the one that the economy suffers if an expansionary fiscal policy is adopted and the economy moves from point *A* to point *C*.

Summary

In this chapter we have introduced the balance of payments into our flexible price model. We have considered the adjustment process following a number of disturbances. In this regard, we have found that there is a distinction to be made between *internal* and *external* disturbances. The effect of internal disturbances on the equilibrium value of a flexible exchange rate is ambiguous in the sense that different results obtain depending on the size of key structural parameters. However, in the case of external disturbances the effect on the exchange rate is clear. In a case study into the effects of an increase in U.S. interest rates we were able to obtain unambiguous predictions concerning the consequences of adopting fixed or flexible exchange rate policies. Finally, in the last section we established that a flexible exchange rate policy offers more protection to the Canadian economy in the face of a decline in Canadian exports than a fixed exchange rate policy. However, given that a fixed exchange rate policy is adopted, we showed that fiscal policy can be used to mitigate the recessionary effects of a decline in exports.

Appendix: An Algebraic Approach

In this appendix an algebraic approach is used to derive some of the key propositions that have been developed in this and the previous chapter. First we examine the effects of (1) an exogenous demand stimulus and (2) an increase in the nominal money supply within the *IS-LM-PEP* model. Then the analysis is extended to the *IS-LM-BP-PEP* model.

The *IS-LM-PEP* Model

An important proposition that was developed in Chapter 11 is that given the monetary authority maintains a constant nominal money supply, the equilibrium position of the economy must be characterized by zero inflation. The equilibrium level of income must be at the point where the *PEP* curve intersects the output axis. We designate this level of output Y^*. The product-market clearing condition requires that the level of output be equal to the sum of the expenditure components. The following equations describe two possible equilibrium positions:

$$C_0 + I_0 + G_0 + (X - M)_0 = Y^*$$

$$C_0 + I_1 + G_1 + (X - M)_1 = Y^*$$

Note that the levels of output and consumption are equal to Y^* and C_0 in both cases (we assume that consumption depends only on the level of income). Now subtract the first equation from the second:

$$\Delta I + \Delta G + \Delta(X - M) = 0 \qquad (12A.1)$$

Equation 12A.1 says that in comparing one equilibrium with another, following a disturbance in any component of autonomous demand or a change in the money supply, the sum of the changes in investment spending, government spending, and net exports must be zero. Another useful result can be obtained from the *LM* curve:

$$\ell P_0 R_0 = -\$_0^S + kP_0 Y^*$$

and

$$\ell P_1 R_1 = -\$_1^S + kP_1 Y^*$$

Again, these two equations represent two alternative equilibrium positions; in both cases the equilibrium level of income is Y^*. Note that the change in a product such as *PR* can be approximated by

$$\Delta PR = P_0 \Delta R + R_0 \Delta P$$

Consequently, subtracting the first *LM* equation from the second gives

$$\ell(P_0 \Delta R + R_0 \Delta P) = -\Delta\$^S + kY^* \Delta P$$

Now collect together the ΔP terms:

$$\Delta P(kY^* - \ell R_0) = \Delta\$^S + \ell P_0 \Delta R$$

The term in parentheses is simply the demand for real money balances which in equilibrium must equal the supply of real money:

$$\left(\frac{\$_0^S}{P_0}\right)\Delta P = \Delta\$^S + \ell P_0 \Delta R \qquad (12A.2)$$

Equation 12A.2 shows how the changes in the price level, the nominal money supply, and the interest rate are related between one equilibrium position and another, regardless of the type of exogenous shock that caused the economy to move from one equilibrium position to another.

A Fiscal Stimulus

Suppose the government increases its expenditures by an amount ΔG. Net exports will not change from one equilibrium to another since we initially assume that exports X are exogenous and that imports M depend only on the level of income which remains unchanged at Y^*, where the *PEP* curve cuts the horizontal axis. The role of relative international prices in determining net export flows is incorporated later in this appendix. Under these assumptions, $\Delta(X - M)$ of Equation 12A.1 is zero following an increase in government spending. Equation 12A.1 reduces to

$$\Delta G = -\,\Delta I$$

This demonstrates the proposition that an increase in government spending will eventually crowd out an equal amount of investment spending. This is achieved through an increase in the interest rate. From the investment equation (5.1) we have

$$\Delta I = -\,e\Delta R$$

Given the increase in government spending ΔG we can use the last two equations to determine by how much the interest rate must rise in order to crowd out an equal amount of investment spending:

$$\Delta R = -\frac{1}{e}\Delta I$$

or

$$\Delta R = \frac{1}{e}\Delta G$$

As we have seen, the interest rate rises because the excess demand created by the increase in government spending causes a bout of inflation which in turn reduces the real stock of money. Using Equation

12A.2 we can determine exactly how much prices will increase following a permanent increase in government spending. Note that the nominal money supply is unchanged so Equation 12A.2 reduces to

$$\left(\frac{\$_0^S}{P_0}\right)\Delta P = \ell P_0 \Delta R$$

We have just seen that the change in the interest rate given the demand stimulus ΔG is $\Delta G/e$. Consequently:

$$\left(\frac{\$_0^S}{P_0}\right)\Delta P = P_0\left(\frac{\ell}{e}\right)\Delta G$$

This can be rearranged to show the effect of the demand stimulus on price levels:

$$\frac{\Delta P}{P_0} = \frac{\ell \Delta G}{e(\$_0^S/P_0)}$$

where $\Delta P/P_0$ represents the proportionate change in the price level. Note that, given the size of the demand stimulus ΔG, the percentage change in the price level depends directly on ℓ and inversely on e. Recall that in the new equilibrium, investment expenditures will be reduced by exactly the same amount as the increase in government spending. The more sensitive investment is to changes in the interest rate (the larger e is), the "easier" it is to displace investment expenditures. The larger is e, the smaller is the required increase in the price level and decline in the real stock of money. On the other hand, if the demand for money is very interest-elastic (ℓ is large) it will take a very large decline in the real stock of money, and therefore a large increase in the price level, to raise the interest rate by the required amount.

An Increase in the Nominal Money Supply

Now suppose the government increases the nominal money supply by an amount $\Delta\$^S$. Consider first Equation 12A.1. Since neither net exports, which depend only on the level of income, nor government spending, which is exogenous, will change in response to an increase in the nominal money supply (again the price effects on net exports are ignored temporarily) it follows that

$$\Delta I = 0$$

In other words, an increase in the nominal money supply has no effect whatsoever on the real variables in the model. Since investment depends on the rate of interest it must be that the rate of interest is unchanged following an increase in the nominal money supply:

$$\Delta R = 0$$

Using Equation 12A.2 we can establish the effect on prices of an increase in the nominal money supply of $\Delta\$^S$:

$$\left(\frac{\$_0^S}{P_0}\right)\Delta P = \Delta\$^S + 0$$

or

$$\frac{\Delta P}{P_0} = \frac{\Delta\$^S}{\$_0^S}$$

This demonstrates that the proportionate rise in the price level is identical to the proportionate rise in the nominal money supply. The real money supply does not change.

The *IS-LM-BP-PEP* Model

The extension of the model to include the balance of payments constraint that net capital inflows plus net exports must sum to zero in equilibrium and the effect of relative international prices on net exports does not invalidate Equations 12A.1 and 12A.2, but it does provide an additional equation representing the *BP* curve:

$$R = R^{US} + \frac{s\pi P + n - X_0 - p}{q} + \left(\frac{m}{q}\right)Y \qquad (BP\ \text{curve}) \qquad (6.6)$$

It will be convenient to rearrange this equation as follows:

$$qR_0 - qR_0^{US} - s(\pi_0 P_0) - n + X_0 + p - mY^* = 0$$

where the subscript $_0$ refers to the initial equilibrium position and Y^* is the long-run equilibrium level of output. A new equilibrium will be established if an exogenous shock disturbs the economy. The new equilibrium is:

$$qR_1 - qR_1^{US} - s(\pi_1 P_1) - n + X_0 + p - mY^* = 0$$

Note that the level of income remains unchanged at Y^*, where the *PEP* curve cuts the horizontal axis. We have also assumed that the parameters n, X_0, and p remain unchanged. This is simply because the exogenous disturbances that we consider below do not involve these parameters.[8] Subtracting the first equation from the second, we obtain the relationship between the change in the ratio of the Canadian price level to the foreign price level $\Delta\pi P$ and the change in the interest rate ΔR when comparing one equilibrium with another:

$$q\Delta R - q\Delta R^{US} - s\Delta(\pi P) = 0$$

or

$$q\Delta R - s\Delta(\pi P) = q\Delta R^{US} \qquad (12A.3)$$

An Increase in Domestic Demand: A Fiscal Stimulus

In this section we consider the effects of an increase in government spending on the important endogenous variables within the model. Before we even introduce the issue of what exchange rate policy the government is following, Equations 12A.1 and 12A.3 can be used to solve for ΔR and $\Delta(\pi P)$, given the increase in government spending ΔG. It is convenient to reproduce these equations here:

$$\Delta I + \Delta G + \Delta(X - M) = 0 \qquad (12A.1)$$

$$q\Delta R - s\Delta(\pi P) = q\Delta R^{US} \qquad (12A.3)$$

First, recall that the change in investment expenditures is always determined by the change in the interest rate, $\Delta I = -e\Delta R$. In addition, the equation for net exports (see Equation 6.5 in Chapter 6) shows that the change in net exports is determined by the change in the ratio of Canadian to foreign prices, $\Delta(X - M) = -s\Delta(\pi P)$. Using this information, Equation 12A.1 can be rewritten:

$$-e\Delta R + \Delta G - s\Delta(\pi P) = 0$$

or

$$e\Delta R + s\Delta(\pi P) = \Delta G \qquad (12A.1a)$$

Equation 12A.3 can also be modified, since in the present case there is no reason to expect the U.S. interest rate to change, $\Delta R^{US} = 0$:

$$q\Delta R - s\Delta(\pi P) = 0 \qquad (12A.3a)$$

---

8 If, however, we wanted to consider the effect of a sudden increase in imports that is unrelated to the level of income and to the ratio of domestic prices to foreign prices we would allow the parameter n to rise.

Equations 12A.1a and 12A.3a form a two-equation system in ΔR and $\Delta(\pi P)$. The solutions are:

$$\Delta R = \frac{\Delta G}{q + e} > 0 \tag{12A.4}$$

$$\Delta(\pi P) = \frac{q\Delta G}{s(q + e)} > 0 \tag{12A.5}$$

These equations show that a permanent increase in government expenditures, or any component of autonomous expenditure, will raise both the interest rate and the ratio of Canadian to foreign prices. The increase in the interest rate crowds out private investment expenditures. The increase in the ratio of Canadian to foreign prices crowds out net exports. The actual increases in the rate of interest and the ratio of Canadian to foreign prices are independent of the government's exchange rate policy. However, the ratio of Canadian to foreign prices has two components: the Canadian price level P and the exchange rate π. How the total change in πP is broken down between a change in π and a change in P does depend on the nature of the government's exchange rate policy. We will examine the flexible and fixed exchange rate cases in turn.

Flexible Exchange Rate

In this case the money supply is exogenously determined by the government. When government expenditure is increased, the money supply is assumed to remain fixed, $\Delta\$^S = 0$. From Equation 12A.2 we have

$$\left(\frac{\$_0^S}{P_0}\right)\Delta P = \ell P_0 \Delta R$$

so, using Equation 12A.4,

$$\left(\frac{\$_0^S}{P_0}\right)\Delta P = \frac{\ell P_0 \Delta G}{q + e}$$

$$\frac{\Delta P}{P_0} = \frac{\ell \Delta G}{(q + e)(\$_0^S / P_0)} > 0 \tag{12A.6}$$

Equation 12A.6 shows that under a flexible exchange rate policy an increase in government spending will lead to an increase in the domestic price level. We now determine the effect on the foreign exchange rate. The total change in the ratio of Canadian to foreign prices πP has two components:

$$\Delta(\pi P) = P_0 \Delta\pi + \pi_0 \Delta P \tag{12A.7}$$

Substituting Equations 12A.5 and 12A.6 into Equation 12A.7 we have

$$\frac{q\Delta G}{s(q+e)} = P_0\Delta\pi + \frac{\pi_0 \ell P_0 \Delta G}{(q+e)(\$_0^S/P_0)}$$

This can be solved for $\Delta\pi$:

$$\Delta\pi = \frac{\Delta G}{(q+e)}\left[\frac{q}{sP_0} - \frac{\pi_0\,\ell}{(\$_0^S/P_0)}\right] \tag{12A.8}$$

Since all the parameters and initial values in this expression are positive, the sign of $\Delta\pi$ depends on the specific parameter values. For example, if q is large, meaning that capital flows are very sensitive to the interest rate, and s is very small, meaning that net exports are insensitive to the ratio of Canadian to foreign prices, then the exchange rate will appreciate following an increase in government expenditure. However, if s is sufficiently large, or if q is zero, $\Delta\pi$ will be negative. Note that the slopes of the *BP* and *LM* curves, m/q and k/ℓ, respectively, are independent of s so that the slopes of these two schedules alone do *not* determine whether the exchange rate will appreciate or depreciate following an expansionary fiscal policy. The parameter s determines the sensitivity of net exports to changes in the ratio of Canadian to foreign prices and therefore the speed with which the *IS* and *BP* curves shift leftwards when the ratio of Canadian to foreign prices rises.

Fixed Exchange Rate

Under a fixed exchange rate policy $\Delta\pi = 0$, but the money supply becomes endogenous. From Equation 12A.7 we have

$$\Delta(\pi P) = \pi_0 \Delta P$$

and from Equation 12A.5,

$$\pi_0 \Delta P = \frac{q\Delta G}{s(q+e)}$$

or

$$\Delta P = \frac{q\Delta G}{s\pi_0(q+e)} > 0 \tag{12A.9}$$

Comparing Equations 12A.9 and 12A.6 we have

$$\Delta P(\pi \text{ fixed}) - \Delta P(\pi \text{ flexible}) = \frac{\Delta G}{(q+e)}\left[\frac{q}{s\pi_0} - \frac{\ell P_0}{(\$_0^S/P_0)}\right]$$

$$= \frac{\Delta G P_0}{(q+e)\pi_0}\left[\frac{q}{sP_0} - \frac{\ell \pi_0}{(\$_0^S/P_0)}\right]$$

so, using Equation 12A.8

$$= \Delta\pi\left(\frac{P_0}{\pi_0}\right)$$

or

$$\frac{\Delta P}{P_0}(\pi \text{ fixed}) - \frac{\Delta P}{P_0}(\pi \text{ flexible}) = \frac{\Delta\pi}{\pi_0}$$

This demonstrates that if the exchange rate appreciates (depreciates) following an increase in government spending, then domestic inflation will be greater (less) under a fixed exchange rate policy than under a flexible exchange rate policy.

An Increase in the Nominal Money Supply

Equations 12A.3a (derived from the *BP* curve) and 12A.1a (derived from the crowding-out equation (12A.1)) apply as equally to an increase in the nominal money supply as to an increase in exogenous spending. However, since there is no increase in government spending, Equation 12A.1a reduces to Equation 12A.1b:

$$e\Delta R + s\Delta(\pi P) = 0 \qquad (12A.1b)$$

$$q\Delta R - s\Delta(\pi P) = 0 \qquad (12A.3a)$$

Adding one equation to another reveals that $\Delta R = 0$ provided that $q \neq -e$, which we assume to be the case. This in turn implies $\Delta(\pi P) = 0$.

Since $\Delta R = 0$ it follows that $\Delta I = 0$ because investment depends only on the interest rate. Equation 12A.1 shows that with $\Delta I = \Delta G = 0$, it follows that $\Delta(X - M) = 0$. Hence, an increase in the nominal money supply has no effect on real variables Y, I, C, $(X - M)$.

Finally, combining $\Delta R = 0$ with Equation 12A.2 and $\Delta(\pi P) = 0$ with Equation 12A.7 gives

$$\frac{\Delta \$^S}{\$_0^S} = \frac{\Delta P}{P_0} = -\frac{\Delta\pi}{\pi_0}$$

which demonstrates that a given proportionate increase in the nominal money stock leads to an equal proportion *rise* in the price level and *decline* in the value of the Canadian dollar in the foreign exchange market.

An Increase in U.S. Interest Rates

In this section we examine the effects of an increase in U.S. interest rates on the Canadian economy. As we saw in the last section, some headway can be made even before we consider what exchange rate policy the government is following. Again, Equations 12A.1 and 12A.3 form the basis of the preliminary analysis. In the present case, there is no increase in government spending and so Equation 12A.1a, which was derived from Equation 12A.1, reduces to

$$e\Delta R + s\Delta(\pi P) = 0 \qquad (12A.1b)$$

For ease of reference we reproduce Equation 12A.3:

$$q\Delta R - s\Delta(\pi P) = q\Delta R^{US} \qquad (12A.3)$$

Equations 12A.1b and 12A.3 form a two-equation system that can be solved for ΔR and $\Delta(\pi P)$:

$$\Delta R = \frac{q}{(q+e)}\Delta R^{US} > 0 \qquad (12A.10)$$

$$\Delta(\pi P) = \frac{-eq}{s(q+e)}\Delta R^{US} < 0 \qquad (12A.11)$$

Equation 12A.10 shows that the increase in the U.S. interest rate will lead to a rise in the Canadian interest rate *regardless of the exchange rate policy*. However, the Canadian interest rate rises by less than the U.S. interest rate because $q/(q + e)$ is less than unity. The more sensitive net capital inflows are to the Canadian–U.S. interest rate differential (the larger q is), the closer the ratio $q/(q + e)$ will be to unity. In the limiting case that q tends to infinity, capital is perfectly mobile and the Canadian interest rate is equal to the U.S. interest rate. In this limiting case the *BP* curve is horizontal and cuts the vertical axis at R^{US}. Note that $q/(q + e)$ also tends to unity in this limiting case so that $\Delta R = \Delta R^{US}$.

The second factor that determines how the Canadian interest rate responds to changes in the U.S. interest rate is the sensitivity of investment spending to changes in the interest rate, measured by the parameter e. As we have seen, the Canadian interest rate rises by a smaller amount than the U.S. interest rate. Consequently, net capital inflows will be smaller in the final equilibrium position compared with the initial equilibrium position. This means that net exports must rise to maintain balance-of-payments equilibrium. However, an increase in net exports must be exactly offset by a decline in investment spending since total aggregate demand must be equal to Y^* in all equilibrium positions.[9] It is the rise in the interest rate that reduces investment spending. If investment is highly interest-elastic (e is large), only a small increase in the Canadian interest rate is required to induce the necessary decline in investment.

Equation 12A.11 shows that regardless of the government's exchange rate policy, an increase in the U.S. interest rate will reduce the ratio of Canadian to foreign prices. As we pointed out in the previous paragraph, this is necessary because in the new equilibrium net exports will be greater.

Now we turn to examine how exchange rate policy determines the breakdown of the decline in the ratio of Canadian to foreign prices into a Canadian price level adjustment and an exchange rate adjustment.

Flexible Exchange Rate

In this case the money supply is exogenously determined by the government, $\Delta\$^S = 0$. Equation 12A.2 reduces to

$$\left(\frac{\$_0^S}{P_0}\right)\Delta P = \ell P_0 \Delta R$$

We can use Equation 12A.10 to substitute for the change in the interest rate:

$$\left(\frac{\$_0^S}{P_0}\right)\Delta P = \frac{q\ell}{(q+e)} P_0 \Delta R^{US}$$

$$\frac{\Delta P}{P_0} = \frac{q\ell}{(q+e)}\left[\frac{\Delta R^{US}}{(\$_0^S/P_0)}\right] > 0 \qquad (12A.12)$$

In order to find the change in the exchange rate we use Equations 12A.7, 12A.11, and 12A.12:

$$\frac{-eq\Delta R^{US}}{s(q+e)} = P_0 \Delta\pi + \pi_0 \left[\frac{q\ell P_0 \Delta R^{US}}{(q+e)(\$_0^S/P_0)}\right]$$

---

[9] Note that Equation 12A.1 implies $\Delta(X - M) = -\Delta I$.

Solving for $\Delta\pi$, we have

$$\Delta\pi = \frac{-q\Delta R^{US}}{(q+e)P_0}\left[\frac{e}{s} + \frac{\pi_0 \ell P_0}{(\$_0^S/P_0)}\right] < 0$$

Here we can state unambiguously that a rise in the U.S. interest rate will cause a depreciation of the Canadian dollar. We have already seen that the Canadian price level rises under a flexible exchange rate policy and that the ratio of Canadian to foreign prices must *fall.* The depreciation must be sufficiently large to offset the rise in the Canadian price level.

Fixed Exchange Rate

Under a fixed exchange rate policy, all the adjustment in the ratio of Canadian to foreign prices is achieved through a decline in the Canadian price level. From Equation 12A.7 we have

$$\Delta(\pi P) = \pi_0 \Delta P$$

Using Equation 12A.11:

$$\Delta P = \frac{-eq}{\pi_0 s(q+e)}\Delta R^{US} < 0$$

Unlike the flexible exchange rate case, in which the Canadian price level rose, when the exchange rate is fixed, higher U.S. interest rates cause the Canadian price level to fall. The level of output will be *below* Y^* throughout the adjustment phase. In order to maintain the fixed exchange rate, monetary policy must be very restrictive to force down the Canadian price level. The Canadian economy therefore approaches the new equilibrium via a recession rather than a period of excess demand.

In this section we have looked at the effects of both internal and external shocks on the Canadian economy. The case of a decline in Canadian exports was considered in the main body of the chapter. We leave it to the interested student to develop the algebraic details of this and other disturbances.

Key Concepts

domestic demand
internal and external disturbances
fixed and flexible exchange rates

the relationship between exchange rate policy and the breakdown of a change in the ratio of the Canadian price level to the foreign price level into an exchange rate adjustment and a price level adjustment

Review Questions

1. Use the *IS-LM-BP-PEP* model to analyze the effects of a decline in autonomous investment under both fixed and flexible exchange rate regimes.
   (a) Does the particular exchange rate policy that the government adopts influence the final equilibrium values of net exports, net capital inflows, the interest rate, the real money supply, the nominal money supply, the price level, and the ratio of the Canadian price level to the foreign price level?
   (b) What factors determine whether the exchange rate will appreciate or depreciate when the exchange rate is floating?
   (c) If the exchange rate is subject to upward pressure, which exchange rate policy will minimize the unemployment problem during the adjustment period?
2. Suppose the federal government adopts long-term policies that encourage Canadian ownership of resource industries. If this reduces net capital inflows over the long term, what will be the effects of these policies on the economy as a whole? What exchange rate policy would you recommend the government adopt as it pursues its "Canadianization" program?
3. One effect of an increase in U.S. interest rates is to cause Canadian interest rates to rise. What factors determine by how much Canadian rates will rise, *given* the size of the increase in U.S. rates?

CHAPTER 13

The Unemployment–Inflation Trade-Off Reconsidered

> *There is always a temporary trade-off between inflation and unemployment; there is no permanent trade-off.*
>
> *Milton Friedman*[1]

In Chapter 11 it was demonstrated that the equilibrium income/output level in the *IS-LM-PEP* model is determined in the labour market and production sector of the economy. If the government attempts to increase the level of income and employment by a good dose of fiscal policy, the economy will automatically gravitate back to its original equilibrium income position (the natural rate of output). The only permanent effect of an increase in government expenditures is a higher price level and a higher interest rate, which will crowd out an equivalent amount of new investment to offset the increase in government expenditures. The best that the government can hope for is a *short-run* effect on output. As discussed in Chapter 11, the duration of the short-run effect following an expansionary fiscal policy depends on the characteristics of the Phillips curve. The steeper the *PEP* curve and/or the faster the adjustment of inflation expectations, the shorter the short-run adjustment period and the less the potential for even a temporary gain in output and employment from an expansionary fiscal policy.

In this chapter and the next we wish to probe further the policy implication of the *IS-LM-PEP* model. During the 1960s and early 1970s, Keynesian policymakers thought that they could "beat the Phillips curve at its own game." By continually expanding the money supply, the government *might* be able to *perpetuate* the short-run adjustment period and therefore bring about a *permanent* increase in the level of

---

1 Milton Friedman, "The Role of Monetary Policy," *American Economic Review*, March 1968, p. 11.

output and employment. The price that the government would have to pay for such a *permanent* increase in output and employment would be an *enduring* inflation rate. This possibility brings us face-to-face with the now-famous inflation–unemployment trade-off.

In this chapter we analyze the nature of the elusive inflation–unemployment trade-off, from both Keynesian and monetarist perspectives. Since the inflation–unemployment trade-off is basically a *long-run* issue (*perpetuate* the short run, a *permanent* increase in output, an *enduring* inflation rate), it should come as no surprise that monetarists, the denizens of the *long run*, hold the upper hand in this chapter. *In the long run*, there is *no* trade-off between inflation and unemployment; the government cannot permanently decrease the unemployment rate by implementing expansionary Keynesian policies. However, the government can permanently lower the inflation rate. In the now-famous words of Milton Friedman, "Substantial inflation is always and everywhere a monetary phenomenon . . . inflation occurs when the quantity of money rises more appreciably more rapidly than output, and the more rapid the rise in the quantity of money per unit of output, the greater the rate of inflation."[2] By restricting the growth rate of the money supply, the government can control the inflation rate in the long run.

Although there is no *long-run* trade-off between inflation and unemployment, there is an important *short-run* relationship between inflation and unemployment when the macroeconomic system is in disequilibrium. In Chapter 14 we explore the *short-run* inflation–unemployment path that the economy might travel during the *disequilibrium adjustment* period accompanying the implementation of an anti-inflationary, restrictive monetary policy. As we shall see, the *short-run* adjustment costs of a *long-run* anti-inflationary monetary policy may be very severe. Even though the *long-run* inflation–unemployment trade-off curve is dead, a *short-run* relationship between inflation and unemployment is very much alive.

Trying to Beat the Phillips Curve at its own Game

In Figure 13.1 we have replicated our basic *IS-LM-PEP* diagram from Chapter 11 (to simplify the analysis we ignore the balance of payments *BP* curve). We assume that the labour, goods, and money markets are all in equilibrium and that the economy is initially at Y^*, R^*, and U^*, with a zero inflation rate and zero inflation expectations (the *PEP* curve corresponds to $\dot{P}^e = 0$). The economy is at point *A* on the IS_0 curve in the upper panel of Figure 13.1.

---

2 Milton and Rose Friedman, *Free to Choose* (New York: Harcourt Brace Jovanovich, Inc., 1980), p. 254.

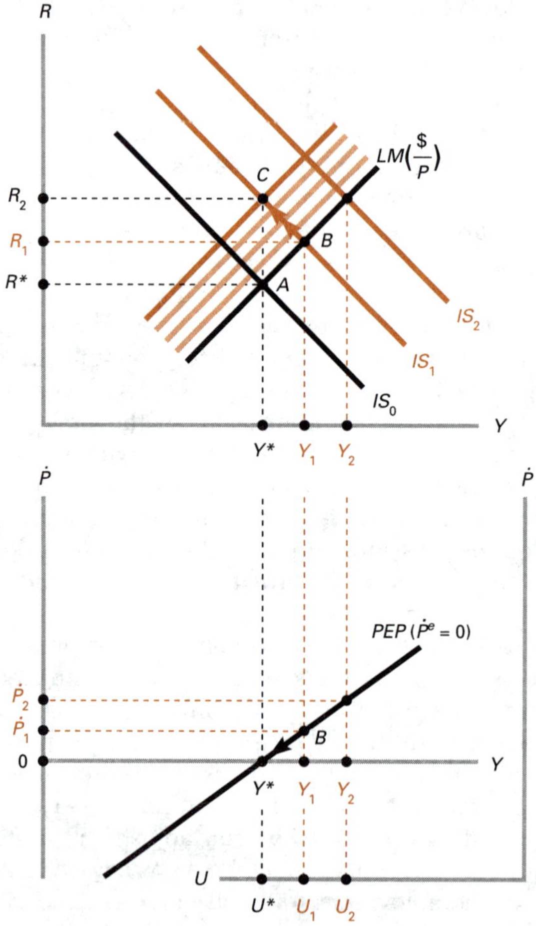

Figure 13.1 Monetary validation

Now assume that the IS_0 curve shifts rightwards to IS_1, say from an expansionary fiscal policy, and the economy moves from point *A* to point *B*. Income/output increases to Y_1, interest rates rise to R_1, the unemployment rate decreases to U_1, and the inflation rate rises to $\dot{P}_1$. As discussed in Chapter 11, the inflation generated at Y_1 will erode the real money supply, causing the *LM* curve to drift upwards to the left (see the coloured *LM* curves in Figure 13.1). The economy will slide down the *PEP* curve as the *LM* curve climbs up the new IS_1 curve (see arrows in Figure 13.1), with the economic system eventually returning to its original equilibrium position at Y^* and U^*, but with a higher interest rate R_2

(point *C*). An expansionary fiscal policy cannot permanently increase the level of income, nor can it permanently decrease the unemployment rate.

While the mechanics of the adjustment process described above are undeniable, our analysis has overlooked one important point. Is the government necessarily a captive of this adjustment process? In other words, must the government idly sit by and watch the real value of the money supply decline and the economy return to Y^* and U^*? Obviously not. The government controls the nominal money supply. Each period of time the Bank of Canada can change the nominal money supply by any amount it chooses. If a 10 percent inflation rate erodes the *real* value of money by 10 percent, the Bank of Canada can increase the *nominal* money supply by 10 percent, or by any other amount it wishes.

What would happen if the Bank of Canada were to adopt a policy whereby the nominal money supply was allowed to increase by an amount exactly equal to the inflation rate? Under such circumstances, the real money supply $\$/P$ would not change, since both the numerator \$ and the denominator P would be rising at the same rate. If the real money supply does not change, the *LM* curve will not shift. The adjustment process will be thwarted.

Returning to Figure 13.1, we now assume that the government couples its expansionary fiscal policy with such a "clever" increase in the nominal money supply. The *IS* curve is again shifted rightwards to IS_1, but the nominal money supply is also increased by an amount exactly equal to the inflation rate $\dot{P}_1$ generated at Y_1. As long as the percentage increase in the nominal money supply is equal to the percentage increase in the price level, namely $\dot{P}_1$, the real money supply will remain constant and the *LM* curve is prevented from shifting backwards. The economy will stay at Y_1 and U_1, with an inflation rate $\dot{P}_1$ (point *B* in Figure 13.1).

It is important to note that in each subsequent period of time the Bank of Canada must further increase the *nominal* money supply by $\dot{P}_1$ to match the inflation rate that will be generated by this higher output level Y_1. To keep the *LM* curve permanently anchored under such inflationary circumstances, a continual expansion of the nominal money supply is required. Each round of inflation must be matched with a new issue of money. Henceforward we will refer to a monetary policy that increases the nominal money supply by an amount exactly equal to the inflation rate as a **monetary validation policy**. The existing inflation rate is validated by an increase in the *nominal* money supply, thus preserving the *real* value of the money supply. By following a **monetary validation policy** it would appear that the government can override the shifts in the *LM* curve (which carry the economy back to Y^* and U^*) and achieve a permanent increase in output and a permanent decrease in the unemployment rate.

The possibility of such a permanent increase in output from an expansionary fiscal policy coupled with a monetary validation policy suggests the concept of a policy trade-off between inflation and unemployment. Each point along the *PEP* curve conceivably represents a potential inflation–unemployment rate combination that could be achieved and sustained by an appropriate expansionary fiscal policy and monetary validation policy. For example, in Figure 13.1 the government could just as easily shift the IS_0 curve out to IS_2 by using a larger dose of fiscal policy and increase the rate of monetary expansion to $\dot{P}_2$. Such a policy would sustain an income level of Y_2, an unemployment rate of U_2, and validate an inflation rate of $\dot{P}_2$. Again the *LM* curve remains anchored against the economic system's self-correcting adjustment mechanism, and the economy does not revert to the natural rate of output Y^*.

Given an entire range of unemployment–inflation rate possibilities along the Phillips curve, Keynesian government policymakers *thought* that they could choose any particular unemployment rate, such as U_2, and live with the implied inflation rate $\dot{P}_2$. Since the slope of the underlying Phillips curve appeared to be relatively flat, policymakers assumed that they could trade off a modest amount of inflation for a permanently lower unemployment rate. Subject to the Phillips curve constraint, Keynesian fiscal and monetary policy still appeared to offer a permanent cure for the unemployment problem.

The Monetarist Rebuttal: There is No Lasting Trade-Off Between Inflation and Unemployment

In his 1967 American Economics Association presidential address, Milton Friedman pointed out a *basic defect* in attempting to beat the Phillips curve by using expansionary fiscal and monetary policies: "Implicitly, Phillips wrote his article for a world in which everyone anticipated that nominal prices would be stable and in which that anticipation remains unshaken and immutable whatever happened to actual prices and wages."[3]

Returning to Figure 13.1, suppose that the government attempts to move up the *PEP* curve to Y_1 by continually validating the inflation rate $\dot{P}_1$. If this policy were successful, the economy would experience a permanent increase in output ($Y_1 > Y^*$) and a permanent inflation rate $\dot{P}_1$. However, the *PEP* curve in Figure 13.1 only holds for an expected inflation rate of zero — that is, "stable prices." For Y_1 and $\dot{P}_1$ to be a long-run equilibrium position, people must continually expect zero inflation

3 M. Friedman, "Monetary Policy," p. 8.

even though the actual inflation rate is always $\dot{P}_1$! As Abraham Lincoln once noted, "While the government may be able to fool *all* of the people *some* of the time, it cannot fool *all* of the people *all* of the time." Sooner or later, people will realize that the prevailing inflation rate $\dot{P}_1$ is *not* what they expected and will revise their inflation expectations upwards (from $\dot{P}^e = 0$ to $\dot{P}^e = \dot{P}_1$). But as soon as people revise their inflation expectations upwards, the *PEP* curve will shift upwards, creating a new disequilibrium adjustment period. The position $(Y_1, \dot{P}_1)$ is *not* a final equilibrium position for the economy.

As Friedman pointed out, the "basic defect" in attempting to use the Phillips curve as a trade-off curve is the assumption that inflation expectations are "unshaken and immutable" regardless of the inflation rate that the government chooses to validate. Any attempt by the government to increase output permanently by moving along the *PEP* curve will cause the *PEP* curve to shift upwards as inflation expectations will be adjusted upwards. In short, the Phillips curve does *not* provide the government with a *stable* trade-off curve that can be exploited to lower the unemployment rate.

To illustrate this key monetarist proposition that Keynesian policies *cannot* beat the Phillips curve in the long run, we reconsider the expansionary policy depicted in Figure 13.1. Initially our economy is in equilibrium at Y^* and U^* with both $\dot{P}$ and $\dot{P}^e$ equal to zero. The government then employs an expansionary fiscal policy to shift the *IS* curve rightwards to IS_1 and validates the resulting inflation rate $\dot{P}_1$ by increasing the nominal money supply by $\dot{P}_1$ each period. With price levels and the nominal money supply increasing at the same rate $\dot{P}_1$, the *real* money supply is constant and the *LM* curve is stationary. The self-correcting inflation adjustment forces (*LM* curve shifts) are neatly thwarted.

However, there is a second set of inflation-adjustment forces at work in the labour market. Recall from Chapter 10 that the size of wage changes depends on both the unemployment rate and the expected inflation rate. In Figure 13.2 we have reproduced our basic inflation-expectations-Phillips wage relationship. A decrease in the unemployment rate causes a movement up the Phillips curve, whereas an increase in inflation expectations causes an upward shift in the Phillips curve. Both factors lead to a higher rate of wage inflation. Given an unemployment rate of U^* and zero inflation expectations (from Figure 13.1), wage inflation will initially be running at $\dot{W}_0$ (point *A* in Figure 13.2). Now when the government stimulates output by implementing an expansionary fiscal policy (see Figure 13.1), the new lower unemployment rate U_1 will cause the rate of wage inflation to increase to $\dot{W}_1$. Initially the economy moves from point *A* to point *B* in Figure 13.2. However, this higher rate of wage inflation will be "marked up" by firms and the rate of price inflation will rise to $\dot{P}_1$ (in Figure 13.1).

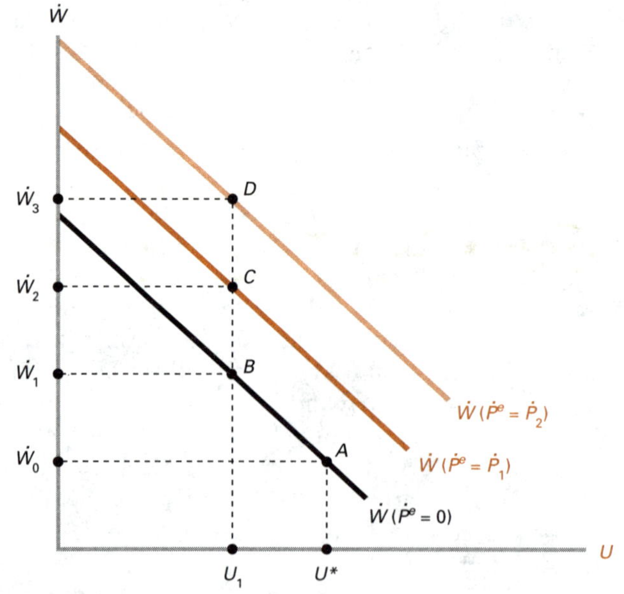

Figure 13.2 The effects of unemployment changes and revised inflation expectations on wage adjustments

Rather than letting this new inflation rate erode the real money supply, the government steps in and validates the $\dot{P}_1$ inflation rate by increasing the nominal money supply by $\dot{P}_1$ each period. Although the "Keynesian" story ends at this point, the "monetarist" story is just beginning.

With inflation now running at $\dot{P}_1$, sooner or later people will revise their inflation expectations upwards from zero to $\dot{P}_1$. It would be a very strange world if people continued to expect a zero inflation rate when the prevailing inflation rate was always $\dot{P}_1$! When people adjust their inflation expectations upwards to $\dot{P}_1$, the original wage Phillips curve corresponding to $\dot{P}^e = 0$ in Figure 13.2 will shift upwards to the $W(\dot{P}^e = \dot{P}_1)$ curve. The economy moves from point B to point C. Both the lower unemployment rate U_1 (due to the expansionary fiscal policy) and the higher expected inflation rate $\dot{P}_1$ (due to the monetary validation policy) will cause the rate of wage inflation to increase to $\dot{W}_2$ in Figure 13.2. Again, firms will mark up this second round of wage increases ($\dot{W}_2$) and the rate of price inflation will rise beyond $\dot{P}_1$. The *PEP* curve will shift upwards reflecting this higher expected inflation rate $\dot{P}_1$.

In Figure 13.3 we have replicated our diagram from Figure 13.1, and have added this new higher PEP_1 curve corresponding to an expected inflation rate of $\dot{P}_1$. Based on an unemployment rate U_1, corresponding to the IS_1-LM intersection point Y_1, and an expected inflation rate of $\dot{P}_1$, the new inflation rate will now be $\dot{P}_2$ (point C in Figure 13.3). The upward revision of inflation expectations from zero to $\dot{P}_1$ in the labour market has pushed the rate of price inflation up from $\dot{P}_1$ to $\dot{P}_2$ in the goods market (from point B to point C in Figure 13.3).

However, our "monetarist" story is by no means over. Point C in Figure 13.3 is clearly *not* a final equilibrium point either. The expected inflation rate $\dot{P}_1$ is again less than the actual inflation rate $\dot{P}_2$ and the actual inflation rate $\dot{P}_2$ exceeds the change in the nominal money supply (recall $\dot{\$} = \dot{P}_1$). Thus, the *real* money supply will be decreasing and the LM curve will again start to drift upwards to the left.

We consider two *possible* disequilibrium adjustment paths premised

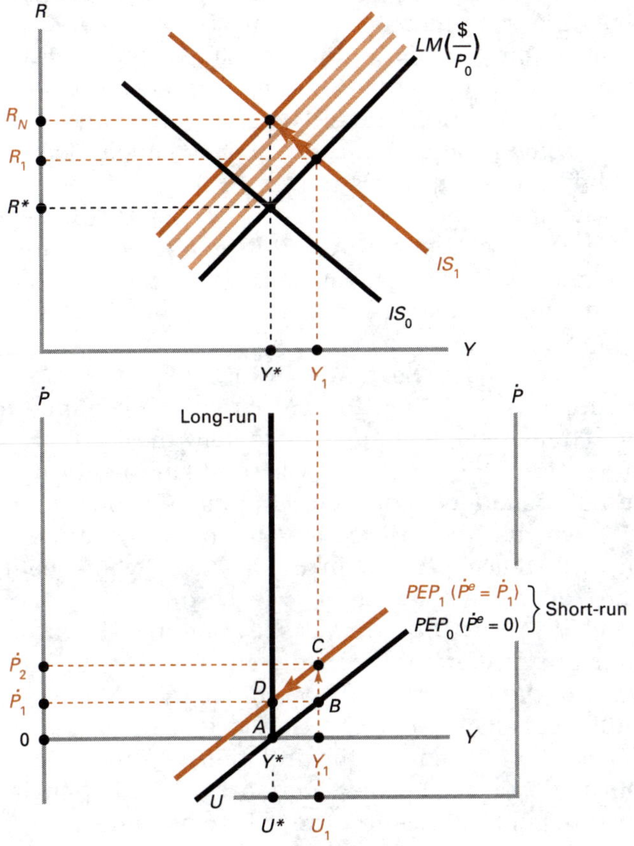

Figure 13.3 Expansionary fiscal policy with a constant increase in the nominal money supply

on two very different assumptions about monetary policy. First, we assume that the government continues to increase the *nominal* money supply by a *constant* $\dot{P}_1$ each period, even though the actual inflation rate exceeds $\dot{P}_1$. Second, we assume that the government validates whatever inflation rate materializes, for example, the government increases the nominal money supply by $\dot{P}_2$ in the second period. As we shall see, these two different monetary policies give radically different macroeconomic results.

A Constant Increase in the Nominal Money Supply

Returning to Figure 13.3, if the government maintains a *constant* increase in the *nominal* money supply of $\dot{P}_1$ per period, then at point *C* the *real* money supply must start to decline. The numerator \$ is rising by $\dot{P}_1$ whereas the denominator *P* is rising by $\dot{P}_2$, where $\dot{P}_2 > \dot{P}_1$. With the real money supply eroded by this new higher inflation rate, the *LM* curve will start to shift upwards (see the coloured *LM* curves in Figure 13.3) and our standard inflation-adjustment mechanism will start to lower output/income levels. As the real money supply declines, interest rates are pushed further upwards (beyond R_1), investment expenditures decline, and income levels decrease. The economy will begin to slide down the PEP_1 curve and climb up the IS_1 curve (see arrows in Figure 13.3). The output and employment gains from an expansionary fiscal policy coupled with a *constant* increase in the nominal money supply ($\dot{\$} = \dot{P}_1$) begin to disappear.

How far will the economy slide down the PEP_1 curve? As long as the *real* money supply is declining, the *LM* curve will continue to shift upwards, interest rates will continue to rise, and the level of income will continue to decline. The *LM* curve will continue to shift upwards until the inflation rate generated along the PEP_1 curve is brought down to $\dot{P}_1$, the rate at which the *nominal* money supply is increasing. Eventually the economy will reach point *D* in Figure 13.3, where both the price level and the nominal money supply will be growing at the same rate $\dot{P}_1$ each period. At point *D* the *real* money supply \$/*P* will be constant, because both the numerator and denominator are increasing at the same $\dot{P}_1$ rate, and the *LM* curve will be stationary.

Point *D* in Figure 13.3 must be exactly above point *A*. At point *D*, which is on the $PEP_1(\dot{P}^e = \dot{P}_1)$ curve, the inflation rate is $\dot{P}_1$. Given the increase in inflation expectations from zero to $\dot{P}_1$, the PEP_1 curve is exactly $\dot{P}_1$ units higher than the PEP_0 curve (recall from Chapter 10 that a one-percentage-point increase in $\dot{P}^e$ shifts the *PEP* curve upwards by exactly one percentage point). If the *PEP* curve shifts upwards by $\dot{P}_1$ and point *D* has an inflation rate of $\dot{P}_1$, then point *D* must be exactly above point *A* (which has a zero inflation rate and is on the $PEP_0(\dot{P}^e = 0)$ curve). The economy has returned to its original equilibrium income level Y^*.

Finally, we note that at point D the expected inflation rate $\dot{P}_1$ is equal to the actual inflation rate $\dot{P}_1$. There is no *un*expected inflation; no one is being fooled by the actual inflation rate $\dot{P}_1$. Point D represents the final resting point for the economy, assuming that the government continues to increase the *nominal* money supply by $\dot{P}_1$ each period. The *real* money supply is constant, the LM curve is stationary, and the actual inflation rate corresponds to the expected inflation rate.

In summary, if the government attempts to increase the level of output from Y^* to Y_1 by shifting the IS curve outwards to IS_1 and increasing the nominal money supply by $\dot{P}_1$ each period, inflation expectations will be adjusted upwards to $\dot{P}_1$ and the economic system will eventually return to its original equilibrium income level Y^*. In the words of Milton Friedman, "There is always a temporary trade-off between inflation and unemployment; there is no permanent trade-off."[4] The government cannot permanently increase the level of output (and permanently reduce the unemployment rate) by implementing an expansionary fiscal policy coupled with a constant increase in the nominal money supply.

A Monetary *Validation* Policy

The "problem" with the policy described above is an eroding *real* money supply. After inflation expectations are adjusted upwards to $\dot{P}_1$, the actual inflation rate $\dot{P}_2$ exceeds the growth rate in the *nominal* money supply ($\dot{\$} = \dot{P}_1$), the *real* money supply $\$/P$ declines, the LM curve shifts upwards, interest rates rise, investment and output levels decline, and the economy slides down the new higher PEP_1 curve to point D, where the actual inflation rate equals the increase in the nominal money supply. Given that the problem is an erosion of the *real* money supply and an upward-shifting LM curve, what would happen if the government decided to anchor the LM curve by *validating* whatever inflation rate materializes? Replicating the basic features of Figure 13.3 in Figure 13.4, suppose that the government steps up the growth rate of the *nominal* money supply to $\dot{P}_2$ each period when inflation expectations are adjusted upwards to $\dot{P}_1$ and the economy moves from point B to point C. With both prices and the *nominal* money supply now increasing by $\dot{P}_2$ per period, the *real* money supply will remain constant and the LM curve will be stationary.

Even though the government can anchor the LM curve by validating the new $\dot{P}_2$ inflation rate (with $\dot{\$} = \dot{P}_2$), this new position C cannot be a final equilibrium resting point for the economy. Point C is on the PEP_1 curve, which assumes that the expected inflation rate is $\dot{P}_1$. For point C to be a final equilibrium resting point, people must continually expect

4 *Ibid.*, p. 11.

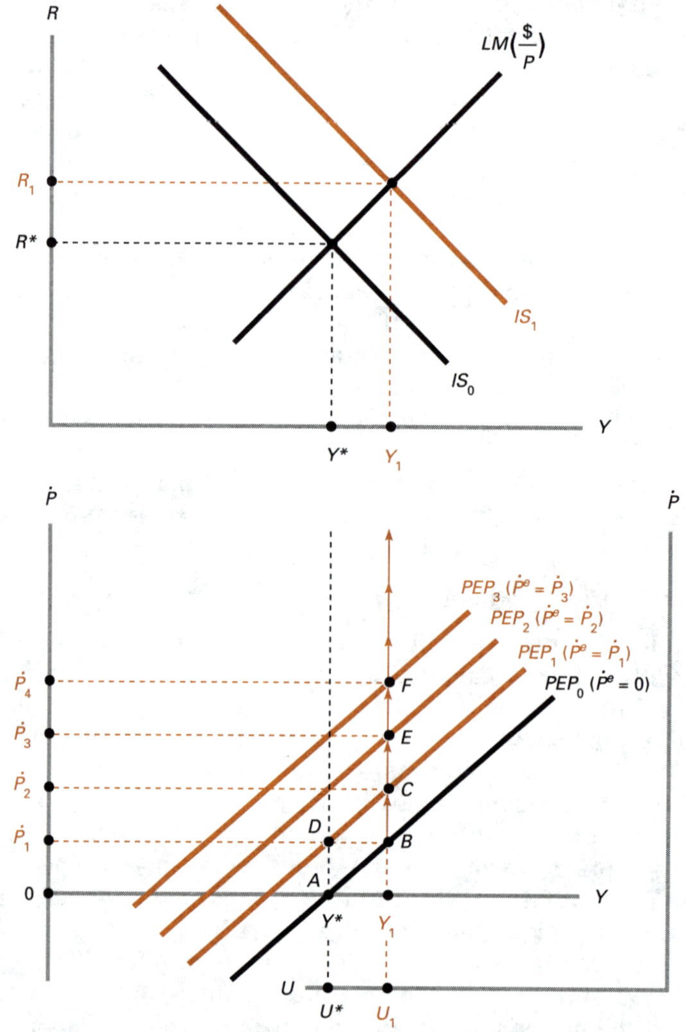

Figure 13.4 Expansionary fiscal policy with a monetary validation policy

an inflation rate of $\dot{P}_1$ even though the actual inflation rate is $\dot{P}_2$! Sooner or later people will "catch on" to the fact that the actual inflation rate, validated by the government, is $\dot{P}_2$ and will again revise their inflation expectations upwards. Of course, when inflation expectations are adjusted upwards from $\dot{P}_1$ to $\dot{P}_2$, the wage Phillips curve will shift up in Figure 13.2 and the *PEP* curve in Figure 13.4 will shift up to $PEP_2(\dot{P}^e = \dot{P}_2)$. On the basis of increased inflation expectations, workers will bargain for larger wage settlements ($\dot{W}_3$ in Figure 13.2) and firms will pass on these higher labour costs in the form of a higher rate of price inflation ($\dot{P}_3$ in Figure 13.4). In terms of Figure 13.4, a monetary validation policy will cause the economy to move from point C to point E after inflation expectations are revised upwards from $\dot{P}_1$ to $\dot{P}_2$.

Having adopted a monetary validation policy, the government must further increase the rate of expansion of the nominal money supply to $\dot{P}_3$, to validate the new higher inflation rate at point E. But again point E cannot be a final equilibrium resting point for the economy. At point E on the PEP_2 curve, people are expecting an inflation rate of $\dot{P}_2$ but the actual inflation rate, validated by the government, is $\dot{P}_3$! Again inflation expectations will be adjusted upwards, the PEP_2 curve will shift upwards to $PEP_3(\dot{P}^e = \dot{P}_3)$ and a new higher inflation rate $\dot{P}_4$ will emerge (point F in Figure 13.4). As long as the government continues to validate each new inflation rate with a further increase in the rate of expansion of the nominal money supply, inflation expectations will continue to rise and the rate of wage and price inflation will continue to spiral upwards (see vertical arrows in Figure 13.4).

In summary, the only way that the government can permanently increase the level of output beyond Y^* (say to Y_1 in Figure 13.4) is to continually increase the growth rate of the nominal money supply. Under such conditions, the economic system will experience an *ever-accelerating* inflation rate, $\dot{P}_1$, $\dot{P}_2$, $\dot{P}_3$, $\dot{P}_4$, and so on. As discussed later in this chapter, the nominal interest rate will also spiral upwards as rising inflation expectations are incorporated into interest rates. Again, there is no permanent trade-off between unemployment and a *stable* inflation rate. The cost of a permanent reduction in the unemployment rate (say to U_1 in Figure 13.4) is an *ever-accelerating* **wage–price inflation spiral**.

Short-Run *PEP* Curves and Long-Run Inflation–Output Curves

As our analysis clearly demonstrates, it is very important to distinguish between *short-run disequilibrium* positions (such as points B, C, E, and F in Figure 13.4) and *long-run equilibrium* positions (such as points A and D in Figures 13.3 and 13.4). For the macroeconomic system to be in *long-run equilibrium*, the following conditions must hold:

1. the labour market must be in equilibrium
2. the goods market must be in equilibrium
3. the money market must be in equilibrium
4. the actual inflation rate must equal the expected inflation rate (that is, there is no unexpected inflation).

In terms of the *IS-LM* diagram, the first three conditions require that the equilibrium income level Y^* (the amount of output produced by the equilibrium quantity of labour) coincide with the intersection point of a stable *IS* curve and a stationary *LM* curve. Provided that the government *validates* the actual inflation rate with a corresponding increase in the *nominal* money supply ($\dot{\$} = \dot{P}$), the *LM* curve will be stationary. However, there is no unique inflation rate associated with a stationary *LM* curve because any particular inflation rate can be validated. The final equilibrium condition asserts that whatever inflation rate the government chooses to validate (say $\dot{P}_1$ in Figure 13.3), that particular inflation rate must be correctly anticipated. In the long run, people cannot be permanently fooled by a validated inflation rate that is different from what they expected. There can be no unexpected inflation in long-run equilibrium.

Although in the long run inflation expectations must be brought into line with the actual validated inflation rate, inflation expectations may not be adjusted immediately. For a short-run period of time, inflation expectations may diverge from the actual inflation rate. Labour market participants may not be sure whether a new unexpected inflation rate (perhaps caused by a new government policy) will be permanent and may prefer to wait awhile to see if the new inflation rate (and new government policy) persists before revising their inflation expectations. During this short-run period prior to any revision in inflation expectations, the economy will move along a particular **short-run *PEP* curve**. For a given rate of expected inflation, there is a *short-run* positive relationship between the actual inflation rate and the level of output. Our original *PEP* curve (Equation 10.7) describes this *short-run* relationship between inflation and output levels under the assumption of *constant* inflation expectations:

$$\dot{P} = \dot{P}^e - jvY^* + jvY \qquad \text{(Short-run)} \qquad (10.7)$$

As long as inflation expectations (and Y^*) remain unchanged, the economy will simply move along a given *short-run PEP* curve, depending on movements in the *IS* and *LM* curves.

However, in the long run, inflation expectations must be brought into line with the actual validated inflation rate. Again, people cannot be permanently fooled by an inflation rate that is consistently different from what they expected. If we substitute this final equilibrium condition ($\dot{P}^e = \dot{P}$) into Equation 10.7, we find

$$\dot{P} = \dot{P} - jvY^* + jvY$$

The two inflation terms cancel out and the equation reduces to

$$0 = -jvY^* + jvY$$

or

$$Y = Y^* \qquad \text{(Long-run)} \qquad (13.1)$$

where Y^* is the amount of output produced when the labour market is in equilibrium and the unemployment rate is at its equilibrium level U^*.

In the long run, when expectations concerning inflation are correct, the level of output and the unemployment rate will equal their equilibrium values Y^* and U^*, regardless of what the validated inflation rate happens to be. In the long run, output and unemployment are independent of the growth rate of the money supply and the inflation rate.

This is an extension of the result we obtained in our earlier analysis of the aggregate demand and supply model (see Chapters 7 and 8). Allowing sufficient time for wage and price adjustments to take place, money is neutral in the long run. An increase in the money supply has no long-run effect on the equilibrium level of output or on the equilibrium unemployment rate. The only lasting effect of an increase in the money supply is to raise wage and price levels.

In this chapter we have extended this argument to an inflationary economy and have shown that there is no relationship between the level of output (or the unemployment rate) and the *rate of growth* in the money supply. This proposition is often referred to as the **superneutrality of money**. Output is not only independent of the stock of money (the neutrality proposition), but it is also independent, in the long run, of the *rate of growth* of the money supply (the superneutrality proposition). There is no lasting trade-off between inflation and unemployment that the government can exploit. The equilibrium output level Y^* and unemployment rate U^* are independent of the validated inflation rate, and are determined in the labour market and production sector of the economy.

The absence of a *long-run* relationship between inflation and output (or unemployment) was the major conclusion of Figure 13.3. If the government tries to validate the inflation rate $\dot{P}_1$ in the hope of permanently increasing output levels to Y_1, once this new validated inflation rate became anticipated, the economy would return to its original income level Y^*, but with a higher inflation rate $\dot{P}_1$ (point *D* in Figure 13.3). Validating a higher inflation rate does not change the long-run equilibrium values for output Y^* and unemployment U^* after inflation expectations have been brought into line with the new higher validated inflation rate. Diagrammatically, the long-run equilibrium relationship between inflation and output is a *vertical* straight line at Y^* and U^* (passing through points *A* and *D* in Figure 13.3). At every point along this vertical long-run relationship, expected inflation is equal to actual inflation. Each upward-sloping short-run *PEP* curve (corresponding to a given level of inflation expectations, such as $\dot{P}_1$) has just one point where actual and expected inflation are equal (the point at which the upward-sloping short-run *PEP* curve intersects the vertical long-run line). Case Study 7 identifies the key assumption for this vertical long-run inflation–output relationship and looks at the demise of the inflation–unemployment trade-off curve.

In his 1967 presidential address to the American Economics Association, Milton Friedman referred to the equilibrium unemployment rate U^* as the **natural rate of unemployment**. Friedman's choice of words is regrettable, as U^* is obviously not an immutable act of nature. Economists who do not like the connotations of the word "natural" frequently refer to U^* by the mnemonic NAIRU. A key property of U^* and Y^* is a constant inflation rate. As discussed above, any attempt by the government to permanently increase output beyond Y^* will lead to an *ever-accelerating* inflation rate (the wage–price spiral of Figure 13.4). Thus U^* represents the unique unemployment rate that in the long run will have a *non-accelerating* inflation rate; U^* is the non-accelerating inflation rate of unemployment — NAIRU.

Case Study 7: Whatever Happened to the Inflation–Unemployment Trade-Off Curve?

The conclusion that there is no long-run relationship between inflation and output (unemployment) can be traced back to the wage-change equation (10.6) presented in Chapter 10:

$$\dot{W} = PR\dot{O}DT + \dot{P}^e + j(U^* - U) \qquad (10.6)$$

The crucial assumption in this wage-change equation is that the coefficient on the expected inflation variable $\dot{P}^e$ is unity: an x percent increase in the expected inflation causes an x percent increase in wages.

What would happen if we relax this crucial assumption? Suppose that only a fraction, say g, of expected inflation is incorporated into wage increases. With this new assumption, the wage equation becomes:

$$\dot{W} = g\dot{P}^e + PR\dot{O}DT + j(U^* - U) \qquad (10.6a)$$

When Equation 10.6a is combined with our price equation from Chapter 10,

$$\dot{P} = \dot{W} - PR\dot{O}DT \qquad (10.4a)$$

and the unemployment–output equation from Chapter 11,

$$(U^* - U) = -v(Y^* - Y) \tag{11.1}$$

the new *PEP* curve becomes

$$\dot{P} = g\dot{P}^e - jvY^* + jvY \tag{11.2a}$$

Equation 11.2a differs from the original *PEP* curve equation (11.2) in Chapter 11 in only one respect: the expected inflation rate has a coefficient "g" instead of unity.

To find the long-run relationship between inflation and output, we impose the long-run equilibrium condition that actual inflation must be equal to expected inflation. By replacing the expected inflation rate $\dot{P}^e$ in Equation 11.2a with the actual inflation rate $\dot{P}$ and rearranging terms, the following long-run equilibrium equation connecting inflation and output is obtained:

$$\dot{P} = -\left(\frac{jv}{1-g}\right)Y^* + \left(\frac{jv}{1-g}\right)Y \tag{13.2}$$

The slope of the long-run equilibrium inflation–output relationship is determined by the slope of the short-run *PEP* curve, jv, and by the parameter g. If the parameter g is positive but less than one, the factor $1/(1-g)$ will be larger than one and the slope of the long-run inflation–output curve will be steeper than the slope of the short-run *PEP* curve (by this $1/(1-g)$ factor). If wages incorporate only a small part of expected inflation, then g will be relatively small and the long-run inflation–output curve will not be much steeper than the short-run *PEP* curve. As g approaches unity, the long-run inflation–output curve gets steeper and steeper until it becomes vertical (when g is unity, the slope of the long-run inflation–output curve becomes infinitely large, that is, vertical).

The relationship between the short-run *PEP* curve and the long-run inflation–output curve is illustrated in Figure 13.5. The long-run inflation–output curve (the solid coloured line) passes through point *A* on the horizontal axis where inflation is zero and output is Y^*. There is also a flatter short-run *PEP* curve passing through point *A*, corresponding to a zero expected inflation rate. If the government maintains a constant money supply, there will be no inflation and the economy will remain at point *A*.

Suppose that the government decides to increase the money supply by 5 percent each year. Initially, the expected inflation remains at zero, and the economy moves along the black short-run $PEP(\dot{P}^e = 0)$ curve. Both output and inflation increase. But expectations cannot be wrong forever, and ultimately the expected rate of inflation will match the ac-

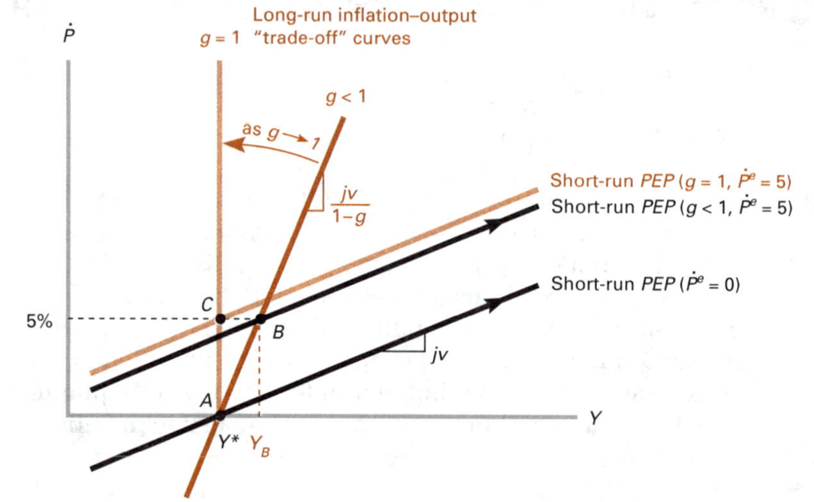

Figure 13.5 Short-run *PEP* curves and long-run inflation–output trade-off curves

tual validated inflation rate of 5 percent. When expectations adjust to this new higher 5 percent validated inflation rate, the short-run *PEP* curve will shift upwards by a vertical distance equal to g times 5 percent (when g is less than unity, workers do not receive wage increases to fully compensate for inflation). For g less than unity, the long-run equilibrium output–inflation position is given by point B, where the actual and expected inflation rates are both equal to 5 percent (the growth rate of the money supply). Notice that the long-run equilibrium level of output Y_B is greater than Y^*.

This example illustrates that when wage increases do not fully incorporate expected inflation (the parameter g is less than unity), the long-run output level depends on the inflation rate that the Bank of Canada validates. By transposing Equation 13.2, the long-run equilibrium output level can be expressed in terms of the validated inflation rate:

$$Y = Y^* + \left(\frac{1-g}{jv}\right)\dot{P} \qquad (13.2a)$$

When g is less than one, the long-run equilibrium output level depends positively on the validated inflation rate; the long-run equilibrium level of output is no longer independent of monetary policy (money is no longer superneutral).

When the parameter g equals one (wage increases fully reflect expected inflation), the coefficient on the validated inflation rate in Equation 13.2a is zero and the long-run equilibrium output level is Y^* (as in Equation 13.1). In Figure 13.5, when g is equal to unity the long-run equilibrium relationship between inflation and unemployment is given by the vertical broken coloured line at Y^*. Notice that when $g = 1$, workers receive a full 5 percent wage increase when inflation is 5 percent and there is a higher short-run *PEP* curve ($\dot{P}^e$ = 5 percent) passing through point *C* (at 5 percent) on the vertical long-run line.

A positively-sloped long-run equilibrium relationship between inflation and output requires a value for the parameter g less than unity. For there to be a persistent long-run trade-off between inflation and unemployment, workers must be willing to accept wage increases that do *not* fully reflect the expected inflation rate.

In his presidential address to the American Economics Association, Milton Friedman dismissed the possibility that the parameter g might be less than unity on purely theoretical grounds. As discussed in Chapters 7 and 10, what matters in the labour market is the *real* wage, not the *nominal* wage. Workers will bargain for wage increases that maintain their *real* wage regardless of the expected inflation rate and firms will be willing to pay such wage increases because they expect their product prices to rise accordingly. If workers do not receive full compensation for expected inflation, then higher rates of expected inflation will erode the *real* wage. Why should workers voluntarily accept a lower real wage simply because the expected inflation rate is 10 percent rather than 5 percent? Labour market theory forcefully argues that the nominal wage should fully reflect expected inflation.

Even though economic theory predicts that this crucial price inflation expectations coefficient in the wage-change equation should be unity, early empirical evidence suggested that this g parameter might be less than unity. For example, an influential 1966 study for the Economic Council of Canada reported price inflation coefficients in the wage-change equations from 0.44 to 0.60, well under unity.[5] On the basis of these estimates for the parameter g, the Economic Council of Canada strongly promulgated the view that a *long-run* inflation unemployment trade-off curve existed in Canada:

> Even after full allowance for qualifications, the central analysis of this special study strongly confirms the existence of an inherent reconciliation or trade-off problem between the goals of high employment and reasonable price stability in Canada in the post-war period.[6]

---

5 R.G. Bodkin et al., *Price Stability and High Employment: The Options for Canadian Economic Policy* (Ottawa: Economic Council of Canada, 1966), p. 124.

6 *Third Annual Review: Prices, Productivity and Employment* (Ottawa: Economic Council of Canada, 1966), p. 143.

Most economists in the 1960s and early 1970s shared similar views concerning the possibility of an inflation–unemployment trade-off. Since nearly all of the initial wage studies reported price inflation coefficients less than unity, it appeared possible for the government to decrease the unemployment rate by accepting a higher validated inflation rate. Much of the policy debate in macroeconomics during the 1960s revolved around the trade-off concept. How much inflation should be traded off to lower the unemployment rate? For example, the 1966 study for the Economic Council of Canada concluded that "when the unemployment rate is 3 percent, the Consumer Price Index can be expected to rise at 4 percent per year."[7] Should Canada accept a 4 percent inflation rate in order to lower the unemployment rate to 3 percent?

In retrospect this 1960s trade-off debate reads like a chapter from *Alice in Wonderland*. By the mid-1970s the Canadian inflation rate was into the double-digit range and the unemployment rate was hovering around 7 percent. The inflation–unemployment trade-off curve had vanished, and embarrassed economists were scrambling for an explanation.

As it turns out, the mystery of "whatever happened to the trade-off curve" has a relatively straightforward solution: the econometricians did it. The "low" estimates for the crucial g parameter in wage-change studies (which went against theoretical priors) were unreliable. Subsequent wage studies, which incorporate data from the 1970s and 1980s, report price inflation expectations coefficients in the wage-change equation that are *not* less than unity. For example, Professor Reid of the University of Toronto found that over the 1967 to 1978 period "the coefficient on $\dot{P}^e$ exceeds one but is not significantly different from its theoretical expected value of unity."[8] Based on empirical evidence drawn from the 1970s and 1980s, this crucial price inflation expectations coefficient in the wage-change equation is not less than unity, which in turn leads us to conclude that there is *no* long-run trade-off between inflation and unemployment. The possibility of a permanent inflation–unemployment trade-off was an econometric *hoax*, based on unreliable statistical estimates for the parameter g.

Having solved the mystery by declaring that the alleged victim — the trade-off curve — never existed, we consider briefly those unreliable initial estimates for the parameter g. Although there are many possible explanations for these low estimates for g,[9] it must be remembered that this early time period was characterized by relative price stability. From 1953 to 1965 (the time period of the Economic Council of Canada study), the average inflation rate in Canada was only 1.5 percent per

---

7 R.G. Bodkin et al., *Price Stability*, p. 217.

8 F. Reid, "The Effect of Controls on the Rate of Wage Change in Canada," *Canadian Journal of Economics*, May 1979, p. 218.

9 See D.A. Wilton, *Wage Inflation in Canada, 1955–75* (Ottawa: Economic Council of Canada, 1980).

year! In fact, in 9 of these 13 years the annual inflation rate was below 1.5 percent. Given this period of unusual price stability, the estimated coefficient on inflation expectations may give a very misleading indication of wage behaviour during periods of high and/or unstable inflation. For example, when inflation is typically less than 1.5 percent per year, wage bargaining may not pay much attention to inflation, which is barely perceptible. Econometric estimates should only be used to predict economic behaviour under similar circumstances. Estimated wage parameters derived from a period of very low, stable inflation should not be used to predict the nature of wage behaviour in an unstable, inflationary environment. As "high" inflation observations from the 1970s were added to wage-change regressions, estimates for the crucial g parameter quickly rose to unity, putting to rest any possibility of a lasting trade-off between inflation and unemployment.

In retrospect, the 1960s inflation–unemployment trade-off debate was perhaps the sorriest chapter in macroeconomics. Most macroeconomists (who were around in the 1960s) now regret the fact that they let "poor" econometric estimates override "good" economic theory. Unfortunately, even though the possibility of a permanent trade-off between inflation and unemployment has been discredited, the *trade-off* dogma continues to live on in non-economic circles. One cannot help but recall J.M. Keynes's closing remarks in the *General Theory*:

> The ideas of economists and political philosphers, both when they are right and when they are wrong, are more powerful than is commonly understood. Indeed the world is ruled by little else. Practical men, who believe themselves to be quite exempt from any intellectual influences, are usually the slave of some defunct economist. Madmen in authority, who hear voices in the air, are distilling their frenzy from some academic scribbler of a few years back.[10]

Inflation, Interest Rates, and Monetary Policy

As shown above, the long-run equilibrium output level and unemployment rate are independent of the growth rate of the money supply. However, the long-run inflation rate and nominal interest rate depend crucially on the growth rate of the money supply. By continually increasing the nominal money supply, the government dictates that inflation and high nominal interest rates will prevail. Before we analyze this crucial link between changes in the nominal money supply and inflation, we briefly reconsider the important distinction between nominal and real interest rates.

---

10 J.M. Keynes, *General Theory*, p. 383.

Nominal Versus Real Interest Rates: A Brief Digression

As discussed in Chapter 3, the interest rate paid on financial assets (bonds, guaranteed investment certificates, and savings accounts) will incorporate an additional premium to cover the inflation rate that is expected to prevail during the term of the financial asset. Returning to our earlier illustration in Chapter 3, if I am willing to lend you $1,000 at a 5 percent interest rate when there is zero inflation, then I would want to charge you 15 percent when the inflation rate is expected to be 10 percent. To the extent that inflation is correctly anticipated, the 10 percent inflation premium contained in the interest rate will preserve the real purchasing power of my $1,000 loan. You will be willing to pay the 15 percent interest rate because you also expect inflation to be 10 percent and realize that you will be able to repay the $1,000 loan in dollar bills that have been eroded by inflation to 90 cents.

Economists distinguish between the market, or *nominal*, interest rate (15 percent in the above illustration) and the *real* interest rate (5 percent). The real interest rate RR is simply the market interest rate R minus the expected inflation rate $\dot{P}^e$:

$$RR = R - \dot{P}^e \tag{13.3}$$

Alternatively, the nominal interest rate will equal the real interest rate plus the expected inflation rate. The higher inflation is expected to be, the higher nominal interest rates will be. The evidence presented earlier in Figure 1.4 clearly supports the proposition that Canadian interest rates are systematically related to (expected) inflation.

To incorporate this key distinction between nominal and real interest rates into the *IS-LM-PEP* model, one additional refinement must be introduced. As we will see in Chapter 17, investment decisions depend on the real interest rate RR, not the nominal interest rate R. Business people know that product prices and sales revenues rise with general inflation, thus allowing the firm to pay the inflation expectations premium contained in nominal interest rates. Profit-maximizing firms will make investment decisions by comparing *real* rates of return with the *real* cost of borrowing. Thus, our simple investment function of Chapter 5,

$$I = I_a - eR \tag{5.1}$$

must be recast in terms of the real interest rate RR:

$$I = I_a - eRR \tag{13.4}$$

Recasting our investment function into *real* interest rate terms implies that our *IS* curve should be reconstructed in terms of the real interest rate *RR*. But to do so raises an obvious problem in the *IS-LM* diagram, as the vertical axis of the *IS-LM* diagram is based on the nominal interest rate *R*. Furthermore, the demand for money depends on the nominal interest rate (the opportunity cost of holding money in an inflationary world) and thus the *LM* curve remains a function of the nominal interest rate. In short, the *IS* curve depends on *real* interest rates and the *LM* curve depends on *nominal* interest rates. How can we fit a *real* interest rate *IS* curve and a *nominal* interest rate *LM* curve into the same diagram? Fortunately, Equation 13.3 can be used to solve our problem. By making use of this relationship that connects nominal and real interest rates to the expected inflation rate, we can convert our *real* interest rate investment function (Equation 13.4) back into *nominal* interest rate terms:

$$RR = R - \dot{P}^e \qquad (13.3)$$

$$I = I_a - eRR \qquad (13.4)$$

$$I = I_a - e(R - \dot{P}^e)$$

$$I = I_a + e\dot{P}^e - eR \qquad (13.4a)$$

In an inflationary world, real investment expenditures depend negatively on the nominal interest rate corrected for the expected inflation rate (for further discussion, see Chapter 17). Holding the nominal interest rate constant, an increase in the expected inflation rate (which means lower *real* borrowing costs) leads to an increase in investment expenditures. In Equation 13.4a, investment expenditures depend positively on the expected inflation rate, holding the nominal interest rate constant. For a given expected inflation rate, investment expenditures depend negatively on the nominal interest rate.

The *IS* curve must be rederived using this new investment function (Equation 13.4a). For ease of reference, the other equations used in the derivation of the *IS* curve are reproduced from Chapter 4:

$$AE = C + I + (X - M) + G \qquad (4.1)$$

$$C = C_a + b(Y - T) \qquad (4.2)$$

$$T = T_a + tY \qquad (4.5)$$

$$M = mY \qquad (4.4)$$

$$AE = Y \qquad (4.7)$$

As done in Chapter 5, we can substitute Equations 13.4a, 4.2, 4.3, 4.4, and 4.7 into Equation 4.1 to obtain a new *IS* curve which will contain inflation expectations:

$$Y = AE = C_a + b(Y - T_a - tY) + I_a + e\dot{P}^e - eR + G + X - mY$$

or

$$Y(1 - b + bt + m) = (C_a - bT_a + I_a + e\dot{P}^e + G + X) - eR$$

Rearranging with R on the left-hand side and Y on the right-hand side produces the following equation for the *IS* curve:

$$R = \frac{1}{e}(C_a - bT_a + I_a + e\dot{P}^e + G + X) - \frac{1}{e}(1 - b + bt + m)Y$$

$$= \dot{P}^e + \frac{1}{e}(C_a - bT_a + I_a + G + X) - \frac{1}{e}(1 - b + bt + m)Y \qquad (13.5)$$

After the algebraic dust has settled, recasting the investment function into *real* interest rate terms produces only one change in the equation for the *IS* curve. As shown in Equation 13.5, the expected inflation rate $\dot{P}^e$ now enters the intercept of the *IS* curve with a coefficient of unity. For a given level of income, a one-percentage-point increase in the expected inflation rate will cause the *IS* curve to shift upwards by exactly one point on the R axis. Alternatively, for a given nominal interest rate, an increase in the expected inflation rate will cause the *IS* curve to shift horizontally to the right. For a given nominal interest rate, a higher expected inflation rate implies a lower real interest rate (lower *real* borrowing costs), which would prompt more investment expenditures and higher income levels. In the next section of the chapter we illustrate the mechanics of the *IS-LM-PEP* model with an *IS* curve containing inflation expectations.

A Famous Proposition: Inflation is a Monetary Phenomenon

Although the long-run equilibrium unemployment rate U^* and output level Y^* are independent of monetary and fiscal policy, the long-run inflation rate and nominal interest rate depend very much on government policy. The long-run equilibrium solution to the *IS-LM-PEP* model accords with a fundamental monetarist proposition. In the long run, **inflation is a monetary phenomenon**. There can be no lasting inflation unless the nominal money supply is growing, and continual increases in the money supply will guarantee that there is enduring inflation.

To illustrate this famous monetarist proposition, in Figure 13.6 we have reproduced our basic *IS-LM-PEP* model and have assumed that our hypothetical economy is initially in equilibrium at an output level Y^* (position A in both panels of Figure 13.6), with a price level P_0, a zero inflation rate, zero inflation expectations, and a zero growth rate in the nominal money supply. Notice that both the black *PEP* and *IS* curves depend on this zero expected inflation rate, and have been labelled

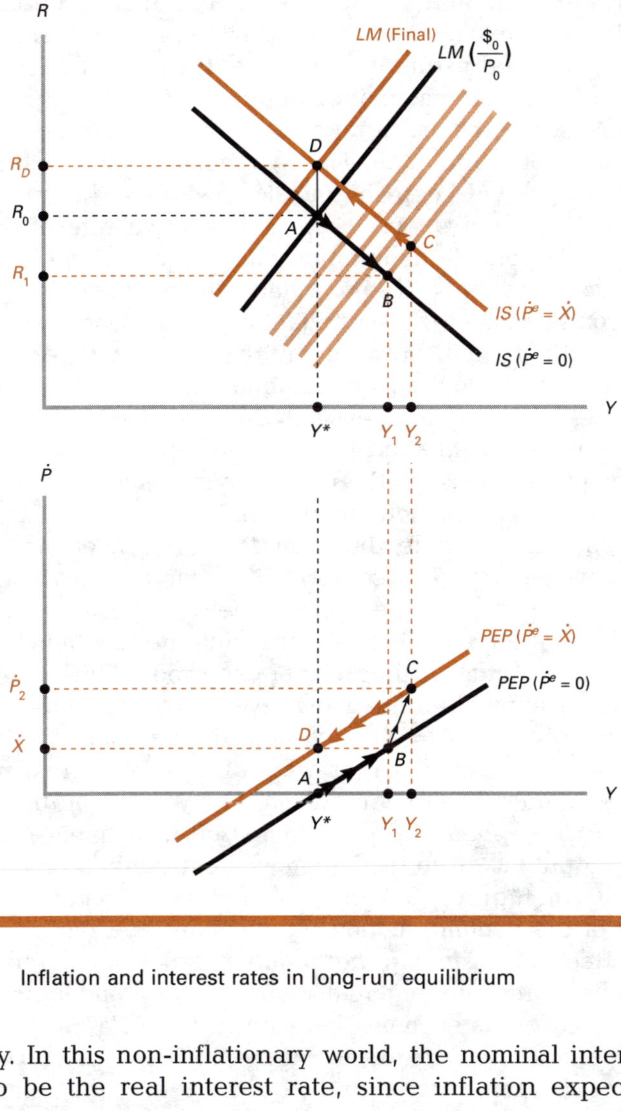

Figure 13.6 Inflation and interest rates in long-run equilibrium

accordingly. In this non-inflationary world, the nominal interest rate R_0 would also be the real interest rate, since inflation expectations are zero.

Now suppose that the government decides to increase the growth rate of the nominal money supply from 0 to $\dot{X}$ percent. To simplify the macroeconomic story, we discuss the various adjustments that will take place in a sequential fashion. In the real world, many of these adjustments will be taking place simultaneously.

Given an initial zero inflation rate and a zero expected inflation rate, an increase in the nominal money supply will cause an increase in the real money supply, a rightward shift in the *LM* curve, a decline in both the nominal and real interest rates (which are identical when inflation expectations are zero), and an increase in investment and output levels. *Assuming inflation expectations temporarily remain at zero*, during the first phase of the adjustment process following an increase in the growth rate of the nominal money supply from 0 to $\dot{X}$ percent, a sequence of *LM* curve shifts will take the economy from point *A* to point *B* in both panels of Figure 13.6. The real money supply will keep rising (and the *LM* curve will keep shifting downwards to the right) until the inflation rate is pushed up to $\dot{X}$, the new growth rate of the nominal money supply. At point *B* the inflation rate is equal to the growth rate of the nominal money supply ($\dot{X}$), but inflation expectations are still zero.

In the second phase of the sequential adjustment process, we assume that everyone throughout the economy realizes that government monetary policy is now validating an inflation rate of $\dot{X}$. Workers demand wage increases to cover this new expected inflation rate and firms incorporate an expected inflation rate of $\dot{X}$ into both their labour market and investment decisions. Both the *PEP* curve and the *IS* curve shift upwards by exactly $\dot{X}$ percent (both the *PEP* curve and the *IS* curve have intercepts that include the term $\dot{P}^e$ with a coefficient of unity). Given this new higher coloured $IS(\dot{P}^e = \dot{X})$ curve, the economy moves from point *B* to point *C* in the upper panel of Figure 13.6 as business people realize that the real costs of borrowing are now much lower than the nominal interest rate R_1 (because of expected inflation) and increase their investment expenditures. In the lower panel, the *PEP* curve shifts up to the coloured $PEP(\dot{P}^e = \dot{X})$ curve and the inflation rate jumps to $\dot{P}_2$ (point *C*). Workers demand larger wage increases for two reasons: (1) inflation expectations have been adjusted upwards from 0 to $\dot{X}$ percent (a higher *PEP* curve), and (2) given increased investment expenditures, the level of output has risen to Y_2 (a movement up the *PEP* curve).

At point *C* in Figure 13.6 the inflation rate $\dot{P}_2$ now exceeds the growth rate of the *nominal* money supply $\dot{X}$ and the *real* money supply will start to decline. *Assuming that inflation expectations remain at* $\dot{X}$ (a key assumption), the eroding real money supply and upward-shifting *LM* curve will carry the economy back down the $PEP(\dot{P}^e = \dot{X})$ curve from point *C* to point *D* (see arrows in Figure 13.6). At point *D* the actual inflation rate has been lowered to the growth rate of the nominal money supply $\dot{X}$ and the real money supply is once again constant. Furthermore, the actual inflation rate $\dot{X}$ is now correctly anticipated by workers and firms. Thus the *LM*, *IS*, and *PEP* curves will all remain stationary and the economy is once again back in long-run equilibrium, at the natural rate of output Y^*.

In the *IS-LM* panel of Figure 13.6, the upward-shifting *LM* curve has carried the economy up to point *D* with a nominal interest rate of R_D. Since the *IS* curve shifted upwards by exactly $\dot{X}$ (the intercept of the *IS* curve rose by $\dot{P}^e = \dot{X}$), the distance *AD* must equal $\dot{X}$. The final equilibrium interest rate R_D must be $\dot{X}$ percent higher than the initial interest rate R_0. The long-run equilibrium interest rate will fully reflect the validated, expected inflation rate $\dot{X}$.

To summarize, both the long-run inflation rate and the long-run equilibrium nominal interest rate in the *IS-LM-PEP* model are monetary phenomena. Whatever growth rate $\dot{X}$ the government chooses for the nominal money supply, it will eventually be reflected in the inflation rate and nominal interest rate. The higher the growth rate of the nominal money supply, the higher the inflation rate and interest rate will be. By controlling the growth rate of the nominal money supply, the government can control the long-run inflation rate, as well as the equilibrium interest rate. It is continual increases in the nominal money supply that fuel inflation, reinforce inflation expectations, and drive up interest rates.

As the Governor of the Bank of Canada has acknowledged, the short-run interest rate effects from monetary policy must be clearly distinguished from the long-run interest rate effects:

> In a market-oriented economy there is a direct interaction between monetary expansion and interest rates. A reduction in the rate of monetary expansion will, other things being unchanged, push up short-term interest rates, and vice versa. In the longer term the relationship is different. A reduction in the rate of monetary expansion will over time lead to a lower rate of inflation than would otherwise have existed and interest rates will be lower than they would otherwise have been. But the first effect on interest rates is in the other direction.[11]

If the government permanently increases the rate of monetary expansion, we can confidently predict that *in the long run* both inflation and nominal interest rates will rise. However, the short-run movement of interest rates following a change in the growth rate of the money supply is more difficult to predict.

Given the inherent lags in the economic system and slowly adjusting inflation expectations, an increase in the growth rate of the money supply may *initially* produce a *decline* in nominal interest rates (from *A* to *B* in the *IS-LM* panel of Figure 13.6), as well as an initial increase in output and employment. But one should not be lulled into believing that an increase in the rate of monetary growth will generate permanent interest rate reductions, or permanent gains in output and employment. Once inflation expectations are adjusted upwards to reflect the higher rate of inflation, nominal interest rates will start to rise. In terms of the upper panel in Figure 13.6, once inflation expectations are revised upwards the economy will begin to loop up and around (from *B* to *C* to *D*),

---

[11] Bank of Canada, *Annual Report, 1980*, p. 6.

heading back to the equilibrium output level Y^* and to a higher nominal interest rate R_D. The shorter the lags in the economic system and the faster the adjustment of inflation expectations, the faster the economy will move to its new long-run equilibrium position (point D) and the less likely it becomes that an expansionary monetary policy will generate temporary interest rate reductions, and temporary output and employment gains.

Case Study 8: Is Inflation Really a Monetary Phenomenon?

Our theoretical *IS-LM-PEP* model leads us to predict that in the long run the rate of price inflation will be directly related to the growth rate of the nominal money supply. Since this is an extremely important prediction of economic theory, the empirical validity of this prediction must be verified. Do data from the real world support the theoretical conclusion that the long-run inflation rate is directly related to the growth rate of the nominal money supply, that inflation is a monetary phenomenon?

Figure 13.7(a) presents a scatter diagram for the rate of price inflation and the rate of change in the money supply. Inflation is measured on the vertical axis by the annual percentage increase in the GDP deflator, the most comprehensive measure of prices available. On the horizontal axis we plot the percentage change in the money supply M1 (see Chapter 15 for a definition of M1). The lower left point indicates that in the year 1990 there was a 3.1 percent inflation rate and a negative 1.9 percent change in the money supply. The only other year in which the money supply actually declined was 1982 (M1 fell by 0.1 percent), a year in which the inflation rate was 8.7 percent!

As is obvious, Figure 13.7(a) is all scatter. There is *no* statistical relationship between the change in prices and the change in the money supply. For any given change in the money supply there are widely divergent inflation rates. For example, in the years 1963, 1980, and 1988 the Canadian money supply increased by approximately 6 percent; the corresponding inflation rates for these three years are 2.0, 10.8, and 4.8 percent. There is little indication that the current inflation rate is influenced by the current change in the money supply.

However, much of the breadth of the scatter of points in panel (a) can be explained when we allow for the lags in the economic system. An increase in the growth rate of the money supply initially causes interest rates to decline. In response to lower interest rates, investment expenditures increase and there is a multiplier effect on output. Rising output and falling unemployment put upward pressure on wages and then on prices. Each step (lower interest rates, increased investment, increased output, lower unemployment, higher wage increases, and higher price inflation) takes time to complete. The full inflation effects from a change

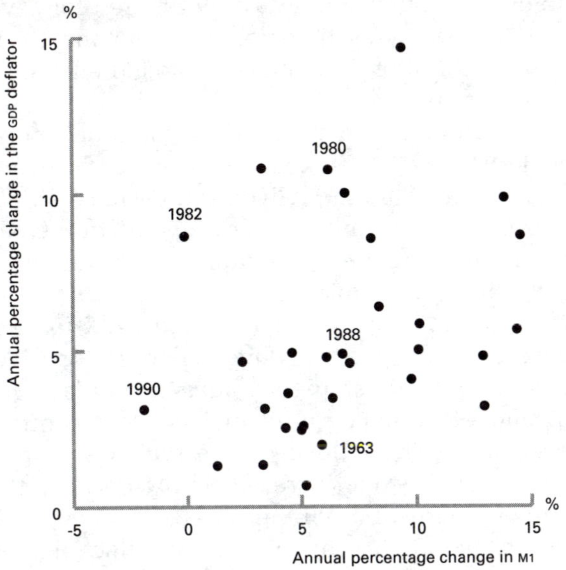

(a) Current percentage change in the money supply

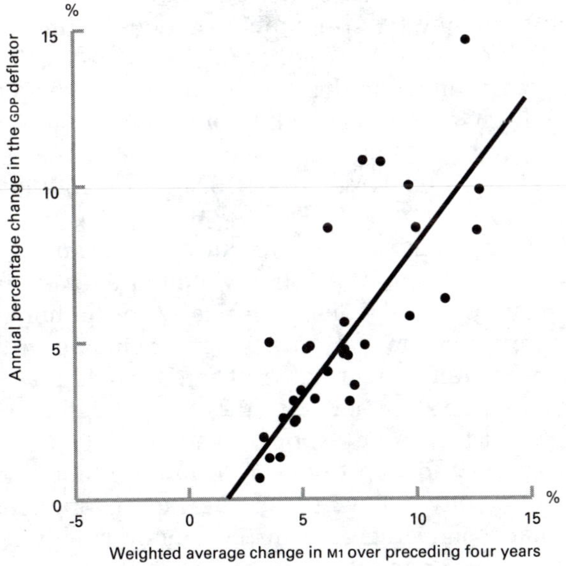

(b) Average percentage change in the money supply over the preceding four years

Figure 13.7 Inflation and the growth rate of the money supply, 1960–90

in the growth rate of the money supply will not be felt for several years. In terms of Figure 13.3, it takes time for the economy to move from point *A* to *B* to *C* to *D*. In Milton Friedman's words, the lags in monetary policy are "long and variable."

The response of investment expenditures to changing interest rates is likely to be particularly slow — it takes a year or two to plan and build a new factory or apartment building. Given the basic lags in the investment (construction) process, output will slowly start to increase following a decrease in interest rates, and unemployment will slowly start to decline. A slowly declining unemployment rate may have little effect on current wages and prices. Almost one-half of the work force is covered by collective agreements that fix the wage schedule for several years. Unionized workers cannot adjust their wages upwards to reflect this new expansionary monetary policy until their current contract expires. In the non-union sector, most employees have their wages adjusted annually, and do not receive a wage increase simply because the monthly unemployment rate decreases. For all these reasons, it may take several years for a change in monetary growth be fully reflected in the rate of inflation.

Given the lags in monetary policy, the inflation rate in any particular year will depend on past changes in the money supply. Statistical investigation suggests that the current inflation rate is best explained by a weighted average of money ($W\dot{A}M$) supply changes during the preceding four years, with the following weights, 0.272, 0.304, 0.219, and 0.150 applied to the lagged changes in the money supply (these weights were determined by the least squares estimation procedure):

$$W\dot{A}M_t = 0.272\dot{M}_{t-1} + 0.304\dot{M}_{t-2} + 0.219\dot{M}_{t-3} + 0.150\dot{M}_{t-4}$$

In Figure 13.7(b) we again plot the current inflation rate on the vertical axis, but this time we plot $W\dot{A}M$, the weighted average increase in the money supply over the preceding four years, on the horizontal axis. The statistical improvement in the price inflation change in the money supply relationship is quite remarkable. There is a highly significant positive statistical relationship between the current inflation rate and the average change in the money supply over the four previous years. The four lagged weights add up to 0.945, a number that is not significantly different from unity. Allowing for the lags in monetary policy, each extra percentage-point increase in the money supply leads to an extra percentage point of price inflation.

It should also be noted that the least squares line cuts the horizontal axis to the right of the origin. An average increase in the money supply of 1.2 percent produces a zero inflation rate. Given the underlying real growth in the economy, one would expect a positive intercept. As the economy grows, the transactions demand for money increases and interest rates will rise if the money supply is not increased. To maintain stable interest rates and stable prices, the money supply must increase by the real growth rate of the economy. Our horizontal intercept estimate of 1.2 percent suggests that the Bank of Canada increased the money supply by considerably less than the real growth rate of the economy (which averaged 4.2 percent per annum over this period), which implies that interest rates had to increase (real interest rates rose from 3–4 percent in the early 1960s to 7–9 percent in the late 1980s).

Of course, there is still a scatter of points around the upward-sloping line in Figure 13.7(b). There are many other factors (such as changes in the GST, oil price shocks, and changes in agricultural commodity prices) that affect the inflation rate. Perhaps the surprising result of Figure 13.7(b) is the importance of past changes in the money supply in determining the current inflation rate. Statistically speaking, a weighted average of past changes in the money supply explains about 60 percent of the variation in the inflation rate.

The Outbreak of Double-Digit Inflation in 1974: A Retrospective Analysis

Case Study 8 clearly demonstrates that there is a strong positive relationship between past changes in the money supply and the current inflation rate. Thus, we should be able to trace the outbreak of double-digit inflation in 1974 back to monetary policy in the years preceding 1974.

In 1971 the Canadian money supply began to grow at a record rate. Compared to a 2.5 percent increase in the money supply in 1970, the nominal money supply increased by 12.8 percent in 1971, 14.0 percent in 1972, and 14.4 percent in 1973. The average annual increase in the money supply over the three years 1971–73 was an incredible 13.9 percent, which compounds to a 48 percent increase over this three-year period!

Economic theory and the empirical relationship presented in Case Study 8 predict that if the government increases the money supply by 14 percent per year for three successive years, then in the fourth year (1974) the inflation rate will be in the double-digit range. The fact that the GDP deflator increased by 14.7 percent in 1974 (and the CPI increased by 10.9 percent) is hardly surprising. Although there were extenuating circumstances and aggravating external events, the excessive expansion of the money supply in the early 1970s was the root cause of a double-digit inflation problem that lasted for ten years.

Even though economic theory can explain the outbreak of double-digit inflation in the mid-1970s, it *cannot* explain *why* the government pursued such an expansionary monetary policy in the early 1970s. Five years later, the Department of Finance admitted that its earlier expansionary policies were wrong: ". . . in retrospect it is clear that the aggregate demand policy in the period 1971–73 was excessively expansionary."[12]

To understand the government's "excessively expansionary" policies during the early 1970s, we have to go back to the 1960s, a decade of unprecedented economic growth and a gently rising inflation rate. In 1969 Prime Minister Trudeau instituted a very restrictive monetary and fiscal policy, designed to "wrestle inflation to the ground." The real growth rate in the economy was cut in half and the unemployment rate climbed to 5.7 percent in 1970 and 6.2 percent in 1971. This government-engineered recession partially achieved its anti-inflation objective, as the inflation rate dropped from 5 percent in 1969 to 3 percent in 1971.

Perhaps in anticipation of the 1972 federal election, in 1971 the Trudeau government abruptly switched back to a very expansionary policy. Fighting unemployment rather than inflation became the number one priority. In the words of John Turner: "Mr. Speaker, my first words to this House as Minister of Finance last February were that the most urgent priority was jobs. This remains my first priority."[13] The federal government surpluses of 1969 and 1970 were converted into deficits in 1971 and 1972. At the same time, the Bank of Canada flooded the economy with dollar bills (a 48 percent increase in the money supply during the years 1971–73). The fiscal brakes were released, the heavy "Keynesian" foot of the government stomped on the monetary accelerator, and the Canadian economy sped away to double-digit inflation.

One explanation for this "excessively expansionary" monetary policy was the government's unwillingness to let the Canadian dollar appreciate on foreign exchange markets. As Finance Minister Benson stated in his budget of 18 June 1971,

> I have said on many occasions that the government did not wish to see the Canadian dollar appreciate. A higher dollar works with increasing effect against our exporters and against domestic producers who must try to meet foreign competition. Since the appreciation affects the economy in this way, it works against our policy of trying to expand employment opportunities in Canada.[14]

As discussed in Chapter 6, the Bank of Canada can prevent the Canadian dollar from appreciating by demanding foreign currencies (in exchange for Canadian money) and maintaining a low interest rate (to

---

12 *Canada's Recent Inflation Experience*, Department of Finance, Ottawa, November 1978, p. 14.

13 *Hansard*, 8 May 1972, p. 1998.

14 *Hansard*, 18 June 1971, p. 6904.

discourage capital inflows). As Professor Courchene of Queen's University has noted:

> The policy error over this period (the early 1970s) arose from the authorities' belief that Canada could simultaneously achieve a less-than-world inflation rate and an unchanged exchange rate. . . . The policy error during this period is obvious — the money supply was allowed to grow far too rapidly. In turn the principal reason why this rate of monetary expansion occurred was that the Bank and the government attempted to stabilize the exchange rate at or near parity with the U.S. dollar.[15]

Although rapid monetary expansion prevented the Canadian dollar from appreciating, such rapid monetary growth eventually led to an accelerating domestic inflation rate, a subsequent deterioration in Canadian international competitiveness, and a dramatic decline in the value of the Canadian dollar during the late 1970s and early 1980s.

With the advantage of 20/20 hindsight, it is clear that the government seriously underestimated the inflationary consequences of its policies of the early 1970s. Most economists and policymakers of the early 1970s still subscribed to an *incorrect* inflation–unemployment *trade-off* view of the economy, believing that expansionary policies could permanently lower the unemployment rate with only modest increases in the inflation rate. Friedman's *natural* rate of unemployment hypothesis, advanced in 1967, was not well understood in the early 1970s and the possibility that the inflation rate might continually accelerate if the unemployment rate was pushed below the *natural* rate was dismissed as theoretical speculation. Mistaking the relatively flat *short-run* Phillips curve for a *long-run* inflation–unemployment *trade-off* curve, the Canadian government expanded aggregate demand rapidly in 1971 and 1972 in an attempt to lower the 6.2 percent unemployment rate, *incorrectly* presuming that only a modest increase in the inflation would materialize.

As discussed in Case Study 5 in Chapter 10, fundamental structural changes in the labour market had caused an increase in the natural rate of unemployment in the early 1970s.[16] The government's expansionary

---

15 T.J. Courchene, *Money, Inflation, and the Bank of Canada* (Montreal: C.D. Howe Research Institute, 1976), pp. 13–14.

16 During the 1960s and 1970s the demographic composition of the labour force shifted to younger, less experienced, secondary workers, with a resulting increase in frictional and structural unemployment. In addition, the government substantially liberalized the unemployment insurance program in 1971, which significantly altered the incentive structure within the labour market (particularly for secondary workers). As a consequence of this enriched unemployment insurance program, the more heavily subsidized unemployed exercised more discretion over the choice of jobs that they would accept (longer job search). The combination of demographic shifts and an enriched unemployment insurance program increased the natural rate of unemployment by one or two percentage points in the early 1970s (for further discussion, see Case Study 5 in Chapter 10).

fiscal and monetary policies were driving the economy to an unemployment rate below the new natural rate of unemployment. Even though government policymakers may or may not have understood the implications of Friedman's *natural* rate concept, they certainly would have rejected the notion that the Canadian *natural* rate of unemployment was in excess of 6.2 percent, the prevailing Canadian unemployment rate in 1971–72.

In retrospect, the government and the Bank of Canada committed a series of grave macroeconomic policy errors in the 1971–73 period, such as attempting to run the economic system with an unemployment rate below the natural rate and trying to prevent the Canadian dollar from appreciating. In concert, these policy errors manifested themselves in an "excessively expansionary" monetary and fiscal policy, which led to double-digit inflation.

In fairness to the government of the day, it should be noted that academic economists of the early 1970s were not criticizing the government's "excessively expansionary" policies. Most economists still clung to a mistaken belief in a *long-run* inflation–unemployment *trade-off* curve. Opposition critics in Parliament were demanding even more expansionary policies. In criticizing the February 1973 Liberal budget, the Progressive Conservative finance critic James Gillies stated:

> The really fundamental question one has to ask in considering this budget and its effect on employment in the economy is: is the deficit large enough? . . . I would argue, that it is not. . . . If a Progressive Conservative government had been in power . . . [the] budget would have been substantially more expansionary.[17]

The NDP, which held the balance of power in Parliament throughout most of the 1972–74 period, were even more vocal in demanding expansionary policies. In terms of the academic and political commentary of the day, it would not have been obvious to the 1971–73 Canadian government that its macroeconomic policies were "excessively expansionary" or incorrect.

Echoing the words of the Governor of the Bank of Canada, "there is no great mystery about the nature and origins" of the emergence of double-digit inflation in Canada in 1974. Average increases in the money supply of 13.9 percent for three successive years (1971–73) guaranteed the emergence of double-digit inflation (in 1974–75). Unfortunately, once double-digit inflation has existed for several years, fuelled by excessively expansionary monetary policy, people will come to expect double-digit inflation to continue. Canadian inflation expectations of 3 to 4 percent in the early 1970s were undoubtedly revised upwards

[17] *Hansard*, 22 February 1973, pp. 1559–60.

to 10 percent in the mid-1970s, shifting the Canadian short-run *PEP* curve upwards. As discussed in the next chapter, once the inflation genie is let out of the bottle, it is very difficult to get it back into the bottle. Once inflation expectations and the *PEP* curve shift up into the double-digit range, its very hard to get inflation and the *PEP* curve back down.

Summary

Assuming that wages fully reflect the expected inflation rate, there is no lasting inflation–unemployment trade-off that the government can exploit. The long-run equilibrium unemployment rate (the NAIRU or the *natural* rate of unemployment) is determined in the labour market and is independent of monetary and fiscal policy. If the government attempts to use expansionary monetary and fiscal policies to lower the long-run unemployment rate, larger and larger increases in the money supply will be called for, and a wage–price inflation spiral will be triggered. If monetary growth is stabilized at some particular rate, the level of output and the unemployment rate will return to their unique equilibrium (natural rate) values. The long-run independence of output from the rate of monetary growth is referred to as the *superneutrality* property of money.

Although the long-run equilibrium unemployment rate is independent of monetary and fiscal policies, the long-run inflation rate and nominal interest rate depend crucially on monetary policy. In the long run, the inflation rate and the nominal interest rate will mirror the growth rate of the money supply. Unlike the difficult problem of long-run unemployment, inflation and interest rates are controllable in the long run. However, getting a relatively high inflation rate down to a low inflation rate may entail a prolonged and painful short-run adjustment period of high unemployment and high interest rates. The analysis of anti-inflationary policy options is taken up in the next chapter.

Key Concepts

monetary validation policy
wage–price inflation spiral
short-run *PEP* curve versus long-run inflation–output relationship
superneutrality of money
natural rate of unemployment
NAIRU

inflation as a monetary phenomenon
real versus nominal interest rates

Review Questions

1. How does a monetary validation policy affect labour market behaviour? Under a monetary validation policy, explain why an attempt by policymakers to hold the unemployment rate below the natural rate will cause the Phillips curve to shift.
2. Assuming that the monetary authorities continually validate whatever inflation materializes, carefully explain why an expansionary fiscal policy will lead to an accelerating inflation rate. How can this wage–price inflation spiral be halted? What are the output and unemployment ramifications of halting this inflation spiral?
3. Using the *IS-LM-PEP* model, analyze the short-run and long-run inflation and output effects if the nominal money supply is allowed to increase from 5 percent per year to 10 percent per year.
4. What are the key determinants of the long-run equilibrium output level and unemployment rate?
5. Under what conditions will the equilibrium output level be independent of the inflation rate and independent of monetary and fiscal policy? Do you think there is a sustainable inflation–unemployment trade-off available to policymakers? Explain.
6. What role can Keynesian fiscal policy play in lowering the unemployment rate?
7. In the long run, what determines the inflation rate? Explain using an *IS-LM-PEP* diagram.
8. If inflation is theoretically a monetary phenomenon, why is the current inflation rate often unrelated to current monetary policy? How do you explain the fact that a 2 percent growth rate of the nominal money supply might produce a zero inflation rate in the real world?
9. Why will the *IS* curve shift when there is a change in the expected inflation rate? Explain.
10. Using an *IS-LM-PEP* model, illustrate that the nominal interest rate will reflect the rate of increase in the nominal money supply.
11. Suppose that the government decreases the rate of expansion of the nominal money supply. Explain why interest rates might initially rise before they start to fall.
12. Why did the Canadian inflation rate rise to more than 10 percent in 1974? Why did the government implement such a policy?

CHAPTER 14

Anti-Inflationary Policy

. . . short-term pain for long-term gain . . .

John Crosbie, former Finance Minister

As discussed in the previous chapter, to lower the *long-run* equilibrium inflation rate the government must restrict the growth rate of the nominal money supply. Unfortunately, the *short-run* adjustment costs of an anti-inflationary monetary policy may be very painful. Gearing the economy down from a high inflation rate to a low inflation rate may entail a prolonged period of high unemployment and high interest rates. Even though the *long-run* inflation–unemployment trade-off curve may be dead, the *short-run* Phillips curve relationship between inflation and unemployment is "dangerously" alive. In the words of John Vanderkamp,

> Ultimately the rate of monetary expansion determines the rate of inflation in this model, but the Phillips curve plays a very important role in the adjustment process . . . in the downward direction the path of *adjustment* is likely to be tortuous. . . . If price change expectations are slow to adjust, then the unemployment experience along the adjustment path is likely to be very prolonged and severe . . . an incomes policy may well be a useful tool when it is employed together with a restrictive monetary policy to aid in the downward adjustment from an established inflation rate. The incomes policy would then reduce the unemployment burden resulting from the transition to a lower inflation rate. . . this model suggests that the Phillips curve is not dead, but that it is in fact a more dangerous device than the simple trade-off approach implies. The danger lies in the costs of reducing inflation, which may

not be realized when the economy is moving to higher inflation rates.[1]

In this chapter we return to an analysis of the *short-run* properties of the *IS-LM-PEP* model. The first half of this chapter explores the "tortuous" *short-run* unemployment–interest rate path that the economy travels during the adjustment period accompanying an anti-inflationary monetary policy. Given the likelihood of a "very prolonged and severe" recession accompanying an anti-inflationary monetary policy, a number of economists (such as Vanderkamp) have advocated the use of *temporary* wage and price controls to "reduce the unemployment burden" associated with a restrictive monetary policy. As discussed in the middle section of this chapter, *temporary* wage and price controls might be implemented to minimize the "short-term pain" associated with a restrictive monetary policy. The chapter concludes with a case study evaluation of the 1975–78 imposition of wage and price controls in Canada and a discussion of the Bank of Canada's "monetarist" monetary policy during the 1975–90 period.

The Costs of an Anti-Inflationary Monetary Policy: "Short-Term Pain"

To illustrate the costs of lowering the inflation rate, Figure 14.1 reproduces our standard *IS-LM-PEP* model. We assume that the economy is in long-run equilibrium at point *A* with an income level of Y^* and a "high" inflation rate of $\dot{P}_H$, say 10 percent. For whatever reason, the government has allowed the nominal money supply to increase by 10 percent each year and people have come to expect an inflation rate of 10 percent each year. Both the *PEP* curve and the *IS* curve reflect an expected inflation rate of 10 percent.[2] Now suppose that the government decides to reduce this high 10 percent inflation rate to a lower inflation rate $\dot{P}_L$, say 5 percent. From our analysis in the previous chapter the policy prescription is obvious: the government must restrict the growth rate of the nominal money supply to 5 percent each year. The arrows in Figure 14.1 depict the short-run adjustment path that our hypothetical economy *may* follow once the growth rate of the nominal money supply is lowered to 5 percent. This adjustment path is premised

---

1 J. Vanderkamp, "Inflation: A Simple Friedman Theory with a Phillips Twist," *Journal of Monetary Economics*, January 1975, pp. 120–22. (John Vanderkamp died in June 1991.)

2 As discussed in the previous chapter, investment decisions depend on the real interest rate. Assuming a given nominal interest rate, the *IS* curve will shift horizontally to the right (left) if the expected inflation rate increases (decreases).

on a *delayed* one-step reduction in inflation expectations from 10 to 5 percent.

In the first phase of the adjustment period, inflation expectations will likely remain high. People may be unsure whether the government is serious about lowering the inflation rate and may wait for evidence that the actual inflation rate does indeed decline before lowering their inflation expectations. Even though everyone wants lower price inflation, no one wants to be the first to accept a lower wage increase. There is no guarantee that the government will continue its anti-inflationary monetary policy and that other workers will also accept lower wage increases in subsequent wage contracts. Staggered long-term wage contracts (that is, two- and three-year contracts signed at different times) likely impart

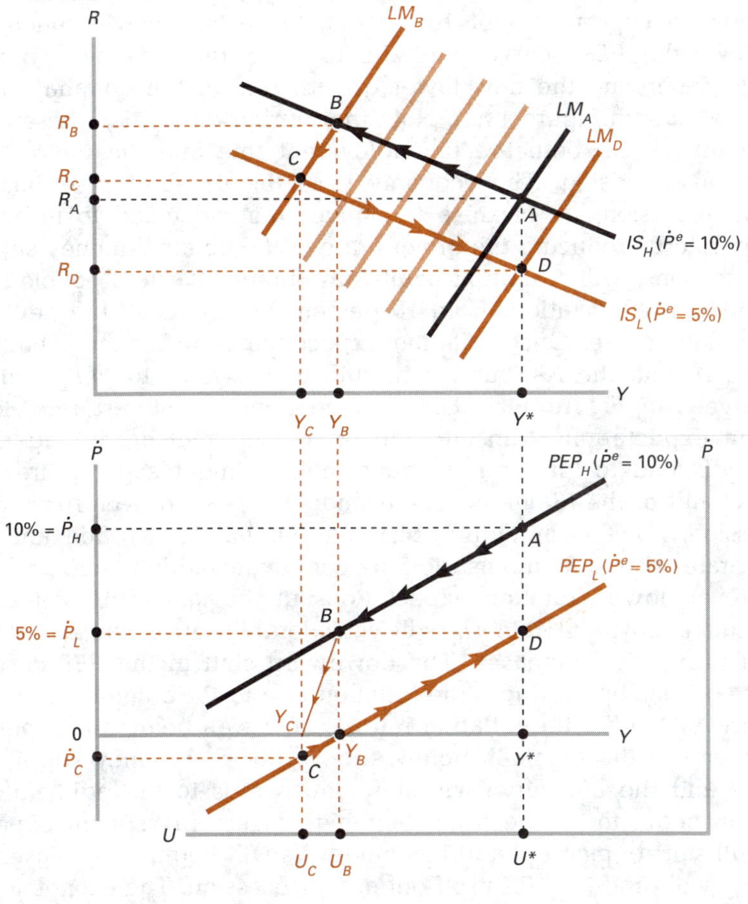

Figure 14.1 Effects of an anti-inflationary restrictive monetary policy

a considerable degree of persistence to inflation expectations and wage increases. With inflation expectations and the actual inflation rate initially remaining high (at 10 percent), the new lower 5 percent growth rate in the nominal money supply will cause the real money supply to decline and the *LM* curve to shift upwards to the left. This reduction in the growth rate of the nominal (and real) money supply will push interest rates upwards, leading to a decrease in investment expenditures and a decline in income levels. The economy will begin to slide down the PEP_H curve to a lower income level and a lower inflation rate.

In this section of the chapter, we assume that inflation expectations remain high (at 10 percent) for several periods of time following the reduction in the growth rate of the nominal money supply. (The next section considers a more complicated case in which inflation expectations adjust each period to the actual inflation rate in the preceding period.) Given high inflation expectations of 10 percent, the economy will continue to slide down the PEP_H curve until the inflation rate has been brought down to 5 percent, the new lower growth rate in the nominal money supply (point *B* in Figure 14.1). Note that during this initial phase of the adjustment period, both the unemployment rate and the interest rate are continually rising. The economy is in the midst of a serious and growing recession, all because the government decided to lower the inflation rate by reducing the growth rate of the nominal money supply.

The economy will remain at point *B* in Figure 14.1 until people lower their inflation expectations from 10 percent to 5 percent, the new validated inflation rate. Once inflation expectations are lowered, both the PEP_H curve and the IS_H curve will shift downwards, to PEP_L and IS_L, respectively, in Figure 14.1. For a given nominal interest rate, lower inflation expectations translate into increased *real* borrowing costs, which will lead to further reductions in investment expenditures (the leftward shift of the *IS* curve). The economy is pushed even further into a recession, point *C* in Figure 14.1. Output falls to Y_C and and *real* interest rates rise to R_C minus the 5 percent expected inflation.

However, lower inflation expectations in the labour market and a higher unemployment rate U_C will considerably lower wage increases and, in turn, price increases. The downward shift in the *PEP* curve to $PEP_L(\dot{P}^e = 5$ percent) reduces the inflation rate to $\dot{P}_C$, a negative number in Figure 14.1. With the inflation rate $\dot{P}_C$ now well below the 5 percent growth rate in the nominal money supply, the real money supply will increase and the *LM* curve will shift downwards to the right. Interest rates will begin to recede from their high levels, investment expenditures will start to pick up, and income levels will begin to increase. The economy will gradually lift itself out of the recession. The economic system will climb up the new lower PEP_L curve, eventually returning to the long-run equilibrium point *D* in Figure 14.1 (where $\dot{\$} = \dot{P} = \dot{P}^e = 5$ percent). At point *D*, the level of output and the unemployment rate have returned to their original equilibrium values (Y^* and U^*) and the prevailing inflation rate has been lowered from 10 to 5 percent (which is fully expected and validated). As discussed in the previous chapter, the nominal interest rate will be 5 percent lower at point *D* than point *A* and the real interest rate will be back to its original long-run equilibrium level.

Lowering the inflation rate requires excess supply conditions in the goods market, which can be generated either by reducing demand relative to supply (as in Figure 14.1) or possibly by increasing supply relative to demand. Since aggregate supply is the product of a demographically determined labour force, a capital stock accumulated over many decades, and technology (which determines labour productivity), it is not easy for the government to affect aggregate supply, at least in the short-run. Any government-induced increase in aggregate supply designed to dampen the inflation rate is likely to be "too little, too late":

> An extreme, and currently very popular, version of supply-side economics is that the way to tackle the inflation problem is from the supply side, especially by cutting taxes. The argument is simply that inflation results from an excess demand over supply, and there is no sense in correcting that by the painful method of restricting demand when it could be done by the pleasant way of raising supply. The answer is of course equally simple. What we can do on the supply side is not big enough to solve the problem. We have demand growing by about 12 percent a year and supply growing by about 2 percent a year, which yields a 10 percent inflation (in 1980–81). To increase the rate of growth of supply by 50 percent from 2 percent to 3 percent a year, which is a difficult task, would still leave an enormous inflation, especially if the increase of supply is accomplished by means like cutting taxes which at the same time increase demand.[3]

As a consequence, to generate excess supply conditions to lower the inflation rate, the government has to restrict aggregate demand.

Thus the term "anti-inflationary" monetary policy should be understood as a euphemism for reduced aggregate demand, higher interest rates, and higher unemployment rates. Unfortunately, the cutting edge of an anti-inflationary monetary policy is a larger pool of unemployed workers that will increase the competition for jobs and thereby restrain wage (and price) increases. The economic cost of a lower *long-run equilibrium* inflation rate is a *short-run disequilibrium* increase in interest rates and unemployment rates. Both Keynesians and monetarists tend to agree on this fundamental, if discouraging, point:[4]

---

3 H. Stein, "Some 'Supply-Side' Propositions," *Wall Street Journal*, 19 March 1980.

4 As discussed below, new classical macroeconomists assume that inflation expectations are formed in a "rational" manner and believe that an anti-inflationary monetary policy is relatively costless.

Richard Lipsey:

> I don't believe our policy of so-called monetary gradualism will bring down the inflation rate without a major recession.[5]

Milton Friedman:

> I know of no example of a country that has cured substantial inflation without going through a transitional period of slow growth and unemployment.[6]

In the immortal words of former Finance Minister John Crosbie, Canadians must endure "short-term pain for long-term gain."

The magnitude and duration of the "short-term pain" depends crucially on how quickly prices and wages adjust to changing economic circumstances. If wages and prices are relatively insensitive to changing demand conditions, then the short-run disequilibrium adjustment period will be prolonged. On the other hand, if wages and prices are very flexible (in a downward direction), then the short-run will be very short and the costs of an anti-inflationary monetary policy minimal.

As discussed in Chapter 11, the length of the short-run adjustment period depends on the nature of the underlying price-expectations Phillips (*PEP*) curve. We can identify three different factors that affect the length of the short-run adjustment period in response to an anti-inflationary monetary policy.

First, the existence of long-term wage contracts may prevent wages from adjusting to a new lower inflation rate. Existing long-term contracts, signed prior to the implementation of the new anti-inflationary monetary policy, will likely contain large second- and third-year wage increases (based on a high expected inflation rate). Smaller wage increases, consistent with the government's new anti-inflationary monetary policy, must wait until the current set of contracts expires, perhaps one or two years into the future. Given the institutional feature of long-term wage contracts containing deferred wage increases, any increase in unemployment will initially have minimal effects on reducing wage increases and price inflation.

Second, even when contracts expire and wages are adjusted, the change in wages may not be that large. As discussed in Chapter 10, the slope of the wage change–unemployment relationship in Canada is estimated to be 0.8; each extra point of unemployment lowers wage increases by only 0.8 of a percentage point. It takes a 5 percent

---

5 *The Financial Post*, 6 December 1980.

6 *Newsweek*, 12 November 1979.

point increase in the unemployment rate to lower wage settlements by 4 percent. If the short-run *PEP* curve is relatively flat, an increase in the unemployment rate from an anti-inflationary monetary policy will have a relatively small effect on moderating the rate of wage and price inflation. If the rate of inflation does not decline very quickly, then it will take a considerable length of time and/or a substantial amount of unemployment to bring the inflation rate down to the new lower validated rate (and move the economy from point *A* to point *B* in Figure 14.1).

Third, the speed with which inflation expectations are adjusted downwards is critical in determining the length of the short-run adjustment period. In analyzing the cost of an anti-inflationary monetary policy in Figure 14.1, we assumed that inflation expectations do not decline until the economy has reached point *B* (with an inflation rate of 5 percent). If inflation expectations begin to moderate as the inflation rate declines (as the economy moves from point *A* towards point *B*), then the short-run adjustment process will be speeded up. In the next section of the chapter we analyze an anti-inflationary monetary policy under the assumption that inflation expectations are revised each period. Both adaptive and rational inflation expectations models will be considered. As shown below, when inflation expectations adjust rapidly to a new lower inflation rate, the recession accompanying an anti-inflationary monetary policy will be less as severe than when inflation expectations adjust slowly.

To summarize, a reduction in the growth rate of the money supply will lower the inflation rate in the long run. However, there are costs associated with an anti-inflationary monetary policy. During the entire short-run adjustment period, the unemployment rate and the real interest rate are higher than they would have been (if anti-inflationary monetary policy had not been implemented). Given existing long-term wage contracts and slowly adjusting inflation expectations, the lags for an anti-inflationary monetary policy will be quite long, and the "short-term pain" will last for a number of years.

In addition to the short-run costs of an anti-inflationary monetary policy, there may be long-run costs as well. As discussed in Chapter 11, a prolonged negative demand shock may have a permanent effect on the unemployment rate, a *hysteresis* effect. Persistent short-run unemployment may lead to an erosion in "human" capital and a permanent increase in the equilibrium unemployment rate. Insider–outsider models have also been advanced to explain how a short-run increase in unemployment can lead to a permanent increase in unemployment. To the extent that *hysteresis* effects exist, the new long-run equilibrium position following an anti-inflationary monetary policy might have a higher unemployment rate, albeit with a lower inflation rate.

The Effects of an Anti-Inflationary Monetary Policy Under Adaptive and Rational Inflation Expectations

As discussed in Chapter 8, two different expectations models have been used by macroeconomists: adaptive and rational expectations. The *adaptive* expectations model was first introduced into macroeconomics by Phillip Cagan in the mid-1950s and quickly became part of the monetarists' arsenal in their early attack on Keynesian economics. The *rational* expectations model, which can be traced back to a 1961 paper by John Muth, did not take hold in macroeconomics until the mid-1970s. Once the striking implications of rational expectations were fully appreciated, a whole new school of *new classical* macroeconomic thought emerged in the late 1970s.

Adaptive Inflation Expectations

An adaptive expectations model assumes that people base their predictions of a particular variable, such as the inflation rate, on past experience with that particular variable. People "adapt" their expectations of future inflation in light of recent movements in the inflation rate. The adaptive expectations model assumes that future inflation rates are predictable from current and past inflation rates. (For further discussion of adaptive expectations models, see Chapter 8.)

Although sophisticated adaptive expectations models employ complicated moving averages of current and past inflation rates to predict the future inflation rate, we illustrate the macroeconomic implications of adaptive inflation expectations by using the simplest possible model. We assume that people believe that next year's inflation rate can be predicted from this year's inflation rate (the moving average contains only one term, the current inflation rate). People adjust their inflation expectations each period to the actual inflation rate that prevailed in the previous period. For example, if the actual inflation rate fell from 10 percent in year 1 to 8 percent in year 2, we assume that people lower their inflation expectations to 8 percent in year 3.

Following our earlier analysis, we assume that a hypothetical economy is in long-run equilibrium at Y^* with a fully anticipated and validated inflation rate of 10 percent (point A in Figure 14.2). Now suppose that the government decides to lower this 10 percent inflation rate to 5 percent and therefore reduces the rate of nominal monetary growth to 5 percent. In the first period following the reduction in the growth rate of the nominal money supply, people will still base their inflation expectations on the previous period's actual inflation rate of 10 percent. Consequently, inflation expectations will remain at 10 percent for the first period and the original (solid black line) *IS* and *PEP* curves correspond-

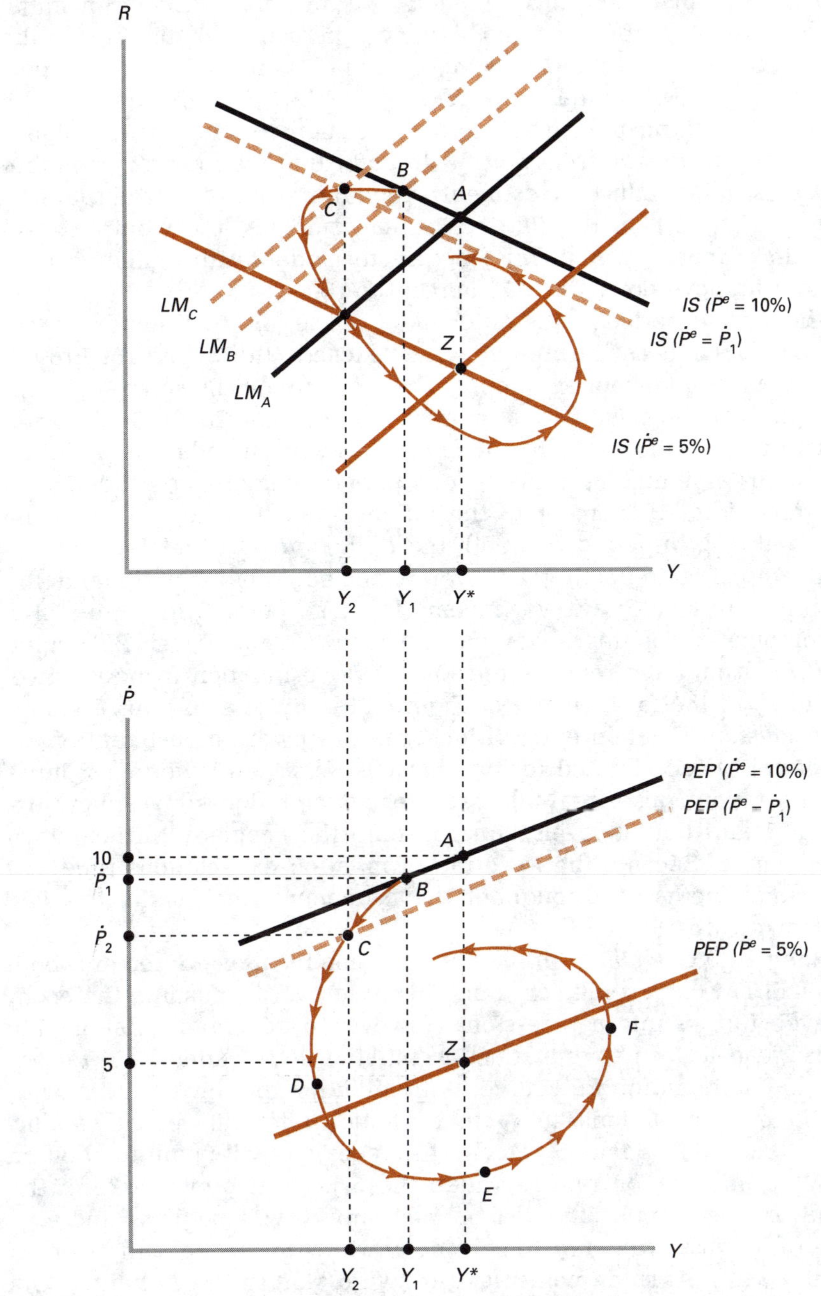

Figure 14.2 Effects of an anti-inflationary restrictive monetary policy under adaptive inflation expectations

ing to 10 percent inflation expectations will not move. Given an initial inflation rate of 10 percent and a new 5 percent growth rate of the nominal money supply, the real money supply will decline (by 5 percent) causing a substantial upward shift in the *LM* curve (to LM_B in Figure 14.2). During the first period of the short-run adjustment phase, the economy will move from point *A* to point *B* in Figure 14.2, as higher real interest rates reduce investment expenditures and lower output levels (from Y^* to Y_1). In the *PEP* curve diagram, this lower output level (and higher unemployment rate) begins to moderate the inflation rate, causing it to move down from 10 percent to $\dot{P}_1$.

In the second period of the adjustment phase, the real money supply will again decline as the inflation rate exceeds the 5 percent growth rate of the nominal money supply. The *LM* curve will again shift upwards (to LM_C), although by a smaller amount than in the first period (because the inflation rate has declined). Given our adaptive inflation expectations assumption, in the second period inflation expectations will be lowered from 10 percent to the inflation rate that prevailed in the first period ($\dot{P}_1$). In period two both the *PEP* curve and the *IS* curve will shift downwards (reflecting a lower expected inflation rate) and the economy will move to a lower income level Y_2, point *C* in Figure 14.2. The combination of this lower income level Y_2 and lower *PEP* curve ($\dot{P}^e = \dot{P}_1$) substantially reduces the rate of price inflation in period two, down to $\dot{P}_2$ in the lower panel of Figure 14.2. By relaxing our assumption of *constant* inflation expectations, the downward adjustment of the inflation rate is accelerated for two reasons. First, the lowering of inflation expectations raises real interest rates which reduces investment expenditures and output levels, thus pushing the economy further down the *PEP* curve. Second, the lowering of inflation expectations produces lower wage increases throughout the economy, which shifts the *PEP* curve downwards.

As long as the *declining* inflation rate remains *above* 5 percent, both the *IS* and *LM* curves will continue to shift leftwards, pushing the economy even further into a recession. However, a declining inflation rate will also lead to further reductions in inflation expectations and further downward shifts in the *PEP* curve. With falling output levels and declining inflation expectations, the actual inflation rate will decline rapidly. Once inflation falls *below* 5 percent, the recession will begin to "bottom out." With an inflation rate less than the 5 percent growth rate of the nominal money supply, the real money supply will begin to increase and the *LM* curve will start to shift downwards to the right (not shown in Figure 14.2). At some point this rightward shift in the *LM* curve will dominate the leftward (downward) shift of the *IS* curve (reflecting declining inflation expectations). Once this happens, say at point *D* in the lower panel of Figure 14.2, real interest rates will begin to decline and investment expenditures and income levels will start to increase. The economy will begin to recover and move back towards its equilibrium income level Y^*.

The pace of the recovery will accelerate as the inflation rate declines further below 5 percent: the lower the inflation rate, the greater the increase in the real money supply and the larger the rightward shift in the *LM* curve. However, as income levels increase and unemployment decreases, the economy will be moving upwards on a *PEP* curve. This upward movement *along* the *PEP* curve will tend to offset the *downward* shifts in the *PEP* curve (reflecting lower inflation expectations). At some point, such as point *E* in the lower panel of Figure 14.2, the *positive* inflation effects associated with higher income levels will outweigh the *negative* inflation effects from the declining inflation expectations, producing a *net increase* in the inflation rate. In the labour market, wage increases have begun to rise as the positive effects from a (large) decline in the unemployment rate outweigh the negative effects from a (small) decline in inflation expectations. Notice that at point *E* in Figure 14.2, the level of income has passed the equilibrium income level Y^*.

Given a rising inflation rate, the increases in output will become smaller and smaller. As the inflation rate rises towards 5 percent, the real increases in the money supply, and the associated rightward shifts in the *LM* curve, become progressively smaller and smaller. In addition, a rising inflation rate prompts people to increase their inflation expectations, shifting both the *IS* and *PEP* curves upwards, which further accelerates the increase in the inflation rate. In short, the inflation rate is rising at a faster and faster pace while the increases in output are becoming smaller and smaller. Once the inflation rate *exceeds* 5 percent, the real money supply will once again begin to decline and the *LM* curve will shift upwards to the left. At some point, such as point *F* in the lower panel of Figure 14.2, the *leftward* shift in the *LM* curve (because the real money supply is falling) will exceed the *rightward* shift in the *IS* curve (because inflation expectations are rising) and the level of income will begin to fall. As the inflation rate rises further and further above 5 percent, the decreases in the real money supply will become larger and larger, and the *LM* curve will shift to the left by greater and greater amounts. Income levels will continue to decrease as rising real interest rates reduce investment expenditures. The economy will accelerate back towards its equilibrium income level Y^*, with a moderating inflation rate.

Having traced through one complete output–inflation cycle for an anti-inflationary monetary policy under the assumption that inflation expectations adjust to the actual inflation rate in the previous period, we end our analysis of Figure 14.2 at this point. Assuming that the economy is stable in a dynamic sense, this cyclical adjustment path will continue to repeat itself as the economy "spirals" into its new equilibrium position, labelled as point Z in Figure 14.2.

If we compare the adaptive expectations adjustment path in Figure 14.2 with the adjustment path in Figure 14.1, two important points emerge. First, if inflation expectations are formed adaptively (that is, if they adjust each period), the recession that accompanies an anti-inflationary monetary policy is not as deep. Successive downward adjustments in inflation expectations repeatedly shift the *PEP* curve down, reinforcing the decline in inflation associated with rising unemployment rates. Much less unemployment is required to drive wage and price inflation down to a new lower rate (say 5 percent). Similarly, under the assumption of adaptive inflation expectations, increases in interest rates are not as large, because declining inflation expectations shift the *IS* curve downward.

Second, although the economy does not undergo as deep a recession following the implementation of an anti-inflationary monetary policy under the assumption of adaptive inflation expectations, the adjustment path will *overshoot* its equilibrium position and *oscillate* around the natural rate Y^*. Instead of the rather simple parallelogram path analyzed in Figure 14.1, the adjustment path for an adaptive inflation expectations model consists of a rather complicated set of dynamic inward spirals. The assumption of adaptive inflation expectations reduces the magnitude of the recession from an anti-inflationary monetary policy, but creates a recurring business cycle as the economic system oscillates around its equilibrium position.

Rational Expectations

As discussed in Chapter 8, the rational expectations model assumes that people efficiently use all available information to make the best possible forecast of the inflation rate. A "rational" forecaster would look not only at past inflation rates (the adaptive expectations model), but would use all relevant information to come up with the best possible forecast of the inflation rate.

Rational expectations do not imply that people always make correct forecasts. Even though people will make forecast errors, rational expectations imply that there will be no systematic pattern to forecast errors. In the adaptive expectations inflation path described in Figure 14.2, from point *A* to point *E* people continually *over*predict the inflation rate (for example, at point *B* the expected inflation rate is 10 percent and the actual inflation rate is $\dot{P}_1 < 10$ percent). However, if people use all available information, they will be aware of their past forecast errors. Self-interest dictates that any tendency to overpredict the inflation rate will be corrected. The rational expectations model assumes that people, acting in their own best interests, extract all of the systematic information out of past forecast errors; future forecast errors are random or unpredictable.

Part of the information available to people for forecasting purposes is the structure of the economy. John Muth, the father of rational expectations, suggested that people will use their knowledge of economics to forecast economic variables. In Muth's words: "I would like to suggest that expectations, since they are informed predictions of future events, are essentially the same as the predictions of the relevant economic theory . . . we shall call such expectations 'rational'."[7] Rational expectations imply that people base their expectations of the inflation rate on the predictions of economic theory.

Returning to Figure 14.1, the equilibrium inflation rate in our model is determined by the growth rate of the nominal money supply. If the government lowers the growth rate of the nominal money supply from 10 percent per annum to 5 percent, the equilibrium inflation rate will decline from 10 percent to 5 percent. The rational expectations model assumes that people immediately revise their inflation expectations to the new equilibrium inflation rate and base their economic decisions on this new 5 percent equilibrium inflation rate. Why should rational firms and workers sign wage contracts based on a disequilibrium inflation rate (higher than 5 percent) that guarantees that the economy will be thrown into a recession (such as points *B* and *C* in Figure 14.1)?

If firms and workers immediately lower their inflation expectations to the new equilibrium inflation rate of 5 percent, then the *PEP* curve will immediately shift down to the lower $PEP_L(\dot{P}^e$ = 5 percent) position in Figure 14.1 and the actual inflation rate will drop to 5 percent (equal to the new 5 percent increase in the nominal money supply, thereby preventing the *LM* curve from shifting back to the left). The economy moves directly from point *A* to point *D* without having to endure a recession with output levels less than Y^* and unemployment rates higher than U^* (such as points *B* and *C* in Figure 14.1).[8] New classical, rational expectations macroeconomics predicts that lowering the inflation rate is costless to society.

There are two key assumptions implicit in this "costless" rational expectations adjustment path to a lower inflation rate: (1) the assumption of completely flexible wages and (2) the assumption of a "credible" government policy.

To illustrate the importance of these two key assumptions, suppose that an economy has had an annual inflation rate of 10 percent for several years. People have come to expect 10 percent inflation each year, and the government validates this 10 percent inflation each year with a 10 percent increase in the nominal money supply. The economy is sitting at point *A* on the $PEP(\dot{P}^e = 10$ percent) curve in Figure 14.3. On

---

[7] J. Muth, "Rational Expectations and the Theory of Price Movements," *Econometrica*, July 1961, p. 316.

[8] As discussed in Chapter 8, in a rational expectations, new classical macroeconomic model, an expected change in monetary policy will have no effects on output or employment levels.

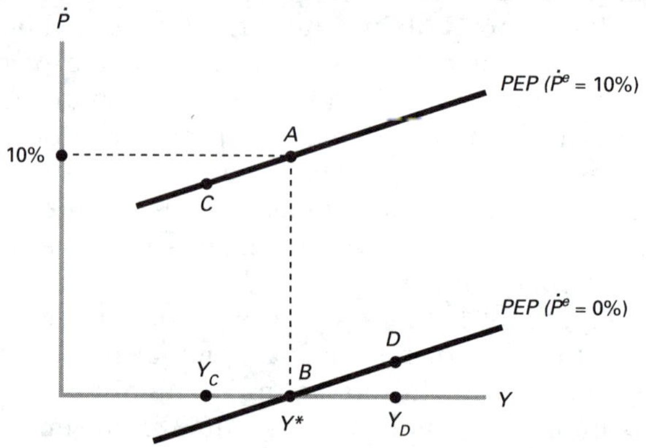

Figure 14.3 Lowering the inflation rate

New Year's eve, the prime minister goes on national TV to announce a new "zero inflation" monetary policy. Starting on January 1 the government will no longer increase the money supply by 10 percent each year; the money supply will be held constant. With a 0 percent increase in the nominal money supply, the new equilibrium inflation rate will be 0 percent. Thus, people can now revise their inflation expectations down from 10 percent to 0 percent. If firms and workers will reduce wage (and price) increases by 10 percent, the government's new "zero inflation" monetary policy will work, without raising the unemployment rate. The economy will move directly from point *A* to point *B* in Figure 14.3, with no short-run decrease in output. The prime minister urges workers to lower their inflation expectations and wage demands by 10 percent, promising a happy "inflation-free" new year.

For the prime minister's new "zero inflation" monetary policy to work, two conditions must be met: (1) wages must be flexible on January 1 and (2) the prime minister and his monetary policy announcement must be "credible."

Wage Flexibility and the Existence of Wage Contracts

If all wage contracts expire on December 31, then firms and workers would at least be in a position on January 1 to reduce the rate of wage increases by 10 percent, which would allow price increases to fall from 10 percent to 0 percent. However, Canadian union wage contracts are typically two to three years long. Most existing wage contracts will not expire for another year (or two) and workers will continue to receive double-digit annual wage increases contained in existing long-term contracts signed prior to December 31 (based on the assumption of a 10 percent expected inflation rate). Given second- and third-year inflationary wage increases contained in existing long-term contracts, price inflation will continue to run at around 10 percent.

Thus, when the government lowers the growth rate of the nominal money supply from 10 percent to 0 percent on January 1, continuing price inflation will decrease the real value of the money supply and shift the *LM* curve back to the left, causing interest rates to rise, investment and output to decline, and unemployment to increase. In terms of Figure 14.3, the economy moves from point *A* to point *C*, with output Y_C less than Y^*. Contractual wage rigidities prevent the economy from moving directly from point *A* to point *B*. For a short-run period of time (at least until all wage contracts expire), the economy will be pushed into a recession with inflation still close to 10 percent. To achieve a zero inflation rate without going through a recession, wages must be completely flexible.

The Credibility of the Government

Suppose that all wage contracts *do* expire on December 31. Will wage increases decline by 10 percent on January 1? For the government's new "zero inflation" monetary policy to work, people must believe that the government will do what it says it is going to do (namely, hold the nominal money supply constant), and the government must actually do what it says it is going to do. To have any hope of success, the government must convince people that it has changed its policy: it is now going to fight inflation, rather than cause (validate) inflation by increasing the money supply each year. Then, the government must actually carry out this new restrictive monetary policy, and not revert to its old expansionary ways. The announcement of a new "zero inflation" monetary policy must be credible.

Unfortunately, the public may not believe that the government will actually implement its new policy. Without wishing to belabour the point, governments and prime ministers have been known to "flip-flop" on policy issues; to say one thing and then do the opposite (see, for example, the implementation of wage and price controls in 1975, discussed below).

In fact, there may be short-run economic benefits if the government does *not* implement its new policy. To illustrate, suppose that the government convinces everyone to lower their inflation expectations from 10 percent to 0 percent and to settle for 10 percent lower wage increases. Once firms and workers have committed themselves to lower wage increases, the *PEP* curve will shift down to $PEP(\dot{P}^e = 0 \text{ percent})$ in Figure 14.3. Given this new lower *PEP* curve (which will last for the length of the new wage contract), there may be a strong temptation for the government *not* to implement its new constant money supply policy. By continuing its old policy of increasing the nominal money supply when the inflation rate is near zero (on the new lower *PEP* curve), the government can move the economy up the relatively flat short-run $PEP(\dot{P}^e = 0$ percent) curve to a higher output level, say point *D*. With an increase in the real money supply (a rightward shift in the *LM* curve), interest rates and unemployment rates will decrease. The government simultaneously produces an economic boom and a much lower inflation rate (compared to 10 percent at point *A*). Having convinced people that it is going to change its monetary policy, there are substantial short-run benefits if the government does *not* implement its new policy. In fact, the government could continue with its old expansionary monetary policy and claim that its new policy (which it did not implement) is working; inflation has fallen from 10 percent to almost 0 percent.

If people think that the government might succumb to this temptation and not implement its new monetary policy, they will be unwilling to lower wage settlements. If the government keeps increasing the money supply by 10 percent each year, the equilibrium inflation rate remains at 10 percent (point *A* in Figure 14.3).

The "catch-22" of an anti-inflation monetary policy is getting people to lower their inflation expectations and to accept lower nominal wage increases *in anticipation of the new policy working*. Governments that have caused or validated inflation in the past may have great difficulty convincing people that they have changed their ways and that their new policies will work (unlike their old policies). People may not believe that the government will change its policy and that the inflation rate will actually fall. People may want to see the inflation rate actually decline before they are willing to commit themselves to lower wage increases in long-term contracts. If the government has a credibility problem, rational workers and firms may negotiate wage contracts *as if* they formed their inflation expectations adaptively; they may base next year's wage increase on this year's inflation rate (see Figure 14.2).

If the new anti-inflationary monetary policy is not "credible," workers and firms will not lower their inflation expectations (the *PEP* curve will not shift down), and wage and price increases will continue at their existing inflationary rates. Under such circumstances, if the government implements its new anti-inflationary monetary policy, the real money supply will decrease, the *LM* curve will shift to the left, interest rates will rise, output will fall, unemployment will increase, and the inflation rate will still remain close to 10 percent. The implementation of the new anti-inflationary monetary policy will throw the economy into a serious recession (as analyzed in Figures 14.1 and 14.2). Given the recession costs of implementing its new policy (because the government was unable to convince people to lower their inflation expectations and accept lower wage increases in anticipation of the new policy working), the government may decide *not* to implement its new anti-inflationary monetary policy and continue with its old expansionary monetary policy, creating even further "credibility" problems for itself in the future.

Temporary Wage and Price Controls

Rather than waiting for workers and firms to revise their inflation expectations downwards and settle for lower wage and price increases, the government could impose *temporary* wage and price controls to expedite its anti-inflationary monetary policy. The government could directly intervene within the economy to control the size of wage and price increases, and thereby force the inflation rate down to a new lower rate. Under such a policy it would be illegal to raise wages and prices by an amount that exceeded the government's prescribed legal norm or guideline. Anyone who violated the legal norm would be prosecuted and "excessive" wage and price increases would be "rolled back" by the government.

The rate of inflation would be lowered initially by a legal instrument (controls) rather than by using the blunt economic instrument of a recession engineered by a restrictive monetary policy. By lowering the inflation rate quickly, the government may be better able to overcome any credibility problems it may have, thus speeding up the lowering of inflation expectations. Once inflation expectations have been brought down to the new lower target inflation rate (validated by a new lower growth rate of the money supply), wage and price controls can be removed. The sole purpose of a *temporary* wage and price controls policy is to ease the economy down to a new lower inflation rate without the costs of a painful recession.

To illustrate the theoretical case for imposing *temporary* wage and price controls along with a restrictive monetary policy, we assume that the economy is initially in long-run equilibrium (at Y^*) with a validated and expected inflation rate of 10 percent (point *A* in Figure 14.4). Suppose that the government decides to lower the inflation rate from 10 percent to 5 percent, and therefore restricts the growth rate of the nominal money supply to 5 percent. In addition to a restrictive monetary policy, the government also imposes *temporary* wage and price controls to immediately limit the inflation rate to 5 percent.

In our previous analysis of an anti-inflationary monetary policy (in Figures 14.1 and 14.2), it took a considerable length of time for the inflation rate to fall to 5 percent. However, given the imposition of wage and price controls, the inflation rate will fall to 5 percent immediately. The *PEP* curve ($\dot{P}^e$ = 10 percent) will now be *kinked* at point *B* in Figure 14.4. Wage and price controls have *no* effect if the inflation rate is *below* 5 percent and the original *PEP* curve ($\dot{P}^e$ = 10 percent) remains valid for all output levels *below* Y_B. But inflation rates *above* 5 percent

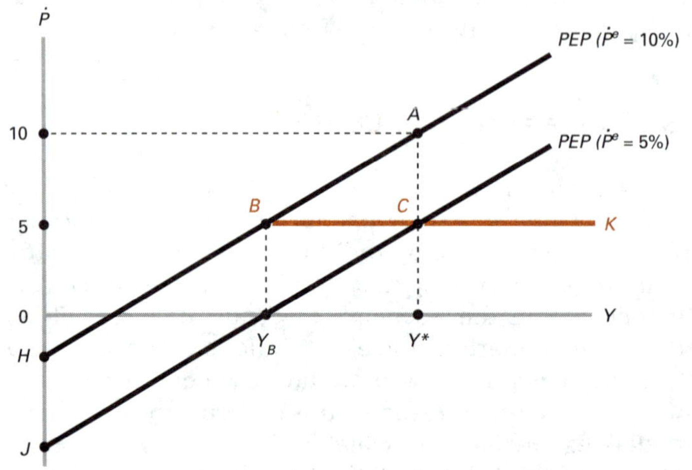

Figure 14.4 Temporary wage and price controls

(associated with output levels greater than Y_B) are now *illegal* under the new controls program. The original *PEP* curve ($\dot{P}^e$ = 10 percent) rotates downwards at point *B* to a *horizontal* line as the government has imposed a 5 percent ceiling on the inflation rate. The new *controlled PEP* curve ($\dot{P}^e$ = 10 percent) is represented in Figure 14.4 by the *kinked* line *HBK*.

With wage and price controls effectively limiting the inflation rate to 5 percent, the economy will move directly from point *A* to point *C* in Figure 14.4. Since the nominal money supply has been restricted to a 5 percent growth rate (equal to the 5 percent legal ceiling on the inflation rate), the real money supply will be constant, the *LM* curve will be stationary, and output levels will remain at Y^*. The economy has at least temporarily achieved a new lower 5 percent inflation rate without a recession.

However the economy is not yet in long-run equilibrium. Even though the new *legally enforced* 5 percent inflation rate is validated by a 5 percent growth rate in the nominal money supply, inflation expectations remain at 10 percent. To achieve a permanently lower inflation rate, wage and price controls must remain in force until people lower their inflation expectations to 5 percent. Once inflation expectations have been reduced to 5 percent, the *PEP* curve shifts down to *PEP* ($\dot{P}^e$ = 5 percent) and the *kink* in the *controlled PEP* curve (*JCK*) now appears at point *C*. Again wage and price controls prevent inflation rates from *exceeding* the 5 percent legal ceiling, but have no effect on inflation rates *below* 5 percent. With inflation expectations now lowered to 5 percent, point *C* represents the long-run equilibrium position for the economy. The 5 percent inflation rate is fully expected and validated; the economy is at the natural rate of output Y^*.[9]

Once inflation expectations have been lowered to 5 percent, wage and price controls are no longer required. Given the lower *PEP* curve ($\dot{P}^e$ = 5 percent), the inflation rate will be 5 percent at Y^* *without the need for legal controls*. Wage and price controls are required only until inflation expectations have been lowered to 5 percent. If wage and price controls are removed before inflation expectations are lowered, then the economy would revert to its original 10 percent inflation rate (point *A* in Figure 14.4) and would have to rely on the recession generated by the restrictive monetary policy to bring the inflation rate down to 5 percent. The success of a *temporary* wage and price control program depends crucially on inflation expectations falling to the new lower inflation rate (which monetary policy is now validating).

It is important to point out that the imposition of *temporary* wage and price controls does not remove the necessity for monetary restraint. If the government chooses to impose wage and price controls along with an expansionary monetary policy (as U.S. President Richard Nixon did in 1971–73), controls will not work. An expansionary monetary policy would generate pent-up aggregate demand during the controls period, which in turn would create a price explosion as soon as controls were lifted. To be effective, wage and price controls must (1) be accompanied by a reduction in nominal aggregate demand (monetary restraint) and (2) lower both wages and prices by the same degree (to preserve the equilibrium real wage rate). If wage and price controls are accompanied by monetary restraint and if there is no erosion in the real wage rate during the controls period, there is no reason for a wage–price explosion when controls are removed.

Temporary wage and price controls, implemented in conjunction with a reduction in the growth rate of the money supply, represent a potential policy instrument that might be used to ease the economy down to a lower long-run inflation rate. The sole purpose of *temporary* wage and price controls is to lessen the "short-term pain" associated with lowering the inflation rate. The economic benefits of *temporary* wage and price controls are measured in real opportunity cost terms: less unemployment, fewer bankruptcies, lower interest rates, and more output during the adjustment period as the economy gears down to a new

9 There is one additional complication. When inflation expectations are lowered to 5 percent, the *IS* curve will also shift downwards (see Figure 14.1), which will produce an output level below Y^* and an inflation rate below 5 percent (a mini-recession). Given a 5 percent increase in the nominal money supply, the real money supply will increase, the *LM* curve will shift downwards to the right and the economy will return to Y^* with a 5 percent inflation rate.

lower inflation rate. Wage and price controls do not remove the necessity for monetary restraint, nor do they lower the long-run inflation rate. At best, wage and price controls alleviate some of the economic hardship associated with an anti-inflationary monetary policy. Temporary wage and price controls are best thought of as a "recession analgesic," not as an "inflation cure."

In one of the most dramatic and breathtaking policy reversals of all time, in 1975 Prime Minister Trudeau imposed a three-year program of wage and price controls. During the 1974 federal election campaign, he had vigorously campaigned against the Progressive Conservatives' key election promise to bring in wage and price controls. On 25 May 1974 Prime Minister Trudeau is reported to have said that controls are "a proven disaster looking for a new place to happen." But on 13 October 1975 he went on national television to announce that wage and price controls "will take effect at midnight tonight," but failed to add his famous 1974 election campaign one-liner: "Zap, you're frozen!" Case Study 9 provides a postmortem on this three-year controls program, Canada's first peacetime attempt to legally control wage and price increases. As we shall see, what may be good in theory does not always work out well in practice.

Whether a government should use temporary wage and price controls is a highly controversial issue. Citizens generally favour wage and price controls and economists oppose them.[10] Much of economists' opposition to wage and price controls stems from their belief in the free market system. In general, economists are opposed to any attempt by government to legislate or regulate a price for a market commodity, be it minimum wages, rent controls, or oil prices. Not only do price controls involve substantial administrative costs, government controlled prices tend to quickly part company with "free market" prices, leading to shortages and resource misallocation problems. When the Canadian government introduced wage and price controls in 1975, most economists opposed the policy. The front-page headline in the 3 December 1975 issue of *The Globe and Mail* proclaimed "17 economists say controls won't work." Leading the charge against wage and price controls was Richard Lipsey, perhaps Canada's most influential economist. We quote from Lipsey's 1976 address to the Canadian Economics Association.

> The themes of this paper are that both theoretical reasoning and historical experience teach three important lessons concerning

---

10 The 6 December 1980 issue of *The Toronto Star* reported the results of a Canadian Gallup poll that found that 51 percent of those polled were in favour of the imposition of wage and price controls by the federal government (34 percent were opposed and 15 percent did not know). In a 1979 survey of American economists, 72 percent were generally opposed to wage and price controls and only 6 percent were generally in favour of such controls (see J.R. Kearl et al., "A Confusion of Economists," *American Economic Review, Papers and Proceedings*, May 1979).

> wage–price controls. First, the benefits they yield are entirely of a temporary nature; and even these benefits are almost negligibly small. Second, the policy of attempting to contain inflation by wage–price controls is unlikely, when it has been tried once, to be confined to situations of extraordinary economic crises. It is more likely to be resorted to frequently, increasing in its degree of severity with each subsequent application, until it threatens to become a permanent and serious feature of the economy. Third, the indirect and long-term effects of wage–price controls are almost totally on the cost rather than on the benefit side. The effects on the economy are almost always harmful, and the political consequences on the organization of society are potentially disastrous. This leads me to the general conclusion that wage–price controls should be opposed under virtually all peacetime circumstances since they produce at best small and transitory short-term benefits in return for large and persistent long-run costs. . . . The obvious costs are the administrative costs, and they are borne both by the public and private sectors. The less obvious costs concern the distortions that are introduced into the economy by any centrally administered set of prices and wages. These costs, of course, get larger the longer the controls are in place . . . I say, therefore, that *now* is the time to stand up and be counted. Now is the time to say loudly and clearly that wage–price controls are ineffective in their main objective and extremely harmful in all of their other effects. Now is the time to do everything that we can to influence public opinion. In doing this economists will be fighting for the integrity of their own subject, since economic analysis clearly shows that the price level cannot be permanently determined by legislation.[11]

However, during the late 1970s and early 1980s many macroeconomists became much more willing to consider the use of temporary wage–price controls to ease the painful adjustment down to a lower inflation rate. Double-digit inflation expectations seemed to be very firmly entrenched during the 1974–82 period, and the 1982 recessionary effects of an anti-inflation restrictive monetary policy were all too obvious (see below).

Perhaps the most surprising convert to the use of controls was Richard Lipsey. In 1979 Lipsey conceded to a group of Australian economists that "wage and price controls might be used to force the rate of inflation down" and that if he were prime minister he would "cut the rate of monetary expansion to 3–5 percent within months; slap on a six months wage–price freeze . . . and wear a bulletproof vest every time I showed myself in public."[12] Five years after rousing Canadian economists to

---

[11] R.G. Lipsey, "Wage–Price Controls: How to do a lot of harm by trying to do a little good," *Canadian Public Policy — Analyse de Politiques*, Winter 1977, pp. 1–13.

[12] R.G. Lipsey, "World Inflation," *The Economic Record*, December 1979, p. 295.

"stand up and be counted" against wage and price controls, in his 1981 presidential address to the Canadian Economics Association, Lipsey (sans vest) outlined a six-point anti-inflation program that included wage–price controls.[13]

Even conservative monetarist economists concede that controls can have a role to play in complementing monetary restraint. As the following 1977 quotation from Tom Courchene, one of Canada's leading monetarists, makes clear, wage and price controls can reduce the "real cost of defusing inflationary expectations":

> In order for economic agents to be willing to revise their expectations downward, they must first and foremost be convinced that the Bank of Canada intends to stand firm in its commitment to a gradual reduction in the rate of money supply growth and, hence, to an unwinding of inflation. . . . It is precisely in this context that controls acquire an economic rationale, and probably their only rationale. Controls in themselves, will not provide a lasting solution to the inflation problem. . . . However, they can have a role to play in complementing monetary restraint in order to minimize the real (employment and output) cost of defusing inflationary expectations.[14]

Both Richard Lipsey, a Keynesian, and Tom Courchene, a monetarist, concede that wage–price controls coupled with monetary restraint can reduce the short-run unemployment costs associated with lowering the long-run inflation rate. Both economists would undoubtedly point out that wage–price controls entail substantial administrative costs and the potential for resource misallocation problems, which must be balanced against the potential benefits of controls (less unemployment while the economy is gearing down to a lower inflation rate).

Case Study 9: Canadian Wage and Price Controls, 1975–78

In October 1975 the Canadian government created the Anti-Inflation Board (AIB) to administer wage and price controls. AIB "guidelines for responsible social behaviour" established ceilings for wage increases consisting of the sum of the following three elements:

1. a basic protection factor of 8 percent in the first program year, 6 percent in the second year, and 4 percent in the third year;

---

13 R.G. Lipsey, "The Understanding and Control of Inflation: Is there a crisis in macroeconomics?" *Canadian Journal of Economics*, November 1981.

14 T.J. Courchene, *The Strategy of Gradualism: An Analysis of Bank of Canada Policy from Mid-1975 to Mid-1977* (Montreal: C.D. Howe Research Institute, 1977), p. 65.

2. a national productivity factor of 2 percent per year; and
3. an experience adjustment factor that varied between plus and minus 2 percent per year depending on a group's experience relative to the rise in the CPI over the past two or three years.

All Canadians were expected to comply with these wage compensation guidelines; major employer/employee groups[15] were legally bound by these guidelines and had to submit to the AIB details of their wage settlements.

With respect to AIB price and profit margin guidelines, "the general principle is that increases in prices should be limited to amounts no more than required to cover net increases in costs."[16] Profit margins were to be controlled. Over the life of the AIB, there were 882 cases in which firms were found to have increased their profit margins; in each case, the firm was forced to divest itself of "excess revenues" by lowering prices or giving customers refunds. If wage increases could be brought down to more reasonable amounts and if firms were prevented from increasing profit margins,[17] then price inflation would be restrained.

The restraint of wage increases was crucial to the success of the AIB. If the AIB had no effect on lowering wage increases, then it would be impossible for the AIB to have any effect on reducing the rate of price inflation. Before examining the quantitative effect of the AIB on wage increases, a brief review of AIB procedures is useful. First, workers and the firm had to agree on a proposed wage contract, which was then submitted to the AIB for approval. Table 14.1 indicates the number of employees for whom wage compensation plans were submitted to the AIB in each program year. Contracts that provided wage increases at or below AIB guidelines required no formal AIB decision. Approximately two-thirds of all employees signed wage contracts that did not exceed the government's guidelines.

Turning to the minority of cases that required an AIB decision (cases where wage increases exceeded the guidelines), the AIB would typically recommend a wage "rollback." If the firm and union refused to amend their wage contract to reflect the AIB rollback, the matter was referred to the government Administrator who had full legal powers to *enforce* a wage rollback.

The AIB and the Administrator (the "enforcer") adopted a "soft cop–

---

15 The groups included firms with more than 500 employees, firms in the construction industry with 20 or more employees, firms thought to be of strategic importance, professionals, and all government employees.

16 Canada, *Attack of Inflation: A Program of National Action*, Policy statement tabled in the House of Commons by the Honourable Donald S. Macdonald, Minister of Finance, 14 October 1975, p. 16.

17 The AIB also monitored firms to make sure that firms did not increase discretionary expenditures, such as landscaping or advertising.

Table 14.1 Compensation Increases Submitted to the AIB and AIB Decisions

	Program Year 1 October 14/75 to October 13/76	Program Year 2 October 14/76 to October 13/77	Program Year 3 October 14/77 to October 13/78
Total number of employees submitting plans	3,256,604	3,983,999	1,682,790
Percentage of employees for whom compensation increases were at or below guidelines	59.1	69.6	65.7
Number of employees for whom AIB decisions were taken	1,463,929	1,343,398	538,080
AIB Decisions:			
i) Average % increase submitted	12.1	8.6	6.3
ii) Average % arithmetic guideline	9.1	7.1	5.5
iii) Average % increase allowed	10.1	7.5	5.7
iv) Average % rollback recommended	2.0	1.1	0.6
Estimate of average size of AIB recommended rollback in terms of all employees submitting compensation plans	0.8	0.3	0.2

Source: AIB *Third Year Report*, pp. 8–9.

tough cop" stance. The AIB was often prepared to be somewhat lenient in interpreting the guidelines whereas the Administrator enforced the letter of the law. In many instances the Administrator rolled back wage increases even further than the AIB. For example, the Cyprus Anvil Mining Company signed a two-year contract calling for wage increases of 36.5 percent in the first year and 10.4 percent in the second year. When the AIB recommended rollbacks that reduced the wage increases to 14 percent and 10 percent, the United Steelworkers union appealed the AIB decision to the Administrator, who promptly *enforced* a settlement of 8 percent plus 10 percent. It quickly became apparent that any appeal to the Administrator ran the risk that the "tough cop enforcer" would impose a wage rollback even more severe than the "soft cop" AIB. As of September 1978, only 277 wage compensation plans were referred to the Administrator, representing only 1 percent of all AIB decisions.

Table 14.1 also provides information on the average size of wage increases submitted to the AIB, the average wage guideline, the average wage increase allowed by the AIB, and the average size of the AIB wage rollback for each program year. Perhaps the most surprising feature of Table 14.1 is the modest size of the average AIB wage rollbacks (2 percent in the first program year). Most wage increases submitted to the AIB were relatively close to the guidelines. If the average AIB wage rollback is weighted with the majority of cases which did not involve an AIB wage rollback, an estimate for the average size of the wage rollback in terms of *all* employees submitting wage compensation plans to the AIB can be obtained. As shown in the bottom line of Table 14.1, the average size of the wage rollback in terms of *all* employees was very small, totalling only 1.3 percent over the life of the entire controls program. This is not meant to imply that particular groups of workers may not have suffered very large wage rollbacks (recall the Cyprus Anvil Mining Company workers), but rather suggests that in aggregate the *direct* effect of controls on wage increases was not very large.

Even though *direct* wage rollbacks were the most visible aspect of the controls program, a less obvious and more important *indirect* effect on wage increases may have occurred. The existence of legal wage guidelines and the presence of the AIB and Administrator may have altered the size of negotiated wage increases *before* they were submitted to the AIB for formal approval. Given the threat of a legal wage rollback, firms and unions may have lowered wage increases to the guidelines, much the same way that radar traps and the threat of a speeding ticket slow down the traffic flow along a highway. The possibility of being caught by the AIB for breaking the law may have caused a change in wage behaviour, a slowdown in wage increases along the inflation highway. If such a change in wage behaviour did occur, the actual size of the AIB rollbacks would give a very misleading indication of the "controls-induced" reduction in wage increases. The success, or failure, of an anti-speeding highway patrol program is *not* measured by the number of speeding tickets issued but rather by the average speed of traffic (compared with what it would have been in the absence of an anti-speeding program).

Although the *direct* rollback effects can be easily tabulated, an entirely different methodology must be used to quantify the *indirect* wage effects attributable to the presence of controls. To measure this indirect effect, one has to forecast what wage increases *would have been in the absence of controls* (in terms of our highway illustration, one has to forecast the average speed of traffic in the absence of radar traps). Having obtained a *hypothetical* forecast for the size of wage increases in the absence of controls, one can then compare the *actual* size of wage increases to these *hypothetical "no controls"* forecast values. The difference between the *actual* wage increase and the *hypothetical* forecast value provides a measure of the *indirect* effect of controls on wage behaviour.

A number of empirical studies have examined the size of the *indirect* controls effect on wage increases.[18] All of these studies conclude that controls exerted a significant effect on wages; wage increases were approximately 3 percent per annum below the level that likely would have prevailed in the absence of controls. Given the existence of long-term contracts, however, the effect of controls on aggregate wage increases accumulated very slowly, as many workers were locked into (inflationary) pre-controls wage contracts for much of the early life of the AIB. On the basis of the existing bargaining cycle, Christofides and Wilton estimated that

> the cumulative impact of the AIB on private sector wage rates was only about 0.8 percent after one year and 3.2 percent after two years, but rose quite dramatically to 6.1 percent after three years and 7.2 percent after four years. . . . In short, the existence of the AIB and the Administrator appears to have substantially moderated wage inflation over levels which might have prevailed assuming that the wage structure in the decade prior to the imposition of the AIB would have continued to exist throughout the remainder of the 1970s.[19]

The moderating effects of controls on Canadian wage settlements are obvious when one reviews the pattern of wage increases during the 1970s. In Figure 14.5 we have plotted the average annual wage increase in new union wage contracts (without COLA clauses) signed each year. For comparison purposes, we have also plotted the annual percentage change in the consumer price index (CPI). There is a clear deceleration in the rate of wage inflation during the controls period (see the shaded area in Figure 14.5). As the Department of Finance noted in 1978,

> During the controls period both money supply growth and real growth declined, and the unemployment rate rose. These factors would have exerted some downward pressure on wage and salary increases even in the absence of controls. Inflationary expectations may also have been declining prior to the imposition of controls. However . . . these forces by themselves would not have been adequate to reduce the rate of increase of base wage rates

---

18 See, for example, L.N. Christofides and D.A. Wilton, *Wage Controls in Canada (1975:3–1978:2): A Study of Their Impact on Negotiated Base Wage Rates* (Ottawa: Anti-Inflation Board, 1979); F. Reid, "The Effect of Controls on the Rate of Wage Changes in Canada," *Canadian Journal of Economics*, May 1979, pp. 214–27; and P. Fortin and K. Newton, "Labour Market Tightness and Wage Inflation in Canada," in M.N. Baily, ed., *Workers, Jobs and Inflation* (Washington: The Brookings Institution, 1982).

19 Christofides and Wilton, *Wage Controls*, pp. 88–89.

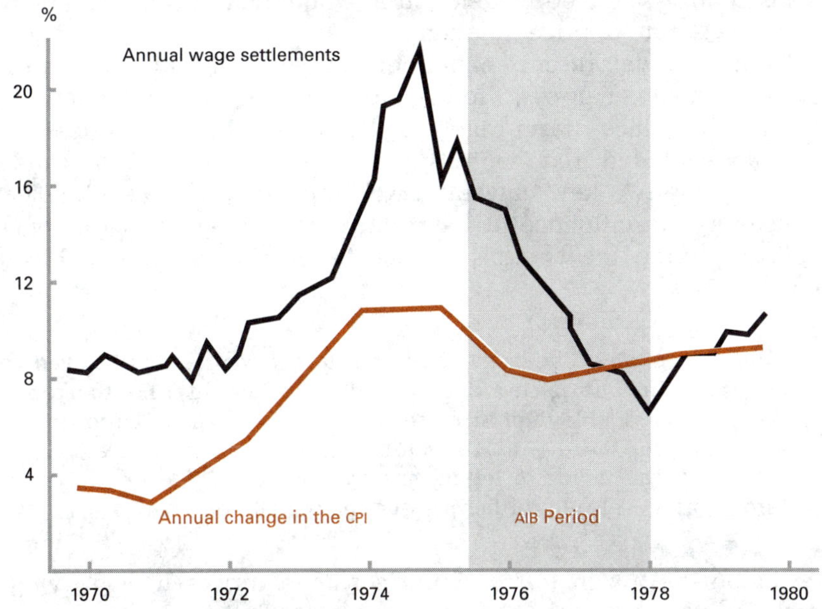

Figure 14.5 Wage and price inflation in the 1970s

from over 20 percent in 1975 to a little over 12 percent in 1976 and to 8 percent in 1977.[20]

In summary, all empirical evidence points to the fact that controls exerted a moderating influence on the rate of wage increases, with a total *cumulative* controls effect of 6 to 8 percent on wage rates. Despite predictions of a post-controls wage rebound effect (to recapture "lost" wage increases during controls), there were no obvious signs of such an effect. As shown in Figure 14.5, new wage settlements negotiated during the first two years after controls were terminated barely kept pace with the inflation rate, compared to very large *real* wage gains in the early 1970s. Not only was there no obvious sign of a post-controls wage rebound effect, post-controls wage settlements (measured in real terms) were extremely moderate in comparison to wage settlements in the pre-controls period.[21] Since there is no evidence that aggregate profit margins rose during the controls period (in fact, the ratio of profits to GDP fell slightly, from 0.117 in 1975 to 0.111 in 1978), one would surmise

20 *Canada's Recent Inflation Experience*, Department of Finance, Ottawa, November 1978, pp. 51–52.

21 See L.N. Christofides and D.A. Wilton, "Wage Determination in the Aftermath of Controls," *Economica*, February 1985.

that this controls-induced moderation in wage increases must have produced a lower rate of price inflation.

In Table 14.2 we present annual percentage changes for labour compensation, consumer prices, the GDP deflator, and the government's inflation targets. Since "farm gate" food prices and energy prices were specifically excluded from controls, we have also included CPI changes excluding these two key "uncontrolled" components. Table 14.2 clearly demonstrates the influence of food and energy price increases on the overall CPI during the controls period. As the Department of Finance noted,

> In the first program year, the 8-percent target was easily achieved because of an unexpected decline in food prices. In 1977 the re-emergence of double-digit increases in food prices was in large part responsible for the CPI growth rate's exceeding the target rate. In both years, the policy of letting energy prices continue to rise towards world levels put further pressure on the all-items CPI.[22]

If we judge the AIB in terms of the consumer prices it was trying to control, the CPI excluding food and energy, the inflation rate decreased from about 10 percent to 6 percent during the controls program. In terms of the more comprehensive GDP price deflator (which also in-

Table 14.2 Annual Percentage Changes in Inflation Indicators

	Labour Compensation*	Total CPI	CPI Excluding Food	CPI Excluding Food & Energy	GDP Deflator	AIP Targets
1971	7.5	2.9	3.4	n.a.	3.2	
1972	7.1	4.8	3.7	n.a.	5.6	
1973	10.1	7.6	5.1	n.a.	8.7	
1974	13.6	10.9	8.8	n.a.	14.7	
1975	14.1	10.8	10.1	9.6	9.9	
1976	12.7	7.5	9.4	8.8	8.6	8
1977	6.7	8.0	7.9	7.4	6.4	6
1978	5.4	8.9	6.4	6.1	5.8	4
1979	7.0	9.1	7.9	7.6	10.0	

* Labour compensation per person employed in all commercial non-agricultural industries.

Source: Department of Finance, *Economic Review.*

22 *Canada's Recent Inflation Experience*, p. 53.

cludes capital goods and public sector goods and services), a similar picture emerges.

Unfortunately uncontrolled food prices and the government's oil-price policy shocked the inflation rate by almost 3 percent. Given that most people form their inflation expectations in terms of the expected price increase for *all* goods and services they purchase (even the heartiest Canadian must "eat and heat"), the controls program had very little effect on lowering inflation expectations. Entering the 1980s, the actual and expected inflation rate remained stubbornly at about 10 percent (what it was in 1975). Since the *raison d'être* of controls was to lower actual *and* expected inflation, the AIB obviously failed to achieve its major objective. Even though the AIB may have won the battle on the wage front, it lost the war against price inflation.

Nevertheless, the AIB should not be deemed a total failure. Without wage and price controls in place, the food and energy price shocks would have pushed the Canadian CPI inflation rate to about 11 percent in 1978. With wage and price controls, the 1978 inflation rate was a little less than 9 percent, about 2 percent lower than what it would have been in the absence of controls. Furthermore, in the absence of any food and energy price shocks the AIB would likely have lowered the actual CPI inflation rate to about 5 percent.[23] Even though the AIB failed to achieve its inflation targets, it at least prevented any further acceleration of the inflation rate that would have occurred because of rising energy prices and double-digit food price increases. In the words of Wilson and Jump, "we could have done far worse" without the AIB.[24]

In conclusion, all empirical studies agree that wage controls significantly reduced the rate of wage inflation (by about 3 percent per annum). The major benefits of a *temporary* controls program are measured in real terms. Lower wage increases can be accomplished without having to endure a severe painful recession with high unemployment rates, high real interest rates, and a substantial loss in output. Assuming the slope of the Canadian Phillips curve is 0.8 (see Chapter 10), to accomplish the same degree of wage restraint achieved by the AIB *without controls* would have required unemployment rates of 10 to 11 percent. The economic benefits of imposing *temporary wage* and price controls translated into approximately 400,000 more jobs. Even though the AIB undoubtedly imposed some administrative and resource distortion costs on the Canadian economy, these costs likely fall far short of the substantial economic costs associated with a major recession engineered by the government to generate the same degree of wage restraint.

---

23 See D.A. Wilton, "An Evaluation of Wage and Price Controls in Canada," *Canadian Public Policy — Analyse de Politiques*, June 1984, pp. 167–76.

24 T.A. Wilson and G. Jump, *The Influence of the Anti-Inflation Program of Aggregate Wages and Prices* (Ottawa: Anti-Inflation Board, 1979).

Monetary Policy During the 1975–90 Period

Having spent most of the early 1970s stimulating the economy with an "excessively expansionary" monetary policy (see the end of Chapter 13), in mid-1975 the Bank of Canada abruptly switched to a more restrictive *monetarist* policy. The government's major objective was to lower the inflation rate and the centrepiece of this new policy was a reduction in the growth rate of the money supply. The Bank of Canada's conversion to a monetarist policy approach was announced by the Governor of the Bank of Canada in a Saskatoon speech, and was fully endorsed by leading monetarists.

> In thought and word, the Bank of Canada probably qualifies for the designation of the world's most monetarist bank. The Saskatoon manifesto and the 1975 Annual Report embody an articulation of the monetarist approach that is second to none. Even Milton Friedman has conceded as much. Referring to the Governor's Saskatoon speech, he asserted: "It is a marvellous speech. It is the best speech I have ever heard a central banker give . . . I could have written it myself." Hence, 1975 will go down in the annals of Canadian central banking as a most significant year — the year in which the Bank of Canada . . . embraced a monetarist philosophy.[25]

In his Saskatoon "manifesto," the Governor of the Bank of Canada clearly identified inflation as the number one priority of the government and a restrictive monetary policy as the major weapon in the battle against inflation:

> it is very much in the public interest that the drift into deepening inflation in Canada be halted and reversed. . . . whatever else may need to be done to bring inflation under control, it is absolutely essential to keep the rate of monetary expansion within reasonable limits. Any programme that did not include this policy would be doomed to failure. There is no way of preserving its value if money is created on an excessive scale.[26]

Coming from the Governor of the Bank of Canada who had allowed the Canadian money supply to increase by an average rate of 14 percent for the previous five years (1971 through 1975), this is indeed a remarkable admission that the Bank of Canada's previous monetary policies were "doomed to failure."

Although the government was firmly committed to lowering the infla-

---

[25] T.J. Courchene, *Monetarism and Controls: The Inflation Fighters* (Montreal: C.D. Howe Research Institute, 1976), p. 111.

[26] Reprinted in *Bank of Canada Review*, October 1975, pp. 23–24.

tion rate, the government thought that the best way to achieve a lower inflation rate was by *gradually* reducing the rate of monetary expansion and supplementing this restrictive monetary policy with wage and price controls. In the words of the Governor of the Bank of Canada,

> It is useful to supplement financial discipline by direct action to restrain increases in incomes and prices. . . . This approach can bring about the needed adjustment at less cost in terms of unemployment and lost output, with less serious inequities, than would result from the sole reliance on monetary and fiscal policies.[27]

Going "cold turkey" from a 14 percent annual increase in the money supply to a zero increase in the money supply was considered to be "too disruptive in economic and social terms to be sensible or tolerable."[28] By *gradually* reducing the rate of monetary expansion and imposing temporary wage and price controls, it was hoped that the inflation rate could be lowered to about 4 percent without Canadians having to endure a painful recession.

In an attempt to give its new policy greater credibility, the Bank of Canada announced annual target ranges for the growth rate of M1, the narrowest definition of money (see Chapter 15). As shown in Table 14.3, the Bank of Canada *gradually* lowered the M1 target ranges from 10–15 percent in 1975–76 to 4–8 percent in 1981. It should be noted, however, that the period over which the target was to be achieved did not begin on the announcement date but rather on the base date (the first column of Table 14.3), and that the base and announcement dates are *not* the

Table 14.3 Canada's Monetary Targets

Base Date*	Announcement Date	Target Range M1	Actual Growth in Year Following Base Date M1
May 1975	November 1975	10–15%	9.7%
March 1976	August 1976	8–12	6.9
June 1977	October 1977	7–11	9.0
June 1978	October 1978	6–10	9.0
May 1979	October 1979	5– 9	3.4
September 1980	January 1981	4– 8	–0.3

*The base money stock is calculated as a three-month average around the month indicated.

27 Bank of Canada, *Annual Report, 1975*, p.11.

28 *Ibid.*, p. 10.

same each year. The practice of selectively choosing base and announcement dates each year clearly made it easier for the Bank of Canada to achieve its "announced" targets (the Bank of Canada knew the actual change in M1 between the base date and the announcement date).

Nevertheless, the Bank of Canada was only 50 percent successful in achieving its M1 targets. The fourth column of Table 14.3 lists the actual growth rate of M1 during the 12 months following the base date. In the first, third, and fourth year the actual growth of M1 fell within the *target* range. In the second, fifth, and sixth year the growth rate of M1 fell below the target range. Having missed the target range (which was 4 percentage points wide) by a wide margin in 1981, the Bank of Canada abandoned the practice of announcing target ranges for monetary growth.

To assist our analysis of monetary policy during the 1975–90 period, Figure 14.6 presents annual data on the growth rate of the *nominal* money supply (M1), the growth rate of the real money supply (M1/CPI), the annual inflation rate (as measured by the consumer price index), and the prime interest rate charged by banks in both Canada and the United States.

As noted above, the primary objective of this new monetarist monetary policy was to reduce the double-digit inflation of 1975. Unfortunately, success on the inflation front did not occur for eight years! After a temporary dip in 1976, the inflation rate rose steadily, reaching a new peak of 12.4 percent in 1981. This escalation in inflation was largely due to supply-price shocks, which were beyond the control of the Bank of Canada. During the five years 1976–80, world commodity prices and world food prices increased by average annual rates of 17 and 19 percent, respectively. In addition, the Canadian government was *phasing in* world oil price increases and the price of gasoline jumped by 19 percent in 1980, 36 percent in 1981, and 21 percent in 1982. Nevertheless, after six years of a *gradualist* monetary policy (including wage and price controls during the 1975–78 period), the 1981 inflation rate was 1.5 percentage points higher than it had been in 1975 when the Bank of Canada converted to monetarism!

As early as 1980, the Governor of the Bank of Canada began to express doubts about the merits of a *gradualist* approach to lowering the growth rate of the money supply:

> The battle against inflation is never easy. It has not been easy over the past five years during which we have been pursuing monetary targets, and I confess that I am disappointed by the results to date. . . . In retrospect, given some of the largely unpredictable economic and financial developments that occurred over that period, it might have been better if the moderation of excessively rapid

growth since 1975 had been less gradual so that the moderating effect on inflation would have been greater.[29]

While the Governor of the Bank of Canada was publicly questioning the merits of his *gradualist* approach (perhaps a "less gradual" approach would have had a greater moderating effect on inflation), many critics questioned whether the Bank of Canada was really pursuing a monetarist policy. Why did the the money supply increase by 10.1 percent in 1978? Why was the money supply still growing by over 6 percent in 1979 and 1980 (see Figure 14.6(b))?

With inflation still running at more than 10 percent in the early 1980s, the Bank of Canada abandoned its *gradualist* approach. In 1981 the *nominal* M1 money supply increased by only 3.3 percent and in 1982 the *nominal* money supply actually decreased by 0.1 percent. In *real* terms, the money supply (M1/CPI) fell by 9.1 percent in 1981 and by 11 percent in 1982 (see Figure 14.6(b)). We note, in passing, that in 1981–82 the Trudeau government rejected the use of *temporary* wage and price controls, opting to fight inflation solely with a tight monetary policy.

Given these very substantial *real* reductions in the money supply, interest rates soared to unprecedented heights. The prime interest rate charged by banks to their best customers averaged 19.3 percent in 1981 and 15.8 percent in 1982, causing nonresidential investment expenditures to decrease by 5.1 percent in 1982 and by 7 percent in 1983. Five-year mortgage rates reached 18 percent in 1981–82 and new housing starts fell by 29.3 percent in 1982. This severe dose of monetary restraint plunged the economy into the worst recession in 35 years. Real GDP fell by 3.2 percent in 1982 and the unemployment rate rose from 7.5 percent in 1981 to 11 percent in 1982 and to 11.8 percent in 1983. With double-digit unemployment rates, the inflation rate fell to 5.7 percent in 1983 and to 4.4 percent in 1984, the lowest annual inflation rate in 13 years. Although a restrictive monetary policy will indeed lower the inflation rate, there is a considerable amount of short-term pain (unemployment and bankruptcies) to be endured along the way to a lower inflation rate.

It is important to put this very restrictive Canadian monetary policy of the early 1980s into an international perspective. Canadian monetary policy of the late 1970s and the first half of the 1980s was a mirror reflection of U.S. monetary policy. As shown in Figure 14.6(c), from 1978 to 1985 Canadian interest rates simply followed the course of U.S. interest rates. In the early 1980s the U.S. Federal Reserve Board implemented a very tight monetary policy, and the Bank of Canada followed suit.

29 Remarks by G.K. Bouey to The Empire Club of Canada, Toronto, 13 November 1980, reprinted in *Bank of Canada Review*, November 1980, pp. 3–11.

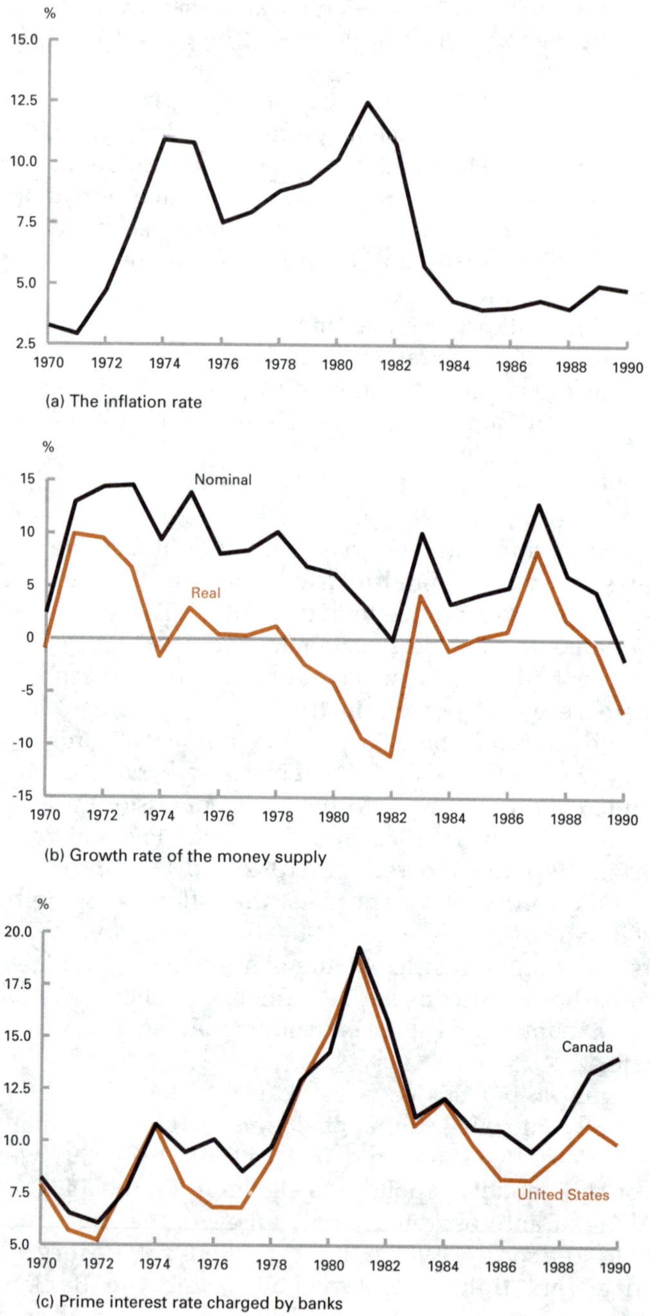

Figure 14.6 Inflation, the growth rate of the money supply, and interest rates, 1970–90

Did the Bank of Canada have to follow U.S. monetary policy in the early 1980s? What would have happened if the Bank of Canada had chosen a less restrictive monetary policy in 1981–82, in an attempt to keep Canadian interest rates below soaring U.S. interest rates? With relatively higher interest rates in the United States, capital would have flowed out of Canada to the United States, putting tremendous downward pressure on the value of the Canadian dollar in foreign exchange markets. A falling value for the Canadian dollar raises the price of imported goods and stimulates the demand for Canadian exports, which would lead to an even higher inflation rate in Canada. Since the government was desperately trying to lower double-digit inflation during this period, the Bank of Canada was very reluctant to let the value of the Canadian dollar fall on foreign exchange markets, with its accompanying inflationary pressures. To prevent the Canadian dollar from declining in value (given an increase in U.S. interest rates), the Bank of Canada had to reduce the real money supply and move Canadian interest rates up in tandem with U.S. interest rates. In effect, high U.S. interest rates were "exported" to Canada, as the Bank of Canada raised interest rates to prevent a decline in the value of the Canadian dollar (which would have triggered additional inflationary pressures).

The Bank of Canada continued to mirror U.S. monetary policy for the next several years. When U.S. interest rates continued to fall in 1983, the Bank of Canada substantially increased the nominal money supply (by 10.1 percent) to keep Canadian interest rates in line with falling U.S. interest rates. Faced with a post-Depression record high Canadian unemployment rate of 11.8 percent, the Bank of Canada chose *not* to maintain its monetarist policy. If the Canadian nominal money supply had remained constant in 1983 (not increased by 10.1 percent), Canadian interest rates would have risen substantially above U.S. interest rates, which would have caused the value of the Canadian dollar to appreciate on foreign exchange markets. An appreciating Canadian dollar depresses Canadian exports and encourages imports, which would have pushed the Canadian economy deeper into an already severe recession.

In 1984 the Bank of Canada reduced the rate of monetary expansion back down to 3.4 percent and rising U.S. interest rates were again "exported" to Canada. By stepping up the rate of monetary expansion in the 1985–87 period (to 12.9 percent in 1987), Canadian interest rates fell along with U.S. interest rates. However, a weakening value of the Canadian dollar in foreign exchange markets (the value of the Canadian dollar fell to $0.69 U.S. in February 1986) prevented the Bank of Canada from lowering Canadian interest rates to the same extent as U.S. interest rates (see Figure 14.6(c)). A positive differential between Canadian and U.S. interest rates was needed to attract foreign capital inflows and prevent the Canadian dollar from falling even further (which would have put upward pressure on the inflation rate).

Towards the end of the 1980s, the Bank of Canada began pursuing a more independent, and more monetarist, policy. The new Governor of the Bank of Canada, John Crow, seemed determined to achieve price stability. Canadian monetary policy was tightened up and the differential between Canadian and U.S. interest rates widened to over 4 percent in 1990 (see Figure 14.6(c)). As Canadian interest rates rose relative to U.S. interest rates, Canada became an attractive place for foreign investment and the value of the Canadian dollar rose (reaching $0.87 U.S. in 1990), which helped the Bank of Canada in its battle against inflation. In 1990 the Bank of Canada decreased the *nominal* money supply by 1.9 percent. With less money in the system, the prime interest rate charged by banks rose to over 14 percent in 1990 (4 percent higher than in the U.S.) and the Canadian economy was once again plunged into another recession. As of April 1991, real GDP had fallen for two successive quarters and the rising unemployment rate had reached 10.5 percent.

Both the 1981–82 recession and the 1990–91 recession were caused by a restrictive monetary policy. As Figure 14.6(b) reveals, in both cases the real money supply declined substantially and interest rates increased sharply. Although both recessions were engineered in Ottawa (one by a Liberal government and one by a Conservative government), only the 1990–91 recession was a truly made-in-Canada recession. Unlike the 1981–82 recession, in the 1990–91 recession Canadian interest rates were increased substantially above U.S. interest rates. Although U.S. interest rates fell by approximately one percentage point in 1990, the Bank of Canada continued to push Canadian interest rates upwards. The 1990 inflation rate of 5 percent must be eliminated.

On 26 February 1991 the Bank of Canada issued the following press release, entitled, *Targets for reducing inflation:*

> The Governor of the Bank of Canada, John W. Crow, in a joint announcement today with the Minister of Finance, set out targets for reducing inflation and reaching price stability in Canada.
>
> These targets are designed to provide a clear indication of the downward path for inflation over the medium term. The path provides for gradual but progressive reductions of inflation until price stability is reached. The range of public policies besides monetary policy can make a significant contribution. However, since inflation cannot persist over an extended period without monetary accommodation, for price stability to be reached it is essential for monetary policy to work firmly and consistently to that end.
>
> The specific targets for the year-over-year rate of increase in the consumer price index are as follows:
>
> - 3 percent by the end of 1992
> - 2 1/2 percent by the middle of 1994
> - 2 percent by the end of 1995

> Thereafter the objective would be further reductions in inflation until price stability is achieved . . .
>
> In view of the lags involved in the effect of policies on inflation, no explicit target has been set for inflation in 1991. However, this target path is consistent with a year-over-year increase in the CPI of about 5 percent (less than 4 percent excluding the impact of the GST) by the end of the year.
>
> In the actions it takes to implement these targets, the Bank will, for practical reasons, focus on the consumer price index excluding the volatile food and energy components, as published by Statistics Canada.[30]

Only time will tell whether the Bank of Canada is more successful in achieving its inflation targets in the 1990s than it was in achieving its targets of the 1970s and 1980s.

Summary

The economic costs of an anti-inflationary monetary policy are likely to be severe and prolonged. To reduce the double-digit inflation of the 1970s to 4–5 percent in the mid-1980s required a very severe recession in the early 1980s, with double-digit unemployment rates and record high interest rates. Given the substantial economic costs associated with an anti-inflationary monetary policy, a theoretical case can be made for combining a reduction in the growth rate of the money supply with *temporary* wage and price controls. The sole purpose of the controls program would be to alleviate some of the unemployment and high interest rate costs associated with an anti-inflationary monetary policy. Canada's experience with various anti-inflationary policies in the 1970s, 1980s, and 1990s suggests that eliminating inflation is easier said than done.

Review Questions

1. Carefully analyze the short-run adjustment costs of an anti-inflationary monetary policy (using an *IS-LM-PEP* diagram).
2. How would these adjustment costs be affected if people form their

[30] Reprinted in *Bank of Canada Review*, March 1991, pp. 5–6.

inflation expectations in an adaptive manner? Explain using an *IS-LM-PEP* diagram.

3. Distinguish between adaptive and rational expectations. How do rational expectations forecast errors differ from adaptive expectations forecast errors (as illustrated in your answer to Question 2)?
4. Suppose people form their inflation expectations in a rational manner. How would your answers to Questions 1 and 2 change? In what way does the credibility of the government affect your answer? Explain.
5. Are the benefits of a lower inflation rate worth the likely costs of an anti-inflationary monetary policy? Discuss.
6. What is the economic rationale for imposing temporary wage and price controls? Do you think that the potential benefits from imposing temporary wage and price controls outweigh the costs of controls? Explain.
7. Suppose that the government implements a tough three-year program of wage and price controls but fails to restrict the growth rate of the nominal money supply. What do you predict will happen? Explain using an *IS-LM-PEP* diagram.
8. Evaluate Canada's use of wage and price controls during the 1975–78 period.
9. Given U.S. monetary policy in the early 1980s, do you think that Canadian monetary policy was justified? Discuss.
10. Do you think that the Bank of Canada's monetary policy since 1975 qualifies the Bank of Canada as a "monetarist" institution? Discuss.

Part 5

CHAPTER 15

The Supply and Demand for Money Balances

I find that the high prices we see today are due to some four or five causes. The principal and almost the only one (which no one has referred to until now) is the abundance of gold and silver which is today much greater in this Kingdom than it was four hundred years ago.

Jean Bodin (1568)[1]

In this chapter we will be concerned exclusively with the money market, where the supply and demand for money balances determine the rate of interest. There are three parts to this chapter. The first is concerned with the nature of money itself and the way in which the stock of money is measured in Canada. A discussion of the nature and functions of money leads naturally to the development of theories that can explain what quantity of money balances the public wants to hold, that is, the demand for money balances. This is taken up in the second part. Finally, we turn to the supply side of the money market. Here we will be concerned with how the Bank of Canada exercises its influence over the Canadian money market.

The Functions and Definitions of Money

Perhaps the best way to think about the role that money plays in our modern economy is to imagine what it would be like if money did not exist. An important feature of any economy, other than the most primi-

1 Jean Bodin, "The Dearness of Things," in A.E. Monroe, ed., *Early Economic Thought* (Cambridge, Mass.: Harvard University Press, 1924), p. 127.

tive subsistence economies, is that people trade with each other — labour services are supplied to firms so that in return people can obtain the goods and services that are produced by firms. If there were no money, payments would have to be made in kind. For example, farm workers would be paid in agricultural products. This would clearly be very inefficient: imagine being paid in peaches, which are bulky and perishable. How would you arrange to buy a car if all your income came in the form of fresh peaches? You would have to find a car salesperson who needs a truckload of fresh peaches! Money solves these awkward trading problems, since it is neither bulky nor perishable and can be used in any exchange. This is the first and single most important function of money: it serves as a **medium of exchange**. Money balances that are kept for the purpose of making payments are often referred to as transactions balances.

A closely related issue is that of pricing and accounting. Suppose that our imaginary, moneyless economy produces only four different items (A, B, C, D). There are six different pairs of items that can be traded in a 4-item economy (AB, AC, AD, BC, BD, CD). This means there would be six rates of exchange between pairs of goods, or six prices. In a 15-item economy, the number of 2-item exchanges exceeds 100 (105 to be exact), and in a 100-item economy the number of 2-item exchanges that are possible rises to 4,950. Obviously, keeping track of all the prices in a moneyless economy would be exceedingly difficult. In a monetary economy, each product and service has just one dollar price, so that it is possible to add up the value of a number of different items by expressing their value in terms of the unique monetary unit. This in turn greatly simplifies accounting procedures and points to the second function of money, which is to provide a **unit of account**.

Another feature of modern economies is the phenomenon of borrowing and lending. For example, a mortgage contract requires the borrower to pay specific sums of money on specific dates, say $500 on the first of each month for 15 years. In this instance, money acts as a **means of deferred payment**.

The fourth function of money is related to its durable nature. Money is a **store of value**, or wealth. There are many kinds of assets that people can own; stocks, bonds, and real estate being just three examples. Money is another kind of asset that can be part of an overall portfolio of wealth. An interesting question to ask is: What are the factors that determine the share of total wealth that people should keep in the form of money? Obviously, if stock prices are about to fall it is better to hold money than stocks. But this question brings us to the demand for money balances itself, which will be discussed more fully later. Let us first look at how the stock of money is measured in Canada.

Four definitions of money that are regularly reported by the Bank of Canada are presented in Table 15.1. Two of the functions of money we

Table 15.1 Measures of the Stock of Money, February 1991 (Millions of Dollars, seasonally adjusted)

Currency	Currency + Demand Deposits (M1)	Currency + all Chequable Notice and Term Deposits (M2)	M2 + deposits at trust companies (M2+)	M2 + non-personal deposits (M3)
19,325	39,302	265,403	455,000	315,269

have just described motivate these definitions. First, money's major function is to serve as a medium of exchange. With this as a guide, everything that can be used to make payments (transactions balances) should be included in a definition of money. The most narrowly defined concept of money, labelled M1, is an attempt to conform to this criterion. M1 includes the currency in circulation and chequable demand deposits held at chartered banks, both of which can be used directly to make payments. However, there are other types of deposits that can be used to make payments. In recent years daily interest savings accounts have become increasingly popular. Many of these accounts are chequable, which means the funds can be used for transactions purposes. In 1990 Canadians held over $30 billion in chequable savings accounts. Many other types of accounts cannot be used directly for settling transactions, but the funds can be withdrawn relatively quickly, which makes these accounts very close substitutes for transactions balances. Examples include personal nonchequable savings accounts and nonpersonal (firms') notice deposits. To capture these broader notions of money, the Bank of Canada regularly publishes data on a series called M2. As Table 15.1 shows, M2 is over six times larger than M1.

Possibly an even more important difficulty in measuring spendable deposits is the exclusion of chequable deposits held at financial institutions other than banks. The importance of this omission is illustrated by a comparison of the growth rates of M1 and chequable deposits held at trust and mortgage loan companies; call this latter quantity MTM for short (money at trust and mortgage companies). Over the ten-year period from 1980 to 1990, M1 grew 48 percent while MTM grew by a factor of 7.6, that is, a huge 656 percent. At the beginning of this ten-year period MTM was only 6.4 percent of the size of M1, but ten years later MTM had grown to 29.4 percent of the size of M1. Clearly the growth of M1 has understated the growth of spendable deposits in recent years for two separate reasons. First, chartered banks have created new kinds of chequable deposits and these are not included in M1. Second, institutions other than banks have been increasingly successful at competing for the public's chequable deposits, and these are not included in M1.

The continuously changing financial system has made it impossible to define a single measure of the stock of money that accurately reflects total spendable deposits over a lengthy period of time and the Bank of Canada has had to modify its monetary definitions as circumstances have changed. In recent years the Bank of Canada has recognized the growing importance of trust and other financial companies and now refers to a quantity called M2+, which includes all of M2 as well as the deposits held at financial institutions other than banks.

The wider definitions of the stock of money, M2 and M3, go beyond the concept of transactions balances (immediately spendable deposits). For example, M2 includes personal term deposits, that is, deposits that are left with a bank for a specific term and that can be liquidated only at some cost. These deposits are stores of wealth that are considered closer to money than to other kinds of financial assets such as long-term bonds or stocks, both of which have the potential for large capital gains or losses. A still more comprehensive monetary aggregate is M3, which includes nonpersonal term deposits and foreign currency deposits of Canadian residents booked in Canada. These wider definitions, nevertheless, do not include the term deposits and guaranteed investment certificates offered by trust companies, which serve essentially the same purpose as term deposits at chartered banks.

In summary, defining the stock of money is not a simple task. The difficulty is not merely an abstract one. Over the period 1975 to 1982, M1 was the centrepiece of monetary policy. At the time, the Governor of the Bank of Canada clearly believed that M1 was the most appropriate concept of money on which to base Canada's monetary policy:

> This aggregate [M1] . . . moves with the trend of aggregate spending in the economy in a fairly predictable manner and is susceptible to control by the central bank through the adjustment of short-term interest rates without causing great instability in financial markets. Our experience to date in using M1 has confirmed in my mind its usefulness as a proximate target in the conduct of monetary policy. Those money supply aggregates that are appreciably broader in their coverage than M1 do not appear in Canada's present circumstances to meet the requirements noted above as well as M1.[2]

But in 1984 the Governor was considerably less enthusiastic:

> One technical difficulty that arises in implementing monetary policy . . . is that there are no aggregate measures or indicators of the rate of monetary expansion in Canada that are sufficiently reliable at

---

[2] Bank of Canada, *Annual Report 1978*, p. 15.

> present to be used as targets for policy, or that are uniquely helpful in the task of explaining the impact of monetary policy.[3]

With these practical difficulties in mind, we turn now to the theories of the demand for money balances.

Demand for Money Theories

The alternative theories of the demand for money focus on the most important functions of money. As discussed earlier, the usefulness of money as a medium of exchange creates a transactions demand for money. We will examine below the variables that are important determinants of the transactions demand for money. A somewhat broader view of money is that it provides one form in which wealth can be held. The distinguishing feature of money in this context is that it is liquid; its money value is certain (unlike bonds, stocks, and real estate) and it can be exchanged for other assets, goods, or services with little or no transactions cost. We begin our discussion of the demand for money with the transactions approach, which focuses on the medium of exchange function of money.

The Transactions Demand for Money

The **transactions demand** for money arises because the receipt of income by individuals and firms is not perfectly synchronized with the payments that they have to make. If, in fact, all household payments could be made on the same day that the monthly paycheque is paid into the bank, there would be no need to keep either cash or chequable deposits. All bills could be settled on pay day and the surplus (savings) could be invested in some interest-bearing asset. In practice, of course, individuals do need to make payments between paycheques and they hold money for this purpose.

To illustrate the costs and benefits of holding money, consider two extreme strategies. The first is to exchange the monthly paycheque for an interest-bearing asset (for example, a savings account or a bond) as soon as the paycheque is received. Appropriate amounts are then cashed in whenever a payment has to be made. This approach will maximize the individual's interest income, but substantial transactions costs will be incurred (such as repeated trips to the bank to transfer funds, or commission charges that would have to be paid if bonds were sold). These transactions costs are often simply referred to as brokerage

[3] Bank of Canada, *Annual Report 1984*, p. 8.

costs. The other extreme strategy is to avoid brokerage costs altogether by keeping the entire month's cash requirements in the form of cash at all times. The cost of this strategy is the interest that could have been earned on the idle cash. The optimal strategy is to hold a level of money balances that minimizes the sum of brokerage costs and foregone interest.[4]

Suppose, for example, that the total value of transactions a household makes in a month is T and that these payments are spread evenly throughout the month. The decision that has to be made is the following: how many times per month should transfers be made between interest-earning assets (say bonds) and money? Figure 15.1 illustrates two possibilities. The first involves two transfers. On pay day half of the month's cash requirements is kept as cash and the other half is invested in a bond, at a cost of b (the brokerage fee). During the first half of the month cash balances are gradually run down to zero, and on the middle

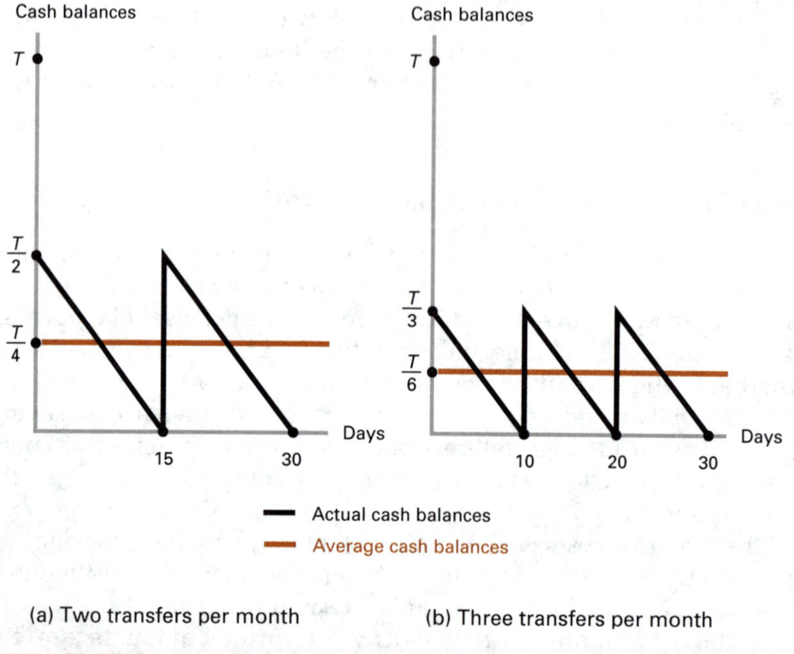

Figure 15.1 The average level of cash balances depends on the frequency of transfers between bonds and cash

[4] This approach to the transactions demand for money was first developed by W. Baumol in "The Transactions Demand for Cash: An Inventory Theoretic Approach," *Quarterly Journal of Economics*, November 1952, pp. 545–56.

day of the month the bond is cashed in, again at a cost of b. The coloured line in Figure 15.1 represents the average level of cash held during the entire month, which is $(T/2) \div 2 = T/4$. Notice that for half the month (the first and third quarters) cash balances are above $T/4$ and during the other half of the month cash balances are below $T/4$. The loss of interest income can be represented by R times $T/4$, where R is the monthly interest rate. The total cost of holding this particular level of average cash balances is therefore the sum of the two brokerage charges and the foregone interest, $2b + RT/4$.

Figure 15.1(b) shows the household's cash position throughout the month when three financial transactions are made between bonds and cash. The day the paycheque is received, two-thirds are put into bonds. Cash balances steadily run down to zero by the tenth day of the 30-day month. Bonds are then cashed (again at a cost b) to provide enough money to last another one-third of a month, at which point the remainder of the bonds are cashed. Three financial transactions between money and bonds have been made at a cost of $3b$. Average cash balances are only $(T/3) \div 2 = T/6$, implying foregone interest of only $RT/6$. The total cost of this strategy is $3b + RT/6$. In general, if the individual makes n financial transactions the brokerage and lost-interest costs amount to

$$nb + \frac{RT}{2n}$$

The astute individual will be concerned with the value of n that minimizes this total cost. If n is treated as a continuous variable rather than as a whole number, then it can be shown that the optimal level of average money balances is[5]

$$\$^D = \sqrt{\frac{bT}{2R}} \tag{15.1}$$

It is interesting to compare this demand function with Equation 5.3:

$$\$^D = kY - \ell R \tag{5.3}$$

In Chapter 5 it was argued (with empirical support) that the demand for real money balances depends directly on the level of real income Y and inversely on the interest rate R. The linear specification (Equation 5.3) proved to be a convenient form for our algebraic manipulations and is broadly consistent with the theoretically based Equation 15.1. For example, when the price level is fixed, Equation 15.1 can be interpreted as

[5] Students familiar with the calculus can demonstrate this by differentiating the total cost expression with respect to n. Setting the first derivative to zero (the first order condition for total cost minimization) and substituting the optimal value of n in the expression $\$^D = T/2n$ gives Equation 15.1.

the demand for real money balances. In this case T varies with the volume of transactions and is therefore likely to be highly correlated with the level of real income. Equation 15.1 is therefore consistent with the view that the demand for real money balances varies directly with the level of real income. Second, in both Equations 5.3 and 15.1, an increase in the rate of interest R leads to a reduction in the demand for real money balances.

When the price level is flexible, the $\$^D$ of Equation 15.1 must be interpreted as the demand for nominal money balances and T is the value of transactions. How does the demand for nominal money balances vary with the price level? Suppose the price level doubles but all real magnitudes remain unchanged. Since both the value of transactions T and the price of brokerage fees b will double, the product bT quadruples. However, $\$^D$ depends on the square root of bT so that the quadrupling of this product leads to only a doubling of the demand for nominal money balances. This argument shows that Baumol's transactions demand for money approach predicts that a doubling of the price level will lead, *ceteris paribus*, to a doubling of the demand for nominal money balances.

Keynesian Liquidity Preference

Keynes recognized the transactions motive behind the demand for money and, in fact, broke it down into two components: the demand due to regular, planned transactions (which Baumol considered in detail) and a demand for precautionary purposes. The precautionary demand accounts for the money balances that are held in order that unforeseen transactions can be made. But more important than this distinction is Keynes's recognition that money also serves as a store of liquid wealth. Money is an asset just as real estate, stocks, and bonds are assets. But because the prices of most assets vary considerably and/or substantial transactions costs are incurred when they are bought and sold, it is sometimes advantageous to hold money rather than income-earning assets. In particular, just before bond and stock prices fall, it would be convenient to hold money rather than bonds and stocks. Financial analysts are certainly aware of this role of money: Investors should keep a substantial part of their portfolio in short-term debt or cash to be able to move in and out of the stock market, a report from McLeod Young Weir Ltd. of Toronto says.[6]

To capture the essence of the problem Keynes confined his analysis to a situation in which wealth can be held in two forms: money and long bonds. The choice between these alternatives depends on their

---

6 *The Globe and Mail*, 6 October 1980.

relative rates of return. Of course in nominal terms, money pays no return at all. Long bonds, on the other hand, can give either positive or negative returns over a period of, say, one year. Bonds pay a fixed annual interest payment, usually referred to as the coupon. But the market price of a bond can change dramatically from one year to the next. The bondholder therefore stands to lose or gain (in any given year) depending on how bond prices move. In general the price of an asset, such as a bond, depends on the flow of income that it generates and the market interest rate. Let us consider in more detail the determination of bond prices. When the government (or a corporation) issues a bond it undertakes to pay the bondholder an annual interest payment C — the coupon — and to redeem the face value F of the bond on the maturity date. For example, Table 15.2 gives some information on an 11¾-percent Government of Canada bond that will mature in February 2003. The 11¾-percent refers to the size of the annual coupon payment. If the face value of the bond is \$100, the annual coupon payment is \$11.75. The table also shows that the market price of the bond in July 1981 was \$67.88. In other words, at that time investors were prepared to pay \$67.88 for the right to receive \$11.75 every year up to the year 2003 (the coupon payment) and an additional \$100 in the year 2003 (the face value of the bond). The price that individuals (or pension funds) are prepared to pay for the bond is often referred to as the bond's present value. To see what determines the present value or price of this bond let us consider the general case in which the annual coupon C is to be paid for N years. In the Nth year the bond matures and the bondholder receives the face value F. The present value of the bond is the value of this stream of income. We will consider the problem in several stages. Suppose the present value of the first coupon payment (which will be received in one year's time) is PV_1. That is, an individual is prepared to pay PV_1 now in order to receive C in one year's time. What alternatives does the individual have? If the annual rate of interest is currently R, then the individual could invest the sum PV_1, say in a savings account, and receive $PV_1(1 + R)$ in one year's time. The individual will be indifferent between these two alternatives only when the sum accumulated

Table 15.2 Bond Yields and Bond Prices

	Long Bond		Short Bond	
	(11¾%, due February 2003)		(10.5%, due October 1984)	
Date	Price	Yield	Price	Yield
July 1981	67.88	17.5%	82.0	18.2%
July 1983	96.73	12.2%	99.6	10.1%

in the savings account is equal to the coupon C, that is, when $PV_1(1 + R) = C$. This can be rearranged to give

$$PV_1 = \frac{C}{1 + R}$$

This equation says that at the annual interest rate R, the present value of C (to be paid in one year) is $C/(1 + R)$. To illustrate this formula consider the present value of \$10 (to be paid in one year) when the annual interest rate is 8 percent ($R = 0.08$). The formula indicates that it is \$10/(1 + 0.08) or \$9.26. Note that if \$9.26 is placed in a savings account that pays 8 percent per annum the accumulated sum after one year will be \$9.26 (1 + 0.08) or \$10. Paying \$9.26 for the right to receive C (\$10) is just as profitable as placing these funds in a savings account. No one would pay more than \$9.26 now for \$10 next year because even \$9.27 will accumulate to more than \$10 in one year at 8 percent interest. If the annual interest rate were 12 percent rather than 8 percent, the present value of next year's \$10 would be \$10/(1.12) or \$8.93. No one would pay more than \$8.93 to receive \$10 next year because at 12 percent per annum a greater sum could be accumulated by putting the funds into a savings account. This example illustrates the inverse relationship between the present value of an asset and the rate of interest. We will say more on this later. Now let us turn to the present value of the coupon payment that will be received in two years' time, PV_2. The alternative to receiving the coupon is to place the funds in a savings account that pays an annual interest rate R. The accumulated value in the account after one year would be $PV_2(1 + R)$. If this is left in the account for a second year it becomes

$$[PV_2(1 + R)](1 + R) = PV_2(1 + R)^2$$

The individual will be indifferent between paying PV_2 for the coupon C (to be paid in two years) and putting PV_2 into the savings account if $PV_2(1 + R)^2 = C$. This can be rearranged to give the present value in terms of the coupon and the interest rate:

$$PV_2 = \frac{C}{(1 + R)^2}$$

Again, suppose C is \$10 and the interest rate is 8 percent ($R = 0.08$). At this interest rate, the present value of \$10 (which will be paid in two years' time) is $\$10/(1 + 0.08)^2$ or \$8.57. This is less than the present value of the first coupon payment (\$9.26) and in general the further into the future is the date that the \$10 will be paid, the less will be its present value. In fact, similar calculations to those above show that the present value of the coupon to be received N years from now is:

$$PV_N = \frac{C}{(1+R)^N}$$

Consider again the bond that pays C in each of N years and F in the Nth year. This bond has a present value equal to the sum of the present values of all the coupon payments as well as face value F:

$$PV_N = \frac{C}{(1+R)} + \frac{C}{(1+R)^2} + \dots + \frac{C+F}{(1+R)^N} \qquad (15.2)$$

Equation 15.2 shows that the present value of a bond depends on the size of the stream of payments and the interest rate. As the interest rate R rises the present value of the bond falls. The sensitivity of the present value to changes in the interest rate depends on the term to maturity N. When N is large, a small change in R can cause a large change in $(1 + R)^N$ and therefore a large change in the present value. This is well illustrated in Table 15.2. The 11¾-percent bond that sold for $67.88 in July 1981 had a market value of $96.73 two years later, an increase of $28.85 or 43 percent. Over this period the long-term interest rate (measured by the yield on long bonds held to maturity) fell from 17.5 to 12.2 percent, a decline of 5.3 percentage points. If you had bought one of these bonds in July 1981, by July 1983 you would have received two coupon payments worth $11.75 each and seen the price of your bond rise in value by $28.85, giving a total return of $52.35. This works out to a 77 percent return on an initial outlay of $67.88. Of course, these spectacular gains are far from assured. It is equally possible to suffer large capital losses by investing in long-term bonds. This happened between March 1979 and March 1980, when long-term bond prices fell 25 percent during the rapid increase in long-term interest rates.

In 1981, the long-term bond illustrated in Table 15.2 had 22 years to go before its maturity date. In contrast, the short bond illustrated in the same table was to mature in 1984. As of July 1981, it had a much shorter life of just over three years. Over the next two years, short-term interest rates fell sharply from 18.2 to 10.1 per cent, a drop of 8.1 percentage points. Although short rates fell more than long rates, the capital gain on the short bond was much less — just $17.60 on an initial outlay of $82. Had you bought one of these bonds in July 1981, your total yield over the next two years would have included two coupon payments of $10.50 each and a capital gain of $17.60, giving a total return of $38.60; that is, an overall yield of 47 percent on an outlay of $82.

These examples illustrate that during periods of falling interest rates, bond prices rise, and the longer the term to maturity the more sensitive bond prices are to changes in the rate of interest. This works the other way. When interest rates rise, bond prices fall. Huge capital losses can be suffered on long bonds when long-term rates rise.

Keynes's theory of **liquidity preference** stresses the role of potential capital gains or losses in the individual's portfolio decision. If long-term interest rates are expected to fall, then the individual expects to earn capital gains by holding bonds. In these circumstances the demand for money will be low (there is little preference for liquidity). However, if long-term interest rates are expected to rise sufficiently far, then capital losses will wipe out the interest income and the individual will be better off if he holds cash rather than bonds (there is a great preference for liquidity). Keynes argued that long-term interest rates follow a cyclical pattern around a normal interest rate. The higher are long-term interest rates, the greater will be the number of people who anticipate that interest rates will fall and therefore that bond prices will rise. Most people will prefer to hold bonds rather than money when interest rates are high. On the other hand, the lower are interest rates, the greater will be the number of people who expect rates to rise and bond prices to fall. Therefore, the lower are interest rates, the greater will be the demand for money. Thus, Keynes argued that the demand for speculative money balances varies inversely with the current rate of interest.

Tobin's Analysis of Liquidity Preference

A much more persuasive and influential approach to the analysis of how individuals decide how to allocate their wealth between alternative financial assets was pioneered by Professor James Tobin.[7] Tobin's approach can be applied to the general problem of determining the optimal combination of assets in a portfolio, as well as providing a rationale for the inverse relationship between the demand for money and the rate of interest. Here we want to focus on the latter, so our discussion will again be confined to the choice between two assets: money and bonds. Tobin assumes that the owners of wealth want to increase the value of their wealth by investing in assets that have a high expected yield. However, such assets are often risky in that while the expected yield is high there is also a high probability that the actual yield will differ considerably from the expected yield. The second assumption is that individuals prefer to avoid risk rather than to take risk. Thus, of two equally risky assets, individuals typically prefer the one with the higher expected yield, and of two assets with the same expected yield, individuals typically prefer the less risky of the two.

Money has an expected yield of zero, but is also riskless. Bonds on the other hand usually have a positive expected yield, although there is some risk because future bond prices are unknown and there is a possi-

[7] J. Tobin, "Liquidity Preference as a Behaviour Towards Risk," *Review of Economic Studies*, February 1958, pp. 65–86.

bility that a large capital loss will be incurred. The individual's problem is how to allocate his or her total wealth (which is given) between the two alternative forms. A portfolio of money is riskless, but yields no return. A portfolio made up entirely of bonds, on the other hand, has both a maximum expected yield and maximum risk because of potentially large capital losses. The riskiness of the overall portfolio can be reduced by replacing bonds with money, but the cost of reducing risk is the loss in expected yield. The optimal portfolio is one in which any further reductions in risk are simply not worth the cost in terms of lower expected yield. Tobin showed that under reasonable assumptions the optimal portfolio will include both money and bonds. Thus, some liquidity (money) is preferred to none because individuals generally seek to avoid risk. Moreover, if the expected yield on bonds rises without any change in their riskiness, then the individual has an incentive to increase the proportion of bonds in the portfolio and reduce the size of money holdings. Consequently, an increase in expected bond yields (without any change in risk) leads to a reduction in the demand for money. To the extent that an increase in the actual interest rate leads to an increase in the expected yield on bonds but no change in their riskiness, the demand for money is a decreasing function of the interest rate on bonds.

Tobin's approach demonstrates that there will be a portfolio demand for money balances despite the fact that money pays no interest precisely because money is riskless whereas all other assets are risky. However, in practice, savings accounts can be thought of as riskless assets and they do pay interest. This poses a problem: if money is held only because it is riskless, but some kinds of riskless money pay interest and others don't, Tobin's theory predicts that no one will hold the non-interest-bearing money. Tobin's theory can therefore explain why interest-bearing deposits are held, but not cash and demand deposits. The theories of Baumol and Tobin are complementary rather than alternatives. Baumol's transactions demand model is intended to explain the holding of M1, which corresponds to transactions balances. Tobin's theory is able to explain the holding of those components of M2 that are not included in M1.

The Quantity Theory of Money, Old and New

The origins of the traditional **quantity theory of money** go back to the beginnings of economics as a discipline. The fundamental identity that underpins this approach to the demand for money is Irving Fisher's equation of exchange:[8]

8 I. Fisher, *The Purchasing Power of Money* (New York: Macmillan Co., 1911).

$$\$^S V = PY$$

The equation of exchange is in fact an identity that defines the velocity of money V: $V = (PY)/S^S$. In this expression P is the aggregate price level, Y is the level of real annual income (GNP) so that PY is the value of nominal GNP. As we learned in Chapter 2, this is simply the annual value of all transactions involving the exchange of final goods and services. By dividing this total volume of transactions by the stock of money $\$^S$, we find how many times the typical dollar changes hands during the year (the velocity of money).[9]

Quantity theorists argue that both the velocity of money and real income are, in the long run, determined by factors other than the stock of money. Velocity, the rate at which money changes hands, is in large part determined by institutional and technological factors such as the frequency with which paycheques are issued and the speed with which financial institutions settle accounts. Thus, while velocity may change slowly over the long run, these changes are unrelated to changes in the stock of money. Similarly the level of real income is determined by the supplies of the factors of production, land, labour and capital, and the state of technology. Changes in the supply of money have no bearing on the capacity of the economy to produce real goods and services.

Having assumed that both the velocity of money and the level of real income are independent of the stock of money, the quantity theorist is now able to demonstrate that a given percentage change in the stock of money will, of itself, ultimately cause an equal percentage change in the aggregate price level. This is shown by rearranging the equation of exchange to read

$$P = \left(\frac{V}{Y}\right)\$^S$$

Given that the ratio V/Y does not depend on the stock of money, a doubling of $\$^S$ will lead, *ceteris paribus*, to a doubling of the aggregate price level. Second, because velocity is slow to change, the level of nominal income PY will bear a stable relationship with the quantity of money. This is shown by the equation of exchange itself.

$$PY = V\$^S$$

The modern quantity theory developed by Professor Milton Friedman

---

9 Fisher's original equation of exchange defined the transactions velocity of money; that is, all transactions were included, not just those involving final goods and services. Modern economists have found the income velocity concept more useful because it relates the stock of money to the level of nominal GDP rather than to the total volume of transactions.

embraces both of these conclusions, and has become the cornerstone of the monetarist approach to macroeconomics.

Friedman's view of money is similar to Tobin's in that money is seen as an asset. But rather than treating money simply as a riskless financial asset, Friedman regards money as a durable good that yields its return solely in kind, in the usual form of convenience, security, etc.[10] From the point of view of firms, money is a factor of production, or capital good. Friedman has analyzed the key variables that determine households' and firms' demand for money balances and concludes that these are sufficiently similar that no distinction needs to be made between them. Consequently, the total demand for money balances can be written as:

$$\frac{\$^D}{P} = f(\pi, r_b, r_e, Y, w) \qquad (15.3)$$

First, note that Friedman defines the demand for money in terms of the demand for real money balances, $\$^D/P$, because it is through its purchasing power that money yields its benefit. As in Tobin's analysis, the arguments of the demand function include the rates of return that can be earned on alternative assets. Friedman classifies these alternatives into three types. The first category is physical goods. The relevant rate of return is the rate of price inflation, π. Thus, the higher is the rate of inflation, the greater is the incentive to buy physical goods and reduce one's holdings of real money balances. The second and third alternatives are bonds and equities, which have rates of return r_b and r_e, respectively. The greater are the rates of return on bonds and equities, the lower is the demand for real money balances. The fourth variable, Y, represents permanent income.[11] This is a proxy for Friedman's all-encompassing return on wealth. Friedman's concept of wealth includes both financial wealth (stocks, bonds, and physical assets such as land, houses, and consumer durables) and human wealth. The latter concept recognizes that, for example, just before Wayne Gretzky started his professional hockey career he may not have been financially wealthy. However, his personal skills amounted to wealth in that they were about to earn him a high income and are expected to do so for many years to come. Compared with an individual who has considerable financial wealth or capital, an individual with an equal amount of wealth, but most of it in the form of human capital, will tend to hold a smaller proportion of his wealth as money. Consequently, it is not only total wealth that determines the demand for money, but also the form that the wealth takes. Accordingly, Friedman includes w, the ratio of human to nonhuman wealth, in his demand for money function.

---

10 Milton Friedman, "The Quantity Theory of Money, A Restatement," in Milton Friedman, ed., *Studies in the Quantity Theory of Money* (Chicago: University of Chicago Press, 1956), pp. 3–21.

11 See Chapter 16 for a more extensive discussion of permanent income.

The key distinguishing feature of Friedman's demand for money function lies in the presence of the rate of return on physical assets in the demand function. Unlike Keynesians who emphasize the substitutability of money for financial assets such as bonds and stocks, monetarists argue that physical assets are also direct substitutes for money. This has important implications for the transmission mechanism of monetary policy. The traditional Keynesian view is that an open market purchase of treasury bills, for example, will bid up the price of treasury bills (and depress interest rates). Firms find that the funds they might need for expansion purposes are now less costly to obtain and as a result, firms have an additional incentive to undertake investment projects, so aggregate demand increases.

Monetarists accept this traditional Keynesian chain reaction from declining interest rates to increasing investment expenditures, but argue that it is not the only route through which monetary policy affects aggregate demand. The open market purchase of treasury bills by the Bank of Canada will increase the supply of money. The public's portfolios will be out of balance; these portfolios will include too much money in relation to other assets, including physical goods. The public will not only purchase financial assets as their portfolios are put in order, but will also purchase physical goods such as cars and television sets. Hence, there is a direct link between changes in the stock of money and aggregate spending. By emphasizing this direct link, monetarists are able to argue that changes in the nominal stock of money have a strong influence on aggregate demand. Indeed, monetarists believe that the impact of changes in the stock of money on nominal aggregate demand is much greater than the effect of fiscal measures such as a change in income taxes or government spending.

At the foundation of these views is the belief that velocity is stable over the long term. This can be interpreted to mean that the demand for money is a **stable** function. From Fisher's equation of exchange we have

$$\frac{\$^S}{P} = \frac{Y}{V}$$

Setting the left-hand side equal to the demand for real money balances, we have

$$f(\pi, r_b, r_e, Y, w) = \frac{Y}{V}$$

or

$$V = \frac{Y}{f(\pi, r_b, r_e, Y, w)}$$

The velocity of money is simply the ratio of real income to the demand for real money balances. Monetarists argue that over the long term central banks cannot influence the level of real income, nor the real return on bonds and equities. As long as the demand for money is a stable function of these variables, the velocity of money will be stable and there will be a direct link between the stock of money and both the price level P and the level of nominal income PY. In the next section we will look at some of the empirical evidence on the properties of the demand for money function.

Empirical Evidence on the Demand for Money

The theories of the demand for money that were discussed in the previous section suggest several hypotheses that can and have been tested empirically. A fairly general specification of the demand for money that allows these hypotheses to be tested is the following:

$$\$^D = AP^aY^bR^c \tag{15.4}$$

In this equation $\$^D$ represents the demand for nominal money balances, P is the aggregate price level, Y is the level of real income, and R is an interest rate that measures the opportunity cost of holding money. The symbols A, a, b, and c are parameters that are estimated by fitting Equation 15.4 to actual data. This is a particularly useful functional form since the parameters a, b, and c can be interpreted directly as elasticities. That is to say, c, for example, is the interest elasticity of demand for money. All of the theories of the demand for money that we discussed earlier are consistent with the hypothesis that the demand for nominal money balances is proportional to the aggregate price level or, in other words, that the demand for money should be expressed in real terms. In terms of Equation 15.4, this amounts to saying that a is unity, in which case both sides of the expression can be divided by P to give

$$\frac{\$^D}{P} = AY^bR^c \tag{15.5}$$

Although many empirical studies have taken an equation such as 15.5 as the starting point for the analysis, there is strong empirical support for the hypothesis that the demand for money balances is proportional to the price level. For example, White[12] estimated equations very similar to 15.4 and found that the Canadian data are consistent with the hypothesis that a is unity. Other important issues raised by the theoretical literature, which have been tested empirically, include the following:

---

12 W.R. White, *The Demand for Money in Canada and the Control of Monetary Aggregates: Evidence from the Monthly Data*, Bank of Canada Research Study, 12 (Ottawa: 1976).

1. Does the rate of interest influence the demand for money?
2. Are there economies of scale in holding money; that is, is the income elasticity of demand less than unity?
3. Is current income or wealth the appropriate variable to include in the demand for money function?
4. Should money be defined in a narrow (M1) or a wide sense (M2)?
5. Is the demand for money a stable function of a few variables?

The most important question that concerned the early literature is that of the role of the interest rate in the demand for money function. As we saw in Chapter 5, the initial debate between Keynesians and monetarists concerned the slopes of the *IS* and *LM* schedules. Monetarists argued that the demand for money is not influenced greatly by the rate of interest. Although Friedman's theoretical reformulation of the quantity theory allows for interest rate effects, as an empirical matter, Friedman found that permanent income alone determines the demand for money over the long term and that even during business cycles when current income deviates from permanent income, movements in interest rates do not affect the demand for money.[13] Consequently, monetarists such as Friedman believe that the *LM* curve is very steep, if not vertical, and that fiscal policy is ineffective because increases in government spending inevitably raise interest rates and crowd out private spending.

However, Friedman's empirical work on the role of interest rates stands alone, as the evidence is now overwhelming that interest rates do indeed affect the demand for money. While the size of the interest rate elasticity does depend on the precise specifications of the model, the literature has come to a broad consensus. In studies that have used a narrow definition of money, the interest elasticity is found to be in the range of 0.1 to 0.2.[14] Investigators who have used a wider definition of the stock of money such as M2, which includes interest-bearing deposits, have found somewhat weaker interest rate effects on the demand for money. Goldfeld[15] claims that it is not sensible to specify the demand for money in terms of M2. The holding of non-interest-bearing deposits satisfies the transactions motive and the two key variables are income and the opportunity cost of holding money, say the rate paid on savings accounts. A rise in the savings account interest rate will reduce the demand for cash and demand deposits,

[13] Milton Friedman, "The Demand for Money: Some Theoretical and Empirical Results," *Journal of Political Economy*, August 1959, pp. 327–51.

[14] Both White, in *Demand for Money*, and Goldfeld (see note 15 below) found the short-term interest rate elasticity to be close to 0.15. In both cases a narrow definition of money was used.

[15] M. Goldfeld, "The Demand for Money Revisited," *Brookings Papers on Economic Activity*, vol. 3, 1973, pp. 577–638.

and raise the demand for savings deposits. Consequently, M1 will show a negative relationship with the rate of interest paid on savings accounts, but the relationship between M2 and this rate of interest is ambiguous; one component rises (savings deposits) and one component falls (M1) as interest rates rise. Consequently, one would expect to find clearer and larger effects of changes in short-term interest on the demand for M1 than on the demand for M2. This is exactly what the data show.

As we have seen, the transactions motive for holding money suggests that the level of current income is an important determinant of the demand for money because the total volume of transactions is likely to be related to the level of income. Studies that have found the current level of income to be a significant determinant of the demand for money have confirmed the prediction of Baumol's theoretical approach that there are economies of scale in holding money balances. That is to say, as real income rises, the demand for real transactions balances also rises but by a smaller proportion. While both White and Goldfeld were concerned with the total demand for real money balances, their studies confirm this prediction since income elasticities were found to be between 0.6 and 1.0.

We turn now to the issues of the stability of the demand for money function. If the demand for money can be shown empirically to be a function of only a few variables and if the effect of each of these variables on the demand for money does not change over time, then we can say that the demand for money is stable. The stability of the demand for money has assumed some importance for monetarist policy prescriptions. As we saw in the last section, the monetarist position has been that the velocity of money is stable. This is critical to the proposition that the stock of money bears a stable relationship to nominal income and to the price level and, therefore, that by controlling the rate of growth of the money supply, central banks can ultimately control the rate of inflation. But we also saw in the last section that the velocity of money is simply the ratio of real income to the demand for money. The argument that, over the long term, velocity is stable boils down to the argument that, over the long term, the demand for money is stable. The large amount of empirical evidence that had been accumulated by the 1970s confirmed the existence of stable demand for money functions in many countries. Goldfeld found that the demand for M1 was more stable than the demand for M2. White, in his 1976 study, also determined that in Canada the demand for M1 was stable. The Canadian results provided a foundation for the use of M1 as the central indicator of monetary policy over the period from 1975 to 1982, when growth targets for this narrow measure of the stock of money were set annually.

In the mid-1970s, however, Goldfeld detected a sudden downward shift in the demand for M1 in the United States.[16] The U.S. economy appeared to be functioning with far less money than the estimated demand curves predicted, given the existing levels of output and interest rates. Only a part of this shift could be attributed to changes in banking legislation. What had earlier seemed to be a solid and well understood relationship between the demand for narrowly defined money and its determinants turned into a controversial area once again as researchers sought to solve the puzzle of what Goldfeld called the case of the missing money.

Subsequently, in Canada, similar difficulties were experienced with the use of M1 as the principal measure of monetary policy. From mid-1981 to the end of 1982, M1 grew so slowly that it fell well below the lower limit of the Bank of Canada's target range. The shifts in the demand for money were so substantial that at the end of 1982 the Bank of Canada abandoned its seven-year experiment with monetary targets. The demand function for money seems to have been a casualty of the turbulent 1970s and has presented researchers with a new set of challenges in an area that was previously thought to be well understood.

The Money Supply Process

To complete our discussion of the money market we turn now to the supply side of the market. We will focus on the two major institutions that are involved in the money supply process, namely the Bank of Canada and the chartered banks.

The Role of the Chartered Banks

The greater part of the money supply, M1, is made up of demand deposits held at chartered banks. In this section we examine the role of chartered banks in the money creation process. The chartered banks in Canada are privately owned, profit-making institutions which are in the business of financial intermediation. That is to say, banks (and other financial institutions such as trust companies and caisses populaires) act as intermediaries between those who want to lend funds and those who want to borrow funds (the ultimate lenders and borrowers). For this to be a profitable enterprise the banks must offer services to the borrowers and lenders that they bring together. Let us examine some of the more important services.

---

[16] M. Goldfeld, "The Case of the Missing Money," *Brookings Papers on Economic Activity*, vol. 3, 1976, pp. 683–730.

An important role of financial intermediaries, such as banks, is that of reducing risk in financial markets. Take, for example, the case of an individual who is considering holding (investing in) a mortgage. If the going mortgage rate is 11 percent, the lender has a chance of either earning 11 percent on his investment or something far worse; the borrower may default and the lender may not even recover the principal of the loan. Holding a mortgage is clearly much more risky than leaving the money in a savings account where the chance of not being able to withdraw the funds due to bank failure is so remote as to make the investment essentially riskless. Unlike the individual lender, a bank is able to hold thousands of mortgages simultaneously. Even if each of these mortgages is as risky as the one we discussed above, the portfolio of mortgages as a whole is far less risky. The bank can be almost certain that some mortgages will be defaulted, but it can be equally certain that the vast majority will be repaid in full with interest. Unlike the individual mortgage holder, the bank does not care which of the mortgages goes into default as long as it can predict roughly what proportion of the total will be defaulted. This is because the losses can be spread over the whole portfolio. If 2 percent of the portfolio yields a return of zero but 98 percent of the portfolio yields a return of 11 percent, then the portfolio as a whole will yield (0.98×11) or 10.8 percent. Because the bank can be quite sure that the actual return on the portfolio will be close to this figure, the bank can guarantee to its deposit holders that they will be paid, say, 7 percent on their savings account. The margin of 3.8 percent covers the expenses of the bank as well as the return to the owners of the bank, its stockholders.

The purpose of this example has been to illustrate how financial institutions can reduce the risks associated with lending by pooling together the relatively small savings of individuals. This pooling of loanable funds has other important advantages. First, the pooling together of small amounts of savings allows huge projects to be financed more easily than if the ultimate borrower had to deal directly with hundreds of small investors. Second, because of the vast size of their lending operations, financial institutions are able to accumulate the information and expertise necessary for the proper evaluation of the creditworthiness of borrowers, be they individuals or firms. Third, financial intermediation offers ultimate borrowers and lenders a greater flexibility in choosing the term of the debt or the loan than would be possible if ultimate borrowers and lenders had to deal directly. Let us develop this last point in more detail.

Table 15.3 shows the assets and liabilities of the chartered banks at the end of September 1990. Notice that loans and mortgages make up a large proportion of total Canadian-dollar assets. On the other side of the ledger, deposits are the most important component of Canadian-dollar liabilities. The banks are channelling the "liquid" funds that firms and individuals have placed in savings and notice accounts into longer-term assets, for example, loans and mortgages that fall into the less liquid category. The term *liquid* has a specific meaning in this context. Assets whose prices show little fluctuation and which can be readily (without significant transactions costs) exchanged for money (M1) are described as liquid. Oil stocks and gold can be readily converted into money but their prices show considerable variability over time and for this reason these assets are not described as liquid. The variability of price means that at any particular time the price of the asset may or may not be favourable for cashing in. Consequently, such assets are unlikely to be desirable forms for holding wealth if there is a high probability they may have to be cashed in at a moment's notice. Government bonds are more or less liquid depending on the term to maturity. As we have seen, the price of a financial asset is inversely related to its rate of return. Moreover, the asset price is more sensitive to changes in the rate of return the longer-lived is the asset. The prices of bonds and securities with very long terms to maturity show considerable variability, and are certainly less liquid than treasury bills, which mature in a matter of months and do not have wildly fluctuating prices.

The data of Table 15.3 show clearly that banks tend to borrow short

Table 15.3 Chartered Bank Assets and Liabilities, September 1990 (Millions of Dollars)

Assets		Liabilities	
Liquid assets		Deposits	
Bank of Canada notes		Demand	22,362
and deposits	4,731	Personal saving	196,553
Treasury bills	16,148	Nonpersonal term and notice	66,498
Other liquid assets	5,996	Government of Canada	232
Total liquid assets	26,875	Total deposits	285,646
Less liquid assets			
General loans	173,844	Bank of Canada advances	202
Mortgages	107,474	Shareholder's equity	30,550
Canadian securities	18,907	Other liabilities	74,678
Total less liquid assets	300,225	Total Canadian-dollar liabilities	391,076
Other assets	75,927		
Total Canadian-dollar assets	403,027	Foreign currency liabilities	197,819
Total foreign currency assets	185,868		
Total assets	588,895	Total liabilities	588,895

and lend long. In this way, the funds that individuals or firms wish to lend for only a short period of time are in fact loaned out for longer periods than suit the original lender. Suppose, for example, that you deposit $1,000 in a savings account. The bank may lend it to someone who wants to buy a car and the car loan may extend over a period of four years. If you turn up a month later and ask for your $1,000, is the bank going to be able to pay you? One possibility is that another individual (or individuals) will deposit $1,000 at the bank, allowing the bank to pay you. In this way the bank can finance the car loan by a sequence of deposits. It does not matter to the bank who owns these deposits; what is important is that there are sufficient deposits at all times to cover the loans that the bank has made. Of course, in practice no bank will invest all its liabilities (deposits) in long-term assets such as bank loans because if the total value of deposits were to fall the bank would have to call in loans to pay its depositors. Consequently, banks keep a sufficiently large share of their assets in the form of cash reserves to ensure that such temporary reductions in deposits can be accommodated.

The cash reserves of the chartered banks are made up of Bank of Canada notes held in the vaults of chartered banks plus the deposits that chartered banks hold at the Bank of Canada. Table 15.3 shows that at the end of September 1990 all chartered banks together held cash reserves of $4,731 million. Neither vault cash nor deposits at the Bank of Canada earn interest, and it is a matter of convenience how individual chartered banks decide to hold their cash reserves. Some must be kept in vaults to allow the public to withdraw cash. The deposits at the Bank of Canada are used to settle accounts between the chartered banks. For example, when an individual writes a cheque on his demand account held at bank A, his account will be reduced by $100. The person who receives the cheque may deposit it at bank B, where his account will be credited with $100. However, bank B must somehow obtain the funds from bank A. This can be done simply by reducing bank A's deposits at the Bank of Canada by $100, and crediting bank B's account at the Bank of Canada by $100 (the Bank of Canada is the chartered banks' bank). In this example the total volume of cash reserves is unchanged, but the effect of the transaction is that bank B gains cash reserves at the expense of bank A.

What volume of cash reserves should a prudent bank hold? This depends on the size of its deposits and the variability of these deposits. In fact, federal legislation dictates the minimum cash reserves that chartered banks must hold. This minimum level of cash reserves not only protects the public but also provides the means for the Bank of Canada to manipulate the size of the stock of money. We will examine this latter point in more detail below. Under the present Bank Act, for every dollar of demand deposits banks must hold 10 cents in the form of cash reserves and for every dollar of savings or notice deposits banks must hold 3 cents in the form of cash reserves. The value of savings and notice deposits is much greater than the value of demand deposits (see Table 15.3) so the required reserve ratio, averaged over all deposits, is usually close to 0.04. In order to be sure of meeting the **reserve requirements**, banks tend to keep reserves in excess of the minimum. These excess reserves do not earn interest for the bank and are usually very small (typically less than one-tenth of one percent of total deposits).

Should a bank have difficulty in meeting the reserve requirements, perhaps because of a large unexpected cash drain, the bank can obtain a cash loan from the Bank of Canada. Such loans are short-term. They are shown in Table 15.3 under the heading "Bank of Canada Advances."

A Simple Model of the Money Supply

The basic objective of the chartered banks is to generate profits by using depositors' funds to make loans and to buy corporate or government securities and other interest-bearing assets. The major constraint that banks face is that the public may wish to withdraw funds that have been tied up in the form of less liquid assets (loans and securities). Consequently, banks keep, and are required by law to keep, cash reserves that can be used when deposits decline. In this section we develop a model of the supply of money for a simplified financial system. We begin with an equation that defines the supply of money $\$^S$, which is the sum of deposits D and cash held by the public C:

$$\$^S = D + C \tag{15.6}$$

The Bank Act specifies the minimum level of the ratio of reserves to deposits, which we call r (the reserve ratio). The quantity of required reserves R depends on the reserve ratio and the volume of banks' deposit liabilities,[17]

$$R = rD \tag{15.7}$$

Since banks earn no interest on cash reserves there is an incentive for banks to keep reserves as low as possible. As we saw above, it is not much of a distortion to assume that banks keep no excess reserves at all, so that the actual level of reserve holdings is equal to required reserves. In addition, we assume that banks hold just two kinds of assets: reserves R and loans L, and only one kind of liability: deposits D. For

[17] The reader will be aware that R has been used elsewhere to represent the rate of interest. In this section alone, R represents the quantity of required reserves.

each bank, and therefore all banks together, total assets must equal total liabilities,

$$D = R + L \tag{15.8}$$

Reserves can be thought of as cash held in chartered bank vaults, although in practice some reserves are held as deposits at the Bank of Canada. The remainder of the Bank of Canada's notes circulate throughout the economy as cash held by the public, C. The total amount of cash issued by the Bank of Canada is called **high powered money**, and we will use the symbol H to represent this quantity. Since the quantity of cash issued by the Bank of Canada, H, must either be held by the banks as required reserves R or by the nonbank public as currency C, it follows that:

$$H = C + R \tag{15.9}$$

The four equations we have just discussed make up our model of the money supply. The four endogenous variables are D, L, R, and $\$^S$. The variable that we are most interested in is $\$^S$, the money supply. Of secondary interest is L, the value of loans, since this is a more direct measure of the volume of credit within the economy. The exogenous variables in our model are H and C. Cash is just one way for the nonbank public to hold its wealth and this model does not attempt to explain the level of cash holdings; we simply take C as given.[18] The quantity of high powered money H is controlled by the Bank of Canada. We leave to the next section a discussion of the mechanisms available to the Bank of Canada for controlling this quantity. Our immediate task is to establish the reduced-form equation for $\$^S$.

First, substitute Equation 15.7 for D in Equation 15.6:

$$\$^S = \frac{R}{r} + C$$

Using Equation 15.9, we can substitute for R. This gives us the reduced-form equation for $\$^S$:

$$\$^S = \frac{H - C}{r} + C \tag{15.10}$$

or

$$\$^S = \frac{H}{r} - \frac{C(1 - r)}{r}$$

---

18 One way to convert C into an endogenous variable is to assume that cash balances are a constant proportion of deposits ($C = cD$), where c is the ratio of cash to deposits. This implies that when the money stock doubles, so too does the level of deposits and the level of cash holdings.

We have noted in earlier chapters that the coefficients of reduced-form equations can be interpreted as multipliers. Accordingly we have

$$\frac{\Delta \$^S}{\Delta H} = \frac{1}{r}$$

This multiplier indicates that a one-dollar increase in high powered money leads to an increase in the money supply of $(1/r)$ dollars. Before looking at a numerical example, let us discuss the reduced-form equation for bank loans. First, rearrange Equation 15.8 and then substitute for R using Equation 15.7:

$$L = D - R$$

$$= D(1 - r)$$

To eliminate D, note that Equation 15.6 implies $D = (\$^S - C)$, and using the reduced-form Equation 15.10 we have

$$L = \frac{(H - C)(1 - r)}{r}$$

The multiplier effect on loans of a change in the quantity of high powered money is therefore

$$\frac{\Delta L}{\Delta H} = \frac{1 - r}{r}$$

The numerical example shown in Table 15.4 illustrates how this expansion of loans and deposits comes about after an increase in high powered money. In the initial situation the total level of deposits is 100. Assuming that the required reserve ratio is 0.1 (to keep the arithmetic simple) and that banks keep no excess reserves, the level of reserves will be 10. The volume of loans is initially at 90. Now suppose that two units of cash are injected into the system and that these are deposited at a chartered bank (the public's cash holdings remain unchanged throughout the exercise). Table 15.4 shows that deposits rise to 102. Total reserves have risen by the same amount, to 12, but required reserves rise only to $(0.1 \times 102) = 10.2$. This means the bank has vault cash of 1.80 that is earning no interest and is not needed as a reserve to back up deposits. The chartered bank is likely to loan out these excess reserves in order to increase profits. Step 2 of the table shows that the effect of this is to increase loans by 1.80 to 91.80. How does a bank extend loans? The bank simply credits the borrower's account with an amount equal to the size of the loan. In this case, deposits rise by the stroke of a pen to 103.80 from 102.00. The borrower will typically spend the money he has just borrowed, but as he does so the account of some other individual will be credited with 1.80 (recall that the nonbank public's cash holdings are assumed to be constant).

Since deposits of 103.80 require reserve holdings of only 10.38, banks will again want to increase loans. The excess reserves (1.62) will be loaned out and both loans and deposits expand together dollar-for-dollar. This process will come to a stop only when excess reserves are back to zero. Since vault cash is 12, deposits have to be 120 before excess reserves are driven to zero. Thus, comparing the final position with the initial situation we find deposits have risen by 20. Two units of these extra deposits come from the injection of cash and the remaining 18, created as excess reserves, are put to work in the form of loans. In this numerical example it is assumed that the required reserve ratio is 0.1, implying a monetary multiplier of $1/r = 10$ and a loan multiplier of $(1 - r)/r = 9$. Note that the increase in reserves of

Table 15.4 Effect of an Increase in High-Powered Money on Chartered Bank Assets and Liabilities

	Assets		Liabilities	
Initial Situation	Reserves:		Deposits	100
	Required	10		
	Excess	0		
	Total	10		
	Loans	90		
		100		100
Injection of Cash	Reserves:		Deposits	102.00
	Required	10.20		
Step 1	Excess	1.80		
	Total	12.00		
	Loans	90.00		
		102.00		102.00
	Reserves:		Deposits	103.80
	Required	10.38		
Step 2	Excess	1.62		
	Total	12.00		
	Loans	91.80		
		103.80		103.80
Final Position	Reserves:		Deposits	120.00
	Required	12.00		
	Excess	0.00		
	Total	12.00		
	Loans	108.00		
		120.00		120.00

two units leads to a monetary expansion of 20 and an increase in loans of 18, confirming the multipliers we derived algebraically.

The **money multiplier** process we have described does not require that banks extend loans at each stage. In practice banks may purchase income-earning assets such as government bonds. However, this will also cause deposits to rise in exactly the same way because banks will credit the bond seller's chequing account with the value of the bonds. No other deposits are reduced so the net effect is for each bank's deposits to rise by an amount equal to the increase in its bond holdings. Equation 15.7 above reminds us that the total of bank assets always equals total liabilities. An increase in reserves will result in an equal expansion of both liabilities (chiefly deposits) and bank assets (reserves, loans, securities).

The Role of the Bank of Canada

The model of the money supply that we have just developed indicates how the stock of high powered money, required reserve ratios, and the behaviour of the banks and the public interact to determine the supply of money and bank credit. In this section we discuss the means used by the Bank of Canada to control the supply of money. In the words of the Governor of the Bank of Canada, "I should point out that the technical means available to the Bank of Canada for slowing down the growth of the money supply is to restrict the quantity of cash reserves it makes available to the banking system."[19] In order to see how the Bank of Canada changes the quantity of reserves let us first examine the balance sheet of the Bank of Canada as it stood at the end of September 1990. This is shown in Table 15.5.

Table 15.5 Bank of Canada Assets and Liabilities, September 1990 (Millions of Dollars)

Assets		Liabilities	
Government of Canada securities:		Notes in circulation	20,506
Treasury bills	13,535	Canadian dollar deposits:	
Other maturities	9,605	Government of Canada	824
Advances*	232	Chartered banks	1,590
All other assets	687	All other liabilities	1,139
Total assets	24,059	Total liabilities	24,059

*Advances to the members of the Canadian Payments Association (primarily chartered banks).

[19] Comments made by the Governor of the Bank of Canada to the Fredericton Chamber of Commerce, June 1976.

The first item on the liabilities side is notes in circulation. These are the Canadian dollar bills that are either held by chartered banks (part of their reserves) or by the nonbank public (part of M1). The second item is Canadian dollar deposits, the most important component of which is the deposits of chartered banks (the remaining part of banks' cash reserves). As we mentioned above, these deposits are used to settle transactions between individual chartered banks. The Government of Canada also keeps deposits at the Bank of Canada, although these are small and are not the government's working balances. Generally, the Government of Canada uses its deposits at chartered banks for its transactions with the private sector.

Open Market Operations

The assets of the Bank of Canada consist largely of government securities such as treasury bills and longer-term bonds. It is through the purchase and sale of treasury bills and other government securities on the open market that the Bank of Canada controls the quantity of high powered money. These financial transactions are called **open market operations**. Suppose, for example, that the Bank of Canada sells treasury bills valued at $100 in the open market. If the purchaser is a corporation, then the firm will pay for the treasury bills by writing a cheque on its account at a chartered bank. The Bank of Canada will present this cheque to the chartered bank for payment. Payment can be made by simply reducing the chartered bank's deposits at the Bank of Canada by $100 (the Bank of Canada now owes the chartered bank $100 less than before). The net result of these transactions is that the corporation now has treasury bills worth $100 and a reduced bank account while the Bank of Canada has reduced both its assets (treasury bills) and its liabilities (chartered bank deposits). The chartered banks collectively have also reduced equally their assets (reserves in the form of deposits at the Bank of Canada) and their liabilities (deposits held by corporations). However, a $100 reduction in both reserves and deposit liabilities leaves the chartered banks with insufficient reserves. Banks are not likely to call in loans to get the extra cash they need to meet the required reserve ratio. Rather, chartered banks will typically sell liquid assets such as treasury bills in an attempt to obtain cash reserves. The increased supply of treasury bills will put downward pressure on their price and therefore upward pressure on interest rates. As the nonbank public purchases the treasury bills, they do so with cheques drawn on demand deposits and consequently the volume of deposits falls. The process will come to an end when deposits have fallen sufficiently to bring reserve ratios into line with the legal requirements.

The effect of open market sales of treasury bills by the Bank of Canada is to raise short-term interest rates and reduce banks' holdings of liquid assets as well as the stock of money. Ultimately the effect of the policy will be felt in the market for loans since banks will want to restore their liquidity position. As bank loans are paid off, banks will acquire more liquid assets rather than extend new loans, resulting in higher interest rates on bank loans. Open market purchases of securities by the Bank of Canada have the reverse effects. Chartered bank reserves are increased and an expansion of chartered bank assets and liabilities ensues. The pressure on interest rates is in the downward direction.

Transfers of Government Deposits

As we mentioned earlier, the Government of Canada keeps deposits at both the chartered banks and the Bank of Canada. A transfer of deposits from the Bank of Canada to the chartered banks has the effect of increasing the quantity of cash reserves. A transfer in the opposite direction leads to a reduction in cash reserves. Suppose, for example, that the federal government moves $100 from the Bank of Canada to the chartered banks. One way to visualize how this process works is to assume the government withdraws cash from its Bank of Canada account and deposits this cash with the chartered banks. The federal government has exchanged one asset for another: deposits at chartered banks for deposits at the Bank of Canada. The Bank of Canada has exchanged one liability for another (government deposits are down $100 and notes outstanding are up $100). The chartered banks find both assets (cash reserves) and liabilities (government deposits) are up $100. Since the reserves required to back the $100 of government deposits amount to just $12, the chartered banks have excess reserves that will be put to work. The result will be a multiple expansion of bank assets and liabilities.

The procedure that we have just described is the second stage of a process that is sometimes referred to as the "monetization of government debt." In Chapter 5 we discussed the alternative ways that the government can finance its spending on goods and services and on transfer payments. The first is through tax revenue. The difference between total government spending and total tax receipts is called the government deficit (if tax revenues exceed government spending the difference is referred to as a budget surplus). The government has two choices in its decision on how to finance a deficit. The first is to sell bonds to the public. But, to persuade the public to buy bonds, a sufficiently high rate of return has to be offered. Sales of large volumes of government bonds will cause market interest rates to rise because the government has to compete for funds along with the private sector (corporations and individuals). The second method of financing the deficit avoids the competition for private sector funds. In this case the government sells its bonds to the Bank of Canada and receives in return bank deposits at the Bank of Canada. In order to spend these deposits they are transferred to the chartered banks. In effect the government has monetized the debt (bonds) by selling the bonds to the Bank of Canada and receiving cash in return. Put differently, the government has simply printed money to pay for its spending. The relationship between the government's budget deficit, *DF*, and the two methods of financing can be represented algebraically:

$$DF = \Delta B + \Delta H$$

This identity says that a government deficit must be reflected in either an increase in government bonds ΔB or an increase in high powered money ΔH. Since a deficit requires the government to sell bonds to the public or to the Bank of Canada, a deficit must increase the total indebtedness of the government; that is, it increases the size of the national debt. The national debt is simply the accumulation of all previous government deficits. In order to reduce the size of the national debt the government must run a budget surplus;[20] if taxes exceed government spending, the difference can be used to retire (buy back) part of the national debt.

One further point can be made from the deficit equation. Note that if the government's budget is balanced the deficit will be zero and

$$\Delta B = -\Delta H$$

In this case the equation describes the result of open market operations. As the Bank of Canada, acting on behalf of the government, sells government bonds (ΔB is positive but not because of a government deficit) the quantity of high powered money falls by the same amount. Open market operations simply change the composition of the national debt — more bonds for less high powered money or vice versa but not the size of the national debt. The shuffling of the composition of the national debt can also take the the form of changing the types of bonds that are issued (long or short bonds, for example). This shuffling is referred to as debt management.

Other Bank of Canada Activities

The Bank of Canada is not only charged with the responsibility of maintaining orderly domestic financial markets, but also has the responsibility of carrying out government policy in the foreign exchange market. As we saw in Chapter 6, it is in this market that the value of the Canadian dollar in terms of other currencies is determined. From time to time

20 The reader is reminded that all the quantities in this discussion are in nominal terms. The real value of the national debt will fall as long as the rate of inflation exceeds the growth rate of the nominal national debt.

the Bank of Canada intervenes in the foreign exchange market, either buying or selling foreign exchange. The Canadian dollar funds that the Bank uses are federal government deposits at the Bank of Canada. As these are spent (when foreign exchange is purchased) cash is injected into the banking system, and the stock of high powered money increases. Unless the Bank of Canada takes offsetting action, a purchase of foreign exchange by the Bank of Canada leads to an increase in the stock of high powered money and a sale of foreign exchange leads to a reduction in the size of this stock. In Chapter 6 we discussed more fully the foreign exchange rate, the balance of payments adjustment mechanism, and monetary and fiscal policy in an open economy.

Our discussion in this section has focused entirely on the ways in which Bank of Canada actions influence the size of cash reserves. As our earlier quote of the Governor of the Bank of Canada indicates, this is the principal channel of Canadian monetary policy. However, there are other discretionary instruments available to the Bank of Canada that we do not explore further. These include the bank rate, secondary reserve requirements, and moral suasion. The student is referred to other sources for an analysis of these monetary policy instruments.[21]

Summary

In the first part of this chapter we discussed the four functions of money: medium of exchange, unit of account, means of deferred payment, and store of wealth. We also looked at the way in which the Bank of Canada actually measures the stock of money. The narrow definitions are motivated by the medium of exchange function of money; that is, bank balances that are immediately spendable (transactions balances). The wider definitions take into account the store of value function of money. From this point of view, savings deposits, for example, which are not immediately spendable, are considered to be money. Two practical problems in defining money are: repeated changes in the type of bank deposits made available by banks and the growing importance of nonbank financial institutions in providing banking services.

In the second section we considered several theories of the demand for money balances. These theories imply hypotheses about the nature of the demand for money which have been tested empirically. Briefly put, these studies have confirmed that the demand for nominal money balances is inversely related to the rate of interest, directly related to the level of real income, and proportional to the price level.

---

[21] *Money, Financial Markets and Economic Activity* by Norman E. Cameron (Don Mills, Ontario: Addison-Wesley, 1991) gives a full description of the instruments of monetary policy in Canada.

In the final section we turned to the supply side of the money market. In the most general models of the money supply process, the stock of money is determined by the behaviour of the chartered banks, the nonbank public, and the Bank of Canada. In the simple model developed in this chapter, the key factors are the stock of high powered money and the required reserve ratios that are prescribed by the Bank Act. An implication of this model is that the supply of money does not depend on the rate of interest; it is interest-inelastic. This is precisely the assumption that was made in Chapter 5 where the *LM* curve was first introduced. There the supply curve for money was shown as a vertical line. Because the Bank of Canada ultimately controls the quantity of high powered money, the Bank of Canada can control the stock of money. The major instrument of control is the open market operations of the Bank.

Key Concepts

the four functions of money:
1. medium of exchange
2. unit of account
3. means of deferred payment
4. store of value

definitions of the stock of money: M1, M2, M2+, M3
the transactions demand for money
liquidity preference
bond prices and bond yields
the quantity theory of money
the stability of the demand for money
required reserves
high powered money
the money multiplier
open market operations

Review Questions

1. Why are there so many definitions of the stock of money?
2. Are Baumol's transactions demand for money and Tobin's theory of liquidity preference substitutes or complements?
3. Why are long-term bond prices more sensitive to changes in long-

term interest rates than are short-term bond prices to short-term interest rates?

4. What is meant by the "transmission mechanism" of monetary policy?
5. How have Keynesian and monetarist views differed on this transmission mechanism?
6. Chartered banks make profits by lending individual A's money to individual B. Why do A and B not get together, split the bank's profit, and eliminate the need for the bank?
7. Use the money supply model that is developed in this chapter to answer the following.
   (a) State all the assumptions required to derive the money and loan multipliers that are given in the text under the heading "A Simple Model of the Money Supply."
   (b) If the required reserve ratio is 0.2, what will be the size of the money and loan multipliers?
8. How does the Bank of Canada influence the money supply through its open market operations?
9. State all the assumptions underlying the money supply model that is developed in the text and use this model to analyze the effects of the following events. In each case state the effect on the money supply and show the final balance sheets. Begin each part with the following initial balance sheets:

Nonbank Public

Assets			*Liabilities*
Treasury bills	50	58	Loans
Demand deposits	100		
Cash	10		
	160	58	

Chartered Banks

Assets			*Liabilities*
Reserves	12	100	Demand deposits
Treasury bills	50	20	Government deposits
Loans	58		
	120	120	

Bank of Canada

Assets			*Liabilities*
Treasury bills	42	22	Notes outstanding
		20	Government deposits
	42	42	

(a) What is the initial money supply?
(b) The government transfers two units from its deposits at the Bank of Canada to the chartered banks.
(c) The government spends two units of its (i) chartered bank deposits, (ii) Bank of Canada deposits. Why are the government's working balances kept at the chartered banks?
(d) The Bank of Canada buys two units of treasury bills from (i) the nonbank public, (ii) the chartered banks. When the Bank of Canada undertakes open market operations to influence the money supply, does it matter who the other participant in the open market transaction is?
(e) The nonbank public withdraws two units of its demand deposits to hold as extra cash. How can the Bank of Canada offset the effects of this event on the money supply?

CHAPTER 16

The Theory of Consumption

> *The study of the consumption function has undoubtedly yielded some of the highest correlations as well as some of the most embarrassing forecasts in the history of economics.*
>
> *Franco Modigliani and Richard Brumberg*[1]

The consumption function is the centrepiece of Keynes's *General Theory*. It formed the basis of Keynes's analysis of why unemployment is likely to be a characteristic of capitalist economies and it also played the key role in the theory of the multiplier process. The simplicity and importance of the aggregate consumption function was so compelling that it soon became the focal point of a vast amount of statistical and theoretical research. In the 1940s and early 1950s a large body of data on consumption patterns was collected and the theory of the aggregate consumption function was pushed forward to meet the challenge of the new observations. In this chapter we will discuss these theoretical developments as well as more recent issues such as the implications of rational expectations for the theory of consumption. In addition, we will consider the effects of fiscal policy measures that have a direct effect on personal consumption. There have been several examples of this kind of fiscal policy during the past two decades. A temporary personal income tax surcharge was imposed in 1968, and in 1975 consumers benefitted from a temporary tax cut. More recently, the Reagan administration introduced a permanent tax cut in the early 1980s. As we shall see, the

---

1 Franco Modigliani and Richard Brumberg, "Utility Analysis and the Consumption Function: An Interpretation of Cross-section Data," in K. Kurihara, ed., *Post-Keynesian Economics* (New Brunswick, N.J.: Rutgers University Press, 1954), p. 388.

effect of a tax cut on personal consumption is likely to be very different, depending on whether the cut is *temporary* or *permanent*.

Facts About Consumption

When researchers first investigated the consumption function, a curious paradox was noticed. This paradox is illustrated in Figure 16.1. First, time-series data collected over a relatively short period of time, say 20 years, result in consumption functions that are relatively flat, that is, the short-run marginal propensity to consume is relatively low and by implication the short-run marginal propensity to save is high. This is illustrated by the line labelled $C = a_0 + bY_d$ in Figure 16.1. Short-run variations in income during the ebb and flow of the business cycle are associated with movements up and down this flatter consumption function. As the economy moves up the short-run consumption function, the ratio of consumption to disposable income, C/Y_d, rises. This consumption ratio is equal to the slope of the broken line that connects the origin to the economy's position on the short-run consumption function. As income rises during a short-run economic expansion, the broken line becomes flatter and the consumption ratio declines. Another way to describe this behaviour is in terms of the **saving ratio**, which is the ratio of saving to disposable income. Since disposable income is the sum of consumption and saving, the consumption and saving ratios always add up to unity. Consequently, when the economy expands and the consumption ratio falls, the saving ratio must be rising. Conversely, during an economic downturn the saving ratio tends to fall.

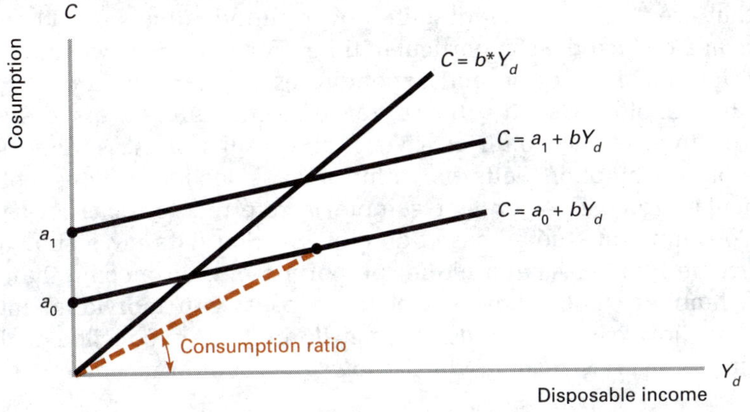

Figure 16.1 Short-run and long-run consumption functions

Keynes, who was the first to write about the consumption function, explained the short-run procyclical[2] behaviour of the saving ratio in terms of people's consumption habits, which he argued are fixed in the short run. Because people are creatures of habit, in the short run, they will not fully adjust their consumption to a new higher level of income. Rather, a part of the extra income will be saved, at least initially. The relatively flat consumption function is consistent with Keynes's view of consumer behaviour.

The second empirical fact associated with consumption is that the short-run consumption function drifts upwards over time, that is, the intercept parameter a becomes larger as the block of observations moves forward in time. In Figure 16.1, the line $C = a_1 + bY_d$ represents a more recent set of data than the parallel but lower line.

The third empirical fact is that if all available data over a very long period of time are considered together, the fitted consumption function is (1) steeper than the short-run functions and (2) passes through the origin. In Figure 16.1 the long-run consumption function is labelled $C = b^*Y_d$. It passes through the origin and has a slope, b^*, which is steeper than the short-run consumption functions. Because the long-run consumption function passes through the origin, the consumption ratio, C/Y_d, *does not* vary with income; it is always equal to b^*. Over the long run, the proportions of income that are consumed and saved are essentially constant, despite short-run cyclical variations. Canadian estimates of **short- and long-run consumption functions** are presented in Figure 16.6, which will be discussed later in the chapter.

The statistical results presented in Figure 16.6 are based on **time-series data** that are collected over time. In a time-series sample there is just one observation on each variable — income, consumption, etc. — at a given time. Usually time-series data are based on economy-wide measures that are necessarily aggregated over all individuals. Another kind of data are collected at a particular time. For example, we may have survey data on the income and expenditures of a large number of individual households. Usually the survey questionnaire covers a specific period of time, say a month or a year. The results of the survey give a picture of consumption patterns within a cross-section of households at a particular time. This kind of sample is referred to as **cross-section data**. Consumption studies based on cross-section data have shown that high-income families save a higher proportion of their income than low-income families, that is, the saving ratio rises with individual income levels. But how can these cross-section findings be reconciled with the long-run time-series results which show that, as real incomes rise over

---

2 Economic variables that rise during business cycle expansions and fall during downturns are said to be "procyclical." The saving ratio is therefore procyclical, but the unemployment rate, which decreases during economic expansions, is countercyclical.

time, the average saving ratio remains essentially stable? Answers were provided in the mid-1950s by two influential theoretical developments. The first is the life-cycle theory proposed by Franco Modigliani and his associates. The second is the famous permanent income hypothesis developed by Milton Friedman. Both approaches are able to account for the apparent contradictions in the cross-section and the short- versus long-run time-series findings. In addition, both approaches have significant policy implications which will be taken up in a later section. More recently, the rational expectations revolution has had an effect on research into aggregate consumption behaviour and these issues will also be addressed. Our first task, however, is to deal with some preliminaries concerning the definition of consumption, which we have already alluded to in Chapter 2.

The Measurement of Consumption

As we discussed in Chapter 2, the National Income and Expenditure Accounts record the total value of goods and services that consumers purchase each year. These data form the basis of time-series studies of the aggregate consumption function. Unfortunately, the data in their raw form do not correspond to the economist's concept of personal consumption, which focuses on the flow of consumption services rather than the flow of expenditures. The difficulty concerns durable goods that are purchased in a particular year but consumed gradually over several years. Take, for example, the case of an automobile that sells for $10,000. Obviously the automobile yields a flow of services to the owner during the whole life of the automobile. For simplicity we may assume that the car lasts for ten years and that each year the consumer receives $1,000 worth of services from the car. After ten years the car is rusted-out and has no value. The purchaser has consumed all the services that were initially embodied in the car at the rate of $1,000 per year.[3]

The National Income and Expenditure Accounts record the spending of $10,000 on the car (under personal expenditure on durable goods) in the year when the purchase is made. This figure greatly overestimates the individual's actual consumption of car services during the first year. In fact, in our illustration, the individual bought a new car for $10,000, but only $1,000 of this is actually consumed in the first year. At the end of the year the purchaser has an asset, in the form of a car, worth $9,000. Since the purchase of assets, such as stocks, bonds, and term deposits is referred to as saving, it reasonable to say that the purchaser

3 In practice, the car is not consumed at an even rate. The annual consumption is initially very high and then diminishes as the car ages. We have ignored this complication in our illustration.

of the car consumed $1,000 of new car services and saved $9,000. In the second year of car ownership, the individual makes no outlays under the heading of "car purchases," but consumption is again valued at $1,000 per year. At the end of the second year the wealth that the individual has in the car has declined to $8,000 (the consumption is "paid for" through dissaving as the asset value of the car is reduced).

An implication of this argument is that the flow of consumption services derived from a car is much smoother than the individual's flow of spending on new cars. Spending takes place in discrete lumps, while consumption is maintained at a more or less even level. It is true that this argument becomes much weaker when we aggregate over a number of individuals because not all individuals replace their durable goods at the same time. Nevertheless, the replacement of durable goods tends to coincide with the expansion phase of the business cycle. A large part of this spending on durable goods is not consumption but it is in fact saving. In empirical studies of consumer behaviour, typically the objective is to explain consumption, not expenditures. The problem that the data refer to expenditures rather than consumption is tackled in one of two ways. The first approach involves adjusting the actual data on durable goods expenditure in order to get a better measure of the flow of services from the *stock* of durables. Milton Friedman tried to follow this approach as closely as possible in his time-series work: "[We] treat expenditures on major consumer durables in excess of their use value in services rendered by them as savings and include in consumption only the estimated value of their services."[4] The second approach is to simply exclude expenditure on durables from the study, that is, to focus exclusively on the consumption of nondurable goods and services.[5]

The Life-Cycle Hypothesis

The **life-cycle theory** of consumption was first proposed by Modigliani and Brumberg in 1955. The central feature of this theory is that the individual's current consumption and saving decisions are part of a lifetime plan that recognizes that the typical individual does not have a constant flow of income throughout his lifetime. How much is consumed and how much is saved out of current income does not depend only, or even chiefly, on the level of current income. In retirement, for example,

4 Milton Friedman, *A Theory of the Consumption Function* (National Bureau of Economic Research, 1957), p. 116.

5 Two recent examples of research that focused on nondurables are: Robert E. Hall, "Stochastic Implications of the Life-cycle–Permanent Income Hypothesis: Theory and Evidence," *Journal of Political Economy*, vol. 86 (December 1978), pp. 971–87 and Alan S. Blinder and Angus Deaton, "The Time Series Consumption Function Revisited," *Brookings Papers on Economic Activity*, vol. 2, 1985, pp. 465–521.

income usually falls well below the pre-retirement level. Few individuals would plan their affairs so that their level of consumption would fall dramatically as soon as they retire. It is much more likely that an individual would prefer to maintain a fairly constant level of consumption. This can be achieved by saving during the high-income years and dissaving during the low-income years.

Figure 16.2 illustrates a typical lifetime profile of income and consumption. The income profile is shown in colour and the consumption profile is shown in black. Throughout his working life the individual consumes less than his income. Savings accumulate steadily up until retirement in year *N*. At this point the individual's wealth, which is at its lifetime peak, is represented by the coloured area. As soon as he retires his income likely falls sharply, but consumption is maintained at a steady level as the individual's wealth is gradually reduced during retirement. By the end of his life in period *L*, the total amount of dissaving during retirement is equal to the grey area.

Central to the life-cycle hypothesis is the argument that the level of consumption in any particular period depends much more on an individual's expected lifetime resources than on his current income, which for one reason or another may be unusually low or unusually high in relation to the average income expected over a lifetime. This proposition clearly contradicts the hypothesis that underlies the simple

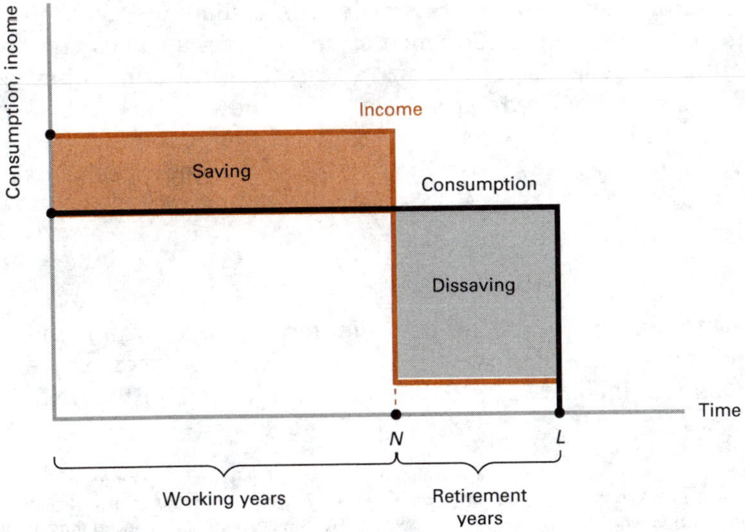

Figure 16.2 Lifetime consumption and income profiles for the typical individual

conventional Keynesian consumption function, namely that *current* consumption is a function of *current* disposable income. As we shall see, Modigliani and Brumberg's theoretical analysis leads them to include two more variables, other than current income, in the aggregate consumption function. The analysis begins, however, at the level of the individual.

The Individual Consumption Function

Consider an individual who expects to retire at the end of year N. He plans to accumulate sufficient wealth during his working life that his consumption will remain constant throughout both his working life and retirement years. Suppose he expects to live to the end of year L so that the total number of retirement years is $(L - N)$. Assuming that he expects no income during retirement, and that he plans to maintain a constant level of consumption c_t (where the subscript indicates year t), the amount of wealth he must accumulate by the end of his working life, W_N, is the product of the number of retirement years $(L - N)$ and the annual consumption c_t:[6]

$$W_N = (L - N)c_t \tag{16.1}$$

Suppose we observe this individual at the beginning of year t, sometime during his working life. The amount of wealth that he has already accumulated by the end of period $(t - 1)$ is W_{t-1} and his current income is y_t. During the rest of his working life, which amounts to $(N - t)$ years after the current year, the sequence of annual real incomes can be represented by the symbols $y_{t+1}, y_{t+2}, \ldots, y_N$. The individual himself may think of this possibly irregular stream of income in terms of an average annual income that he expects to earn over the remaining $(N - t)$ years of his working life. We will use the symbol y_t^e to represent this expected average income:

$$y_t^e = \frac{(y_{t+1} + y_{t+2} + \ldots + y_N)}{(N - t)}$$

At the beginning of year t, the total lifetime resources of this individual consist of his accumulated wealth W_{t-1}, his current income y_t, and the average annual income y_t^e he expects to earn in each of the next $(N - t)$

[6] Throughout our analysis of the life-cycle model of consumption we will ignore the problems of uncertainty. In practice, people do not know when they will actually die or even when they will retire so the numbers L and N are at best estimates. The implications of this uncertainty are ignored in the present discussion. In addition, we will assume that the rate of interest is zero. This assumption greatly simplifies the algebra because it allows us to combine incomes from different periods without having to worry about discounting or the cumulative effects of compound interest. This simplification allows the essence of the theory to be explained most simply.

years. His total lifetime resources, as they appear at the beginning of year t, amount to

$$W_{t-1} + y_t + (N - t)y_t^e$$

To compute the annual consumption level that can be maintained throughout his working and retirement years he must divide his total lifetime resources by the number of years he expects to live. Since he expects to die at the end of year L and it is now at the beginning of year t, he expects to live another $(L - t + 1)$ years. By dividing the number of remaining years into total lifetime resources, we can calculate the value of annual consumption. Thus, the life-cycle hypothesis leads to the following individual consumption function:

$$c_t = \frac{[W_{t-1} + y_t + (N - t)y_t^e]}{(L - t + 1)} \qquad (16.2)$$

The first point to note is that the quantity of wealth appears in the consumption function. From Equation 16.2, the marginal propensity to consume out of wealth is $1/(L - t + 1)$, which clearly depends on the age of the individual. As the individual gets older, $(L - t + 1)$ becomes smaller so that the change in consumption becomes larger for any given change in wealth. For example, when $t = L$ the individual is at the beginning of the last year of his life. In this case the marginal propensity to consume out of wealth is unity; any increase in wealth is consumed entirely. However, when $t = L - 1$ the individual is at the beginning of his penultimate year. The marginal propensity to consume out of wealth is 0.5, which means that one-half of any windfall increase in wealth at this time will be consumed in each of the two remaining years. At the other extreme, an individual who expects to live another 50 years will have a marginal propensity to consume out of wealth of only 0.02.

The marginal propensity to consume out of current income MPC_y cannot be determined uniquely from Equation 16.2 because a change in current income y_t may induce the individual to change his expectations concerning his future average income. For example, a promotion and a salary increase will very likely lead to an upward revision of future earnings. The sensitivity of expectations about future income to changes in current income influences the size of the MPC. In general, we have

$$\Delta c_t = \frac{[\Delta y_t + (N - t)\Delta y_t^e]}{(L - t + 1)}$$

For purposes of illustration, suppose that the change in current income is assumed by the individual to be a permanent change in income so that $\Delta y_t^e = \Delta y_t$. In this case, the marginal propensity to consume out of income is

$$MPC_y = \frac{\Delta c_t}{\Delta y_t}$$

$$= \frac{(1 + N - t)}{(L - t + 1)}$$

As age increases, MPC_y declines. To illustrate, suppose that the typical working life is 40 years ($N = 40$) and that the retirement period lasts for 10 years ($L = 50$). At the beginning of the tenth year of work ($t = 10$), MPC_y is (1 + 40 – 10)/(50 – 10 + 1), which is approximately 0.75. By the beginning of the thirtieth year of work, MPC_y has fallen to (1 + 40 – 30)/(50 – 30 + 1), which is approximately 0.5. The common sense of this arithmetic is that a young person who receives a permanent increase in income has many years over which to accumulate savings for her retirement. She can therefore afford to consume a large proportion of any increase in income. An older person has fewer years left to save for retirement and must therefore consume less of any increase in income if a higher level of consumption is to be maintained throughout the working and retirement years. Modigliani and Brumberg cite cross-section statistical evidence that shows the marginal propensity to consume does indeed decline with age.

Cross-Section Studies

Cross-sections of the general population show that the personal saving ratio tends to rise with the level of income. As we have seen, this means that an aggregate consumption function that is estimated from cross-section data has a positive intercept on the vertical axis. More careful analysis of different sub-groups within society reveals some interesting differences in behaviour. For example, cross-section analysis of groups whose individual members have highly unstable incomes, such as farmers, shows that the saving ratio has a great deal of variation within the cross-section compared to the general population; the consumption function for a group with unstable incomes is relatively flat and has a positive vertical intercept. This is illustrated in Figure 16.3. In contrast, for groups that have very stable incomes over time, such as teachers and college professors, the saving ratio is essentially constant and independent of the level of income, that is, the intercept of the aggregate consumption function is close to zero. This case is also illustrated in Figure 16.3.

In order to demonstrate how the life-cycle hypothesis can account for these apparently puzzling cross-section findings, it is useful to introduce the notion of "life-cycle" equilibrium for the individual. There are two aspects to this concept. The first condition for equilibrium is that the

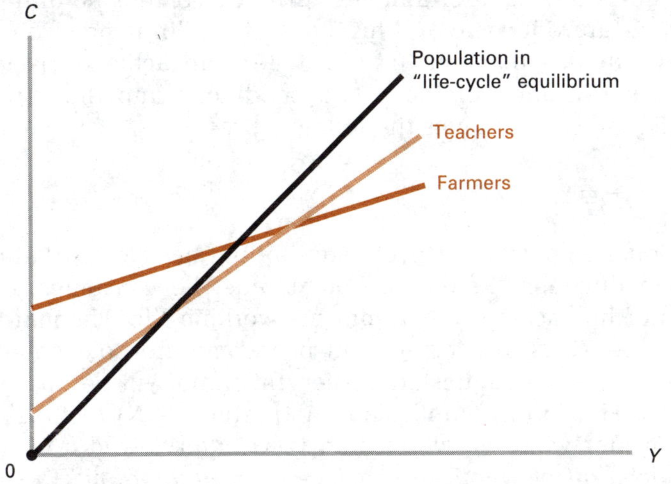

Figure 16.3 Cross-section consumption functions

individual's current income must be identical to current expectations about future income,

$$Y_t = Y_t^e \tag{16.3}$$

The second condition concerns the individual's stock of wealth. As we have seen, the individual plans to accumulate sufficient wealth after working for N years so that his current level of consumption can be maintained throughout his working and retirement years. Equation 16.1 shows that the required amount of wealth that must be accumulated by the end of his working life is $W_N = (L - N)c_t$, where c_t is the constant level of consumption. At the beginning of year t, the individual has already worked for $(t - 1)$ of his total N working years. If the savings plan is on schedule, his wealth at the end of year $t - 1$ (or the beginning of year t) must be a fraction $(t - 1)/N$ of the final objective W_N:

$$W_{t-1} = \frac{W_N(t-1)}{N} \tag{16.4}$$

$$= \frac{(L-N)c_t(t-1)}{N}$$

If Equations 16.3 and 16.4 are both satisfied, the individual can be said to be in "life-cycle" equilibrium. His current income is no different from his expected future income and his stock of wealth is precisely where it ought to be at this point in his life if he is to achieve his long-term goals. The substitution of these two conditions into the consumption function, Equation 16.2, gives the following result:[7]

$$c_t = \frac{N}{L} y_t \tag{16.5}$$

The individual who is in life-cycle equilibrium has a remarkably simple consumption function. Regardless of his age, he consumes a constant proportion of his income throughout his working life. His marginal and average propensities to consume out of income are both equal to N/L. Using the figures we suggested earlier, this ratio will be approximately 40/50 or 0.8. This in turn implies a saving ratio $(L - N)/L$ of 0.2.

Now consider what we would find if we interviewed a cross-section of individuals, *all of whom are in life-cycle equilibrium*. To the extent that every person has approximately the same values for N and L, their saving ratios will all be approximately the same and equal to $(L - N)/L$ *regardless* of age and income level. The aggregate consumption function for such a group would be identical to Equation 16.5. It would pass through the origin and have a slope equal to N/L (see Figure 16.3). In practice no social group consists of individuals who are all in equilibrium. However, such groups as teachers and professors have very modest fluctuations in their annual incomes compared to the population as a whole. The current income of a teacher is very likely to be close to his expected annual income. In addition, the stability of his income makes it more likely that his actual wealth will be close to the desired level, given the individual's lifetime goals. Consequently, individuals with stable incomes are likely to come close to satisfying the two equilibrium conditions described by Equations 16.3 and 16.4. The prediction of the life-cycle hypothesis that the aggregate cross-section consumption function for a group with stable incomes will pass through the origin is confirmed by the facts.

---

7 Multiply both sides of Equation 16.2 by $(L - t + 1)$ and then subsititute Equations 16.3 and 16.4. This gives

$$(L - t + 1)c_t = \frac{(t-1)(L-N)}{N} c_t + y_t + (N - t)y_t$$

Multiply throughout by N and collect terms in c_t and y_t.

$$[N(L - t + 1) - (t - 1)(L - N)]c_t = N(1 + N - t)y_t$$

or

$$L(1 + N - t)c_t = N(1 + N - t)y_t$$

which reduces to

$$c_t = \frac{N}{L} y_t$$

Let us turn now to consider the savings behaviour of an individual whose income differs from his expected lifetime average. Suppose that he is initially in equilibrium, but suddenly experiences an unexpected increase in his current income. This raises his lifetime resources and therefore his lifetime consumption.[8] Since retirement consumption will also be increased, the amount of wealth that must be accumulated by the retirement age W_N is correspondingly increased. The current level of wealth is now too low given the upward revision in W_N, so the individual must raise his saving ratio to build up his wealth to the appropriate level. Once this is done, and if there are no further changes in income, the individual will be back in equilibrium and the saving ratio will return to the equilibrium value $(L - N)/N$. The conclusion of the analysis is that an individual whose current annual income is above his expected annual income will save a higher proportion of his current income than others who are in equilibrium, regardless of their age or income level. Conversely, an individual with a current income that is below his expected lifetime average will save a smaller share of his current income than those who are in equilibrium.

As we have seen, cross-section analysis of the farming population reveals a positive correlation between the level of income and the saving ratio. The consumption function for this group is flat and has a positive vertical intercept; it does not pass through the origin. According to the life-cycle hypothesis, the reason for this is that, at any given time, most individuals are not in equilibrium. Because incomes fluctuate from year to year, the high-income group within the cross-section will have a large share of individuals who have incomes that are above their lifetime average. As a result, the high-income group will consist of a large share of individuals whose saving ratios are above the equilibrium value of $(L - N)/N$. Similarly, the low-income group in the cross-section will have a relatively large share of individuals whose saving ratios are below the equilibrium value of $(L - N)/N$. It is not surprising that in cross-section studies of farming communities, investigators have found a positive correlation between the level of income and the saving ratio, and determined that the aggregate consumption function has a positive intercept and is relatively flat.

Within the population as a whole, most individuals experience considerable fluctuations in their annual incomes, perhaps on a smaller scale than farmers or salespeople but more than teachers and college professors. According to the life-cycle hypothesis, it is the variability in income *over time* that gives rise to the positive relationship between

---

8 We continue to make the key assumption that consumption will be maintained at a constant proportion of lifetime resources until death.

income and the saving ratio *within a cross-section*. If each individual's income were always equal to his expected lifetime average, everyone would save the same proportion of his income, regardless of age and income. For such a group, the aggregate cross-section consumption function would pass through the origin.

Time-Series Studies

The major difficulty with the simple Keynesian consumption function is that the intercept a must be positive to account for the short-run procyclical behaviour of the saving ratio, but must be zero to explain the tendency of the saving ratio to be constant in the long run. To resolve the paradox, note that Equation 16.2 suggests that the aggregate consumption function can be represented by

$$C_t = \alpha W_{t-1} + \beta_1 Y_t + \beta_2 Y_t^e \tag{16.6}$$

where C_t and Y_t are aggregate consumption and aggregate disposable income, respectively, in period t.[9] Aggregate average annual expected future income as perceived in period t is Y_t^e, and W_{t-1} is the value of real wealth that is carried over from the previous period.

A major difficulty in using time-series data to estimate the unknown parameters α, β_1, and β_2 in Equation 16.6 is that there are no published data for the variable Y_t^e, since this variable exists only in the minds of consumers. In practice it is necessary to measure expected future income indirectly. Ando and Modigliani consider a number of possibilities; the simplest is to assume that expected future income is proportional to current income,[10]

$$Y_t^e = \gamma Y_t$$

The substitution of Y_t^e in Equation 16.6 gives the following consumption function:

$$C_t = \alpha W_{t-1} + (\beta_1 + \beta_2) Y_t$$

or

$$C_t = \alpha W_{t-1} + \beta Y_t, \tag{16.7}$$

9 In Equation 16.2 the coefficients on wealth and current income are identical. However, when the model is fitted to aggregate data, investigators are likely to estimate the coefficients separately. Using statistical methods, it would be possible to test the hypothesis that the coefficients are equal in the aggregate consumption function.

10 Alternatively, expected income may be a weighted average of current and past levels of income. See the permanent income hypothesis, which is discussed below.

where

$$\beta = \beta_1 + \gamma\beta_2$$

Note that as far as the current period is concerned, the quantity of real wealth that is left over from the previous period is given. Equation 16.7 shows that the product of the wealth parameter α and the lagged value of wealth W_{t-1} is the positive intercept in the short-run consumption function.

First, consider the consumption function in period one, which is labelled C_1 in Figure 16.4. Total consumption can be broken down into two components. The first of these depends on the value of accumulated real wealth αW_0, which is fixed in period one. The second component depends on the level of current income in period one, Y'_1. Total consumption in period one can take any number of potential values depending on the level of current income. These possible values all lie on the short-run consumption function. For example, if income in period one is relatively low due to a cyclical downturn, say Y'_1, the ratio of consumption to income will be relatively high and the saving ratio will be relatively low. Conversely, if income in period one is at a cyclical peak, say Y'_2, the saving ratio will be relatively high. As we saw earlier in this chapter, it is the positive intercept in the short-run consumption function that guarantees that the saving ratio follows a pro-cyclical path. In the life-cycle hypothesis it is the presence of real wealth in the aggregate consumption function that determines the positive intercept.

Over time, however, the level of real wealth increases and the vertical intercept αW_{t-1} shifts upwards. In Figure 16.4 the short-run consumption function for period two is above and parallel to the short-run consumption function for period one. Although the level of real wealth is taken as given in the short run, in the long run real wealth grows steadily. In fact, over the long term, real wealth and real incomes have grown at approximately the same rates, which means that over the long term these two variables are roughly proportional to each other:

$$W_{t-1} = \delta Y_t$$

The substitution of W_{t-1} in Equation 16.7 gives the following long-run consumption function:

$$C_t = (\alpha\delta + \beta)Y_t \qquad (16.9)$$

In the long run, consumption is proportional to income and the saving ratio is constant at all levels of income. According to Equation

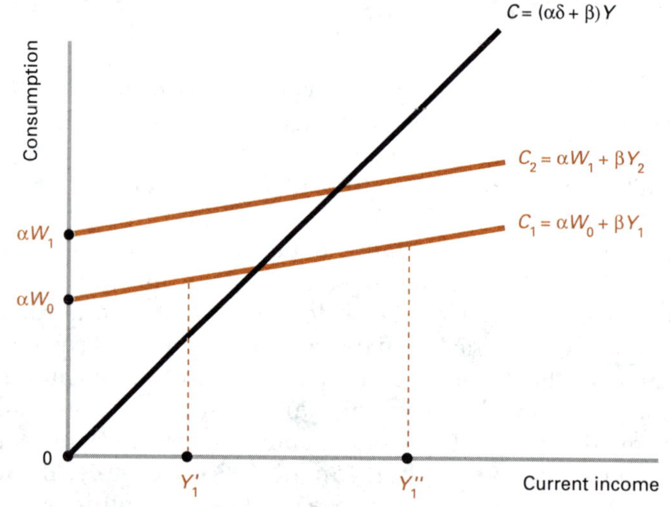

Figure 16.4 Short-run and long-run consumption functions — the life-cycle hypothesis

16.9, the long-run marginal propensity to consume is $\alpha\delta + \beta$, which exceeds the short-run marginal propensity to consume by the positive quantity $\alpha\delta$. The empirical evidence presented by Ando and Modigliani[11] suggests that the short-run marginal propensity to consume β is approximately 0.7. The short-run marginal propensity to consume out of wealth α is approximately 0.04. Finally, the ratio of wealth to income δ is approximately 5 over the long term. These rough figures suggest a long-run marginal propensity to consume out of income of about 0.9.

The Permanent Income Hypothesis

The **permanent income hypothesis**, which was proposed by Professor Milton Friedman in 1957, is also capable of explaining the cross-section and time-series findings on the behaviour of aggregate consumption. The permanent income hypothesis differs only in its details from the life-cycle hypothesis that we have already discussed. Both hypotheses share the important point that current consumption depends not on current income but rather on a longer-run concept of income which Friedman termed "permanent income." Although Modigliani and Brumberg

---

11 A. Ando and F. Modigliani, "The 'Life-Cycle' Hypothesis of Saving: Aggregate Implications and Tests," *American Economic Review*, March 1963, pp. 55–84.

also wrote of the permanent component of income, this term is now almost exclusively associated with the name of Friedman. In developing this concept, Friedman began with a definition of income that was first proposed by Sir John Hicks.

According to Hicks, an individual's real annual income is the maximum amount that he could consume while maintaining intact his stock of real wealth. Suppose, for example, that an individual's wealth amounts to $100,000. If this wealth is invested in a variety of assets that yield an average real rate of return of 5 percent per annum, this individual could consume $5,000 per annum in real terms without eroding the real stock of wealth, which will remain at $100,000 in real terms. Accordingly, this individual's real income is defined to be $5,000 per year.

Friedman pointed out that there are two distinct types of wealth, human and nonhuman. Human wealth reflects the individual's capacity to earn income. Suppose that an individual's current and future annual earned incomes are $y_0, y_1, y_2, \ldots, y_N$. The present value of this stream of future incomes constitutes his human wealth W_H:

$$W_H = y_0 + \frac{y_1}{(1 + RR)} + \frac{y_2}{(1 + RR)^2} + \ldots + \frac{y_N}{(1 + RR)^N}$$

In addition to human wealth, an individual may own some nonhuman wealth W_{NH}, such as stocks, bonds, and durable goods. The individual's total wealth W is the sum of human and nonhuman wealth:

$$W = W_H + W_{NH}$$

Friedman defines the individual's real permanent income to be

$$y^p = RR \times W$$

where RR is the representative real rate of return earned on all forms of wealth.

In any given year, an individual's actual income is likely to be different from his permanent income. There are many possible reasons for this. It may be that a worker has been temporarily laid off so that his current income y is below his permanent income y^p. The difference between the two is called transitory income, $y^t = y - y^p$, which in this case is negative. Throughout an individual's lifetime there will be periods when transitory income is positive and periods when it is negative. However, the central assumption of the permanent income hypothesis is that consumption is proportional to permanent income and is quite unrelated to transitory income. This means that the worker who has just been temporarily laid off will not reduce his consumption unless being laid off causes him to change his views about his permanent income. Similarly, a temporary income tax cut will lead to a temporary increase in disposable income. Since permanent income will be essentially unchanged, Friedman would argue that a temporary tax cut will do nothing to stimulate consumption. A temporary tax cut, according to the permanent income hypothesis, will lead to a temporary increase in the saving ratio.

The permanent income hypothesis that the individual's consumption is proportional to his permanent income can be written in the form of an equation,

$$c_t = ky^p \tag{16.10}$$

Since y^p is not directly observable, empirical research requires an additional assumption about the way in which individuals form expectations of their future incomes. The two distinct alternatives are rational and adaptive expectations, which were discussed in Chapter 8. The implications of rational expectations for the theory of consumption were first recognized by Robert Hall.[12] This is taken up in the next section. We will then turn to the more traditional adaptive expectations approach.

Rational Expectations and Permanent Income

The most important feature of expectations that are formed rationally is that they do not consistently over- or under-forecast the target variable. Forecast errors made under rational expectations must be purely random and therefore cannot contain any forecastable component. For example, if an individual consistently over-forecasts the hours he or she will be able to work in the upcoming week, the rational thing to do is to modify the forecast rule to correct this systematic error. As soon as the systematic errors are eliminated, the forecast errors will then be truly random.

In order to estimate the value of human wealth, it is necessary to forecast the flow of future income. In making the rational forecast, all available relevant information must be taken into account. From one period of time to another, events may occur that will require the forecasts to be modified. The essence of the rational expectations assumption is that only unexpected (random) events will cause a revision in the forecasts of future income and hence in the estimate of total wealth. All other events that are anticipated with certainty — for example, graduation, job promotion, or marriage — will already enter into the calculations before they actually occur. Given that these events are anticipated with certainty, then their actual occurrence at some later date will not

---

[12] Robert E. Hall, "Stochastic Implications of the Life-cycle–Permanent Income Hypothesis: Theory and Evidence," *Journal of Political Economy*, vol. 86 (December 1978), pp. 971–88.

result in changes in expectations about the future, nor the estimate of total wealth. In short, if life's plan unfolds according to previously held expectations, then there will be no need to modify the plan. Only *unforecastable, random* events, such as an unexpected long-term illness or disability, will lead to revisions in the estimate of total wealth. This in turn means that any subsequent changes in the estimate of wealth must themselves be random and unforecastable. This proposition can be expressed simply in mathematical terms. Using subscripts to denote the time period and assuming the real interest rate is constant, we can write permanent income in periods t and $t + 1$ as

$$y_t^p = RR \times W_t \quad \text{and} \quad y_{t+1}^p = RR \times W_{t+1}$$

Subtracting values in period t from those in period $t + 1$ gives

$$\begin{aligned} y_{t+1}^p - y_t^p &= RR(W_{t+1} - W_t) \\ &= RR \times u \end{aligned}$$

where u represents the random, unforecastable change in total wealth between periods t and $t + 1$. The implication is that permanent income also changes in a random and unforecastable manner through time. In the special case in which no random events occur to disturb previously held expectations, then u would be zero and permanent income would remain constant through time.

The importance of this argument for consumption is revealed by Equation 16.10, which implies

$$c_{t+1} - c_t = k(y_{t+1}^p - y_t^p)$$

$$c_{t+1} - c_t = k \times RR \times u \qquad (16.11)$$

or, taking c_t to the right-hand side we have:

$$c_{t+1} = c_t + k \times RR \times u \qquad (16.12)$$

The interpretation of Equation 16.11 is that changes in consumption from period t to $t + 1$ are random because u is itself random. This proposition is usually expressed by the statement that consumption follows a *random walk*. Equation 16.12 illustrates a second point, namely, that the best and rational forecast for consumption in period $t + 1$ is simply the observed level of consumption in period t since the other component on the right-hand side is random and unforecastable. This is bad news indeed for those who make their living by selling "sophisticated" economic forecasts!

The rational expectations model of consumption therefore has two related implications that are testable. The first is that consumption follows a *random walk* and the second is that the only relevant information for forecasting *next period's* level of consumption is the *current* level of consumption. If the rational expectations model is correct, then it should be impossible to find additional information that will improve this simple forecast.

There has been a considerable amount of empirical work on the rational expectations hypothesis. On balance the empirical studies tend to support the permanent income theory of consumption but reject the strict rational expectations hypothesis. As Equation 16.10 indicates, rational expectations theory implies that the change in consumption from one period to the next should be random and therefore the change in consumption should be unrelated to information that is available in period t. A study by Marjorie Flavin[13] found that changes in consumption are *not* purely random, but are correlated with current income — a clear rejection of the permanent income/rational expectations hypothesis. In a more recent study, Blinder and Deaton[14] came to the same conclusion. However, in discussing Blinder and Deaton's paper, Robert Hall[15] argued that the case should not yet be closed because the models used by Flavin and by Blinder and Deaton may be deficient. Properly specified rational expectations models may yet be shown to be consistent with the data.

Adaptive Expectations and Permanent Income

In many empirical applications of the permanent income hypothesis the adaptive expectations formulation of permanent income has been used. The principal feature of the adaptive expectations approach is that expectations about the future are assumed to be modified in the light of recent experience. It seems perfectly plausible that if current events are at variance with previously held expectations, then expectations are likely to be changed. For example, if current income is repeatedly below permanent income, then it is very likely that permanent income will be revised downwards. A simple equation illustrates the adaptive expectations interpretation of permanent income:

$$y_t^p = (1 - a)y_{t-1}^p + ay_t \qquad (16.13)$$

where $0 < a < 1$. The first point to notice about Equation 16.13 is that permanent income remains unaltered as long as actual income contin-

13 Marjorie A. Flavin, "The Adjustment of Consumption to Changing Expectations about Future Income," *Journal of Political Economy*, vol. 89 (October 1981), pp. 974–1009.

14 Blinder and Deaton, "The Time Series Consumption Function Revisited," pp. 465–521.

15 *Ibid.*

ues to equal permanent income. This can be demonstrated by setting current income, y_t, equal to the previous level of permanent income, y^p_{t+1}. However, if current income differs from the previous value of permanent income, then permanent income will change. The parameter a represents the speed with which permanent income is altered when actual and permanent income are different. In the extreme case that a equals zero, permanent income never changes, that is, expectations never adjust. In the other extreme case, when $a = 1$, permanent income instantly adjusts to equal the current level of actual income. For values of a between zero and unity, permanent income is a weighted average of its previous value and the current value of actual income with high values of a corresponding to rapid adjustment in expectations.

The adaptive expectations assumption has played an important role in empirical studies of the consumption function because it allows us to express *unobservable permanent income* in terms of *directly observable actual income*. This can be demonstrated by noting that Equation 16.13 holds for any given time. In period $t - 1$, for example,

$$y^p_{t-1} = (1 - a)y^p_{t-2} + ay_{t-1}$$

By substituting y^p_{t-1} into Equation 16.13, we obtain

$$y^p_t = ay_t + (1 - a)ay_{t-1} + (1 - a)^2 y^p_{t-2}$$

By repeating this process a total of n times the current level of *permanent income* can be expressed in terms of previous levels of *actual income*:

$$y^p_t = a[y_t + (1 - a)y_{t-1} + (1 - a)^2 y_{t-2} + \dots + (1 - a)^n y_{t-n}] \qquad (16.14)$$

$$+ (1 - a)^{n+1} y^p_{t-n-1}$$

Notice that because a and $(1 - a)$ are fractions, the size of the coefficients on distant income levels is small. In particular, the process of repeatedly substituting for permanent income on the right-hand side steadily reduces the coefficient on permanent income towards zero, that is, $(1 - a)^{n+1}$ tends to zero as n gets larger. It is also interesting to note that when a is close to unity, the coefficient on current income, y_t, is large and the coefficients on the lagged levels of income decline very rapidly because $(1 - a)$ is close to zero. Thus, when a is large, and expectations adjust very quickly, permanent income is primarily determined by current and very recent levels of actual income. On the other hand, when a is small, and expectations adjust slowly, permanent income depends less on current income and more on the long history of actual income levels.

As mentioned above, the significance of the adaptive expectations assumption is that it makes the permanent income hypothesis operational by allowing the parameters of the consumption function to be estimated using data on consumption and actual income. Equations 16.10 and 16.14 can be combined to give

$$c_t = b_0 y_t + b_1 y_{t-1} + b_2 y_{t-2} + \ldots \qquad (16.15)$$

where the parameters b_0, b_1, etc., depend on k and a. Theoretically, there are an infinite number of terms on the right-hand side, but because the coefficients b_0, b_1, b_2, . . . decline towards zero, only the first few need be considered in empirical work. In Milton Friedman's original analysis of the aggregate consumption function, 17 terms were included on the right-hand side, but the first 4 coefficients accounted for 80 percent of the total (the sum of all 17 coefficients). In the next section we will illustrate how the adaptive expectations version of the permanent income hypothesis is able to explain time-series data.[16]

Permanent Income and Time-Series Studies

The purpose of this section is to describe how the adaptive expectations version of the permanent income hypothesis can explain the relationship between the short- and long-run time-series consumption functions. Our starting point is Equation 16.14. But to simplify the analysis, consider an example in which only three terms appear on the right-hand side. Specifically, suppose that aggregate permanent income, Y_t^p, is estimated by a weighted average of current income and income during the last two years (with weights of 1/2, 1/3, and 1/6):

$$Y_t^p = \frac{1}{2}Y_t + \frac{1}{3}Y_{t-1} + \frac{1}{6}Y_{t-2} \qquad (16.16)$$

Note that the weights sum to unity. This ensures that if actual income remains constant for an indefinite period, permanent income will be equal to actual income. However, an increase in current income of \$1 raises permanent income in our example by only 50¢ in the current period. This is because the individual is not sure that the increase in Y is indeed permanent. If the increase in income persists for another period, permanent income is raised by another 1/3 of \$1 or 33¢. Finally, if

[16] The manner in which the permanent income hypothesis accounts for the positive relationship between the level of income and the saving ratio that is found in cross-section studies is similar to the explanation offered by Modigliani and Brumberg. Essentially, the high saving ratio of the high-income group within a cross-section reflects the relatively large number of individuals within this group who have positive transitory incomes. Since transitory income is saved, the high-income group has a high saving ratio. Similarly the low-income group has a large number of individuals who have negative transitory income and who therefore have low saving ratios.

the increase in current income is maintained into the third period, permanent income will be adjusted by another 1/6 of $1 or 17¢. In our simple illustration it takes three periods for a change in permanent income. The substitution of Y into the long-run consumption function, Equation 16.10, gives the following short-run consumption function:

$$C_t = k\left(\frac{1}{3}Y_{t-1} + \frac{1}{6}Y_{t-2}\right) + \frac{k}{2}Y_t \qquad (16.17)$$

From the point of view of the current period, the income levels Y_{t-1} and Y_{t-2} are given. The relationship between current income and current consumption is therefore linear. The term $k[(1/3)Y_{t-1} + (1/6)Y_{t-2}]$ is the intercept and the term $k/2$ is the short-run marginal propensity to consume out of current income. The intercept of the short-run consumption function is determined, in part, by the levels of income in the two previous periods. Since the marginal propensity to consume out of current income is just $k/2$, the short-run consumption function is relatively flat. The fundamental reason for this, as we have seen, is that increases in current income are not considered to be permanent. Individuals therefore consume only a small fraction of any increase in current income. The following numerical example illustrates the relationship between the short-run and long-run consumption functions.

Friedman estimates that the long-run marginal propensity to consume out of permanent income k is about 0.9 and this is the figure we will use in our example. Suppose that the level of income is 100 in periods one, two, and three; $Y_1 - Y_2 - Y_3 - 100$. Using Equation 16.16 we have

$$Y_3^p = \left(\frac{100}{3} + \frac{100}{6}\right) + \frac{100}{2}$$

Figure 16.5 shows that consumption in period three (point C_3) lies on both the short-run and the long-run consumption functions. For example, the long-run consumption function, Equation 16.10, gives

$$C_3 = (0.9)(100) = 90$$

Similarly, the short-run consumption function, Equation 16.17, gives

$$C_3 = 0.9\left(\frac{1}{3}Y_2 + \frac{1}{6}Y_1\right) + 0.45Y_3$$

$$= 0.9\left(\frac{100}{3} + \frac{100}{6}\right) + (0.45)(100)$$

$$= 45 + 45 = 90$$

Now suppose that in period four income rises to 110. The short-run consumption function shows the effect on current consumption:

$$C_4 = 0.9\left(\frac{1}{3}Y_3 + \frac{1}{6}Y_2\right) + 0.45Y_4$$

$$= 0.9\left(\frac{100}{3} + \frac{100}{6}\right) + (0.45)(110)$$

$$= 45 + 49.5 = 94.5$$

The increase in income of 10 leads to an increase in consumption of 4.5, which confirms that the short-run marginal propensity to consume is 0.45. If the higher income level is maintained through period four to period six, permanent income will gradually be adjusted upwards until it too is equal to 110. Meanwhile consumption will also be adjusted upwards as the short-run consumption function shifts vertically. By period six, the short-run consumption function will have an intercept of 49.5:

$$C_6 = 0.9\left(\frac{1}{3}Y_5 + \frac{1}{6}Y_4\right) + 0.45Y_6$$

$$= 0.9\left(\frac{100}{3} + \frac{100}{6}\right) + 0.45Y_6$$

$$= 49.5 + 0.45Y_6$$

By period six, actual consumption C_6 lies on both the short-run and the long-run consumption functions, as shown in Figure 16.5. According to the short-run function,

$$C_6 = 49.5 + 0.45(110) = 99$$

Similarly, given that permanent income in period six is 110, the long-run consumption function gives the same value:

$$C_6 = 0.9(110) = 99$$

The permanent income hypothesis is therefore able to explain both the short-run and the long-run reactions of consumption to a change in income. According to the adaptive expectations version of the perma-

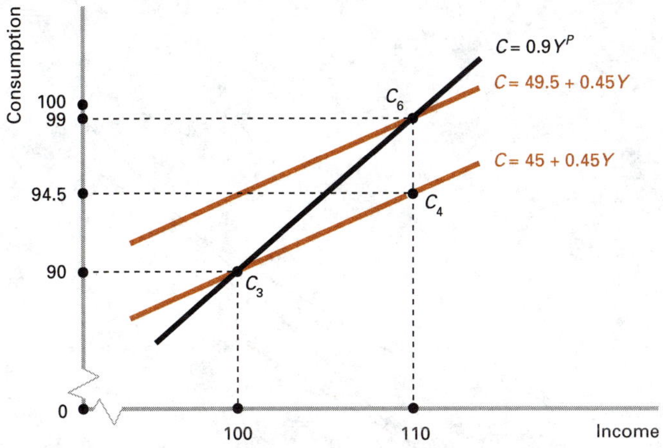

Figure 16.5 Short-run and long-run consumption functions — the permanent income hypothesis

nent income hypothesis, the intercept of the consumption function depends on lagged values of income, whereas under the life-cycle hypothesis the intercept depends on the quantity of real wealth. However, in both cases the short-run *MPC* out of current income is considerably lower than the long-run *MPC*.

An Empirical Illustration

Figure 16.6 presents estimates of the Canadian consumption function using annual aggregate time-series data for the period 1949 to 1990. The horizontal axis plots personal disposable income, PDI, per person in constant 1986 dollar terms. To arrive at this quantity, total Canadian personal disposable income was divided by the Canadian population. A constant 1986-dollar series was obtained by dividing by the consumer price index (scaled to be unity in 1986). Constant 1986-dollar consumption per person is plotted along the vertical axis. The scatter of points lies closely around a linear long-run consumption function that was fitted by least squares.[17] The slope of the long-run consumption function is estimated to be 0.84.

Each point of the long-run consumption function has a flatter short-run function passing through it. Figure 16.6 illustrates short-run con-

---

[17] The estimates are based on a first order autoregressive model of consumption; namely $C_t = a + bC_{t-1} + cY_t + e_t$. The estimation procedure accounts for first order serial correlation in the error term, e_t.

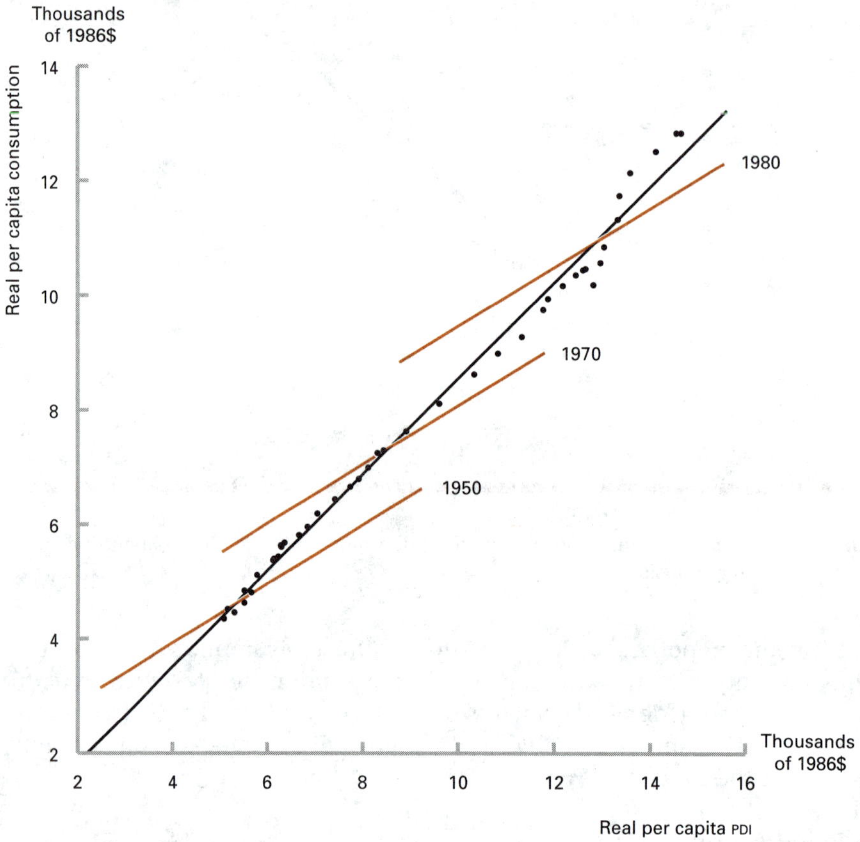

Figure 16.6 Short-run and long-run consumption functions

sumption functions for three years: 1950, 1970, and 1980. Given the method of estimation, the slopes of these short-run consumption functions are all identical and equal to 0.57.

Fiscal Policy and the Consumption Function

There have been numerous examples, in the United States and Canada, of tax changes that might have potentially affected the level of personal consumption. In the United States in 1968, a temporary tax surcharge was introduced. The increase in taxes was to last one year. However, it was announced later that the surcharge would be extended for a second year, but at a lower rate. In 1975, under the Nixon administration, consumers benefitted from a one-shot tax rebate. Finally, under the Reagan administration, there was a series of permanent tax cuts that were phased in over the 1981–84 period. The life-cycle and permanent income theories predict that the effects of temporary tax cuts will be very different from the effects of a permanent tax cut. The next two sections present the arguments and the empirical evidence.

In Canada, income tax surcharges were introduced in the late 1980s. Although these surcharges are calculated over and above the normal rate of tax as determined by the standard income tax brackets, the surcharge is income-related. Hence, the Canadian surcharges have really been equivalent to tax rate increases. Moreover, the surcharges are not necessarily temporary, nor were they introduced in order to directly influence consumption behaviour. In Canada, the federal government and provincial governments have tried to increase spending in economic slumps by temporarily lowering sales taxes on selected goods, and in one case, across the board. We will consider these examples of fiscal policy below.

A Temporary Income Tax Cut

Modern theories of consumption predict that current consumption depends on lifetime or permanent income rather than on current income. Consequently, the effect of a cut in the rate of income tax will have an effect on consumption only to the extent permanent income is increased. Clearly, if the tax cut is known or believed to be temporary, the effect on permanent income will be negligible and consumption will be largely unaffected. The additional income resulting from a temporary tax cut will probably be saved, wealth will be increased and to the extent that this raises permanent income, consumption will also rise. However, the stimulus that this will give to aggregate demand is not likely to be particularly large. For example, if the temporary tax cut gives each household an additional $100 in the form of a one-time tax rebate, household wealth will rise by $100. Assuming a real interest rate of 5 percent, household permanent income rises by only $5 per year. If the marginal propensity to consume out of permanent income is 0.8, consumption will rise by only $4 per year. Thus, in the year of the tax rebate, the household's consumption will rise $4 and its annual saving will rise by $96. In short, temporary changes in the tax system are not likely to provide an effective means of influencing the level of aggregate demand.[18]

18 However, saving can take many forms. The household may simply place the $96 in a bank account to earn interest. But the purchase of durable goods involves a considerable amount of saving because the good lasts much longer than one year. Although buying a videocassette recorder is mostly saving, the entire purchase is a contribution to current aggregate demand. The point is that some forms of saving do directly affect aggregate demand.

A Permanent Tax Cut

On the other hand, a permanent tax cut is likely to lead to a much greater increase in consumption. Provided the public believes the government's promise that the tax cut will not be reversed at some later date, there will be an upward revision in the estimate of both *present* and *future* disposable income, that is, permanent income will rise. This in turn will result in an increase in consumption both in the present and in the future. Consequently, a permanent income tax cut has a much greater effect than a temporary income tax cut on consumption and aggregate demand. Using the same example as before, a permanent tax cut that increases a household's disposable income by $100 per year will also raise permanent income by $100 per year. Assuming a marginal propensity to consume of 0.8, consumption will rise by $90 per year. Saving will rise by $10 per year.

Clearly the permanent tax cut has a greater effect on consumption than the temporary tax cut. However, it is important to note that if the government tries to gain greater fiscal leverage by repeatedly announcing permanent tax cuts that actually turn out to be temporary, the government will soon lose credibility and the announcement of further permanent tax cuts will have little effect on consumption.

Empirical Evidence on Income Tax Cuts

Theoretically, the marginal propensities to consume out of transitory and permanent income are very different. However there is conflicting empirical evidence on precisely how large the difference is. In two separate studies, Okun and Springer[19] analyzed the 1968 temporary tax increase in the United States. Okun's empirical estimates contradicted the strict theoretical result that the surcharge should have virtually no effect on consumption, but Springer found support for this proposition. In a later study, Blinder looked at the 1975 American temporary tax cut.[20] He concluded that "a temporary tax cut is about half as effective as a permanent tax cut in the first year, rising to about three-quarters as effective in the second year." To illustrate Blinder's empirical results, suppose that an individual receives a tax cut of $1 in the first quarter of the year. If the tax cut is expected to be permanent (income is to rise by $1 per quarter forever), Blinder's results imply that after one year the individual will have spent $0.51 of the first dollar. By the end of the second year $0.81 of this first dollar will have been spent. But if the tax

---

[19] Arthur M. Okun, "The Personal Tax Surcharge and Consumer Demand, 1968–70," *Brookings Papers on Economic Activity*, vol. 1, 1971, pp. 167–211; William L. Springer, "Did the 1968 Surcharge Really Work?" *American Economic Review*, September 1975, pp. 644–59.

[20] Alan S. Blinder, "Temporary Income Taxes and Consumer Spending," *Journal of Political Economy*, vol. 89, no. 1, 1981, pp. 26–53.

cut of $1 is thought to be temporary, the consumer will have spent just $0.30 of it one year later and a total of $0.65 two years after the one-shot $1 tax cut.

These estimates suggest several points. First, permanent tax cuts have a greater effect on spending than temporary tax cuts. Second, the effect of tax cuts is surprisingly strong in the second year, which means that they will not give the economy a sharp boost right away, but rather a gentle stimulus over a long period of time. This may be the opposite of what policymakers want. They would prefer the control and precision that would come with an immediate and once-and-for-all effect. Stimulating the economy two years after it needs boosting may amplify the business cycle rather than dampen it. Third, the fact that $0.65 out of every dollar of a temporary tax cut is spent (even though it takes two years to see all this spending) is evidence against the theoretical implication of the permanent income hypothesis that virtually all of a temporary tax cut will be saved. However, the more recent study by Blinder and Deaton[21] supported the view that temporary tax cuts have no effect on consumption. They suggest that the "source of the discrepancy [between the two studies] is an intriguing question for future research."[22]

Sales Tax Cuts

The stimulation of aggregate demand through temporary cuts in sales taxes became a popular fiscal tool in Canada during the 1970s. In 1975 the Ontario government reduced the provincial sales tax from 7 percent to 5 percent between April and December. In addition, the provincial sales tax on new cars was removed entirely between July and December of the same year. More recently, in 1978 the federal government encouraged the provinces to temporarily reduce their sales taxes when it offered to compensate the provinces for the lost tax revenue by transferring federal government income tax revenues to the provinces. The federal offer allowed those provinces that levy sales taxes (Alberta is the only province that does not levy such a tax) to reduce their tax rates by either three percentage points for six months or two percentage points for nine months. In November 1980, the Ontario government, encouraged either by the success of its earlier program or by the upcoming election, finally removed the sales tax from a wide selection of durable goods until June 1981.

There are two channels through which cuts in sales taxes stimulate consumer spending and aggregate demand. First, by directly reducing

21 Blinder and Deaton, "The Time Series Consumption Function Revisited," pp. 465–521.

22 *Ibid.*, p. 497.

the market prices of consumer goods, real disposable income is increased. According to the modern theories of consumption we would not expect this to provide much stimulus to consumer spending because the modest increase in real disposable income is temporary and contributes very little to lifetime or permanent income. The second effect of a temporary sales tax cut is to change the intertemporal relative price of a product. This intertemporal relative price effect provides a strong incentive to buy now what might otherwise be bought in the near future. This is particularly true of durable goods. The very fact that the sales tax cut is temporary gives it a powerful influence over current spending. Consumers can take advantage of the tax cut only if they spend during the tenure of the program. While a *permanent* sales tax cut will raise lifetime real income, and therefore lifetime consumption, there is no intertemporal price effect. The real income effect of a permanent sales tax cut will be spread out over all the future years and the immediate effect may be very small indeed.

Peter Gusen has undertaken a study of the Ontario government's 1975 auto sales tax rebate.[23] Gusen estimates that the suspending of the 5 percent retail sales tax during the second half of 1975 stimulated additional car sales to the tune of 46,000 vehicles in 1975. However, most of these sales were borrowed from 1976. Gusen estimates that car sales in 1976 were lower by 41,000 than they would otherwise have been in the absence of the sales tax rebate in 1975. Although the program is estimated to have raised car sales over both years by a mere 5,000 units (just over 1 percent of annual sales), Gusen argues that the sales tax rebate proved to be a successful countercyclical policy:

> It can be argued that even a pure shifting forward of demand might in itself have been desirable. The year 1975 was one of decline for the Ontario economy, with real Gross Domestic Product falling by 0.6 percent, whereas in 1976 a short-lived economic recovery took place as evidenced by the 4.9 percent growth in output.[24]

The attractive feature of a temporary sales tax cut is its ability to influence the *timing* of spending decisions by changing intertemporal relative prices. Unlike the temporary income tax cut, the temporary sales tax cut can be expected to provide a substantial stimulus in the current period. It is therefore a potentially useful countercyclical device.

---

23 P. Gusen, "The Role of Provincial Governments in Economic Stabilization: The Case of Ontario's Auto Sales Rebates," *Canadian Studies: No. 52* (Ottawa: The Conference Board in Canada, 1978), p. 115.

24 *Ibid.*

The Permanent Income Hypothesis and the Keynesian/Monetarist Debate

Not surprisingly, the permanent income hypothesis fits neatly into the monetarist arsenal: the economy is essentially stable. Even large demand shocks cause only small ripples because the biggest single component of aggregate demand, personal consumption, depends chiefly on long-term factors and only to a limited degree on current events. This in turn means that the government's countercyclical policies have small effects. What is not so widely recognized is that Keynes himself would have found no argument with the proposition that income tax policies aimed at stimulating consumption spending are likely to be ineffectual. As we pointed out earlier, Keynes believed that through firmly held *habits* consumption patterns are very stable. There is no doubt that Keynes, the discoverer of the consumption function, anticipated the permanent income theory of consumption. We leave the last word to Keynes:

> I doubt if it is wise to put too much stress on devices for causing the volume of consumption to fluctuate in preference for devices for varying the volume of investment. . . . People have established standards of life. . . . A remission of taxation on which people could only rely for an indefinitely short period might have very limited effects in stimulating their consumption.[25]

Key Concepts

the saving ratio
long-run and short-run consumption functions
time-series and cross-section data
the life-cycle hypothesis
the permanent income hypothesis
rational expectations
adaptive expectations
income tax changes, temporary and permanent

---

25 J.M. Keynes, "Activities, 1943–46: Shaping the Postwar World: Employment and Commodities," in D. Moggridge, ed., *The Collected Writings*, Vol. 27 (Cambridge and New York: Cambridge University Press, 1980), pp. 319–20.

Review Questions

1. Discuss the distinction between personal consumption and personal spending.
2. In the life-cycle theory the individual consumption function (Equation 16.4) shows that the marginal propensities to consume out of wealth and income depend on age.
   (a) Explain why the marginal propensity to consume out of wealth rises with age.
   (b) Derive the marginal propensities to consume out of current income under the alternative assumptions that a change in current income results in (i) no change in expected future income *y* and (ii) an equal change in expected future income. Explain why in one case the marginal propensity to consume declines with age and in the other it rises with age.
3. How does the life-cycle theory account for the fact that the short-run consumption function shifts upwards through time?
4. The following questions may be answered either qualitatively or quantitatively. In the latter case, assume the working and retirement periods last 40 and 10 years, respectively.
   (a) Under the life-cycle hypothesis what would you expect the aggregate saving ratio to be in a stable population, that is, one in which every age group remains a constant size through time? (Assume there is no real income growth.)
   (b) How does your answer change when the real income *per capita* of successive generations in a stable population rises by, say, 2 percent per year when (i) there are no income transfers between people of different age groups and (ii) income transfers equalize *per capita* incomes across all age groups?
   (c) What do you expect the saving ratio to be in a population which is growing at, say, 1 percent per year? (Assume there is no *per capita* real income growth.)
   (d) What would be the effect on the Canadian saving ratio of a decline in the rates of growth of both real income and the total population?
5. How do temporary and permanent income tax changes affect aggregate consumption?

CHAPTER 17

The Theory of Investment

The instability of private investment is, of course, at the heart of the problem of the business cycle.

R.A. Gordon[1]

Of all the components of aggregate demand, investment expenditures are by far the most volatile. The wide fluctuations in investment spending are illustrated in Table 17.1, which compares the instability of investment with the relative stability of consumer spending. Since 1960, the largest year-to-year increase in the volume of nonresidential investment was in 1964, when spending in constant dollar terms rose 16 percent over 1963 levels. The largest decline in nonresidential investment spending since 1960 was in 1982, when real expenditures fell 12 percent. Thus, the range of year-to-year changes is 25 percentage points. Investment in the residential construction industry experiences even greater year-to-year fluctuations, spanning a range of 34 percentage points.[2] This is in sharp contrast to consumer spending on goods and services. The largest year-to-year change in real consumer spending was only 7.5 percent and in only one year, 1982, did this component of demand actually fall in real terms. Annual changes in real consumer spending have therefore fallen within the relatively narrow range of 10 percentage points.

The instability of investment spending has led economists to study the determinants of investment expenditures in order to better under-

1 R.A. Gordon, "The Stability of the U.S. Economy," in M. Bronfenbrenner, ed., *Is The Business Cycle Obsolete?* (New York: John Wiley, 1969), p. 13.

2 Changes in inventories are also part of investment spending. The rise and fall of inventory levels also contributes greatly to the instability in total investment.

Table 17.1 The Range of Year-to-Year Changes in Selected Components of Aggregate Demand* (1960-90)

Direction of Change	Nonresidential Investment (%)	Residential Investment (%)	Consumer Spending (%)
Maximum rise	+16.2	+18.0	+ 7.5
Maximum fall	− 9.0	−16.3	− 2.7
Range	25.2	34.3	10.2

*All calculations are derived from constant dollar expenditures.

stand its role in the creation of business cycles. An understanding of what factors influence investment spending is important if successful stabilization policies are to be adopted. Both monetary and fiscal policies have effects on the amount of investment that businesses undertake. Tax rates, for example, influence the net return that an investment project will yield and therefore tax rates enter into the calculations of an investment project's profitability. Monetary policy also has an effect on investment spending through the effect of interest rates on the profitability of investment projects. As we saw in Chapter 5, investment spending is inversely related to the level of interest rates. Residential construction in particular has been shown to be very sensitive to the level of interest rates.

Investment spending is of interest not only because of its key role in business cycles, but also because today's investment plays a large part in determining tomorrow's potential output. It is through net investment that the total stock of capital goods is increased. In the minds of policymakers, net investment means more jobs for the workers who produce the capital equipment and more jobs for the people who will work with the new equipment as soon as it is in place. In addition, improvements in technology are usually embodied in new capital goods so that it is often through net investment that long-term improvements in productivity are achieved. For these reasons, the level of investment has been a popular target of macroeconomic policy initiatives.

We begin our discussion of the theory of investment by reviewing the relationship between net investment, gross investment, and the stock of capital. Next, we will turn to accelerator theories of investment. Theories of this type take for granted that investment expenditures vary considerably from year to year and they try to explain the role that investment plays in the creation of business cycles. Accelerator models of business cycles tend to be associated with the traditional "interventionist" view that effective countercyclical macroeconomic policies can be used to smooth out business cycles. However, in a case study we demonstrate that well-meaning stabilization policies can have the perverse effect of destabilizing the economy if the policy action is only slightly mistimed. Following the case study, we will examine in more detail the determinants of the optimal capital stock. Using the concept of present value, it will be shown that the optimal stock of capital depends on the level of real output and the *real* interest rate. In the final section on the theory of investment, we will discuss the neoclassical approach that emphasizes the profit-maximizing behaviour of firms. The neoclassical theory also gives additional insight into how macroeconomic policies can affect the level of investment. In the last section, we will look at some recent policy initiatives that were aimed at raising the level of investment in the U.S. economy.

Investment and the Capital Stock

The relationship between investment and the capital stock is best shown in the form of an equation:

$$K_t = K_{t-1} + I_t - \delta K_{t-1} \tag{17.1}$$

In this equation, K_{t-1} represents the size of the capital stock at the end of period $t-1$. The level of gross investment during period t is represented by I_t. Recall from Chapter 2 that the National Income and Expenditure Accounts record the total value and volume of gross investment rather than net investment. During the unit time period (say one year) a part of the capital stock is used up through wear, tear, and obsolescence. This quantity we can take to be a constant proportion of the capital stock. We will use the symbol δ to represent the rate of depreciation. The last term in Equation 17.1, δK_{t-1}, represents the quantity of capital that is used up during period t. The net addition to the capital stock (net investment, I_t^N) is therefore:

$$I_t^N = I_t - \delta K_{t-1} \tag{17.2}$$

The quantity of net investment is added to K_{t-1} to obtain the size of the capital stock at the end of period t (K_t). By substituting I_t^N into Equation 17.1 and rearranging it, we obtain the following expression for net investment:

$$I_t^N = K_t - K_{t-1} \tag{17.3}$$

which says that **net investment** is simply the change in the capital stock.

This observation suggests an important point: it is discrepancies between the desired capital stock (we will use the symbol K_t^* for this concept) and the actual capital stock that give rise to net investment. Indeed the theory of investment has two distinct components. The first is a theory of capital that tells us what determines the size of the desired capital stock. The second is a theory of how the economy adjusts the actual capital stock so that it is equal to the desired capital stock. For the economy as a whole, it may take more than one time period to complete the adjustment from the current capital stock to the optimal capital stock. Depending on the type of equipment, delivery and installation of new investment may take only a matter of weeks (typewriters and automobiles) or a matter of years (oil tankers and pipelines). Consequently, the adjustment period that is necessary to reach desired capital stock may be considerably longer than one unit of time. Throughout the adjustment period, net investment will be only a fraction of the difference between the current capital stock and the desired capital stock. However, once the adjustment is complete (the actual capital stock is equal to the desired capital stock) there is no incentive for firms to make net additions to the stock of capital; net investment will be zero. If there are no further changes in the desired capital stock, the level of net investment will continue to be zero. The only investment that will be necessary is **replacement investment** (to replace the continuously depreciating capital stock). In these unchanging circumstances net investment would be zero and gross investment would be equal to replacement investment.

If the capital stock fell below the actual capital stock, firms would let the stock of capital decline. In the most depressed conditions it is theoretically possible that there would not be any replacement investment at all. The stock of capital would simply erode away at the rate of depreciation. In this extreme case, gross investment would be zero (the capital goods industries would be completely shut down) and net investment would be negative. This can be confirmed by Equation 17.2. By setting gross investment to zero, net investment reduces to

$$I_t^N = \delta K_{t-1}$$

To summarize these introductory comments, the theory of investment is related to the theory of capital. The essential ingredient in the theory of capital concerns the determinants of the desired capital stock. Once this desired capital stock is determined, it is clear what net investment is required in order to move the current stock of capital to the desired stock of capital. This second step may well not be completed in one period of time. A theory of investment must specify the factors that determine the speed of adjustment from the current stock of capital to the desired stock of capital.

The Accelerator Theory of Investment

Accelerator theories of investment emphasize that the level of investment spending is determined not by the current *level* of income but by how fast income is *changing*. As we will see below, this dynamic investment function can create considerable instability in the economy. Any change in output that results from an exogenous shock, such as a rise in exports or an increase in government spending, will generate an investment boom because investment depends on the change in output. The investment boom itself reinforces the original disturbance and will create further increases in output and therefore further increases in the level of investment spending. The **accelerator** theory of investment injects a dynamic element into macro models. Disturbances in the current period feed through the accelerator mechanism and have repercussions in future time periods. As we shall see, accelerator models of investment can account for the cyclical behaviour that free enterprise economies exhibit.

We begin with a theory of what determines the size of the desired capital stock. In the simple accelerator theory this is very straightforward: the desired stock of capital K_t^* is assumed to depend upon the current level of income Y_t:

$$K_t^* = kY_t \tag{17.4}$$

The rationale for this simple formulation is the following: to produce a given level of output, certain quantities of inputs (labour, land, capital, and materials) are required. If the level of output increases, then the inputs required to produce this output will also increase. In other words, the quantity of inputs will be approximately proportional to the level of output. In particular, as Equation 17.4 states, the desired capital stock will be proportional to the level of output. Although a number of criticisms can be levelled against this simple specification, we will defer our discussion of these criticisms until later.

The next step in the analysis is to formulate the method of adjustment to changes in the desired capital stock. The simplest assumption is to suppose that any discrepancy between the size of the capital stock that was left at the end of last period and the desired capital stock this period will be made up entirely in the current period. In other words, net investment in the current period will be exactly equal to the difference between the last period's capital stock K_{t-1} and this period's desired capital stock K_t^*:

$$I_t^N = K_t^* - K_{t-1} \qquad (17.5)$$

This implies that the capital stock at the end of a period will always be equal to its desired level. Last period's net investment, for example, was exactly equal to whatever was required to make last period's capital stock K_{t-1} equal to its desired level K_{t-1}^*. Substituting K_{t-1}^* for K_{t-1} in Equation 17.5:

$$I_t^N = K_t^* - K_{t-1}^*$$

Now, substituting from Equation 17.4 we have the accelerator theory of investment that relates the level of investment to changes in the level of output:

$$I_t^N = k(Y_t - Y_{t-1})$$

which can be written as:

$$I_t^N = k\Delta Y_t \qquad (17.6)$$

where ΔY_t is the change in income.

A famous model constructed by Professor Samuelson[3] illustrates the power of the accelerator model of investment to affect the dynamic properties of a macro model.

Samuelson's Accelerator–Multiplier Model

Samuelson's model consists of three equations:

$$Y_t = G_t + I_t + C_t \qquad (17.7)$$

$$C_t = bY_{t-1} \qquad (17.8)$$

$$I_t = \bar{I} + k(C_t - C_{t-1}) = \bar{I} + k\Delta C_t \qquad (17.9)$$

The first equation is the familiar equilibrium condition. The second equation is a simple consumption function: consumption is proportional to last period's income. The third and final equation is Samuelson's version of the accelerator model of investment. The first component of gross investment, $\bar{I}$, is constant and can be interpreted as replacement

[3] P.A. Samuelson, "Interactions Between the Multiplier Analysis and the Principle of Acceleration," *Review of Economics and Statistics*, May 1939, pp. 75–78.

investment. Since additions to the capital stock are small in relation to the existing capital stock, it is not unreasonable to assume that replacement investment is constant. The second component of total investment is net investment, which Samuelson assumes is proportional to the lagged change in income. This can be demonstrated by substituting Equation 17.8 into Equation 17.9. The three equations, 17.7 to 17.9, can be used to obtain an equation that describes the dynamic path of income. The substitution of Equations 17.8 and 17.9 into Equation 17.7 gives

$$Y_t = \bar{I} + G_t + b(1 + k)Y_{t-1} - kbY_{t-2} \tag{17.10}$$

Equation 17.10 describes the path of income through time once the values of replacement investment, $\bar{I}$, government spending G_t, the parameters b and k, and the initial levels of income are specified.

Before we examine the nature of the possible dynamic paths of income, let us first consider the long-run equilibrium properties of the model. Suppose that government spending remains at the level $\overline{G}$ indefinitely. What is the level of income (say $\overline{Y}$) that will persist indefinitely given that $G_t = \overline{G}$ for all time? Since income will be equal to $\overline{Y}$ indefinitely, it follows that

$$\overline{Y} = Y_t = Y_{t-1} = Y_{t-2} = \ldots$$

Substituting $\overline{Y}$ and $\overline{G}$ into Equation 17.10 gives

$$\overline{Y} = \bar{I} + \overline{G} + b(1 + k)\overline{Y} - bk\overline{Y}$$

or

$$\overline{Y} = \bar{I} + \overline{G} + b\overline{Y}$$

Solving for Y gives

$$Y = \frac{\overline{G} + \bar{I}}{1 - b} \tag{17.11}$$

Note that Equation 17.11 is precisely the solution we would get if we solved the following simple two-equation static model:

$$Y = \overline{G} + \bar{I} + C$$

and

$$C = bY$$

The accelerator plays no role whatsoever in determining the long-run solution to the dynamic model described by Equations 17.7 through 17.9. Note that the accelerator coefficient k does not appear in Equation 17.11. This is because the long-run equilibrium solution is characterized by constant values for all variables. When the levels of income and consumption are constant, investment spending is restricted to replacement investment as no new capital equipment is required. Consequently, the accelerator coefficient k does not appear in the long-run solution described by Equation 17.11.

However, the accelerator does play a vital role in the adjustment process that takes the economy from one long-run equilibrium to another. Figure 17.1 illustrates several possibilities. Suppose that the marginal propensity to consume b has the value 0.6, that the level of replacement investment $\bar{I}$ is 10, and that initially the level of government spending $\overline{G}$ is 10. Using Equation 17.11, the long-run income level is

$$\overline{Y} = \frac{10 + 10}{1 - 0.6}$$

$$= 50$$

That this income level actually is the equilibrium value can be demonstrated easily. From the consumption function (Equation 17.8) the level of consumption is $0.6 \times 50 = 30$. The sum of replacement investment $\bar{I}$ and government spending $\overline{G}$ is $10 + 10 = 20$. Consequently, the sum of consumption, replacement investment, and government spending is 50, exactly what the equilibrium condition (Equation 17.7) requires. Net investment is zero in equilibrium.

Now suppose that the level of government spending rises from 10 to 12. The new long-run equilibrium level of income will be

$$\overline{Y} = \frac{10 + 12}{1 - 0.6}$$

$$= 55$$

The two-unit increase in government spending, magnified by a multiplier of $1/(1 - 0.6) = 2.5$, leads to a rise in income of 5. The path that the economy follows as it moves from one long-run equilibrium position to the other depends crucially on the size of the accelerator coefficient k. Three different types of response are illustrated in Figure 17.1. If the accelerator coefficient k is relatively small, such as 0.1, the level of income gradually adjusts upwards as the full multiplier effect works its way through the economy. In this particular case the effect of the accelerator is to speed up the multiplier process. In the first time period following the increase in government spending, the level of income rises by two units, exactly the same as the increase in government spending. In the second time period income rises again as part of the extra income of two units is spent on consumption goods. This is the familiar multiplier process. However, as consumption rises the desired capital stock is also raised and so net investment is increased. This extra boost to total

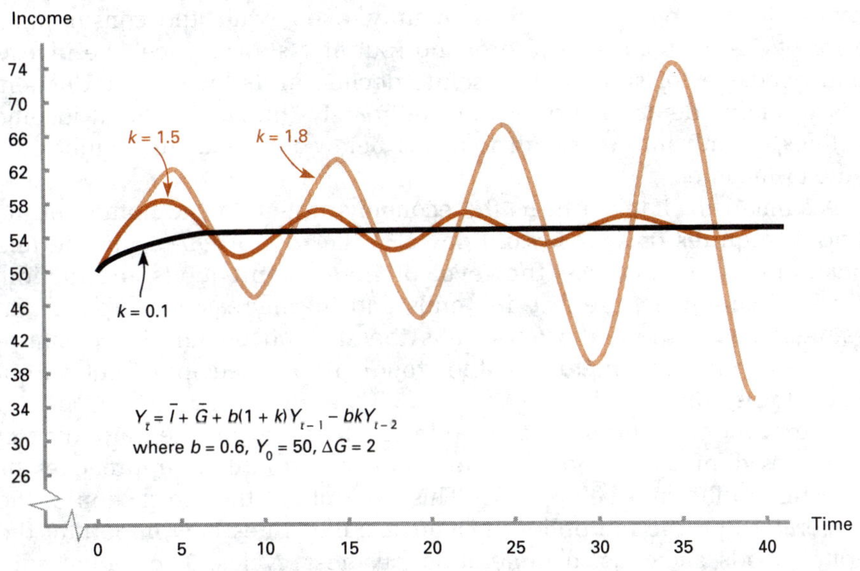

Figure 17.1 The response of income to a change in government spending

demand from an increase in net investment pushes the economy towards the new equilibrium at a faster pace than if the accelerator were not in operation ($k = 0.0$). However, the accelerator does not change the nature of the new equilibrium because the successive rounds of the multiplier effect result in ever smaller increases in income and consumption. Since the level of net investment depends on the change in consumption spending, net investment declines as the changes in consumption get smaller. In the new equilibrium, the levels of income and consumption are both constant. The desired capital stock remains unchanged and so the level of net investment is zero.

In the second example, the accelerator coefficient has a value of 1.5, making net investment much more sensitive to changes in consumption than in the previous case. This creates a cyclical effect in the economy's adjustment to an exogenous shock. As before, the increase in government expenditure raises income and then consumption, but investment responds more sharply than before to the *change* in consumption. As a result, the path of income rises much more steeply than in the previous case and even overshoots the long-run equilibrium value of 55. However, the economy soon runs out of steam and income begins to fall. The reason for this is that investment depends on the *change* in consumption, that is, the growth of consumption. It requires only a decline in the *rate of growth* of consumption to cause a drop in the production *level* of investment goods. Consequently, even while the consumption sector of the economy is still growing (but at a slower pace) the investment goods sector suffers an absolute decline in its level of production. This weakens demand further until ultimately the level of total income declines, falling into a trough that lies below the long-run equilibrium value of income.

A similar mechanism turns the economy around at the bottom of the cycle. It requires only a slowing down of the *rate of fall* of income and consumption to increase the *level* of investment goods production. When this happens, the free fall ends and the increasing output of investment goods gradually outweighs the slowing decline of consumption. Eventually the bottom of the trough is reached and total output begins to rise once again.

The economy continues to cycle in this fashion, but the amplitude of the cycles diminishes and the level of income gradually approaches its long-run equilibrium value of 55. This example of the interaction of the accelerator and the multiplier mechanisms illustrates how important the capital goods sector is in generating business cycles. The model suggests that any slowing down in the growth of the economy will ultimately cause a recession during which total income will fall. This is because the level of investment declines as the growth of the economy slackens off.

For larger values of the accelerator coefficient, net investment may be so sensitive to changes in consumption (or income, depending on the specific formulation of the accelerator equation) that a demand shock creates an unstable sequence of recession and expansions. This is illustrated in Figure 17.1 for the case where k is 1.8. While the new equilibrium level of income is still 55 following the increase in government spending, the economy will never come to rest at this level of income. The accelerator is so powerful that an **explosive cycle** follows the increase in government spending. The income roller coaster races along a cyclical path of ever increasing amplitude.

A fourth mathematical possibility, which we have not illustrated, occurs if the accelerator coefficient is sufficiently large. In this case the economy does not follow a cyclical pattern at all in the wake of an exogenous shock, but simply races off to infinity (if the demand shock is positive). Again, such an economy can be described as unstable in that once it is disturbed the economy can never settle down to its new equilibrium position.

Although the two unstable cases are of mathematical interest, they have no relevance for the behaviour of actual economies. However, the second example that we looked at does illustrate how the accelerator theory of investment can explain why, after a demand shock, the economy's path to its new equilibrium may follow a series of economic booms and recessions. In reality the economy never reaches its long-run equilibrium position because new shocks are continually arising. The actual behaviour we observe is the amalgamation of the effects of a sequence of shocks: some small, some large, some recent, and some in the distant past. The shock waves of all these events combine to produce the actual cyclical path that the economy follows. It is this complex dynamic world that faces government policymakers.

The cyclical instability that the investment sector imparts to the economy as a whole strongly suggests the need for countercyclical government policies. However, given the lags in the policy process itself — recognition of the problem, implementation of policy, and the lagged response of the economy to the policy measures — there is considerable danger that countercyclical policies will actually be procyclical, exacerbating the unavoidable shocks that disturb the economy in the ordinary course of events.

In the following case study we simulate the effects of fiscal policy in a dynamic macroeconomic model. A version of Samuelson's accelerator–multiplier model is used to illustrate how a lack of synchronization between an exogenous shock and the intended countervailing policy response can lead to destabilizing effects.

Case Study 10: Can Fiscal Policy Be Destabilizing?

Figure 17.2 illustrates how the lags involved in implementing fiscal policy can actually result in fiscal policy having a **destabilizing** rather than a stabilizing influence. Suppose that the structure of the economy is described by Samuelson's accelerator–multiplier model (Equations 17.7 to 17.9) and that the marginal propensity to consume b and the accelerator coefficient k are 0.6 and 1.5, respectively. As we saw earlier, this particular model exhibits damped oscillations following a disturbance; that is, the level of income follows a cyclical path as it moves from one equilibrium position to another.

Initially, the levels of exogenous investment $\bar{I}$ and government spending $\overline{G}$ are both equal to 10. Using Equation 17.11, the long-run income level is

$$\overline{Y} = \frac{10 + 10}{1 - 0.6}$$

$$= 50$$

In Figure 17.2 the level of income is shown to be initially equal to 50. Then, in period one a temporary disturbance strikes the economy: exogenous investment declines to 6 from 10 for one period and then returns permanently to 10 in period two. The black line in Figure 17.2 shows

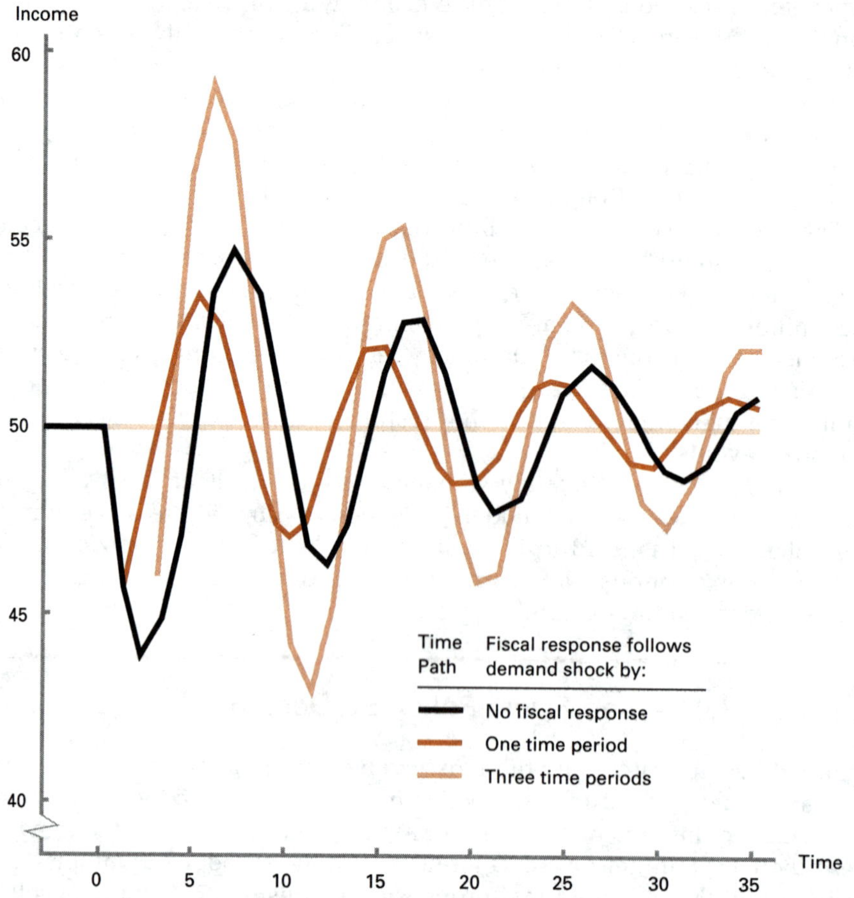

Figure 17.2 The path of income following a temporary demand shock under alternative fiscal policy responses

the path of income following this temporary negative demand shock given that the level of government spending remains at 10 (there is no fiscal response to the demand shock). In period one, income immediately falls by exactly the same amount as the decline in investment, to 46 from 50. The interaction of the multiplier and accelerator then projects the economy along a cyclical trajectory that oscillates around, and gradually converges towards, the long-run equilibrium income level of 50. Note that the long-run equilibrium position is not affected by temporary disturbances.

The ideal fiscal response to this demand shock would be for the government to raise its level of spending in period one by exactly the same amount as the decline in investment. Essentially, the economy would be hit by two offsetting demand shocks in period one. The level of income would remain at 50. In period two, when exogenous investment returns to its earlier level of 10, the government would reduce its spending back to 10. In all periods the sum of $\bar{I}$ and $\bar{G}$ would be 20 so that the level of aggregate demand would remain constant and income would never deviate from its long-run value of 50.

This perfect countercyclical policy is unlikely to be realized in practice. Since government spending levels must be planned, in order to synchronize the increase in government spending with the drop in investment the government must be able to forecast both the exact amount by which investment will decline and the exact time when this decline in spending will take place. Forecasting techniques are simply not good enough for the government to be able to accurately predict either of these two critical factors — the size of the shock and the time when it will hit. Indeed, it may be argued that by their very nature some shocks are impossible to forecast. It is much more likely that the government will simply react to today's crisis. In addition, the effect of the policy may lag behind the implementation of the policy. We will refer to the time between the exogenous shock and the effect of the fiscal response as the **fiscal lag**.

Figure 17.2 illustrates the path that the level of income follows given that the fiscal response takes effect one or three periods after the temporary decline in investment spending. In both cases, the fiscal response is a one-period increase in government spending which is the same size as the one-period decline in investment spending; that is, government spending is raised to 14 from 10 for one period. Consider first the case where the fiscal lag is just one period. As shown in Figure 17.2 the effect of the fiscal stimulus in period two is to avoid the continued decline in the level of income. In the absence of a fiscal response, the level of income falls to 44 in period two. With the fiscal stimulus of four units of additional government spending in period two, the level of income is 48. Even though the fiscal stimulus is one period late, it does reduce the depth of the first recession. Indeed, in all subsequent periods it is clear from Figure 17.2 that a fiscal response with a one-period lag leads to a less volatile cyclical path than if there is no fiscal response whatsoever.

However, in this particular model, if the fiscal lag exceeds one period, then the fiscal policy actually causes the cycle to be more volatile. For example, Figure 17.2 also illustrates the case where the fiscal lag is three periods. In this case the fiscal stimulus actually takes effect when the level of income is below the level of income in period one. The economy is still in a very depressed state. But at this point the natural forces within the economy are pushing the level of income upwards, albeit from a very low level. The fiscal stimulus augments the natural multiplier and accelerator forces and sends the level of income surging upwards well beyond the long-run equilibrium level. Despite the fact that the fiscal stimulus takes effect near the trough of the first cycle, the resulting income cycle is very much more volatile than if no fiscal policy measures at all had been taken. The situation is even worse if the fiscal lag is five rather than three periods (this case is not illustrated).[4] In this case the fiscal stimulus takes effect just before the first cyclical peak is reached. Just as the level of income is about to peak and turn down towards the long-run equilibrium level, the fiscal stimulus pushes the level of income even higher and further away from the long-run equilibrium income level. The economy then embarks on a very volatile cyclical path that gradually converges towards the long-run equilibrium income level of 50.

These examples have illustrated the difficulties that fiscal lags pose for policymakers. The fiscal lag comprises the recognition lag, the policy implementation lag, and the effectiveness lag. The existence of these lags, together with the shortcomings of forecasting techniques, means that it is virtually impossible to guarantee the exact synchronization of the fiscal response and the exogenous shock that it is supposed to offset. As we have seen, this does not rule out the possibility that fiscal policy can be countercyclical, but it does raise the distinct possibility that a fiscal stimulus that takes effect even near the trough of a business cycle will be destabilizing. Monetarists have made much of our ignorance of the lag structures within free enterprise economies, claiming that this ignorance together with unavoidable fiscal lags makes countercyclical fiscal policy a dangerous experiment that is more likely to do harm than good. Keynesians have come to accept the limitations of fine-tuning but do not believe that the best policy in the face of all conceivable exogenous shocks is to do absolutely nothing.

Extensions To the Simple Accelerator

The simple accelerator model of the economy can explain how the instability of investment spending can lead to fluctuations in economic activity, but it has several limitations. For example, within a large range of seemingly reasonable values of the two important parameters — the marginal propensity to consume b and the accelerator coefficient k — the model is unstable, that is, it describes an economy that can never attain equilibrium once it is disturbed by an exogenous shock. Such a model can hardly purport to represent actual economies. For example, a reasonable estimate of the capital/output ratio, which is the accelerator

4 Such a case may arise if the government takes action in period three, but there is a two-period lag before the policy takes effect.

coefficient k, is 3. That is to say, the ratio of the value of the capital stock to the value of annual output is approximately 3. In our illustrations of Samuelson's accelerator–multiplier model we saw that a marginal propensity to consume of 0.6 coupled with a capital/output ratio of only 1.8 results in unstable behaviour. With a capital/output ratio of 3, the marginal propensity to consume would have to be less than 0.33 in order for the model to be stable. But no one would suggest that the marginal propensity to consume out of income is as low as 0.3.

There are a number of factors that are ignored in the Samuelson accelerator–multiplier model that serve to make actual economies more stable than this particular version of the accelerator model suggests. In the case of an unstable economy, a positive demand shock would cause the level of income either to race off towards infinity or to follow a cyclical path of ever increasing amplitude. In both cases supply constraints are likely to prevent the level of income from growing at a rapid rate of growth for anything more than just a few periods. For example, the capital goods industry is of limited size in the short run and it is likely that the increases in the output of capital goods that are called for by the accelerator equation (17.9) simply could not be produced. Since it is the rapid expansion of the investment goods sector that fuels demand, this supply constraint will limit the growth of demand. Similarly, in the recession phase of the unstable cycle the decline in the total spending on capital goods cannot push total investment spending below zero; gross investment cannot be negative. The worst that can happen is that the whole capital goods industry closes down, but the output of capital goods cannot be negative. Yet Equation 17.9, which determines the volume of gross investment, will generate negative figures for gross investment if the decline in consumption from one period to another is sufficiently large, as it will be for an economy that oscillates on a wild cyclical path. If realistic bounds were placed on the range over which gross investment can vary, then the model would be much less unstable.

Two further modifications to the simple accelerator model of investment are the permanent income theory of investment and the partial adjustment model. These are discussed in the next two sections.

Investment and Permanent Income

Since capital goods have the potential to produce output for many years, firms are unlikely to react instantly to a rise in demand by building additional productive capacity. It is more likely that the desired capital stock K^* depends on permanent income Y_t^P than on current income.[5]

---

5 This theory was proposed by Robert Eisner, "A Permanent Income Theory for Investment: Some Empirical Explanations," *American Economic Review*, June 1967, pp. 363–90.

A sudden increase in demand (which may turn out to be short-lived) is more likely to be met by having employees work overtime and by the use of backup equipment. Only if the increase in demand is believed to be permanent will the desired capital stock rise. To illustrate the permanent income approach, suppose that the desired capital stock K^* is proportional to permanent output Y_t^P rather than current output:

$$K_t^* = kY_t^P$$

As demonstrated in Chapter 16, if expectations are formed adaptively, permanent output can be expressed as a weighted average of the current level of output and the previous estimate of permanent output:

$$Y_t^P = (1 - a)Y_t + aY_{t-1}^P$$

By repeatedly substituting the lagged value of Y_t^P on the right-hand side (see Chapter 16) permanent output can be expressed as a weighted average of past levels of output:

$$Y_t^P = (1 - a)(Y_t + aY_{t-1} + a^2Y_{t-2} + \dots) \qquad (17.12)$$

Because the parameter a is less than unity, the most recent levels of output receive larger weights than the more distant levels of output. Thus, in forecasting the future, more weight is given to the recent past than to the distant past. To express the desired capital stock in terms of previous levels of output, substitute for permanent output using Equation 17.12:

$$K_t^* = kY_t^P$$

$$K_t^* = k(1 - a)(Y_t + aY_{t-1} + a^2Y_{t-2} + \dots) \qquad (17.13)$$

Note that current output Y_t has a smaller effect on the desired capital stock than in the simple current output formulation that was discussed earlier. That is, $(1 - a)k$ is smaller than k because $(1 - a)$ is less than unity. One way to interpret this is that a sudden increase in demand, which may turn out to be short-lived, will not cause firms to fully adjust the desired capital stock. In the short run firms are more likely to work with the current stock of capital, for example by having employees work overtime. If the increase in demand turns out to be permanent, firms will gradually revise expectations about the permanent level of output and the desired capital stock will rise accordingly.

To find the implications for net investment, we will continue to assume that net investment in any given period equals the difference between the actual capital stock and the desired capital stock. Net investment is therefore:

$$I_t^N = K_t^* - K_{t-1}^* = \Delta K_t^*$$

From Equation 17.13, the first difference of the desired capital stock ΔK_t^* can be expressed in terms of the first differences of output:

$$I_t^N = b_0 \Delta Y_t + b_1 \Delta Y_{t-1} + b_2 \Delta Y_{t-2} + \ldots$$

Hence, one implication of the permanent income theory of investment is that the current level of net investment depends on both current and past changes in the level of income.[6]

A Partial Adjustment Model

Finally, accelerator models that recognize the production lags in the investment process tend to be less prone to instability than models of the sort we examined earlier. To this point we have continued to assume that any difference between the actual stock of capital and the desired stock of capital will be made up in the current period. As we mentioned earlier, this is probably a reasonable assumption for certain types of capital goods such as office equipment (desks, chairs, and typewriters). But for heavy machinery, office buildings, power stations, oil tankers, and pipelines, the time taken for an increase in the desired stock of capital to be reflected in the actual capital stock may be several years. Given construction and delivery lags, only a proportion of the difference between the actual capital stock that was left at the end of the previous period and the new desired capital stock will be closed by net investment in the current period. Suppose this proportion is τ. An equation that represents a gradual capital **stock adjustment** process is the following:

$$I_t^N = \tau(K_t^* - K_{t-1}) \qquad (17.14)$$

6 The permanent income and current income versions of the accelerator model of investment do not differ in the total response of the capital stock to a permanent change in output. It can be shown that the sum of the coefficients b_0, b_1, . . . is k. Hence, in both models the capital stock rises by the amount $k\Delta Y_t$. However, the manner in which the capital stock is adjusted does differ between the two models. In the current income version it takes just a single period of net investment to achieve the desired change in the capital stock. In the permanent income version the same amount of net investment is spread out over several time periods. Consequently, the permanent income model does not generate the massive swings in net investment that occur when the desired capital stock depends on current income. In the context of accelerator–multiplier models such as the one we discussed earlier, the effect of the permanent income accelerator is to increase the stability of the model given the values of the key parameters — the marginal propensity to consume b and the capital output ratio k.

If the value of the adjustment coefficient τ is 0.5, then 50 percent of the discrepancy between the actual capital stock left at the end of the last period and the desired capital stock this period will be removed by current net investment. It will take four periods before 90 percent of the gap is removed. To illustrate, suppose that in the initial period the capital stock is 100 units and that suddenly the desired capital stock rises to 110 units. The difference between the desired and actual capital stocks is initially 10 units. According to Equation 17.14, with $\tau = 0.5$, one-half of this difference of 10 units will be removed in the first period, and net investment will be 5 units. The actual capital stock rises from 100 to 105. In the second period the gap between the desired and actual capital stocks is 5 units (110 – 105 units). Net investment in the second period will be one-half of this gap, or 2 units. At the end of the second period the actual capital stock will rise from 105 by the amount of net investment (2 units) to 107 units. Consequently, after just two periods, 75 percent of the initial gap has been removed. The process of adjustment will continue indefinitely as the actual capital stock gradually approaches the desired capital stock.

The size of the adjustment coefficient τ determines the speed with which the gap between the actual and desired capital stocks is closed. In the extreme case in which τ is unity, the gap is closed entirely within the current period. This is the assumption that we have maintained up until the present discussion. The greater the production and construction lags in getting net investment in place, the smaller will be the coefficient τ and the slower will be the adjustment towards the net desired capital stock. As Equation 17.14 makes clear, the smaller is τ, the less responsive is net investment to changes in the desired capital stock and implicitly to changes in output. Consequently, the incorporation of a stock adjustment process, such as the one described in Equation 17.14, into the accelerator model of investment will tend to reduce the range of instability in macro models.

In this section we have discussed three modifications to the simple accelerator model of investment. First, supply constraints in the capital goods industries will limit the growth of demand during expansion phases of business cycles and will therefore tend to reduce the chance of the macro model being unstable.[7] Second, lags in the investment process can result from the slowness of the desired capital stock to adjust to changes in output. We saw that if the desired capital stock depends on permanent output rather than the current level of output, net investment will be less sensitive to short-run changes in output. Third, lags in the investment process can arise from production and construction lags.

7 Recall that an unstable economy is one that cannot move from one equilibrium position to another, but will either race off directly to infinity or will embark on a path of explosive cycles as soon as it is disturbed from its initial equilibrium position.

The fact that it takes several periods for some kinds of capital goods to be put in place following an increase in the desired capital stock means that the effect of an increase in the desired capital stock on the level of net investment will be spread out over many periods.

However, we have continued to rely on the assumption that the desired capital stock essentially depends on output alone (either current or permanent). This has allowed us to highlight the role of the accelerator model of investment as a source of instability. But there are a number of other important variables that determine the desired stock of capital and the speed of adjustment towards equilibrium. For example, the rate of interest is likely to influence the size of the desired capital stock and the speed of adjustment towards equilibrium. Consequently, the rate of interest in part determines the level of net investment. Recall that Figure 5.1 shows statistical evidence that suggests investment expenditures tend to be inversely related to the nominal interest rate. In the next two sections we will examine in more detail the variables that determine the desired stock of capital. Since the desired stock of capital will be shown to be the outcome of a rational decision-making process within the firm, we will from now on refer to this concept as the **optimal capital stock**.

The Optimal Capital Stock

Firms make profits by combining factors of production such as labour, materials, and capital to produce output. Unlike labour and materials, which are purchased each period, capital equipment lasts for many periods. Consequently, the calculations that have to be made in order to judge the profitability of a piece of capital equipment involve an assessment of all the profits or losses that can be expected during the whole life of the equipment. This is a complex calculation because it requires an evaluation of a stream of profits that will be spread out over several years. In Chapter 15 we discussed in some detail the concept of present value, which can be thought of as the price one would be prepared to pay today in order to receive a stream of payments over a period of several future years. The concept of present value is an important one for the rational investment decision.

Consider the case of a project that involves the purchase of a piece of capital equipment today at a cost of C. The capital equipment will be combined with labour L to produce real output Y for N periods into the future. At that time the capital will be scrapped and, for simplicity of exposition, we will assume that this scrap value will be zero. In the first period of operation (indicated by the subscript 1) the net profit will be

$$P_1Y_1 - W_1L_1$$

where P_1 and W_1 are the prices of output Y_1 and labour L_1, respectively. Note that we are assuming the production process involves just two factor inputs — capital and labour. As we showed in Chapter 15, the present value of this profit that will be earned one period from the present is

$$\frac{P_1Y_1 - W_1L_1}{1 + R}$$

where R is the rate of interest. The rate of interest is expressed in decimal form; for example, 0.05 represents a rate of interest of 5 percent. The factor $1/(1 + R)$ is used to discount next year's net profit $(P_1Y_1 - W_1L_1)$ in order to evaluate it in terms of today's money. The present value of the entire stream of profits that will accrue over the N periods less the initial cost C of the capital equipment is

$$PV = -C + \frac{(P_1Y_1 - W_1L_1)}{(1 + R)} + \frac{(P_2Y_2 - W_2L_2)}{(1 + R)^2} + \ldots \qquad (17.15)$$

$$+ \frac{(P_NY_N - W_NL_N)}{(1 + R)^N}$$

The cost of the capital equipment is not discounted because it is paid out in the present period. Because this outlay is a cost it has a negative sign, just as the outlays on labour have a negative sign in Equation 17.15. In order to compute the present value of the project, the firm must make some estimate of the output that will be produced from this project, the market price that this output will be sold for, as well as all future labour requirements and wage rates. Although the firm knows the cost of the equipment and the current market interest rate, all of the other elements in the present value calculation have to be estimated. Clearly, expectations about the future are of paramount importance in the investment decision.

Having made its estimates of the future net returns, the firm can calculate the present value of the project. But what decision rule should the firm use in order to judge rationally the viability of the project? The following example illustrates that the optimal strategy for the firm is that it should undertake the investment project if the present value calculation yields a positive number. However, if the present value turns out to be negative, the project should be rejected as the funds that would be needed to purchase the capital equipment could be put to better use by simply loaning out these funds at the current rate of interest R.

Suppose, for example, that the cost of the machine, C, is 100 and that it will produce output for just one period in the future. Suppose further that the value of this output, PY, is estimated to be 210 and that the labour costs, WL, are estimated to be 100. Using Equation 17.15, the present value of the investment project is

$$PV = -100 + \frac{210 - 100}{1 + R}$$

We will evaluate this present value at three different interest rates. First consider 8 percent, or $R = 0.08$. In this case the present value is

$$PV = -100 + \frac{210 - 100}{1 + 0.08}$$

$$= -100 + 101.9$$

$$= 1.9$$

The present value is positive, which indicates that it is better to invest in this new capital project than to lend the funds at 8 percent. Note that if the funds that are needed to purchase the equipment are in fact loaned out at 8 percent, the firm would give up 100 in the present in order to have 100(1 + 0.08) = 108 at the end of the next period. However, the purchase of the equipment would also cost 100 in the current period, but net returns at the end of the next period would be (210 – 100) = 110. This is an alternative way of demonstrating the superiority of the investment project over loaning funds at the prevailing interest rate of 8 percent.

If the rate of interest were 10 percent rather than 8 percent, the present value calculation would yield

$$PV = -100 + \frac{210 - 100}{1 + 0.10}$$

$$= -100 + 100$$

$$= 0$$

At this rate of interest the firm would be indifferent between the investment project and loaning out the funds at 10 percent. Either way, the firm invests 100 in the present period and receives 110 (net) one period later.

At a higher rate of interest the investment project is no longer worthwhile and the present value calculation will yield a negative number. For example, at a rate of interest of 12 percent the present value is

$$PV = -100 + \frac{210 - 100}{1 + 0.12}$$

$$= -100 + 98.2$$

$$= -1.8$$

The firm would be better off if it loaned out its funds at the current interest rate of 12 percent rather than if it invested in the project. At 12 percent, a loan of 100 pays 120 in the next period, but the project yields a net return of only 110 in the next period.

These three calculations demonstrate that the higher the rate of interest, the lower the present value of an investment project. In our example, as the rate of interest rises from 8 percent through 10 percent to 12 percent, the present value of the project falls from 1.9 through 0 to –1.8. The present value of any particular project is inversely related to the rate of interest. This can be seen from Equation 17.15 directly. As the interest rate R increases, each term on the right-hand side that involves R declines. Consequently, the present value PV is a declining function of the interest rate R.

In order to calculate the size of the optimal capital stock it is necessary to consider all potential investment projects. Given all the factors that affect the present values of these potential projects, it is possible in principle to add up the value of all projects that have a positive present value. The total value of these profitable investment projects (which have yet to be undertaken) together with the value of the capital stock currently in use gives the current optimal capital stock. How does the rate of interest affect the size of the optimal capital stock? We have already seen that an increase in the rate of interest reduces the present value of all investment projects. In some cases, a rise in the rate of interest will be sufficient to push the present value of the projects from a positive number to a negative number. At a higher interest rate, some investment projects will no longer be profitable and the optimal capital stock will be smaller. In other words, the optimal stock is inversely related to the interest rate R.

The conclusion that the optimal capital stock and the nominal interest rate R are inversely related is based on the fact that the present value of potential investment projects declines as the nominal interest rate rises. This conclusion is correct as long as expected inflation is zero. However, as we argued in Chapter 13, when expected inflation is not zero, the investment decision depends upon the real interest rate rather than the nominal interest rate. This can be demonstrated here by examining the role of prices in the present value calculation. To keep the analysis simple we will assume that the volume of output and labour inputs remain constant at the levels Y and L, respectively, throughout the life of the new capital equipment. In this case, Equation 17.15 becomes

$$PV = -C + \frac{(P_1Y - W_1L)}{(1+R)} + \frac{(P_2Y - W_2L)}{(1+R)^2} + \ldots + \frac{(P_NY - W_NL)}{(1+R)^N} \qquad (17.16)$$

In order to illustrate the role of prices in the present value calculation, suppose that prices and wages are both expected to rise at a constant and identical rate, π.[8] Let P and W be the level of prices and wages, respectively, at the time the capital equipment is purchased. One period later, when the first output is produced, prices and wages are expected to be

$$P_1 = P(1 + \pi)$$

$$W_1 = W(1 + \pi)$$

The level of profits in this period is expected to be

$$PY(1 + \pi) - WL(1 + \pi) = (PY - WL)(1 + \pi)$$

Similarly, expected profits in the following period are

$$(PY - WL)(1 + \pi)^2$$

The present value of an investment project that is expected to give profits N periods into the future is represented by

$$PV = -C + \frac{Z(1 + \pi)}{(1 + R)} + \frac{Z(1 + \pi)^2}{(1 + R)^2} + \ldots + \frac{Z(1 + \pi)^N}{(1 + R)^N} \quad (17.17)$$

where $Z = (PY - WL)$. Note, if $\pi = 0$, then Equation 17.17 is equivalent to Equation 17.15, which was derived on the assumption that the expected rate of inflation is zero.

As we argued in Chapter 13, given the nominal interest rate R, the higher the expected rate of inflation, the lower is the real interest rate ($\overline{R} = R - \pi$). It is the real interest rate that is important for investment decisions. This can be demonstrated as follows. The ratio $(1 + \pi)/(1 + R)$ can be approximated by the following expression: $1/(1 + R - \pi)$.[9] Consequently, the formula that gives the present value of the investment project can be written as:

$$PV = -C + \frac{Z}{(1 + R - \pi)} + \frac{Z}{(1 + R - \pi)^2} + \ldots + \frac{Z}{(1 + R - \pi)^N} \quad (17.18)$$

8 Historically, wages have risen at a faster pace than the price of output, that is, the real wage has risen. This has been possible because of gains in productivity. Here we are assuming that labour productivity associated with a particular piece of capital does not change during the life of the equipment. The conclusions of the analysis in the text do not change if we allow for productivity improvements with a given piece of equipment, but the mathematical argument is slightly more complicated.

9 For example, if expected inflation is 5 percent and the rate of interest is 8 percent the first ratio is:

$$(1 + \pi)/(1 + R) = 1.05/1.08$$
$$= 0.972$$

For the same interest rate and expected rate of inflation we have

$$1/(1 + R - \pi) = 1/(1 + 0.08 - 0.05)$$
$$= 0.971$$

where $R - \pi$ is the real rate of interest. An increase in the real rate of interest will reduce the present value of all potential investment projects and lower the optimal capital stock. An increase in the real rate of interest will occur if, for example, the nominal interest rate rises for a given expected rate of inflation or if the expected rate of inflation declines given the nominal interest rate.

Although the nominal rate of interest and the expected rate of inflation both have an effect on the present value of an investment project, the effects of these two factors are subsumed under the effect of the real interest rate on the present value of the project. Since the present value of any particular project decreases as the real interest rate rises, the higher the real rate of interest, the fewer will be the number of projects that have a positive present value and the smaller will be the size of the optimal capital stock.

Finally, Equation 17.18 can be used to show that an increase in future output will lead to an increase in the size of the optimal capital stock. Suppose, for example, that the firm doubles its estimate of the quantity of output Y that can be placed on the market without altering the price of the product. This will require additional inputs. Let us assume a doubling of output requires a doubling of both labour and capital inputs; consequently, both L and C in Equation 17.18 also increase by a factor of two. It is clear from this equation that the present value is also doubled:

$$PV^{**} = -2C + \frac{2Z}{(1+R)} + \frac{2Z}{(1+R)^2} + \ldots + \frac{2Z}{(1+R)^N} \tag{17.19}$$

Given that the original investment project is worthwhile (its present value is positive), an increase in the level of expected future output will lead to an increase in the optimal stock of capital. As we assumed in the case of the simple accelerator, the optimal capital depends positively on the level of expected output. However, we have also shown that the size of the optimal capital stock depends inversely on the real rate of interest. In symbols, this relationship can be expressed as follows:

$$K^* = K^*(Y, \overline{R})$$

where Y is the level of output and $\overline{R}$ is the real rate of interest.

In this section we have considered in some detail the key factors that influence the profitability of potential investment projects. By summing the values of all profitable investment projects (those with positive present values) and adding this total to the capital stock that is currently in use, we obtain the optimal capital stock. It is important to stress the distinction that we have made before between the theory of capital and the theory of investment. The latter is concerned with the volume of net investment that occurs in a particular time period. Generally, this will not be equal to the gap between the optimal capital stock and the actual capital stock because of, for example, the long production and construction lags involved in some types of projects and the uncertainty of future sales. However, to the extent that the level of net investment does depend on the size of the gap between the actual and optimal capital stocks, the level of net investment will be a function of both real output and the real rate of interest.

Tobin's *q*

Professor James Tobin has suggested that the amount of new investment taking place in the economy is related to the ratio of the market value of firms to the cost of replacing their capital.[10] He has called this ratio q. The market value of a firm is equal to the value of its shares on the stock exchanges. This is the price investors are prepared to pay for the firm's assets. If this value is less than the cost of replacing the firm's capital equipment, then the firm is in no position to expand — its q is less than unity. If q is less than unity for the economy as a whole, firms are not presently worth their replacement costs and we would not expect to see much new investment. For example, if all houses have a current market value less than the cost of constructing a new house, it is unlikely that many new houses will be built. The buyers that are in the market will most likely select an existing home rather than have one built. Similarly, when q is less than one, firms that want to expand will probably do so through the acquisition of existing firms rather than through the purchase of new buildings and equipment.

However, when q is greater than unity, the value of existing firms exceeds the cost of replacing their capital. Firms that want to expand will do so by purchasing new equipment that costs less than the market value of existing plant and equipment. Also, if existing homes are selling for prices well above the cost of building new ones, we would expect to see a great deal of construction activity.

The basis of the theory is simply that sales of new equipment are likely to expand when the demand for new equipment exceeds the supply price. As we have discussed above, the demand price of an asset is the present value of an asset. The present value is precisely what an investor is prepared to pay, given market interest rates and expectations of future net revenues. The supply price in a competitive industry, such as the capital goods industry, is determined by the marginal cost of pro-

---

10 James Tobin, "A General Equilibrium Approach to Monetary Theory," *Journal of Money, Credit and Banking*, Vol. 1 (February 1969), pp. 15–29.

ducing additional output. Whenever the demand price of new equipment exceeds the supply price (this is the present value criterion for undertaking the project), the new equipment will be purchased.

We can think of the present value of existing firms as representing the present value of new equipment opportunities, that is, the demand price of capital. The ratio q is therefore a proxy for the ratio of the demand and supply prices for new capital equipment.

The Neoclassical Theory Of Capital and Investment

The neoclassical theory of the optimal capital stock is based on the profit-maximizing behaviour of firms. Unlike the discussion in the previous section, the production function and the choice of factor inputs play central roles. A production function describes in a formal way the relationship between the factors of production (capital and labour) and the quantity of output that these factors produce. Specifically, a production function describes the various combinations of capital and labour that can be used to produce a given level of output. A certain quantity of, say, shirts can be produced in a variety of ways — some relatively labour-intensive and some relatively capital-intensive. The actual technique that is used to produce a given quantity of shirts depends on the relative prices of labour and capital. The lower the price of capital relative to the price of labour, the more capital-intensive will be the technology that is used to produce shirts. The differences in the techniques used to produce shirts in different countries can be explained largely by differences in the relative prices of capital and labour.

The price of labour is usually expressed in terms of an hourly wage rate, or the cost of hiring one unit of labour for one hour. Similarly, the cost of using capital equipment for, say, one hour is referred to as the **user-cost of capital**. Firms generally own the capital goods that they use, but the user-cost of capital can be thought of as the rental cost of using a piece of capital equipment for a certain period of time. For example, there are rental markets for office equipment and trucks. In equilibrium the cost of renting office equipment for, say, one week will be the same as the implicit user-cost that is incurred each week by firms that own their own office equipment. Consider a situation in which the firm intends to produce a certain quantity of output indefinitely. Given this level of output and the relative prices of the two factors of production (labour and capital), the firm will decide on the levels of these inputs that minimize the costs of production. Since the level of output is to be maintained at a constant level indefinitely, the quantities of inputs will also remain constant indefinitely (as long as their relative price remains unchanged).

The first cost associated with capital equipment is due to the fact that funds are tied up in the equipment itself; the funds used to purchase the equipment could have been used to purchase some other income-earning asset, such as a bond. The return that can be earned on the bond is the real rate of interest $\overline{R}$, which is the nominal rate of interest paid out by the issuer of the bond less the rate of price inflation, which cuts into the purchasing power of the income generated by the bond. Again the initial cost of the capital equipment will be represented by the symbol C. Funds equal to C will be tied up in the form of capital equipment indefinitely. Each period a real interest return of $C\overline{R}$ will be foregone by the owner of the capital equipment. This is the interest rate component of the user-cost of capital.

The second component of the user-cost of capital is due to the wear and tear that inevitably takes place as the capital equipment is used. Since the firm is assumed to produce a given level of output indefinitely, the firm's capital requirements remain constant (again assuming there is no change in the relative price of inputs). Consequently, each period the firm will need to replace that part of the capital stock that is eroded away through wear and tear. Suppose that a certain proportion δ of the capital stock is worn out each period. The cost of replacement investment will be $C\delta$, where the proportion δ is expressed in the form of a decimal. For example, if replacement investment per period is 10 percent of the capital stock, then δ will be 0.10.

The interest and replacement costs of capital must be added together to give the total user-cost of capital. In terms of the symbols we have used, the user-cost of capital can be expressed as $C(\overline{R} + \delta)$, where C is the cost of the capital equipment, $\overline{R}$ is the real interest rate, and δ is the rate of replacement investment. To illustrate the calculation of the interest and replacement components of the user-cost of capital, suppose that the cost of the equipment is \$100. If the real rate of interest is 5 percent per annum and replacement investment is 10 percent per annum, then the user-cost per \$100 of capital is \$100(0.05 + 0.10) = \$15 per annum. The user-cost of capital, just like the real interest rate, can be expressed in decimal form. In this example, the user-cost of capital is 0.15. Alternatively, if the firm were to rent the equipment that is worth \$100, then the annual rental cost would be \$15. Of this, \$5 would be compensation for the interest cost incurred by the firm that owns the equipment and \$10 would be compensation for the annual wear and tear, known as depreciation.

Once the firm has determined the user-cost of capital, the price of labour, and the appropriate level of output, the firm will be able to choose that particular production technique which minimizes total cost. One result of this optimizing behaviour is the determination of the optimal size of the capital stock, or the firm's demands for capital. The optimal size of the capital stock is an increasing function of output and a decreasing function of the user-cost of capital. As the user-cost of capital rises relative to a given wage rate, the firm will find that by using less capital and more labour the same output can be produced at a lower total cost.

Our discussion so far has focused entirely on the determinants of the optimal capital stock and nothing has been said about the determinants of net investment, that is, the factors that determine the rate of net investment given that the optimal capital stock differs from the actual capital stock. In this regard the neoclassical theory is not at all special. Typically, in empirical studies of investment, a stock adjustment process of the type we discussed earlier is specified.[11] This specification recognizes that changes in the desired capital stock are not necessarily immediately translated into net investment. Once firms have recognized that the optimal capital stock has increased, it takes time for specific plans to be finalized, orders to be placed, equipment to be delivered and finally, to put the capital equipment in place. The effects of an increase in the optimal capital stock on net investment are therefore distributed over many periods.

The neoclassical theory of capital is a useful framework for analyzing theoretically, and estimating empirically, the effects of monetary and fiscal policies on net investment. There are two distinct ways in which monetary and fiscal policies can influence the volume of investment. The first is through their effects on the size of the optimal capital stock. Any measure that increases the size of the capital stock will result in additional net investment, which is equal to the gap between the original optimal capital stock and the new value. Of course, this investment may take place over a period of many years. The second way in which monetary and fiscal policies influence the volume of investment spending is through their effects on the timing of investment. The government may introduce temporary measures that encourage firms to make investment outlays in the present that would otherwise have been made sometime in the future.

It is through their effects on the user-cost of capital that monetary and fiscal policies have a direct influence on the optimal capital stock and therefore on net investment.[12] An expansionary monetary policy, for example, which reduces nominal and real interest rates, will also reduce the user-cost of capital. This encourages firms to adopt more capital-intensive techniques than they otherwise would. Net investment spending is correspondingly increased as firms move towards more capital-intensive production methods. However, if the decline in the real rate of interest and the user-cost of capital turn out to be temporary, then the

[11] See, for example, R.E. Hall and D.W. Jorgenson, "Tax Policy and Investment Behaviour," *American Economic Review*, June 1967, pp. 391–414.

[12] Monetary and fiscal policies have an indirect effect on net investment via their influence on the level of output.

optimal capital stock will return to its earlier level. The net investment that earlier increased the size of the actual capital stock will be offset by a decline in replacement investment that will continue until the capital stock is restored to the original optimal size.

Alternatively, monetary policy may affect the volume of investment that is currently being undertaken by having an influence on the timing of investment outlays. Net investment may be given a boost when long-term financing is available at below-average interest rates. On the other hand, net investment may slacken off despite the existence of a gap between the optimal and actual capital stocks when the real cost of borrowing is at a cyclical peak. The effect of monetary policy on the timing of investment spending is muted, however, by the fact that the borrowing and spending decisions do not necessarily have to be taken at the same time. A firm that intends to build a new plant next year may well borrow the funds now to take advantage of low interest rates; this does not mean that the firm has to begin building the plant ahead of schedule.

Macroeconomic Policy and Investment

The close connection between capital investment and the growth of productivity, and hence improvements in the standard of living enjoyed by all Canadians, has made investment policies an important component of government's overall economic policy. The two principal levers for providing investment incentives are investment tax credits and the tax treatment of capital cost allowances (depreciation).

Investment tax credits were first introduced in Canada in 1975, at which time firms investing in new buildings or machinery and equipment in manufacturing and processing industries were entitled to tax credits equal to 5 percent of the value of the investment. Since that time the credits have become more generous. In 1985, the general tax credit rate was 7 percent, but higher rates (up to 50 percent) applied in certain regions. Small businesses were also favoured under the program by being entitled to an investment tax credit rate of 35 percent. To illustrate how investment tax credits work, consider a firm that spends $100,000 on a piece of machinery. A tax credit of 10 percent allows the firm to reduce its tax bill by 10 percent of $100,000, that is, $10,000. This is equivalent to reducing the cost of capital equipment by 10 percent and consequently reduces the user-cost of capital. By reducing the user-cost of capital, the investment tax credit encourages the use of more capital-intensive techniques. A permanent tax credit program permanently increases the size of the optimal capital stock.

In the United States, the most recent large-scale attempt to encourage private investment through corporate tax legislation was in 1981 and 1982 when the U.S. economy was in the depths of a recession. The Economic

Recovery Tax Act (ERTA) was signed into law in 1981. It was modified one year later by the Tax Equity and Fiscal Responsibility Act, 1982. These two pieces of legislation covered considerably more ground than the tax law affecting private investment, but a major objective was to make investment in plant and equipment much more attractive than previously.

Prior to the ERTA, the level of tax credits ranged from 3.5 percent for short-lived equipment such as company cars and light trucks, to 10 percent for long-lived capital such as factory buildings and warehouses. The effect of the ERTA was to raise the tax credits available on shorter-lived assets. For example, the tax credit available on light trucks was raised to 6 percent and the tax credit on machinery and equipment was raised to 10 percent from 6.5 percent. These changes effectively lowered the user-cost of capital on a wide range of capital goods.

An alternative way to reduce the user-cost of capital is to increase the rate at which firms are allowed to depreciate their capital equipment for tax purposes. This fiscal tool is known as **accelerated depreciation**. When a firm spends $100,000 on a machine, this is clearly a business expense that must be deducted from gross income in order to arrive at a net income figure. However, since the machine will not be used up entirely during its first year of operation, it is reasonable to allow only part of the initial cost of the machine to be deducted from the first year's gross income. If the machine will last five years, a firm may spread the total cost of $100,000 equally over five years. The annual capital cost allowance or depreciation cost in this case would be $20,000. It is in a firm's interest to depreciate its plant and equipment as quickly as possible, but firms are limited by what the tax laws allow. For example, consider the firm that invests in a machine that costs $100,000. If all of this expenditure could be deducted from gross income in the first year of operation, the firm would reduce its taxes by, say, $50,000 (we are assuming that the corporate tax rate is 50 percent). Under these circumstances, the firm spends $100,000 on the machine and saves $50,000 in taxes. On the other hand, if the firm deducts the cost of the machine over a five-year period ($20,000 per year), the firm will reduce its tax bill by $10,000 per year for five years. To compare this situation with the first, we need to calculate the present value of five payments of $10,000 each. This calculation requires information on the rate of interest. Assuming that the real rate of interest is 5 percent, the present value of $10,000 per year for five years is $45,459. Consequently, the firm would be $4,541 better off ($50,000 – $45,459) if it could deduct the whole cost of the machine from current income compared to deducting one-fifth of the cost in each of five years. This represents just over 4.5 percent of the cost of the machine itself. If the firm were to benefit from such a fast write-off of its equipment, it would be equivalent to reducing the cost of capital equipment by approximately 4.5 percent (compared to a five-year write-off period). The user-cost of capital would be similarly reduced.

The third major fiscal instrument that has been used to stimulate investment spending is the tax rate applied to corporate income. Corporate tax rates differ according to the type of business, the size of business, and the type of ownership. Generally, the tax structure in Canada has been designed to favour manufacturing and processing firms, and particularly small businesses. The rate of corporate income tax influences the after-tax profitability of investment projects. By lowering business income tax rates, projects that would otherwise have been unprofitable, may be profitable. In this way, corporate income taxes affect the optimal capital stock and the rate of net investment.

Summary

Economists have long thought of investment spending as one of the major sources of instability in free enterprise economies. The simple accelerator models of investment, which relate investment expenditures to changes in the level of output, provide a powerful insight into the origins of business cycles. In addition, we have used a simple dynamic model to illustrate how fiscal lag can make an intended countercyclical fiscal policy actually procyclical. The model showed that, contrary to expectations, even a fiscal stimulus that takes effect near the trough of a business cycle can have a destabilizing effect.

Several extensions to the simple accelerator model have been suggested. First, the optimal capital stock is likely to depend on expected output rather than current output. If expectations are slow to adjust, a sudden change in current output may not cause an equal change in expectations about future output. It may take several periods at the new level of output for the change to be fully incorporated into expectations. This implies that the relationship between the optimal capital stock and the level of output will involve long lags. This in turn means that the ratio of the capital stock to the current level of output will not be constant. Eisner's permanent income theory of investment recognizes the importance of expectations in the theory of capital and investment.

Second, simple accelerator models assume that discrepancies between the optimal stock of capital and the current stock of capital will be removed (through net investment) within the current period. Even if the time period of the analysis is one year, this is an unreasonable assumption to make about many kinds of investment projects. The time interval between the point when it is recognized that the optimal capital stock has changed and the point when the capital is in place may be several years. We have seen how the stock adjustment model allows for these delays and how this adds a further complication to the lag structure of investment spending.

Third, the simple accelerator theories of investment do not recognize the role of the real rate of interest in determining the size of the optimal stock of capital. As we have seen, a rise in the real rate of interest will reduce the present value of potential investment projects and will consequently reduce the size of the optimal capital stock. Once this point is recognized, we can see how monetary policy directly influences investment spending through the effect of changes in the money supply on the real rate of interest. However, the Bank of Canada's control of interest rates is largely effected through its control of nominal interest rates such as the treasury bill rate. The Bank of Canada's control of real interest rates is indirect in that it comes through the control of nominal interest rates.

For the neoclassical theory of investment the instability of investment expenditures is not the focal point of the analysis. Rather, the neoclassical theory provides a rigorous treatment of optimal capital accumulation for the profit-maximizing firm. Given the level of output, firms will choose more or less capital-intensive production techniques depending on the relative prices of the inputs into the production process (capital and labour). Thus, in this theory, the price of capital services, the user-cost of capital, plays a major role. A reduction in the user-cost of capital, given the wage rate, will favour more capital-intensive techniques; the demand for capital will rise and therefore the flow of investment will increase.

A great advantage of the neoclassical approach is that it provides a framework for systematically analyzing the channels through which monetary and fiscal policies influence investment spending. Both monetary and fiscal policies affect the user-cost of capital and therefore the relative prices of capital and labour. A reduction in the real rate of interest (monetary policy) reduces the user-cost of capital and encourages the use of more capital-intensive techniques. Investment tax credits and accelerated depreciation (fast write-off) schemes are two examples of fiscal policies that subsidize capital inputs and directly affect the user-cost of capital. In addition, corporate income tax rates influence the overall profitability of investment projects and therefore affect the investment decision.

Key Concepts

net and replacement investment
the accelerator
damped and explosive cycles
fiscal lag and destabilizing fiscal policy

the optimal capital stock
the stock adjustment model
the user-cost of capital
investment tax credits
accelerated depreciation

Review Questions

1. Which of the following investment projects is likely to be most affected by interest rate considerations: a major water diversion scheme, the purchase of railway rolling stock, the construction of a large office tower, or the purchase of a mini-computer? Explain your answer.
2. Explain the role of expectations in the investment decision.
3. Explain the channels through which monetary policy influences investment spending.
4. Discuss two fiscal measures that are aimed at increasing investment spending.
5. What is the motivation for the stock adjustment model of investment?
6. Explain why it is the real rate of interest rather than the nominal rate of interest that determines the profitability of an investment project.

Index

A

G

H

I

O

P

Q

R

S

T

U

Y